Issues and Trends of Information Technology Management in Contemporary Organizations

VOLUME 2

2002 Information Resources Management Association International Conference
Seattle, Washington, USA

May 19-22, 2002

Mehdi Khosrowpour
Information Resources Management Association, USA

IDEA GROUP PUBLISHING
Hershey • London • Melbourne • Singapore • Beijing
http://www.idea-group.com

Information Technology and Business Strategies Alignment—A Model for Its Sustainability and an Analysis of the Big Brazilian Companies' Practices

Aline França de Abreu, Ph.D.
Universidade Federal de Santa Catarina, Florianópolis - SC, Tel: +5 (548) 331-7030, aline@eps.ufsc.br

Denis Alcides Rezende, MSc.
Universidade Tuiuti do Paraná, Curitiba - PR, +5 (541) 333-7400, drezende@netpar.com.br

INTRODUCTION

Business Intelligence is the aim of most of the big companies, regarding their use of information technology to support their business strategies. By achieving it, the companies are aggregating value to their products and/or services through the IT infrastructure, and therefore, obtaining return with the investment made in this area. However, one of the first conditions to reach that is the required alignment between the companies' strategic business and IT plans.

Several models in the literature indicate how to achieve such alignment (TURBAN et. al, 1996; KEARNS & LEDERER, 1997; CIBORRA, 1997), but they do not discuss about the organizational resources needed to sustain this alignment on a daily basis.

Therefore, the objective of this paper is to describe a model for business and IT strategic alignment with emphasis on sustainable resources. The model is being verified through a survey of the major Brazilian big companies' practices in this area.

Besides the authors already cited, others authors (PREMKUMAR & KING, 1992; BOAR, 1993; REZENDE & ABREU, 2000; MINTZBERG & QUINN, 2001) were reviewed regarding business strategic planning, IT strategic planning and the alignment between the two.

THE RESEARCH MODEL

Based on the review of the literature and on the consulting experiences of the researchers, a model of IT and business alignment is proposed (see Figure 1), emphasizing the organizational resources (HENDERSON & VENKATRAMAN, 1993; CIBORRA, 1997; LUFTMAN & BRIER, 1999) which should sustain this alignment.

The rationale behind this research is based on previous studies which indicate that the organizations face several difficulties when trying to align business and IT strategies, especially regarding the necessary resources to achieve such alignment (FERNANDES, ALVES, 1992; IVES, JARVENPAA, MASON, 1993; YETTON, JOHNSTON, CRAIG, 1994; TURBAN, MCLEAN, WETHERBE, 1996; KAPLAN, NORTON, 1996; TALLON et al., 1997; KEARNS, LEDERER, 1997; MEADOR; 1997). Such difficulties are related to human, cultural and technological factors (LYRA, 1991; DAVENPORT; PRUSACK, 1998; CIBORRA; ANDREU, 1998; STRASSMANN; BIENKOWSKI, 1999; LUFTMAN; BRIER, 1999; PUKSZTA, 1999; CARRUTHERS, 2000; SEGARS; HENDRICKSON, 2000; MINTZBERG; QUINN, 2001). Based on these studies and several others (as shown on Table 1), these resources were organized in four groups or constructs: information technology (IT), knowledge and information systems (IS), human capital (HC) and organizational context (OC).

The IT Strategic Planning dimension offers a general overview of IT concepts, models, methods and tools necessary to support and to enable business strategies and decision making and process management. Such planning activities should organize information management at each hierarchical level and by process, integrating information systems, people and infrastructure.

The Business Strategic Planning dimension gives the general overview of concepts, models, methods and tools for the company to go from strategic planning to strategic management. It allows a clear and adequate understanding of the business scenario, regarding its internal and external environments. It indicates its threats, opportunities, strengths, critical success factors, client satisfaction, market positioning and core competencies, among other important factors for the enterprise performance.

The organizational resources to sustain alignment is the dimension that brings the overview of the activities and factors which facilitates such alignment and are divided as shown in Table 1.

Figure 1: Research model overall design

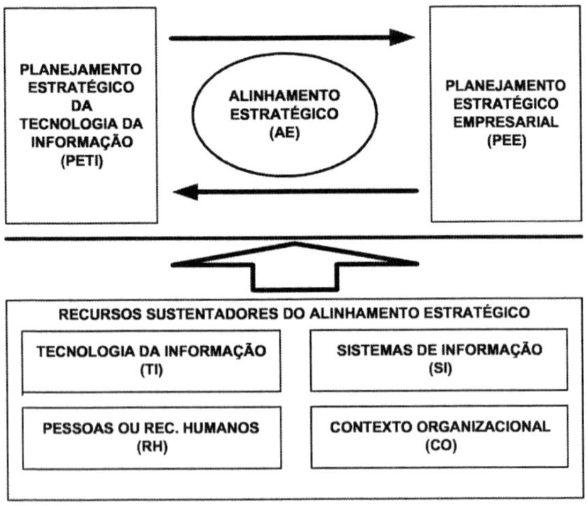

Finally, the alignment between Business Strategic Planning and IT Strategic Planning is a dimension itself which comprises the following elements: synergy of the business' functions, adjustment of available technologies, strategic management, competitive intelligence and business intelligence.

RESEARCH METHODOLOGY AND PRELIMINAR DATA ANALYSIS:

This study is being carried out through a series of phases and steps:

Phase 1:

1. review of the literature;

Table 1: Constructs and variables

Constructs and variables	Authors and respective studies
Information Technology (IT) Hardware, Software, Telecommunications Systems, Information and data management	PARSONS, 1983; ROCKART & MORTON, 1984; BAKOS & TREACY, 1986; ZVIRAN, 1990; HAMMER, 1990; DAVENPORT & SHORT, 1990; MACDONALD, 1991; WALTON, 1993; EARL, 1993; HENDERSON & VENKATRAMAN, 1993; YETTON, JOHNSTON & CRAIG, 1994; McGEE & PRUSAK, 1994; BROWN & MAGILL, 1994; PAPP & LUFTMAN, 1995; TORRES, 1995; REICH & BENBASAT, 1996; KING & TEO, 1996; PAPP, LUFTMAN & BRIER, 1996; CHAN, HUFF, BARCLAY & COPELAND, 1997; EVANS & WURSTER, 1997; KING & TEO, 1997; LUFTMAN, 1998; ARCHER, 1999; LUFTMAN & BRIER, 1999; REZENDE & ABREU, 2000.
Knowledge and Information Systems (IS) Transactional IS, Managerial IS, Strategic IS, Knowledge IS	ZVIRAN, 1990; HAMMER, 1990; DAVENPORT & SHORT, 1990; MACDONALD, 1991; HENDERSON & VENKATRAMAN, 1993; McGEE & PRUSAK, 1994; TORRES, 1995; CHAN, HUFF, BARCLAY & COPELAND, 1997; LUFTMAN & BRIER, 1999; ARCHER, 1999; REZENDE & ABREU, 2000.
Human Capital (HC)), values and behaviors, professional profile, competencies, working plan, communications and social relations, teams and partnership, Climate, motivation, Willingness and commitment	ROCKART & MORTON, 1984; BAKOS & TREACY, 1986; JOHNSTON & CARRICO, 1988; MACDONALD, 1991; WALTON, 1993; EARL, 1993; HENDERSON & VENKATRAMAN, 1993; YETTON, JOHNSTON & CRAIG, 1994; McGEE & PRUSAK, 1994; BROWN & MAGILL, 1994; PAPP & LUFTMAN, 1995; PAPP, LUFTMAN & BRIER, 1996; KING & TEO, 1996; EVANS & WURSTER, 1997; CHAN, HUFF, BARCLAY & COPELAND, 1997; KING & TEO, 1997; REVELL, 1997; LUFTMAN, 1998; LUFTMAN & BRIER, 1999; ARCHER, 1999; SEGARS & HENDRICKSON, 2000; REZENDE & ABREU, 2000; REICH & BENBASAT, 2000; SCALET & LOW, 2001.
Organizational Context (OC), Organizational Image , Mission, objectives and strategies, decision making models, processes and procedures, Culture, philosophy and business policies, organizational structure, investments and costs, organizational Infra-structure l	PARSONS, 1983; ROCKART & MORTON, 1984; BAKOS & TREACY, 1986; JOHNSTON & CARRICO, 1988; ZVIRAN, 1990; HAMMER, 1990; DAVENPORT & SHORT, 1990; MACDONALD, 1991; WALTON, 1993; HENDERSON & VENKATRAMAN, 1993; YETTON, JOHNSTON & CRAIG, 1994; McGEE & PRUSAK, 1994; EARL, 1993; BROWN & MAGILL, 1994; PAPP & LUFTMAN, 1995; TORRES, 1995; REICH & BENBASAT, 1996; PAPP, LUFTMAN & BRIER, 1996; KING & TEO, 1996; CHAN, HUFF, BARCLAY & COPELAND, 1997; EVANS & WURSTER, 1997; KING & TEO, 1997; REVELL, 1997; LUFTMAN, 1998; LUFTMAN & BRIER, 1999; STRASSMANN & BIENKOWSKI, 1999; TAURION, 1999; ARCHER, 1999; SEGARS & HENDRICKSON, 2000; REZENDE & ABREU, 2000; REICH & BENBASAT, 2000; SCALET & LOW, 2001.
Strategic Alignment: business functions synergy, adaptation of available technologies, management of both types of planning, Competitive and Business Intelligence	ROCKART & MORTON, 1984; BAKOS & TREACY, 1986; JOHNSTON & CARRICO, 1988; MACDONALD, 1991; WALTON, 1993; EARL, 1993; HENDERSON & VENKATRAMAN, 1993; YETTON, JOHNSTON & CRAIG, 1994; McGEE & PRUSAK, 1994; BROWN & MAGILL, 1994; REICH & BENBASAT, 1996; KING & TEO, 1996; EVANS & WURSTER, 1997; CHAN, HUFF, BARCLAY & COPELAND, 1997; KING & TEO, 1997; REVELL, 1997; LUFTMAN, 1998; LUFTMAN & BRIER, 1999; STRASSMANN & BIENKOWSKI, 1999; TAURION, 1999; ARCHER, 1999; REZENDE & ABREU, 2000; REICH & BENBASAT, 2000; SCALET & LOW, 2001.

2. meta-analysis of the several cases studies (consolidation of the authors' experiences);

Phase 2:

3. definition of the research model;
4. formulation of a semi-structured interview guide, including quantitative and qualitative data. Both CIO and CEO of each company were interviewed, either by phone, e-mail or personally.;
5. pre-test of the data collection instruments in 2 companies.

Phase 3:

6. elaboration of a pilot study with 8 companies from several sectors to refine the interview guide and the study methodology;
7. selection of the research sample – companies listed in the 500 biggest and best Brazilian companies list, an economic annual directory published by specialized literature. Initially 222 companies were randomly selected to receive the invitation to participate on the study. The presentation letter and the questionnaire were sent by e-mail and by fax. Since the return of these e-mails and faxes were very low, the researchers start to contact them by phone. Every time they accepted to participate, the respondent was asked to indicate another company which in his/her opinion would accept to participate on this study. After the phone contacts, 78 accepted (already taking out the interviews which were not completely fulfilled), representing 35% of response.
8. data collection and analysis. Triangulation was used by the combination of interview, observation and secondary analysis of companies' documents, every time the interview was done face to face. The analysis was both qualitative and quantitative.

The sample studied had the following averages: time of existence of 37,4 years, 5.446 direct employees, 1,81% of the revenue in IT investment. The CEOs had an average age of 41,2 years and had been in the company for about 12,8 years in average. The CIOs had 41,6 years of age in average and 11,1 years in average working for the company.

The percentage for the alignment between business and IT strategy planning was of 79,4%, being IT responsible for 11,1%, IS for 10,84%, HC for 47,05% and OC for 31,0%, indicating that behavioral issues and the organizational context are more effective in achieving the expected alignment than IT and IS, regardless if the planning process is undertaken in an either formal or informal way.

Tables 2 shows the percentage of alignment per business area and the importance of each resource in sustaining this alignment respectively, accordingly to the CEOs and CIOs' perceptions.

CONCLUSIONS

This study reinforces the importance of doing research about strategic alignment of business and IT strategies. Besides the difficulties to realize this research and the fact that the results are related to Brazilian companies, this study indicates that when the 4 constructs are managed as a combined and inter-related set, companies achieve the desired alignment between business and IT strategies. The results will also help the CEOs and CIOs on their decisions regarding IT strategic planning and the implementation of their working plans.

Table 2: Participation of the sustainable resources in the alignment between IT and business

Constructs and Variables	*CEOs' answers*	*CIOs' answers*	*Percentagel*
Information Technology			
- adequation of hardware, software and telecomunications	25	28	
- strategic use of IT	16	12	
Subtotal	*=41*	*=40*	*11,11 %*
Information Systems			
- adequation of transactional systems	25	26	
- strategic use of IS	11	8	
- quality of decion making and knowledge management	4	5	
Subtotal	*=40*	*=39*	*10,84 %*
Human Capital			
- values and pro-active behaviors	26	21	
- adequation of professional profile	15	10	
- competences and training	32	26	
- Formal working plan	12	10	
- Informal planning	15	16	
- communications and relationships	16	15	
- team working and partnership	14	15	
- organization climate and motivation	22	21	
- Willingness and commitment	13	14	
- Conciousness and effective participation	17	13	
Subtotal	*=182*	*=161*	*47,05 %*
Organizational context			
- Positive organizacional image	6	4	
- Business competence and emphasis on performance management	13	9	
- Mission, objectives and strategies well defined	9	8	
- Decision-making models	10	11	
- Process and procedures well defined	5	6	
- Formal planning methodology	35	38	
- culture and clear philosophy and politics	8	9	
- organizational structure	6	5	
- adequacy of investiments, expenses and costs	13	14	
- satisfactory infra=structure	10	7	
Subtotal	*=115*	*=111*	*31,00 %*
Total	378	351	100 %

Finally, further studies need to be done in order to verify the different heights the variables might have and to develop implementation methodologies for IT strategic planning models.

REFERENCES

BOAR, B. H. The Art of Strategic Planning for Information Technology: Crafting Strategy for the 90s. John Wiley & Sons, Inc. USA, 1993.

CARRUTHERS, T. E. Occupational psychology. **Journal of Occupational and Organizational Psychology,** Leicester, v. 73, p. 380-381, Sept. 2000.

CIBORRA, C. De profundis ? Deconstructing the concept of strategic alignment. Proceedings of Twentieth IRIS Conference. Department of Informatics, University of Oslo, Norway. August 9-12, 1997.

CIBORRA, C.; ANDREU, R. Organizational learning and core capabilities development: the role of IT. In GALLIERS, R. D.; BAETS, W. R. J. (Ed.). **Information technology and organizational transformation:** innovation for the 21st century organization. Chichester: John Wiley & Sons, 1998.

DAVENPORT, T. H.; PRUSACK, L. **Ecologia da informação.** São Paulo: Futura, 1998.

FERNANDES, A. A.; ALVES, M. M. **Gerência estratégica da tecnologia da informação:** obtendo vantagens competitivas. Rio de Janeiro: LTC, 1992.

HENDERSON, J. C.; VENKATRAMAN, N. Strategic alignment: Leveraging information technology for transforming organizations. IBM Systems Journal, Vol 32, Num 1, pp. 4-16, 1993.

IVES, B.; JARVENPAA, S.; MASON, R. O. Global business drivers: aligning IT to global business strategy. **IBM Systems Journal,** Armonk, v. 32, n. 1, p. 143, 1993.

KAPLAN, R. S.; NORTON, D. P. Using the balanced scorecard as a strategic management system. **Harvard Business Review,** v. 76, 1996.

KEARNS, G.; LEDERER, A. Alignment of IS plan with business plan: the impact on competitive advantage. Proceedings of AIS 97, Indianapolis, USA, 1997.

LYRA, C. E. **Relatos sobre questões comportamentais na informática do grupo de interesse em qualidade e produtividade.** Curitiba: SUCESU/PR, 1991. Notas prévias.

LUFTMAN, J. N.; BRIER, T. Achieving and sustaining business-IT alignment. California Management Review, Vol. 42, p. 109-122. Berkeley; Fall 1999.

MEADOR, L. C. IT/strategy alignment - identifying the role of information technology in competitive strategy. **Working Paper** n. 9403. Disponível em: <http://www.it-consultancy.com/background/alignment/index.html>. Acesso em: 21 out. 1997.

MINTZBERG, H.; QUINN, J. B. O processo da estratégia. 3. ed. Porto Alegre : Bookman, 2001.

PREMKUMAR, G.; KING, W. R. An empirical assessment of information systems planning and the role of information systems in organizations. Journal of Management Information Systems, v. 9, p. 99; Armonk; Fall 1992.

PUKSZTA, H. Don't split IT strategy from business strategy. **Computerworld,** Framingham, v. 33, n. 2, p. 35, 11 Jan. 1999.

REZENDE, D. A.; ABREU, A. F. Tecnologia da Informação aplicada a Sistemas de Informação Empresariais. São Paulo : Atlas, 2000.

STRASSMANN, P.; BIENKOWSKI, D. Alignment of IT and business: key to realizing business value. **ABT Corp. White Paper**, August 1999. Disponível em: <http://www.strassmann.com/index.shtml>. Acesso em: 21 ago. 1999.

TALLON, P. P.; KRAEMER, K. L.; GURBAXANI, V.; et al. A multidimensional assessment of the contribution of information technology to firm performance. In: ECIS, 1997. **Proceedings eletrônicos...** Disponível em: <http://www.gsm.uci.edu/~ptallon/ecis97.html>. Acesso em: 06 maio 1997.

TURBAN, E.; MCLEAN, E.; WETHERBE, J. Information Technology for Management: Improving Quality and Productivity. New York, John Wiley and Sons, 1996.

YETTON, P. W.; JOHNSTON, K. D.; CRAIG, J. F. Computer-aided architects: a case study of IT and strategic change. **Sloan Management Review,** p. 57-67, Summer 1994.

The Impact of National Culture on the Meaning of Information Systems Success: Implications for IS Standardization in Multinational Corporations

Hafid Agourram and John Ingham
University of Sherbrooke, Quebec, Canada, Email: Hafid.agourram@sympatico.ca, Jingham@adm.usherb.ca

ABSTRACT

Information system success is still one of the most searchable IS topic in the IS discipline. The difficulty of defining IS success was found in a particular context namely the north American context since the majority of IS research has been dominated by north American researchers. As the world globalizes, large organizations namely Multinational organizations sees in IT and IS a crucial and a necessary tool hat glues all the units of the Corporation. Moreover, IS standardization (i.e., the same IS implemented in all the units) has attracted these Corporations because of the economic benefits standard applications can yield to. However, researchers in the international management discipline have assessed that culture is a major factor that influences organizations in general and some researchers in IS have also confirmed that culture does have an impact on IS. As culture is defined as "A shared system of meaning", the success of IS would hold different meanings as we move from a culture to another. We found no research work on how people from different national cultures perceive, define and opertaionalize IS success. The purpose of this research proposal is develop a model of IS success in different national cultures. This paper includes problem definition, research framework and research methodology. The results of the research will be published in subsequent issues of the proceedings.

INTRODUCTION

From the most recent list of IS research mainstream, Marcus (2000) argues that one of the most enduring research topics in the field of information systems is that of information systems success. The importance of, and the urge to cohesively define the dependent variable (IS success) was first called by Keen (1980) when he presented a list of five issues that IS researchers need to resolve (DeLone and McLean, 1992). DeLone and McLean (1992) argued that if information systems research is to make a contribution to the world of practice, a well-defined outcome measure is essential.

Today, managers are still frustrated because the problem of IS success definition and measurement has no definite or clear answer (Myers et al., 1998). This problem of IS definition and measurement has largely been documented in North America. We specify North America because most IS research has been dominated by this continent's researchers. The IS success problem becomes more complicated for large organizations or Multinational Corporations, which conduct business activities in different parts of the globe; that is, in different contexts or cultures. This complexity grows in intensity in case a Multinational Corporation seeks to standardize the IS in all of its subsidiaries. This complexity is largely justified by the impact that culture has on human behavior, attitudes, and beliefs, which in turn influence managerial practices and the variety of systems used in that particular culture.

A Multinational Corporation that decided to standardize an IS in all the subsidiaries faces two major challenges. First, the system needs to be implemented successfully; that is, the system needs to successfully enter the operational phase of its cycle. Second, it needs, at an appropriate time, to measure either objectively or subjectively the success of the system; that is, the outcome from implementing the new system. Both challenges are within a particular context; the subsidiary context or culture.

North American researchers have developed many IS success models. However these models are developed by people whose ideas and propositions reflect, in a way, what North American people believe. Put differently, these researchers know something about the meaning system or constructs systems of people who belong to the North American culture. However, cross-cultural research has largely suggested that it is not obvious to take these made-in-the-USA models and theories and apply them to different contexts or cultures (Hofstede, 1980; Laurent, 1983; Maurice, 1979; Tayeb, 1994; Trompenaars, 1993). Moreover, in reviewing the literature, we could not find any research work on how people in different cultures define, operationalize, or measure IS success. The intent of this dissertation is to fill in the gap and to bring some insight to this issue.

Multinational Corporations are perfect means for conducting cross-cultural research. Until the headquarters of a Multinational Corporation, which seeks to standardize IS, understands what a successful information system means for its employees in a specific subsidiary located in a specific culture, and master the way these people operationalize it so that it can either adapt the new system to their beliefs and their values or take the challenge to act on their values and beliefs and adapt them to the way the corporate office define IS success, the IS implementation and IS success are left to chance.

Our research proposal is structured mainly according to Creswell (1994) recommendations for qualitative research design. However, other recommendations and guidelines from Yin (1984) and Marshall and Rossman (1995) are also taken into consideration.

The following sections provide detailed discussions about:

- The research problem components;
- The purpose of the study;
- The research framework.

The Research Problem Components

IS success. The dependent variable (IS success) is a multidimensional construct and there is no single overarching measure (Pitt and Watson, 1994). A new line of research on IS success has emerged since DeLone and McLean's (1992) work on IS Success. The authors proposed to consider IS success as a process linking six variables: namely, IS Quality, Information Quality, Usage, User Satisfaction, Individual Impact, and Organizational Impact. Three levels of IS success can be deduced from the model. These are the systems level, the individual level, and the organizational level. Figure 1 illustrates these levels.

Figure 1: IS success levels.

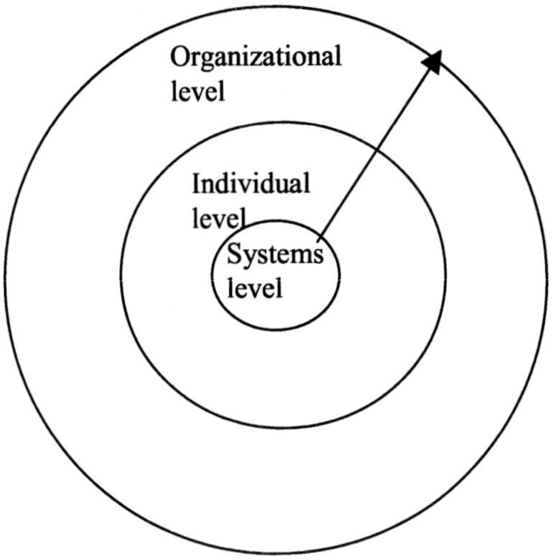

From the authors' conclusions, we can argue that IS Success is neither well understood nor well defined in the American context or culture. We specify the American context because the Meta analysis upon which the article was based concerns only the American research work on IS success. In practice, Marcus (2000) reported on the results of a survey on ERP (Enterprise Resource Planning) implementation projects that KPMG Management Consulting' recent report "Profit-Focused Software Packages Implementation", showed some worrying results. Eighty-nine per cent of respondent companies claimed that their projects were successful, but only a quarter had actually obtained and quantified all the planned benefits. Thus, adds the author, this quotation illustrates a fundamental gap in both practical and academic thinking about information systems lack of consensus and clarity about the meaning of "Success" where information systems are concerned (Marcus, 2000).

In the international context where cultural terms such as values and assumptions are used, Shing-Kao (1997) argues that research has shown that people notice, interpret and retain information based on their values, assumptions and expectations and that different assumptions and values lead to different ways of looking at the same thing.

This international differing perception of the meaning of a phenomenon is considered as a hot topic in International Management or cross-cultural Management disciplines. Do theories and concepts born in North America apply or have the same meaning elsewhere? Hofstede (1981), for example, after a large survey on work-related values in sixty countries, concluded that management theories and findings are not automatically transferable from one context to another.

Shing-Kao (1997) adds that the majority of theories of management have a western and, therefore, generally, an American perspective that is based on the embedded values that influence the ways in which Americans perceive and think about the world, as well as the way in which they behave within that world (Kedia and Bhagat, 1988; Robichaux et al., 1998).

However the majority of North American researchers do not explicitly state the context for which their proposed theory is built. They assume that their findings are culture-free (Kedia and Bhagat, 1988) which is not to be taken for granted (Hofstede, 1993).

Moreover, Rosenzweig (1994) argues that a central concern in scientific research is external validity. That is the extent to which a theorized or observed relationship among variables can be generalized to other settings. The author does not mean external validity within a specific context or culture; rather, he questions the applicability of these relationships to other contexts and other cultures; that is the international dimension of the theory. The author based his argument on the basic definition of science which is "a systematic method of inquiry that consists of several stages, including: 1) definition and operationalization of variables; 2) the emerged relationship among variables; and 3) measurement of variables to test hypotheses. He further argues that the international generalization of management science research encounters obstacles at each of these stages of the scientific process.

In concluding, the author claims that the main question should not be, "Are management science theories that interest us valid elsewhere"? But how can we best understand management, as it exists around the world? (p.37). And this is exactly the main purpose of this research project where we seek to understand the IS Success in different national cultures.

Culture. Culture is a term that was originally developed in the field of Anthropology and has recently become a prevalent research area in organizational studies. Unfortunately, a consistent definition of this ambiguous concept is extremely difficult to find (Lammers and Hickson; 1979). Krant (1975) has even suggested that in light of this difficulty, it would be desirable not to use the term culture in cross-organizational studies of organizations. However, researchers need to deal with culture in cross-cultural organizational studies. It is the only way to help understanding how and why organizations are similar and different (Lammers and Hickson, 1979).

Baligh (1994) argues that there are many ways to describe and define culture and that one may conceive of culture in terms of its parts or its components, and the two are related. According to Baligh (1994), the functional segments or parts are: family, language and communication, religion, government and politics, education, transformation and technology, society, and economic structures and activities (business). Organizations, adds the author, are a part of a number of these, notably the last one. "A culture may be defined in terms of these parts" (p. 16). The components of culture are: truth, beliefs, values, logic, rules, and actions.

Schein (1990) links the cultural concept to the dual pressures upon human beings: to face external adaptation and internal integration and to propose to define culture as:

(a) A pattern of basic assumptions,
(b) Invented, discovered, or developed by a given group,
(c) As it learns to cope with its problems of external adaptation and internal Integration,
(d) That has worked well enough to be considered valid and therefore,
(e) Is to be taught to new members as the
(f) Correct way to perceive, think, and feel in relation to those problems.

Culture is then applied to a group of people who share a common understanding and meaning of things around them. It is a shared system of meaning (Trompenaars and Hampden-Turner, 1998) or the collective programming of the human mind that distinguishes members of one group from another (Hofstede, 1993).

Figure 2: Trompenaars and Hampden-Turner (1998) cultural model

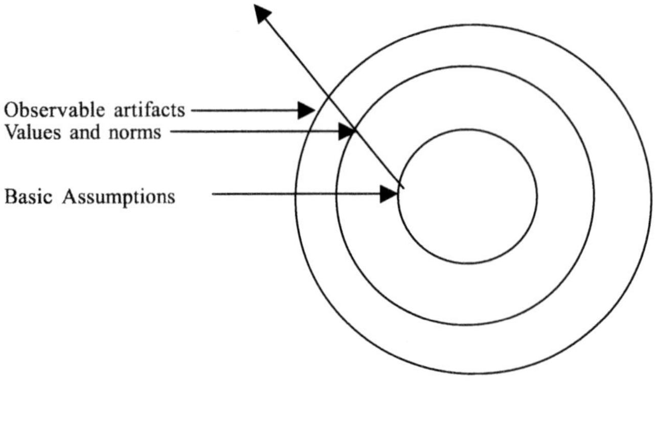

Schein (1990) proposes a cultural model and claims that there are three levels of culture:

(a) Observable artifacts;
(b) Values;
(c) Basic assumptions.

Trompenaars and Hampden-Turner (1998) call these levels "layers" and propose the following framework, which forms the cultural model and shows the relationship between these layers.

The model indicates that the products (observable artifacts) we see everywhere are symbols of the norms and values of the people living in that place which in turn are based on fundamental basic assumptions about human existence and life. The values of people in a particular culture are the most widely used concept or variable in cross-cultural studies (Glenn and Glenn, 1981; Hofstede, 1980; Triandis et al., 1982).

The reason behind the popularity of values as cross-cultural research variables is because the deeper layer of culture; basic assumptions are preconscious (taken for granted) and are powerful because they are less debatable than espoused values (Lachman et al., 1994). Schein (1990) argues that basic assumptions are values that become stronger and are usually taken for granted.

Hofstede's model of national culture is based on work-related values and is one of the most widely used models in cross-cultural management. In addition, Hofstede's framework has been increasingly employed in information system research (Straub, 1994; Watson and Ho, 1994). Hofstede's work on culture is based only on work-related values of people in different cultures.

IS Standardization. Standards are defined as "A set of rules or policies governing the characteristics of software and/or hardware that an organization may purchase or develop" (Gordon, 1992, p. 275).

The benefits of IS standardization in MNC's subsidiaries is the output of a complex equation which includes exogenous variables such as the economical and socio-political environments of the subsidiaries and the cultural gap between the home country and the host country. The endogen variables include the company's structure, strategy, and the built-in assumptions of the information system to standardize. IS built-in assumptions are not well documented in the literature and are believed to be a critical barrier to IS transfer and implementation across cultures (Davenport, 1998).

IS Built-In-Assumptions. "Information systems have built-in values biases reflecting the value priorities of the culture in which they are developed" (Krumar and Bjoin-Anderson, 1990, p. 535). This means that a cultural misfit is likely to occur if an information system or information technology developed in one culture is implemented in an organization in another culture (Leither et al., 1999).

The outcomes and use of IS depend then on the degree of the "fit" between their built-in assumptions which are based on the designers values (Krumar and Bjoin-Anderson, 1990; Watson et al., (1994) and the assumptions and the values of the adopting organisation. Both implementation and success of a standard information system in different national cultures are targeted by the misfit problem. The problem comes from differences in meaning. Here we have two meanings: the shared system of meaning of people living in a particular national culture (e.g. their culture) and the built-in meaning of the system; that is, its built-in assumptions concerning the reason behind its development and the expected impact on its users. When the systems built-in assumptions do not fit the assumptions and the meaning given by its future users, then its built-in success assumptions are likely to differ from the meaning of its success from the perspective of these users. Two types of IS built-in success assumptions emerge then: IS built-in implementation success assumptions, and IS built-in success assumptions. This classification is deduced from Marcus et al., (2000) categories; IS implementation success and IS ongoing success and adapted to IS built-in assumptions. The authors argue that IS success in general can be divided as early success (implementation success) and later success (upward success) of the system and the two constructs are not closely related, that is, even if successfully implemented, the upward success is not guaranteed. Even if an adopting organization judges that both early and later successes are achieved in a particular culture, this is less likely to occur in the case of IS transfers from two different cultures as stated by Leither et al., (1999). "Even if successfully implemented, such systems may not yield the same benefits as they do in the culture from which the systems originally emerge". One probable cause for this is the misfit between IS built-in success assumptions and the meaning of IS success given by the adopting organization.

Multinational Corporations, which aim to standardize information systems in all of its subsidiaries usually, face a challenging problem of both early and later successes (Robey and Rodriguez-Diaz, 1989).

Assuming that many corporate factors may lead to standard IS implementation success (early success), the meaning of the success of

Figure 3: An integrated framework of cultural and IS success layers

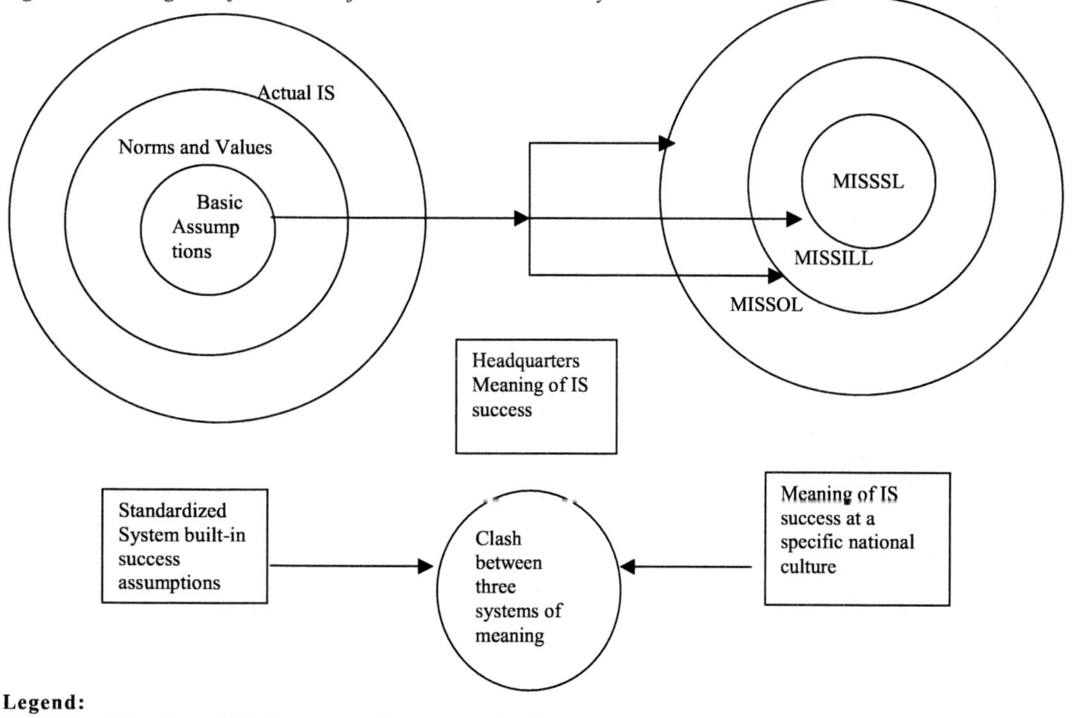

Legend:
MISSSL: Meaning of IS Success at the systems level
MISSIL: Meaning of IS success at the individual level
MISSOL: Meaning of IS success at the organizational level

the standardized system in a particular subsidiary of the MNC which is located in a different national culture is likely to be different from the meaning given by the headquarters and the IS built-in success assumptions. This is mainly due to the existence of many shared systems of meanings and the meaning of the system itself.

The Research Purpose

The purpose of this study is to discover and understand the meaning of IS success in different national cultures using a case study design, resulting in case study research.

The Research Framework

Explanations. The first three circles on the upper left side of the framework show the cultural layers of any subsidiary as proposed by Trompennars and Hampden-Turner (1998). These are: basic assumptions, norms and values, and products layers. In the product layer, we choose the IS as a product. The arrow linking the three layers shows the dependency among them as proposed by Trompennars and Hampden-Turner (1998) and described earlier in this document.

The second set of circles shows our proposed representation of IS success levels. It shows three levels of analyses of IS success: systems level, individual level, and organizational level. For the purpose of our research, the levels are used to show the meaning of IS success at each level.

We argues that the left set of circles (culture) influences the meaning of IS success at the systems level, the individual level and the organizational level. The model also shows the intersection of three systems of meanings: the meaning of IS success in a particular national culture, its meaning as defined by the headquarters office and the built-in success assumptions of the future standard system.

RESEARCH PROCEDURE

Research Questions

Based on the recommendations of Creswell (1994) and Marshall and Rossman (1995) concerning the structure of the research questions, the following are the Grand tour research questions.

- What is the meaning of IS success from the perspective of people living in a different national cultures and how is it operationalized?
- How are the categories at each level of the emerging construct of IS success weighed (i.e. which are more important than others) in each national culture?
- In the case of IS standardization in a Multinational Corporation, what is the gap between the meaning of IS success from the perspective of the headquarters of the MNC, the meaning of IS success from the perspective of each subsidiary, and the built-in success assumptions of the standardized system itself?

Research Approach and Paradigm

We will use the interpretative paradigm and the case study strategy approach in this project. This is mainly linked to the purpose of our research which is to discover the meaning of IS success in different national cultures.

The Case and the Units of Analysis.

Our case is a multibillion-dollar Canadian Multinational Corporation with subsidiaries in many national cultures. The MNC decided to standardize information systems in all of its subsidiaries. The standard system is chosen and a multibillion-dollar contract is signed. The Corporation decided to standardise an ES (Enterprise System) in all of its subsidiaries.

Our units are three subsidiaries of the Multinational Corporation, which are located in Germany, France and Canada. We based our selections of these units on the organizational model of Hofstedee (1981).

Research Technique

We need a research technique that would enable to eliminate the researcher's bias since we are dealing with the very sensitive concept of culture and one that helps to get the system of meaning of each research participant. Kelly's (1955) Repertory Grid is the best tool that responds to our needs. In fact, the Rep Grid interviewing technique allows to almost eliminating the researcher bias and helps to get the constructs system of a person, that is his or her system of meaning about a particular part of the world.

Basic Concepts Associated with the Technique

Elements. These are lists of words, which define the kind of interview you have, by selecting the subject matter. They must be discrete (people, objects, events and activities). They must be homogenous, that is, not a mixture of classes of elements (people with objects) and they should not be subsets of other elements. The researcher can supply them to the participants, or can get them by free responses from the participants.

Construct. This is the bipolar distinction, which represents the dimensions the interviewee uses when he is thinking about the elements.

Construct elicitation. This is the process of getting constructs from elements by asking the interviewee to put two together and separate them from the third. This Triadic-comparison procedure, by asking for both a similarity and a difference gets out both ends of each construct.

The Stages of the Technique

Rep Grid comprises four research stages or procedures (Marsden and Littler; 1998)

- Elements selection
- Construct elicitation
- Elements comparison
- Data analysis

The Application of the Technique In Our Project

The purpose of our research project is to discover and understand the meaning of IS success in different national cultures using an interpretive approach, a qualitative mode of inquiry, a quantitative and qualitative mode of analysis, and a Case study strategy.

It is amazing how large is the quantity of information that can be produced from using Repertory Grid technique. Peters (1994) mentioned that a 6 element Grid might generate on average, thirty constructs per interview. We are expecting to conduct about twenty interviews in each subsidiary.

The respondents. There are three categories of respondents; key informants such as top managers, middle managers, and IS specialists from each subsidiary, the ES project management team at the Headquarters office, and ES vendor.

The elements. Ideally, the elements should identify Information systems. However and for the sake of simplicity and ambiguity avoidance, we will use IS Applications as our elements. Furthermore, the research participants should have a lot of experience in working with various IS Applications. Each participant will be asked to choose or to think of six IS Applications he or she has worked with during the last five to eight years.

Elicitation question. The participant will be asked to first think of six IS applications he has used or worked with in the last five to eight years. Two, which are characterized by a high degree of success, tow which are characterized by a very low degree of success and two, which are characterized by average degree of success. The names of the Applications will be written down on six cards with one name on each card. The participant will then be asked to randomly pick sets of three cards and for each set, he will be asked the following elicitation questions:

- «How are two applications alike yet different from the third in terms of their effectiveness or success at the systems level? » (Systems level)
- «How are the same two applications alike yet different from the third in terms of their impact on a person? » (Individual level).

- «How are the same two application alike yet different from the third in terms of their impact on the organization? » (Organizational level).

The whole process of construct elicitation and the Rep Grid questionnaire will take about an hour and a half. We are expecting to conduct about twenty interviews in each subsidiary. Once all the constructs are elicited, the participant is asked to enter a digit 1 to 5 at the intersection cell of each application and each construct. The digit corresponds to the degree of concordance of the construct to the application.

Data Analysis

At the end of our data collection process, we will end up with about 60 completed Repertory Grid questionnaires. Each Grid will have 6 elements, a number of bipolar constructs and the ranking of each element according to each construct. We will use Software packages such as "Enquire Within" to speed up the analysis process. This package allows us to enter the elements, the construct and the ranking numbers of each Repertory Grid questionnaire, to perform cluster analysis on elements and on constructs. In performing cluster analysis on element, we will be able to see and compare each set of software applications (elements). In performing clusters analysis on constructs, we will be able to identify the relationship between the constructs. Our research purpose is linked to the later analysis (cluster analysis on constructs) rather than to elements analysis. The output of the software package application, which performs cluster analysis, is a graph that shows the relationships between elements on the one hand and between constructs on the other. These relationships are based on the correlation indices. The constructs that are highly correlated are grouped together to form a subset of the graph. The graph does provide excellent information about the relationship between constructs but it is the researcher who needs to interpret these relationships. There is no software package, which allows entering all sets of elements and their associated constructs. Our aim is to emerge the categories of IS success in each national culture. That is, we will need to find the meaning of IS success in France, in Germany and in Canada. However, in conducting only cluster analysis, we would not answer our research Grand tour questions. We will also need to conduct a content analysis on all Grids questionnaires in each country for IS meaning categories development. Beck and Hunter (2000), in their work on what is an excellent systems analyst in Singapore and in Canada, have performed content analyses on all questionnaires in each country.

Frequency counts analysis will allow us to determine the ranking of preferences of each IS success category.

THE SIGNIFICANCE OF THE STUDY.

This study targets both academic and practice communities particularly Multinational Corporations that wish to standardize IS in all the subsidiaries.

Research on the impact of national culture on IS in general has been encouraged (Ein Dor, 1992). We do not know of any research work on national culture and the meaning of IS success. This thesis is aimed to bring some contribution in this area. The world meaning in the last statement is rather than important. Our intent is not to measure the impact of national culture on IS success, as we do not know its meaning elsewhere. The intent is to develop a model, which describes the different categories or constructs of IS success in three national cultures which are described later in the units of analysis section. Further research in this area can test our findings and verify its robustness and use these findings for international IS success measurement instrument development.

This research will also be beneficial for practitioners, especially MNC practitioners. As Multinational Corporations extend their activities world-wide and as the need to optimize the famous balance between the subsidiaries' autonomy to respond to the local market needs and the consistency of the subsidiaries to the headquarters policies, corporate culture and general philosophies, MNC turn to IS standardization as a mean to achieve this goal.

Even if a standardized information system is implemented, its contribution to the performance of the subsidiary and, therefore, to the overall performance of the MNC is not guaranteed.

This project will have two outputs: a theoretical framework of the meaning of IS success in different national cultures as well as a distribution of the relative importance (weight) of each IS success categories and, second, the gap between the meaning of the standardized IS success from the headquarters perspective, the meaning of IS success from the subsidiary perspective, and the built-in success assumptions perspective.

The research findings should be considered as a guide to the implementation team in their effort to implement a standard IS in different national cultures. We propose that the implementation team should provide a set of tools and procedures to fit the meaning of the standardized system success from the Headquarters' perspective, the meaning of IS success from the subsidiary perspective, and the built-in success of the standardized systems.

We argue that the "fit" project will help to achieve a high degree of contribution of the standardized IS to local subsidiary performance and, therefore, the MNC overall performance.

THE LIMITATIONS OF THE STUDY.

This study has many limitations. First, the academic constraints and the budget of the research will not permit conducting the research in more than three national cultures. Second, the site selection will be based on the findings of previous research on work-related values of culture and not on all parts or components of national cultures. Third, as this research is about meaning and perception, researchers' and respondents' biases will occur even if we use a data collection technique, which theoretically allows reducing them to zero.

REFERENCES

Baligh, H.H. "Components of Culture: Nature, Interconnections, and Relevance to the Decisions on the Organization Structure", *Management Science*, Vol. 40, No. 1, 1994, pp. 14-27.

Creswell, J.W. *Research Design: Qualitative and Quantitative Approaches*, Sage Publications, 1994.

Davenport, T.H " Putting the enterprise into the enterprise system" *Harvard Business Review* , Vol. 76, No. 4, (1998).

DeLone, W.H and McLean, E.R. "Information Systems Success: The Quest for The Dependent Variable", in *Information Systems Research*, Vol. 3, No. 1, 1992, pp. 60-95.

Ein-Dor, P, Segev, E. and Orgad, M. "The Effect of National Culture on IS: Implications for International Information Systems", in *Journal of Global Information Management*, Vol. 1, No. 1, 1992, pp. 33-44.

Glenn, E.S. and Glenn, C.G. « *Man and Mankind: Conflict and Communication between Cultures* », Ablex, Northwood, NJ, 1981.

Gordon, S.R. "Standardization of Information Systems and Technology at Multinational Companies", in *IRMA Conference Proceedings*, 1992, pp. 274-278.

Gordon Hunter, M and Beck, J.E " Using Repertory Grid to Conduct cross-cultural Information Systems Research" *Information Systems Research*, Vol.11, No. 1, (2000).

Hofstede, G " *Cultures and organizations: software of the mind*". London, *McGraw-Hill* (1993).

Hofstede, G. "The Interaction between National and Organizational Value Systems", *in Journal of Management Studies*, Vol. 22, No. 4, 1985, pp. 347-357.

Hofstede, G. "Management Scientists Are Human", in *Management Science*, Vol. 44, No. 1, 1994, pp. 4-13.

Hofstede, G. "Motivation, Leadership and organization: do American theories apply abroad?", *Organizational Dynamics*, Vol. 75; 1980, pp. 42-63.

Kedia, B.L and Bhagat, R.S. "Cultural Constraints on Transfer of Technology Across Nations: Implications for Research in International and Comparative Management", in *Academy of Management Review*, Vol. 13, No.4, 1988, pp. 559-571.

Keen, G.W "References Disciplines and a Cumulative Tradition", *Proceedings of the First International Conference on Information Systems*, December, 1980.

Kelly, G.A "*The Psychology of Personal Constructs*", 1955, New York, Norton.

Krant, A..I "Some recent advances in Cross-national management research" *Academy of Management journal,* Vol. 18, 1975, pp. 538-549.

Krumar, k. and Bjrn-Andersen, LA. "Cross-Cultural Comparison of IS designer values" *Communications of the ACM*, Vol. 33. No. 5, May 1990, pp. 528-538.

Lachman, R, Nedd, A and Hinings, B. "Analyzing Cross-national Management and Organizations: A Theoretical Framework", in *Management Science*, Vol. 40, No. 1, 1994, pp. 40-55.

Lammers, C.J and Hickson, D. J "*Organisations alike and unlike: Toward a comparative sociology of organisations"*. London: Routledge and Kegan Paul. 1979.

Laurent. A. "The cultural diversity of western conceptions of management", *International Studies of Management and Organizations,* Vol. XIII, No. 1-2; 1983; ME Shape,Inc., pp. 75-96.

Leidner, D.E, Carlsson, S and Corrales, M. "Mexican and Swedish managers' Perceptions of the impact of EIS on organizational intelligence, decision making and Structure", *Decision sciences*, Vol. 30, No. 3, 1999, pp. 633-658.

Marcus, M.L, Axline, S, Petrie, D and Tanis, C; "Learning from adopters' experience with ERP: problems encountered and success achieved", *Journal of Information Technology*, Vol. 15, 2000, pp. 245-265.

Marshall, C. and Rossman, G.B. *Designing Qualitative Research,* Second Edition, Sage Publications, 1995.

Maurice, M. "*For a study of the societal effect: the universality and specifity in Organizational research*", 1979; in Lammers, C.J and Hickson, D.J (Eds), Organizations alike and unlike, Routledge and Kegan Paul, London.

Myers, B.L, Kappelman, L.A and Prybutok, V.R "*A Comprehensive Model for Assessing the Quality and Productivity of the Information Systems Function: Toward a Theory for Information Systems Assessment*", Idea Group Publishing, Chapter 6, 1998.

Peters, W.L "Repertory Grid as a Tool for Training Needs Analysis" *The Learning Organization,* Vol. 1, No. 2, 1994.

Pitt, Watson and Kavan. "Measuring Service Quality in Information Systems" *Working paper. Department of Management. University of Georgia, 1994.*

Robey, D. and Rodriguez-Diaz, A. "The Organizational and Cultural Context of System Implementation: Case Experience from Latin America", *in Information and Management*, Vol. 17, 1989, pp. 229-239.

Rosenzweig, P.M. "When Can Management Science Research Be Generalized Internationally?" *in Management Science*, Vol. 40, No. 1, 1994, pp. 28-39.

Schein, E.H. "Organizational Culture", in *American Psychologist,* Vol. 45, No. 2, 1990, pp. 109-119.

Shing-Kao, L "*A study of National Culture versus Corporate Culture in International Management"*. Dissertation, Nova South-eastern University, 1997.

Straub, D.W " The effect of culture on IT diffusion: E-mail and Fax in Japan and the U.S.A" *Information systems research*, Vol. 5, 1994, pp 23-47.

Tayeb, M. "Organizations and national culture: methodology considered*", Organizations Studies,* Vol. 15, No. 3, 1994, pp. 429-446.

Triandis, H.C, McCusker, C, Hui, C.H "Multi-method probes of Individualism and Collectivism", *Journal of Personality and Social Psychology*, 1982.

Trompenaars, F.T. and Hampden-Turner, C.H. *Riding The Waves of Culture – Understanding Diversity in Global Business*, McGraw-Hill, 1988.

Trompenaars, F. "*Riding the waves of culture: Understanding Cultural Diversity in Business"*, Economics Books, London, 1993.

Watson, R.T, Ho, T.H and Raman, K.S "Culture: A fourth dimension of group support systems" *Communication of the ACM,* Vol. 37, 1994, pp. 44-55.

Watson, R,T and Brancheau , J,C "Key Issues in information system management: an international perspective*" Information and Management,* Vol. 20, No. 3, 1991.

Yin, R.K "Case Study Research, Design and Methods" in Sage Publication, 1984.

Yin, R, K "Case Study Research: Design and Methods", 1989, *Newbury Park, CA: Sage.*

Web-Based Supply Chain Integration Model

Latif Al-Hakim
Faculty of Business, University of Southern Queensland, Australia, hakim@usq.edu.au

ABSTRACT

This paper discusses various business process supply-chain models and emphasises that firms need to apply CRM concepts and to integrate the Internet within the functions of sales, services and marketing to be able to gain good customer expectations in the era of e-commerce. This paper outlines a framework for developing a web-based supply chain integrating model and attempts to link this model with traditional productivity improvement programs. The paper suggests the development of a website of two levels, the first level is within the public domain and the other is limited to supply chain partners.

INTRODUCTION

Traditionally, firms did not consider the potential for their suppliers or customers to become partners. Instead, they may have competed with their suppliers and customers, fearing that they would be taken advantage of by them [6]. As a result, firms were constrained by their customers' or suppliers' lack of collaboration and unresponsiveness. These attributes prevented firms from responding quickly to changes in the market or to customers' requirements.

The changing conditions of competition have forced organizations to now adopt a different strategy. Lambert and Copper [9] point out that one of the most significant paradigm shifts of modern business management has been that individual businesses no longer compete as solely autonomous entities, but rather as supply chains. Managing the supply chain has become a means of improving competitiveness [5,10]. The association of supply chain management with e-business and the Internet offer new challenges for marketing. This association allows companies to interact with customers and collect enormous volumes of data and manipulate it in many different ways to bring out otherwise unforeseen areas of knowledge [1]. The concept of Customer Relationship Management (CRM) is one of the new ways of interacting with customers[7]. The aim of this paper is to explain the possibility of developing a web-based supply chain integration model that enhances CRM by incorporating the advantages of existing supply chain reference models.

CUSTOMER RELATIONSHIP MANAGEMENT

CRM is about the management of technology, processes, information resources, and people needed to create an environment that allows a business to take a 360-degree view of its customers [7]. CRM environments, by nature, are complex and require organisational change and a new way of thinking about customers and about business in general. Creating such an environment also requires a new form of leadership. Within the framework of supply chain, such an environment is grounded in three core principles: (1) customer satisfaction, (2) collaboration and partnership, and (3) continual improvement and learning. While CRM environments improve business performance, initiatives undertaken in this new management field require sound leadership as well. The current focus of CRM tends to be almost entirely on the front office. Extending CRM into multiple media means interacting the front office (and aspects of back office where appropriate) with different communication channels [4].

Creating the optimal CRM environment within the supply chain is and will increasingly become a rapidly growing critical business challenge. CRM is a major strategic challenge for the twenty-first century [6].

INTERNET AND WEBSITES

The Internet plays a significant role in the development of supply chains. Through the combination of interactivity, networking, multimedia and data processing, the Internet offers a wide variety of new generation e-commerce opportunities. With effective websites, the Internet not only supports application-to-application e-commerce similar to that of traditional electronic data interchange (EDI), but also person-to-person and person-to-application forms of e-commerce. Courier or distribution services such as Federal Express (FedEx) allows customers to track their packages over the Internet [16]. Dell's suppliers share demand and inventory information online with the company . Netscape and Shockwave fill and deliver orders over the Internet through downloads of electronic products [17,18]. Companies can use the Internet for negotiations and auctions to set prices of products and services. Companies like eBay allow people to auction products over the Internet [15].

However, it is not enough for a company to develop websites and provide its customers easy access to its products world wide, while not being able to deliver on time as a result of poor customer service or delay in delivery due to lack of integration between its supply chain elements.

BUSINESS PROCESS MODELS

To achieve a healthy CRM environment and to reap maximum benefits from websites for developing effective supply chain, companies are seeking ways to totally satisfy customers. High quality, competitive prices, and JIT delivery are but three factors among many others that enhance customer satisfaction. While the first two factors require continual improvement of the supply chain processes, the JIT delivery necessitates coordination, communication and collaboration among suppliers. Lee [66] surmises that supply chain complexity grows exponentially since companies use the services of multiple suppliers, and each of them often has their own suppliers. Gunasekaran et. al [8] emphasise that because of the increase in the complexity of the supply chain, companies rarely manage the supply chain without a framework. As a result, such a framework (model) provides the following in addition to the CRM core principles mentioned earlier:

(1) continual improvement of the entire supply chain business processes:
(2) valid line of customers' feedback to orient the improvement;
(3) seamless flow of information along a company's supply chain;
(4) a channel that makes it possible for information to be located at a central source, such as the seller's Web server.

Modelling the processes for the supply chain is also necessary because companies have an overwhelming number of processes that require integration. Modelling will help expose patterns among business units and supply partners [2]. There are several process reference models available in the market. Tthe most well known ones are the Supply-Chain Operations Reference model (SCOR), the Collaborative Planning, Forecasting and Replenishment model (CPFR), and the Demand Activated Manufacturing Architecture model (DAMA).

SCOR was developed by Supply-Chain Council (SCC) in 1996. SCOR is an extension of business process reengineering [13]. It classifies business processes into four basic processes - plan, source, make, and deliver. It classifies these processes into detailed sub-processes and offers benchmark metrics to compare process performance to objective, external points of reference. It also describes the best-in-class management practices. This allows companies to prioritise their activities, quantify the potential benefits of specific process improvement, and determine financial justifications. However, SCOR lacks in the area of external supply chain collaborative planning and long term forecasting. Though, the level 4 of SCOR focuses on implementation, the specific elements of the level are not defined within the industry-standard model [13,14]. SCOR lacks a roadmap for process improvement.

CPFR is a strategic cross-industry initiative designed to improve supplier and retailer partnerships through co-managed processes and shared information. CPFR involves collaboration and joint planning to make long-term projections which are constantly updated based on actual demand and market changes [12]. Most initiatives in CPFR involve external supply chain collaboration. However, CPFR has several barriers [3] which make the system sensitive to the agile environment:

(1) Ineffective replenishment in response to demand fluctuations;
(2) Ineffective planning using visibility of POS customer demand; and
(3) Difficulty to manage the forecast exception/review process (sales and order forecast).

DAMA represents an effort focused on increasing the competitiveness of the fiber, textile, apparel, and retail industries [11]. Similar to CPFR, DAMA focuses on the external supply chain collaboration. In addition, DAMA lacks performance measurements and does not provide any sub-process details of any processes.

Table 1 compares some key features of the three models. The asterisks indicate that the model incorporates the particular feature.

Table 1: Comparisons of the three models

	Feature	Model		
		SCOR	CPFR	DAMA
1	External collaboration / planning	-	*	*
2	Detailed internal processes	*	-	-
3	Performance measurement	*	*	-
4	Benchmarking	*	-	-
5	Best-class practices	*	*	-
6	Techniques / analysis tools	-	*	*
7	POS feedback / analysis	-	*	*
8	Logical information flow	-	*	*
9	Roadmap for implementation	-	*	*
10	Agility	*	-	-
11	Improvement program	-	-	-
12	Website feature	-	-	-

INTEGRATING MODEL

To create a more comprehensive model, we found that it is possible to enhance the SCOR with key features of other models and to link with traditional productivity programs in a way that improves the productivity of the whole supply chain. This can be managed within an integrating website comprised of two levels. The first level of the website is in the public domain. It allows consumers to track their orders in real time and to provide their input on a regular basis. This level can be used to obtain answers to questions such as:

- Which products/services meet your expectations? Which do not?
- What products/services do you need that you are not receiving?

The second level is only accessible to supply chain partners and suppliers. This level allows partners and suppliers to access internal information, POS data, and partners' specific activities. It also helps in identifying the core competence of each partner.

Both levels are used to identify potential processes in the chain with a view to possible improvement of these processes. The implementation of a productivity improvement program requires mapping the logical flow of information in association with best class practices. Figure 1 illustrates such mapping. It is also possible to introduce improvement program such as the traditional Productivity Improvement Program (PIP) suggested by the American Institute of Industrial Engineers . Table 2 demonstrates the relationships between the PIP and SCOR processes. With such relationships, the link between SCOR elements and specific improvement activities could be identified and the program could, with some modification, be applied.

Table 2: Identification SCOR elements related to PIP areas of improvement

Area for Improvement	SCOR Processes
Receiving	S1.2 – S1.4, ES3
Material flow	EM6
Material Handling	ES, EM
Plant layout	EM5
Production control	M1.1 – M1.6, EM3, EM4, EM5
Warehousing	M1.4 – M1.6, EM3, EM6
Shipping	D1.2 –D1.8
Maintenance	EM5

Figure 1: Mapping S1.2

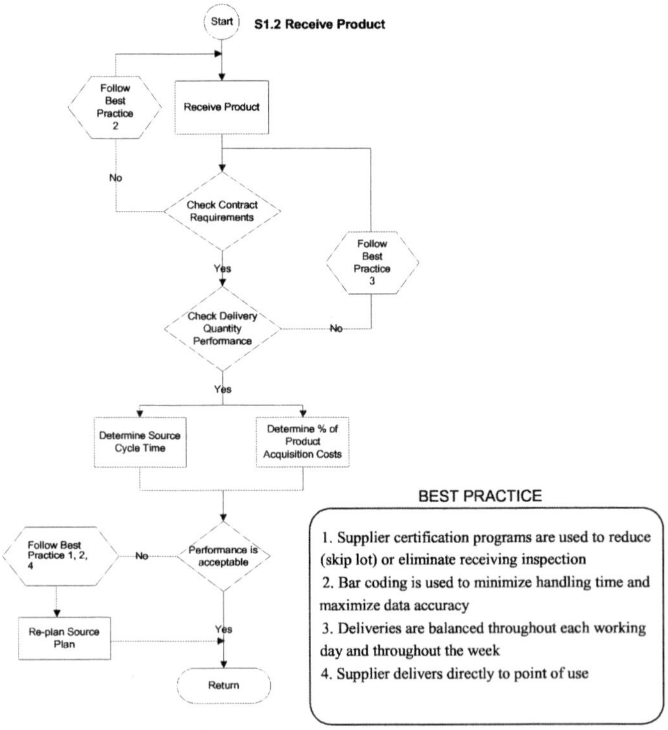

REFERENCES

1. Abbott, J., "Data data everywhere-and not a byte of use?" International Journal of Qualitative Market Research, 4(3), 2001. pp.182-192.

2. Alvarado, U.Y., Kotzab, H., "Supply chain management: the integration of logistics in marketing", Industrial Marketing Management, 30, 2001. pp.183-198.
3. Barrat, M., and Oliveira, A., "Exploring the experiences of collaborative planning initiatives." International Journal of Physical Distribution & Logistics, 31(4), 2001. pp.266-289.
4. Bradshaw, D., and Brash, C., "Managing customer relationship in the e-business world: how to personalise computer relationships for increased profitability." International Journal of Retail & Distribution Management, 29(12), 2001. pp.520-529.
5. Chantra, C., and Kumar, S., "Supply chain management in theory and practices: a passing fad or a fundamental change?" Industrial Management & Data Systems, 100(3), 2000. pp.100-113.
6. Fredendall, L.D., Hill, E., "Basics of Supply Chain Management." CRC Press LLC, Florida, 2001.
7. Galbreath, J., and Rogers, T., "Customer relationship leadership: a leadership and motivation model for the twenty-first century business." The TQM Magazines, 11(3), 1999 pp.161-171.
8. Gunasekaran, A., Patel, C., and Tirtiroglu, E., "Performance measures and metrics in a supply chain environment", International Journal of Operation & Production Management, 21 (1/2), 2001. pp.71-87.
9. Lambert, D.M., Cooper, M.C., "Issues in supply chain management." Industrial Marketing Management, 29, 2000. pp.65-83.
10. Lee, H.L., "Creating value through supply chain integration." Supply Chain Management Review, 14 (4), 2000. pp.30-37.
11. Mitchiner, J., "DAMA Supply Chain Architecture", 1999 Supply Chain World Conference, Chiago, Illinois, April, 1999.
12. Stank, T., Daugherty, P., and Autry, C., "Collaborative planning: supporting automatic replenishment programs." Supply Chain Management, 4(2), 1999. pp.75-85.
13. Stewart, G., "Supply-chain operations reference model (SCOR): The first cross-industry framework for integrated supply-chain management", Logistics Information Management, Vol. 10, Issue 2, 1997. pp.62-67.
14. Supply Chain Council, Inc., "Supply-Chain Operations Reference-model: SCOR Version 4.0".2000; Refer also to http://www.supply-chain.org.
15. www.ebay.com
16. www.fedex.com
17. www.netscape.com
18. www.shockwave.com

Peru's Experience in Electronic Journalism

Antonio Díaz-Andrade and Martín Santana
ESAN—Escuela de Administración de Negocios para Graduados, Peru
Tel: (511) 317-7200, Fax: (511) 345-1328, adiaz@esan.edu.pe

INTRODUCTION

On line journalism dates back to the end of the 70s when Knight-Ridder launched an initiative to develop a videotext service called *Viewtron* which it latter dropped in 1986 after realizing losses of US$50 million. Still, Knight-Ridder's interest in online information services remained unwavering and, in 1988, it made a decision to buy *Dialog Information Services, Inc.*, a leader in information retrieval. Only a year later, the first signs of success already appeared. (Díaz & Meso, 1998).

By the end of the 80s, Gannet -*USA Today's* publisher- launched a daily summary comprising 18 news pieces in text format it called *USA Today Decisionline.* Almost simultaneously, Dow Jones published *The Wall Street Journal* and *Barron's* on Prodigy, or directly on the Internet, with interactive multimedia features (Díaz & Meso, 1998).

In 1992, *The Chicago Tribune* became the world's first daily to launch an electronic version of its newspaper on America OnLine. In 1993, Knight-Ridder started publishing what would eventually become one of the paradigms of international electronic journalism, the *San Jose Mercury Center,* which was in fact something more than the *San Jose Mercury News* printed copy. By 1994, *The New York Times, The Washington Post*, *Los Angeles Times*, *USA Today* and *The Examiner*, among others, offered readers an online version, whether on the Internet, America OnLine, CompuServe, Prodigy, Interchange, Delphi or their own networks (Díaz & Meso, 1998).

Although each type of medium -whether print, radio or television- publishes information in a different way responding to its specific characteristics and peculiarities, their respective approach and the specific type of message receiver, (Romero, 2000), their Internet versions all seek new schemes to refresh their contents and reach their audiences with new formats. Now, Internet-enable readers can read newspapers, listen to the radio, and watch TV from anywhere in the world (McClung, 2001).

OBJECTIVES

We aim at describing the beginnings, evolution, strategies and current state of Peruvian information media focusing on web-based journalism.

CONCEPTUAL FRAMEWORK

After defining journalism as the job of compiling and disseminating information (Gargurevich, 1999), electronic journalism stands out for four features: it uses multimedia resources (text, image, audio, databases and executable programs); it breaks down the sequence of information because it uses hypertext and hypermedia; it breaks down periodicity because it allows to access information at any time without need to wait until the next edition; and it is interactive, allowing users to access information of their interest (Díaz & Meso, 1998). Thus, electronic journalism uses every Internet resource to disseminate information and taps on this medium's unlimited capacity to hold contents and to provide ongoing updating. Moreover, the Internet is the first truly global-reach channel making it possible to disseminate information to the remotest corners of the earth without greater distribution costs (Singer, 2001).

The arrival of the Internet has had a major impact on the way we do journalism. Just like radio and television were milestones in journalism, displaced daily newspapers and led to the closing of some evening newspaper editions (Burnham, 2000), at present the web is becoming a medium that through its interactivity allows readers to disagree with the publishers or contribute to the writers' work by incorporating readers' opinions (Giles, 2000). This is the true journalistic potential of the Internet. Additionally, the Internet makes it possible to deliver news on a permanent basis, so editors must constantly determine how much information to gather (Maynard, 2000).

The arrival of the Internet confronted the printed media with a dual challenge. On the one hand, the risk of disappearing because now users find it easier to access information on the web. On the other hand, this new channel provides them with an opportunity to broaden their readership (Boynton, 2000). Compared to a radio listener or television viewer, readers are individuals with a heightened interest in accessing information they look for through the medium that best suits their specific interests (Romero, 2000). We may therefore wonder if being present on the Internet, may translate into larger readership for the printed media thanks to a "cross-sales" mechanism. For instance, Boston's *The Christian Science Monitor* sells through its web page as many subscriptions for the printed version as through other conventional channels. Remarkably enough though, web subscriber retention rates are double those from other sources (Regan, 2000). Although one fourth of respondents to a US survey performed by Kaye (as cited in McClung, 2001) on reasons to surf the Internet declared they spend less time watching TV, listening to the radio or reading newspapers and magazines since they found out about the web, a later study concluded that the obvious drop in the use of those media cannot be attributed to the Internet's becoming a mass medium in the US (Stempel, Hargrove & Bernt, 2000).

Many sites relating to printed media have evolved from pages that initially were but word-for-word copies of the printed version to a dynamic environment that can be constantly updated (Pack, 2001). In this sense, Internet journalism ethics should not be different from that governing traditional channels to the extent that, until now, online journalists' experience and values are born from the former. The web only gives them an expanded way of displaying information (McNamara, 2000). Digital-era journalists must find the way to reach a global audience without compromising the principles of truthfulness, of reliable sources, independence (Pavlik, 2000) and their originality. However, to the extent journalism moves to the Internet, there is an increased risk of contents plagiarism given the enormous size of the information files that are being put together (Wier, 2000).

Journalism on the Internet poses a number of challenges. On the one hand, news pieces for the printed media are discussed before they are broadcast while, on the Internet, as on radio, journalists are compelled to make very quick decisions, almost in real time (Kansas, 2001). On the other hand, the Internet opens the doors to new, purely virtual media although they must still walk a long way before they gain enough credibility and overcome the stigma that "anybody can publish on the web". Additionally, they must rise to the challenge of a huge infrastructure that has already been put in place by consolidated news groups and overcome limited access to capital (Giles, 2000 and Uy, 2001). Some think that, at least in the first decade of the web, the printed media have overpowered electronic journalism because they are specialized on preparing reports, likely thanks to their large-scale journalistic infrastructure ("Internet won't", 2001), which they use to their own advantage.

On the other hand, as access to the Internet increases and the public gets used to obtaining their information through the web, probably evening new shows will have to create new ways of presenting information. Otherwise, they would blunder if they repeat information the public is already aware of (Brown, 2000). Webmasters of some news media have already identified increased traffic in the early afternoon hours, presumably when office workers are back at their desks after the lunch break (Rainie, 2000).

Given the phenomenon of ethnocentricity -manifest, for instance, in a local medium's web page written by locals for locals who find in the information contents sufficient elements for understanding the news piece (Priess, 2000), publishers may find it convenient to specialize on reporting about a reality that is best known to them, i.e. local reality (Singer, 2001). Although the cost of preparing a news feature has remained almost unaltered, and although presenting news in a multimedia format (Fulton, 2000) may slightly increase costs, it is clearly cheaper to prepare a page and make it available to millions of people around the world over the Internet than to distribute it on a printed format (Small, 2000).

When deciding to move to the Internet world, information media must carefully analyze their project's feasibility, a particularly critical step for those initiatives that lack a prior base in the real world. The collapse of Taiwan's virtual *Tomorrow Times* information medium -despite 1.8 million daily page visits- poses a question about the viability of sustaining the high cost of generating news that must be updated on a permanent basis (Ling & Guyot, 2001), when no journalistic infrastructure has been developed in the physical world. We must remember that the Internet has made people used to obtaining free information while revenue-generation models based on advertising have shown to be unsustainable.

ELECTRONIC JOURNALISM IN PERU

Peruvian information media are no strangers to web journalism. Lima's main dailies publishing on the Internet are Correo *(*www.correoperu.com.pe*),* El Comercio *(*www.elcomercioperu.com.pe*),* El Peruano[1] *(*www.elperuano.com.pe*),* Expreso *(*www.expreso.com.pe*),* Gestión *(*www.gestion.com.pe*),* La República *(*www.larepublica.com.pe*),* Ojo *(*www.ojo.com.pe*), and* Síntesis *(*www.sintesis.com.pe*).*

Two of Lima's radio broadcasters send their news programming over the Internet. They are Radioprogramas del Perú and Cadena Peruana de Noticias, (www.rpp.com.pe and www.cpnradio.com.pe). Television networks on the web are Frecuencia Latina, (www.frecuencialatina.com.pe), América Televisión (www.americatv.com.pe), Panamericana Televisión (www.pantel.com.pe) and Televisión Nacional del Perú (www.tnp.com.pe). Exclusively virtual information media are www.peru.com, www.primerapagina.com.pe and www.gatoencerrado.com.

Internet penetration in Peru -a country with a little over 25 million people- is low. Only 33% of Peruvians have heard about the Internet or used it at all (Chaparro, 2001). In the first quarter of 2000, 130,000 users accessed the Internet through a commuted line while 390,000 used dedicated lines (Araoz and van Ginhoven, 2001). To June 2001, the total figures exceeded 800,000 (Cifras y Datos, 2001). A 2000 survey on technological innovation among 8976 Peruvian companies showed that only 38% had an Internet connection, 36% effectively used the Internet and 4.5% were planning to get a connection in the next 12 months (Instituto Nacional de Estadística e Informática, 2001).

The above figures clearly point to a hurdle for further developing successful news media on the web targeting a Peruvian audience. However, there exists a potential foreign market. Non-official figures show that Peruvian expatriates -who have greater Internet access and typically show a strong community feeling and deeply attached to the roots (Altamirano, 2000)- may reach 2 million.

METHODOLOGY

For this study , we chose those media which, additionally to being published on the Internet -also showed some special features that we describe below.

We chose how the following printed media:

- Lima's best recalled and most widely read daily, *El Comercio*, also has a reputation for being the most truthful, entertaining, and the best at covering local political news events (Actitudes hacia la prensa escrita, 2001). It is read by an average 574,700 people in Lima (Instituto Cuánto, 2001).
- *Gestión* was Peru's first written medium to produce an online version. Its printed edition, targeting the business community, reaches an average 27,500 readers in Lima (Instituto Cuánto, 2001).
- *La República* was Peru's second printed medium to publish an electronic version. It is regarded as the second most truthful and also mentioned as the second most reliable daily in providing local political news coverage (Actitudes hacia la prensa escrita, 2001). It is read by an average 171,300 readers in Lima (Instituto Cuánto, 2001).

Radio broadcasters in this survey comprise those which broadcast over the web but focus on news programming:

- *Radioprogramas del Perú, RPP Noticias,* enjoys a spontaneous recall rate of 27% among all radio broadcasters and 62% among news radio broadcasters. It is the most widely-heard radio broadcaster (23% of listeners) (Radio, 2001). Its annual average half-hour audience in Lima reaches 95,100 listeners (Insituto Cuánto, 2001).
- *CPN Radio,* Radio Cadena Peruana de Noticias, is spontaneously recalled by 6% of listeners of all radio stations (Radio, 2001) and has an annual average half-hour audience of 22,900 listeners in Lima (Insituto Cuánto, 2001).

Rather than displaying full and updated information, Peruvian television networks on the web underscore programming information. Their web sites are closer to an institutional page than to an information page. They were not included in this study.

Of the three Peruvian information media lacking a printed, radio or television matching part, only www.peru.com and www.primerapagina.com.pe participated in this study; www.gatoencerrado.com did not answer.

In all cases, we conducted in-depth interviews on relevant topics for this study with their electronic publishing officials. We also asked them to narrate their areas' operations and work-style when preparing news pieces. As a complement, we describe and analyze each medium's web site.

El Comercio

Founded in Lima in 1839, after 162 years of publication, *El Comercio* is the doyen of Peruvian dailies. It is presently owned by Empresa Editora El Comercio S.A. and a member of Grupo de Diarios de América.[2] In 1996, it published the company's institutional page on the Internet and 1997 it started publishing the www.elcomercioperu.com.pe electronic daily. In May 2001, it organized an independent area charged with the daily's electronic publication. This division comprises 33 staff of which 9 are journalists, 10 are technical experts and the rest manage the daily's portal.

The electronic version is almost completely dependent on the printed version for its contents. News is updated on the web using information provided by the daily's reporters and input from news agencies. The editing companies television operations through *Canal N* cable broadcaster and *Radio Canal N* radio station help in updating news contents. www.elcomercioperu.com.pe publishes not only the news of the day but also *Canal N's* fresh headlines. News is tracked through other information media as it evolves. Occasionally, www.elcomercioperu.com.pe, publishes reports prepared by others *El Comercio* newspapers and supplements. The contents and site design editor is ultimately responsible for all Internet publications.

www.elcomercioperu.com.pe gets an average 3 millions monthly hits, mostly from Peruvian residents in the United States, followed by expatriates residing in Japan. Hits originating in Peru rank third. Both the daily's and its electronic version's target audience is found in the top two income groups, comprised of professionals, students and members of the Armed Forces. Other subscribers to *El Comercio* include a number of foreign universities and organizations, and Peruvian embassies abroad. No "cannibalization" seems to take place between the printed and virtual media.

Information sections in the daily's electronic version include national, city, and world affairs. Business, politics, communities, entertainment, technology, special sports reports and graphic sections, as well as access to past editions are the other options. Its most widely read pages are the front page and local soccer news. In December 2001, the Internet publication of a report prepared by Somos magazine[3] featuring photographs of young Peruvian actresses who had acted in a soap opera, only shortly after its airing got the electronic newspaper a record number of visits.

www.elcomercioperu.com.pe's revenues come from advertising by some announcers. Nevertheless, this revenue generation model fails to pay for the virtual daily's operating costs. Another revenue stream originates in the sale of news to the TIM telephone operator who distributes the news to its cellular telephone customers. Additionally, www.elcomercioperu.com.pe has prepared private circulation newsletters for Profuturo pension fund manager's staff and the JobShark employment agency.

As yet another alternative source of revenues and an attempt to turn the daily's electronic version into a profitable venture, www.ec-store.com.pe has created a portal providing, among other services, the www.ec-store.com.pe virtual shop that reached sales worth US$3 million in 2000. Other portal services include an electronic job hunting agency, postal office boxes in the United States, health and university student counseling, a veterinarian's online office, debate forum, PC world in Spanish for Peru, a public interest services page, a leisure and entertainment feature, a virtual corporate directory, Internet access and a virtual cards site, and a link to www.batanga.com virtual radio broadcast.

As a means to increase traffic to www.ec-store.com.pe and thus enlarge sales, there is a project to put in place Internet public kiosks. However, most purchases through www.ec-store.com.pe do not originate in users who access Internet from a public kiosk but rather from surfers who reach the web from their homes or offices. The www.elcomercioperu.com.pe site publishes the small ads regularly found on the daily's print version. This same site has an option to write and pay for small ads. Subscriptions are available for the daily's crosswords in PDF format.

El Comercio's management has made a decision to make the newspaper a Latin American leader. Comprised in their strategy to reach their goal is the effort to provide Internet-based news services, an irreversible and final decision despite the fact that news electronic publishing in itself may not yield acceptable financial results.

Gestión

An economics, finance and business newspaper, *Gestión* first circulated in 1990 and is owned by Corporación Gestión, a company that seeks to become Peru's information leader by providing a "constant flow of impartial, plural and independent information".

Gestión's economic and business reporting goes hand in hand with information about political events and ongoing debate on business and government proposals and plans. Daily issues include sections on politics, the economy, editorial opinion, business and finance, the stock exchange, data bases and world affairs. Other sections include the latest business comments and other information. Guest writers fill *Gestión*'s pages on industry, taxes, marketing, foreign and international trade. Major Peruvian and international consultants provide opinion on economic, tax, real estate and other issues. In 1995, *Gestión* joined the Ibero-American Financial Dailies' Network [4].

Gestión was Peru's first daily to publish on the Internet when it launched its electronic site www.gestion.com.pe in September 1996 to spread Peru's economic, financial and political news and become a channel for communication among its readers. Its site includes the same sections as the printed publication and also provides links to the other members of the Ibero-American Financial Dailies' Network as well as links to online versions of various international specialized daily publications[5]. From www.gestion.com.pe it is possible to access other media run by the corporation, including *CPN Radio* www.cpnradio.com.pe information broadcast station and its *Gestión Médica*[6] (www.gestion.com.pe/GM) weekly health publication.

Gestión readership comprises mainly members of the business community, government officials and students and faculty from higher learning organizations. It is also the site of choice for economic and financial references for other media. Although it can be found at newsstands, a high percentage of its circulation is by subscription. Although *Gestión*'s circulation has not grown as expected, its presence on the Internet cannot be blamed. Most www.gestion.com.pe visitors are businessmen from the US, Spain, Argentina, Chile and Japan who have business and interests in Peru. Ever since www.gestion.com.pe started publishing, Peruvian embassies abroad have cancelled their subscriptions. Articles on political issues are the most frequently visited, followed by economic reports. *Gestión*'s contents are prepared with materials and interviews gathered by its reporters, together with news from news agencies. Information in www.gestión.com.pe is posted on the web by *CPN Radio* personnel working the late night shift. *CPN Radio* updates the news during the day. *Gestión* also offers a free e-mail news service called *Gestión Mail* that distributes economic, political, financial and business news before 7 a.m. with an update at 3 p.m. with the main news events until that time.

La República

Founded in Lima in 1981, *La República* has as its objective to inform and become an opinion maker for the Peruvian public. Initially, it underscored police reports but later became an overseer for government action. It describes itself as an opinion making daily rather than an impartial and objective medium. Its slogan "our opinion makes news" reflects its style in displaying information.

This newspaper has always been characterized by its technological innovations. Since 1995 it uses satellites to publish local editions in other cities around Peru's[7]. Driven by its commitment to innovation, in October 1996 it launched an electronic version called www.larepublica.com.pe at an investment of US$10,000, without expecting any economic benefit from it. However, the photo reporting of the abduction of a number of personalities who attended a reception at the Japanese ambassador's residency in Lima in December that year brought large windfall revenues when a Japanese newspaper showed interest in buying the photographs published in www.larepublica.com.pe. The sale of that material amounted to several times the investment made to materialize the newspaper's Internet initiative. However, and although *La República* later tried to sell the photographs of various reports to finance its electronic publication, this was possible only intermittently and to a small scale. The project to launch a simultaneous version of *La República* in New Jersey [8] via satellite emerged through contacts with a Peruvian businessman who sells a printed version of www.larepublica.com.pe in Patterson to which he attaches his own business advertising.

The existence of www.larepublica.com.pe is not conditioned to its standalone capacity to create a stream of revenues because it is understood that the electronic version can reach anywhere in the world where there are people interested in its contents. An important consideration for *La República* managers is interaction with its readers. The Internet has strengthened this feature. Since its launching, the number of opinion letters it gets through e-mails from readers outside Peru has grown steadily. Some visitors at www.larepublica.com.pe have become the newspaper's foreign correspondents and they "add a Peruvian flavor" to international reports. Foreign readers account for 70% of the electronic edition's readership.

All of *La República*, including its supplements, is published on www.larepublica.com.pe. The newspaper includes sections on politics, editorial opinion, local news, cultural, economic, police and entertainment, as well as opinion columns, besides the sports, comic strips, and horse racing pages. Its electronic version includes links to the *Líbero* sports newspaper, owned by the same publishing company, and a section called Latinoticias that publishes articles from Argentina's *La Prensa*. Among all these sections, the most visited cover current political affairs and sports. A discussion forum where readers shared their views on Peru's deep political crisis at that moment and the large corruption network within government operated for four months at the end of 2000. A discussion forum has not been totally discarded as a future option.

Information published on www.larepublica.com.pe comes from articles written by the daily's reporters and from writers of both the printed edition and news agencies. News is not updated along the day. Two people are charged with summarizing and entering *La República* contents on the Internet. The electronic version is published daily around 03 a.m., i.e. it is published before the printed edition. At some point, this difference in publication times for the two versions was an issue for *La República*'s regular circulation. Given its critical stand towards President Fujimori in the last year of his administration, the government intelligence agencies decided to purchase large numbers of newspaper copies to prevent investigative reporting about corruption from reaching the public. State security agents read at the beginning of the day www.larepublica.com.pe and, depending on the articles' contents, decided whether to purchase or not *La República.* The upside of this operation for the newspaper was that on those particular days the newspaper was sold out.

At present, the *La República* publishing group has shown interest in buying an open (non-cable) television channel to reach its corporate goals through operations in various media channels.

Cadena Peruana de Noticias – CPN Radio

A news radio chain owned by Corporación Gestión, *CPN Radio* broadcasts from Lima throughout Peru on both the FM and AM bands through a satellite link to Panamsat. *CPN Radio* first broadcast in 1996. It was purchased by Corporación Gestión in 1998, when it renewed its programming and significantly expanded coverage. *CPN Radio* and *Gestión* newspaper share their general information sources, including both from reporters and news agencies. Highly specialized economics, finance and business information is published only by the newspaper.

In June 2000, through an agreement between *CPN Radio* and Terra Networks and at an investment of US$20,000, the www.terra.com.pe/cpn site was launched to give the broadcaster Internet access to the www.terra.com.pe/cpn portal. In September 2001, a new page was launched at the www.cpnradio.com.pe site although it still provided information to Terra. The reason to move into the virtual medium was the radio's interest in positioning itself and creating an image before the public vis-à-vis Radioprogramas del Perú, *CPN Radio's* direct competitor. *CPN Radio's* Internet participation is ensured independently of its economic results. To date, it has not yet become a source of corporate revenues.

To launch the www.cpnradio.com.pe project, professional journalists within the organization were reassigned. Also a network technical expert was hired. At present, two editors alternate shifts until midnight and are responsible for updating headlines along the day. To refresh their news, they rely not only on material supplied by *CPN Radio* and *Gestión* but also on news from other media.

"Information on the spot" is *CPN Radio*'s slogan for its www.cpnradio.com.pe site. Audiences reaching the broadcaster are mostly adults who want to stay abreast of current affairs. Between 60% and 70% of visitors to www.cpnradio.com.pe originate in Peru, half of which come from Lima, while the remaining 30% to 40% come from abroad. Political features are most often followed, with the economy coming next. Visitors can also listen to radio programming in real time. This is done to avoid channel "cannibalization" because a www.cpnradio.com.pe user is also listening to *CPN Radio.* A total one million monthly visits are expected in 2002.

In its publication, www.cpnradio.com.pe includes headlines with photographs, and the political, economic, financial, business, local affairs, national affairs, world affairs, showbusiness, sports and culture sections. It also has a "last minute news" flash section, complete radio programming and links to articles written by the broadcaster's columnists.

Radioprogramas del Perú – *RPP Noticias*

Initially conceived in 1963 as an entertainment radio broadcaster, in 1979 Radioprogramas del Perú became a round-the-clock news broadcaster when it created *RPP Noticias,* building on the concepts of immediacy, objectivity and plurality. At present, it reaches 97% of Peruvians through a network of FM and AM affiliates. *RPP Noticias* seeks to become a Latin American and world telecommunications leader. In 1992, it expanded its broadcasting throughout the region by establishing the Latin American Broadcasting Association[9].

RPP Internet launched its institutional web page in 1996. At the end of 1999 the www.rpp.com.pe site was added to the original product with a view at "making radio broadcast's immediacy and volatile contents a more permanent product, by transforming it into a written medium that would target audiences interested in more exhaustive information without loosing the interactivity characterizing radio broadcasts "a strategy to globalize information through the Internet". After creating www.rpp.com.pe, the RPP Group can call itself a generator of contents that can be encapsulated in various formats[10]. Although *RPP Noticias* provides support in journalistic coverage for information broadcast through www.rpp.com.pe, which saves on content preparation, the Internet area staffs its own four writers, an economics-specialized reporter and another one to cover sports. It also relies on two audio broadcast specialists for Internet news broadcasting.

While *RPP Noticias* focuses on audiences above 18 years of age throughout the socio-economic spectrum, www.rpp.com.pe targets Peruvians of both sexes living in Peru, aged between 23 and 45 and belonging to the middle and high income groups. These readers have Internet access at their work places, universities or Internet public kiosks and they are interested in staying abreast of events. It also targets Peruvians of both sexes living abroad, between 25 and 50 years old and belonging to an intermediate income level. They resort to www.rpp.com.pe as their means to be informed about, communicated with and linked to Peru. At the end of 2001, RPP Internet got an average 3 million monthly visits and hit 4.8 million visits during the Peruvian elections. About 40% of visits to www.rpp.com.pe originate in Peru, closely followed by visitors from the United States, Argentina and Japan. Its most visited pages covered the political, sports, local affairs, entertainment and financial sections.

RPP Internet's information is supplied on both audio and text format, although photographs are attached to the main news features. At www.rpp.com.pe, visitors find the latest news in the "news by the minute" section, as well as local affairs, political, sports, world affairs, finance, cultural, entertainment and special reports sections. There is also the option to participate in opinion surveys. Through the audio on demand service, the comedy,11 gastronomy, interviews,12 and the labor, medical, veterinarian, geriatric and sexuality questions-and-answers sections can be reached. There is also a discussion forum around current affairs. Likewise, the direct *RPP Noticias* audio broadcast can be heard on www.rpp.com.pe. Users can also join the regular chat sessions. Parallel consumption has not been slighted. In the near future, radio announcers may answer telephone calls from both *RPP Noticias* listeners and answer questions from www.rpp.com.pe users.

A new market has opened thanks to www.rpp.com.pe and an effort is underway to increase the number of single-service users and visits to create a stream of revenues from advertising and contents sales. *RPP Internet* announcers can sponsor web-format radio programs and with their banners lure clients to their own web sites. If they do not own a web site, they can design an area providing their own information and piggyback on www.rpp.com.pe's structure. Content sales can be arranged through windows where www.rpp.com.pe contents are shown on clients' windows or by creating direct links to the client's site in the headlines newsletters that are distributed every day on text or HTLM format. Additionally, *RPP Internet* provides contents to the CNN, BBC and www.elarea.com networks and it sells CD-ROM including a summary of the main events of 2001. WAP technology enables Nextel and Telefónica telephone operators' clients to access *RPP Noticias* while Bellsouth's clients get headlines on their short-messaging service.

Although to date *RPP Internet* revenues are below expenses, the www.rpp.com.pe's is here to stay. It is widely held that launching this service has had a positive influence on RPP Group's image-building by creating among both listeners and announcers a perception of leadership, while strengthening the Group's competitive standing in terms of its capacity to reach a wider target audience that comprises both radio listeners and web users.

www.peru.com

www.peru.com site is owned by Interlatin Corporation, -a Peruvian company owning several domains (www.colombia.com, www.bolivia.com and www.futbolargentino.com)- that seeks to develop portals throughout Latin American countries that provide information and specific services adapted to individual countries.

Although www.peru.com has been operational since 1998, this domain was already registered in 1995 and became the company's main tool in luring traffic towards its site. It is totally dedicated to delivering information about and covering topics relating to Peru. The site targets Peruvian expatriates based on the principle that Peruvian residents have a choice of alternative ways to get information. In November 2001, the site got 11 million visits, mostly from the United States (over 50% of the total), followed by visitors from Japan and Spain.

www.peru.com seeks to differentiate its contents through quick publication of information gathered by an in-house team of journalists and wire-fed news. A company policy requires reporters to generate information that is clearly different from what may be available on other media. For this reason interviews about current affairs are avoided while aiming rather for the "exclusive" interview. News must be original and it is the company's perception that this has helped in building credibility among visitors. After being edited, information is published in text, audio, image and/or video formats as soon as possible. Updated headlines based on ongoing reporting appear in the "last minute section". www.peru.com.pe journalists recognize they do not have all the journalistic infrastructure available to traditional media and, therefore, resort to their own inventiveness in finding and publishing the most recent information.

Its press area comprises the soccer and sports section covered by eight reporters; a current political affairs section covered by six journalists and a show business department covered by three reporters. A project is currently being evaluated to recruit senior journalism students to work as correspondents in cities around Peru. Emphasis is placed on current political affairs although the soccer page is the most visited of all sections. A weekly chat session is available covering soccer and show business and exceptionally, political issues.

Besides its news coverage, www.peru.com contents include travel services, a browser, chat rooms, free e-mail addresses, job searches, a Lima city street finder (www.idonde.com), a communication media directory, messaging to cellular telephones, a community of Peruvian expatriates around the world, access to music radio broadcasts, electronic postcards and a virtual shop (www.iquiero.com). It also includes sections on automobiles, jokes, movies, finance, gastronomy, the horoscope, pets, music, and others. Other sections are special reports, the weekly survey, raffles, the day's video, and special culture-oriented articles. Exclusive features are summarized in English.

Interlatin Corporation's sources of revenues are diverse and balanced. However, its www.iquiero.com virtual shop has recorded growing sales in recent months. Products sold range from pastries and cakes through toys to electric household appliances, alcoholic beverages, clothes, books, perfume, music, jewelry and others. Its travel agency, www.peru.com/travel, also contributes to income generation. In a pessimistic scenario, Interlatin management foresees reaching their break event point in June 2003. In the meantime, they continue to generate traffic towards www.peru.com by tapping the site's attractions, in particular news, jokes and e-mail services. Additionally, www.peru.com accepts advertising and provides web page design services. Through agreements with TIM Peru and Nextel, www.peru.com sells news to these telephone operators who then distribute them among their users. Occasionally, they prepare special event reports which are an additional source of income.

Becoming an Internet news leader is www.peru.com's goal. Differently from reporters from other news media that operate through various channels, www.peru.com's journalists focus on the Internet and try to provide "an additional information step". They have even proposed purchasing a fly-away to broadcast directly on the web. Although they recognize their experimental approach in a totally different environment where nothing is yet final, they are also persuaded the Internet cannot be stopped and is here to stay.

www.primerapagina.com.pe

Owned by Chile's iLatinHoldings -which also developed several business pages including www.elarea.com, www.areasalud.com, www.elgolpe.com, www.planetaviajes.com, www.areafinanzas.com, www.viajuridica.com in Argentina, Chile and Colombia, the www.primerapagina.com site provides local contents specifically from Peru. A shareholder restructuring at iLatinHoldings in August 2000 hurt the launching of the site when the marketing budget allowance was cancelled together with the planned promotional initiative. Still, www.primerapagina.com.pe appeared in September 2000 as an online news service with a "last minute" news updating section. Initially, news were provided on video and audio format, as well as text plus photographs. At present, only the last two formats are offered.

News is gathered from international agencies and the site director's personal contacts, plus some information gathered from broadcasts by 2 television channels. In its initial months, www.primerapagina.com.pe counted on a team of 22 writers and four editors, one each for the sections on political and financial affairs, current affairs, sports and another one for entertainment. The site covers the main events of the day, national and world affairs, infographs, specials, opinion columns and surveys on current issues. It also provides links to similar web pages in Argentina, Chile and Colombia, as well as with all other iLatinHolding sites. Hits to www.primerapagina.com.pe border 150,000 every month, 60% of which originate in Peru and another 40% abroad.

Their business plan is based on good, quality writing, aimed at luring traffic to the site and persuade strategic partners to join the venture and sell advertising. However, the publicity-based revenues generation scheme has not yet borne fruit while the attempt to sell www.primerapagina.com.pe to US CNN chain stalled, as did arrangements with Lycos and Yahoo. After investments of one million dollars and returns of scarcely US$10,000, by mid-2001 iLatinHoldings decided to sell its Peruvian www.areafinanzas.com.pe, www.viajuridica.com.pe and www.elgolpe.com.pe sites. All the staff were laid off in August that year while the site's head kept a 30% share. Four freelance reporters are in charge of writing.

Besides, the director has been given a free hand to negotiate the best rescue formula for www.primerapagina.com.pe. Until November 2001, the site prepared an in-house newsletter for TIM Peru, a telephone operator. A further agreement with this telephone company allows www.primerapagina.com.pe to supply news messages for distribution among cellular telephone users. This agreement has been extended to include TIM Bolivia and TIM Venezuela where it is presently in a trial stage. Simultaneously, an option is under study to distribute publications by installments together with a Peruvian publishing group. These installments will provide links to www.primerapagina.com.pe. Another project underway considers preparing a television program in cooperation with *Televisión Nacional del Perú* and www.trabajando.com[13], to cover labor issues.

DISCUSSION

Only a few years have passed since some Peruvians media that had already an established presence in other channels decided to enter the Internet, while others were organized exclusively to serve this channel. Although the last word has not yet been said about electronic journalism, the experiences so far allow us to draw some lessons.

Although the approaches to develop the Internet with a print or radio media basis have moved along different roads, some seem more clearly determined to explore new options to increase their revenues and earnings while others simply wish to expand their readership or number of listeners by drawing international audiences. However, they all seem persuaded that there is no turning back and that they have entered the web never to escape from it. The same thing cannot be said about the new media. Those who do not have a traditional media foundation, have no choice but to yield satisfactory economic results that will allow them to survive.

New pieces and reports prepared for traditional media are the raw material for the articles published by conventional media on the web. To attain the above goal, special staff have been recruited. Exclusively virtual media such as www.primerapagina.com.pe and www.peru.com had to draw a press team out of the blue and have made them responsible for searching news and then publishing their reports. In all cases, Internet reporters staff are very young.

Initial plans had to be modified as Internet media identified difficulties and opportunities along the way. However, it is clear that advertising, no matter how high traffic through the site (Table No. 1), does not constitute in itself a sufficiently sound source of revenues to cover operating costs.

Table 1: Traffic by site

	Approximate Number of Monthly Visits
www.elcomercioperu.com.pe	3.000.000
www.gestion.com.pe	n/a*
www.larepublica.com.pe	n/a
www.cpnradio.com.pe	n/a*
www.rpp.com.pe	3.500.000
www.peru.com.pe	11.000.000
www.primerapagina.com.pe	150.000

* One million monthly hits planned for 2002

Table No. 1 also shows that the medium's reputation has an impact on traffic generated to its site, as is the case of *RPP Noticias* and *El Comercio,* which are the two media with the highest number of listeners and readers in Peru, respectively. Large volume of traffic through www.peru.com.pe may be attributed, in the first place, to its domain name, the first one to pop up on Internet browsers when the word Peru, is typed in. It is also attributable to the varied and interesting range of contents options offered by the site, without disdain for the substantial effort put in by its team of journalists.

All the media rely on text and photograph formats. Radio broadcasting sites www.cpnradio.com.pe and www.rpp.com.pe provide audio for their whole programming while the latter also provides an option to access some of its already broadcast programs through an audio-on-demand option. www.peru.com efforts to provide video over the web is also remarkable as this is the only Peruvian medium to do so. Table No. 2 shows how multimedia resources are used.

A common feature among all studied media -independent of their origin, editorial line or place of origin of its visitors- is that the most visited sections are the Peruvian political current affairs and sports pages, thus leading us to think that Peruvians looking for international news visit other media, most likely foreign ones. Although the media provide international news contents, they do so from a Peruvian perspective. In almost all media, most visits come from abroad which may be explained by two facts. In the first place, low Internet penetration in Peru and, secondly, the strong family, cultural and social ties of almost two million Peruvians living abroad and who have better conditions to access the web.

Table 2: Multimedia resources used in deploying information

	Text	Video	Direct Audio	Audio on Demand	Photographs
www.elcomercioperu.com.pe	x				x
www.gestion.com.pe	x				x
www.larepublica.com.pe	x				x
www.cpnradio.com.pe	x		x*		x
www.rpp.com.pe	x		x*	x	x
www.peru.com.pe	x	x	x**		x
www.primerapagina.com.pe	x				x

* All programming is broadcast directly over the web.

** Only some programs are broadcast directly over the web.

Peruvian Internet media offer a wide range of services. Outstanding among them, www.rpp.com.pe with its news updates, e-mail headlines, chatrooms and discussions fora, as shown in Table No. 3. *La Republica* newspaper does not provide other services beyond information but e-mail may have led to a perceived increased interaction with its readers.

Table 3: Service offerings

	News Updating	e-mail Headlines	Chatting	Discussion Fora
www.elcomercioperu.com.pe	x			x
www.gestion.com.pe	x	x		
www.larepublica.com.pe*				
www.cpnradio.com.pe	x	x		
www.rpp.com.pe	x	x	x	x
www.peru.com.pe	x		x	x
www.primerapagina.com.pe	x			

* Discussion fora provided towards yearend 2000.

An accepted practice among journalists is to provide news prepared with information obtained from other media provided appropriate credit is given to the information source. However, there is concern that the Internet somehow makes it easier to engage in "information piracy".

NEW CHALLENGES

Increasing participation of Peruvian information groups in various channels -including the web- opens the possibility for them not just to strengthen their own image but also to reach a larger number of users and thus develop new businesses in the field of information. To do so, only rigorous environment and trend surveying can contribute to sound decision making regarding the path to follow. A valid approach is to take into account the option to increase Internet involvement while acknowledging the restrictions that apply to the Internet in Peru, and thus help developing traditional channels.

Additionally, purely virtual Peruvian media are hard put to make any short term inroads into traditional channels. Instead, they must try and develop business lines that can sustain the work of their news teams. Using Internet resources to create virtual communities that may be served with alternative products is an option deserving consideration.

Internet reporting display formats combine the advantages of radio, television and printed channels. When easy-to-use, flexible and portable devices are sufficiently developed and widespread, all featuring multimedia capabilities, newsmen will have to be ready to meet the ever faster pace of information needs in modern societies. In the meantime, the number of Peruvians that go to the Internet to stay abreast of events increases constantly.

ENDNOTES

1Peru's oficial gazet.

2 *La Nación* from Argentina, *O Globo* and *Zero Hora* from Brazil, *El Mercurio* from Chile, *El Tiempo* from Clombia, *El Comercio* from Ecuador, *El Universal* from Mexico, *El Nuevo Diario* from Puerto Rico, *El País* from Uruguay and *El Nacional* from Venezuela, on top of *El Comercio* from Peru.

3 Weekly magazine including in *El Comercio's* Saturday edition. The most widely read in Peru.

4 *El Cronista* from Argentina, *La Razón* from Bolivia, *Gazeta Mercantil* from Brasil, *El Diario* from Chile, *La República* from Colombia, *Hoy* from Ecuador, *Prensa Libre* from Guatemala, *El Economista* from México, *El Observador* from Uruguay, *Expansión* from España and el *Diario Económico* de Portugal, on top of Peru's *Gestión*.

5 *The Wall Street Journal*, the *New York Times* and *Washington Post* from US, *Financial Times* and *The Economist* from England and *Nikkei Business News* from Japan.

6 A free, nationwide tabloid published since 1996.

7 The news paper includes local contents for its Piura, Chiclayo, Trujillo, Arequipa and Iquitos editions.

8 This US state is home to the largest community of Peruvian expatriates.

9 A chain comprising *Radio Mitre* from Argentina, *Radio Panamericana* from Boliva, *RCN* from Colombia, *Radio Quito* Ecuador, *Radio RPP Noticias* from Peru and *Caracas Radio* from Venezuela. This broadcasting network reaches 106 million listeners.

10 At present, RPP Group broadcasts news on cable TV.

11 The radio leader in Peru.

12 Only audio broadcasts of the days news are available free of charge. Interviews from previous days are sold at request.

13 Chile's online job bourse.

REFERENCES

Actitudes hacia la prensa escrita. (2001, April). Retrieved December 3, 2001, from http://www.apoyo.com/infor_util/inv_mercados/igm_prensa_042001.html.

Altamirano, T. (2000). Liderazgo y organizaciones de peruanos en el exterior: Culturas transnacionales e imaginarios sobre el desarrollo. Lima: Fondo Editorial PUCP y PromPerú.

Araoz, M. y van Ginhoven, S. (2001). Preparación de los países andinos para integrar las redes de tecnologías de la información: el caso de Perú. Lima: Centro de Investigación de la Universidad del Pacífico.

Boynton, R. (2000). New media may be old media's savior. Columbia Journalism Review, 39(2), 29-34.

Brown, M. (2000, October 2). Bringing people closer to the news. Adweek, 41(40), IQ26.

Burnham, A. (2000). Journalism.com. The Virginia Quarterly Review, 76(2), 203-213.

Chaparro, H. (2001, December 16). Investigación exploratoria en el mundo digital. Semana Económica, 17(801), 10.

Cifras y datos. (2001, August). Retrieved November 15, 2001, from http://www.osiptel.gob.pe/cifydat/frames/fr4.html.

Díaz, J. y Meso, K. (1998). Desarrollo del periodismo electrónico. El profesional de la información, 7(12), 4-11.

Fulton, K. (2000). News isn't always journalism. Columbia Journalism Review, 39(2), 30-35.

Gargurevich, J. (1999). Los periodistas: Historia del gremio en el Perú. Lima: Ediciones La Voz.

Giles, B. (2000). Journalism in the era of the web. Nieman Reports, 54(4), 3.

Instituto Cuánto. (2001, September). Anuario estadístico: Perú en números 2001. Lima: Author.

Instituto Nacional de Estadística e Informática. (2001). Impactos de las tecnologías de información y comunicación en el Perú. Lima.

Internet won't eliminate print media. (2001, August). USA Today, 130(2675), pp. 15-16.

Kansas, D. (2001, July 16). A dot-com editor sheds his five-year 'cocoon', and looks at how journalism has changed in the age of the Internet. New York Times, C-5.

Ling, C. y Guyot E. (2001, February 23). Taiwan newspaper closes web edition, cites funding woes. Wall Street Journal.

McClung, S. (2001). College radio station web sites: Perceptions of value and use. Journalism & Mass Communication Educator, 56(1), 62-73.

McNamara, T. (2000). Defining the blurry line between commerce and content. Columbia Journalism Review, 39(2), 31-35.

Pack, T. (2001, Sep-Oct). All the news that's fit to digitally print. Link-up, 18(5), 16.

Pavlik, J. (2000). The journalist: A disappearing species in the online world? The UNESCO Courier, 53(2), 34.

Priess, F. (2000). Los medios de comunicación en los conflictos armados. In A. Cacua & F. Priess (Eds.), Ética y responsabilidad: reflexiones para periodistas. Bogotá: Editora Guadalupe.

Radio. (2001, February). Retrieved December 4, 2001, from http://www.apoyo.com/infor_util/inv_mercados/igm/igm_2001_2.html

Rainie, L. (2000). Why the Internet is (mostly) good for news. Nieman Reports, 54(4), 17-18.

Regan, T. (2000). Technology is changing journalism. Nieman Reports, 54(4), 6-9.

Romero, G. (2000). Autocontrol de la información. In A. Cacua & F. Priess (Eds.), Ética y responsabilidad: reflexiones para periodistas. Bogotá: Editora Guadalupe.

Small, J. (2000). Economics 101 of Internet news. Nieman Reports, 54(4), 41-42.

Singer, J. B. (2001). The metro wide web: Changes in newspapers's gatekeeping role online. Journalism and Mass Communication Quarterly, 78(1), 65-80.

Stempel, G., Hargrove, T. y Bernt, J. (2000). Relation of growth of use of the Internet to changes in media use from 1995 to 1999. Journalism and Mass Communication Quarterly, 77(1), 71-79.

Uy, E. (2001). Reporters on superhighway meet roadblocks. News Media and the Law, 25(3), 49-50.

Wier, D. (2000). Web journalism crosses many traditional lines. Nieman Reports, 54(4), 35-37.

Elements for a Mobile Community Business Model

Peter Aschmoneit[1] and Dr. Hans-Dieter Zimmerman[2]
Institute for Media and Communications Management, University of St. Gallen, Blumenbergplatz 9, 9000 St. Gallen, Switzerland,
Tel:[1] +41-71-224 3608, [2]+41-71-224 2748, Fax:[1,2] +41-71-224-3523, {Peter.Aschmoneit, Hans-Dieter.Zimmerman}@unisg.ch

ABSTRACT

In both, academia and practice, there is a lively interest and a variety of definitions of the term business model. Most of the definitions are determined by the elements of a business model. With this top-down approach most authors specify generic elements valid in every business context. In this research paper we take a bottom-up approach. After a brief discussion of the understanding of business models and mobile communities, we derive elements of a mobile community business model. By means of this special business context we are able to study the usefulness of our element based research model. To illustrate our approach, we will employ the elements and the terminology of the research model to an operating mobile community in Switzerland

INTRODUCTION

The term business model is widely used in both academia and practice. Importance is usually regarded as high, since a sound business model seems to influence the (potential) revenues and the future success of the business initiative. Business models determine participation of partners, channel conflicts, and revenues etc. However, there are multiple indications that neither the understanding nor the elements of business models are broadly available. Grönroos et al. (2000, p. 243) state that "there is no systematic model available in the literature that would guide marketers in their development of Internet offerings of goods or services."

In this research we take a bottom-up approach to attain a deeper understanding of important elements of business models. Therefore we apply a research model on a special business context, the mobile community business model. We refine and revise the research model by employing it to an operating mobile community case. Thus, the superior research question is: Which are necessary elements of a mobile community business model and which causal relationships do they have? If the revised research model is proven reasonable after applying it to a number of mobile communities, we strive to follow the same structure in other special business contexts.

THEORETICAL UNDERPINDINGS

Business Models

Schmid (2000a, 2000b) argues that we are facing a new industrialization and that in the digital economy the scarce resource shifts from production to communication in a novel way and, therefore, the entire design of value creation systems is challenged. Westland/Clark (1999, p. 89) elaborate the shift from a traditional business model for marketing to a new interactive Electronic Commerce business model. Moore believes that the transition from the multidimensional firm (M-form) to the ecosystem form (E-form) will be at the heart of future success and growth (Moore 1998). Gartner Group expects 'knowledge-oriented' business models to dominate in which a number of hub-like members share and organize knowledge and social relationships (Tunick Morello 1999) PricewaterhouseCoopers expects 'metacapitalistic' business models and predicts that "the century-old business model in which brand-owning companies put a premium on maintaining a huge internal base of physical capital ... will crumble and give way to thinly capitalized brand-owning companies operating with external or outsourced networks" (Means/Schneider 2000). Andersen Consulting (Friedman/Langlinais 2000) develop an intermediate or hybrid model that is customer-centric and "value is created at the relationship level across products and channels rather than at the individual product level". A similar, more detailed model is presented by Österle (2000, p. 37) who defines an intermediary that supports the entire customer process (process portal provider) using a variety of standardized electronic services.

The popular definition of Timmers (1998, p. 1) who conceives business models as "an architecture for the product, service and information flows, including a description of the various business actors and their roles; and a description of the potential benefits for the various business actors; and description of the sources of revenues" strongly influenced our further research.

Mobile Communities

The lively interest and the variety of definitions of business models prompt us to investigate the business model approach in specific business contexts. As there is no common understanding of the term business model, we try to extract important elements of business models through a detailed investigation of mobile communities. Therefore, we first illustrate our understanding of communities and mobile communities.

In general virtual communities are defined as a group of people that are sharing interests or needs through electronic channels. (Hagel III and Amstrong 1997, p. 143). As Bughin and Hagel III (2000, p. 237) or Timmers (1998, p. 6), we consider that a virtual community is a business model in electronic markets itself, especially when the value "is coming from members (customers or partners), who add their information onto a basic environment provided by the virtual community company" (Timmers 1998, p. 6). In addition to that a virtual community is sometimes described as a complementary part of an existing business model, especially when there is no direct source of revenue related to that community. In this research paper we make no distinction between these two archetypes. Direct and indirect sources of revenues are just varieties of the community business model.

Like the virtual communities, a mobile community is a group of people sharing interests or needs, through *wireless* electronic channels. However, the idea of the mobile community is not only an extension of the virtual one with wireless channels. Detecting the impact and value of the mobile context, the use of the wireless electronic channel is not enough. Mobility adds significant value to virtual communities in the first stage, but it reshapes exiting and defines new business models in the future. Drivers of this development are the following mobility-factors that can be identified: localization, identification, immediacy and availability (Mueller and Aschmoneit 2001, p.2). These four characteristics are relative advantages of emerging mobile communication technologies as well as characteristics for the phenomenon of mobility. A Mobile Communities is a group of people sharing interests or needs through wireless electronic channels, using the characteristics of emerging mobile technology as an added value.

PROPOSED RESEARCH METHODOLOGY

To extract important elements for a mobile community business model, we are taking a case study approach. As there is no common understanding of the term business model, there is no universal mobile community business model. However, we derive five elements, from prior research and the interviews with several mobile service provid-

Figure 1: Elements for a mobile community business model

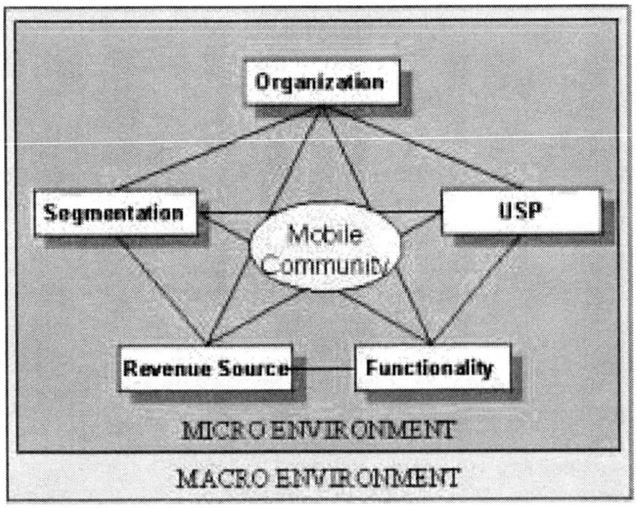

ers, we made so far. These are organization, segmentation, sources of revenue, functionality and customer value and unique selling proposition respectively. In the first draft of the research model, these elements are providing a means for the design of mobile communities from the business-side.

The elements have to be incorporate into the micro and macro environment. While the micro environment of the mobile community concerns the internal resources of an organization, the macro environment can be differentiated in several external conditions.

To test this first draft of a business model phase one will apply the elements to an operating location based service in Switzerland, named "Friend Zone". This mobile community is operated by the countries biggest mobile operator Swisscom. We will illustrate and analyze our approach, following the structure and employing the terminology of the proposed research model. The unit of analysis for this field research is the organization behind "Friend Zone", the application itself as well as the external communication of the organization. Specially, interviewees will be the project manager and lead analyst for the initiative, champions for the projects, and select members of the user groups. This first phase is interpretative to gain an insight concerning the background of mobile communities and factors impacting business models. Propositions will be formulated from the information qualitatively analyzed from the case study and the research model will be revised with findings.

The second phase will entail quantitative methods such as a survey to discern the validity of the proposed research model. It is assumed that by the next year, more mobile communities will be offered. Then, the hypotheses based on the revised research model developed in phase on can be surveyed in a larger number. Survey questions will be developed for the managerial personnel of the operators and the users of the mobile community. If the revised model is proven reasonable after phase 2, we will apply the elements to other business contexts, especially in mobile business.

REFERENCES

Bughin, J. and Hagel III, J. (2000) "The Operational Performance of Virtual Communities – Towards a Succesful Business Model," in: EM - Electronic Markets, 10(4), 237-243.

Friedman, J.P. and Langlinais, T.C. (2000) Best Intentions: A Business Model for the eEconomy, Andersen Consulting. http://www.ac.com/ideas/Outlook/1.99/over_currente2.html, (Accessed September 25, 2000).

Grönroos, C., Heinonen, F., Isoniemi, K., and Lindholm, M. (2000) "The NetOffer model: A Case Example from the Virtual Marketspace," Management Decision 34(4), 243-252.

Hagel, J. and Armstrong, A. (1997) "Net Gain – Expanding markets through virtual communities," in: The McKinsey Quarterly, 1/97, 140-153.

Means, G.E., Schneider, D. Worldwide Capital Market Value Could Explode from $ 20 Trillion to $ 200 Trillion by 2010, PricewaterhouseCoopers. http://www.pwcglobal.com/extweb/ncpressrelease.nsf/DocID/2594EAA15DB1A56A852569130058CBB9, (Accessed: September 25, 2000).

Moore, J.F. (1998) "The New Corporate Form," in Tapscott, D., Lowy, A., Ticoll, D. (Eds.) Blueprint to the Digital Economy, New York: McGraw-Hill, 77-95.

Mueller, C. and Aschmoneit, P. (2001) "Opportunities of customer relationship management and mass customisation in the mobile environment," in: Proceedings of the World Congress of Mass Customization, Hongkong 2001, forthcoming, pages unknown.

Österle, H. (2000) "Enterprise in the Information Age," in: Österle, H., Fleisch, E., and Alt, R. (eds.): Business Networking: Shaping Enterprise Relationships on the Internet, Berlin, Heidelberg: Springer, 18-55.

Saban, K. (2000) " Strategic Preparedness: A Critical Requirement To Maximizing E-Commerce Investments", EM - Electronic Markets, 11(1), forthcoming, pages unknown.

Schmid, B. (2000a) "Was ist neu an der digitalen Ökonomie?" Belz, C.; Bieger, T. (Eds.): Dienstleistungskompetenz und innovative Geschäftsmodelle; Forschungsgespräche der Universität St. Gallen 2000, St. Gallen: Thexis Verlag, 178-196.

Schmid, B. (2000b) "What is new about the Digital Economy?" EM - Electronic Markets, 11 (1), 44-51.

Shipley, T.(1995) IS Needs Multiple Business Models, Research Note Gartner Group, Doc. No. SPA-MGT-1177, August 16, 1995, http://www.gartnergroup.com, (Accessed September 25, 2000).

Timmers, P. (1998) "Business Models for Electronic Commerce", EM - Electronic Markets, 8(2), 3-8. URL: http://www.electronicmarkets.org/netacademy/publications/all_pk/949 (Accessed: 20 September, 2000).

Tunick Morello, D.(1999) "Centrality" as Organizing Principle for E-Business Models, Research Note Gartner Group, Doc. No. SPA-09-7467, December 7, 1999, http://www.gartnergroup.com, (Accessed: September 25, 2000).

Viscio, A. and Paternack, B.A. (1996) "Toward a New Business Model", strategy + business, Issue, 20, second quarter 1996, http://www.strategy-business.com/research/96201/ (Accessed: September 20, 2000).

Westland, J.C., and Clark, T.H.K. (1999) Global Electronic Commerce: Theory and Case Studies, Cambridge, MA: MIT Press.

Personalization via Information Preconditions

Tamara Babaian
CIS Department, Bentley College, 175 Forest Street, Waltham, MA, tbabaian@bentley.edu

INTRODUCTION AND MOTIVATION

Personalization has been identified as a key task to success of many modern systems. However, there are drawbacks in the way personalization is usually performed in these systems

1. Personalization is carried out as a separate process that is taken out of context of the task in which such personal information is used, thus obscuring from the user the purpose and advantages from supplying such information.
2. The amount of potentially useful personal information is sometimes overwhelming, thus the systems are installed with a set of settings that are considered typical. Further customization has to be initiated by the user. However, inexperienced users rarely take advantage of customization even if they are aware of potential benefits, due to lack of information on available options. As a result, as experience demonstrates [3], many users shy away from customization, while they can benefit from it a great deal.
3. As Pednault [4] points out, the underlying representation of personal information at times lacks flexibility to be easily adjustable and reusable.

We propose a new approach to personalization that ensures gradual adaptation of the system to the user's preferences; in our approach the system has the ability to elicit personal information from the user at the time it is processing the task for which such information is critical. The novelty of our approach and its implementation also lies in defining the personalization task declaratively via informational goals and preconditions on the actions that the system would take in response to a user's request. This is enabled by the use of a knowledge base that stores the gathered preference information, and an automated reasoning and planning system that can reason autonomously about knowledge, lack of knowledge and actions that the system may take to acquire necessary missing information. The system performs information gathering autonomously (by inspecting available personal information, such as for example person's Internet bookmarks) as well as by direct user querying.

GOAL-DIRECTED PERSONALIZATION IN WRITER'S AID

Writer's Aid [2] is a system we that works parallel with an author writing a document, helping him with identifying and inserting citation keys, autonomously finding and caching papers and associated bibliographic information from various online sources.

At the core of Writer's Aid is a knowledge base that contains system's knowledge about the state of the world, and an automated planner system. The planner has a description list of actions that Writer's Aid can execute and it can automatically combine the actions into a plan that will achieve a posted goal. Each action is described via preconditions that must be true prior to executing the action, and effects that the action brings about. Plan-generation is accomplished by representing both goals and actions using a logic-based language and using a reasoning engine that can infer what is true after performing a sequence of actions. For an example consider the following action of searching user's personal directories for bibliographic collections:

Action-1: **FindLocalBibliographies**
Preconditions: none
Effects: Knowing locations of all bibliographic collections of a user.

Personalization in the Writer's Aid consists of the **initial tune-up** of the system to the user's parameters and the **dynamic personalization** that occurs while Writer's Aid works on accomplishing a user-posted goal and identifies a need for information.

Initial tune-up occurs at the time of installation. The goal of the initial tune-up is to establish and enter into the system certain user-specific parameters, such as, for example, the user's own locally stored bibliographic collections, his preferred on-line bibliographies, etc.

To direct the system to collect the data about location of local bibliographies it is sufficient to post the following goal on the list of goals to be accomplished during the tune-up

Personalization-goal-1 = Knowing the locations of all of user's bibliographic collections,

and in response, Writer's Aid will generate a plan (in this case consisting of a single Action-1) described above, which accomplishes Personlaization-goal-1, and thus provides Writer's Aid with access to the user's personal bibliographies.

This declarative approach to the initial customization separates personalization from the rest of the code, making personalization design very flexible and more easily adjustable.

DYNAMIC PERSONALIZATION

Imagine the following scenario: Writer's Aid is working to locate a viewable version of a paper that the user requested. The plan for locating the paper includes an action of querying a known paper collection, namely ACM digital library. In order to avoid wasting time on searching collections of papers on subjects unrelated to the user's research field, this action contains a precondition that the paper collection be one of user's preferred collections:

Action-2: **QuerySourceForPaper**(source, paper)
Precondition: source must be User's Preferred Source
Effects: Knowing whether source contains viewable version of paper.

Writer's Aid does not know if ACM digital library is the user's preferred bibliography, so it cannot establish the precondition unless it executes an action (namely Action-3 described below) of asking the user himself to obtain necessary information.

Action-3: **AskUserAboutSource** (source)
Precondition: User permits system to post questions
Effects: Knowing whether source is user preferred source.

The user's response determines whether ACM digital library will be queried; it is also recorded in Writer's Aid knowledge base for future use.

Dynamic personalization occurs gradually, always within a context of a particular task, thus eliciting the user's input at the time it is used and providing the user with knowledge of how the personal information is being used by the system.

DISCUSSION

An important requirement to the underlying knowledge representation and planning system is non-redundancy of information gathering, as it would be annoying if the system could not infer a fact that follows from the user's replies and it would be disastrous for the system if it ever repeated a question to the user. The planning system used in Writer's Aid, PSIPLAN, [1] can infer all the facts that are implied by its knowledge base, and it never discards any valid information, thus ensuring non-redundancy of information gathering.

On the other hand, the user must have access to the same customization data as the system, and be able (and aware of the way) to modify those settings at any time.

CONCLUSIONS AND FUTURE WORK

Representing a personalization task via a set of information goals addresses the problems with the way personalization is approached in most modern systems that are outlined in the beginning of this paper in the following ways:

- It leads to preference elicitation that occurs within the context of the particular task that requires personal information, thus informing the user of their choices, motivating the response and ensuring its accuracy.
- Personalization occurs gradually at the times when the personal information is critical to the satisfaction of a user's goal and is initiated by the computer system, thus relieving the user from potentially time consuming task of specifying all preferences at once.
- Personalization defined declaratively via information goals separates customization of the interface from the overall system architecture, making the interface more easily adjustable and extendable.

We are working on the implementation of semi-automatic preference gathering in Writer's Aid and will perform laboratory user studies to investigate whether use of the proposed mechanism results in improved user satisfaction and system performance, compared to typical offline preference gathering.

REFERENCES

[1] Babaian, T. Knowledge Representation and Open World Planning Using psi-forms, PhD Thesis, Tufts University, May 2000.

[2] Babaian, T., Grosz, B and Shieber, S, A Writer's Collaborative Assistant, In Proceedings of Intelligent User Interfaces'02, January 2002.

[3] Manber,U., Patel, A., Robison ,J., Experience with personalization on Yahoo! Communications of the ACM, v. 43,8. August 2000

[4] Pednault, E. Representation is Everything, Communications of the ACM, v. 43,8. August 2000

Moving E-Business Principles to Government/ Client Interactions: The Development of Interactive Web Sites to Enhance Police/Community Relations

Susan A. Baim
Assistant Professor of Business Technology, Miami University Middletown, 4200 E. University Blvd., Middletown, Ohio
Tel: (513) 727-3444, Fax: (513) 727-3462, baimsa@muohio.edu
Doctoral Student, Organization and Management Program, E-Business Specialization, Capella University

ABSTRACT

This paper discusses research to determine the feasibility of creating virtual communities in the form of two-way interactive Web sites to enhance communications between city police departments and the citizens that they serve. Mail surveys are used to collect Internet usage statistics on randomly-selected residents from three medium-sized Southwestern Ohio cities. Based on an analysis of the data and a review of relevant literature on community-oriented policing initiatives, an hypothesis is stated regarding the criteria necessary to establish successful police/community interactions over the Internet. Research studies to confirm or refute the validity of the hypothesis are suggested.

COMMUNITY-ORIENTED POLICING

It is no longer sufficient for police departments across the country to cruise the streets in squad cars and apprehend criminals when called. Citizens in small and large cities alike are requiring more from their police departments. In a recent article for a sales and marketing journal Betsy Cummings points out that police departments are essentially being asked to enroll in Marketing 101 in order to better sell their services to their constituencies (Cummings, 2001, p. 14). Cummings quotes officials in the New York Police Department as saying that determining what programs will "sell' to city residents and improve the image of the department is no different than a business looking at its marketing strategy to determine what products and services should be on the shelf. Increasingly, one of those products offered by police departments is a city-personalized version of community-oriented policing.

Police department s that have taken advantage of the latest available technologies in terms of communications gear, weaponry, vehicles and other law enforcement equipment are generally well-versed in handling major crimes and emergency situations within their communities. What may not immediately be obvious is that these same departments are also positioned well to move forward with community-oriented policing efforts. Community-oriented policing takes time — time to sit down with residents to understand their concerns and to draw up action plans that could help improve the quality of life in community neighborhoods. Only those departments that are experienced and efficient at handling the major crimes committed within their jurisdictions are likely to have the time and also the patience that it takes to pursue a significant community-oriented policing agenda.

SPECIFIC EXAMPLES OF COMMUNITY ORIENTED POLICING

Although the concept of community-oriented policing has been in existence since the 1960's, little formal evidence of studies exists in the literature prior to the early- to mid-1990's. In one of the earliest published studies, officers of the Merriam Police Department (a suburb of Kansas City, Missouri) developed a brief survey questionnaire that they used in conjunction with personal visits to meet with business owners in the community (Sissom, 1996). The officers' goal was to build a better working relationship with community business leaders across a broad spectrum of the city's economic base.

Results of the Merriam survey project were reviewed personally by the police chief and used to establish a training program to enhance officers' understanding of community-oriented policing principles. Regular contacts with all businesses were instituted as part of the officers' daily patrol duties and a mechanism was set up to track these contacts on an ongoing basis. The survey process was revised and updated to be used on a recurring basis to give an indication of how the operational changes were affecting community/police relations (Sissom, 1996).

Newer studies, such as those described by Hugh Culbertson, focus on identifying the issues that tend to divide police officers from their communities and prevent the successful implementation of community-oriented policing initiatives (Culbertson, 2000). Culbertson notes a variety of turning points in community/police relations, including the 1995 criminal trial of O. J. Simpson and the early 1990's videotaped beating of Rodney King. He stresses that the failure of police departments to understand and address the divisive issues in their communities can thwart any efforts to implement change in a department's operating procedures.

Implementing the fundamental change in police operating procedures that is needed to support community-oriented policing in more than a token sense quickly becomes a delicate balancing act. The planning required to implement an effective community-oriented policing approach exposes officers to the inner-workings of the neighborhoods that they protect and serve. Many problems that these officers will be asked to solve are not exclusively within the sphere of influence of the police. As such, the thought processes used and action plans derived by the officers may appear to be comparatively "un-police-like" as compared to traditional crime-fighting activities. In an intriguing and very recent study, William Rohe, Richard Adams and Thomas Arcury investigated many of the community-oriented policing efforts underway in two North Carolina cities, Asheville and Greensboro. In each case, these researchers identified common themes between the approaches in use by the police and those in use by the cities' planning commissions (Rohe, Adams and Arcury, 2001, p. 78).

RESEARCH CONDUCTED TO DATE

The primary research presented in this paper was originally conducted to assess city residents' satisfaction with four separate governmental agencies in three Southwestern Ohio communities. Table 1 lists the studies conducted and their specific purposes.

Each of the four surveys was conducted using a mail questionnaire format. Questionnaires were developed jointly with the Chiefs of Police and other high-ranking police officials or with individuals at the

Table 1: Studies conducted to assess satisfaction

City	Agency	Study Type
Middletown, Ohio	Police Dept.	Police Customer Satisfaction
Middletown, Ohio	Water Services	Utilities Dept. Customer Satisfaction
Oxford, Ohio	Police Dept.	Police Customer Satisfaction
Trenton, Ohio	Police Dept.	Police Customer Satisfacation

Division Director level in the case of the Middletown Water Services Division. Input from the Oxford Citizens' Advisory Board was also used in formulating the questionnaire employed in that city.

All four surveys focused on issues of general concern to the residents of the communities with special emphasis on the quality of the services provided by the local police or water departments. The questionnaire designs included a number of quantitative ranking questions to provide the best possible statistical assessment of the agencies' performances along with a selection of qualitative questions designed to broaden or "flesh out" the understanding of the issues revealed. Each survey also included a generous selection of demographics questions in order to look for differences of opinion across different age, income, neighborhood or other differentiators. The sample size for each survey was approximately 2000 city residents.

Among numerous other trends, data collected from all three cities shows a widespread range of Internet-readiness among the citizens. City of Middletown residents only demonstrate a 40.1% connectivity rate while City of Oxford residents are much more likely to be connected with a rate of 81.4% among those residents surveyed. City of Trenton residents fall in between with 66.1% connected to the Internet. Table 2 provides an assessment of each city, based on an overall analysis of the demographic data.

Table 2: City assessment based on demographic data

	Middletown	Oxford	Trenton
Age of Residents	Oldest	Close to Middletown	Younger
Internet Access	Lowest	Highest	Middle
Interest in Internet Programs from City Agencies	Lowest	Moderate	High
Length of Residency	Very Long	Very Long	Relatively Short (highly mobile)
Explanation	Low Internet access rate and set Police expectations make Web site use unlikely.	High Internet Access rate (college town) but older population accustomed to police service a certain way	Medium Internet access rate but younger, mobile population willing to try new approaches

RESEARCH HYPOTHESIS

Based on an analysis of the data available from the four surveys conducted to date, it may be hypothesized that police/community interactions over the Internet are likely to be most successful in generating positive community-oriented policing efforts when they are undertaken in fast growing communities that are inhabited by "younger" residents. Stated in question form, this hypothesis states: Are speed of community growth and age of community residents, taken together, accurate and reliable predictors of the success of community-oriented policing efforts conducted over the Internet?

FUTURE RESEARCH STUDIES

From an examination of the research data collected in each of the three cities, it is likely that the City of Trenton is the best candidate for the development of a new, interactive police Web site. If successful, this site could lead to the roll out of an online virtual community for the police department and local citizens to use as an information source and mode of communication. With Trenton's acceptable Internet connection rate and the younger, more mobile population living in that city, it is plausible that receptivity to new forms of community-oriented policing may be good or better. Although a discussion of other data obtained from the Trenton survey is beyond the scope of the present paper, there are additional attributes expressed by city residents that make them seem less set in their ways (and their expectations of the police) than are the residents of Middletown and Oxford.

It is not surprising that Middletown looks like an unlikely candidate for the development of an interactive police Web site and virtual community. Middletown residents have comparatively little familiarity with the Internet and seem relatively set in their ways of doing business. Additionally, they have enjoyed a very well-respected, stable police department under the leadership of Chief Bill Becker for a number of years. The impetus for change simply is not evident.

It is surprising, however, to net out with a relatively low probability of success for the City of Oxford. College communities tend to be more vocal in debating issues and raising concerns than do many other cities of smaller size and one might predict that this could lead to a very high usage of a virtual community associated with the police department. Such communities may also be more liberal in their politics, but the effect of this parameter on the desirability of an interactive police department Web site is not under study at the present time. Additionally, the survey in Oxford, as conducted, surveyed predominantly permanent residents of the city as opposed to students on campus. The older residents of the surrounding city, despite claiming to have a very high rate of Internet access, did not demonstrate a high interest in city government Web sites and thus may be difficult to convince to try something new.

The stated research hypothesis will require significant additional work to establish or refute its validity. Such experimentation is likely to include studies to design and set up interactive Web sites for the cities previously studied. Once this is accomplished, residents' actual usage of the sites may be tracked. Additional studies should include running customer satisfaction studies on police/community relations in other cities where significant Internet activities involving the police are already taking place. Such studies will help confirm the importance of the aforementioned demographic parameters in the ongoing success of interactive police/community Web sites or help elucidate any other factors that may have been overlooked in developing the original hypothesis.

REFERENCES

Culbertson, H. M. (2000, Spring). A key step in police-community relations: identifying the divisive issues. Public Relations Quarterly, 45(1), 13-17. Retrieved March 2, 2001 from EBSCO Industries Inc. Database (Academic Search Elite) on the World Wide Web: http://www.ebsco.com

Cummings, B. (2001, April). NYPD meets marketing 101. Sales and Marketing Management, 153(4), 14. Retrieved September 1, 2001 from EBSCO Industries Inc. Database (Academic Search Elite) on the World Wide Web: http://www.ebsco.com

Rohe, W. M., Adams, R. E. & Arcury, T. A. (2001, Winter). Community policing and planning. Journal of the American Planning Association, 67(1), 78-90. Retrieved June 9, 2001 from EBSCO Industries Inc. Database (Academic Search Elite) on the World Wide Web: http://www.ebsco.com

Sissom, K. (1996, December). Community-oriented policing means business. FBI Law Enforcement Bulletin, 65(12), 10-14. Retrieved March 2, 2001 from EBSCO Industries Inc. Database (Academic Search Elite) on the World Wide Web: http://www.ebsco.com

Intrinsic and Contextual Data Quality: The Effect of Media and Personal Involvement

Andrew S. Borchers
Kettering University, 1700 West Third Avenue, Flint, Minnesota
Tel: 810-762-7983, Fax: 810-762-9944, aborcher@kettering.edu

INTRODUCTION AND LITERATURE

This research in progress examines intrinsic and contextual data quality and how individual perceptions of it are impacted by media (World Wide Web versus print) and personal involvement with the topic. The impact of the Internet revolution on information sharing is widely acknowledged. But this access comes with a challenge as stated by Gilster (as cited in Flanigan, 2000). "One of the challenges of Internet publishing is that it turns our conventional expectations, built upon years of experience with newspapers and magazines, on their head. We can no longer assume that the appearance of a publication is necessarily relevant to the quality of its information."

Data quality has been described in the literature as a multidimensional concept (Wand, 1996). In a rigorous study of the dimensions of data quality, Wang (1996) identifies four major areas of data quality: intrinsic, contextual, representational and accessibility. He further defines intrinsic data quality as including accuracy, objectivity, believability and reputation. Contextual data quality includes relevancy, timeliness and appropriate amount of data. This study focuses on intrinsic and contextual data quality for two reasons. First, the attributes studied were found to be significantly different between WWW and print media by a prior researcher (Klein, 1999). Klein found web based material to be more timely, but less believable and of lower reputation, accuracy and objectivity than printed material. Second, these attributes are also commonly used in the literature by researchers studying internet credibility.

Beyond the information systems literature, there is a body of literature among journalism scholars about the perceptions of internet credibility (Flanagin, 2000 and Johnson, 1998). The major thrust of this literature is in comparing the Internet to traditional sources with respect to credibility. Note that when referring to "credibility", these authors say "the most consistent dimension of media credibility is believability, but accuracy, trustworthiness, bias and completeness of information are other dimensions commonly used by researchers." (Flanagin, 2000, p. 521). Hence, there is a rough correspondence of thinking about "credibility" in the journalism literature to the concept of "intrinsic" and "contextual" data quality in the information systems literature. Flanagin's work focuses in three areas. First, he looks at the relative perceived credibility of television, newspapers, radio, magazines and the Internet. The major finding, unlike Klein, is that there is little difference in credibility between media. Second, Flanagin looks at the extent to which Internet users verify what they receive. Third, and most important to this work, Flanagin looks at whether perceived credibility varies depending on the type of information being sought. Flanagin cites Gunther in suggesting that "greater involvement with the message results in, first, a wider latitude of rejection."

Finally, health care literature forms a final basis for this work. Bates (2000) notes the role of "word of mouth" in providing consumers with health care information. Others have noted the gender difference in many families when it comes to health information. Women are most often the conduit through which health care information is filtered. Further, they are the chief decision maker in health care matters in many families (Looker, 2001).

Using information about cancer from a "reputable" and a "disreputable" source as a vehicle to study these relationships, the author posits the following hypotheses:

H1: Subjects will perceive web based material to be more timely, but less believable and of lower reputation, accuracy and objectivity than printed material.

H2: Individuals with greater personal involvement in cancer will be better discriminators of data quality in viewing reputable and non-reputable cancer information.

H3: Women are better discriminators of data quality in viewing reputable and non-reputable cancer information than men.

Further, since the experiment is premised on a source being "reputable" and "disreputable", the author tested an initial hypothesis (H0) that posits the "reputable" source has significantly greater intrinsic and contextual data quality than the "disreputable" source.

METHODOLOGY

This research involves an experiment in which subjects (n=127) reviewed information on cancer and answered a questionnaire. Subjects were drawn from mid-career students in MBA classes at a Midwestern university. The sample is strongly multi-cultural with significant U.S., Indian and Chinese representation. Subjects were randomly assigned to one of four groups.

These four groups were shown cancer information based on two sources of information presented in two different formats. One source was a website of a highly credible cancer organization. The second source of cancer information was a website of low creditability, a site that touted alternative medical treatments. The third and fourth sources were identical to the first two with the exception that they were presented in printed form by way of a color document. Subjects were then asked about their perceptions of the data that they have viewed using Wang's intrinsic data quality dimensions (accuracy, objectivity, believability and reputation) as well as contextual dimensions (timeliness, relevancy and appropriate amount of information) and ease of use. Further, subjects were asked about their personal and family experience with cancer as well as demographic questions.

FINDINGS

After the data was collected, the author analyzed it using a univariate ANOVA procedure. H0 was tested for all eight measured data quality dimensions using the source reputation (high or low) and media (print or WWW) as fixed factors. H2 and H3 were tested by looking at the product term for source reputation and cancer involvement (H2) or Gender (H3). Table 1 below summarizes the findings:

DISCUSSION

This research in progress has begun a line of work that seeks to understand the underlying factors behind different dimensions of perceived data quality. Do people perceive data quality differently depending on the media that data is presented in? The results of this paper suggest, as Flanigan (2000) did, that media is not a significant factor. Do people become more discriminating of data quality for topics that they are personally involved in? This study would suggest, at least for cancer information, that this is not the case. Finally, does gender play a role in one's ability to discriminate between reputable and non-reputable sources? This study would suggest that this is not so.

Table 1: Hypothesis testing results

Hypothesis	Dimension	F ratio	Significance
H0 – Initial	Believable, accuracy, reputation, objectivity and appropriate amount	10.526 to 24.489	.000 to .002
H0 – Initial	Timeliness, Relevance, ease of use	< 1.4	> .35
H1 – WWW compared to print	Timeliness Believable Reputation Accuracy Objectivity	2.587 1.036 .340 .483 1.132	.110 .311 .561 .489 .290
H2 – Personal Involvement with Cancer	Believable Accuracy Reputation Objectivity Appropriate Amount	All < 4	All > .05
H3 – Gender	Believable Accuracy Reputation Objectivity Appropriate Amount	All < 4	All > .05

There are several limitations in this study and further areas for research. The author intended this work as only a first study and a vehicle to begin to understand the issues. Second, the personal involvement with cancer aspect bears rework. The subject population included mostly younger adults. Fully half of the sample was in the age range of 26-35. It may be that their "involvement" in cancer is so remote that it has little impact on their perception of data quality. Third, the data collection instrument used here (including the Cancer literature), needs to be revisited. Although it was created using the terminology of Wang (1996), it may have lost some of its meaning with the multinational sample used in this work. Finally, this research data was collected in tandem with another survey instrument. The resulting form was four pages long and may have fatigued the participants. This having been noted, there does appear to be a line of research in data quality that crosses between the information systems and journalism disciplines. Further work should be done to better understand the underlying factors behind data quality.

REFERENCES

Bates, D.W. and Gawande, A.A. (2000). The Impact of the Internet on Quality Measurement. (19:6) *Health Affairs*. pp. 104-114.

Flanagin, A. J. and Metzger, M. J. (2000). Perceptions of Internet Information Credibility. *Journalism and Mass Communications Quarterly.* (77:3), pp. 515-540.

Looker, P.A. and Stichler, J. F. (2001). Getting to Know the Women's Health Care Segment. *Marketing Health Services.* (21:3), pp. 33-34.

Johnson, T. J. and Kaye, B. K.. Cruising is Believing?: Comparing Internet and Traditional Sources on Media Credibility Measures. *Journalism and Mass Communications Quarterly.* (75:2), pp. 325-340.

Klein, Barbara D. (October, 1999). Information Quality and the WWW. *Applied Business in Technology Conference.* Rochester, MI: Oakland University.

Smith, Stephen E. (1998) Reliable cancer resources on the Internet. *Information Today* (15:6) p.23,28+.

Strong, Diane M; Lee, Yang W Wang, Richard Y. (1997) Data quality in context. *Communications of the ACM* (40:5) p.103-110

Wand, Yair; Wang, Richard Y, (1996) Anchoring data quality dimensions in ontological foundations. *Communications of the ACM* (39:11), p.86-95

Wang, Richard Y; Strong, Diane M. Beyond accuracy: What data quality means to data consumers. (1996) *Journal of Management Information Systems.* (12:4), p.5-33.

Model-Based Risk Management Using UML and UP

Folker den Braber
Sintef Telecom and Informatics, P.O.Box 83, N-0314 Oslo, Norway, folker.den.braber@informatics.sintef.no

Theo Dimitrakos
CLRC Rutherford Appleton Laboratory, Oxfordshire, OX11 0QX, UK, t.dimitrakos@rl.ac.uk

Bjørn Axel Gran
Institute for Energy Technology, P.O. Box 173, N-1751 Halden, Norway, bjorn.axel.gran@hrp.no

Ketil Stølen and Jan Øyvind Aagedal
Sintef Telecom and Informatics, P.O.Box 83, N-0314 Oslo, Norway, {ketil.stoelen, jan.aagedal}@informatics.sintef.no

ABSTRACT

CORAS is a research and technological development project under the Information Society Technologies (IST) Programme (Commission of the European Communities, Directorate-General Information Society). CORAS started up in January 2001 and runs until July 2003. The main result of the CORAS project is the CORAS framework for model-based risk assessment. It employs UML-oriented modelling for three main purposes. (1) To describe the target of assessment at the right level of abstraction; (2) As a medium for communication and interaction between different groups of stakeholders involved in risk assessment; (3) To document risk assessment results and the assumptions on which these results depend. This paper provides a brief overview of the CORAS framework with particular emphasis on the role of UML and UP.

INTRODUCTION

CORAS [4] aims at an improved methodology for precise, unambiguous, and efficient risk assessment of security critical systems. The focus of the CORAS project lies on the tight integration of viewpoint-oriented UML modelling in the risk management process. An important angle of the CORAS project, is the practical use of UML [15] and UP [10] in the context of security and risk assessment.

CORAS addresses security critical systems in general, but puts particular emphasis on IT security. IT security includes all aspects related to defining, achieving, and maintaining confidentiality, integrity, availability, non-repudiation, accountability, authenticity, and reliability of IT systems [8]. An IT system in the sense of CORAS is not just technology, but also the humans interacting with the technology and all relevant aspects of the surrounding organisation and society.

The CORAS consortium consists of three commercial companies: Intracom (Greece), Solinet (Germany) and Telenor (Norway); seven research institutes: CTI (Greece), FORTH (Greece); IFE (Norway), NCT (Norway), NR (Norway), RAL (UK) and Sintef (Norway); as well as one university college: QMW (UK). Telenor and Sintef are responsible for the administrative and scientific coordination, respectively.

The remainder of this paper is divided into five sections. Section 2 provides and overview of the CORAS framework which is the main result of the CORAS project. Sections 3 - 6 describe the main constituents of the CORAS framework: the risk management process (Section 3), the system documentation framework (Section 4), the platform for tool integration (Section 5), and the integrated risk management and development process (Section 6).

THE CORAS FRAMEWORK

The main CORAS result is the CORAS framework for model-based risk assessment. As illustrated by Figure 1, the CORAS framework has four main anchor-points.

The CORAS risk assessment methodology integrates aspects of HazOp analysis [13], Fault Tree Analysis (FTA) [5], Failure Mode and Effect Criticality Analysis (FMECA) [3], Markov Analysis [11] as well as CRAMM [2]. It is model-based in the sense that it gives detailed recommendations for the use of UML modelling in conjunction with assessment. In fact, it employs modelling technology for three main purposes:

Figure 1: The CORAS framework for model-based risk assessment

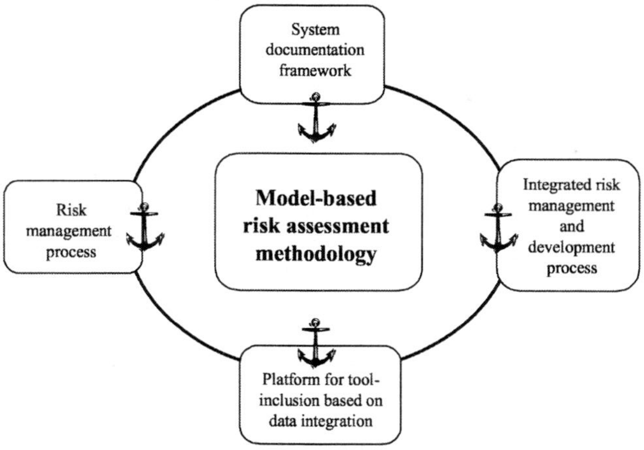

1. To describe the target of assessment at the right level of abstraction.
2. As a medium for communication and interaction between different groups of stakeholders involved in risk assessment.
3. To document risk assessment results and the assumptions on which these results depend.

Model-based risk assessment is motivated by several factors:

- Risk assessment requires correct descriptions of the target system, its context and all security relevant features. The modelling technology improves the precision of such descriptions. Improved precision is expected to improve the quality of risk assessment results.
- The graphical style of UML is believed to further communication and interaction between stakeholders involved in a risk assessment. This is expected to improve the quality of results, and also speed up

the risk assessment process since the danger of wasting time and resources on misconceptions is reduced.

- The modelling technology facilitates a more precise documentation of risk assessment results and the assumptions on which their validity depends. This expected to reduce maintenance costs by increasing the possibilities for reuse.
- The modelling technology provides a solid basis for the integration of assessment methods that should improve the effectiveness of the assessment process.
- The modelling technology is supported by a rich set of tools from which the risk management may benefit. This may improve quality (as in the case of the two first bullets) and reduce costs (as in the case of the second bullet). It also furthers productivity and maintenance.
- The modelling technology provides a basis for tighter integration of risk management and assessment in the system development process. This may considerably reduce development costs and help ensure that the specified security level is achieved.

THE RISK MANAGEMENT PROCESS

The CORAS risk management process is based on AS/NZS 4360: 1999 Risk Management [1] and ISO/IEC 17799-1: 2000 Code of Practise for Information Security Management [9]. Moreover, it is complemented by ISO/IEC TR 13335-1: 2001 Guidelines for the Management of IT Security [8] and IEC 61508: 2000 Functional Safety of Electrical/Electronic/ Programmable Safety Related Systems [6]. As indicated by Figure 2, AS/NZS 4360 provides a sequencing of the risk management process into sub-processes for context identification, risk identification, risk analysis, risk evaluation, and risk treatment. For each of these stages, the CORAS methodology gives detailed advice with respect to which models should be constructed, and how they should be expressed.

Figure 2: The CORAS risk management process and the role of UML

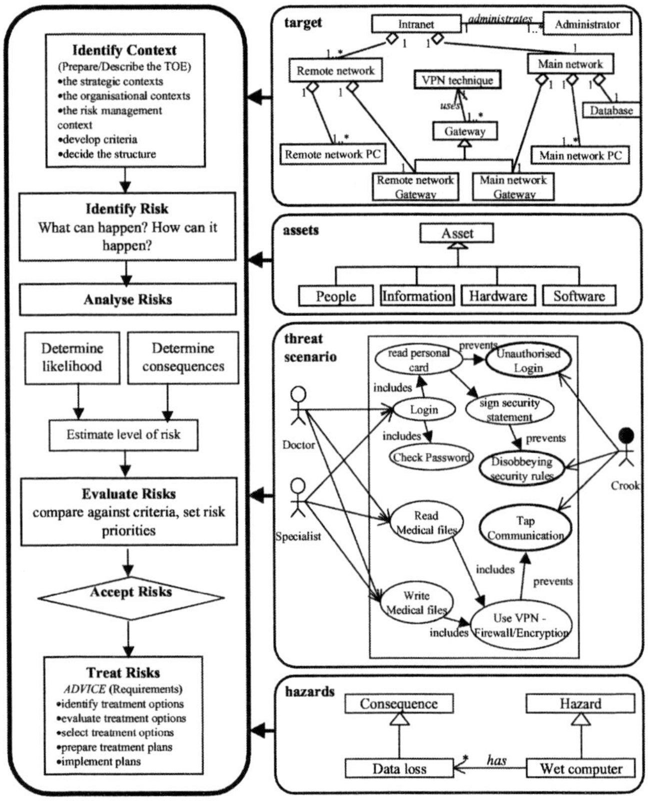

Context identification establishes the strategic, organisational and risk management context. Context identification is supported by models of the following kinds:

- *SWOT:* Describes the relationship between the organisation and its environment, identifying the organisation's strengths, weaknesses, opportunities and threats.
- *Context:* Describes the organisation and its capabilities, as well as its goals and objectives and the strategies that are in place to achieve them.
- *Target:* Describes the goals, objectives, strategies, scope and parameters of the activity, or system to which the risk management process is being applied. Figure 2 illustrates the use of a UML class-diagram to specify some aspects of a potential target.
- *Assets:* Describes the identified assets, their dependencies as well as the results from the asset valuation. Figure 2 illustrates the use of a UML class-diagram to specify relevant assets of a potential target.
- *Security Requirements:* Describes the security requirements needed to preserve the identified assets.
- *Risk Evaluation Criteria:* Describes the criteria against which risk is to be evaluated.

Risk identification is the process of determining what can happen why and how. Risk identification is supported by models of the following kinds:

- *Threat Scenarios:* Describes potential threat scenarios. Threats (and also hazards) to a system may for example be specified with the help of a misuse case diagram inspired from [14] as indicated by Figure 2.
- *Deviations:* Describes potential deviations.
- *Hazards:* Describes potential hazards. The class-diagram at the bottom of Figure 2 captures a consequence-hazard relationship.

Risk analysis is the systematic use of available information to determine how often specified models may occur and the magnitude of their consequences. Risk analysis is supported by models of the following kinds:

- *Consequence Estimates:* Describes consequence estimates for the identified hazards.
- *Hazard Frequencies:* Describes frequency estimates for the identified hazards.
- *Threat Frequencies:* Describes frequency estimates for the identified threats.

Risk evaluation is the process to determine risk management priorities by comparing the level of risk against predetermined standards, target risk levels or other criteria. Risk evaluation is supported by models of the following kinds:

- *Risk Estimates:* Describes risk estimates for the identified hazards.
- *Risk Priorities:* Describes hazard priorities based on the estimated risks.
- *Risk Themes:* Describes how the hazards should be grouped into hazard themes.
- *Risk-Theme Relationships*: Describes the relationships between the hazard themes.
- *Risk-Theme Priorities:* Describes hazard-theme priorities based on the estimated risks.

Risk treatment is the selection and implementation of appropriate options for dealing with risk. Risk treatment is supported by models of the following kinds:

- *Policy:* Describes required changes to policies to handle identified security problems.
- *Security Requirements:* Describes strengthened security requirements to handle identified security problems.
- *Security Architectures:* Describes required changes to security architecture to handle identified security problems.
- *Testing:* Describes requirements to testing to further investigate potential security problems.
- *Monitoring:* Describes requirements to system monitoring to help handling potential security problems.
- *Treatment Priorities:* Describes a list of solutions with priorities.

SYSTEM DOCUMENTATION FRAMEWORK

The CORAS system documentation framework is based on the ISO/IEC 10746 series: 1995 Basic Reference Model for Open Distributed Processing (RM-ODP) [7]. RM-ODP defines a reference model for distributed systems architecture, based on object-oriented techniques.

RM-ODP divides the system documentation into five viewpoints. It also provides modelling, specification and structuring terminology, a conformance module addressing implementation and consistency requirements, as well as a distribution module defining transparencies and functions required to realise these transparencies.

The CORAS system documentation framework extends RM-ODP with

- concepts and terminology for risk management and security;
- carefully defined models within each viewpoint (as already exemplified in Section 3) targeting model-based risk management and assessment of security-critical systems;
- libraries of reusable model fragments targeting risk assessment;
- additional support for conformance checking;
- a risk management module containing the risk management process, relevant standards, risk assessment methodology as well as formats for tool integration.

PLATFORM FOR TOOL INTEGRATION

The CORAS platform will be based on data integration implemented in terms of XML (eXtensible Markup Language) technology. The platform will be built around an internal data representation formalised in XML/XMI (characterised by XML schema). Standard XML tools are supposed to provide much of the basic functionality. This functionality may be used to experiment with the CORAS platform and also support the CORAS crew during two major trials planned for 2002.

Based on XSL (eXtensible Stylesheet Language), relevant aspects of the internal data representation may be mapped to the internal data representations of other tools (and the other way around). This allows the integration of sophisticated case-tools targeting system development as well as risk analysis tools and tools for vulnerability and treat management.

Figure 3: Integrated risk management and development process

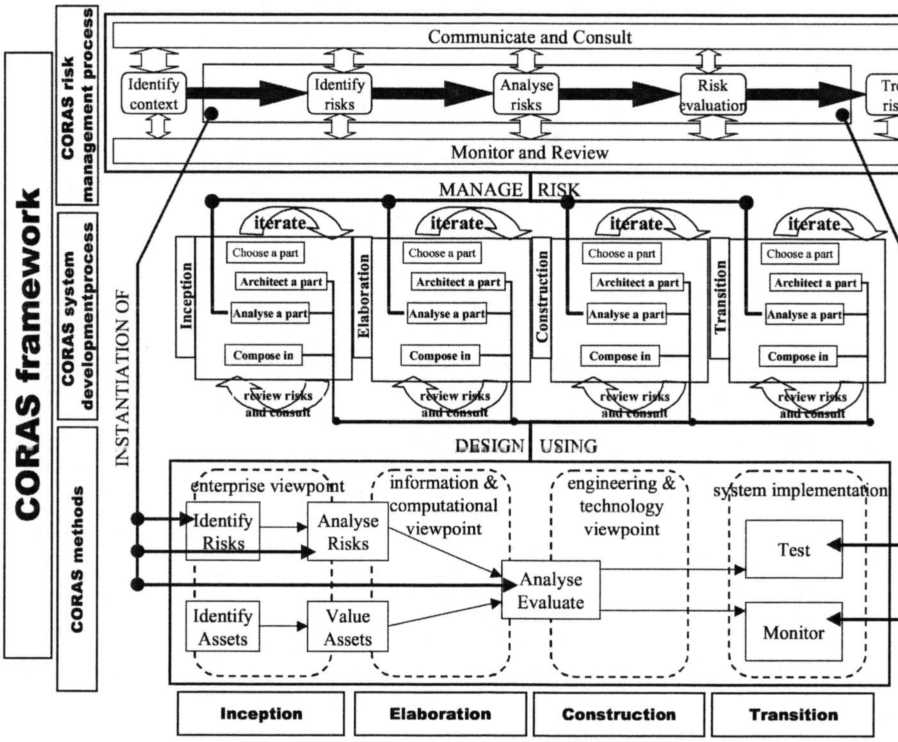

INTEGRATED RISK MANAGEMENT AND DEVELOPMENT PROCESS

The CORAS integrated risk management and development process is based on an integration of AS/NZS 4360 [1] and an adaptation of UP [10] to support RM-ODP [7] inspired viewpoint oriented modelling.

Figure 3 provides an overview of the relationship between the various stages of the risk management process, RM-ODP and the main UP workflows. Emphasis is placed on describing the evolution of the correlation between risk management and viewpoint oriented modelling throughout the systems development and maintenance lifecycle.

As based on the UP, the CORAS process is also both stepwise incremental and iterative. In analogy to the RM-ODP viewpoints, the viewpoints of the CORAS framework are not layered; they are different abstractions of the same system focusing on different areas of concern.

REFERENCES

[1] AS/NZS 4360:1999 Risk management.

[2] Barber, B., Davey, J. The use of the CCTA risk analysis and management methodology CRAMM. Proc. MEDINFO92, North Holland, 1589 –1593, 1992.

[3] Bouti, A., Ait Kadi, D. A state-of-the-art review of FMEA/FMECA. International Journal of Reliability, Quality and Safety Engineering 1:515-543, 1994.

[4] CORAS: A platform for risk analysis of security critical systems. IST-2000-25031, 2000. (http://www.nr.no/coras/)

[5] IEC 1025: 1990 Fault tree analysis (FTA).

[6] IEC 61508: 2000 Functional safety of electrical/electronic/programmable safety related systems.

[7] ISO/IEC 10746 series: 1995 Basic reference model for open distributed processing.

[8] ISO/IEC TR 13335-1:2001: Information technology – Guidelines for the management of IT Security – Part 1: Concepts and models for IT Security.

[9] ISO/IEC 17799: 2000 Information technology – Code of practise for information security management.

[10] Krutchten, P. The Rational unified process, an introduction. Addison-Wesley, 1999.

[11] Littlewood, B. A reliability model for systems with Markov structure. Appl. Stat. 24:172-177, 1975.

[12] Putman, J. R. Architecting with RM-ODP. Prentice Hall, 2001.

[13] Redmill, F., Chudleigh, M., Catmur, J. Hazop and Software Hazop. Wiley, 1999.

[14] Sindre, G., Opdahl, A. L. Eliciting security requirements by misuse cases. In Proc. TOOLS_PACIFIC 2000. IEEE Computer Society Press, 120-131, 2000.

[15] UML proposal to the Object Management Group, Version 1.4, 2000.

Searching for Linkages between Knowledge Management, Learning Organisation and Organisational Culture Within Large Service Enterprises in the United Kingdom: What KM Practitioners Say

Anton Bradburn, Elayne Coakes and Gill Sugden
Westminster Business School, Westminster University, Marylebone Campus, 35 Marylebone Road, London NW1 5LS, England
Tel: 44 (0) 207 911 3033, Fax: 44 (0) 207 911 5839, bradbua@wmin.ac.uk

ABSTRACT

We recognise that in this research in progress we are examining organisational change – change driven by the imperatives of the developing knowledge economy. Organisational change implies the modification of core values in an organisation's cultural paradigm (Hales 2001); it implies the development of a learning organisation (Pedler, Burgoyne and Boydell 1994; Senge 1990; Argyris and Schon 1978) and it implies co-operation between organisational functions (Scarborough et al 1999). Where organisations do not address these issues effectively, attempts to release value from human assets by means of Knowledge Management (KM) carry a high probability of failure (Scarborough and Swan 1999).

In order to confront the challenges posed by the turbulence characteristic of today's operating environments organisational change seems inexorable. To perform successfully in this new era organisations are looking to their intellectual assets and at ways of leveraging them as a source of sustainable competitive advantage.

Due to the low response rate and the resulting size of our sample we recognise that we are unable to generalise from our data. Accordingly, in our paper, we offer an idiographic study of KM practices in UK service organisations.

THE PURPOSE OF THE RESEARCH

Our research interests in this field led us to identify and explore any linkages there may have been between the concepts of knowledge management, the learning organisation and organisational culture from the perspective of KM practitioners. Conventionally, we began with a review of KM literature, which we conducted during the first Quarter of 2001 (Sugden et al 2001). We searched on-line databases, available via our organisation's intranet, covering the years 1995 to 2000 limiting our search to the single term *knowledge management*. We recorded a total of 103 citations distributed as shown in Table 1.

Table 1: KM literature search results (January-March 2001)

YEAR	1995	1996	1997	1998	1999	2000
HITS	0	3	1	11	50	38

Our review of this literature enabled us to map linkages between the concepts in our research focus in two domains - theoretical and empirical - and highlighted ambiguities in the areas of debate surrounding the concepts of knowledge management, learning organisation and culture. We decided to undertake an empirical study focused on individuals involved with and utilising KM in an attempt to resolve some of these ambiguities.

RESEARCH DESIGN AND METHODOLOGY

Our working definition of knowledge management was "any process or practice of creating, acquiring, capturing, sharing and using knowledge, wherever it resides, to enhance learning and performance in organisations," and our research question distilled down to, "Is KM destined for inevitable failure in enterprises whose organisational culture is averse to change and thus resistant to new ways of working and of learning from the outcomes of new working practices?"

We decided to investigate the UK service sector in which there is a mix of private, public and voluntary organisations. We combined methods of research commencing with a survey and are following this up with semi-structured interviews. We drew on a database of KM practitioners for our sampling frame and mailed a self-completion questionnaire to 621-KM practitioners in 332 large service organisations[1] throughout the United Kingdom. These organisations were comprised of airlines, financial services, government - both central and local, healthcare, higher education, insurance, legal services, management consulting and media.

For our research instrument we drew on the work of Allee (1997), Pedler et al (1994) and Johnson and Scholes (1997). Allee (op.cit) starts from the premise that knowledge represents a primary competitive tool and states that survival depends on an organisation's ability to innovate and that to do this knowledge is required that will enable it to learn, adjust and change. Allee offers 12 principles - a checklist really - for KM practice, subsequently adopting the metaphor of maritime navigation within which to provide examples of each of the principles together with examples of organisations noted for using a particular principle. IT is seen as supporting rather than driving KM, in particular corporate intranets (especially for self-directed learning).

Pedler, Burgoyne and Boydell (op.cit) describe a learning organisation as one "that facilitates the learning of all its members and continuously transforms itself" in the process. In non-learning enterprises managers prescribe organisational needs; employees simply operate within these constraints aiming to produce the required outputs and achieve the stated organisational goals. The writers provide a framework comprised of 11 elements with which to assess how close any organisation comes to their learning organisation concept. In developing this concept they provide three descriptors for non-learning, first order and second order learning.

In Hales (2001, 8:163) organisational culture is defined as the values, beliefs and behavioural norms shared by individuals in an organisation. In his view organisational culture operates in one of two modes - weak or strong - in terms of artefacts, values and assumptions about such matters as human nature and the relation of the organisation to the environment. According to Johnson and Scholes (op.cit., 2:60) values, beliefs and assumptions also form the central paradigm of organisational culture - the cultural web. By drawing on frames of reference associated with stories, symbols, power structures, organisational structures, control systems in addition to rituals and routines employees collectively weave their organisation's cultural fabric over time.

Our research instrument in this survey was a questionnaire comprised of 26 variables, intended to generate both quantitative and qualitative data. With the exception of three questions relating to length of service, length of involvement with KM and KM activities in the organisation the remaining 22 variables consisted of statements to which recipients were asked to respond on a seven point Likert scale.

FINDINGS

We received a 6.6 per cent response to our survey (N=41). Of our 41 respondents 20 agreed to an interview at a later stage. Our survey asked respondents to identify KM activities, organisational values and cultural beliefs. KM activities were subsumed into 21 categories, organisational values into 27 categories and cultural beliefs into 10 categories. The most frequent responses to our question about KM activities were concerned with content (26.8% N=22), intranets (23.2% N=19), learning (8.5% N=7), applications (7.3% N=6) and ways of working (6.1% N=5) as shown in Chart 1 below.

The most frequently listed organisation values guiding the way respondents worked in organisations were concerned with best practice (16.2% N=12)), honesty and integrity (10.8% N=8), customer focus (9.5% N=7), team working (9.5% N=7) together with transparency and openness (8.1% N=6). These are shown in Chart 2 below.

The key beliefs most frequently expressed were concerned with excellence (37.5% N=6), customer and employee relations (25.0% N=4), innovation (18.8% N=3) and social networks (18.8% N=3) as illustrated in Chart 3.

Chart 1: Most frequent KM activities

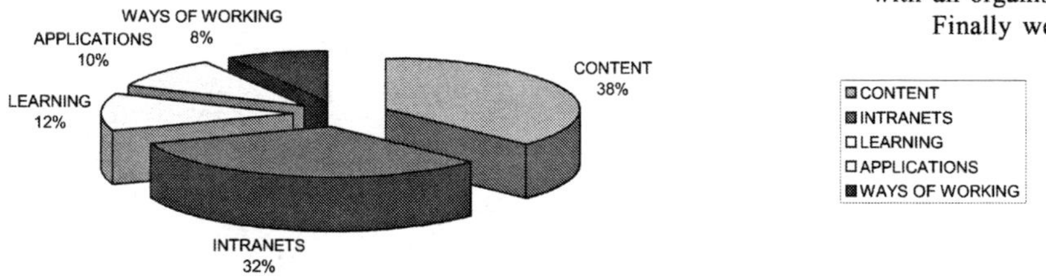

Chart 2: Most frequently cited values guiding ways of working

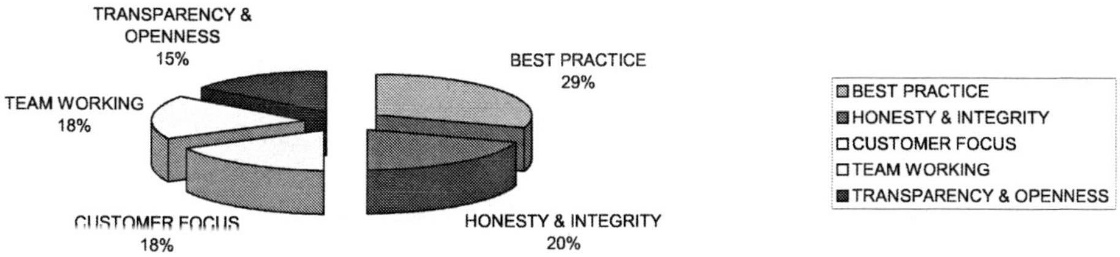

Chart 3: Most frequently expressed key beliefs

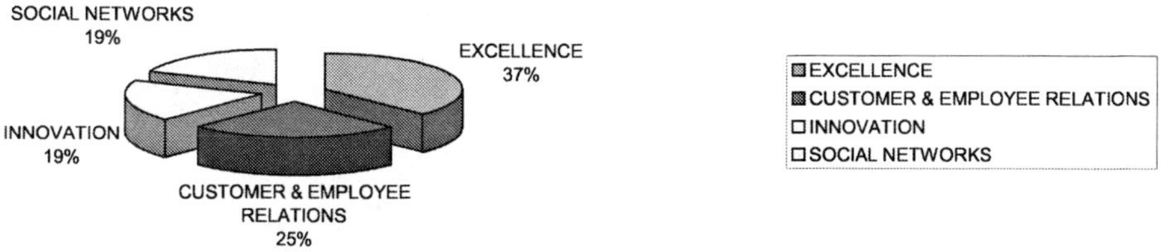

We analysed the quantitative variables in our survey instrument for correlations. We selected the variables and the correlations on the strength of the correlation between them. We chose a cut-off level of 0.50 in the + or – direction considering anything less than 0.50 as representing only a weak relationship.

SOME INTERIM OBSERVATIONS

We found 272 sets of correlations between the pairs of variables we analysed. Defining a correlation coefficient of +/-0.50 to +/-0.74 as moderate and above+/-0.75 as strong within Allee's (1997) principles of knowledge management we noted that there were eight pairs of correlations. Within Pedler et al's (1994) measures of a learning organisation there were 11 such pairs of correlations. This would suggest a degree of internal consistency within each of the sets of variables comprising the KM concept and the concept of the learning organisation.

We observed three moderate sets of correlations between the KM and learning concepts, that is between Allee's work (op.cit) and the work of Pedler et al (op.cit). We noted that the use within an organisation of a particular way of talking about KM correlated with people working together in expert communities, or communities of practice (COPS). We observed that an organisation encouraging the exploitation of organisational knowledge correlated with people working in COPS. We noticed that business strategy developing out of shared knowledge correlated with responsibility for organisational knowledge being vested in one designated individual.

We also noted three such cross-conceptual sets of correlations in variables relating to the learning organisation and organisational culture - the work of Pedler et al (op.cit) and Johnson and Scholes's work (op.cit). Here we observed moderate correlations between employees at all levels being encouraged to participate in formulating their organisations' business policy and the organisational culture supporting KM. A similar moderate correlation was revealed between an organisation's business strategy developing as a result of sharing organisational knowledge and support for KM from the organisational culture. Enhancing organisational knowledge through working collaboratively with other organisations also correlated moderately with an organisational culture supportive of KM.

Finally we report two sets of correlations between the KM and organisational culture concepts. Responsibility for organisational knowledge being vested in one designated individual was moderately correlated with an organisational culture supporting KM and an organisation encouraging knowledge exploitation also correlated moderately with a supportive culture within the organisation concerned.

SOME INTERIM CONCLUSIONS

Given that 241 of the total sets of correlations fell below our reporting threshold may be an indication that the operation of knowledge management within the sample we investigated is not dependent upon the concepts of the learning organisation and organisational culture. However, we have no indicators of operational effectiveness in these cases. The purpose of the semi-structured interviews we are currently undertaking may enable us to report on this aspect subsequently and we are sanguine about having some findings and plausible explanations drawn from our qualitative data to report at the forthcoming IRMA Conference.

ENDNOTES

[1] The European Commission (EC) defines micro, small, medium and large enterprises exclusively by employment, rather than a multiplicity of criteria. Thus a micro-enterprise has between 0 and 9 employees, a small-enterprise has 10 to 99 employees while a medium size enterprise has a workforce of between 100 and 499 employees and a large enterprise employs 500, or more. For the purpose of this study we have adopted the EC's definition of the large enterprise.

REFERENCES

Allee, V. (1997), '12 principles of knowledge management', Training & Development, Vol 51, No 11, pps 71-75.

Argyris, C., Schon, D.A. (1978), 'Organizational Learning: a Theory of Action Perpsective'' Addison-Wesley.

Hales, C. (2001), 'Managing Through Organization' (2nd edition), London, Thomson Learning Business Press

Johnson, G., Scholes, K. (1997), 'Exploring Corporate Strategy', Hemel Hempstead, Prentice Hall.

Pedler, M., Burgoyne, J., Boydell, J. (1994), 'Towards the Learning Company', Maidenhead, McGraw-Hill.

Scarborough, H., Swan, J. (1999), 'Case Studies in Knowledge Management', London, Institute of Personnel and Development.

Scarborough, H., Swan, J., Preston, J. (1999), 'Knowledge Management: a Literature Review', London, Institute of Personnel and Development.

Senge, P.M (1990), 'The Fifth Discipline: the Art and Practice of the Learning Organization', New York, Doubleday/Currency.

Sugden, G., Coakes, E., Bradburn, A. (2001), 'Brains In - Brawn's Out', London, internal paper for Westminster Business School, University of Westminster.

E-mail and WWW Browsers: A Forensic Computing Perspective on the Need for Improved User Education for Information Systems Security Management

Vlasti Broucek[1] and Paul Turner[2]
School of Information Systems, University of Tasmania, GPO Box 252-87, Hobart TAS 7001, Australia
[1]Tel: +61-3-6226 2346, [1]Fax: +61-3-6226 883, [2]Tel: +61-3-6226 2930, [2]Fax: +61-3-6226 2913, {Vlasti.Broucek, Paul.Turner}@utas.edu.au

ABSTRACT

This paper is in two parts. Part One identifies common security and privacy weaknesses that exist in e-mail and WWW browsers and highlights some of the major implications for organisational security that result from employees online behaviours. This section aims to raise awareness of these weaknesses amongst users and to encourage administrators to mitigate their consequences through enhanced security and privacy focused user education and training. Part Two makes recommendations for improved user education as a component of information systems security management practices. These recommendations have been generated from a forensic computing perspective that aims to balance the complex set of issues involved in developing effective IS security management policies and practices. From this perspective these policies and practices should improve security of organisation and the privacy of employees without compromising the potential need for future forensic investigation of inappropriate, criminal, or other illegal online behaviours.

INTRODUCTION

In the age of hactivism, malware and cyber-warfare increasing numbers of publications are being produced by computer security specialists and systems administrators on technical issues arising from illegal or inappropriate online behaviours. Technical advances in the ability of information systems to detect intrusions, denial of services attacks and also to enhance network monitoring and maintenance are well documented and subject to constant research and development.

To date however there has been limited research into a range of other issues impacting on information systems (IS) security and its management. From a forensic computing (FC) perspective IS security management emerges as part of a much broader debate on the risks and challenges posed by digitalisation for legal, technical and social structures (Broucek & Turner, 2001a, 2001b). This perspective highlights that IS security management cannot be addressed by technical means alone. Indeed the development of effective security management relies on recognition of the need to balance a complex set of technical, legal and organisational issues (Lichtenstein & Swatman, 2000).

This paper explores one of these issues, 'user education' and identifies its relevance for and interrelationships with other IS security management issues. This exploration is conducted through an examination of the two most common Internet applications used in organisations: electronic mail (e-mail) and World Wide Web (WWW) browsers. By identifying common security weaknesses in both types of applications the paper examines how the security management problems are compounded by common online user behaviours. Retaining a FC perspective the paper makes recommendations for improving IS security management.

PART ONE

At a technical level systems administrators are very aware of the security risks and security weaknesses prevalent in Internet applications and in particular in e-mail and WWW browsers. Significantly, while technical solutions are available (at a cost) to alleviate most of the major security challenges, the manner in which most users continue to utilise these applications compounds organisational IS security problems. While technical responses may be able to treat some of the symptoms of inappropriate and/or illegal user behaviours, they do little to treat the causes of these or future problematic behaviours (Broucek & Turner, 2002a). The focus here is on 'user education', however, it is important to note that most technical solutions employed to detect intrusions, denial of services attacks and/or to engage in network monitoring/maintenance are not currently designed to collect forensic data (Broucek & Turner, 2002b).

As a result, user education of security risks and weaknesses must be treated as an important element in developing effective IS security management practices. For the purposes of user education of security management issues in an organisational context users can be categorised in three major groups:

1. Employees lacking awareness of the implications of their online behaviours for organisational security;
2. Employees who are security conscious but in taking steps to protect their on-line privacy remain unaware of the implications of these behaviours for organisational security;
3. Employees who may deliberately exploit technical and managerial weaknesses to engage in inappropriate and often illegal online behaviours.

For all three types of users, targeted education, training and awareness raising emerge as central to minimising these risks and improving IS security management practices and policies.

The following section examines some of the major security weaknesses of email, their relationships with employees online behaviours and their implications for IS security.

E-mail

Electronic mail (e-mail) has emerged as a major communication tool in academic, business and social environments. However, e-mail or more technically SMTP as defined by RFC821 (Postel, 1982) and the proposed new standard RFC2821 (Klensin, 2001) remains inherently insecure as a communications medium. As a result e-mail per se is not suitable for the transfer of any information that has to be kept secret. Significantly, most employees and many corporate managers remain unaware that e-mail, unless encrypted, is transferred in plain text and that during its transfer from sender to receiver journeys through numerous computer systems that could provide points of access to the content of the e-mail. More worryingly, most e-mail systems in use still deploy the very efficient, but simple POP3 (post office protocol). In most instances POP3 based e-mail clients send passwords in clear text unencrypted across computer networks thereby enabling sniffing/spoofing type security breaches. These security weaknesses become even more serious given that it has been observed that numerous employees do not bother to have separate passwords for e-mail and other systems that they use in the course of their work. This 'one password for everything' approach means that POP3 e-mail client sniffing/spoofing type security breaches may become access points for all organisational information systems.

Awareness of these security weaknesses in e-mail has led many systems administrators to enhance security and restrict access to organisational e-mail systems. From the users perspective this has led to the perception of organisational e-mail systems as being 'unfriendly'. This is mainly because these systems tend not to be accessible outside the organisational 'firewall' and/or because organisational policy prohibits their utilisation for private communications. As a result of the increasingly important social dimension to e-mail usage most employees solve this 'problem' of lack of anytime/anywhere access to email by subscribing to one of the numerous free web-mail services e.g. hotmail.com, yahoo.com, excite.com, etc. This user response to the need for email access introduces further risks for organisational IS security management.

As was mentioned above the tendency of employees to adopt the 'one password for everything' approach means that the same password is used on organisational e-mail systems as well as on private web-mail accounts. This dramatically increases the possibility of password sniffing/spoofing type security breaches. Web-mail services also appear susceptible to a higher incidence of direct or double-click attachment based viruses that can easily migrate to the organisational information systems as a result of employee on-line behaviours. More significantly most of these free web-mail systems also allow the checking of POP3 e-mail accounts. Employees using these services are rarely aware that in doing so they may be allowing unauthorised access to organisational information.

From the authors own experiences in network administration within a University environment it is evident that more than 70% of current students opt for a free web-mail account in addition to their University e-mail accounts. From class discussions the main reason given by students was the concern that University administrators could gain access to their University e-mail accounts making them feel concern that their personal e-mail would be read. Following open discussions of the security weaknesses and risks of web-mail accounts with a class of 30 post-graduate students, all but one opted to stop utilising web-mail and to use the University e-mail system providing POP3 access internally and SSL protected Web based access from outside of university firewall.

WWW Browsers

Web browsers like e-mail have become central to the development of the information age. But they also exhibit many security weaknesses that combine with users online behaviours to compound IS security management problems. These include:

- Web browser history and cache files being kept on local drives – this is problematic because users are unaware of the implications for their privacy and the ease with which the sites they have visited can be viewed.
- Extensive use of cookies and the fact that many sites now do not work if cookies are disabled in browsers. This is problematic because not just because of the privacy of the user but also because organisational information is disclosed through the TCP/IP address and other details available for WWW browsers.
- Corporate users assuming that being behind corporate firewall/cache/proxy means that their true identity is not exposed to browsed Internet sites. This is often not the case because many corporate installations correctly pass the HTTP_X_FORWARDED_FOR environment variable.

PART TWO

In the context of the above discussion this part of the paper aims to generate recommendations for improving user education as a component of IS security management practices. From a forensic computing perspective these recommendations remain conscious of the need to balance improved security for the organisation and the privacy of employees without compromising the potential for future forensic investigation of inappropriate, criminal, or other illegal online behaviours.

Clearly a major element in any organisational IS security management approach must be to provide detailed explanations and demonstrations to users of how their online behaviours with these two applications could potentially damage the organisation. As part of this education it will be important to address head-on employees privacy concerns and to introduce transparent and documented procedures for any investigations over particular behaviours. Users must also be made aware that using anonymous e-mails, proxies and anonymizers will not prevent future forensic investigations from being able to track and trace their online activities. It is also imperative that the risks associated with computer viruses are explained as well as the potential fallibility of current antivirus software. In particular the importance of not running or opening files received from unknown or even unreliable sources.

In addition to explanations and demonstrations it is important that organisations put in place IS security management policies that balance employee concerns with the need for improved security. These policies must be transparent and developed in cooperation with employees. Where deterrents to inappropriate online behaviours are introduced they should be explained and discussed. If organisations feel the need to have the option of monitoring on line behaviours or conducting forensic investigations then staff should be informed of the procedures and the results of any investigations or monitoring. Creating a 'big brother surveillance' perception amongst employees may well be counter-productive in terms of IS security and/or wider organisational goals. Effective IS security management will increasingly rely on informing users of the risks and allaying privacy concerns they may have as the need for monitoring and forensic investigation become increasingly common.

CONCLUSION

This paper has highlighted series of security problems with e-mail and web browsers, and suggested how improved and targeted user education can significantly improve IS security management within organisations. With the dramatic growth in malware and cyber-attacks that looks set to continue it has become increasingly important that organisations improve their IS security management policies and practices through a balanced and cooperative approach.

REFERENCES

Broucek, V., & Turner, P. (2001a, 11 July 2001). *Forensic Computing: Developing a Conceptual Approach for an Emerging Academic Discipline.* Paper presented at the 5th Australian Security Research Symposium, Perth, Australia.

Broucek, V., & Turner, P. (2001b). Forensic Computing: Developing a Conceptual Approach in the Era of Information Warfare. *Journal of Information Warfare, 1*(2).

Broucek, V., & Turner, P. (2002a, 27-31 May 2002). *Bridging the Divide: Rising Awareness of Forensic Issues amongst Systems Administrators.* Paper presented at the 3rd International System Administration and Networking Conference, Maastricht, The Netherlands.

Broucek, V., & Turner, P. (2002b, 8-11 June 2002). *Risks and Solutions to problems arising from illegal or Inappropriate Online Behaviours: Two Core Debates within Forensic Computing.* Paper presented at the EICAR2002, Berlin, Germany.

Klensin, J. (2001). *RFC2821 - Simple Mail Transfer Protocol.* Available: http://www.ietf.org/rfc/rfc2821.txt?number=2821.

Lichtenstein, S., & Swatman, P. M. C. (2000). *Issues in E-Business Security Management and Policy.* Paper presented at the 1st Australian Information Security Management Workshop, University of Deakin, Australia.

Postel, J. B. (1982). *RFC821 - Simple Mail Transfer Protocol.* Available: http://www.ietf.org/rfc/rfc0821.txt?number=821.

Four Phases of ECommerce[1]: An Analysis of Factors Impacting on SMEs Potential to Derive Benefits from Web-Based ECommerce: 34 Australian Case Studies

Stephen Chau and Paul Turner
School of Information Systems, University of Tasmania, GPO Box 252-87, Hobart TAS 7001, Australia
Stephen.Chau@utas.edu.au, Tel: +61-3-6226 7435, Fax: +61-3-6226 2913
Paul.Turner@utas.edu.au, Tel: +61-3-6226 2930, Fax: +61-3-6226 2913,

INTRODUCTION

Inhibitors to the adoption of electronic commerce (EC) by small to medium sized businesses (SMEs) has been well researched (Freel, 2000; Lawrence & Keen, 1997; Poon 1996). More recently it has emerged that even where EC technology adoption occurs this has often not translated directly into the active utilisation and conduct of EC (Wong & Turner, 2001). Amongst those SMEs who do actively utilise EC, previous research has highlighted that the level and extent of web-based EC can be usefully categorised into four phases[2] (Chau, 2001). Building on the work of Venkatraman (1994) this four phase model has been extended to investigate the relationships between organisational transformation and potential EC benefits (Chau & Turner, 2001). These phases emerge as transitional states in the use of EC that SMEs may establish themselves at directly or migrate to from other phases.

Preliminary case study analysis suggests that the potential to derive benefit from EC activities increases where SMEs have been able to re-align business processes and structures (Chau & Turner, 2001). The ability of SMEs to re-align business processes depends upon a number of factors. To date however, there has been little detailed investigation into the factors that impact on SMEs ability to derive EC benefits within any particular phase of EC activity.

This research paper identifies and explores the range of factors that impact on SMEs potential to derive benefit from EC activities in each of the four phases. The paper develops a framework for exploring these factors that emerge as either internal or external to the SMEs analysed. Preliminary analysis highlights the utility of the framework for revealing the distinct characteristics of these factors within each phase.

THE 34 CASE STUDIES

This research is part of an on-going study investigating the utilisation of EC by Australian SMEs. These 34 case studies investigate the uptake and use of EC amongst SMEs across a broad range of businesses from seven different industries including agriculture, retail trade, hospitality, education, communications, and manufacturing. These businesses vary in age from start-ups to well established businesses. The SMEs that participated in this research were drawn from two States in Australia (Tasmania and Western Australia).

METHODOLOGY

An interpretative epistemology was deployed as the most logical and appropriate approach to capture information about the beliefs, actions, and experiences of SME participants in relation to their use of EC. Data collection consisted of a series of interviews conducted with senior management. Data analysis was conducted through a set of coding procedures. The coding procedures revealed distinct characteristics of factors (internal/external) to each phase of EC utilisation.

DISCUSSION

The data analysis reveals a range of factors affecting the ability of organisations to utilise and incorporate EC. These factors can be categorised into two broad groups, those internal to the organisation and those that are external to the organisation. The internal factors can be divided into three categories: technological; organisational and EC issues (Table 1.)

Table 1: Internal factors influencing the potential to derive EC benefit

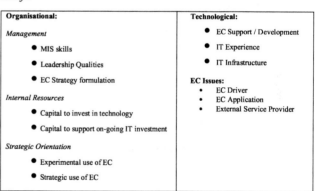

Organisational:	Technological:
Management • MIS skills • Leadership Qualities • EC Strategy formulation *Internal Resources* • Capital to invest in technology • Capital to support on-going IT investment *Strategic Orientation* • Experimental use of EC • Strategic use of EC	• EC Support / Development • IT Experience • IT Infrastructure **EC Issues:** • EC Driver • EC Application • External Service Provider

ORGANISATIONAL FACTORS

Management

Management play a pivotal role in the EC decision-making process. In all 34 cases management viewed EC as providing benefits, however the sophistication of EC implementations and level of benefit varied across phases. Phase 1 businesses use EC in a minimal manner, managers view EC as a support tool as opposed to a mechanism to enhance and extend business processes typical of management support for EC in phases 2,3 and 4.

Internal Resources

Internal resources available for EC varied substantially across all businesses and phases. The ability of SMEs to allocate resources for EC initiatives closely correlates to the business size. Medium sized businesses possess a greater capacity to conduct EC then micro and small businesses. However analysis of the cases shows that the capacity to conduct comprehensive EC activities is not a reflection on actual EC activities executed.

Small and micro businesses that employ few staff find it particularly hard to allocate capital, time and personnel to any venture outside core business activities. Some business owner/managers that could not justify the costs associated with hiring external developers resorted to experimenting with EC development themselves.

Strategic Orientation

Analysis revealed two distinct strategic orientations amongst the cases towards use of EC. Businesses located in Phase 1 and 2 predominantly view EC as an experiment that may prove to be useful for their businesses. In these phases EC is used to complement marketing and sales functions and is utilised independently of existing IS systems. No formal integration with existing office systems is conducted. Businesses in Phases 3 and 4 businesses view EC as a strategic device to extend implicit business strategies to reduce costs, promote greater efficiencies, and enhance customer services. Businesses positioned in Phase 4 rely totally on the Internet to facilitate not only their EC applications but also their whole business infrastructure. EC is used as a strategic platform central to their business operations. Without the Internet these businesses would not exist in their current state.

TECHNOLOGICAL FACTORS

IT/EC Support and Development

Technology infrastructure and support is an integral element of EC utilisation. The analysis revealed three levels of EC support and development skills amongst the cases.

- Businesses designing, developing and maintaining their EC applications in-house, often after hours at home. Small and micro businesses typify this level.
- Businesses that develop their own EC applications internally but seek some external assistance.
- Businesses that exclusively utilise external developers for their EC implementations and support.

IT Experience

Lack of skills and the cost of employing external consultants to build and support EC applications is a major deterrent to SMEs utilising EC. In these cases the decision to embark on an EC initiatives is large financial. In micro and small businesses the owner/manager is often is the first contact for IT support and as a result gains 'hands on' IT experience through necessity. Medium sized business either possess inhouse IT experts or contract in IT expertise.

IT Infrastructure

SMEs do not require ownership of an elaborate IT infrastructure to conduct EC. A computer with Internet access is all that is required for basic EC activities. In 4 cases SMEs used their home computer to develop and maintain their EC applications. The inability to host the EC application has not been a hurdle for SMEs as in Australia hosting costs are small in comparison to those of developing the initial EC application.

EC ISSUES

Driver for EC

The drivers for EC vary considerably across all cases. Access to new customers and suppliers was a common EC driver, although for many providing alternative and convenient trading and communication methods was the key driver. Sophisticated users viewed EC as a strategic tool aimed at reducing operational costs and minimising transaction inefficiencies.

The EC Application

The nature of the EC application relates closely to the driverss and motivations to use EC. Phase 1 and Phase 2 businesses do not significantly alter their core business structure and their use of EC is reflected by their applications which include electronic brochures, online stores and product and service information. Phase 3 businesses exhibit a more comprehensive array of EC applications such as customer information systems, electronic procurement systems and enhanced communication facilities. In Phase 4, EC is fundamental to business' existence. These businesses rely on global and national markets to justify their business strategy. Their EC strategy is synonymous with their business strategy.

External Service Providers

Problems with ISP experience and level of service were identified as a key external factor particularly amongst many small and micro businesses lacking IT skills and experience. The businesses that developed the majority of their EC applications in-house had the least amount of problems with ISPs.

EXTERNAL FACTORS

External factors refer to the environment in which a business operates. These factors do not directly affect the ability of an SME to conduct organisational change however they can strongly influence the potential to derive benefits from EC utilisation. The three external factors that have been identified in the analysis are; the nature of supply chain, the industry in which SMEs operates, the level of government assistance (Table 2.).

Table 2: External factors affecting SME ability to acquire EC benefits

Supply Chain	Industry Influence
• Level of automation in Supply chain • Size and number of participants (Critical Mass) • Other participants internal factors	• Level of industry support for change • Information and Education • Business Champions
Government Support • Policy and EC framework • Type of Sector Strategy • Level of Financial Aid	

Supply Chain

Phone and facsimile remains the primary platform for communication between suppliers and businesses. However, distributors and wholesalers included in the study were keen to push EC technologies on to their respective resellers, but these businesses often lacked the capacity to move on-line. Until a critical mass of EC customers and suppliers are evident, the nature of the supply chain remains a major hurdle to SMEs utilisation of EC. Lack of critical mass may also reduces the benefit to those who engage in EC early on.

Industry

Industry bodies can aid SMEs by supporting and encouraging EC initiatives. None of the SMEs indicated that they had received or sought help from the industry when developing their EC application. One problem identified by business owners was that where large business enterprises dominate the industry body, SMEs often feel powerless to exert any change over the supply chain. However, if a SME is an important customer, they may be able to influence to some degree the supply arrangements.

Government

The government can provide EC assistance in a number of ways. EC education and awareness programs are beneficial to break down the barriers of misinformation and EC adoption fears. Direct injection of capital to help subsidise initial EC efforts would help many of the smaller businesses. The development of role models or EC champions has also proved beneficial.

CONCLUSION

Collectively these factors and their interactions impact on the ability of SMEs to derive benefit from EC. Depending on the nature of these factors they can exert positive or negative forces on the ability of an SME to acquire EC benefit. The relative position of an SME within any phase emerges as being determined by the relative strengths of these factors and their interactions with one another.

ENDNOTES

[1] Chau (2001) Four Phases of ECommerce: A small business perspective – An exploratory study of 23 Australian Small Businesses. *Information Resources Management Association Conference, Toronto May 20-23, 2001.*

[2] The four phases are: Static web prescence; Adjunct to Traditional Business; Substantial re-engineering of business processes; and, Virtual Enterprise.

REFERENCES

Chau, S. B., (2001) "Four Phases of Ecommerce a Small Business Perspective: An Exploratory Study of 23 Australian Small Businesses" *Proceedings of the Information Resource and Management Association Conference,* Toronto, Canada 2001

Chau S.B. & Turner P. (2001) "A Four Phase Model of EC Business Transformation amongst Small to Medium Sized Enterprises: Preliminary Findings from 34 Australian Case Studies" *Proceedings of the 12th Australasian Conference on Information System, Coffs Habour, Australia 5-7 December.*

Freel, M, "Barriers to Product Innovation in Small Manufacturing Firms" *International Small Business Journal* March 2000 (18:2) p60

Lawrence, K. & Keen, C.D. (1997) A survey of factors inhibiting the adoption of electronic commerce by small and medium sized enterprises in Tasmania, *Working paper 97-01*, School of Information Systems, University of Tasmania, Hobart, Tasmania.

Poon, S., Swatman, P. & Vitale, M. (1996) Electronic Networking Among Small Business in Australia– An Exploratory Study, *Ninth International Conference on EDI-IOS, Bled Slovenia.*

Wong, M., & Turner, P. (2001) An Investigation of Drivers/Activators for the

Adoption and utilisation of B2B Electronic Commerce amongst Small to Medium Sized Suppliers to the Tasmanian Pyrethrum Industry, *Proceedings of the 3rd Information Technology in Regional Areas Conference*, Central Queensland University, Rockhampton, Qld. 5-7 September, 2001

Assimilation of Internet Based Technologies in Small and Medium Sized Manufacturers

Prayush Bharati
MSIS, College of Management, University of Massachusetts, Boston, Boston, MA
Tel: 617-287-2418, Fax: 617-287-7877, Pratyush.Bharati@umb.edu

Abhijit Chaudhury
Bryant College, 1150 Douglas Pike, Smithfield, RI, achaudhu@bryant.edu

INTRODUCTION

E-commerce is impacting the way the small and medium sized firms conduct business. They are increasingly being subjected to competition from firms located in different parts of the world. General Electric (GE) has had a big rise in bids from Chinese manufacturers to supply to U.S. plants. GE has, therefore, developed new capacity to handle these suppliers (The Economist, 2000). Thus, e-commerce is exploiting the combined power of the Internet and information technology to fundamentally transform key business strategies and processes (Jones, 2000). This transformation has commenced. For example, the percentage of new Internet Business-to-Business (B2B) projects by small and medium sized firms in supply chain and procurement will rise from less than 25% in 1999 to more than 75% in 2003 (The Economist, 2000). In Denmark, Netherlands and Australia Internet penetration is more than 50% amongst medium sized businesses (The Economist, 2000). These facts show the speed at which change is taking place in small and medium sized firms. Therefore it is pertinent to investigate the impact of e-commerce on small and medium firms.

The research project will examine the factors influencing the assimilation of Internet based technologies and the penetration of these technologies in small and medium sized manufacturers.

Other questions that will be investigated are:

- How are Internet based technologies impacting small and medium sized manufacturers?
- What elements or components of Internet based technologies are they using and for what purpose?
- What factors have played a major role in their move to adopting these technologies?

BACKGROUND

The Internet Economy now directly supports 3.1 million workers. It grew by 62% in 1999 to $523.9 billion and by 58% in 2000 to an estimated $830 billion in 2000. The Internet related revenue growth was 15 times the growth rate for the US economy (Center for Research in Electronic Commerce, University of Texas Austin, 2001). Since 2001 the Internet Economy has slowed down but it still is an important part of the economy.

Small companies constitute a surprisingly high 90% of all U.S. exporters and account for about 30% of the total value of U.S. exports (US Alliance for Trade Expansion, Washington). There is considerable empirical evidence that the employment share of traditionally large-business-dominated industries is declining and that of traditionally small-business-dominated industries is increasing (Cordes, Hertzfeld and Vonortas, 1999). Despite these facts, the implications of this new technology for small sized enterprises have not received much attention to date.

Bill Clinton, former president of U.S.A., in his 1998 directive on electronic commerce urged the United States Government Working Group on Electronic Commerce to "facilitate small business participation in electronic commerce" (US DOC, 1998). The Working Group on Electronic Commerce in its second annual report recommended "The Secretary of Commerce and the Administrator on the Small Business Administration shall develop strategies to help small businesses overcome barriers to the use of the Internet and electronic commerce" (US DOC, 1999). Some studies were launched by these governmental agencies but no systematic data has been collected relating to small and medium firms.

A recent, though limited, survey by Inc (Winter, 2000) shows that about 47% of small businesses are using the Internet in some form or the other for purchasing. A more elaborate empirical study is required to establish how the Internet based technologies are being assimilated and used by small enterprises. We intend to conduct such a study amongst small and medium sized manufacturers in Massachusetts with the possibility of expanding it nationwide.

RESEARCH MODEL

Internet based technologies are complex organizational technologies. Complex organizational technologies impose substantial knowledge burden on would-be adopters (Attewell, 1992). Most theories of innovation incorporate communication of new information about innovations in one way or another. Attewell's work (1992) on organizational learning and innovation diffusion differentiates between the *kinds* of information involved and the *mechanisms* by which information is acquired and propagated. Attewell's research (1992) draws a clear distinction between the communication of "signaling" information about the existence and potential gains of the innovation, versus know-how and technical knowledge. It argues that the acquisition of this technical knowledge and know-how " ... plays a more important role in patterning the diffusion process of complex technologies than does signaling ...[and] should move to center stage in any theory of complex technology diffusion" (1992, p. 5).

The absorptive capacity of the organization for an innovation is largely a result of the organization's pre-existing knowledge in areas related to the focal innovation and the diversity of knowledge in general (Cohen and Levinthal, 1990). These theories have been used to develop a model for the assimilation and diffusion of innovation (Fichman, 1995). The model of assimilation and diffusion of innovations was validated using data from firms undergoing assimilation of software process innovations. The model uses the learning related scale, related knowledge, and diversity together with several control variables like host size, IT size, specialization, education, environmental complexity and government to explain the assimilation and diffusion of innovation. We have used this model as the starting point, although, we have made changes so that the model is more relevant to Internet based technologies and to small and medium sized manufacturers. This model will be used to investigate the assimilation and diffusion of Internet based technologies in small and medium sized manufacturers in Massachusetts.

The hypotheses of our research are:

Hypothesis 1: Learning-Related Scale is positively related to E-Commerce Assimilation Stage.

Hypothesis 2: Related Knowledge is positively related to E-Commerce Assimilation Stage.

Hypothesis 3: Diversity is positively related to E-Commerce Assimilation Stage.

The research study will investigate what Internet technologies are small and medium sized manufacturers using. For the small and medium sized manufacturers who are utilizing these technologies, the research will investigate in what way and for what purpose are they using Internet technologies. The research plans to study the firms who are at the forefront of usage of these Internet based technologies and how can organizations adopt these technologies to strategically benefit themselves. This will shed light on the practices that are becoming best practices in the industry. Thus the research will develop an understanding of how Internet based technologies are relevant to small and medium sized manufacturers, how does it impact them and what can they do about it.

METHODOLOGY ADOPTED

The model of assimilation and diffusion of Internet based technologies was used to develop the research hypotheses. The model was also operationalized in the form of a survey instrument. This survey instrument was used to collect the data for the pre-test of the survey. For the pre-test, the survey was sent to small and medium sized manufacturers in Massachusetts. The survey is currently being analyzed and the preliminary results will be presented at the conference. The Greater Boston Manufacturing Partnership (GBMP), which is based in the College of Management, is helping in administering the survey.

After the surveys have been analyzed, if need be, follow up questions will be asked of the survey respondents. We are also currently exploring the possibility of conducting a few case studies in order to revise the model. After we have collected all the survey data we will be using several statistical techniques to analyze the data. The statistical techniques that will be used are correlation analysis, multiple regression analysis, factor analysis, and structural equation modeling. The statistical analysis will help in developing explanatory models that would shed more light on the relationships that are the subject of research.

Figure 1: Assimilation and diffusion model

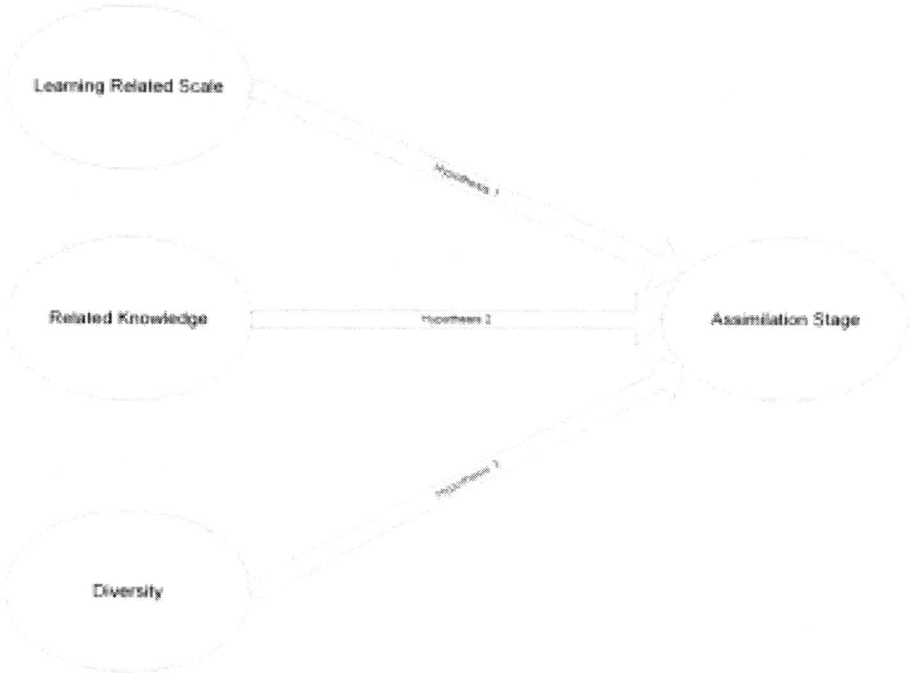

REFERENCES

Attewell, W. B. (1992), "Technology Diffusion and Organizational Learning: The Case of Business Computing", *Organization Science* (3:1), pp. 1-19.

Center for Research in Electronic Commerce (2001), "Measuring the Internet Economy", University of Texas Austin, June (www.internetindicators.com).

Cohen, W. M. and D. A. Levinthal (1990), "Absorptive Capacity: A New Perspective on Learning and Innovation", *Administrative Science Quarterly* (35), March, pp. 128-152.

Cordes, J. J., H. R. Hertzfeld, and N. S. Vonortas (1999), "A Survey of High Technology Firms", *U. S. Small Business Administration.*

Fichman, R. G. (1995), "The Assimilation and Diffusion of Software Process Innovations", *Doctoral Dissertation*, Massachusetts Institute of Technology.

Jones, Frank (2000), "E-Business Transformation in the Manufacturing Industry", *Manufacturing Institute*, National Association of Manufacturers.

NAM Survey of Small Manufacturers, 1999.

The Economist (2000), The Economist E-Management Survey, *The Economist*, November 11.

U. S. Department of Commerce (1998), "The Emerging Digital Economy Report" (www.ecommerce.gov).

U. S. Department of Commerce (1999), Second Annual Report of the Working Group on Electronic Commerce (www.ecommerce.gov/ecommerce.pdf).

Course Development for Introduction to Computer Information Systems: A Modulization Approach

Kuan C. Chen
Assistant Professor, Department of Information Systems and Computer Programming, Purdue University Calumet, Hammond, IN
Phone: (219) 989-3195, Fax: (219) 989-3187, E-mail: kchen@calumet.purdue.edu

ABSTRACT

Teaching the first information technology/system course faces different challenge. A new modularization instructional material design method is demonstrated. In this approach, defining the course goals and arranging the course content are two important issues for the instructors. Course goals will be specified within the context of the course. Justify the course to the instructors. How will students be better for the experience? The instructors must decide what knowledge and skills to teach their students. Is there consensus in their discipline on the knowledge and skills that should be learned by completing an introductory course in computer information system? The instructor must select goals decisively, let instructors lead their students aimlessly. The process of the thinking through essential knowledge and skills in the course can be a valuable synthesizing experience for the instructors. The content of the course can be arranged in many ways, but the modularization approach may be preferable to the students with a variety of background. This paper offers the guiding principles of the modularization content arrangement that some instructors use. A general strategy of these principles and applications in a case study is discussed in this paper as well.

PROBLEM STAEMENT

All the universities and colleges in US provide the introductory course in the computer information systems for either computer major or non-major students. In general, this is the first course to outline the computer concept and information systems development in addition to some hands-on software practices. The course objective is very obvious and straightforward. However, for the instructors and course developers, the structure of this course content is very difficult to arrange because of the big gap of students' background.

There are a number of significant changes in learning computer today, such as the learning style and age. A lot of students start in very early age to use computers. Most high schools also provide the computer application course for students range from typing class to basic software development. Some students even start to use the computers since the childhood by using game software for fun. During the whole growing process, they learn how to use the system, how to use different input and output, how to process data to turn into information, etc. Furthermore, some students even have the capability to write their own program, design their own web site, or build their own computers. The students we mentioned about here are "a lot of them" or "some of them". It implies that not all of students have the strong background. Some may good at the hardware, some may have strong knowledge in software or some may be at home in both. But, some may have very limit knowledge in the computer information system area. However, introduction to computer information system, in general, is a required course and needs to be fit in a variety of students' background.

In this paper, an overview of the computer information course contents, knowledge and skills and trends is presented. A variety of course developments and instructional models are discussed. Because the appropriate course development approach for the pedagogical context depends on the characteristics and scope of the class and student background, special attention is given to identifying the types of situations for which each approach is most suited.

MODULE INSTRUCTIONAL DESIGN

This paper presents the key components and methods of module instructional design (MID), and it shows you how to apply a MID approach to the design of instruction for the course of Introduction to Computer Information Systems. The concept of MID is often misunderstood as involving only the design of teaching materials or the selection of certain courses for the time concerns. However, MID is a broad concept that provides a systematic, problem-solving approach to planning and designing learning experiences.

Modulation is that separate programs are produced that work together as on "system". Two main principles of MID are that course modules should be designed so they are (1) independent of the other modules and (2) each module accomplishes one clear task. The first principle is that each module to be designed and later modified without interfering with the performance of the other modules. The second principle strives to help students and learners easy to understand what each module does. In other words, the MID is to evaluate students' performance in different setting. Students

There are eight planning steps in module instructional design. They are:

1. Determining a purpose
   a. Articulating the goals, e.g., the broad, end-result, real-world performance.
   b. Writing the learning outcomes by specifying what students will be able to do upon completion of the course/program and by deciding what would be accepted as evidence that the desired learning outcomes have been achieved.
   c. Considering the rationale and any assumptions, learning theories, changing/emerging societal conditions, etc., that stimulates and justifies curricular change/innovation/emphases.
2. Determining the content
   a. Organizing the subject-matter content by consulting research, experts, learners, needs assessment results, etc.
3. Determining the sequence
   a. Organizing the content logically and making functional decisions about the curricular structure.
   b. Each module should follow the sequence based on the key knowledge areas and skills requirements.
4. Defining the learners
   a. Considering learners' characteristics, such as their goals, abilities, extra-academic responsibilities, etc.
   b. Creating effective learning environments for all students by using emerging knowledge.
5. Identifying instructional resources
   a. Choosing/developing learning materials.
   b. The available of the instructors, times and spaces.

6. Identifying instructional processes
   a. Choosing activities/strategies/instructional modalities.
   b. Providing the instructional model
   c. Coordinate all modules with the instructors to define the instructional processes
   d. Modules should not be chosen which appear to duplicate the subject matter studied in other modules.
7. Determining assessment/evaluation techniques
   a. Identifying learning outcomes assessment methods (if not determined in #1).
   b. Measuring the degree students has achieved learning outcomes. In this stage it can decide the students' ability to take certain modules.
   c. Well defined the pre-assessment.
   d. The number of credits that may be taken as optional modules at each level.
8. Making adjustments
   a. Using instructors' feedback to improve the planning process and the curricular plan.
   b. Using the students' feedback to change the contents each module.

CASE STUDY

The following case is a general MID for CISB 100 Introduction to Computer Information Systems, which was designed for Lansing Community College in Lansing, Michigan.

Introduction to computer information systems is the first and basic course for any IT major or non-major students. The following standards are defined to server the criteria to observe the students' learning outcome:

1. Students' knowledge about computing processing related to computer technology.
2. Students have the fundamental knowledge about the network and Internet to meet today's working environment.
3. Students have skills to use a personal computer and its software applications to carry out everyday tasks.
4. For IT major students, they should know the concepts of database management, information systems development and computer language selections.
5. For IT major students, the e-commence concepts and basic web development also need to be studied.

The design phases were referenced the program overview and syllabus 3.0 of International Computer Driving License (ICDL) — Training & Certification Program in the United States from Association for Computing Machinery. Originally there are 7 modules in the syllabus. The course is designed for IT major and non-major students so that there are 8 modules in the course. Due to the space limitation, each module's title is just listed.

Module 1 – Computing Process and Computer Technology
Module 2 —Network, Internet and E-mail
Module 3 – Word processing
Module 4 – Spreadsheets
Module 5 – Databases Usages
Module 6 – Graphics and Presentations
Modules 7 – Database Management and Information Systems Development
Modules 8 – Basic E-commence and Web Development

IMPLEMENTATION

For this case, 8 modules can be implanted to Information Technology/system major or non-major students. Each module, also, designed 50 multiple questions and 3 hands-on projects to allow students to take. The test modules can be taken in any sequence. Getting score at 90% for the test and fully complete projects will be waived from that module. Module1 to module 6 are required for non-major IT students to take. For IT major they have to complete the whole 8 modules. In the class setting we suggest that different instructors can teach each module. For students, at their option, an individual can take the course for one, some or all of the modules.

SUMMARY

Modularization approach in instructional design has been widely applied a variety of course development. It also has been used in IT curriculum development for students and learners. In this paper, the main purpose is to follow the module instructional design approach to Introduction to Computer Information Systems. This course always has different backgrounds students in the class. Some of them have strong computer background and they take this course due to the requirement. Some of them take this course because of personal interest. From the instructor perspective, it is very hard to provide the general instructional materials to fit in all the students. From the student standpoint, the course may be distractive and waste time and money.

Incorporating the modularization approach in the course will reduce the gap. Students can go through pre-design evaluation methods to choose their own module to accomplish their educational goal. All of the students may get the same credit but go through different discipline setting and method.

REFERENCES

Association for Computing Machinery and the International Computer Driving License Foundation. (2001). *Syllabus of International Computer Driving License – Training & Certification program in the United States.* Internet: http://www.acm.org/icdl-us.

Eble, Kenneth E. (1988). *The Craft of Teaching: A Guide to Mastering the Professor's Art (2nd edition).* San Francisco: Jossey-Bass.

Hyman, Ronald T. (1974). *Way of Teaching (2nd edition).* New York: J.B. Lippincott Company.

Kathy Shaffer. (2001). *Step-by-Step Curriculum Development.* Lansing: Lansing Community College.

McKeachie, Wilbert J. (1986). *Teaching Tips: A Guidebook for the Beginning College Teacher (8th edition).* Lexington, MA: D.C. Heath.

Norton, Peter (2001). *Introduction to Computers (4th edition).* New York: McGraw-Hill.

Satizinger, John W., Jackson, Robert B. and Burd, Stephen D. (2000). *System Analysis and Design – in a Changing World,* Cambridge: Course Technology.

Shelly, Gary B., Cashman, T. J. and Vermaat, Tim J. (2002). *Discovering Computers 2002 Complete Concepts for a Digital World, Web Enhanced.* Cambridge: Course Technology

Stark, Joan S. & Lattuca, Lisa R. (1997). *Shaping the College Curriculum: Academic Plans in Action.* Boston: Allyn and Bacon.

Training on Management of Information Resources in Small Enterprises: Challenges and Paradigms in Post Communist Developing Countries

Dimitar Christozov
American University in Bulgaria, Blagoevgrad 2700, Bulgaria, Tel: (359-73) 88443, Fax: 9359-73) 80828, dgc@aubg.bg

INTRODUCTION

This paper addresses the assessment of two models of training the course "Information Resources Management" (IRM), which were applied in the MBA-MIS program of the Faculty of Economics and Business Administration at Sofia University "St. Kliment Ohridski". The assessment is based on comparison of performance of students, trained by the two models, both in class and in their professional carrier after graduation. The objectives of training remain unchanged:

- To develop understanding about the role of information in a social institution as a valuable resource, critical for successful management, which need to be managed as well as any other resource;
- To clarify that information as a resource is not limited to data, but it includes also technologies of data processing, organizing, and using effectively for decision making;
- To define information needs for decisions made on different levels in company's hierarchy, and the basic forms of support an information system has to provide;
- To shape the role of Computer Based Information Technologies.

The MIS MBA program was established in 1997 and during the first three years of this period the author had used a "standard" lecture-type training model, following a western textbook (see Kan 1994, some lectures were based on Buc 1991 and Sch 1990) and using cases drawn from other western sources (as Bea 1992, etc.). The students have learned to interpret theory and to analyze cases from the textbooks. Some students, with broader experience, expressed their concern about difficulties in applying that knowledge in Bulgarian business practice. In response, to achieve course objectives and to build practical skills to identify and solve problems, in the last three years a seminar-type model was applied, which explores students' personal background and business experience. In class, cases, presented by students and drawn from their own experience, were analyzed, using brainstorming and other group techniques.

The primary objective of this research is to collect feedback about how students apply the IRM principles and to adjust the course content and training model. As a secondary benefit the students achieved broader understanding of the current business practices, in the particular time of the process of transition to market economy. This period is also characterized with exponential grow of use of computer based information technologies. The two processes are going on simultaneously and impact heavily each other.

WHY THE TRAINING MODEL NEEDS REVISION?

The past twelve years were characterized by transition to market oriented economy. In the countries, like Bulgaria, the collapse of centrally planned economy was followed by unregulated business environment, partially following market principles partially preserving high level of governmental regulation, monopolies, and key influence of the state's bureaucracy. In such environment "standard" managerial models do not work properly. That is true particularly to the small businesses. The following characteristics, related to IRM, of the Centrally planned economy still impacts the behavior of people engaged in business activities:

- Infrastructure for collecting and distributing information was organized hierarchically, and people had very restricted access to reliable sources. Official sources are suspicious, partially by inertia, partially because of the conflict of interests with state's officers engaged in providing services;
- People had used to rely on shared interpersonal information, instead of information provided by the specialized institutions, as Statistical Agency and therefore they have not developed skills of dealing with such sources;
- Managerial experience was obtained in a monopolistic type of enterprises, without proper competition and market driven rewards, where the role of information was neglected.

Currently, the factors, which have impact on the "success" of training IRM, can be classified in two groups:

A. Environmental factors:

- Information infrastructure in the country is extremely underdeveloped and students had limited experience of dealing with information in their practice;
- Social practices show that a successful business makes managerial decisions based more often on intuition and general knowledge, or on personally delivered internal information, and not on applying theoretical models and market research, as studied in the universities;
- Entire business environment lacks of proper regulation, which is changing frequently and heavily depends on Government, bureaucracy, and monopolies.

B. Personal Factors:

- Business background and experience is accumulated in small companies with guaranteed customers in given region or area, run in conditions of shortage on the market with absence of real competition;
- In small, family type, businesses information is shared free among the employees, without even an attempt to organize it. This leads to:
  o The role of proper administration is highly underestimated;
  o Information is not presented in a well structured manner and therefore it is not helpful enough in the decision making process, and of course, its role and importance is not visible;
  o The lack of proper documentation leads to the lack of history. Repeating mistakes are not analyzed, the outcome is nor measured, and management is considering as a kind of art;
  o A single person makes decisions usually and his information processing abilities are the bottleneck of the company.

All this creates a skeptical attitude toward the content of the course and potential practical benefits in mastering the material.

There is no literature, which provides training materials (theoretical models, cases, studies, etc.) relevant to the current situation in Bulgaria. Also, it is no worthy to develop such literature, because it is needed only for the transitional period, when situation is changing rapidly. Finally, the current students are the people who are intended to transfer economy – they must be trained to perform successfully in the current business environment with clear understanding of the principles and benefits of the modern management.

A flexible training approach is needed, which is highly sensitive to current students expertise and the state in the business environment.

DESCRIPTION OF THE ADOPTED MODEL

The training passes in two stages:

- Lecture dominated stage: presentation of basic IRM principles with intensive discussion on problems, benefits, and difficulties. Applying problem driven approach. This part takes the first one third of the duration of the course.
- Case study seminars: every student has to present a snapshot of a real or virtual company, based on his/her own experience. S/he must be able to answer any questions related to business processes, administrative structure and practice, information flows, decision-making processes, etc. The other students are invited to analyze how the IRM principles are or can be implemented in the company. This discussion:
  o starts with highlighting the hierarchy of decisions made in the company;
  o information needed to make any type of decisions, specifying information sources, how to access, and how to interpret information;
  o persons engaged in decision making;
  o what kind of IT technologies can be useful,
  o evaluation of the price of implementation of such procedures and technologies, including training of the personnel;
  o assessment of the overall performance of company if it applies these procedures comparing with existing practice;
  o feasibility assessment and defining recommendations.

DESCRIPTION OF THE PERFORMED RESEARCH

This approach was applied for the first time in 1998/1999 year. Some students from this class shared last year that they have implemented the recommendations reached in class discussions with a significant success. This encouraged us, first to continue with the same training model next year and second to initiate a research on alumni performance.

A group of students, trained according to "standard" model, working for companies similar to those, in which the five above mentioned students are engaged, with similar key managerial positions in them, were identified and approached. This actually excludes, large or even medium size enterprises, state's owned institutions, and branches of international companies. Further, research includes identifying and applying to both groups a set of measurable criteria, which will allow more clear identification of the benefits of the two approaches and will serve the improvement of the training model. The criteria have to reflect the objectives of IRM course. Finally, eight small size companies were selected, where former IRM students play a key managerial role and can influence the way of organizing the administration. The students in the first group of four companies have studied according to the "standard" model, and in the second group – to the "new" model. Companies in the two groups were selected with similar type of activities:

Table 1: Types of activites for each model

Type of activities		"Standard" model	"New" Model
S1:	Providing intellectual services	Consulting: assets evaluation for enterprises privatization	Consulting: Personnel Agency
S2:	Providing material services	Garage	Home renovation
T:	Trade	Species for meat production	Electrical supplies
P:	Production	Software	Software

Comparison was performed according to the following criteria:

C1: Existing of proper organization of internal information: facts, suppliers and supplies, delivery, claims, etc. to allow traceability of events.

C2: Existing of proper organization of collecting and evaluation of relevant external information.

C3: Existing of predefined procedures and distribution of responsibilities, related to information processing and decision-making (the best case is to have written procedures, but, because of the size of the company, informal by default knowledge is well enough).

C4: Use of Information Technologies, computers, and Internet.

For a given company every criterion is evaluated according to a six-level scale, where "0" means "not at all", and "5" – "best possible". In some cases, especially for companies in the second group, a higher grade was given, when implementation of a proper organization is planed, but still not implemented. I have graded higher understanding about what is needed and why, instead of simply copy of the best practice in the branch, without considering the particular specific needs of the company.

Table 2: The six-level scale

	"Standard" model				"New" Model			
	S1	S2	T	P	S1	S2	T	P
C1	3	0	2	1	3	2	4	5
C2	1	0	3	2	4	2	4	4
C3	3	1	4	1	5	3	5	5
C4	4	0	3	5	4	2	5	5

CONCLUSION

The above table together with personal observations on the organization and administration of these businesses, shows that the students from the "standard" group have not initiate any particular activities toward implementation of IRM principles, but follow closely the main stream of development in the sector. They know what is needed, but don't believe that it is possible to be done here and now. The other group has initiated implementation of IRM principles, in one case literary the recommendations reached in class discussion, willing to demonstrate the benefits of well managed information. They behave as people who trust in what they are doing.

REFERENCES

Jerome Kanter, Managing with Information

Michael Buckland, Information and Information Systems, PRAEGER, 1991

Schoderbck, Schoderbck and Kefalas, Management Systems: Conceptual Considerations, BPI IRWIN, 1990

Beaumont and Sutherland, Information Resources Management, Butterworh-Heinemann Ltd, 1992

Teaching IT Development Using Live Versus Case Projects: A Comparative Analysis

Earl Chrysler
Quinnipiac University, Mount Carmel Avenue, Hamden, Connecticut, Tel: (203) 582-8799, Fax: (203) 582-8664, earl.chrysler@quinnipiac.edu

ABSTRACT

Many MIS/CIS/IS/IT programs incorporate a course in which student teams perform a system development project. Some professors use case studies from texts, some develop their own hypothetical projects and some use live projects from local off-campus organizations and/ or campus units. The advantages and disadvantages of each methodology are presented and discussed.

BACKGROUND

MIS faculty frequently feels that some required MIS course should require students to undertake a system-related project of some consequence. This typically means that a course such as Project Management provides the home for this type of project. The instructor for the course has the following options as to how to select the project(s) for the teams of students:

- Locate a text that contains case studies and assign the same case to all groups or a different case to each group;
- Design a group of projects and assign one case to all groups or a different case to each group;
- Locate "live" cases in terms of an off-campus organization that is in need of having a system project completed and assign the same case to all groups or a different case to each group;
- Locate "live" cases in terms of a campus unit that is in need of having a system project completed and assign the same case to all groups or a different case to each group; and/or
- Locate "live" cases in terms of both off-campus organizations and campus units in need of having systems projects completed and assign some teams to off-campus organization cases and some teams to campus unit cases.

COMPARATIVE ANALYSIS

Each of the methods listed above will now be presented and the advantages and disadvantages of each method presented based upon the authors firsthand experiences.

1. Locate a text that contains case studies that are appropriate and assign the same case to all groups

Advantages: There are no "up front" costs to the instructor, i.e., he/she does not have to develop a hypothetical system design or re-design problem.

Since all groups/teams will have the same project, comparing deliverables from the teams allows grading against a common desired output.

Disadvantages: Many text authors have limited experience in the design, documentation and implementation of actual corporate information systems. Therefore only general guidelines may be provided, requiring the instructor to have the actual experience that allows him/her to provide detailed instruction to the students, or having the students to approach the project from an academic viewpoint, giving general rather than detailed, specific deliverables. The result may be a student experience that has less transferability to industry than one would like.

2. Locate a text that contains case studies that are appropriate and assign a different case to each group

Advantages: The advantages are the same as those described in method #1 above, but with one additional item. Using different cases discourages the groups/teams from "cooperating" in the development of their deliverables.

Disadvantages: The disadvantages of this approach are the same as those described in method #1 above. Also, using different cases means that the instructor needs to develop, or have supplied by the text author, several different case solutions.

3. Design a group of projects that are appropriate and assign one case to all groups

Advantages: The instructor can design a basic case to present specific issues to be addressed. By couching the case in different types of firms the instructor can make each case seem unique, when in fact each is designed to introduce the students to the same set of issues that require the same types of skills and problem-solving abilities. Since the instructor has designed the basic case, the desired deliverables are known in advance and a common grading scheme can be developed.

Disadvantages: In order to be able to design a basic case, and then be able to superimpose the "template" of that case over different types of business enterprises it is most appropriate that the instructor have significant experience with corporate systems.

4. Design a group of projects that are appropriate and assign a different case to each group

Advantages: The instructor can make each case seem unique, when in fact each is designed to introduce the students to the same set of issues that require the same types of skills and problem-solving abilities. In addition, the potential for "cooperation" is virtually eliminated.

Disadvantages: The disadvantages associated with #3 also apply here. An additional disadvantage is that the instructor is faced with attempting to develop a set of grading "standards" that will apply across all cases.

5. Locate a "live" case in terms of an off-campus organization that is in need of having a system project completed and assign the same case to all groups

Advantages: In these types of situations students are exposed to working with actual users and, in many cases, attempting to design a system that interfaces with existing systems, required to develop programs that must be "production ready", i.e., tested and documented, and are faced with deadlines that are not imaginary. Since all teams would be attempting to solve the same processing issues, there would doubtless be multiple proposals that could be compared as to their relative strengths and weaknesses. As to grading, if all teams attempted to solve the same processing assignment, the grading should be manageable.

Disadvantages: There may be constraints imposed regarding when and for what length time periods students may interview employees. Also, there would have to be representatives from all teams present during user interviews.

There is another issue that is rarely considered. Although academicians may look upon this type of project as primarily a student learning experience, the deliverables developed will, in many cases be implemented. It is not unreasonable to understand that there are business organizations that perform these same tasks for a livelihood that are less than enthusiastic about having competition that gives its services free of charge.

6. Locate "live" cases in terms of off-campus organizations that are in need of having systems projects completed and assign a different case to each group

Advantages: The advantages to this option are the same as those for #5 above.

Disadvantages: The disadvantages to this method include those in #5 above. In addition to developing grading standards that can be applied to projects of various types, the instructor must spend considerable time attempting to identify organizations that both have systems projects to be addressed and will also open their doors to a student team and accept some disruption of their work environment.

7. Locate a "live" case in terms of a campus unit that is in need of having a system project completed and assign the same case to all groups:

Advantages: The advantages include those listed for #5. Also, the campus location makes for easy and frequent client access without transportation problems. The instructor can also establish campus credibility for the department's curriculum and enhance faculty-administration rapport by providing free consulting services.

Disadvantages: The disadvantages related to this method are almost the same as presented in #5 above. However, local system consulting firms would probably not be concerned with the student teams performing tasks for a campus, since the campus is rarely a potential client.

8. Locate "live" cases in terms of campus units that are in need of having a systems project completed and assign a different case to each group

Advantages: The advantages that apply to #7 are relevant here also.

Disadvantages: In addition to the disadvantages related to #7, the instructor must now develop grading criteria that apply across a diverse set of projects. Also, the instructor must spend considerable time locating campus units that have system project needs and who are willing to accept the products developed by students, even though under supervision of a faculty member.

9. Locate "live" cases in terms of both off-campus organizations and campus units in need of having systems projects completed and assign some teams to off-campus organization cases and some teams to campus unit cases.

Advantages: The advantages associated with #5 and #7 apply here.

Disadvantages: The disadvantages that apply to #5 and #7 are also applicable here.

OBSERVATIONS

The author has experimented over time with different methods in the undergraduate courses Software Project Management and Systems Development Practicum and an MS in MIS course, Hardware and Software Selection.

Software Project Management

For this course I have developed a new project each semester the course is offered. The project retains the same issues and student team requirements. The grading of the project deliverables is very time-consuming, but manageable since the deliverables for all of the project "problems" from semester to semester are comparable. All teams have the same project, making the grading less onerous than having multiple projects. The issue of "cooperation" has rarely come up since the teams develop a competitive spirit - attempting to outscore the other teams on each deliverable, even though there is no grading "curve".

Many students have stated that this is the most demanding, and the most valuable, course in the MIS curriculum since it consolidates almost all functions of the system development life cycle and allows them to understand how all of the individual courses they have had fit together.

Software Development Practicum

For the Practicum I located campus organizations that were interested in having small-scale projects developed. I would allow each team to select their assignment from a list of projects available. First the class covered how to interview users and how to document the existing system processing logic. The next topic covered was analyzing an existing system for simplification and/or improvement of the entire system, both manual and automated portions. Each team then designed a revised or new system for the client and developed a client presentation. Finally, each team developed the proposed system, revised as required by the users. The system was then tested and user documentation prepared. The complete system documentation was then provided to the user and user training conducted to finish the project.

According to their comments, the touch of realism in this course impressed upon students the realities of dealing with actual users. One student wrote on a course evaluation form, "Just like Dr. Chrysler said, the users keep changing their minds!"

Due to the variety of the types of projects, grading was somewhat time-consuming. While the exams and presentations made up some of the final grade, the final deliverables also had to be graded.

Hardware and Software Selection

The semester this course was offered provided a fantastic experience for all concerned, myself included. I decided to use actual business firms as case studies for the course. In order to obtain a set of possible projects, I visited the Business Editor of the largest local newspaper. I explained that a class of MIS graduate students were interested in performing hardware and software selection studies for small firms as a class project, but I wanted it understood we were not in competition with professional consulting firms. An article that described the situation and gave our MIS department telephone number appeared in the business section of the Sunday edition of the newspaper.

When the department secretary came to the department office at 7:45 Monday morning the phone was already ringing. There were more projects than we needed. The firms not selected as clients were told they were having their names put on a list and they would be contacted in future semesters.

There were various types of business with software requirements ranging from student enrollments in Medical Technician courses to inventory control for a small retail firm. At the end of the semester all projects had been completed and I attended final presentations at all client firms. All client firms were impressed by the thoroughness and professionalism shown by the student teams. Grading was easy - all A's! The students gave the course the same grade!

Metrics and DSS: Do We Have the DSS Cart Ahead of the Measurement Horse?

William K. Holstein
D. Hollins Ryan Professor, School of Business Administration, the College of William and Mary, Williamsburg, Virginia
Tel: (757) 221-2920, Fax: (757) 221-2937, William.Holstein@business.wm.edu

Jakov Crnkovic
Associate Professor, School of Business, University at Albany, State University of New York, Albany, New York
Tel: (518) 442-5318, Fax: (518) 442-2568, yasha@albany.edu

INTRODUCTION

The past decade has seen tremendous progress in systems for information support – flexible and adaptable systems to support decision makers and to accommodate individual needs and preferences. These model- or data-driven or hybrid systems incorporate diverse data drawn from many different internal and external sources. Decision support and DSS have entered our lexicon and are now increasingly common topics of discussion and development in large, and even in medium-sized, enterprises.

But recent economic conditions, particularly the downturn in the fortunes of e-commerce, suggest that the road ahead for DSS may be fraught with problems. In our view, many of those problems have to do with inadequate procedures and metrics for measuring business and management performance.

As expected in economic hard times, we observe the problem first in increased pressure for more formal justification of new IT investments. Although most of the discussion in the literature deals with metrics related to IT investments, we will take a broader view. But we begin with some brief data on IT investment metrics.

Many large investments in enterprise systems and e-commerce infrastructure have been made without clear justification from traditional measures such as Return on Investment (ROI) or Payback, or even newer measures such as Total Cost of Ownership or Economic Value Added.

> *Most don't know what the ROI is on CRM [and other large IT investments]. They're making big, expensive, politically risky blind faith investments.*[1]

An InternetWeek survey reported in October 2001 that 82 percent of 1,000 managers surveyed said they expect their company's overall "e-business operations" to be profitable in 2001. Yet only 34 percent said their company had developed an ROI model to measure the success of those operations. A Jupiter Media Metrix survey reported in the same article indicates that most companies use ROI metrics that are inconsistent from one project to another, making it "nearly impossible to correctly choose which projects should be funded and which should be killed."[2]

The times when any investment related to Internet-enabling the enterprise was considered too strategic to require detailed justification are over. But what metrics are valid and useable? The Internet Week survey suggests that more than half of IT investment projects related to e-business have problems in measurement:[3]

> 25% Don't have the time or budget to conduct detailed justification studies
> 19% Available metrics are not satisfactory
> 13% ROI doesn't apply

We are convinced that the problem goes beyond metrics to justify and support IT investments and extends, as we noted above, to broader questions of methods and metrics for measuring business and management performance. Answers to these questions will have an important impact on decision support systems.

BUSINESS, RATHER THAN IT METRICS

Decision support means supporting managers who are running the business. Increasingly, it refers to supporting middle-level managers who rely on a mix of internal and external data that is steadily tilting towards external data on customers, markets, competitors, the political, regulatory and economic environment. If we define the process of control as tasks undertaken by middle- and lower-level managers to ensure that plans come true, we see clearly the role of data and information in decision support: managers use data and convert it into information to monitor the implementation of plans to ensure that strategic goals are met. If the monitoring indicates that plans will not be fulfilled, corrective action must be taken in time to ensure that the plan is, in fact, met. If the information from a decision support system cannot serve as the basis for action (i.e. cannot first help the decision-maker to decide to do something, and then help to decide what to do) the information will not be used and the system will therefore be useless.

The key words in the previous paragraph that lead to action are monitoring and time. Monitoring is the management function that is the primary target for DSS implementation. Timeliness is crucial. Advance warning without enough time to steer around the iceberg, or to make the necessary changes to ensure that strategic plans are successful, is not the kind of decision support that managers seek.

In this environment, IT-related metrics related to uptime, downtime, response time and peak capacity mean little to managers under pressure to make plans come true. They are trying to formulate and monitor plans that reflect the strategic mission and goals of the business, i.e. accomplish strategic tasks. They need IT that can add value to the business in ways that they can clearly understand.

The Balanced Scorecard Collaborative, an organization that promotes the Balanced Scorecard approach to measuring business and management performance, presents discouraging data if the objective for DSS is to support strategic tasks:[4]

> Only 5% of the workforce understands their company strategy
> Only 25% of managers have incentives linked to strategy
> Only 40% of organizations link budgets to strategy

These data suggest that business metrics, clearly related to strategy, are far more important than metrics related solely to IT investments or even to IT and systems performance.

DSS AND BUSINESS METRICS

Pulling together what we have stated thus far, we see a situation that precludes significant progress in the development and implementation of decision support systems unless:

- new metrics that focus more clearly on business and management performance are developed and implemented

- more attention is given to metrics that focus on monitoring strategic activities, or activities that will have an important effect on the outcomes of strategic initiatives and high-level company goals

It is widely recognized that traditional business metrics rely too heavily on financial and accounting measures. Financial measures tend to be hard, historical, and internal, rather than soft (including judgmental data and estimates that, while 'inaccurate,' are vital to future planning), future-oriented (and therefore, by definition, soft), and external (related to the customer, the market and the environment).[5] We see, therefore, that an important question is not just what to measure, but how to measure and in which areas of the business to seek meaningful metrics.

Consider a metrics example from the world of professional sports. The Portland Trail Blazers basketball team[6] has implemented an aggressive eCRM strategy to increase fan involvement and change the mix of audience demographics. ROI metrics used to determine the effectiveness of the eCRM strategy indicate it that is paying off handsomely, but that is only part of the story. According to Jim Kotchik, senior vice president and CFO of the Trail Blazers:

> *We can measure things like overall revenue, but that wouldn't tell us if we've got more fans because of how we service them or because the team just pulled in two new superstars. We needed to develop other metrics to analyze the impact. One metric is season ticket sales, which reduce dependency on transitory and more labor-intensive box-office sales. The eCRM system helps the Trailblazers target and service season ticket holders, and the results are clear. Season ticket sales increased by 5.4 percent in the first year after introduction of the system, and 7.3 percent the following year.*

All of the Trailblazers' measurements are proprietary, but team managers say they indicate conclusively that the eCRM strategy is a keeper. "We ask ourselves continually if we had to do this all over again, would we," says CFO Kotchik. "The answer is yes – even if it had cost twice as much."[7]

As another example, consider a service (as opposed to product) company in the current difficult business environment. Following a historic strategy of developing a continuing stream of new and innovative services may not be appropriate at this time. What if management enunciates a strategy of operational excellence – doing things faster, better and cheaper – to support a traditional range of services? How do you measure speed, excellence, and simplicity? Cost per service might be a simple measure, but how do you incorporate complexity of the service provided, the cost of support required, after-sales costs? and how would you benchmark your performance against competitors for whom your cost, timeliness and quality data estimates are sketchy at best?

The questions raised by this example are all answerable, individually, one at a time, by individual or small groups of managers. But in reality, that is not the answer. These questions need to be answered in a total, systematic manner that spreads the idea of different measures, and then different business processes and structures to achieve results against the new metrics, throughout the organization. Earlier, we said that information that does not lead to action is useless. Here we paraphrase that comment by observing that new measurements and metrics that do not lead to significant organizational change are useless.

IMPLEMENTATION ISSUES

Much of the literature on measurement and metrics focuses on the measurement of IT accomplishments derived from business strategy. This is an important issue, certainly for those of us who promote the application of IT and systems to business problems. However, the terrain is connected to far more than just traditional IT tasks. Managers are trying to enhance customer service, shorten time to market, increase productivity, reduce costs, organize customers into meaningful segments and then develop unique programs to serve them better, etc. These tasks, earlier referred to as strategic tasks, are the stuff of which our systems, and our metrics, should be created. It is also important to note that metrics serve not only to support and measure performance, but also as the basis for communication within the organization – communication that helps to frame discussions in business, not IT, terms. We turn now to implementation issues surrounding these ideas and suggest some guidelines for DSS development incorporating new metrics.

Implementation Guidelines

A first guideline, as we have discussed, is that breadth in measurement (beyond financial and accounting measures) is important. The ideas behind the Balanced Scorecard should be understood and implemented in decision support systems. Breadth, however, does not imply complexity.

A second guideline is simplicity. Metrics must be easy to understand and communicate. They must relate to relevant activities and tasks, and be 'drivable,' i.e. managers must be able to use the measures to determine actions that will affect the outcome of future measures.

Our third suggestion relates to simplicity: DSS designers must avoid the impulse to measure everything. The focus must be only on the most important metrics from the user's (the decision maker's) point of view. Metrics should be built in hierarchies, with more details for lower-level managers, and fewer, more summarized measures for higher-level managers.

Fourth, DSS design should emphasize data and data collection, not for reporting, evaluation and auditing, but for research and learning, for finding exceptions, for learning the causes of exceptions and for exploring alternative courses of remedial action.

As a fifth guideline, we cannot overemphasize the importance of benchmarking against credible external targets. Benchmark analysis can identify problems and suggest solutions and can serve as an excellent idea bank for new metrics. New organizational forms, alliances and cooperative arrangements such as the implementation of supply chain management across several companies present excellent opportunities for benchmarking. For example, is a given manufacturer's frequent late delivery an inventory-level issue or is it caused by slow order reaction time on the part of one or more of the supply chain's participants? Benchmarking can help to target on the exact answer, which can then lead to needed adjustments.

As a sixth and final guideline, we suggest careful consideration of collapsing time. Speeding up of business processes and reaction times has become almost a cliché, but time is the most important element in most new metrics to support decision making. Consider this example from the supply chain literature[8]:

> *Take one standard supply chain metric: order fulfillment lead time. Its meaning remains the same as always, but the effective unit of measure applied (time, in this case) has been moving from months down to weeks, from weeks to days, and, in this "e-" era, to hours.*

Another example cited in the same article is a benchmark metric called "upside production flexibility," meaning the number of calendar days to achieve an unplanned, sustainable 30 percent increase in production—perhaps prompted by a sudden change in a supply chain partner's requirements.

> *If I said today that I need 30 percent more of something, how fast can my suppliers, and their component suppliers, deliver that? [Only] Part of the answer is in manufacturing lead time, [The other, equally important] part is administrative lead times—getting the information, sharing it, and synchronizing it.*

This quote deftly summarizes our implementation guidelines for the development of metrics for decision support systems:

- Think beyond financial measures

- Focus only on the most important, but not necessarily obvious, issues and collect relevant data to support understanding
- Benchmark outside the organization and build relevant knowledge to support change, and
- Do it fast.

INDICATIONS FOR FURTHER RESEARCH

We have only scratched the surface in this paper. Much more needs to be done to categorize and delineate metrics for decision support and to tie metrics more closely to system architecture and concepts. Metrics for reporting performance, for example, differ significantly from metrics for improving performance. We need a better understanding of how these different types of metrics can be incorporated in decision support systems.

We all agree that contemporary systems must include more external, soft data. But such data is often 'dodgy' as the British would say – unreliable, inaccurate, judgmental. While some data might not be unusable for reporting and management performance evaluation, it could be invaluable for suggesting avenues for change and for improving performance. What DSS architecture can accommodate these differences in role and data quality and still meet simplicity and transparency requirements?

There are many unknowns, but one thing is sure: rapid progress in DSS will be made, with or without those of us in the academy who are interested in contributing. We must sharpen our understanding and clarify our communication if we hope to influence the future of metrics and DSS.

ENDNOTES

1 Aaron Zornes, VP Meta Group, quoted in ENT Magazine, December 13, 2000

2 InternetWeek.com, October 1, 2001

3 ibid

4 From an August 20, 2001 advertisement. See bscol.com

5 The Balanced Scorecard initiative (See bscol.com) has done much to raise awareness of this point, but we believe that much more must be done, particularly to connect Balanced Scorecard-like ideas to DSS.

6 www.nba.com/blazers

7 ROI: Mad to Measure, eCFO Magazine, September 17, 2001

8 Advanced Performance Metrics for the e-Era, Technology Edge, June 2001. The subtitle of the article is instructive: Your old gauge for measuring and meeting operational and profitability goals may need recalibration.

Surf School For Older People: A Special Graduate Information Systems Course

Dr. Georg Disterer
Department of Business Administration, University of Applied Sciences and Arts, Hannover, georg.disterer@wirt.fh-hannover.de

ABSTRACT

Many elderly people (age of 60+) are keen on getting familiar with the Internet. At the same time end-user training gets more and more important for IT management. Therefore we implement a graduate Information Systems course, where students have to design, organize, manage, and run (!) a training session where elderly people could see and try the usage of the Internet. The students learned to design a teaching curriculum and teaching materials, to set up and maintain the technical infrastructure, to organize end-user training and - most important - to teach and to train end-user.

INTRODUCTION: INTERNET NEEDS OF OLDER PEOPLE

In the countries of the western hemisphere we observe a growing elderly population (60+), where many older people are smart and clever enough to focus their attention on the management for productive elder years. They are keen to get to know and to use modern tools and techniques, but some circumstances and barriers hinder them to reach a promising starting point. For example, within the population of the users of the Internet, elderly people are by far not represented proportional to their part of all inhabitants. For Germany the situation is like shown in Figure 1.

46 % (24,2 Mio) out of 52,5 Mio people in Germany between 14 to 69 years old have access to the Internet and do use it at least some times [source: GfK Online Monitor 2001]. But only 5 % of the more older population (60 - 69) are using the Internet. For instance, while two out of three juniors (14 to 19 years) are using the Internet at least occasionally, only one out of eight older people (60 to 69 years) do so [source: GfK Online Monitor 2001].

Various reasons cause this different usage patterns. Some reasons why elderly people are not using the Internet like younger people are:

- Older people have Internet access seldom at home or at work. Therefore they are missing possibilities to test and to train the usage of the Internet.
- Older people often are too shy to test newer technologies for the first time.
- Probably, the current generation of older people is the last generation, which did not get any experience in using a PC; following generations necessarily get into touch with PCs at school or at work.
- Therefore, older people have minor handling skills with PCs and with the Internet; this implies that useful and promising ways to use the Internet could not be recognized by them.
- There may some language problems, because in Germany the common language of Data Processing is full of English idioms (e.g. Browser, World Wide Web, Joystick, Display, Windows, Icon, Click, Desktop, Button, Service Provider, Cursor, Download, Homepage, Link, Newsgroup, online, Client, Server, Update) and abbreviations (e.g. PC, WWW, PS/2, MS, USB, VGA, LCD, GB, DVD, ROM, RAM, ISDN, ISP, SMS, BIOS, DFÜ, PDF, SCSI, SSL). But the language skills of elderly people are probably weaker than the skills of younger people. The lack of understanding the language will increase their uncertainty with the technology.

Figure 1: Inhabitants and Internet users by age

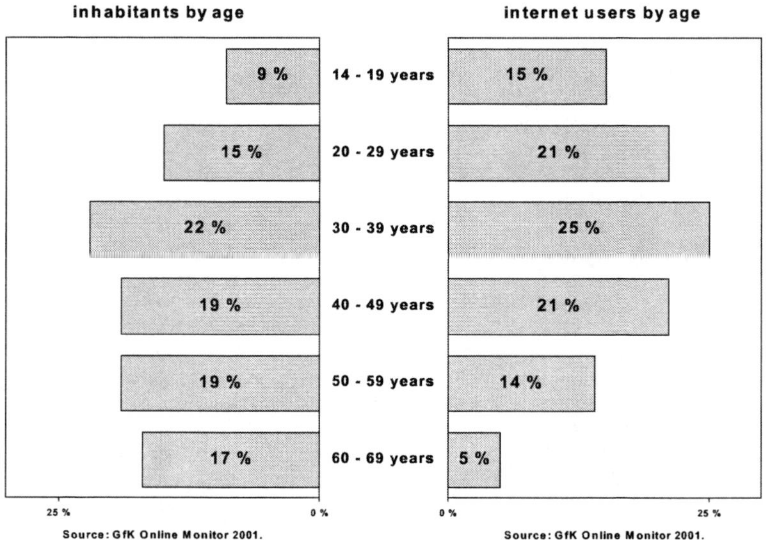

END-USER TRAINING WITHIN IT MANAGEMENT

With modern software architectures such as Enterprise Resource Planning (ERP) more and more workplaces are integrated into the companies' information technology infrastructure, by networking many workplaces and work flows and the vertical and horizontal integration of ERP systems, users' skills to handle the software are critical, because technology networks are more errorprone than standalone systems.

As the money spent on end-user training adds up to 10 or 20 % of the implementation costs, it gets more and more important to spend that money effectively and efficiently [cf. Olfman/Pitsatorn (2000) p. 129]. Therefore, end-user training - its design, organization, and management - is an important topic for future IT manager.

End-user training is also an important point of contact between professionals from the IT department and users from other departments of a company. In addition, end-user training has to cover various aspects: technical aspects of the software, organizational aspects of the situation where the software should be used, motivational aspects when the implementation of the software should change the way people work etc. Therefore the management of end-user training is an important part of the managerial skills in IT organizations.

For this reasons, we designed a special graduate Information Systems course, where students of the Department of Business Administration at the University of Applied Sciences Hannover in their (approx.) third year had to train elderly people how to handle and use the Internet. Older people should have the opportunity to test the Internet - especially World Wide Web (WWW) and Electronic Mail

(Email) - without fear and risk. At the end of the training, they should be able to send and receive Emails, to handle a standard browser, to make a simple search using a search engine, to know basics about PCs and the Internet. In total, the skills of the elderly people in handling and using new media - here: the Internet - should be improved significantly. Barriers which hinder them to use new media and modern technologies should be lowered. A systematic performance evaluation was conducted in order to measure how good the older people and trainers (students) reach those goals.

From this point of view, Internet training for older users is a good simulation of some responsibilities graduates will have in their future working environments when designing and conducting end user training. The skills and training needs of the trainees are not clear, there are certain barriers to use the application, and there social and communication problems between trainer and trainees.

Finally, the "Surf School for Older People" was conducted by 6 students at the end of the semester on three afternoons from 3 to 6 p.m.; every of the 33 (older) participants, grouped by 8 to 9 people, get 9 hours intensive training using the Internet.

COURSE DESIGN

There are various Information Systems courses with different structures and scopes required for our students. One special form of a course is called "project", which means, that students in groups of 4 to 12 people work together on a given task. The volume of their work for a project like this during the semester is calculated as (approx.) 12 hours a week, which adds up to approx. 200 hours of work per person. There is no fixed schedule for this work, because the students have to organize all of their work by themselves - with some guidance and support from the lecturer. They can use all (technical) infrastructure of the university but must observe some procedural conditions and rules of the organization.

For the students two courses of this special form are required. Normally, they participate in these projects in their third or fourth (and last) year. Their participation is graded on a normal scale. The responsible lecturer for a project defines the project task, gives support and guidance, shows adequate tools and techniques, helps to adjust problems. Often the lecturer will play the role of a steering committee in a project organization. The project tasks are often defined together with some cooperation partners from outside the university, who have realistic and practical interests in the results of the project.

In the course documented here, the task was to train users in handling and using a new technology, for instance elderly people in using the Internet. This is a realistic simulation of future tasks and responsibilities of the graduates when they are heading IT management. We choose the context of "older people" and "Internet" because the technical environment is available at the university and well known to the students, and the target group is not familiar with the handling and has barriers to use the technology - so a very realistic context. The training event was named "Surf School for Older People". The main tasks of the students were:

- define detailed goals and rules of the "Surf School for Older People", define and maintain target dates and time limits
- manage the participants (attraction, invitation, registration etc.)
- design and develop the structure and program of the surf school
- design and develop all training materials (teachers guide, handout for participants etc.)
- manage resources (rooms, technical equipment, supplies, spare parts etc.)
- evaluation: design and manage a performance evaluation system
- project management: manage time and division of labor, report to steering committee, document all activities etc.
- conduct the training as teachers.

Some organizational prerequisites were set as follows:

- The whole project should be finished within the semester (5 months).
- The training of the surf school should take place in rooms and with the technical equipment of the university. Regular courses and other events should not be disturbed. The volume of the Internet training should be 25 to 50 hours.

DETAILED GOALS OF THE SURF SCHOOL

After starting the projects the students had some intensive discussions with key people of the target group, some older people we know from a division of the biggest labor party in Germany. Before this analysis together with key people of the target group it was quite an open question, which skills elderly people have and the school can be based on. To conduct an end-user training successfully it is essential to consider the prerequisites the target group brings into the training situation and furthermore the training needs the group have.

Finally, some foundations of the surf school were documented as follows:

- The target group are older people (60+) who have no skills and experiences in using a PC or using the Internet. They are interested and keen to see and to learn how to handle the Internet. This is the reason why motivation of the end-user is not a major topic within this course.
- The content of the training should clearly focus on the Internet services World Wide Web (WWW) and Electronic Mail (Email). Today, these two Internet services build by far the most applications of Internet Technology. For most of the non-experts, Internet and WWW are synonymous. Rather than giving a detailed introduction "How to use a PC", the content of the training should focus on skills which are absolutely necessary to handle a browser.
- The training should focus on "doing" rather than "showing". The participants should spent most of the time using and handling WWW and Email. The trainees should practice using WWW and Email as much as possible.
- One direct consequence was, that each participant should sit in front of one terminal and that the groups should be rather small (8 to 10 people) in order to give good and intensive support by the trainer.

In detail the participants should learn

... to recognize structure and diversity of the Internet
... to realize and understand examples using WWW
... to recognize possible and useful ways using WWW
... to handle the WWW in general
... to use search engines, catalogs, meta search engines
... to understand Electronic Mail as an Internet service
.. to handle incoming and outgoing Emails
... to lower their shyness testing and using newer technologies
... start and finish working with a PC, handling a browser
... to use keyboard and mouse as input devices
... to know important components of a PC to be able to make buying decisions
... to know the connections between PC and telecommunication networks
... to understand the different roles of Internet Service Provider, Internet Presence Provider, Internet Content Provider

To support the participants, a detailed handout (booklet) should be prepared and produced, in order to prevent the participants from writing down tips and tricks during the training sessions.

TEACHING PROGRAM OF THE SURF SCHOOL

While developing the program it got clear that some topics have to been taught in rooms with more advanced technology; otherwise online-Banking, animations with flash technology, 3-dimensional pictures would be too slow on medium-sized PCs. For that reason these topics should be presented in a larger class room with all participants and the other topics in several smaller PC laboratories with 8 to 10 people in each group. Finally, the program was outlined and scheduled as shown below, where the grey shaded boxes show topics presented in the plenary room with all participants together, the non-shaded boxes show topics presented in groups.

Table 1: Outline of teaching program

time	1. day	2. day	3. day
15:00 - 15:15	check in	3D-presentation	online banking
15:15 - 15:30	welcome, organizational details	accessing the WWW	finance
15:30 - 15:45	introduction, history and structure of the Internet	regional information (2)	ticketing
15:45 - 16:00	PC hardware	travel	shopping
16:00 - 16:15	assigning training groups	free training session	free training session
16:15 - 16:30	coffee break	coffee break	coffee break
16:30 - 16:45	handling the mouse	search engines	weather
16:45 - 17:00	PC desktop, browser	search engines	information services
17:00 - 17:15	Electronic Mail	culture	elderly people
17:15 - 17:30	Electronic Mail	politics	health care
17:30 - 17:45	regional information (1)	free training session	free training session
17:45 - 18:00	security issues	animations with flash	webcams; discussion; goodbye

Some special features should be outlined: To get acquainted with a PC desktop, participants were shown and explained the user interface. Because many experiences show that beginners have special problems in handling a mouse as an input device, a separate "mouse training" was held: with a special program from the WWW (www.gemeinsamlernen.de) participants had to follow a light point with the cursor. They also had to click on certain boxes, to paint something on the screen etc.

All participants got an Email-address and -account right on the first day - using an Internet Service Provider which gives access to Email features immediately after signing in (web.de). With the own Email-account, the participants could start right from the first day sending and receiving Emails.

HANDOUT / BOOKLET

To support the learning progress of the participants a booklet was prepared, which summarized all necessary information and contained all tips and tricks (and web addresses). Additionally the booklet gave some basic hints to buy a PC in order to surf the WWW from home and how to get access to the WWW via phone, ISP etc. The booklet consists of more than 50 pages and contains paragraphs like: history and structure of the Internet, PC hardware/input/output devices/buying hints, operating system, browser, security issues, Internet Service Provider, Email Provider, access to the WWW, search engines, links, glossary. The buying hints use the picture of an ordinary advertisement from newspaper, which lists the important components of a PC and its technical details. With this ad the components are described and explained in order to support the reader buying a PC.

ORGANIZATION

There were various organizational tasks the students had to concentrate on:

- Project management: time management, division of labor, task scheduling, reporting, documentation; especially the cooperation of students, lecturer, administration of university and key people of the target group had to be coordinated
- Management of participants: attraction and invitation of participants, registration, registration fees
- Preparation and production of teachers guide and handout (booklet)
- Design and organization of the environment: rooms, technical equipment, supplies, refreshments etc.
- Composing training groups.

EVALUATION

In order to measure systematically how the older people and trainers (students) reach the goals of the "Surf School for Older People", a performance evaluation survey was necessary. The survey was designed in order to sample some demographic data of the participants and to get their feedback. A pretest of the questionnaire was conducted, where some older people tested its meaningfulness as well as its clarity, length, and general appearance. Then, the questionnaire was handed out to the participants before and after attending the school to evaluate training and learning.

Before attending the surf school, the trainees were asked to scale their skills and experiences with the Internet on 5-point Likert scales, after the school we asked the same questions to measures the differences caused by the surf school.

Other questions addressed the barriers, which were assumed to hinder Internet usage by older people (see above) and the detailed goals of the school to lower these barriers. So the older people were asked anonymously, to what extent they have skills to handle a PC (PC literacy) and to surf in the WWW (Internet literacy). Additionally, they were asked if they see clear purpose in using the Internet during their daily life, if they have had enough possibilities trying the Internet to get acquainted with it and if they feel that they can handle the Internet without fear. All answers were measured on 5-point ordinal scales where low values stand for low extent of skills, possibilities etc.

Figure 2 shows the answers which the participants of the "Surf School for Older People" gave **before** the school started. Obviously, there was room to improve on all dimensions; the strategic objective of the school was to address all five dimensions and to increase the respective values.

After attending the school the respondents were asked to answer the same questions again. The answers are summarized in Figure 3 and show significant improvements on all dimensions.

Some of the assumption concerning the school design got confirmed by the results of the survey. So the teaching program was - because of the lack of time - not focused on PC literacy but directly on Internet literacy. Corresponding to this the empirical results which

Figure 2: Skills and opportunities before attending the school (low values ~ low skills, low changes, etc., n= 27 to 32)

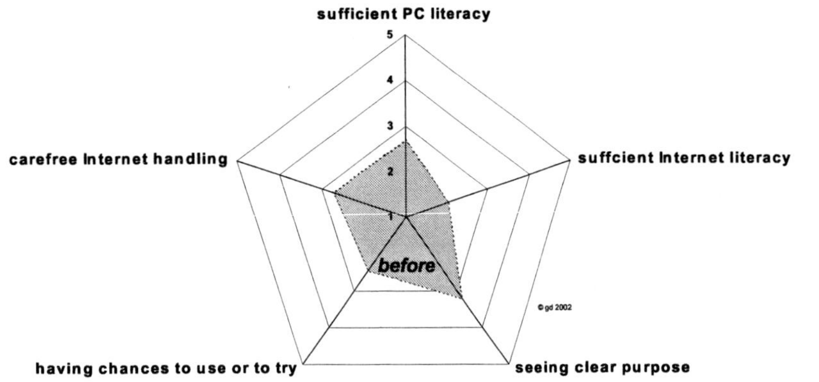

Figure 3: Skills and opportunities before and after attending the school

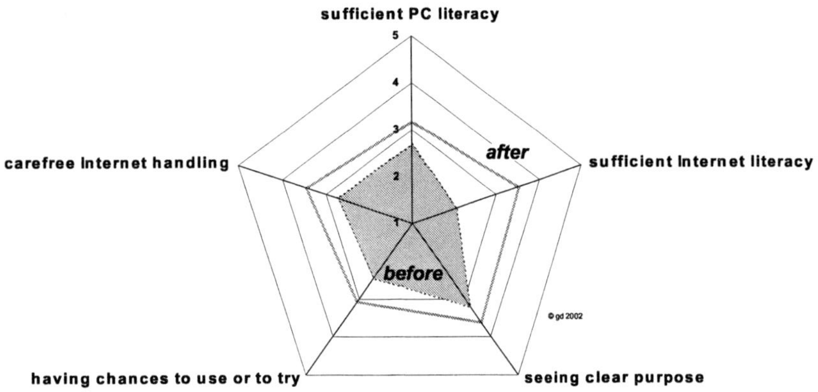

Figure 4: Overall ratings after attending the school (n= 29 to 30)

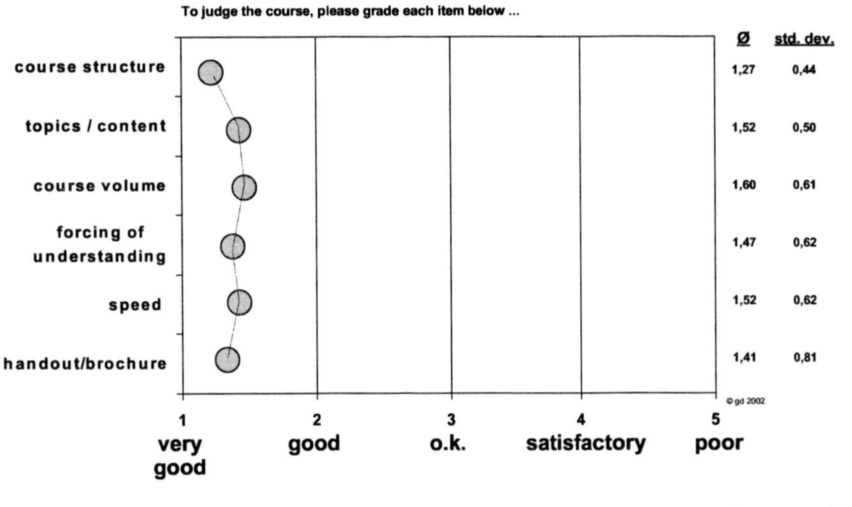

show the improvements along the dimension "Internet literacy" were quite higher than along the dimension "PC literacy".

Additionally, the participants were asked to judge the school in total, the program, the trainer and the organization. All grades were outstanding, Figure 4 shows some results of the survey.

Similar excellent ratings got items like "atmosphere", "interesting topics", "organization", "help and support". In total, 73 % of the respondents *totally* agree with the statement that they will recommend the school. Furthermore 27 % agree with this statement. 97% of the participants said that there expectations were (at least) met, 2 out of 3 said that their expectations were excelled.

CONCLUSION

The project "Surf School for Older People" were an assignment for graduate students of Information Systems at the University of Applied Sciences in Hannover. The students had to design, organize, manage, and run a training event where elderly people could see and try the usage of the Internet. This scenario is a realistic simulation of future tasks and responsibilities for graduates when they are heading IT management, because end-user training gets more and more important for IT management.

During the course, the students had to manage various tasks like recognizing goals and approaches in teaching the Internet, identifying detailed training needs of the target groups, developing training methods and a teaching program, organizing the environment, designing an evaluation performance survey, and finally, conducting the training acting as teachers of the school.

As the discussions with the participants of the "Surf School for Older People" and the empirical results show, the students were able to improve the level of competence of the older people in handling and using the Internet. Additionally, they got excellent grades on all dimensions and a very positive feedback referring to items like atmosphere, organization, help and support. At the end of the school all participants were very happy and would recommend the school to others.

Beside these direct results the special setting of the "Surf School for Older People" provoked some "strange" situations and curious observations:

- Young teachers (~ 25) had to train old end users (60+); normally, only within families, there is intensive contact between two generation so far apart - if ever.
- Students had not only to make a concept or suggest some actions, but they had to implement their suggestions and actually run the school.
- Thoroughly, deep language problems between younger and older people were discovered, because the common languages of the groups differ significantly.
- Students were surprised how eager and enthusiastic the older people were; they seemed to absorb the information the students disseminated.

Some specific lessons learned by the students involved in this project were

- End user training needs a considerable amount of preparation. There some aspects of the course content and some organizational topics which need much attention and which consume substantial work.
- Even with a small group of 8 to 9 trainees, without a detailed sched-

ule and some discipline of trainers and trainees a training session will end up very "dynamic" - but without any learning results. There is no "muddling through" when various trainees ask questions or discuss problems the same time.

- To teach a group of people for a considerable amount of time is an important experience: to stand before "the crowds", to recognize what the trainees get right and what not, to vary the speed sensing if the trainees can follow, to talk to people over 3 hours in free speech.

The success of the school, the experiences, and some of the sociological phenomena made the school an exciting experience for all.

REFERENCES

Olfman, L., Pitsatorn, P., End-User Training Research: Status and Models for the Future, in: R.W. Zmud (Hrsg.), Framing the Domains of IT Management, Cincinnati, 2000, S. 129-146.

GfK Gesellschaft für Konsumforschung, Online Monitor, Nürnberg, 2001.

Assessing Computer Literacy: Are Our Students Getting More Proficient?

George Easton[1] and Annette Easton[2]
Information and Decision Systems Department, College of Business Administration, San Diego State University, California
[1]Tel: (619) 594-2759, [2]Tel: (619) 594-2664, {George.Easton, Annette.Easton}@sdsu.edu

INTRODUCTION

With the increasing prevalence of computers and computer usage throughout society, one might hypothesize that there would be an increase in overall computer literacy among our students. Trends in education show that students are being exposed to and using application software at relatively early ages. Students in primary grade school, for example, are using PowerPoint to produce class presentations, and using word processing to generate and edit their homework. Middle School students create worksheets and charts in Excel. The most pervasive early exposure computer experiences seem to be coming from the Internet and web surfing.

Given their exposure and experience with computers at a relatively early age, many students arrive at college feeling sufficiently computer literate. Interestingly, most students' self-perception of their computer competency, at least currently, doesn't match the skill sets often expected in their college study program, or in the business world.

Most business schools provide computer literacy skills via their 'Principles of Information Systems' or 'Introduction to Computers' class. This class usually serves two main purposes: 1) to teach students fundamentals of information technology, and 2) to teach students various business-oriented software applications. This course is typically offered at the freshman/sophomore level and is usually required of all business majors.

This study proposes to assess university business students' actual computer literacy and to measure the difference between the students' perception of their computer literacy and their actual computer literacy using an objective assessment of their computer knowledge. This measure of actual computer literacy is thought to be particularly valuable as a tool to help business schools and MIS departments make informed curriculum decisions and to provide a mechanism for tracking the evolving computer skills of beginning business students. Comparisons between self-perceptions and actual skills will be helpful in determining strategies for educating and motivating students whose self-perceptions are higher than their actual skills.

CONCEPTUAL BASIS OF STUDY

Over time the definition of computer literacy has evolved from simply a basic understanding of terminology, to understanding how to program, to understanding how to use specific computer applications. Certainly defining a specific level of computer literacy is dependent on the specific context of the situation in which it is applied. Van Vliet, Kletke and Chakraborty (1994) conducted a study to determine if self-appraisal tests are a valid predictor of computer literacy. They defined computer literacy as "the ability to use microcomputers confidently for obtaining needed information, solving specific problems, and performing data-processing tasks. This includes a fundamental understanding of the operation of microcomputers in general, as well as the use of several types of applications software packages." What they reported was that self-appraisal tests were more lenient indicators of a person's computer proficiency than were objective tests. In addition, they concluded that self-leniency decreased as computer expertise increased.

Our primary research goal is exploratory: we want to focus on assessing computer literacy to determine the appropriate level and content of the information technology training/education that a typical business student will need. Rockart and Flannery (1983) and Mackay and Elam (1992) have demonstrated that training is more likely to be effective when differentiated among different levels of user types. Most professors have experienced classes of wide proficiency levels that have made it difficult, if not impossible, to effectively reach all of their students. Experienced students are bored with the introductory-level material, while novice students are overwhelmed with the more advanced content. In the end, most are not satisfied with the resulting experience. If we can understand what levels of proficiency exist within our classes, we may have a better opportunity to deliver a better educational experience.

Further impetus for this study can be found in reviewing the guidelines set forth by the Association to Advance Collegiate Schools of Business (AACSB), the accrediting body or Schools of Business. AACSB has stated the importance of having students understand and apply concepts of management information systems including computer applications. Accreditation standards mandate that Colleges of Business assess not only how and where these skills are addressed across the curriculum, but also the effectiveness of the curriculum. Evaluating curriculum design and student learning can help business schools make progress on addressing AACSB accreditation.

Given the specific purposes of this study we have broadened Van Vliet, Kletke and Chakraborty's definition of computer literacy to include a basic understanding of information technology concepts. This definition has been operationalized in the self-assessment and objective assessment tests.

RESEARCH DESIGN

Approximately 500 students in the Principles of Information Systems course will participate in this study as part of their course. During the first week of the semester they will be required to complete an online self-assessment questionnaire about their general knowledge of information technology and computer concepts and specific knowledge about primary business applications such as word processing and spreadsheets. The self-assessment questionnaire includes an "I don't know" choice for each question in an attempt to avoid having the students guess the answer. Immediately following the self-assessment, during the first few weeks of the term, all students in this introductory course will be required to take an objective MOUS-based (Microsoft Office User Specialist) assessment of their basic operating system, word processing and spreadsheet skills, and a general objective test about their knowledge of information technology and computer concepts.

Students will then participate in the normal semester class activities and assignments. The current structure of our Principles of Information Systems course is comprised of approximately 50% of the time spent on computer concepts, 25% of the time spent on spreadsheet skills, and 10% of the time spent on database, 10% Internet/ HTML, and 5% presentation software skills. The concepts components will include more general discussions of how many of these applications can be used and integrated into organizations. At the end of the semester students will again repeat the self-assessment questionnaire followed by another objective assessment of their computer and application skills.

The students will be drawn from three class sections. Two different instructors taught the sections, but the syllabi and textbooks were identical. Assignments and lab exercises were selected from a common pool to ensure that relevant skills were taught across all sections. Class sizes differed (between 130 and 250 students each), but all were considered large-section courses and the instructors coordinated their approach and content.

PRELIMINARY RESEARCH QUESTIONS

The research is designed to help us understand the level of students' proficiency within the introductory computer class and how students' self-perceptions match actual proficiency. To that end the study examines the following general hypotheses:

H1. Self-appraisal scores from the initial test will be inflated predictors of actual computer literacy scores determined by the initial objective-appraisal score.

H2. As students' computer expertise and skills increase, their self-appraisal score will more closely match their objective-appraisal score as determined by the second round of testing.

H3. Students who spend more time than their classmates each week using the Internet will have an inflated self-appraisal score of their computer proficiency.

In addition to the results of these hypotheses, what may be more interesting is what we can learn through the exploratory part of this study. The actual results from the objective-appraisal scores can inform us of the true levels of computer literacy. Additionally, we will be investigating the specific results related to the different areas of competency studied. This can provide detailed measures of literacy related to specific competency skills.

RESULTS

Given the timeline of the study, results were not available prior to the proceedings publication. Complete results from the research study will be presented at the conference. In discovering what level of computer literacy our students actually have, and pinpointing areas where students lack proficiency, we can look to develop curriculum to address the weaknesses. Our goal would be to look at developing a curriculum model that provides flexibility in tailoring content to accommodate the evolving literacy of students, ultimately providing a richer educational experience for our students.

REFERENCES

Association to Advance Collegiate Schools of Business (AACSB). 1991. *Achieving quality and continuous improvement through self-evaluation and peer review: Standards for Accreditation, Business Administration and Accounting.* Adopted 1991, Revised May, 2000.

Born, R.G. & Cummings, C.W. (1994). An Assessment Model for Computer Experience, Skills, and Attitudes of Undergraduate Business Students. *The Journal of Computer Information Systems*, 35(1), pp. 41-53.

Mackay, J.M. & Elam, J.J. (1992). A comparative study of how experts and novices use a decision aid to solve problems in complex knowledge domains. *Information Systems Research*, 3(2), 150-172.

Rockart, J.F., & Flannery, L.S. (1983). The management of end user computing. *Communications of the ACM*, 26(10), 776-784.

Van Vliet, P., Kletke, M. and Chakraborty, G. (1994). The measurement of computer literacy: A comparison of self-appraisal and objective tests. *International Journal of Human-Computer Studies*, 40(1), pp. 835-857.

Framework of Knowledge Management Systems Acceptance

Fredrik Ericsson[1] and Anders Avdic[2]
Department of Informatics, Örebro University, Örebro, Sweden
[1]Tel: +46 19 30 35 23, [2]Tel: +46 19 30 31 20, [1,2]Fax: +46 19 33 25 46, {fredrik.ericsson, anders.avdic}@esi.oru.se

INTRODUCTION

In order to succeed with a knowledge management system (KMS) development process, some requirements have to be fulfilled. The most crucial aspect in the development process is implementation. Implementation is much a process of acceptance. In this paper we address the issue of acceptance by answering the following question: *What are the requirements of acceptance of a knowledge management system?*

In order to systemize the requirements we put forward a framework called Requirements of Acceptance Model (RAM).

The empirical research represented in this paper has been conducted through a case study using interviews and conceptual analysis. The unit of analysis is a Swedish small to medium-sized manufacturing company. A knowledge management system concerning operational disturbances has been developed using prototyping (Ericsson and Avdic, 2002) and in this paper we elaborate on how this system is to be used by organizational practitioners in their working environment in order to utilize organizational knowledge embedded in the system.

According to Langefors (1966) and Yourdon (1989) information systems can include either operative or directive/decision support information. Operative systems provide the user with necessary knowledge while directive systems provide the user with knowledge that improves quality of a decision.

IT can support knowledge management through a number of supporting technologies (for example intranets, extranets, data warehouses, DBMS) (e.g. Davenport and Prusak, 1998, Scarbrough and Swan, 1999, Borghoff and Pareschi, 1998, Tiwana, 2000, Ericsson and Avdic, 2002). Systems developed to manage knowledge directly or indirectly to give support for organizational performance are referred to as knowledge management systems (KMS). A KMS is typically directive. The user can deliberately refrain from using the KMS therefore user acceptance is crucial for the degree of usage of the KMS. From our empirical findings we see acceptance as a function of perceived relevance, systems accessibility, and management support, which is to be elaborated below. We call this the *Requirements Acceptance Model* (RAM)

REQUIREMENTS ACCEPTANCE MODEL

In this section we describe the Requirements Acceptance Model (RAM) outlined in Figure 1. RAM shows some resemblance with Davis, Bagozzi and Warshaw (1989) Technology Acceptance Model (TAM) and later TAM2 (Venkatesh and Davis 2000). TAM is an explanative model explaining use of a system. Our model is descriptive in nature and we focus on implementation as a mean to acknowledge factors important for knowledge management systems acceptance.

Perceived Relevance

The user has to perceive the KMS as relevant. Since it is possible to work without consulting the IS, it has to be obvious that usage of the IS implies *adding value to the work result.* Another aspect of relevance is how the KMS should be *integrated in running work.* In our case the reduction of disturbances is the aim of the KMS. The user perceives this as positive since it relieves him from unnecessary problems. (Still it has to be proven that this really is the case and that it is not just an unrealistic idea from the management that is made in order to increase control and tempo in the working situation.)

Figure 1: The requirements acceptance model (RAM)

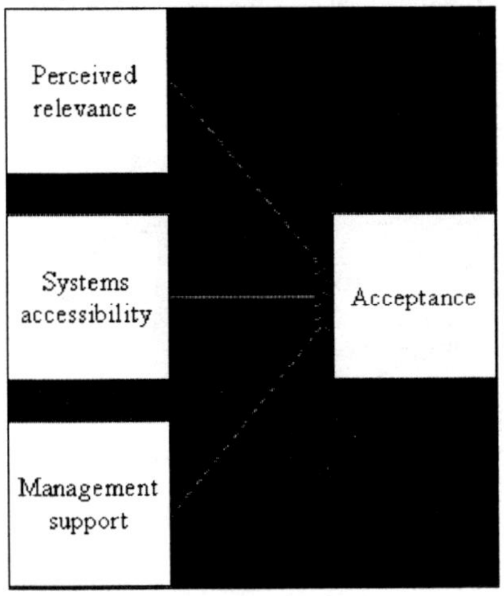

Accessibility

If the system is to be accepted *accessibility* has to be satisfactory. This could be discussed by asking answering four questions. Who? What? Where? When? How?

Who is to be the user? Is it the worker, the supervisor or some administrative personnel? This is a question about if the worker should enter the unique knowledge by himself or if he should have someone else to do it. In our case the strategy has been to make it possible for the worker himself to enter information in order to make it as accurate as possible. This has to be done with considerations to the following aspects though.

What actions are to be performed? The nature of the actions determines the possibilities to develop a KMS. The actions must be possible and meaningful to systemise. The working tasks must not be too routinised and not too unstructured. The task must not be too difficult and not too easy. (Turban 1993) In our case the actions in question are setting up and operating hydraulic presses.

The physical location is a crucial decision that affects how the system can be used and that is affected by who should be the user. If the worker is supposed to be the system user, the system has to be physically placed close to the working place. If the working environment is dirty and noisy, which often is the case in manufacturing industries, special measures has to be taken. In our case the computers where the KMS is implemented are to be located close to the workers.

The system must not be put into operation before a certain degree of usage is secured. The *time of usage start* is therefore dependent of the implementation, which is an iterative phase in the prototyping project. During daily practice there is a choice between using the system in real time mode (i.e. entering information whenever a disturbance occurs) or in batch processing mode (e.g. entering information at the end of the week).

Another important issue is to decide how the *interface of the system* should be designed in order to fulfil the goals of the system. This decision is dependent of who is to use the system and when. In our case the workers are to use the system continuously, which implies simple design and relevant concepts. One should also decide how the KMS should be technically implemented. Existing hardware and software should be used in order to make users make the users familiar with the technical environment.

Management Support

Management support is vital according to many models on systems development, especially when the system is directive/decision support. (Yourdon, 1989) In our case the project is more or less initiated by the management. This implies that resources are available in order to perform a thorough implementation. See further discussion below.

IMPLEMENTATION AS A PROCESS OF ACCEPTANCE

There must be a fit between technology and task and between individual and organizational characteristics and the technology to get acceptance of knowledge management systems. The implementation is a critical activity where the requirements of acceptance are accounted for. The foundation for acceptance has been made during the implementation of the KMS. In our case users have been engaged in an early stage of the development process. This has been done in order to make the users acquainted with the KMS and the purpose of it. This phase has also been a major opportunity for the users to influence the system in design and content. During this phase the choice and meaning of crucial concepts have been decided.

To emphasize the implementation of the KMS we use the prototyping systems development methodology (Smith, 1991, Andersen, 1991, Carey, 1990). Prototyping is usually a mean to develop a model of and identify a requirements specification of the final system and includes collaboration between users and developers in an iterative manner. In our case, we have an evolutionary mode of prototyping where the prototype at some stage is considered to have the qualities worthy to be implemented on a full scale.

The KMS development process is iterative in nature in different development paths consisting of design, implementation, and user testing of the system. Preceding development paths have the proceeding development paths as an input in order to trace changes made in the system back to prior paths.

The process involves management and users of the system. It should be noticed that the managers are not direct users of the system. The aim of the system is to manage knowledge about operational disturbances in production. Therefore the system must be in line with the users in order to be used since it is their knowledge about operational disturbances that is to be systematized into the system. The system's success or failure is determined by users' acceptance.

At first, a pilot group consisting of users where selected. A first version of the system was developed before the pilot group got introduced. The KMS development initiative originates from management and the system was broadly designed in order to raise critical issues relevant for management to consider before the development started involving users, e.g. consider economical effects of undertaking a systems development process and other effects on organisational performance.

Having management support, regularly meetings between users and developers take place after each development path. Since design, implementation and user testing occurs iterative the system is, the more paths, more and more integrated into the pilot groups work practice. In that way the issue of integrating systems use into work is acknowledged, before the process evolves including all users, i.e. implementing the system on a full-scale basis.

Working this way, highlighting the users importance by a collaborative approach, can also set pressure on management to take responsibility for their actions in initiating development of a knowledge management system in terms of investment in computers easily accessed by the user in their working environment.

At the moment the pilot group is in a final stage where final refinements are in focus.

CONCLUSIONS

Findings of the research project reveal that implementing a KMS by prototyping in the way we have described above, supports the three aspects outlined in RAM. Perceived relevance and accessibility is supported by iterations where users in the pilot group are getting acquainted with the KMS step by step. Developing a preliminary design of the system before the actual development process starts highlights the managerial support aspect.

REFERENCES

Andersen E S (1994) *Systemutveckling –Principer, metoder och tekniker* [in Swedish]. Studentlitteratur, Lund

Borghoff U M and Pareschi R (Eds.) (1998) *Information Technology for Knowledge Management.* Springer-Verlag, Berlin Heidelberg

Carey J M (1990) Prototyping: Alternative Systems Development Methodology. Arizona State University, *Information and software technology.* Vol. 32, No. 2

Davenport T and Prusak L (1998) *Working Knowledge: How Organizations Manage What They Know.* Harvard Business Scholl, Boston

Davis F D, Bagozzi R P and Warshaw P R (1989) User acceptance of computer technology: A comparison of two theoretical models. *Management Science.* Vol. 35, No. 8, pp 982-1003

Ericsson F and Avdic A (2002) Information Technology and Knowledge Acquisition in Manufacturing Companies: A Scandinavian Perspective. In Coakes E, Willis D and Clarke S (Eds.) *Knowledge Management in the SocioTechnical World. The Graffiti Continues.* Springer-Verlag, London

Langefors B (1966) *Theoretical Analysis of Information Systems.* Studentlitteratur, Lund.

Scarbrough J and Swan J (Eds.) (1999) *Case Studies in Knowledge Management.* Institute of Personnel and Development, London

Smith M (1991) *Software prototyping –Adaptation, practice and management.* McGRAW-HILL Book Company, London

Tiwana A (2000) *The Knowledge Management Toolkit. Practical Techniques for Building a Knowledge Management System.* Prentice Hall, Upper Saddle River

Turban E (1993) *Expert Systems and Applied Artificial Intelligence.* MacMillan, New York, NY.

Venkatesh V and Davis F D (2000) A Theoretical Extension of the Technology Acceptance Model: Four Longitudinal Field Studies. *Management Science.* Vol. 46, pp 86-204

Yourdon E (1989) *Modern Structured Analysis.* Prentice-Hall, Englewood Cliffs, NJ.

Does Quality Ensure Success in Internet-Based Distance Education in the Philippines: A Formative Study

Sheila B. Bato, Bea V. Espejo and Marlene P. Mana
Department of Information Systems and Computer Science, Ateneo de Manila University, The Philippines
Tel/Fax: (632) 426-6071, sheilabs@hotmail.com, {bea, marls}@admu.edu.ph

The quality of a system is measured with the use of benchmarks, which cover the essential features that a system should have in order for it to be successful. Determining these benchmarks is a difficult task, which is often one sided, meaning that the benchmarks are determined by people or organizations according to their judgement and their definitions of quality. Quality and success are notoriously subjective concepts highly dependent on who is doing the viewing and the judging. Their definitions change over time and between subjects. (Harris, 1995, p. 344) Developing benchmarks and measuring success therefore is an attempt to objectify a subjective matter in the name of standardization.

The rapid growth of Internet-based distance education worldwide has prompted organizations to develop benchmarks designed to apply to a wide variety of institutional contexts, covering aspects such as institutional support, course development, teaching and learning processes, course structure, student support, faculty support, and evaluation and assessment. (Institute for Higher Education Policy, 2000, p. 1) These benchmarks were used to measure the quality of some Internet-based distance education institutions in the United States of America.

This study aims to measure the quality of Philippine Internet-based distance education with the benchmarks for success in Internet-based distance education developed by the Institute for Higher Education Policy to determine if these institutions are at par with their American counterparts. In conjunction with Marshal and Shriver's five levels of evaluation, Kirkpatrick's four levels of evaluation, and the Van Slyke framework to determine if these benchmarks that measure quality are enough to guarantee the success of a distance learning venture.

It is hypothesized that the quality of Philippine institutions will be at par with that of their American counterparts, but that these benchmarks alone are not guarantees for success. Specifically, the benchmarks focus on the quality of the course from the development end, while other methods of evaluation cite that a qualitative investigation of not just the developers end but other factors such as a society's impact on distance education will best determine success in distance education.

First and foremost for any venture to be successful, it should gain acceptance and participation from its target audience. This target audience is the people who wish to study but due to circumstances cannot physically attend classes. Unfortunately, in the Philippine setting, there are many variables that prevent students from enrolling. This research aims to measure the success of Internet-based distance education as how it is accepted. This is determined by the number of enrollees in Internet-based distance education institutions in the Philippines.

This paper describes a research in progress that answers two questions: How do Philippine Internet-based distance education institutions fare as compared to the benchmarks and their American counterparts? And, are distance education institutions that meet these benchmarks guaranteed success?

THEORETICAL FRAMEWORK

The research will be using the benchmarks developed by the National Education Association in measuring the quality of web-based distance learning programs of key institutions in the United States.

There are seven aspects to the benchmark: (Institute for Higher Education Policy, 2000, pp. 2-3)

(1) Institutional Support covers the activities of the institution that helps to ensure the creation of an environment that is conducive to developing and maintaining quality in distance education.
(2) Course Development covers the benchmarks for developing the actual courseware be it produced by an individual or a group of individuals such as faculty, subject experts or commercial enterprises.
(3) Teaching and Learning Process constitutes the activities that pertain to pedagogy. Including issues such as: interactivity, collaboration and modular learning.
(4) Course Structure addresses policies and procedures that support the learning process.
(5) Student Support is the series of student services found in any campus such as: admissions, financial aid, and student expectations.
(6) Faculty Support covers the criteria that assist the faculty in teaching online, plus policies for faculty transition and continued assistance.
(7) Evaluation and Assessment are the policies and procedures that address how the institution evaluates internet-based distance learning, including assessment and data collection.

There are other principles that work in collaboration and support these benchmarks.

Marshall and Schriver's Five Levels of Evaluation assesses if the instructor is able to transfer knowledge and skills to the learner through the quality of course material and course curriculum, the order and structure of course modules, and application of learning experience expounded by Kirkpatrick's Four Levels of Evaluation below. It supports the idea that the assessment of the quality of distance learning is not limited to the technology or communication media used by the instructors but is also determined by the factors mentioned above. (Belanger and Jordan, 2000, p.190)

Kirkpatrick's Four Level of Evaluation is often used to evaluate the impact of learning experience at the affective, cognitive, behavioral and organizational levels. The Learner Reaction level evaluates the learner's personal opinion or view to the instruction that they are receiving. The Knowledge Transfer level measures what the participants have actually learned, both cognitively and in acquired skills. The Behavior Transfer level assesses the observations and measure on behavioral changes in the student. Lastly, the Organizational Impact level measures the relationship between the student's expectation of the institution and if or how the institution responds to these expectations. (Belanger and Jordan, 2000, p.191)

The Van Slyke framework suggests that multiple variables must be taken into account concurrently in looking at their effect in distance learning. The framework looks at determinants of success and evaluation criteria. The determinants of success include, first, Institutional Characteristics, which deals with the variables in objectives, delivery mechanisms and support structure of the institution. Second is Learner Characteristics that relates to the variables on learner objectives and skills. Third is Course Characteristics, which focuses on variables in characteristics of a course that should be taken into account before conversion into an on-line format. Last is the Distance Learning Characteristics, which deals with the variable of use of technology and the learner environment. (Belanger and Jordan, 2000, pp.187-190)

The evaluation criteria takes into account the impact of the interactions of the determinants of success mentioned above on the learner, instructor, institution, and society. The framework suggests that the analysis results in two levels of outcomes and two levels of measures. One for the student and another for the institution. (Belanger and Jordan, 2000, pp.187-190)

The three evaluation frameworks mentioned above supports the Institute for Higher Education Policy in some of its criteria. Other determinants of success of Internet-based distance education, such as knowledge and behavioral transfer, learner's personal reaction to the learning experience, and course curriculum are not covered by the benchmarks. In addition the impact of learner characteristics, learner motivation, and learning style, which may be affected by the learner's culture, environment, and economic situation are not touched by the benchmarks and the evaluation's framework.

The benchmarks exclude economic situations that are prevalent in the Philippine setting. The Philippines is a developing nation, as such there is a limited amount of resources allocated for education. Included in that limited budget is the amount allocated for the use of technology-enhanced education. In comparison with a developed nation where approximately US$430 is spent on the education of each child, developing nations spend approximately only US$5 per child. (Lewin 2000, 313-321) As a result many provincial and even urban public schools do not have concrete floors, furniture, electricity and water. Even if these basic amenities were met, the budget allocated to these schools cannot cover the cost to provide computers and Internet access which are required to engage in Internet-based education. (Beauchamp 1995, 193-201)

In a survey completed in 1988 only 63% of Philippine schools had computers, of these 70% were private schools.(Roxas, et al 1989) This lack of computers is not only prevalent in schools but in the Philippine home as well due to the lack of substantial income. The Family Income Expenditure Survey (FIES) conducted by the National Statistics Coordinating Board in the year 2000 shows that the average family income in the urban area is approximately US$4,766 while US$1,716 in the rural area. The average cost for a computer in the Philippines is approximately US$500, this, in conjunction with the average rate of internet access of around US$20, makes the computer and the Internet luxury items that the average Filipino household cannot afford. (National Statistics Coordination Board, 2000)

Out of the 63% only 30% used computers as teaching aids, this lack of the use of computers to aid in education stems from a lack of documentation, information, cooperation between the public and private education sectors, as well as a lack of government support. (Rodrigo 2001, 129) These are some of the reasons why Internet based distance education is not seen as a viable alternative to traditional classroom education inspite of its many advantages.

METHODOLOGY

The instruments used in this study are surveys and interviews. For a comprehensive view, the survey will be distributed to three different groups: The students, who will be taking the course, the faculty, who design develop and teach the course, and the administration, who are the individuals involved in the planning, development and implementation of the course. The survey will consist of two parts. One section of the survey seeks to determine if that benchmark is indeed being practiced, the other, how important the surveyed individuals consider that benchmark to be. This quantitative analysis will be measured using the Likert scale.

At the same time select individuals from each group will be interviewed using open ended questions to obtain the qualitative aspect of the study, answering the question: Does quality ensure success?

The institutions selected to participate in the survey range from universities offering regular classroom courses on-line to non-educational institutions that offer on-line training and seminars. This range is essential to capture the overall quality of Internet-based distance education in the Philippines and the factors for success.

LIMITATIONS

A limitation of this study is the fact that the institutions involved are not on the same instructional level. Some offer courses on-line that are also available as traditional university courses, while others focuses on giving seminars on-line. Therefore we cannot have what is considered to be a true sample. But this study aims to measure the quality of web-based distance learning in the Philippines and their factors for success, so all these institutions must be included.

STATUS OF THE STUDY

As of this point the research for the theoretical framework has been completed. The survey questionnaires have been completed and are awaiting distribution by mid October to participating institutions. The interview questions are under development. All responses are expected to be in by December and the study should be completed by March.

REFERENCES

Belanger, France, and Dianne H. Jordan. 2000. *Evaluation and Implementation of Distance Learning: Technologies, Tools and Techniques.* Hershey: Idea Group Publishing.

The Institute For Higher Education Policy. 2000. *Quality on the Line: Benchmarks for Success in Internet Based Distance Education.* [Online]. http://www.ihep.com

Chambers, Ellie. 1995. *Course Evaluation and Academic Quality.* Open and Distance Learning Today. ed. Fred Lockwood. London: Routledge.

Lewin, K.M. 2000. *Compare: A Journal of comparative Education.* [Online]

Beauchamp, A.P. 1995. Uganda's Schools: Do These Need Computers? In *World conference on Computers in Education VI: WCCE 95 Liberating the Learner: Proceeding of the Sixth IFIP World Conference on Computers in Education,* J.D. Tinsey & T.J. Van Weert, Eds. London: Chapman & Hall.

Rodrigo, Ma. Mercedes T. 2001. Information and Communication Technology Use in Philippine Public and Private Schools. In *The Loyola Schools Review.* Vol. 1. Manila: Office of Research and Publications, Ateneo de Manila University

National Statistics Coordination Board. 2000. *Family Income Expenditure Survey* [Online] http://www.nscb.gov.ph

Roxas, P.S., B.O. Marinas. 1989. *SEAMO-RESCAM Computers in Education Project: Country Report Philippines.* SEAMO Regional Centre for Education in Science and Mathematics. Malaysia.

State of the Art of Biometrics—A Review

Stewart T. Fleming
Department of Computer Science, University Otago, New Zealand
Tel: (643) 479-5728, Fax: (643) 479-8529, stf@cs.otago.ac.nz

ABSTRACT

The use of biometrics is an important new part of the design of secure computer systems. However, many users view such systems with deep suspicion and many designers do not carefully consider the characteristics of biometrics in their system designs. This research aims to review the current state of the art in biometrics and to conduct detailed study of the available technologies and systems and to examine end-user perceptions of such systems. The research aims to establish guidelines for the design of interactive systems that adopt biometrics.

INTRODUCTION

The upsurge in popularity of biometric devices in recent years prompts many questions regarding their application. While biometric devices can enhance the security of a system, they do not provide a "silver bullet" to guarantee absolute security. This research sets out to investigate the state of the art in biometric devices, to identify risks, possible uses and abuses and user perceptions of the technology.

An effective security system is one in which at least two out of the following three elements are present: something you have, something you know, or something that you are (Schneier, 2000). Biometrics can provide only one of these elements. How the remaining elements of security are to be provided is an open design question. The aim of this research is to provide guidelines for the design of interactive systems that adopt biometrics as part of their design.

STUDY OF BIOMETRICS

There are many forms of biometric data for which capture and verification is possible via some device. Fingerprints, voice recognition, retinal, face or hand scanning are all feasible with current technology. However, the nature of biometric data is such that there are significant risks associated with its capture and use in a secure environment (Schneier, 1999).

Whatever data is used, a biometric security system generally relies on the enrollment of biometric data and subsequent authentication against a sample provided by the same individual. This research will address three aspects of biometric security – the accuracy of the verification, protection of the biometric data and user perceptions of the process.

Verification of Manufacturer's Claims

Two characteristics of any biometric device that have a bearing on usability and security are the false acceptance rate (FAR) and false rejection rate (FRR). If the false acceptance rate is too high, then *unauthorised* individuals may be able to gain access to the system; if the false rejection rate is too high, then *authorised* individuals may have to submit several candidate biometrics before gaining access.

This aspect of the study aims to verify manufacturer's claims for FAR and FRR. This involves the capture of a large number of biometrics, various measurements of similarities between templates and a large number of comparisons to determine actual error rates with real users. This work will provide a protocol for the independent verification of acceptance and rejection rates for biometric devices.

Biometric Encryption

There are various methods of combining biometrics with encryption. The Bioscrypt technology described by (Tomko, 1998) uses optical technology to combine a biometric scan with a pass-phrase known only to the user in order to provide authentication. Asymmetric cryptography can be used to achieve the same ends.

This part of the study aims to develop scenarios in which biometrics and cryptography techniques are combined to guarantee confidentiality, integrity, authentication and non-repudiation – the classic characteristics of a secure system (Clarke, 1998).

User-Perception of Biometric Devices

In an earlier study (Fleming, 1998), users who were not familiar with technology showed reluctance to use a system that captured biometric data. It is expected that many users will have suspicions about the use of biometric devices. This part of the study will investigate potential barriers to the use of a biometric system and develop procedures that could address the concerns.

SCENARIOS

We aim to construct prototype systems to illustrate various scenarios in the use of biometrics.

Non-repudiation – in asymmetric cryptography, a digital signature can be used to provide an assurance that a particular individual sent a particular message. The addition of biometrics reinforces the principle of non-repudiation by providing an assurance that the real, live individual who sent the message was in fact present at a particular time and location.

End-user authentication – many actions in interactive applications may occur automatically, without the explicit consent of the user. A system where authorisation was required from a real, live user before critical actions could take place, would be an important step forward in ensuring the integrity of the user's information resources.

Biometric encryption – many of the biometric systems proposed for use require the biometric data to be stored or registered in some database and keyed to a particular, identified individual. Such a system is prone to a replay attack and introduces significant privacy risks. By encrypting the biometric data with a private key and storing the encrypted template in the database, these risks are reduced. This principle also enables *authentication* without *identification*, which can be a desirable characteristic.

CONCLUSIONS

While biometrics do have an important part to play in the design of secure systems in which a user has confidence, their use requires careful consideration in the design of such systems. By developing various scenarios for the use of biometrics and examining user perceptions of such systems, the researchers aim to provide guidelines for the design of biometric systems that incorporate biometrics.

REFERENCES

R. Clarke, 1998. Cryptography in Plain Text. *Privacy Law & Policy Reporter* 3(2). May 1996, pp 24-27. Available online: http://www.anu.edu.au/people/Roger.Clarke/CryptoSecy.html Accessed: 15th October 2001.

Fleming, S. T. and D. Vorst, 1998. *Putting your finger on it – Patient identification in a multi-name society*. Proceedings of IRMA 1999 International Conference. Information Resource Management Association, Hershey, PA. May 1999.

B. Schneier, 1999. Biometrics : Uses and Abuses. Inside Risks 100. *Communications of the ACM*, 42(8), August 1999.

B. Schneier, 2000. *Secrets and Lies : Digital Security in a Networked World*. Wiley, 2000.

G. Tomko, 1998. *Biometrics as a Privacy-Enhancing Technology: Friend or Foe of Privacy?* Privacy Laws & Business Privacy Commissioner's / Data Protection Authorities Workshop. Santiago de Compostela, Spain, September 1998. Available online: http://www.dss.state.ct.us/digital/tomko.html Accessed 15th October 2001.

Motivating Authors to Share and Re-Use Pedagogical Documents

Emmanuel Fernandes, Fabrice Holzer, Maia Wentland Forte and Bahram Zaerpour
University of Lausanne, Switzerland, {Emmanuel.Fernandes, Fabrice.Holzer}@centef.unil.ch, mwf@unil.ch, Bahram.Zaerpour@rect.unil.ch

Computer based training (CBT) and Computer Aided Learning (CAL) applications have been around for more than thirty years. Conceived as rigid integrated stand-alone pieces of software, they never turned out a real success although they costed a huge amount of human and financial efforts. Thanks to the dazzling deployment of information and communication technologies (ICT) coupled with the tenfold increase of computer power, new and promising opportunities for open and distance education opened up. New paradigms were born, amongst which those of *learning citizen* and *share-and-reuse* are worth mentioning. If properly taken into consideration, these concepts influence greatly the way on-line teaching and training could be handled, in turn modifying the way the production of electronic documents for education and training should be dealt with. In this paper, because we firmly believe it to be one of the main issues, we will concentrate on the share-and-reuse paradigm.

Lots of efforts (ARIADNE, Dublin Core, IMS, eBioMED.ch, IEEE-LTSC, CEN-CENELEC, Medline Mesh tree, etc.) have been invested in defining a proper indexation schema, resulting in an appropriate descriptor or *header*, for describing pedagogical documents. The difficulty stems from the following paradox: the header should be as detailed as possible to get, when querying the knowledge pool, an adequate set of documents, and as light as possible to make sure that indexation will be performed. So whatever the international standard might be, it will achieve its aim of fostering share-and-reuse only if the majority of the involved persons accept to use it!

The question therefore is: "How to convince an author to index a document?" In order to try and answer this question, we are investigating what are the key factors of motivation for an author. The work in progress, detailed hereafter, intends to detect (i) what could motivate or impede authors from sharing and/or re-using educational documents, and (ii) what could be proposed to increase their willingness to do so. A representative panel of authors, belonging to the academic world, will be determined that will answer a survey for discovering what are these key factors. At this stage we exclude the professional world assuming that the objectives and underlying motivations for share and reuse are quite different from those of the academic world (Confidentiality considerations, Strategic information, Institutional policies...).

RESEARCH ASSUMPTIONS AND OBJECTIVES

According to the above mentioned context, it appears that authors' - persons involved in the production and drafting of electronic documents dedicated to the academic training - motivation to share, use and re-use documents is a determining factor when aiming at improving the quality of shared/sharable documents, thus contributing to increase their production. Our assumption is that studying both the related variables, we will be able to deduce which of these endogenous and exogenous factors should be considered to help increase the authors' motivation.

The main endogenous factors retained so far are:

(i) confidence in the quality of what is produced both by oneself and by others ;
(ii) trust in reciprocation, meaning that when one shares its production with others they, in turn, will do the same defeating the belief that "I always give and never receive" ;
(iii) the conviction that by feeding a cooperative database and contributing to it scaling up, the whole community will benefit from it ;
(iv) the wish to belong to a network, so that the combined efforts alleviate a burden that otherwise might be to heavy : investing efforts, time and money to rediscover what already exists ;
(v) the personal intention in sharing with third parties ;
(vi) the ability to consider its specific research and curricular field like forming part of a broader network of general disciplines.

Regarding the exogenous factors, we will consider:

(i) the financial and temporal constraints ;
(ii) the institutional capacity to support transdisciplinarity ;
(iii) the increased visibility of the resulting curriculum ;
(iv) the possibility of developing new collaborations ;
(v) the reluctance towards technological constraints.

We thus propose to examine some dimensions intervening in the motivation process and to interpret them in the light of the variables of the here above mentioned. In order to justify a lack of co-operation, authors often mention exogenous factors, however we believe that endogenous factors are likely to impact the tendency more strongly when being taken in to account in a cooperative model.

Endogenous factors of first level (authors' intention) must be understood according to the model of coalition presented by Foray and Zimmermann.

A population ***I*** involved in producing pedagogical contents, of cardinal *N*, which can influence the individual decision of taking part or not in the collective efforts of sharing these contents. It is considered that these collective efforts generate, for each ***N*** individuals (authors) of ***I***, an externality of use resulting from the improvements made to the first teaching step of production. We represent this externality in the ***f(n)*** function of the number of cooperating authors, where ***f(n)*** is increasing and strictly concave.

In a simplified way, we initially assume that the individual cost of participation per unit of time is uniform and is indicated by *CP*, as well as for the expected effects in term of reputation and competence, indicated by *KR*. Thus we can derive that the cumulated profit for any individual author, for each unit of time, depends whether to whether he cooperates or not:

With regard to the exogenous factors, we subdivide them in 3 categories of dimension: (i) the institutional constraints (existing network, transdisciplinarity, etc.), (ii) the technological constraints (reluctance towards technology) and finally (iii) the academic and linguistic traditions to which belong the institutions where the authors work (Latin language speaking European, German speaking European, English speaking European and North American, etc.).

Motivations of the authors in the step of use, sharing and re-use of electronic documents. A study about these motivations implies to target the underlying endogenous and exogenous factors (psychosocial perspective) acting in this process.

METHODOLOGICAL ASPECTS

It should be noted that the endogenous factors to study are divided into 2 dimensions: (i) dimension of intentionality (above mentioned) and (ii) social factors (gender and age). With regard to the exogenous factors, we subdivide them in 3 categories of dimension: (i) the institutional constraints (existing network, transdisciplinarity, etc.), (ii) the technological constraints (reluctance towards technology) and finally (iii) the academic and linguistic traditions to which belong the institutions in which authors are in function (Latin language speaking European, German speaking European, English speaking European and North American, etc.).

Figure 1

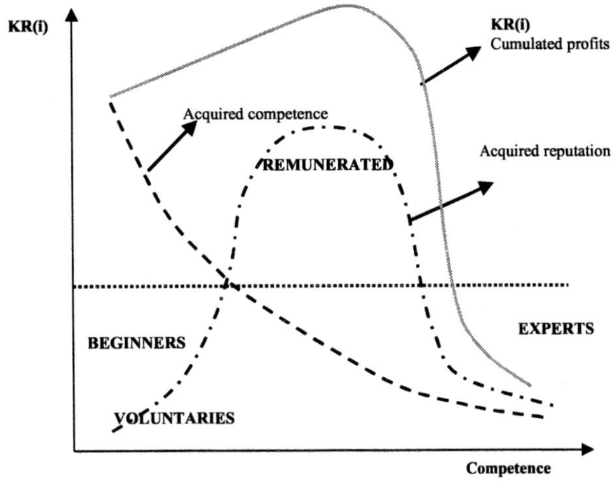

Experimental Conditions

1. Preliminary questionnaire in order to target a representative sample of population (authors involved in production and drafting of electronic documents dedicated to the academic training, independently of their motivations).
2. Determination of the sample (Determining the sample size for a factor or effect in an **AN**alysis **O**f **VA**riance between groups is usually difficult because of the need to specify all of the treatment means in order to calculate the non-centrality parameter of the F-distribution, on which power depends)
3. Dividing this sample into equal and significant (F-distribution) groups (regarding to gender, age, language and academic tradition, etc).
4. Multivariate questionnaire suitable for informing us about all above mentioned dimensions, factors and correlations between the studied variables.
5. Factor analysis of correspondences. 1, 2 and 3 way interaction effect (ANOVA), correlations (multiple regression if necessary), etc.
6. Interpreting the results and offering a grid of understanding.

QUESTIONNAIRE

The questionnaire is being prepared. We can already describe its general schema. The questionnaire will allow the detection of nowadays and past practices of the population sample, regarding sharing and re-use of electronic documents for education (do they share documents? did they share documents in the past? do they re-use documents produced by third parties? in which way? in which context?, etc.). The second part of the questionnaire aims at detecting various dimensions of motivation underlying the past and current practices:

- What factors can/could increase the motivation to share documents (visibility, recognition, altruism, practice imposed by the institution, the possibility to access - in its turn - to documents produced by others etc).
- What are the inhibiting factors for document sharing (lack of recognition, loss of control on its own work, copyright and other legal problems, technical and organisational problems, lack of human and/or financial resources, lack of information, specificity of produced documents to a particular situation etc),
- What are the factors that justify the use of documents produced by others (time saving, lack of competences and/or resources to produce its own documents, the need to diversify resources placed at the disposal of learners, institutional policy etc),
- What are the factors inhibiting the re-use of documents produced by others (inadequacy with the needs, difficulties to find appropriate documents, poor quality of scientific content, technical problems, copyright problems, language and translation problems, price of the documents, the inappropriate granularity of the documents, impossibility to modify and adapt documents, the too large specificity of available material).

FUTURE WORK

This study will detect factors allowing share and re-use of the electronic documents for education. First of all we will categorize the population sample according to their present and past practices. Ability of sharing and re-using documents will constitute the two main dimensions used in order to extract this sample (those sharing documents, those re-using them, those doing both). We will then try to detect the motivations underlaying each type of practice regarding the sharing and re-use of documents. The main factors, highlighted by this inquiry will then be studied, more intensively, in a second article. Obviously the model is not strictly defined, and should be completed by including other factors like the relation between the number of documents re-used and the number of documents shared.

REFERENCES

"L'économie du logiciel libre : organisation coopérative et incitation à l'innovation" D. Foray, JB. Zimmermann in Flash Informatique spécial été 2001.

"Accessing and expanding the science and technology knowledge base", David P. et Foray D. (1995), STIReview, no16, OCDE, Paris, p.13-68

" A Knowledge Pool System of Reusable Pedagogical Elements", K. Cardinaels, K. Hendrikx, E. Vervaet, E. Duval, H. Olivie, F. Haenni, K.Warkentyne, M. Wentland Forte & E. Forte, in Proc. of CALISCE'98, June 15-17th 1998, Göteborg, Suède.

" Managing Digital Educational Resources with the ARIADNE Metadata System" E. Duval, E. Vervaet, B. Verhoeven, K. Hendrikx, K. Cardinaels, H. Olivié, E. Forte, F. Haenni, K. Warkentyne, M. Wentland Forte, and F.Simillion, in Journal of Internet Cataloging (2000).

Linux: l'explosion du phénomène des logiciels libres, M. Ganagé et R. Bonnet, in L'Ordinateur Individuel, No 97, Juillet-Août (1998).

Communication norms and the collective cognitive performance of 'invisible colleges', P. David in G.B. Navaretti (ed.), Creation and transfer of knowledge: institutions and incentives, Physica Verlag Series (1997).

IEEE P1484.12 Learning Object Metadata Working Group, http://ltsc.ieee.org/wg12/index.html

Business Modeling For E-Collaboration Networks: The Path from Entrepreneurial Strategy to Customer-Oriented Business Modeling

Tomaso Forzi and Peter Laing
Research Institute for Operations Management (FIR) at Aachen University of Technology (RWTH Aachen)
E-Business Engineering Department–Pontdriesch 14/16, 52062 Aachen, Germany
Tel: +49(0241)47705-243, Fax: +49(0241)47702-199, {fol, la}@fir.rwth-aachen.de

ABSTRACT

The Internet and web-based E-Business solutions play a crucial enabling role for the design and implementation of new Business Models. This implies high chances, but also remarkable risks for enterprises that choose to pursue a new Business Model, since the implementation of a strategically not appropriate Business Model would critically undermine the long-term success of a company. Hence, we present a new approach for a customer-oriented (E-) Business Modeling, with a specific attention on inter-organizational co-operative networks and re-intermediation.

THE INTERNET TRIGGERS NEW BUSINESS MODELS

The fast development of new Information and Communication Technologies (ICTs) has been revolutionizing the market arena and it extended the horizon of competition [4]. New ICTs allow enterprises to design leaner *intra-* and especially inter-organizational processes by supporting *co-operation* within *entrepreneurial networks* as well as by enabling their *co-ordination* – by means of Internet-based Business Collaboration Infrastructures (BCIs) [5], [13]. Web-based ICT solutions play hence a crucial *enabling role* both for new Business Models and for those models that, up until now, had a higher value on a theoretical than on a practical level (e.g. Virtual Organizations) [8]. Lately, Business Models tend to involve different networked enterprises with the goal of bringing higher profits to each of the participants [1], [8]. The development of such co-operative E-Business Models represents a significant challenge, since there are no appropriate methods to tackle systematically such modeling issue [10]. We developed a *customer-oriented business modeling* approach for intermediaries within dispersed manufacturing networks.

BUSINESS MODELING AND ENTREPRENEURIAL STRATEGY

In the management literature there are different and discrepant definitions of the term *Business Model*, which can be classified according to different criteria, such as the functional integration, the collaboration focus or the involved actors [1], [11], [13].

The core objective of each company is a long-term creation of *added value* [9] and the entrepreneurial *strategy* defines how such a target has to be fulfilled. A sustained profitability is achieved through a successful strategic positioning, an own value proposition, a distinctive value chain and an entrepreneurial fit [9]. Hence, according to our understanding, a *Business Model is an instantiation of an entrepreneurial strategy related to a specific business* and it encompasses: markets (customers and competitors), outputs, revenues, production design, partner network and financing [7].

CUSTOMER-ORIENTED BUSINESS MODELING FOR COLLABORATIVE NETWORKS

Up until now, the development and adjustment of Business Models has been performed by companies mostly in a creative way. In the state-of-the-art there is hardly any holistic methodical support [1]. We are convinced that a successful approach to tackle this methodical lack must focus on the *customer's needs*. As a matter of fact, the fulfillment of the customers' needs is an essential precondition to generate turnover [6]. With this motivation, we have developed the *House of Value Creation (HVC),* a method to design customer-oriented and sustainable Business Models [7] (Figure 1). This method suits explicitly the design of Internet-based BCIs.

Our institution has a proved experience with SMEs of the German manufacturing and machinery industry. Since we identified a remarkable *need for "e-action"* in this traditional and static industrial branch, we decided to develop a *customized Business Model* for an intermediary transaction platform to support the collaboration in this industrial sector. Thus, we started a public founded two year consortial project with 10 SMEs to develop an approach to customize an *Exchange and Communication Platform* within the above-mentioned branch to validate our HVC. More precisely, the case study focuses on the field of *manufacturing networks for metallic material.* As a matter of fact, the generation and mailing of so-called *paper-based test reports* for metallic material, which documents and guarantees to the buyer specific material properties, is nowadays accompanied by several serious problems. For instance, the open issues concern the archiving of reports, the specification check of corresponding material standards or norms referenced in a test report [2].

The HVC is a meta-method and it consists of *three logical pillars* (input, method, and output) and of *six layers.* The HVC illustrates the correlation between a set of significant leverages (first pillar of the HVC), the Customer-oriented Business Modeling process (second pil-

Figure 1: The house of value creation [7]

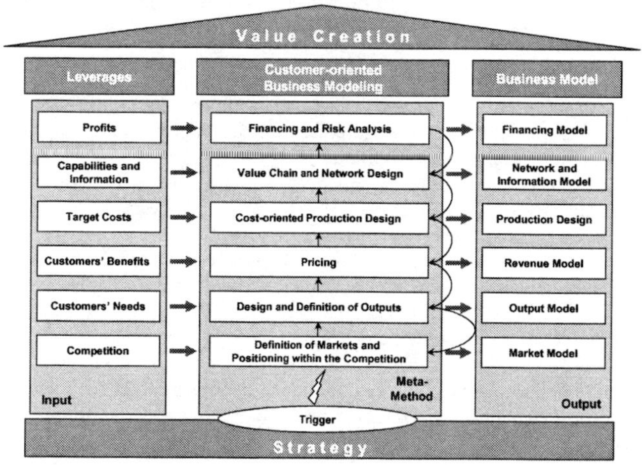

lar), and the resulting Business Model (third pillar). Furthermore, the six layers correspond to six following steps of the method. Each of the process steps requires a suitable method and the corresponding targets must be fulfilled. If one step is not fulfilled, then the process should go back to a prior phase as long as the issue is tackled – with an iterative approach.

The first HVC phase is triggered either by the inside or by the outside of the company – through a new idea, invention, innovation or modifications of the economical environment. The innovative trigger for the case study was the world-wide dissemination and acceptance of the Internet and its suitability for an efficient exchange and storage of material test reports. Thus, we proposed a Business Model for the exchange of *electronic material reports* on an Internet-based BCI, as the result of the use of our HVC modeling approach [7].

1. **Definition of the markets and positioning within the competition.** The initial decision regards the category of products or services to deal with. Hence, a consequent monitoring of all strong players has to be done [9]. This phase deals with the branch profitability and with the rivalry among existing and potential competitors. More concretely, in the case study we identified similar solutions to manage and exchange material reports (e.g. document management systems), but none of them fulfills all relevant requirements. Thus, we decided to develop a BCI for the exchange of standardized electronic material reports in cooperation with experts in the field of material science. In the resulting *market model* there are no direct competitors, while the potential customers are manufacturing enterprises that exchange metallic products with specified and guaranteed properties.
2. **Definition and design of the outputs.** In the product design, a well-proven method is the Quality Function Deployment (QFD). With this approach, a customer-oriented product development can be successfully realized [12]. Therefore, the outputs (physical products or services) have to be shaped in order to maximize the customers' benefit according to a QFD-like method. In the *output model* of the case study, the most relevant customers' needs which were identified are the operating efficiency and flexibility in terms of exchanging metallic material test reports, security (e.g. transmission and privacy), and system availability. Hence, the output services had been designed to fulfill the requirements, e.g.: electronic transaction of standardized reports with high security level.
3. **Pricing.** The identification of prices for the planned outputs should be more the result of a strategic positioning than of a cost-oriented approach [4]. The price calculation should take into consideration the customers' surplus constraint as well as the strength of the competition (existing barriers of entry, such as industry property rights) [6]. For the *revenue model*, we conducted an analysis of the customers' benefit. Nowadays, the cost for the processing of a single report amounts up to about 50 US $. With the use of the electronic transaction platform, the process costs for a test report transmission and specification check drops drastically. Therefore, we proposed a price per transaction significant lower than the present report processing cost to achieve a critical mass in terms of traffic, as well as to ensure a wide dissemination of the standard. This heightens the barriers for market entry for possible competitors.
4. **Cost-oriented production design.** According to the guidelines of the revenue model, the target costs for the output model will be calculated. Hence, the requirements to the value chain will be detailed. In the case of the *"production" design* for the transmission of material reports, the attention was paid to the fixed costs (i.e. target costs for the infrastructure) since direct costs (i.e. cost for the report transmission) tend to zero. Hence, the result is a platform with a targeted low fixed cost (e.g. hardware, software and mainly personnel costs). The lower the fixed costs are, the sooner the critical mass in terms of participants and transactions will be reached.
5. **Network and information.** In this phase, starting from the requirements on performances and from the capabilities (e.g. core competencies, capacities and ICT infrastructure) of the potential partners, the striven value chain will be designed and a specific network will be instantiated. The gathering of all information regarding the potential network participants represents what we define as *capabilities and information* and it is one of the tasks of a network broker. According to the requirements previously identified within the *production design*, a crosscheck with the capabilities of all potential partners helps to define a set of suitable partners. As a result, the instantiation of a *specific network configuration* can be identified. Furthermore, the definition of inter-organizational blue prints and branch-specific process standards is necessary to enable lean and efficient *inter-organizational processes and work-flows*. The result is the *network model*. The most relevant aspect for the following phase is that the inter-organizational processes determine the *sources* and the *sinks* of distributed information. The *information model* focuses on the management of the information within such entrepreneurial networks and inter-organizational value chains (Figure 2). Within the case study, it was decided that the collaboration platform should *not* be managed by one of the manufacturers of metallic material, but that a *third party operator* with know-how of the industrial branch should maintain the platform. Within the *information model*, the crucial issue is the *modeling of processes and the management of shared information*. Some of the most interesting aspects which were taken into consideration within the above-mentioned HVC level are the definition of *process standards* for inter-organizational processes and work-flows and the branch-specific development of a *shared standard* for electronic test reports.
6. **Financing and risk analysis.** Eventually, based upon the expected profits and a suitable scenario analysis for future developments, the risk-level as well as the need for working capital must be calculated to start the search for investors [3]. According to the *financing model*, investors should be willing to bear both losses during the initial phase and risks related to the critical mass. Anyhow, there is a high probability for a scenario with long-term value creation.

Figure 2: The fifth level of the HVC

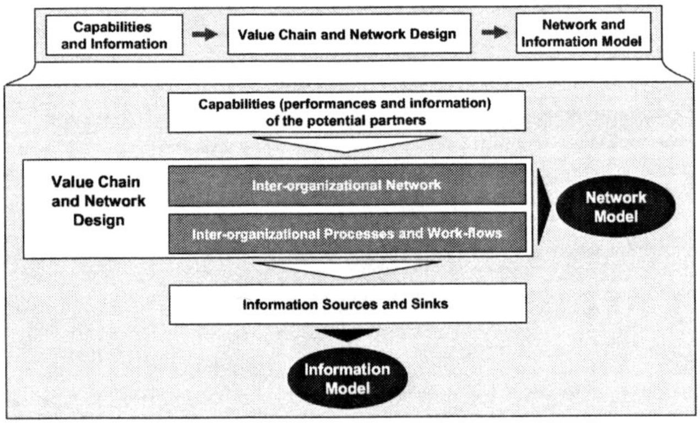

REFERENCES

[1] Afuah, A, Tucci C.L. "Internet Business Models and Strategies: Text and Cases". New York: McGraw-Hill/Irwin, 2001.
[2] DIN (publisher) 10 204. "Metallic products – Types of inspection documents" (German version). Beuth Verlag, 1990.
[3] Fink A., Schlake O., Siebe A. „Wie Sie mit Szenarien die Zukunft vorausdenken". In: Harvard Business Manager, 2000 (2), 34-47.
[4] Hagel III J., Singer M. „Unbundling the Corporation". In: Harvard Business Review, 1999, 77(2), 133-141.
[5] Hoeck H., Bleck S. „Electronic Markets for Services". In: E-Work and E-Commerce, volume 1, Stanford-Smith & Chiozza Edt., Amsterdam, Berlin, Oxford: IOS Press, 2001, 458-464.
[6] Kim C., Mauborgne R. "Knowing a Winning Business Idea When You See One". In: Harvard Business Review, 2000, 78(5), 129-138.
[7] Laing P., Forzi T. "E-Business and Entrepreneurial Cooperation". In: First International Conference on Electronic Business (ICEB 2001), Hong Kong, 2001.

[8] Picot A., Reichwald R., Wigand R.T. „Die grenzenlose Unternehmung – Information, Organisation und Management“, 4th edition. Wiesbaden: Gabler Verlag, 2001.
[9] Porter M.E. “Strategy and the Internet”. Harvard Business Review 2001, 79(3): 63-68.
[10] Rayport J. F. “The Truth about Internet Business Models”, 1999. Retrieved on September 27th, 2001, from the Web-site: www.strategy-Business.com/briefs/99301/page1.html.
[11] Timmers P. “Electronic Commerce – Strategies and Models for Business-to-Business Trading”. John Wiley & Sons, Ltd, 2000.
[12] Warnecke H.J., Melchior K.W., Kring J. „Handbuch Qualitätstechnik: Methoden und Geräte zur effizienten Qualitätssicherung“. Landsberg/ Lech: Verlag Moderne Industrie, 1995.
[13] Wirtz B. W. „Electronic Business“. Dr. Th. Gabler Verlag, 2000.

A Project Management, Costing and Controlling System for Small and Medium-Sized Enterprises

Bardo Fraunholz
Institute for IS Research, University of Koblenz, Germany
Tel: +49 (261) 287-2536, Fax: +49 (261) 287-100 2536, bardo.fraunholz@uni-koblenz.de

INTRODUCTION

With growing popularity of Project Management there have been an increasing number of software products, claiming they qualify as all-inclusive project management tools [Frit00]. Turning to the web, one realises that there seems to be a perception on what project management should be. However when we focus on a business that entirely works project oriented and therefore aims at a piece of software to assist with the organisation of projects and the business as a whole, there do not seem to be a lot of tools available in the marketplace. This is even more so if we look at the demands of Small and Medium sized Enterprises (SMEs) [Gray00].

As we got involved in a project concerned with the introduction of project management in SMEs, especially German trade businesses, we found there is an increasing demand for information technology (IT) support covering all aspects of the business [Hand01] thus requiring us to analyse business processes. The method adopted for calculating cost is the rule of thumb for most of the time, while, if ex post calculation existed, it could hardly be described as satisfactory because it only exists with an aim to account for the profitability of a project [Frau01]. Other findings are not realised and therefore do not enter into future calculations. In addition to that the crucial task of providing customer quotes creates a state of panic because there is usually no - up to date - data available and therefore it creates a repeatingly overwhelming effort. The impact this practice has on businesses and also on customer satisfaction can only be speculated on but is sure to be of financial relevance.

PROJECTS VERSUS BUSINESS PROCESSES

There are apparent similarities between projects and some of the business processes in SMEs; therefore it seems appropriate to be looking for approaches that can be used in both domains. Literature on business process (re-)engineering focuses on organising business processes and - from an information systems perspective – on designing/implementing IT support [Sche94]. In order to derive a fully integrated system we also need a comprehensive controlling concept for the whole project organisation. There are many controlling concepts to be used or adapted for business processes [Horv01] which however typically do not take the specific organisational and technological aspects into account.

I addition to those business processes that can also be described as projects there are many which are not directly related to the revenue creating core competencies businesses perform. However these processes also resemble necessary issues that must be accounted for. Ideally we are looking at an integrated system allowing us to use traditional project management skills – and project management software – but at the same time will support us in organizing and keeping track of the other processes necessary for business.

This triggered an idea to expand and adapt conventional project management tools to the demands and specific requirements of project driven SMEs, enhancing them by adding a financial controlling and cost calculating component. The aim is to provide the business with accurate up to the minute ex-post information of past projects and with the feature of drafting a project calculation for a future project just by sketching a rough project plan.

REQUIREMENTS

The idea is that a system will assist a project oriented SME with the organisation of its business and provide fully integrated project management functionality. To make such a system practical and easy to use in a SME environment which typically does not have an IT department and where employees have hardly any IT skills, it is important to provide a user interface that will make it feel familiar and easy to use.

In order to achieve this, we need to focus on those individuals involved in the businesses processes. These would be the group of employees, the business owner and possible contractors involved with the business. At the same time we should aim at providing a system that will allow for new employees or externals to understand the company and its structure.

The Project Management, Costing and Controlling System (PMCC) should offer a structured template of businesses processes which is easy to follow and adopt to be suitable for any task necessary. This requires a thorough understanding, analysis and description of the enterprise and also has to take a number of interlinked concepts like business strategy or employees into account. With the PMCC it should be possible to disseminate answers to questions like:

- How would a plan for a particular type of project look like?
- What is the cost involved?
- What resources are necessary over time?
- What are the tasks to be performed by John Lamb over time?

To make the system more useful it is important to find the right terminology. For the normal project plan, task lists and resources we recommend the proven concepts as described in various project management textbooks [Dunc96]. I addition it is necessary to provide a format to make the financial plans available and comply with legal requirements. We want to be able to re-use data that might have been acquired in a different context such as bills or wages therefore we need an interface that will ensure the accurate acquisition of data. Also it must be possible to improve the overall quality by ensuring that new concepts used are incorporated in the system.

In order to support different users and different tasks at all levels of the business the PMCC must be able to represent all business processes. However to make the system more manageable the system should offer different levels of detail and complexity. This in many ways is possible with conventional project management tools, too, but we also want the functionality to provide us with a view on all processes currently undertaken in the whole of the business independent from individual projects, while at other times it might be appropriate to just see the utilisation of one machine. Complexity increases further when we are looking at inter business usage of resources in a cooperative setting.

THE ARCHITECTURE

The design and implementation of such an integrated system requires the timely evaluation of organisational and technological options. Our experience within projects where we need detailed knowledge about SMEs in general and also project orientation in trade indicates that a qualitative approach is appropriate. An action research approach has proved the best results – both for the participating companies and the academic appreciation of the transition processes.

During the analysis supported by the use of conceptual models [MyLE85], we established that there is need for additional abstraction and support of multiple perspectives because sometimes it might be sufficient to just describe associations of tasks, while on other occasions it is required to get a detailed description of all tasks and resources used to be able to understand the cost and performance of significant activities and trace activities to final cost objectives. The system should provide us with information on projects in general and indicate activities that are non-value adding or in turn identify the most efficient way to perform a project. The aim is to identify cost drivers in advance and assist with the calculation of a specific customer request. Additionally there is the option to do ex post calculations of all projects with the added benefit of a "learning" system that will incorporate changes to the calculating base when circumstances have changed.

At the same time we need a system that can be used for more than one enterprise. Therefore it is necessary to introduce different levels of abstraction in order to be able to map general project, controlling and accounting concepts with the specific domain of the individual business and provide the business with an intuitive user interface. Preferably using an already familiar project management tool. This can be achieved by introducing different layers that provide information and concepts particular to the necessary abstraction.

Inspired by a method for multi-perspective enterprise modelling named MEMO [Fran99] which differentiates the three perspectives strategy, organisation and information system with the fife aspects resource, structure, process, goal and environment for each perspective (see figure 1), we differentiate between a norm level (providing general principles of e.g. projects or accounting), the domain level (describing certain categories of businesses) and the business level (that is tailor made for the individual business). The three level architecture in figure 2 depicts this concept. The norm level is there to provide general concepts valid for all businesses. The second level, the domain level will make domain specific concepts available for a certain category of businesses while the third level as the business level provides the user interface that utilises and accumulates business data. However such a system can not solely rely on internal data because there is information that might be stored in other areas of the business that are only indirectly project related. Such areas could be the personal department where all data on the cost of individual workers is keep and updated. This kind of data is crucial for financial planning and must be made available, on the other hand there are security issues that must also be addressed. Therefore it must be guarantied that data is available for calculation but can not be trace back to an individual.

In order to implement such an architecture it is possible to fall back on a large variety of well established and proven concepts of software engineering and conceptual modelling respectively [Fran00]. In addition we aimed at using a project management tool as our front end, which with the additional requirements forced upon conventional project management, poses an interesting research problem.

CONCLUSION AND FUTURE WORK

Inspired by the findings in our research project we conducted in SMEs and the requisite requirements we introduced a three level architecture. We have developed a prototype and reached the testing stage for one particular class of businesses, the building trade. However specification and even more implementation faces a number of subtle problems. On the norm level we need to be able to store information in a standardised way to make it possible to utilize without ambiguity. For the domain level we have to be sure about the classification of busi-

Figure 1: The MEMO framework

PERSPECTIVES \ ASPECTS	Resource	Structure	Process	Goal	Environment
Strategy	Human Resource Capital Assets	Strategic Business Unit	Generic Strategy Value Chain	Competitive Advantage Margin	Competitor Customer Supplier Politics
Organisation	Employee Equipment Machinery	Organisation Structure	Business Process Task	Operational Goal	Customer Supplier
Information System	Platform Application Tool	IS Architecture Object Model	Transaction Workflow	Requirement Metrics	Interfaces Standards

Figure 2: Levels of the architecture

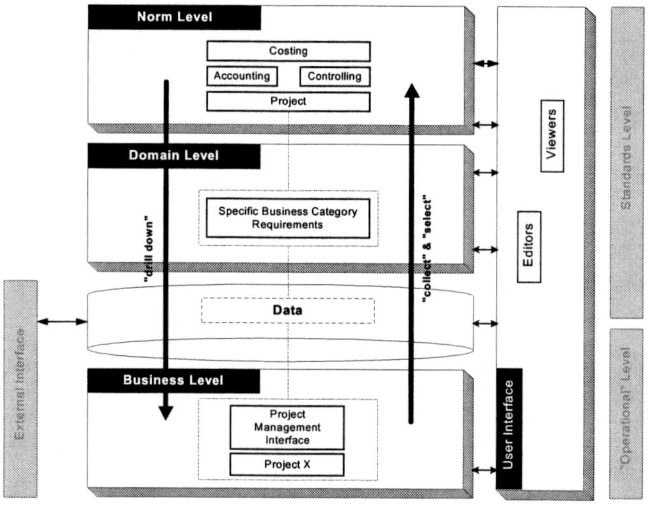

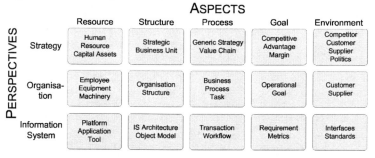

nesses and the domain must be represented in an accurate but at the same time flexible way. However this proves difficult to implement with common programming languages. Additionally we committed ourselves to build on a project management tool for the business level which needs to be expanded and integrated so as to be compatible with the other two levels and at the same time we require base data that can be utilized on all levels but also from outside the system.

Our future research on the PMCC will take us in several directions. Firstly we will be working on refining the norm level. In addition we need to enhance our understanding on domains by investigating and classifying more businesses but also at the same time continue to investigate and analyse business processes and further develop the MEMO Process Modelling Language (PML).

REFERENCES

[Dunc96] Duncan, W. R.: A Guide to the Project Management Body of Knowledge, Newtown Square 1996.

[Fran99] Frank, U.: Visual Languages for Enterprise Modelling. Arbeitsberichte des Institut für Wirtschaftsinformatik der Universität Koblenz-Landau, No. 18, 1999.

[Fran00] Frank, U.: Multi-Perspective Enterprise Models as a Conceptual Foundation of Knowledge Management Systems. In: Proceedings of the Hawaii International Conference on System Sciences, Los Alamitos, Ca. 2000.

[Frau01] Fraunholz, B.: Project Management in the German Trade Sector - A (preliminary) Framework for the introduction of Computer Assisted Management of Projects in Small and Medium Sized Enterprises. In: Proceedings of the Australasian Conference on Information Systems, Coffs Harbour, NSW 2001.

[Frit00] Fritz, S.: Effektive EDV-Werkzeuge für integrierte Projektbearbeitung. In: Projektmanagement, No 1, 2000, p 21-28.

[Gray00] Gray, Clifford F./Larson, Eric W.: Project Management, Newtown Square 2000.

[Hand01] Handwerkskammer Koblenz: Konjunkturbericht Herbst 2001, Koblenz: HWK, 2000.

[Horv01] Horvath, P.: Controlling, 8th ed., Munich, 2001.

[MyLe85] Mylopoulus J., Levesque H. J. (1985) "An Overview of Knowledge Representation". In: Brodie M. L., Mylopoulos J., Schmidt J. (Eds.) On Conceptual Modelling. Perspectives from Artificial Intelligence, Databases and Programming, Hamburg, pp 3-17.

[Sche94] Scheer, A.-W.: Wirtschaftsinformatik. Referenzmodelle für industrielle Geschäftsprozesse. 4th ed., Berlin, Heidelberg etc. 1994.

Instructor-Student Communication in a CyberEd Environment

Stuart Freedman and David Lewis
College of Management, University of Massachusetts Lowell
Tel: (978) 934-2776, Fax: (978) 934-3035, Stuart.Freedman@uml.edu
Tel: (978) 934-2758, Fax: (978) 934-4034, David.Lewis@uml.edu

ABSTRACT

Internet-based instruction, or "CyberEd" as it is commonly called, is becoming an increasingly popular approach to delivering academic courses (Saba, 2000). At one mid-size university in the northeast, for example, the number of students taking CyberEd courses has been increasing steadily over the past several years, as has the range of courses offered and the number of faculty participating. Between the Fall 1996 and Fall 2001 semesters, the number of students rose from sixty-four to 1,700, and the number of courses offered increased from five to eighty. Given the growth of CyberEd, and the likelihood that this growth will continue as Internet use increases, it is important to understand how best to design and deliver Internet-based instructional material in ways that facilitate both student learning and satisfaction with the overall CyberEd experience.

COMMUNICATION BARRIERS

As in traditional classroom settings, CyberEd course delivery takes place through instructor-student communication. However, unlike the traditional classroom, CyberEd communication takes place primarily electronically and in writing. This poses some unique problems regarding communication quality that CyberEd instructors must overcome. For example, how can one communicate clearly and completely when there is no direct, face-to-face interaction? How does one know whether students received a message from the instructor as it was intended? How can students be involved in a course in which they rarely, if ever, meet anyone else in the class? What instructor communication style will increase the likelihood that students feel involved in the course, and believe that their educational needs are being met?

Research on the design and implementation of CyberEd courses has suggested a number of variables likely to influence course effectiveness. These include class size and prior experience with computer-mediated communication (Vrasidas and McIsaac, 1999); availability of technical and instructor support (Daughery, 1998); instructor attentiveness to student needs, and the extent to which there is synchronous, i.e. real-time, interaction (Lara, Howell, Dominquez and Navarro, 2001). Even with the greatest of care, however, courses do not always run smoothly. Hara and Kling (1999), for example, suggest that student frustration with web-based courses can result from insufficient instructor feedback and ambiguous instructions regarding course procedures and requirements, often producing feelings of isolation.

In general, this research suggests that CyberEd course effectiveness is determined in part by the type, quality and frequency of communication that takes place between students and instructor. To the extent these electronic interactions are poorly designed and managed, communication barriers are likely to arise that impede the achievement of course objectives (George and Jones, 2002). There are at least four types of barrier that can negatively affect student performance and satisfaction in a CyberEd environment that must be overcome. These are: 1) the *barrier of social distance*, resulting from overly formalistic instructor communication that reinforces student-instructor status differences; 2) the *barrier of conceptual confusion*, resulting from poorly organized and presented course material; 3) the *barrier of fear and mistrust*, resulting from instructor communication that is perceived by students as non-supportive, indifferent to student needs or, in extreme cases, overtly hostile; and 4) the *barrier of isolation and disconnectedness*, resulting from insufficient speed and frequency of instructor communication. This paper explores ways to reduce these barriers and improve the student-instructor communication process.

Communication in CyberEd courses takes place, in part, through (1) the posting of online lecture notes that typically accompany textbook reading assignments, and (2) electronic responses to individual student messages communicated in the form of emails or Discussion Board postings. This paper explores how instructors can approach these two general methods of communication in ways that reduce the communication barriers suggested above, and increase the likelihood that student learning and satisfaction goals are achieved.

ONLINE LECTURE NOTES

How can a CyberEd instructor create lecture notes in a way that, apart from lecture content, reduces the *barrier of social distance*, and facilitates student learning and course satisfaction? It is suggested that an approach to electronic communication that simulates informal face-to-face interaction will more likely be experienced by students as *spoken* communication. This is likely to improve the perceived "readability" and value of online lecture material and, as a result, enhance learning and satisfaction (i.e., lecture note *context*). There are several approaches that will tend to facilitate this experience. These are:

- Using contractions common in spoken language ("It's likely that..." versus "It is likely that...");
- Using spoken expressions at the beginning of written sentences, to create a tone and feeling of informality (e.g., "Well, what this means to me is that...");
- Writing in the first person, and in the active, rather than passive, voice. For example, compare the following two sentences: (1) "What I'm saying is that if you reduce resistance, you'll more easily change an employee's behavior." (2) "In general, if resistance is reduced, employee behavior will more easily be changed."
- Occasionally using what sound like incomplete sentences, as one often encounters in the dialogue of good novels (e.g., "That's a fact. Hard to believe, isn't it?");
- Using "friendly" expressions that make it easier for students to perceive the instructor as approachable, and as someone with whom they can take intellectual risks (e.g., "That's a fact, folks. Hard to believe, isn't it?) (compare to the previous example); and
- Making consistent use of color, bold face and italics to communicate where emphasis of various kinds would be if a given statement were spoken, rather than written. For example, use red and/or bold face to highlight important points in prose text, and italics to symbolize verbal emphasis (e.g., "*Now*, do you see the **importance** of what I'm saying?")

Regarding the content and structure of lecture notes, it is hypothesized that the *barrier of conceptual confusion* can be reduced, and the understanding and perceived value of online lecture material enhanced, by:

- Creating lecture material that complements or supplements the course textbook (if a text is being used) rather than "rehashes" it;
- Drawing heavily on "real world" examples of course concepts, particularly if the students are practically-minded working adults (although this option depends considerably on the course subject);
- Developing a bulleted outline or PowerPoint graphic for each lecture topic within each weekly lesson that reflects or summarizes the flow of lecture material, and gives students a "bigger picture" of how the details of lecture content "hang together";
- Systematically reducing font size as the outline moves from main title, to headings, to sub-headings, to bulleted points;
- Using one text color, background or font for lecture outlines and another for lecture notes in order to visually distinguish the two, and possibly reduce the "monotony" of what would otherwise be perceived as a monochromatic presentation;
- Dividing a large lecture into several smaller "pieces" that give students a sense of making progress when they reach closure on a "piece of the pie" (i.e., part of the online lecture), even though they may still have a lot further to go before the "pie" is fully "consumed"; and
- Using italics and boldface consistently to highlight key concepts and ideas.

INDIVIDUAL STUDENT MESSAGES

The *barrier of fear and mistrust* may be reduced through more personalized, supportive communication with students. It is important to recognize that the CyberEd customer is often "buying" more than just course content. They are often time-constrained, working adults who are also seeking flexibility and responsiveness from both the instructor and educational institution.

It is suggested that there are several ways in which instructors can convey to students that: they are respected; their unique concerns, uncertainties and pressures are understood; and that the instructor is willing to work with them as individuals to solve both anticipated and unexpected problems (e.g., an unforeseen business trip) that arise over the course of a semester. This more subtle message from instructor to student may be conveyed through the exchange of email messages, and possibly Discussion Board postings. It forms the "between the lines," or "context," message in instructor communications about such issues as course administration; student performance; Internet access problems; student requests for "special treatment" due to unavoidable job constraints; and so on. It is suggested that supportive context messages will be communicated to students when instructors directly or indirectly exhibit *flexibility and responsiveness* in their online communications. Instructors may send these messages in the following ways:

- If a student asks that a particular message be re-sent because the student "never received it," send the message out again "with a smile" (e.g., "sure, I'll send it right out."). It is easy for an instructor to communicate to students "between the lines" that he or she is annoyed at having to do this. It might even be sent inadvertently. If this type of negative message is communicated, the student will most likely "pick it up," and begin to perceive the student-instructor relationship as hostile and defensive, rather than friendly and supportive;
- If a student cannot take an examination, or finish an assignment, at the scheduled time (e.g., due to temporary job overload), permit the student to complete it at a different time, if the explanation for the requested delay appears reasonable and honestly communicated. Always be aware that the goal of the instructor is to evaluate what students have learned, rather than how they respond to time pressure;
- If a student does poorly on an exam, and asks for help, give as much of it as is reasonable and possible, without communicating annoyance "between the lines" (e.g., "Sure, (student's first name), what would you like some help with?" versus "O.K., but you're really expected to learn this material on your own.");
- Begin each email to a student with "Hi (first name)", or "Hello (first name)". This will tend to personalize, and "de-formalize" an electronic message. If the message is an unpleasant one (e.g., to report a poor grade to a student), "hello" rather than "hi" might be a more congruent message introduction. Also, the instructor should use his or her first as well as last name in all communications to reduce "social distance";
- Anticipate what is going to confuse or create uncertainty for students, and address these matters as early in the semester as possible (e.g., "I can't attend your Chat hour because of a conflict with another class. Will this hurt my grade?");
- Respond quickly to emails and other messages from students. Until the instructor responds, students with questions or problems will have no idea what to assume or expect regarding the issue in question. If the instructor does not, or cannot, respond quickly, the instructor should apologize when he or she does respond (e.g., "Sorry for the late response..."), and tell the student why the response was later than it should have been (if appropriate). This type of instructor response is also likely to reduce the *barrier of isolation and disconnectedness*" by creating a "classroom climate" in which students will feel informed and secure.

An effective CyberEd instructor finds ways to electronically simulate the experience of direct face-to-face interaction with students, and recognizes the unique problems that can arise in a CyberEd as compared to traditional classroom environment. It is our hypothesis that student learning and satisfaction with the overall CyberEd experience will be enhanced by creating a "virtual classroom" that is creative in the presentation of course content, flexible with the "rules" and responsive to student needs.

REFERENCES

Daughery, M., "University faculty and student perceptions of web-based instruction," Journal of Distance Education, 1998, 13 (1), 21-39.

George, J. and G. Jones, Organizational Behavior, Upper Saddle River, N.J.: Prentice-Hall, 2002.

Hara, N. and R. Kling, "Student's frustrations with a web-based distance education course," First Monday, 1999, 4(12), at http://www.firstmonday.org/issues/issue4_12/hara/index.html.

Lara, L., R. Howell, D. Jeronimo, and J. Navarro, "Synchronous and asynchronous interactions of bilingual Hispanic pre- and in-service teachers in distance learning," American Journal of Distance Education, 2001, 15(3) 50-79.

Saba, F., "Online education and learning," Distance Education, 2000, 4(1), 1-12.

Vrasidas, C. and M. McIsaac, "Factors influencing interaction in an online course," American Journal of Distance Education, 1999, 13 (3). 22-37.

Effects of Humor and Realism in Hypermedia

Yuan Gao
Assistant Professor, School of Administration and Business, Ramapo College of New Jersey
Tel: (201) 684-7819, Fax: (201) 684-7957, gaoy@hotmail.com or ygao@ramapo.edu

INTRODUCTION

Hypermedia is multimedia. Structural features such as graphics, color, animation, video and audio that were studied in traditional media have also been found in the online environment (Rodgers & Thorson, 2000). Factors related to consumer behavior, attitude, and perceptions in the online environment have been gradually explored in the academic literature (Ducoffe, 1996; Chen & Wells, 1999; Eighmey, 1997; Koufaris, 2000; Coyle & Thorson, 2001). Perceived informativeness and entertainment were critical perceptual antecedents to consumer assessment of the value of a commercial message (Ducoffe, 1996), and attitude toward the site (Ast) (Chen & Wells, 1999). Recent literature has started exploring the effects of interactive features on website appeal (Ghose & Dou, 1998), and that of e-store characteristics on e-store sales and traffic (Lohse & Spiller, 1998). Some experimental studies have also examined the effect of animation and image maps on perceived telepresence and consumer attitude (Coyle & Thorson, 2001), and that of the use of pop-up windows on consumer decision-making processes (Xia & Sadharshan, 2000). This paper examines the effects of two specific presentation attributes — the use of product-related humor and interactive product demos — on perceived informativeness and entertainment, as well as a visitor's overall attitude toward the site (Ast).

REALISM

According to Steuer (1992), teleprence is the perception of direct experience through virtual reality, which in turn is a simulated environment in which the user feels present. Such a telepresence fulfills the needs of "escapism, diversion, or aesthetic enjoyment" (Ducoffe, 1995, p. 3), where the value of entertainment lies (McQuail, 1983).

Nielsen (1995) believes that product demos through animation or video clips are good for showing things that move and are well suited for the Internet medium. This interactive capability allows the user to choose what she wants to see (Rodgers & Thorson, 2000).

A picture is worth a thousand words. A "true picture" of a product is information a consumer values (McQuail, 1983; Ducoffe, 1996). Animated product displays not only provide the consumers an opportunity to see the product from multiple angles, but also enhance the directness of their product experience, which has been found to produce more confidently held and more enduring attitudes (Coyle & Thorson, 2001; Smith & Swinyard, 1983). Such direct product experience is also informative because it is relevant and truthful.

Summarizing the above, the use of such animation fulfills the purpose of providing the visitors an experience that has a higher level of realism. We hypothesize:

H1: Entertainment is positively related to the use of animated product demos.

H2: Informativeness is positively related to the use of animated product demos.

HUMOR

Humor is "an incongruous comment that is recognized by the receiver as an attempt to amuse and that succeeds at amusing" (Morkes et al., 1999, p.403). Research has shown that humor attracts attention and seems effective promoting purchases (Weinberger et al., 1995). In a series of field studies, Scott et al. (1990) found that humorous fliers increased attendance at social events.

Wells et al. (1971) found that humor was a major perceptual dimension in user response profiles to TV commercials. Humor fulfills the needs of escapism, diversion, and emotional release, which was the base for Ducoffe's (1996) entertainment scale.

Humor is intended to amuse and entertain people, to make them laugh, and to convey light-hearted enjoyment. Humor was also found to enhance the likeability of the computer interface and had a positive effect on user cooperation (Morkes et al., 1999). The above leads us to hypothesize:

H3: Entertainment is positively related to the use of humor.

Humor also helps gain attention and comprehension (Speck, 1991). Both related humor – integration of humor with product claims – and unrelated humor have been found to influence reader or viewer recall and comprehension (Chapman & Crompton, 1978). Nonetheless, related humor was found to be superior to unrelated humor when direct comparison studies were conducted (Kaplan & Pascoe, 1977). Recall and comprehension reflect the ad's effectiveness at getting product-related messages across to the viewer, which implies a more informative message to the visitor. Thus we hypothesize:

H4: Informativeness is positively related to the use of humor.

RESEARCH METHODOLOGY

This study adopted a 2x2 factorial design. Fixed factors used to define groups included a humorous ad related to products sold at the site and two prominent links to interactive product demos. The website is a real commercial site manufacturing and selling personal digital assistants (PDAs). This study only peripherally manipulated the above two factor to produce four version of the site. This approach ensured that both internal validity and external validity were high. Voluntary participants were recruited from a northeastern college campus, through a gift incentive and several cash prizes. Participants were randomly assigned to four experimental groups. Sessions of the study were conducted in a computer lab. Each participant completed a survey after a visit to the site. Web experience, age, and gender were taken as potential control variables.

MEASURES

Adapting existing scales in the literature, perceived informativeness and entertainment were measured through 3-item scales developed by Ducoffe (1996). Ast was measured through three pairs of adjectives: like-dislike, favorable-unfavorable, and good-bad (Coyle & Thorson, 2001). Considered a significant predictor of consumer attitude and behavior in e-commerce (Coyle & Thorson, 2001; Koufaris, 2000), product involvement using the Revised Personal Involvement Inventory (RPII) (Zaichkowsky, 1985) was taken as a potential covariate.

RESULTS

One hundred and twenty substantially complete surveys were collected, with 30 data points in each cell. Participants' overall attitude toward the site (Ast) was high, with a mean score of 5.66 on the 7-point scale. Reliability coefficients measured through Cronbach's alpha were .8319, .8668, .9137, and .9278, respectively, for informativeness, entertainment, Ast, and product involvement. Manipulation checks via one-way ANOVAs showed significant, and thus successful, effects ($p < .001$) of manipulated factors on participants' acknowledgement of receipt of said feature.

Normal P-P plots and Levene's tests showed satisfaction of MANOVA assumptions. A multivariate analysis of variance (MANOVA) was performed. $F[1,116]$ statistics for the effects of product realism were 5.259 ($p= .024$) and 9.409 ($p= .003$) on informativeness and entertainment, respectively. The effect of humor on entertainment was marginally significant with $F[1,116]= 2.871$ and $p= .093$. Humor had no effect on perceived informativeness ($F[1, 116]=.079$, $p=.779$). No interaction effect emerged.

Product involvement was included as a covariate in the second run due to its strong linear (sig. $< .001$) correlation with both dependent variables, at $r= .406$ and .437, respectively. No violation of homogeneity of regression slopes assumption was detected. Results of the second run with the covariate included showed similar effects with the F statistics of realism on informativeness and entertainment at $F=4.368$ ($p= .030$) and $F=8.393$ ($p= .003$), respectively. Humor again had marginal effect ($F= 3.651$, $p= .059$) on entertainment. Hence, hypotheses H1 and H2 were supported in this study. Hypothesis H3 received partial support, and hypothesis H4 was not supported.

Additionally, a separate ANOVA model, treating Ast as the dependent variable, showed that access to product demos had a significant effect on Ast ($p< .01$). The effect of humor was not significant ($p > .10$). Lastly, we ran a regression analysis on Ast with informativeness and entertainment as independent variables. Model had good fit with low VIFs and no collinearity or heteroscedasticity. Results showed that both were significant predictors of attitude with p values less than .001. Model explained 59.8% of the variance in Ast. This result validated a proposition that theories and findingss in traditional advertising research would apply to the new medium

DISCUSSIONS AND FUTURE RESEARCH

This study examined the effects of humor and realism on perceived informativeness and entertainment of a website. Product realism achieved through the use of prominent links to product demo pages showed significant effect on both perceived informativeness and entertainment, suggesting to practitioners the potential benefits of using such features widely. No effect of humor was found in this study, possibly due to the dose of humor (only one cartoon was used) employed or the amount of information that already existed at the site, which made further differentiation of informativeness difficult. Future studies should replicate at differing level of information amount.

Though students are deemed appropriate subjects in that they make a significant portion of the Internet population (GVU's 10th Survey), whether the general public will respond in the same way as the student sample did in this study is unknown. The study needs to be replicated through a broader population.

Web marketing research in profiling user reactions to websites or home pages has been largely observational (e.g., Chen & Wells, 1999; Eighmey 1997). To answer the question whether any causal relationship between a website attribute and attitudinal outcomes exists requires experiments in which the differences in dependent variables can be reasonably attributed to factors manipulated. This study represents another step in that direction.

REFERENCES

1 Chapman, A.J., and Crompton, P. (1978). Humorous presentations of material and presentations of humorous material: a review of the humor and memory literature and two experimental studies. In *Practical Aspects of Memory*, M.M.Gruneberg, ed. New York: Academic Press

2 Chen, Q., and Wells, W.D. (1999), Attitude toward the site. *Journal of Advertising Research*, 39(5), 27-38

3 Coyle, J.R., and Thorson, E. (2001). The effects of progressive levels of interactivity and vividness in Web marketing sites. *Journal of Advertising*, (forthcoming)

4 Ducoffe, R.H. (1995). How consumers assess the value of advertising. *Journal of Current Issues and Research in Advertising*. 17(1), 1-18

5 Ducoffe, R.H. (1996). Advertising value and advertising on the Web. *Journal of Advertising Research*. 36(5), 21-34

6 Eighmey, J. (1997). Profiling user responses to commercial Web site. *Journal of Advertising Research*, 37(3), 59-66

7 Ghose, S., and Dou, W. (1998). Interactive functions and their impact on the appeal of the Internet presence sites. *Journal of Advertising Research*. 38(2), 29-43

8 GVU's 10th Survey (1998). *GVU's 10th WWW User Survey*. [Available at http://www.cc.gatech.edu/user_surveys/survey-1998-10/]

9 Kaplan, R.M., and Pascoe, G.C. (1977). Humorous lectures and humorous examples: some effects upon comprehension and retention. *Journal of Educational Psychology*, 69(1), 61-65

10 Koufaris, M. (2000). *System Design and Consumer Behavior in Electronic Commerce*. Doctoral Dissertation, New York University, New York

11 Lohse, G.L., and Spiller P. (1998). Electronic shopping. *Communications of the ACM*, 41(7). 81-86

12 McQuail, D. (1983). *Mass Communication Theory: An Introduction*. London: Sage

13 Morkes, J., Kernal, H.K., and Nass, C. (1999). Effects of humor in task-oriented human-computer interaction and computer-mediated communication: a direct test of SRCT theory. *Human-Computer Interaction*, 14, 395-435

14 Nielsen, J. (1995). Multimedia Guidelines, *Jakob Nielsen's Alertbox*, December, 1995, available at http://www.useit.com/alertbox/

15 Rodgers, S., and Thorson, E. (2000). The interactive advertising model: how users perceive and process online ads. *Journal of Interactive Advertising* (accessed online)

16 Scott, D., Klein, D.M., and Bryant, J. (1990). Consumer response to humor in advertising: a series of field studies using behavioral observation. *Journal of Consumer Research*, 16, 498-501

17 Smith, R.E., and Swinyard, W.R. (1983). Attitude-behavior consistency: the impact of product trial versus advertising. *Journal of Marketing Research*, 20, 257-267

18 Speck, P.S. (1991). The humorous message taxonomy: a framework for the study of humorous ads. In *Current Issues and Research in Advertising*, J.H.Leigh and C.R.Martin, Jr., eds. The University of Michigan

19 Steuer, J. (1992). Defining virtual reality: Dimensions determining telepresence. *Journal of Communication*, 42 (4), 73-93.

20 Weinberger, M.G., Spotts, H., Campbell, L., and Parsons, A.L. (1995). The use and effect of humor in different advertising media. *Journal of Advertising Research*, 35(2), 44-56

21 Wells, W. D., Leavitt, C., and McConville, M. (1971). A reaction profile for TV commercials. *Journal of Advertising*, 11(6), 11-17

22 Xia, L., and Sudharshan, D. (2000). An examination of the effects of cognitive interruptions on consumer on-line decision processes. Paper presented at the *Second Marketing Science and the Internet Conference*, USC, Los Angeles

23 Zaichkowsky, J.L. (1985). Measuring the involvement construct. *Journal of Consumer Research*, 12(3), 341-352

An OO Methodology Based on the Unified Process for GIS Application Development[1]

Jesús D. Garcia-Consuegra and Alfonso Garcia
Departamento de Informática, Universidad de Castilla-La Mancha, Spain
Tel: +3 (496) 759-9200, Fax: +3 (496) 759-9224, jdgarcia@info-ab.uclm.es

ABSTRACT

The aim of our research is to propose an OO methodology to develop applications in the Geographical Information System (GIS) domain. This methodology must involve productivity increase and quality improvement with faster development and deployment, but at the same time requires the software to be built in a repeatable and predictable fashion. This paper shows the first version of this methodology, and also the first approach to adapt and extend the Unified Process to support it.

INTRODUCTION

The Geographical Information System (GIS) applications are sufficiently large, complex and important to warrant Software Engineering skills being set to work on their development. GIS application developments face the same risks or problems as the software developed in other domains:

- Inaccurate understanding of end-user needs
- Inability to deal with changing requirements
- Modules that do not fit together
- Software that is hard to maintain or extend
- Late discovery of serious project flaws
- Poor software quality
- Unacceptable software performance
- Team members in each other's way, making it impossible to reconstruct who changed what, when, where and why
- An untrustworthy build-and-release process

On the other hand, businesses demand increased productivity and improved quality with faster development and deployment, but the building of software in a repeatable and predictable fashion.

Software engineering addresses a wide diversity of domains (e.g., banking, transportation, manufacturing), tasks (e.g., administrative support, decision support, process control) and environments (e.g., human organizations, physical phenomena). A specific domain/task/environment may require some specific focus and dedicated techniques. This is the case for geographical information systems (GIS). In particular, activities like domain analysis as well as requirement elicitation and specification are the main topics of research carried out in the GIS domain.

In order to make an OO Methodology proposal to solve the aforementioned problems, the GIS Enterprises and their developments have been studied. Then, those OO methodologies proposed by Software Engineering as a solution to their software development processes have also been identified. Finally, the modifications and extensions needed to cover the GIS development have been proposed. Thus, our methodology makes full use of the best ideas currently available in Software Engineering as a foundation, extending them to take into account the peculiarity of the GIS domain.

GIS ENTERPRISE CLASSIFICATION

As in the majority of domains, the software developments in GIS can be divided into two categories:

- Software Component Development. ESRI [3] and Intergraph [6] would be two enterprise examples. They develop generic software components (COTS-Commercial-Off-The-Shelf). Software Engineering (SE) proposes methodologies like Catalysis [2], Business Component Factory [5] or Unified Process [8].
- Developments based on previous software components. This category can be divided into two new subcategories:
  - Developments that basically focus on the component integration.
  - Developments that focus on building new components and are highly dependent upon previous COTS, either because they are not on the market or because they are their business case.

In Spain, TAO, GIM or Absys are good examples of enterprises involved in this kind of development. Methodologies, such as Off-The-Shelf Option (OTSO) [7], COTS-based Integrated Systems Development (COTS CISD) [10], Infrastructure Incremental Development Approach (IIDA) [4] or IusWare [9], provide them with a solution.

On the other hand, in the GIS domain we can conclude that the granularity of the software components is equivalent to the Business Component [5]. Furthermore, the granularity suitable for reusing matter must be thought of in terms of a business component, since reusing their distributed components involves a high economical and computational cost.

OUR METHODOLOGY

A methodology must treat the root causes of the problems of software development in order to eliminate their symptoms. That is, the methodology must be a conjunction of the software best practices. This involves: developing software iteratively, managing requirements, using component-based architectures, visually modelling software, continuously verifying software quality, controlling changes to software, etc.

At present, the iCASE tool that supports a methodology is as important as the methodology itself. So, when we thought of the definition of a methodology to develop GIS applications, we also considered developing an iCASE, or adapting an existing iCASE. iCASE complexity demands a great effort for its development and maintenance. The extension or adaptation of an existing iCASE is therefore the more suitable option. In this case, the Rational Enterprise Suite has been selected to implement OOMGIS. This selection takes advantage of the following:

- The Software Component Development is covered due to Rational Enterprise Suite implements RUP [8].
- It provides the mechanisms to extend and modify the process.
- It supports UML as the modeling language as well as the mechanisms to extend it.
- Finally, like every commercial package, its evolution involves OOMGIS evolution as well.

As can be seen in Fig. 1, OOMGIS is an iterative and evolutionary process. OOMGIS plays particular attention to those matters relating to the iterative Requirements Acquisition and Product Evaluation/Selection process. Furthermore, those OOMGIS parts that must be adapted to support the peculiarities of the GIS domain [1] like requirement specification and system modeling, have been identified.

There is a great amount of research taking place in the GIS domain. In general, the research is mainly focused on providing solutions for particular problems or limitations, instead of proposing a full

Figure 1: The OO methodology (OOMGIS) for COTS based development in the GIS domain

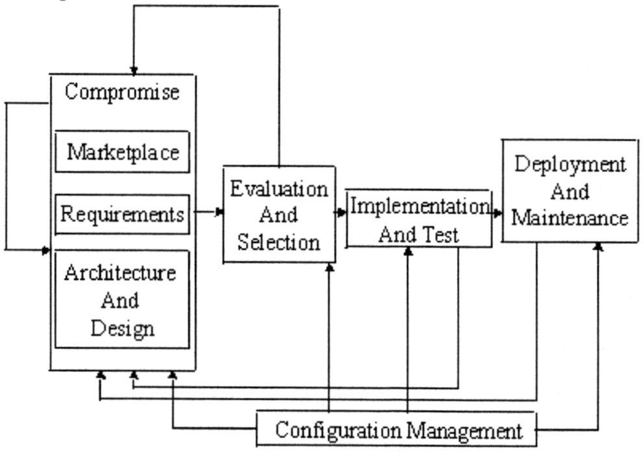

lifecycle software engineering process. OOMGIS tries to cover this gap. Thus, OOMGIS covers the basic activities associated to a COSTBD methodology:

- The requirements, marketplace, and architecture and design activity sets operate concurrently and in cooperation with one another, in order to obtain a compromise in the COTS selection.
  - The requirements activity set defines, prioritises, and constrains the CBS to be fielded, accounting for functional and non-functional requirements, end user processes, business drivers, the operational environment, and constraints (such as policies, schedules, and budgets).
  - The marketplace activity set bounds the COTS marketplace elements.
  - The architecture and design activity set captures decisions about the structure of the components, interfaces, and relationships of a system's components, and the principles and guidelines governing their design and evolution.
- The evaluation and selection activity set examines and selects COTS products and technologies.
- The implementation and test activity set addresses implementation of custom components, COTS integration, and system integration and test. This stage composes and integrates a COTS-based system from available parts.
- The Deployment and maintenance activity set encompasses initial and continuing delivery of a COTS-based system to end users and system maintenance.
- The configuration management activity set establishes and maintains system artefact integrity and traceability throughout the CBS's lifetime.

To carry out the OOMGIS implementation on Rational Suite Enterprise, methodologies like Model-Base Architecting and Software Engineering (MBASE) [11] or Information Technology Solutions Evolution Process (ITSEP) [12] will be taken into account. The MBASE approach is a unified approach that considers four types of models for a system: success, process, product and property. MBASE extends spiral model for integrated product and process development. It uses four guiding principles to develop value-driven, shared-vision-driven, change-driven, and risk-driven requirements. MBASE is compatible with Integrated Capability Maturity Model (CMMI) and Rational Unified Process. ITSEP relies on the A/A PCS Process a framework for COTS Based Engineering and on the Rational Unified Process (RUP). The A/A PCS Process supports simultaneous trade-offs among requirements, preferences, marketplace offerings, architecture, design, and business processes. The process is a spiral approach, where the incremental accumulation of knowledge is used to reduce the risk.

In addition to a methodology, a modeling language with a sufficiently large expressive wealth for supporting the model elements is needed. Therefore, an UML extension to support spatiotemporal characteristics, in Rational Rose, is being carried out in our research group.

CONCLUSIONS AND FUTURE WORK

In this work, research in progress to develop an OO Methodology (OOMGIS) for COTS based development, in the Geographical Information System (GIS) domain, has been shown. OOMGIS makes the maximum possible use of the best ideas of currently available methodologies, especially those based on COTSBD, as a foundation. As the next step, we plan to extend and adapt UP in Rational to support OOMGIS. Both UP and Rational have been chosen due to their capabilities for adaptation, as well as their strong component in SQA, especially in the management of configuration, a critical part of the COTSBD.

ENDNOTE

1 This work is partially funded by the Spanish CICYT project MetaSIG (TIC2000-1106-C02-02)

REFERENCES

[1] The European Commission: BEST-GIS: Best Practice in Software Engineering and methodologies for developing GIS applications. *ESPRIT Programme. Project number 21580.* http://www.gisig.it/best-gis/guides/main.htm (2000)

[2] D. F. D'Souza, A.Wills: Objects, Components and Frameworks with UML, *Addison-Wesley* (1999).

[3] ESRI, http://www.esri.com

[4] G. Fox, S. Marcom and Lantner, K.: A Software Development Process for COTS-based Information System Infrastructure. *Proceedings of the 5th International Symposium on Assessment of Software Tools and Technologies (SAST'97)*: 133-143, (1997) .

[5] P. Herzum and O.Sims: Business Component Factory. *John Wiley & Sons Inc* (2000).

[6] INTERGRAPH, http://www.intergraph.com/gis

[7] J. Kontio: OTSO: A Sysmatic Process for Reusable Software Component Selection. *Technical Report Number CS-TR-3478*, University of Maryland, USA (1995).

[8] P. Kruchten: The rational unified process an introduction, *Addison-Wesley*, 2nd. edition. (2000).

[9] M. Morision, C.B. Seaman, V.R. Basili, A.T. Parra, S.E. Kraft and S.E. Condon: COTS-Based Software Development: Processes and Open Issues. *Journal of Systems and Software*, accepted for publication (2001).

[10] V. Tran and D. Liud: A Procurement-centric Model for Engineering Component-based Software Systems, *Proceedings of the 5th International Symposium on Assessment of Software Tools and Technologies (SAST'97)*: 70-80 (1997).

[11] B. Boehm, D. Port, M. Abi-Antoun, and A. Egyed: Guidelines for the Life Cycle Objectives (LCO) and the Life Cycle Architecture (LCA) deliverables for Model-Based Architecting and Software Engineering (MBASE), *Technical report USC-CSE-98-519, USC-Center for Software Engineering*, (1998).

[12] C. Albert: Meeting the Challenges of Commercial Off-the-Shelf (COTS) Products: The Information Technology Solutions Evolution Process (ITSEP), *International Conference on COTS-Based Software Systems ICCBSS2002*, Orlando, Florida, USA, (February, 2002).

Extending UML To Support Spatiotemporal Characteristics[1]

Jesús D. Garcia-Consuegra and Yago Oseguera
Departamento de InformáticaUniversidad de Castilla-La Mancha, Albacete, Spain
Tel.: +34 967 599 200 Ext. 2444, FAX. +34 967 599 2241, jdgarcia@info-ab.uclm.es

ABSTRACT

The aim of this work is to study the UML extension as the modeling language in application development in the Geographical Information System (GIS) domain. The spatial and temporal components of the real World features[2] are the most important characteristics of the GIS. Therefore our work has been focused first on studying the spatiotemporal models proposed; secondly, on extending the UML with the selected spatiotemporal model; and, finally, on extending the Rational Rose tool to support it.

INTRODUCTION

From the viewpoint of Software Engineering, quality application development in the domain of the Geography Information System (GIS) must be achieved by following some of the methodologies proposed. In addition to a methodology, a modeling language is needed with a sufficiently large wealth of expression expressive wealth to support the model elements.

In recent years, software developers have made full use of the OO paradigm which they have adopted for their developments. Geographical Information System (GIS) applications are no exception to this trend. Therefore, the methodology and the modelling language must take the same approach.

GIS applications fall into the spatiotemporal applications, whose differences from other domains are centred on the support of complex objects and their relationships, together with long transactions. The two most salient characteristics of the GIS are the spatial and temporal components of the real World features to be modelled. So, GIS applications can process:

- Moving objects, which change their position in time, such as a truck on a road.
- Objects located in space, whose characteristics and position may change in time; blocks or parcels in a cadastral information system can change their shape but they do not move.
- Objects with the previous behaviours, such as an oil slick in environmental disasters.

In the scientific community, different temporal, spatial and spatiotemporal models can be found: TEMPOS [10], MADS [6], TOOBIS [9], RDNSAAE [1], ScanGIS [8], EGSV [2], STER [4], GeoOOA [5], Fuzzy-UML [11] and ST-UML [7]. The majority of these were proposed from the database perspective. The spatiotemporal model is the best one to cover GIS needs, since it integrates the spatial and temporal aspects.

Table 1 tells us which model to select in order to carry out the UML extension. The ST-UML selection is based on its design as a UML extension, and also, on its capabilities. However, ST-UML does not cover its implementation. This stage can follow the EGSV or TOOBIS models.

EXTENDING UML

Two important questions arise in this work. First, why UML?. UML was selected as the best OO modelling language, due to its high level of acceptance, understandability, and its flexibility to be extended. And secondly, why is a UML extension necessary to model spatiotemporal characteristics?. As proposed in [3], spatial and temporal properties can be added to an object class definition by associating it with temporal and spatial object classes. In [7], Price reports that this approach is not suitable for representing temporal or spatial variation at the attribute level as the timestamp and spatial locations are defined only at the object component level. Furthermore, these diagrams, when presented in this fashion, were visually highly complex, which gave them an unnatural feel and made them difficult to follow.

Table 1: A comparison of the spatiotemporal models

	Object-Oriented	UML	Simple Annotation	Dates with Spatio-Temporal Data	Relations with Spatio-Temporal Data	Capacity of Defining Restrictions in the Objects and Relations.	Covers the Analysis and Design Stages
TEMPOS	-	-	-	-	-	-	-
MADS	-	-	☑	☑	-	-	-
TOOBIS	☑	-	☑	-	-	☑	☑
RDNSAE	☑	-	-	☑	-	-	-
ScanGIS	☑	-	☑	☑	-	-	☑
EGSV	☑	-	-	☑	-	-	-
STER	-	-	☑	☑	☑	☑	☑
GeoOOA	☑	-	☑	-	-	☑	-
Fuzzy-UML	☑	☑	☑	☑	-	-	☑
ST-UML	☑	☑	☑	☑	☑	☑	☑

Figure 1: Class diagram of a health example using UML

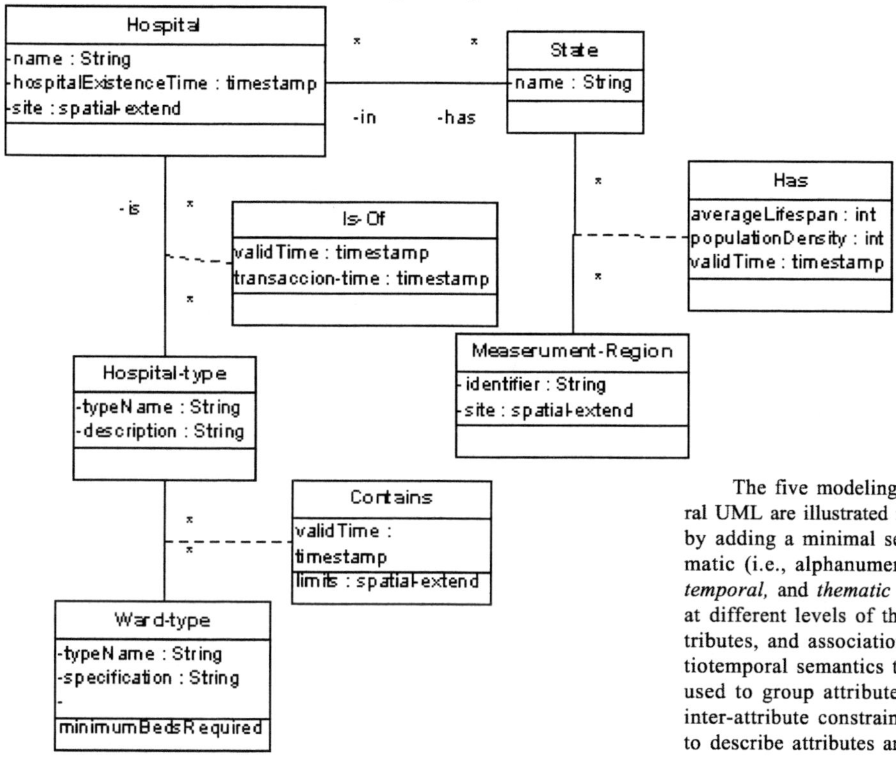

In [7], to illustrate the complexity of the class diagram when UML is used to model spatiotemporal data, a health example is shown. This example deals with health statistics of different states, in terms of average lifespan, as related to the location, size (i.e., number of beds), accessibility, and surrounding population densities of state hospitals of different types. This example considers, among others characteristics:

- Data values may change over time: information about the time periods when a given value is valid (i.e. valid time) or current (i.e. transaction time) is recorded.
- Accessibility is assessed by defining a zone around a hospital that represents travel times to the hospital of no more than half an hour.
- Hospital type definitions may differ between regions due to local regulations.
- Population densities and average lifespans across states vary with respect to time and space, where both values are recorded yearly at the same time and for the same regions.

These last three characteristics cover the three previously defined spatiotemporal concepts of the geographical information. Figure 1 shows its representation using the core constructs of UML. To accomplish this task, each spatiotemporal attribute of a class is promoted to a separate, but associated, class with the appropriate timestamps and spatial extents as attributes. Temporal classes and associations are treated similarly, by adding timestamp attributes to the class or to the association class respectively, after promoting the association to an association class in the latter case.

As Figure 1 shows, this kind of alternative complicates the schema diagram even for simple models. On the other hand, there is no single and easily visible notation to indicate temporal or spatial components.

Furthermore, in the COTS and Component Based Development methodologies, a technology change (for example a ESRI COTS new version or a change to Intergraph technology) involves a high cost (model evolution and/or increment of the glue or wrap code) in the maintenance of the models.

The alternative solution is to extend the UML class diagram in order to model the spatiotemporal characteristics without discarding the simplicity of diagrams. UML provides the "stereotypes" as the usual way to make domain-specific extensions to its core constructs, which can be used as if they were of UML's original meta-model or definition. The way in which this extension is carried out and the advantages that it involves are shown in the following sections.

EXTENDED SPATIOTEMPORAL UML: SPATIAL, TEMPORAL, AND THEMATIC SYMBOLS

The five modeling constructs used in the Extended Spatiotemporal UML are illustrated in Fig. 2. The basic approach is to extend UML by adding a minimal set of constructs for spatial, temporal, and thematic (i.e., alphanumeric) data, represented respectively by *spatial, temporal,* and *thematic* symbols. These constructs can then be applied at different levels of the UML class diagram (i.e., object classes, attributes, and associations) and in different combinations to add spatiotemporal semantics to a UML model element. The *group* symbol, used to group attributes with common spatiotemporal properties or inter-attribute constraints, and the *existence-dependent* symbol, used to describe attributes and associations dependent on object existence.

Figure 2: Extended spatiotemporal UML symbols

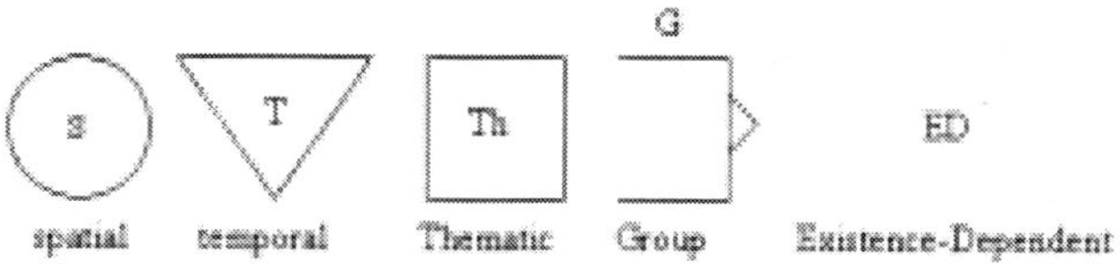

RATIONAL ROSE

In Rational Rose, add-ins allow customisations and automation of several Rose features to be included through the Rose Extensibility Interface (REI) in one package. An add-in is a collection of certain characteristics. In this case, our interest is focused on the following characteristics:

- Properties. Rose model properties allow us to extend Rose model elements through additional properties and their values. This characteristic is used to implement the Specification Box, since it involves a set of properties to be added to the elements of the model.
- Stereotypes. Rose stereotypes allow us to customise the look of different model elements as makes sense to your add-in. So, this is the natural way to add the characteristics proposed in ST-UML.
- Functionality. Some code can be programmed in order to provide the dialog boxes and other functionality desired. It is used to adapt the code to cover our interests.

CONCLUSIONS AND FUTURE WORK

The definition of a modeling language is a critical step in supporting the modeling stage of an OO Methodology. In this case, the ST-UML model will be the modeling language of an OO Methodology for COST based development, in the Geographical Information System domain, which is being developed by the authors. The proposal makes full use of the best ideas of currently available methodologies, especially those based on COSTBD, as a foundation. Extended RUP is then used to support it. The selection of RUP is based on its capabilities to be extended and adapted.

ST-UML requires the definition of new "stereotypes" that consider the spatial and temporal properties at different levels of granularity. The next step, therefore, is to define a basic core of stereotypes and implement them, as a translation to UML, in Rational Rose. Then, they ought to be adapted to industrial models like ArcObjects (ESRI) y Geomedia (Intergraph). Finally, their relationships with GML-Geography Markup Language (OpenGIS) will be studied.

ENDNOTES

1 This work is partially funded by the Spanish CICYT project MetaSIG (TIC2000-1106-C02-02)

2 In this paper the meaning of the term *feature* is the same as that proposed by OpenGIS.

REFERENCES

[1] Michael Böhleny, Christian S. Jensen and Bjørn Skjellaug: Spatio-Temporal Database Support For Legacy Applications, *Proc. ACM symposium on Applied Computing, Atlanta, GA*: 226-234 (February 27 - March 11998).

[2] M. Erwing, R.H. Güting, M. Schneider and M. Vazirgiannis: Spatio-Temporal Data Types: An approach to Modeling and Querying Moving Objects in Databases. *GeoInformatica* 3 (3): 269-296 (1999).

[3] G. Faria, C. B. Medeiros, and M.A. Nascimento: An Extensible Framework for Spatio-Temporal Database Applications, *Time Center Technical Report TR-27*: 1-15, (1998).

[4] T. Hadzilacos, N. Tryfona: Evaluation of database modeling methods for Geographic Information Systems, *Australian Journal of Information Systems* 6 (1), (1998).

[5] G. Kösters, B.-U. Pagel, H.-W.Six, GIS-application development with GeooAA, *Int. Journal Geographical Information Science* 11 (4):307 (1997).

[6] C. Parent, S. Spaccapietra, E. Zimanyi: Spatio-Temporal Conceptual Models: Data Structures + Space + Time, *7th ACM Symposium on Advances in GIS,* Kansas City, Kansas, (November 5-6, 1999).

[7] Rosanne Price, Nectaria Tryfona, Christian S.Jensen: A Conceptual Modelling Language for Spatiotemporal Applications, *Technical report CH-99-20* (1999).

[8] Agnar Renolen: Conceptual Modelling and Spatiotemporal Information Systems: How to Model the Real World. *ScanGIS'97* (June 1 – 3, 1997).

[9] TOOBIS - Temporal Object-Oriented Databases in Information Systems. EEC-funded project of the ESPRIT-IV framework. June 1999. http://www.mm.di.uoa.gr/~toobis/

[10] TEMPOS: A Temporal Database Model Seamlessly Extending ODMG http://citeseer.nj.nec.com/21283.html, (1999).

[11] Adnan Yazici, Qinwei Zhu and Ning Sun: Semantic Data Modelling of Spatiotemporal Database Applications, *International Journal of Intelligent Systems* 16(7): 881-904 (July 2001).

A Transaction Cost Viewpoint of E-Commerce Deployment and Use

Michael L. Gibson[1], Zhangxi Lin[2] and James R. Burns
Department of ISQS, The Rawls College of Business Administration, Texas Tech University
[1]Tel: (806) 742-1925, [2]Tel: (806) 742-1926, [2]Fax: (806) 742-3193, {mgibson, zlin}@ba.ttu.edu, ODBUR@ttacs.ttu.edu

INTRODUCTION

It is clear from recent history that companies who benefit most in e-commerce (EC) business activities are those who either provide a fundamental e-commerce service or brick-n-mortar companies who approach e-commerce more judiciously. Already successful in conducting business in standard ways, these brick-n-mortar companies approach EC with the same sound practices they apply in expanding their businesses in other ways. A close look at how they initiated EC reveals that aspiring to ventures into cyber space need to apply many of the tenets described in a previous investigation by the researchers.

This investigation constitutes a theory-building exploratory study to identify important aspects of EC influenced by transaction cost theory (Williamson 1985). The previous theoretical investigation using the structuration method of collecting data (Beath & Orlikowski, 1994) paved the way for this additional empirical investigation.

PRELIMINARY FINDINGS

From the previous data collection, three major areas of importance regarding EC activities are identified: 1) Fundamental Requisites of Cyber-Commerce, 2) Fundamental Business Operations Within E-commerce, and 3) Important E-commerce Legal Issues. The following depict the findings of this preliminary study.

Fundamental Requisites for E-Commerce

1) Technology Requisites
- Web Servers
- Application Servers
- Database Servers
- Mail Servers
- Procurement Systems
- IT Networks
- Routers/Firewalls
- Ad Serving Sys.
- Intra/Extranets
- Security Systems
- Backup Systems
- Content Management Systems
- Catalogs/Directories
- Messaging Systems
- Certification Systems
- Databases
- Development/Test Environment
- Application Systems
- Help Desk Systems
- Traffic Reporting Systems
- Storage Systems
- Relationship Management Systems
- Seamless Data Access
- Data Warehouse

2) Capability Requisites
- Procurement
- Billings/Payments
- Community Creation
- Data Mining
- Store-Front/Auction/Market
- Site Monitoring
- Customer I/O Support
- Site Data Collection
- Advertising
- Identity Recognition
- Site Searching
- EC Business Content
- Seamless B/M-EC
- Operations

3) Human Resource Requisites
- Web-Masters
- Network Mgrs/Staff
- Application Developers
- Artists/Editors
- Business Analyst
- Financial Managers/Staffs
- Database Managers/Staffs
- Marketing/Advertising Managers/Staffs

Fundamental Business Operations Within E-Commerce

- EC Supplier/Purchaser Location
- EC Procurement Support
- EC Procurement
- Process Improvement
- EC Product/Service Cataloging
- EC Customer Ordering Process
- EC Customer Help Process
- EC Inbound/Outbound Logistic
- EC Billing/Payment Process
- EC Customer Relationship Management

Important E-Commerce Legal Aspects

1) Assimilate Legal Team with Proper Characteristics
- Business Strategy Ability
- Know Business Venture Legalities
- Copyright Research Ability
- Trademark and Patent Ability
- Know Trade Secret/Intelligent
- Property Laws
- Know Internet Patents
- Understand Employment Laws
- Know Domain Name Registration Laws
- Know Customer Data Laws
- Know EC Ownership Laws
- Know EC Business Contract Laws
- Know Proprietary Info. Laws
- Know Geographic Scope Laws
- Know Comp. Sys. Innovation Laws
- Know Time Period Legalities
- EC venture Experience
- Know Customized Software Laws

2) Proactive Legal EC Actions

- Register EC Domain Name
- Establish Developer Contracts
- Obtain Usage Permission
- Establish Future Use Rights
- Establish Intellectual Property Ownership
- Establish Hosting Agreements
- Identify Tax Liabilities
- Establish Customer Privacy Protection
- Set up Advertising Agreements
- Identify Business Method Patents
- Establish Click-through EC Contracts
- Identify Profiling Legalities
- Identify Territory/International
- Law Differences

IMPACTS OF E-COMMERCE ON SUPPLY CHAINS

All business activities are either directly part of supply chain activities, off-line activities that contribute to the supply chain, or back-office activities that perform follow-up supply chain activities. EC potentially impacts the threads of activities all along the supply chain. For example, EC often impacts supply chains with cyber support for procurement of products and services, which is defined as "any purchasing-related activity that involves electronic communication, the Internet, and related software to help companies achieve increased value" (Elliff 2001).

Through EC, the development of new network organizational forms has brought into practice transaction cost economics, inter-organizational collaborations, and strategic alliance (Wang 2000). A growing number of companies are explicitly replacing bureaucratic internal resource allocation with internal markets (Ellig 2001). The businesses of brick/mortar EC companies will penetrate these markets because disappearing market boundaries generate greater business opportunities. Stapleton et al. (2001) explains the concept of such a virtual integration. The tenants of transaction cost economics used to explain conventional vertical integration governance might also be used to explain virtual integration for brick/mortar EC companies. A framework to explain the variety of trading relationships that exist between firms has been presented by Kerrigan et al (2001), using game theory and transaction cost economics. This framework forms the basis for studying virtual integration for e-commerce supported activities.

THE INFLUENCE OF THE PREVIOUS E-COMMERCE RESEARCH PROJECT

Venturing into EC involves tremendous organizational change. The process of the transition is suggested to have three phases: readiness for change, adoption of change, and institutionalization of the change (Armenakis et al 1993). The specific requisites for venturing into EC identified within the Fundamental Requisites of Cyber-Commerce provide preliminary evidence to access readiness for change involved in e-commerce ventures. The deployment of these fundamental requisites in fundamental business operations within EC corresponds to the adoption of the change. Initiating the legal aspects of EC will help to institutionalize the changes instigated when deploying and using EC. These preliminary findings provide guidance relative to this research project.

Using our preliminary results is consistent with the practice of using experts and consultants for important business ventures. Experts and consultants typically bring skills and experiences to new ventures that are not completely proven, but nonetheless considered important to those endeavors. In the next research phase, we will investigate two distinctly different perspectives relative deployment and use of EC. We will perform case studies to investigate the two major cost viewpoints. This research will help construct a model for deploying and using e-commerce.

A TRANSACTION COST VIEWPOINT (TCVP)

Two prominent perspectives exist within the TCVP: 1) that units within an organization interact with participants within a transaction from the standpoint of what is good for the organizational unit and not necessarily the whole of the organization, and 2) that units within an organization interact with participants within a transaction from a stand point of what is good for the entire organization, not just what is good for the organizational unit. The theory is based upon the fundament principles of self -reservation. The first TCVP implies that the organizational unit practices self-preservation of the unit, which can sometimes conflict with the self-preservation of the whole organization. The second TCPV implies that organizational units practice self-preservation of the organization, which can sometimes conflict with the self-preservation of the organizational unit.

The adoption of client/server computing technology has been the key for the popularization of network-based management information system for organizations in 1980s. Today, as the Internet becomes the underpinning technology for EC, organizations further adopt both intranet and extranet infrastructures. The immediate benefit from the expanded network from internal network to the world-wide connection is the reduction of transaction cost, which has finally changed and will continue to change the way organization units operate.

This research project will study cases within EC wherein the organizational units acted within the two opposing TCVPs. We hope to illustrate how the interests of the whole organization should be the main perspective under which EC is deployed and used. We also hope to illustrate how the most prominent TCVP is the one wherein the self-preservation of organizational units dominate, and in which many EC ventures fail. The researchers believe that case study analysis will best serve the purpose of the research objectives. From the research outcomes, we will pose a model of EC deployment and use that encourages the local perspective of the first TCVP within the more important TCVP of the second TCVP that encourages an enterprise-wide perspective for EC deployment and use.

REFERENCES

Armenakis, A.A., S.G. Harris, and K.W. Mossholder, "Creating Readiness for Large-Scale Change," *Human Relations*, 46, 6 (1993), 681-703.

Beath, C., and W. Orlikowski, "The Contradictory Structure of Systems Development Methodologies: Deconstructing the IS-User Relationship in Information Engineering," *Information Systems Research*, Vol. 5, No. 4, September, 1994.

Elliff S.A., "New Dimensions in EC and SCM Part 1: The Benefits of E-Procurement General Electric," *TechnologyEvaluation.com*, February 14, 2001.

Ellig, J., "Internal Markets and the Theory of the Firm," *Managerial & Decision Economics* 22, no. 4,5 (Jun/Aug 2001): 227-237.

Kerrigan, R., Roegner, E. V., Swinford, D. D., and Zawada, C. C., "B2B Basics," *McKinsey Quarterly* no. 1 (2001): 44-53.

Stapleton, D., Gentles, P., Ross, J., and Shubert, K., "The Location-centric Shift from Marketplace to Marketspace: Transaction Cost-inspired Propositions of Virtual Integration via An E-commerce model," *Advances in Competitiveness Research* 9, no. 1 (2001): 10-41.

Wang, S., "Organizational Visualization of Electronic Commerce," *Human Systems Management* 19, no. 4 (2000): 285-294.

Williamson, O., "The Economics Institutions of Capitalism," New York: Free Press, 1985.

Implementing E-Government: Impact on Business Processes and Organizational Structure

Matt Poostchi and Dr. Gerald Grant
Eric Sprott School of Business, Carleton University, Canada
Tel: (613) 520-2600 Ext. 8006, Fax: (613) 520-4427, Gerald_Grant@Carleton.ca

INTRODUCTION

New models of doing business have emerged with the advent of the Internet and the World Wide Web. Companies have experimented with these models with varying degrees of success. Governments are not immune to these changes and are under increasing pressure to change their traditional business model to what is commonly referred to as "E-government" or "Electronic Government", with ready access to information, increased self-service options for citizens and business, and increased accountability and democracy.

In 1999, the Canadian federal government announced that it would become a model user of information technology and the Internet, and become known around the world as the government most connected to its citizens. Certain targets (See Appendix A) were set in a phased approach to be completed by 2004 and others beyond that (Treasury Board of Canada, 2000). Most of these targets, however, were transactional in nature (for example, downloadable forms and ability to submit forms electronically), and did not address improvements in the democratic process or increasing input into the decision making and policy setting of the government nor increasing the accountability of government.

RESEARCH FOCUS

The main research objective is to determine the potential impact of e-government on the structure and operational processes of government departments. E-government implementation is predicated on the deployment of integrated enterprise IT systems. Such deployments have been shown, in the private business context, to require significant transformation in business processes and structures (Davenport, 2000; Markus and Tanis, 2000). In the e-government context, similar transformation is expected if governments are to achieve the goal of better serving citizens, businesses and partners. This research looks at e-government in the Canadian federal government context.

Two studies are planned. One study, based on a mailed questionnaire to Canadian Federal Government department heads, will assess the- impact E-Government has had or will have on department's business processes and organization structures as reported by respondents. Approximately 80-90 Canadian federal organizations of various sizes will be picked for this study. The questionnaire will be 12 pages long and will have 25 questions. It will have four sections covering "IT Practices", "Government On-Line Initiative", "Potential Impact on Processes & Organization Structure", and "Cost Savings".

The second study is a quality assurance (QA) study. It will test the query-response process. The study will test the electronic mail capability and automated acknowledgements of those Canadian federal departments who claim (as filled out in the questionnaire) to have completed this phase of the Government On-line targets.

Recommendations will be made where appropriate. Whereas one study takes a snapshot of the current state of readiness of the departments for one facet of E-government (Query-Response), the second study looks at broader impacts on departments as a result of e-government.

THEORETICAL FRAMEWORK

The theoretical framework given above presents one view of implementing e-government. In this research we only look at e-government as an independently-influencing variable which requires many changes in the organization for its implementation. This would include strategic, operational and technological changes. While there are many changes that merit consideration, this proposal focuses on two key areas: business process change and organization structure change. Other issues such as the need for enhanced IT infrastructure, enhanced network security, employee training, among other changes are outside the scope of this research. We propose that changes in business processes and organizational structure will lead to an increase in short-term costs (less than 5 years) and a decrease in long-term costs (greater than 5 years).

Figure 1: Theoretical framework

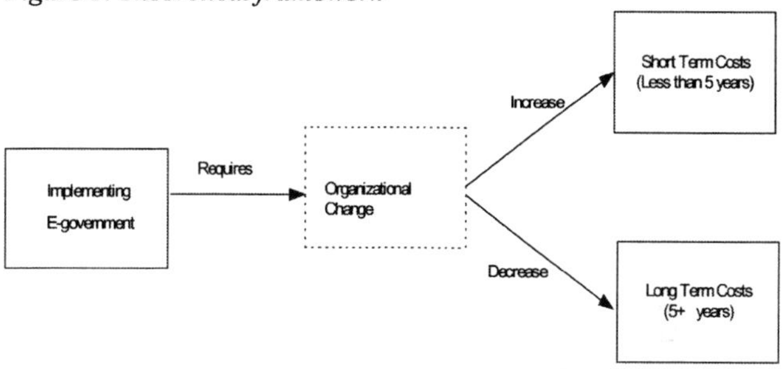

Measurement of change in organization processes and structure is as reported by respondents. For process change, we will report on whether it will be automated, re-engineered or totally transformed, and the degree of change within each. For organizational change, we will report on whether or not respondents think e-government will lead to a flatter organization. Cost decreases and increases are based on respondent's perception of these costs based on their organization's base budgets for the various areas being tested (HR, Finance, Program Delivery etc.).

HYPOTHESES

We propose the following hypotheses:

H1: E-government will lead to flatter organizations within departments

H2: E-government will require government departments to significantly re-engineer key business processes such as those associated with human resources management

H3: Cost savings arising from the implementation of e-government will be little to non-existent in the short term (less than 5 years)

Inter-department processes are out of scope for this study, although inferences can be made from responses received.

BENEFITS

By testing the Query-Response process we can gauge the readiness and progress of departments in meeting the Government On-Line (GOL) goals set by the government. GOL is an important first step towards e-government. This will give us a snapshot of the current state of affairs. By studying the impact or potential impact of e-government, departments can start preparing long-term goals and plans with appropriate resources to fund these initiatives. Since we expect the impact of e-government to be extensive, it may require massive organizational and process changes for which departments and their workers must prepare themselves.

As other countries embark on their journey to e-government, there will be many pages from the Canadian experience from which to borrow and pitfalls to avoid and processes that they can expect to go through to achieve e-government. We expect that this research will provide a basis for future studies on the impacts of e-government.

LIMITATIONS OF STUDY

The potential for insufficient responses from the departments is a concern. This can be either because department heads are too busy or don't care to respond. Another limitation is the potential lack of knowledge of the departments in answering the questionnaire. Since e-government is a new concept, the department may not be aware of its wide reach, but potentially only focus on GOL, which has a narrower transaction-oriented focus.

To mitigate these limitations, we have picked one department that is very active in the area of Government On-line to act as the pilot. We also plan to approach the CIO of Canada, with overall responsibility for Government On-line to partner with us in this study and become a sponsor, thus ensuring a higher participation rate from the departments.

EXPECTED RESULTS

For the first hypothesis (change in organization structure), we expect a lack of awareness or reluctance on the part of departments to acknowledge this impact. Although there are initiatives under way to steam line and centralize many back-office functions such as Human Resources and Information Technology, the feeling seems to be that it will take many years before it will impact organization structure.

For the second hypothesis (change in business processes), we expect departments to be aware of the impact on their business processes at a high level. The expectation for the third hypothesis (short term costs) is for departments to be fully aware of the short term costs involved in making e-government happen and hence will delay its implementation unless extra funding is provided specifically for e-government activities. The QA test with the email should provide us with insight into the quality of responses both in terms of timeliness and automated acknowledgements.

REFERENCES

Davenport, T. (2000) Mission critical: realizing the promise of enterprise systems, Boston: Harvard Business School Press.

Markus, M. L. and C. Tanis. The enterprise system experience- from adoption to success. in Zmud, R. *Framing the Domains of IT Management: Projecting the future through the past*, Cincinati, Ohio: Pinnaflex, (2000), 173-207.

Treasury Board of Canada, CIO's Office (2000a) "A Framework for Government Online" accessed at: http://publiservice.cio-dpi.gc.ca/gol-ged/framework/2000-02/framework-cadrepr_e.asp

APPENDIX A

Government On-Line Targets

	Target
1	Current and reliable information on programs and services is available
2	Forms related to key programs and services are downloadable and printable
3	Ability to e-mail organization is available with an automatic electronic acknowledgement
4	Search capability to find services and programs is available
5	Clients are able to complete transactions on-line in a secure and interactive fashion
6	Secure, interactive electronic forms are available
7	Technical and content support is provided through various help services (online, phone etc.)

Using Industry Certification Courses as Part of the IS Curriculum

Jairo A. Gutiérrez
Management Science and Information Systems Dept., The University of Auckland, New Zealand
Tel: (649) 373-7599 Ext. 6851, Fax: (649) 373-7430, j.gutierrez@auckland.ac.nz

ABSTRACT

This paper discusses the experience of introducing the Cisco Networking Academy Program (CNAP) as part of two data communications courses taught in the School of Business and Economics at the University of Auckland. A detailed description of the implementation of the program is being prepared as a case study paper. Feedback obtained informally through conversations with students and formally by using end-of-semester surveys and by reviewing students assignments and tests indicates that students have enthusiastically received the program and that the combination of traditional "sage-on-the-stage" lectures plus hands-on lab experiments enriches the educational experience. The availability of online curricula and testing is also considered an important element in the learning process.

INTRODUCTION

The courses studied in this paper, Data Communications and Advanced Data Communications, are taught on the second and third years of a three-year Bachelor of Commerce (BCom) degree in Information Systems. The courses can also be taken by BSc (Computer Science) and BTech (Information Technology) students. The second year course typically has enrolments of approximately 360 students roughly distributed in three classes of about 120 students each. Around 130 students take the third year paper. In the past the material has been delivered by lecturing three hours per week (12 weeks per semester) and by making available to students one optional tutorial hour per week during 8 weeks. The coursework assessment consisted of two tests; two research assignments, a laboratory assignment (running CACI's Comnet III networking simulation software), and a group design project.

The third year course had enrolments of around 130 students in one stream during the second semester of each year. The course dealt with detailed descriptions of the seven layers of the OSI Reference Model concentrating on the primitives used among the different layers, and studying the object oriented aspects of the standards. Students were formally introduced to the syntax notation used with this type of modelling and the applications of these techniques were discussed. Anecdotal feedback from students had clearly identified that they found this course to be highly theoretical. Unlike our second year course there was no lab component or group-based assignments.

In late 1999 a casual contact with Cisco's New Zealand's country manager led our Department (Management Science and Information Systems) to consider the possibility of becoming a Regional Academy and of introducing the CNAP as part of our data communication courses. The CNAP is a web-based program with curricula accessed through a web browser and comprises significant practical experience carried out within a lab environment. On completion of the training, the students will be prepared to sit the Cisco Certified Networking Associate (CCNA) and Cisco Certified Networking Professional (CCNP) accreditation tests at any of a number of independent testing centres (Cisco, 2000).

This study will describe the issues associated with the addition of the CNAP to our teaching and learning activities and with the integration of the program with our university courses. It will discuss the advantages and disadvantages encountered in the administration and delivery of the combined (i.e. our traditional content plus the Cisco-based content) material. The research will also try to analyse the impact of the program on the learning outcomes and objectives of our existing courses.

It is difficult to find the proper balance between the introduction of general concepts and the teaching of more pragmatic skills that many students feel they need. This fact has been recognised for IT education (Banks, 2001) and for tertiary students regardless of their discipline (Beyrouty, 2000; Shulman, 1997). It is equally challenging to pitch courses at a level that will keep students interested (Fallows and Ahmet, 1999). This paper argues that there is a need to combine theoretical learning, lab experimentation, and group mini-projects (challenges) with traditional study techniques and testing in order to achieve a deeper level of understanding and learning.

REFERENCES

Banks, David (2001), Reflections on Interpretivist Teaching with Positivist Students. Proceedings of the Informing Science 2001 Conference, Challenges to Informing Clients: A Transdisciplinary Approach, Krakow, Poland, June 19-22. Alka Harriger (Ed.), 80-87

Beyrouty, Craig (2000). Retrieved on 7 December, 1999 from the World Wide Web: http://www.uark.edu/misc/tfscinfo/TFSC.html

Cisco Systems (1999). Retrieved on 16 February, 1999 from the World Wide Web: http://www.cisco.com/training/

Fallows, Stephen and Aahmet, Kemal (1999). Inspiring Students: Case Studies in Motivating the Learner. Kogan Page Limited, London, and Stylus Publishing, Sterling, Virginia, U.S.A.

Shulman, Lee (1997). Professing the Liberal Arts. Education and Democracy: Reimagining Liberal Learning in America. Robert Orrill (Ed.). The College Board.

Developing a Framework for Managing Organizational Influences on IS Component Specialization

Marc N. Haines
University of Wisconsin-Milwaukee, UWM, School of Business Administration, Tel: (414) 229-3773, mhaines@uwm.edu

RESEARCH SUMMARY

Introduction

Enterprise Systems (ES) packages are at the core of the information system (IS) portfolios of many, especially large, organizations. ES implementations are enormous and costly undertakings, often entailing considerable organizational changes (Davenport, 2000). While some organizations have realized substantial benefits from ES implementations, there have also been many disappointments and costly failures (Davenport, 1998; Nash, 2000; Wilder and Davis, 1998). The configuration and customization activities related to adapting a generic ES software package to the particular requirements of an organization is an important part of the implementation process and can take up a considerable amount of time and resources (Weston, 1997; Zeitz, 1996). Understanding the influences that prompt the specialization of IS components and how to manage these influences is therefore a key ability for IS professionals and managers involved in ES implementations.

The purpose of the research project is to develop a framework, which helps to better understand these influences and provides guidance on how to manage these influences with the goal to improve overall ES implementation outcomes. The preliminary framework of influences on IS component specialization is based on the qualitative analysis of evidence from five case studies. In a subsequent phase of the project a survey instrument is being developed to evaluate the current framework on a broader basis and with quantitative methods.

Methodology

The current framework (see Figure 1) is based on empirical evidence collected in five case studies of organizations that have implement ES packages. The cases include four manufacturing firms and one non-profit organization. The organizations referred to as LuminaCo, WoodCo, and TransCo implemented systems by SAP. LightCo implemented a system by Oracle, and NonProfitOrg a system by Peoplesoft. In each organization up-to 8 interviews were conducted with IT directors, senior managers, project managers, and system analysts. The evidence consisted of interview transcripts, field notes, and other textual documents provided by the participants. The analysis was performed according to the case study research methodology outlined by Eisenhardt (1989) and incorporated initial open coding and eventually axial coding as suggested by Strauss and Corbin (1998). The analysis process was carried out using the qualitative analysis tool NVivo (Richards, 1999).

Results

The current framework includes sixteen factors that influence IS component customization. The numbers on the arrows indicate the number of codings - or text passages - that suggest a relationship between an influence factor and IS component specialization. The framework further includes arrows that indicate relationships among the sixteen factors.

Each of the factors is categorized either as a constraint, a manageable influence, or as unknown. The three categories are described in Table 1. The categorizations shown in Figure 1 reflect the experiences made in the LightCo case and should not be regarded as universal. In contrary, each organization needs to carefully assess which factors are constraints, manageable, or unknown, for a particular implementation project. Taking the relationships stated in the framework into account a project team would then be able to identify anchors to decrease potential negative influences and reinforce positive influences. In the scenario shown in Figure 1 below, resistance to change is an unknown factor that can have significant influence on IS component specialization. In the current framework three manageable factors influence resistance to change. These factors are user involvement and preparation, specialization request management, and project team configuration. All three factors are potential anchors for the project management to manage resistance and avoid potential negative influence on IS component specialization through resistance.

Table 1: Manageability of factors

Category	Description	Examples
Constraint	Influences that are known but difficult to manipulate by managerial decisions.	Standard Solution Maturity, Parent Company and Business Partners
Manageable Influence	Influences that are amenable to manipulation by managerial decisions.	Implementation Partner Involvement, Specialization Request Management
Unknown Influence	Influences that are unknown and therefore elude manipulation by managerial decisions.	Resistance to Change, Future IS Developments

Limitations and Further Research

A key limitation that is inherent to case-based research is its generalizability. In a subsequent effort the author is now developing a survey instrument to evaluate the current framework and test its assertions on a broader basis with quantitative methods. The results of this survey are expected to provide insights into the validity of the current framework, the importance of the individual factors and the relationships among the factors. This in turn has the potential to provide improved guidance on how to manage the influences on IS component specialization to contribute to a successful outcome of an ES implementation.

REFERENCES

Davenport, T.H. "Putting the Enterprise into the Enterprise System," *Harvard Business Review* (76:4), 1998, pp. 121-131.

Davenport, T.H. *Mission Critical - Realizing the Promise of Enterprise Systems*, Harvard Business School Press, Boston, Massachusetts, 2000.

Eisenhardt, K.M. "Building Theories From Case Study Research," *Academy of Management Review* (14:4), 1989, pp. 532-551.

Nash, K.S. "Companies Don't Learn From Previous IT Snafus," *Computerworld* (34:44), 2000, pp. 32-33.

Figure 1: Influences on IS component specialization

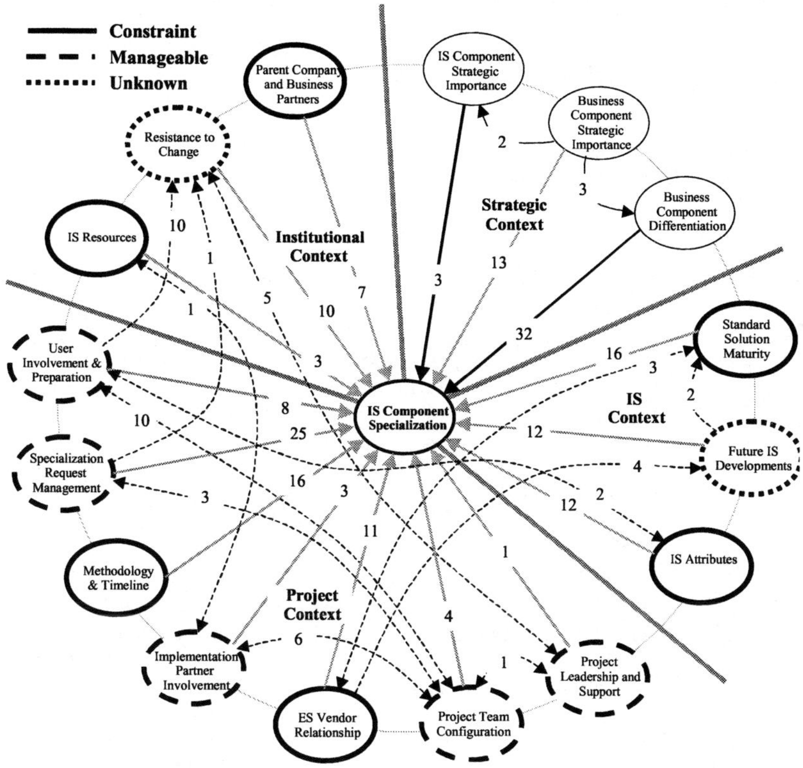

Richards, L. *Using NVivo in Qualitative Research*, SAGE Publications Inc., Thousand Oaks, CA, 1999.

Strauss, A. and Corbin, J. *Basics of Qualitative Research*, SAGE Publications Inc., Thousand Oaks, CA, 1998.

Weston, R. "SAP recasts R/3 for out-of-box use," *Computerworld* (31:1), 1997, pp. 14.

Wilder, C. and Davis, B. "False starts, strong finishes," *Informationweek* (7111998, pp. 41-53.

Zeitz, W.A. "SAP R/3: Dream or nightmare?: Don't jump on the SAP bandwagon," *Computerworld* (30:5), 1996, pp. 101-103.

Comparing I.S. Ethics in the USA with I.S. Ethics in the Arab World

Husain Al-Lawaitia and Thomas Hilton
Business Information Systems Department, Utah State University
Tel: (435) 797-2342, Fax: (435) 797-2351, {HMA, Hilton}@cc.USU.edu

INTRODUCTION

The past two decades have shown a rapid though unequal spread of computers throughout businesses worldwide. Despite this spread, the information systems (I.S.) field is still considered relatively young (Pierce & Henry, 2000). One result of this youth is a general dearth of I.S.-related laws and clear-cut codes of conduct to regulate this challenging, fast expanding sphere (Udas, Fuerst, & Paradice, 1996). Thus, ethical issues in the I.S. field are highly influenced by less obvious factors such as a nation's general legal system and other disciplines such as business law, internal organizational policies, culture, social etc. (Pierce & Henry).

Research suggests that cultural values and traditions have a substantial influence on many I.S. ethics issues (Whitman, Townsend, & Hendrickson (1999). As a consequence, what is considered 'right' I.S. use by one culture may be considered 'wrong' by another culture. This cultural factor may often supersede internal policies and codes that multinational corporations have issued to guide their personnel in using information systems consistently, ethically, and legally. Certainly such internal policies are necessary, but they are often perceived as ineffective (Loch, Conger, & Oz, 1998).

In our opinion, unauthorized copying of software has received a lot of research attention due to its huge negative effect on developers. Other I.S. ethical issues, however, have not received a similar level of attention.

This study aims to explore similarities and differences in I.S. ethics between two different cultures: the USA and the Arab World. The authors hope to begin identifying specifics of how these two cultures vary in deciding what is 'right' and what is 'wrong' in I.S. ethics issues.

LITERATURE REVIEW

In the interest of brevity, the full literature review is not included here; however, it is available at http://cc.USU.edu/~Hilton/IRMA2002.htm. The review is summarized as follows:

Questions of right and wrong in Information Systems use, then, are hardly isolated from outside influences. As Kimberly & Jonathan (1999) write, "Ethics is humanistic, personal, and dependent on one's conscience" (Ethics and the Law section 2). Therefore, laws or organizationally defined policy codes are not enough by themselves to maintain ethical behavior; such relatively public statements must be supported by personal values derived from morals based on experience interpreted through the lens of culture. And it must be understood that religion, although ostensibly minimized in U.S. ethics, plays a major, even preeminent, role in Arabian akhlaq. Wienen (1999) reinforced this point with his finding that the influence of religion is obvious as a cultural influence on management in the Muslim world.

However, having said that, the literature also shows that cultural factors other than religion contribute to the development of personal ethics. Moreover, individual differences play a major role: personal codes of ethics develop variously according to individual experience with law, employment, profession, etc.

In conclusion, literature supports the view that culture has a substantial influence on personal ethical decisions and contributes significantly to the ethical framework through which any act is judged right or wrong, ethical or unethical. Based on this review, the authors hypothesize significant divergence in ethics opinions between U.S. and Arab computer users.

RESEARCH QUESTION

This pilot study investigates and explores similarities and differences in ethics between the American culture and the Arabian culture as they manifest in the BIS field. The specific research question is:

How does the American culture differ from the Arabian culture in their views regarding I.S. ethical issues?

METHODOLOGY

Instrument

After considerable review of the instruments in the area of I.S., the researchers decided to develop an instrument deemed appropriate and suitable for the purpose of the study. Thus, the instrument is based on a series of vignettes illustrating various computer uses. Three types of I.S. ethical issues that are likely to face computer users in any business setting were adopted as the backbone of the survey. These areas are employee's use of company I.S. resources and time for personal use and entertainment; employee's use of company I.S. resources (hardware, software, and or information) for personal, friend's, and or relatives' gain; and finally, the company's use of non-trust systems—either manual or computerized—to monitor its employees. The questions in all three parts of the survey are derived from the studies of Lewellyn, (1996), Loch et al. (1998), and Whitman et al.(1999).

The respondents were asked to judge each ethical issue in the survey on a five-point Likert-type scale (Pierce & Henry, 2000) from usually ethical to usually unethical. Instructions were provided to respondents stating that their answer should reflect their personal opinion. Also, they were asked to respond to all issues even if they were unsure of their opinion. Every effort was made to obtain unbiased responses. To assure anonymity to subjects, the surveys were not coded or numbered. Also, the subjects were informed before giving answers that the data would only be reported in an aggregate form.

Data Collection Procedure and Sample

Unlike other ethics research that used mail surveys in obtaining data (Pierce & Henry, 2000), the unique situation of this study forced the researchers to approach the subjects personally. The reason for using this approach was because the number of Arab students in the two universities that were selected for conducting this study was small. Therefore, Arab students were approached outside the classroom setting. On the other hand, all U.S. undergraduate and some graduate students were approached in the classroom. Other U.S graduate students were approached personally. Additionally, the number of U.S. undergraduate respondents was higher than the number of Arab respondents. In order to avoid problems that might arise concerning equal variance and make the t-tests more robust, surveys of 33 U.S undergraduate students were randomly dropped from the study making the number of respondents of both groups equal.

All computer users across both cultures, not only I.S. or computer science (CS) professionals, were deemed appropriate for this study. A convenience sample of students from two U.S. universities was used. The demographic characteristics of the entire sample are shown in Table 1, available at http://cc.USU.edu/~Hilton/IRMA2002.htm.

RESULTS

To check the survey's reliability, Chronbach's alpha was calculated for each part of the survey. Results generated from this test were, part 1 (.86) part 2 (.84), & part 3 (.77). These results suggest that the instrument appears to be acceptably reliable.

Setting the rejection criterion of significance at 0.05, the following tests were conducted to obtain results from the data collected. First, a t test was used to analyze the difference in survey responses of the two cultures. Results obtained were t (df =134) = 1.423, p = .157, which indicates no significant differences between cultures.

Second, t tests were used to analyze the mean difference between the two groups for each question. Results in Table 2 (available at http://cc.USU.edu/~Hilton/IRMA2002.htm) revealed that 8 out of the total 24 questions were found to have significant differences between the two groups.

Third, a t test was carried out to assess the mean difference between the two groups for each of the three parts of the survey. Results in Table 3 (available at http://cc.USU.edu/~Hilton/IRMA2002.htm) show that only the first part of the survey concerning employee's use of company computers for personal use and entertainment was found to be significantly different (t (df=134) = 2.189, p = .030). However, the other two parts, employee use of company I.S. resources for personal, relatives, and or friends gain (p = .801); and the company use of non-trust systems to monitor employees (p = .138), were not found significantly different.

DISCUSSION AND CONCLUSIONS

Despite the fact that research indicated that culture has a significant influence on personal ethical decisions including some aspects of I.S., the results of this study indicate that there is no overall significant difference between subjects from the Arab World and those from the United States in their views regarding I.S. ethical issues.

Personal Use of Organization Computers

However, when each of the three parts of the survey was independently examined, the first part, which is about the use of company computers for personal matters and entertainment, revealed statistically significant differences (p = .030): while both groups viewed the practice as unethical, Arab respondents viewed this practice as more unethical than did the non-Arab Americans. As discussed in the literature, these results are consistent with the findings of Whitman et al., 1999: (Singapore and Hong Kong, both eastern cultures, were found to be less tolerant of the use of company resources and time for personal matters than most of western cultures including that of the United States.)

This finding is clarified by another interesting result in Part 1 that was revealed when survey questions were examined independently. Questions 2, 4, and 6 evaluate the morality of using company computers for personal use and entertainment after working hours, and questions 1, 3, and 5 ask about using company computers during working hours. There was no significant difference between the two groups regarding use of company computers for personal matters during working hours; the difference became statistically significant only when considering computer use after working hours.

Use of Organization Resources for Non-Company Gain

Comparison of the overall mean responses to the questions in Part 2 revealed no significant difference between Americans and Arabs. However, analysis of individual questions did reveal significant differences.

Questions 9, 10, and 12 appraise the morality of installing or using company-licensed software off-premises by the employee, by friends of the employee, or by relatives of the employee for non-company purposes. The outcome of these questions showed Americans to be more conservative than Arabs. While both cultures agree the above acts are unethical, American subjects viewed these acts as significantly more unethical than their Arabs counterparts. Again, this outcome is consistent with the results of Whitman et al. (1999) who found that Americans are significantly less tolerant of copyright infringement than all other countries.

Question 17 assesses the morality of disclosing potentially damaging personal information to an authorized third person. Responses to this question indicate that Arab respondents consider this unethical while American respondents considered it less unethical. However, the authors find these results counterintuitive (since authorized persons would presumably be justified in receiving information) and therefore did some informal checking with respondents. These informal checks reveal a possible wording problem in the question that, if verified, would invalidate this result.

Monitoring Employee Computer Use

Analysis of Part 3 of the survey as a whole, which asked about monitoring employee computer use, revealed no significant difference between Arab and American respondents. However, question-by-question analysis did reveal one significant difference. Question 19 assesses the morality of monitoring employee email by the company without informing employees of the monitoring. While both groups considered the practice unethical, the Arab respondents considered it to be worse than did American respondents.

CONCLUSIONS

In conclusion, there appear to be two main points identified in this study. First, there is a remarkable consistency between Arabs and non-Arab Americans in their answers to questions: in no case did one group consider ethical an act that the other group considered unethical. Second, there were statistically significant differences between the groups on eight individual questions, suggesting a different level of concern for some issues between the two groups as discussed above; again even these differences were always on the same side of the response scale. Thus, although culture presumably remains a primary determinant of ethics, there seems to be no more than a modest differentiating effect of these two particular cultures on I.S.-related ethics opinions of their members. This is generally in conformity with the literature.

LIMITATIONS AND RECOMMENDATIONS FOR FUTURE RESEARCH

Limitations and recommendations are available at http://cc.USU.edu/~Hilton/IRMA2002.htm.

REFERENCES

References are available at htt://cc.USU.edu/~Hilton/IRMA2002.htm.

Electronic Authentication Initiatives in the IRS *e-file* Program: Enabling E-Government Through Electronic Signatures

Stephen H. Holden, PhD
Assistant Professor, Department of Information Systems, University of Maryland Baltimore County
Tel: (410) 455-3936, Fax: (410) 455-1073, Holden@umbc.edu

INTRODUCTION

Electronic government (e-government) is being touted as a solution for many of the perceived, and in some cases real, problems facing government organizations such as lack of responsiveness, lack of efficiency, and lack of trust (Council for Excellence in Government 2000). E-government makes it possible for public agencies to inform, serve and interact with the public in a myriad of ways, generally more conveniently, often less expensively, and with higher customer satisfaction than is possible by traditional service delivery (University of Michigan 2001, Accenture 2001). While e-government offers many advantages to traditional service delivery, it suffers one potentially debilitating challenge. How do users (i.e., individuals, businesses, government employees and other stakeholders) complete transactions that require either a signature or some form of authentication by law, policy or tradition?

The need for electronic authentication solutions is well documented. Models of e-government maturity assume that government agencies make the shift from just displaying information about public programs to actually enabling transactions (Layne and Lee 2001). There are a number of studies that point out the public is concerned about issues of securing e-government transactions (Holden and Ha 2002). Congress's oversight organization, the General Accounting Office (GAO), also identifies ensuring the privacy and security of transactions to be a major challenge to federal agencies wishing to enable e-government (2000).

To date, no research has documented and evaluated the implementation of electronic authentication for an e-government program. This paper provides one possible response to the challenge of how federal agencies might sign electronic transactions based the experiences of one of the longest-running and arguably most successful e-government programs in the United States. The Internal Revenue Service (IRS) *e-file* program represents an example of an operational e-government program that serves millions of customers each year, has begun to overcome the barriers of electronic authentication through several delivery channels, and has done so without relying on the public key cryptography (Lacijan and Crockett 2000 and IRS 2000a).

BACKGROUND: THE IRS E-FILE PROGRAM

Through its market research efforts, the IRS has found that the public has concerns about the privacy and security of e-government in general and filing taxes electronically in particular (2000a). IRS's annual strategic plan for Electronic Tax Administration cites other research that points to paper-based authentication for the program as an inhibitor to e-file adoption due to costs for preparers and complexity for taxpayers (IRS 2000). Despite these barriers to adoption, the IRS accepted nearly 40 million e-filed returns in 2001, with approximately one third (13.3 million) signed electronically (Corridore 2001, IRS 2001). The IRS has pursued a variety of product offerings, including electronic authentication, to reach this level of market penetration compared to paper filing. Two electronic authentication initiatives launched for the 1999 filing season are the subject of this paper.

Prior to the 1999 filing season, taxpayers who e-filed using tax preparation software (on-line channel) or a tax preparer (preparer channel) had to complete a "jurat" document to satisfy the legal requirement that the tax return be signed. The jurat is actually an IRS Form 8453, U.S. Individual Income Tax Declaration for an IRS *e-file* Return, which includes selected tax return information, the taxpayer identification number (s), and other data elements normally found on the mailing label to help tie the signatures to the return. Depending on the channel, either the taxpayer or the preparer had to mail the jurats to designated IRS service centers within 48 hours of successful e-filing.

Taxpayers who used tax preparation software in filing season 1998, regardless of whether they filed electronically or on paper, received a postcard for the 1999 filing season with an e-file customer number (ECN). When it came time to transmit the return to a third-party transmitter and subsequently to the IRS, the taxpayer(s) entered the ECNs issued by the IRS in order to sign the return. IRS validated other pieces of data (e.g., date of birth, taxpayer identification number, name control), sometimes referred to as "shared secrets," in conjunction with the ECN to authenticate the transaction. The use of the ECN by the taxpayer obviated the need for the submission of the jurat document to the IRS by the taxpayer.

The IRS also instituted a pilot with selected preparers for the 1999 filing season to obviate the need to mail in a paper signature document. Preparers approved to participate in the pilot had their clients who were interested in paperless filing select a PIN that was then recorded on a worksheet that the tax preparer and taxpayer both kept. The worksheet, while similar to the jurat document described above, was retained by the preparer and taxpayer(s) and did not have to be submitted to the IRS. The PIN, or PINs in the case of jointly filed returns, signed the return. Since the IRS had not issued this PIN, it was not used to authenticate the return transaction.

METHODS

This preliminary research is a descriptive case study of the IRS's two electronic authentication initiatives in 1999. The case study is grounded in literature of electronic government and relies on IRS analysis of its market research and surveys of participants in the preparer PIN and taxpayer ECN pilots. The IRS market research of customers was a phone survey of a random sample of 1,000 taxpayers, who are representative of the US taxpaying public (IRS 2000c: 10). For the preparer survey, the IRS used a mail survey of preparers that participated in the PIN pilot although the IRS survey report does not detail the number of preparers survey, sample selection technique or response rates (IRS 1999a). For the ECN customer survey, the IRS mailed out surveys to 2,500 taxpayers who were supposed to have gotten the ECN postcard, but the IRS report on this survey does not explain the sample selection process. Of those surveys mailed, 764 were completed and 15 were undeliverable (IRS 1999b: 4). Other descriptive elements of the case study rely on the author's role as an IRS executive leading these initiatives in 1999.

RESULTS

Program results for filing season 2001 show mixed results for the two new electronic authentication efforts begun in 1999. The proportion of signed electronically through the on-line channel nearly doubled from the previous year (62.91 percent for 2001 vs. 31.46 percent for 2000). For the preparer channel, the proportion of returns signed electronically declined from the previous year (16.37 percent for 2001 vs. 21.48 percent for 2000). Both efforts had shown increases in the proportion of electronically signed returns between 1999 and 2000. All Telefile returns, 4.4 million in 2001, are signed electronically (Corridore 2001).

An IRS analysis of survey data gathered in 1999 from preparers participating in the preparer PIN pilot found that they reacted positively to the pilot and would like the IRS to make it permanent. In the IRS report, survey respondents cited multiple benefits including increased productivity of staff, reduced paper burden, and relative ease of incorporating the PIN process into their business operations. Despite these perceived benefits, 75 percent of preparers responding to the survey believed that the use of the PINS did not increase e-file returns while 15 percent answered yes and the remaining ten percent were not sure. Certain pilot program requirements, namely that taxpayers had to physically come to the preparers' office to sign the return, were reported to create new logistic barriers for preparers (IRS 1999a).

The IRS also did an analysis of survey data gathered in 1999 from taxpayers participating in the ECN initiative and found taxpayers liked that electronic signature effort and would use it in the future. Over 60 percent of those responding to the survey reported they would use an ECN in the future. Unlike the preparer survey results above, the IRS reported that nearly two-thirds (64.6 percent) of taxpayers survey had filed using paper the previous year. The IRS reported an interesting finding that over 32 percent of those that responded said that they did not get the ECN postcard or were not sure if they did (IRS 1999b).

ANALYSIS

The IRS's use of electronic authentication appears to have achieved several intended program results. Since the authentication pilots started, the number of returns signed electronically each year has increased. For taxpayers and preparers that used the electronic authentication programs, they reported a willingness to use the product feature in the future. For preparers, it achieved the goal of reducing cost and burden of participating in the e-file program. Taxpayers, preparers and the IRS all avoided the need to process paper signature forms when the return was signed and authenticated electronically. However, the use of electronic authentication did not seem to induce taxpayers to switch from paper to electronically filing in the minds of preparers, while there is some indication that many taxpayers using ECNs had filed on paper the previous year.

The IRS's use of PINs and "shared secrets" to sign and authenticate electronic government transactions on a relatively large scale demonstrates that public organizations may be able to address what is generally reported to be a major problem facing e-government. Because of limitations of this preliminary study, it is difficult to gauge whether other federal agencies can expect similar results. One weakness of the analysis is the use of a variety of surveys, which employed different data sources and methodologies. Additionally, the analysis does not address other kinds of empirical results relating to pilot results such actual cost savings per transaction or changes in taxpayer or preparer attitudes about privacy and security.

CONCLUSION

Because of the sensitivity of the personal information filed with the IRS each year and the perennial public and Congressional scrutiny of the IRS, it stands to reason that other government organizations should be able to utilize some of these techniques. More research, however, is needed to completely assess the effectiveness of IRS's electronic authentication. In particular, there is a need to evaluate whether the public and preparer communities perceive the use of the electronic authentication capabilities addresses concerns about privacy and security in the IRS e-file program. More systematic research might also help provide clues whether other federal and public agencies can benefit from the kind of electronic authentication used by the IRS.

REFERENCES

Accenture. 2001. *Governments Closing Gap Between Political Rhetoric and eGovernment Reality.* New York, NY.

Corridore, Mary Ellen. 2001. E-mail correspondence with author containing 1999- 2001 filing season PIN program results, 19 June.

The Council for Excellence in Government. 2000. *E-Government: The Next American Revolution.* Washington, D.C.

Government Accounting Office. 2000. *Electronic Government: Federal Initiatives are Evolving Rapidly But They Face Significant Challenges.* Statement of David L. McClure. GAO-T-AIMD/GGD-00-179. Washington, D.C.

Holden, Stephen H., and Lidan Ha. 2002. *Do the Facts Match the Hype: Public Demand for, and Government Attitudes About, E-Government.* Public Administration Times 25, no. 1: 3.

Internal Revenue Service. 1999a. *Practitioner PIN Pilot Study.* IRS Publication 3597. Washington, DC.

Internal Revenue Service. 1999b. *e-file Customer Number (ECN) Pilot Survey.* IRS Publication 3596. Washington, D.C.

Internal Revenue Service. 2000a. *A Strategy for Growth.* IRS Publication 3147. Washington, D.C.

Internal Revenue Service. 2000b. *Findings from the 2000 Wave of ETA Taxpayer & Preparer e-file Satisfaction Research.* IRS Publication 3491. Washington, D.C.

Internal Revenue Service. 2000c. *Presentation of Findings from the 2000 Wave of ETA Attitudinal Tracking Research.* IRS Publication 3492. Washington, D.C.

Internal Revenue Service. 2001. *IRS Filing Season One of the Best Ever; E-Filing Hits Record, Taxpayer Service Improves.* Release No. IRS-2001-49. Washington, D.C.

Lacijan, Chuck and Alix Crockett. 2000. *Making Electronic Filing a Value Proposition for Tax Practitioners.* Tax Practice and Procedure, vol. 2, No 2 (April-May): 25-30.

Layne, K. and Lee, J. 2001. *Developing Fully Functional E-government: A Four-Stage Model.* Government Information Quarterly 18: 122-136.

University of Michigan Business School. 2001. *American Customer Satisfaction Index: Special Report: Government Satisfaction Scores.* Ann Arbor, MI: University of Michigan. Accessed 14 January 2002. Available from http://www.bus.umich.edu/research/nqrc/government.html.

Information Systems and Small Business: Lessons from the Entrepreneurial Process

M. Gordon Hunter
Management Information Systems, Faculty of Management, The University of Lethbridge, Canada
Tel: 1 (403) 329-2672, Fax: 1 (403) 329-2038, ghunter@uleth.ca

Wayne C. Long
Emeritus Professor of Management, The University of Calgary, Canada

ABSTRACT

This document suggests the adoption of the Theory of Entrepreneurship by researchers who investigate the use of information systems by small business. The majority of existing research into this area tends to adopt results determined from investigations of larger business. Thus, the uniqueness of small business is not considered. Concepts such as strategic orientation, decision-making, and resource poverty contribute to the unique situation and approach taken by small business managers. The Theory of Entrepreneurship responds to these concepts. The framework suggests that organizations evolve and that entrepreneurs throughout this evolution face various challenges. While it is noted the entrepreneurship and small business are different, there are components of the Theory of Entrepreneurship that apply equally to the small business manager. These components are described here in concert with the challenge to researchers to consider adopting this framework when conducting investigations into how information systems may be employed to support small business.

INTRODUCTION

Information Systems (IS) are creating a significant impact on the roles and work of individuals, and IS enabled change is revolutionizing businesses processes (Coghlan, 2001). There has been a consequent plethora of research into how business can best use IS or adapt to the IS precipitated change. Unfortunately, this research adopts a generic definition of "business" and there is very little attempt to differentiate businesses based upon size. In deed, where a differentiation is made, Cragg and King (1993) found that most research regarding IS and small business mainly attempts to confirm the research results determined from investigations of larger firms. Thus, it is incumbent upon IS researchers to explore how the unique aspects of small business may impact their use of IS.

The small business sector represents an important segment of most economies. In Canada, for instance, most recent figures indicate that 43% of total economic output is generated by 2.3 million businesses with fewer than 100 employees (Industry Canada, 1997). There is considerable variation in the definition of "small business". Some definitions employ a measure of annual revenue, size of investment, or number of employees. This latter characteristic seems to be the generally accepted term (Longnecker et al, 1997).

The objective of this document is to proffer the possible adoption of a framework, which may prove to be beneficial in the investigation of the use of, IS by small business. To begin, the context of the small business is outlined with respect to its uniqueness. Then, the suggested framework is introduced and described. This discussion presents the Entrepreneurial Process as developed by McMullan and Long (1990) and applies the various challenges depicted by their Process to the use of IS by small business. The document will conclude with suggestions for future research projects, which may adopt the proposed framework.

SMALL BUSINESS CONTEXT

The work of Stevenson (1999) may be used to develop a conceptual interpretation of the managers of businesses. According to Stevenson (1999), as presented in Table 1, managers in small businesses tend to be oriented toward the "promoter" end of a continuum, whereas managers of large businesses tend to take a "trustee" orientation.

From a strategic orientation, then, managers of small businesses will emphasize responding to opportunities, while managers of large businesses will focus on efficient use of resources. Further, with regards to resources, the small business manager will respond quickly to the environment, with a minimum commitment of resources in a multi-staged approach. However, the manager of a large business will take the time to follow formal procedures to make a one-time decision regarding a long-term commitment.

Table 1: Approaches to business practice

ASPECTS OF BUSINESS PRACTICE	PROMOTER ◄	► TRUSTEE
Strategic orientation	Capitalize on an opportunity	Focus on efficient use of current resources to determine the greatest return
Resource commitment and control decisions	Act in a very short time frame	Long time frame, considering long term implications
	Multi-staged	One-time up-front commitment
	Minimum commitment of resources at each stage	Large scale commitment of resources at one stage
	Respond quickly to changes in competition, market, and technology	Formal procedures of analysis such as capital allocation systems

Another concept, "resource poverty", (Thong et al, 1994) may also be employed to provide further elaboration of the difference between managers of large and small businesses. Resource poverty refers to the lack of both financial and human resources. Managers of small businesses must continually conduct their affairs with limited amounts of money. This situation tends to increase the manager's focus, as indicated above, on a minimum and multi-staged commitment process. Further, limited human resources may mean either fewer available employees or employees without the appropriate skills. In either case, the manager of a small business will be limited in what activities can be initiated and completed. Hence, there will be a focus on the near term, with an emphasis on allocating these scarce resources only to what is considered top priority activities. Further, as presented later in this document, the scope of activities and the consequent required IS support will evolve as the small business expands.

Unfortunately, the deployment of IS requires the development of a long-term plan and a large one-time commitment of both financial and human resources. As shown above, this is anathema to the manager of a small business. How can this conundrum be addressed? First, the currently available research into this question will be presented. Then, a proposed framework will be discussed.

RELATED RESEARCH

Pollard and Hayne (1998) investigated the information systems issues identified by small business managers across Canada. Via a two-round modified Delphi technique 34 useable responses were obtained.

Further, 12 follow-up interviews were conducted. The results indicate that the issues being faced by small business managers are different than those faced by large business. Also, in the area of IS the issues are in a continual state of change. This will require constant vigilance by the various stakeholders.

Belich and Dubinsky (1999) applied information theory to investigate the information processing among a group of small business exporters. They determined that information processing of the small businesses was not the same as that found in larger firms.

Taylor (1999) investigated the implementation of enterprise software in small businesses. The results of this research indicate that neither the businesses themselves, nor the software vendors are fully cognizant of the unique problems encountered by small business managers. Taylor (1999) presents a number of challenges that specifically address the implementation of enterprise systems for small business. The overall contention is that a successful implementation of an integrated system will provide significant benefits.

Hunter et al (forthcoming) identified two major themes regarding small business use of IS. These themes are "dependency" and "efficiency". The authors suggest that the adoption of IS increased the small business' dependency on an internal champion, and a series of external entities, including consultants and suppliers. This increased dependency, Hunter et al (forthcoming) suggest, results from the approaches to business (Stevenson, 1999) taken by the manager and the resource poverty (Thong et al, 1994). The efficiency theme suggests that IS is primarily used by small business managers as an operational tool to help complete daily activities.

Bridge and Peel (1999) found that medium sized businesses used computer software more than small businesses. They defined small businesses as those having less than 100 employees and medium firms as those having 100 – 500 employees. These size definitions are based on those employed by the European Commission (Storey, 1994). Bridge and Pell (1999) also determined, which is supported by Hunter et al (forthcoming) that small businesses employed computers mainly to support daily operations and tended not to use them to support decision-making or long term planning.

Dandridge and Levenburg (2000) investigated Internet use by small (fewer than 25 employees) businesses. They determined that very few small businesses were moving to this next step in the use of IS. While they found that IS were being employed for daily operations, there was little use of computerization for competitiveness aspects.

As the above research results indicate, there are differences when comparing the IS needs of small versus medium and large businesses. Thus, it is incumbent upon the IS and small business research community to adopt an approach which recognizes these differences.

Further, the above reported research, even when the uniqueness of small business use of IS is acknowledged, presents a snapshot view of the small business as though it were spatially and temporally constant. However, the underlying theme of the ideas presented in this document is that the dynamism of the small business, which dictates the ever changing requirements, which must be satisfied from the perspective of the business' on-going development. That is, the needs of the small business change as the process evolves from conceptualisation of the business opportunity through start-up and growth. This idea is supported by the research of McMullan and Long (1990) who suggest that small businesses continue to evolve, as they become self-sustaining entities.

McMullan and Long (1990) developed a Theory of Entrepreneurship, which considers embryonic, small, medium, and large businesses as ventures in progress. They suggest that entrepreneurs are engaged in a creative act of, "... impressing their vision on their chosen medium – the venture". (McMullan and Long, 1990:133). Therefore, differing IS requirements will evolve from the dynamics of a developing business. The challenge for the IS researcher is to recognize the changing context of the small business. The next section presents an overview description of the Theory of Entrepreneurship.

ADOPTING ASPECTS OF ENTREPRENEURIAL CHALLENGES

The McMullan and Long (1990) Theory of Entrepreneurship include five building blocks. The activity of entrepreneurship involves 1) risk taking, 2) business management and 3) innovation, and the entrepreneur is committed to 4) strategic, 5) venture development. In other words, the entrepreneur is creatively involved in applying his/her business management skills in developing a business venture, and by virtue of anticipating future uncertain outcomes is bearing risk. All five building blocks are employed in an integrated theory of entrepreneurship, the model of which is shown in Figure 1.

Figure 1: Modelling the entrepreneurial process

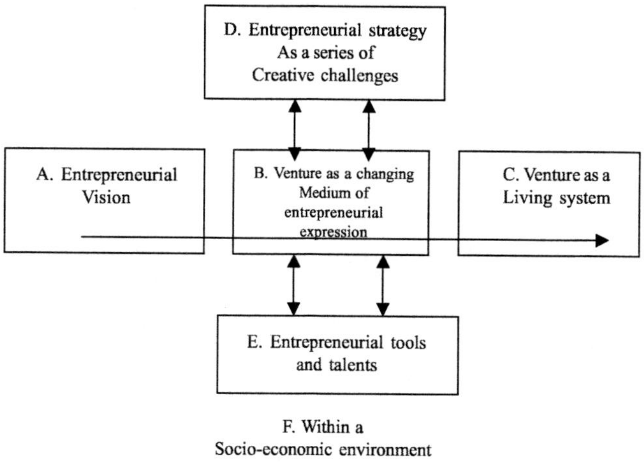

Adapted from McMullan and Long (1990:135)

Further, the entrepreneur undertakes strategic decisions in response to a series of challenges to developing the venture. Implementing these strategic decisions ultimately structures and defines the venture.

The components of the model may be described as follows:

A. Entrepreneurial Vision. The process commences with a vision of a desired venture outcome i.e. a business opportunity.

B. Venture as a Dynamic Medium of Expression. As an artist puts colour and form to the canvas to express his vision, the entrepreneur brings resources and people together who commit to a set of relationships in pursuit of the vision. The entrepreneur's action and the context of both the socio economic environment and the dynamics of the venture itself shape the venture.

C. Venture as a Living System. The above venture elaboration/structuring continues until it becomes a "living system no longer needing the entrepreneur's contribution to survive and prosper". (McMullan and Long, 1990, p.138) The vision is complete.

D. Self-Sustaining Organization or Living System. The organization is complete. The entrepreneur has succeeded in structuring the capacities common to living systems. The entrepreneurship process is complete.

E. Entrepreneurial Strategy. "The entrepreneur's strategies are in response to a series of creative challenges for developing a self-sustaining venture". (McMullan and Long, 1990:139). These strategies appropriately focus attention.

F. Entrepreneurial Tools and Talents. The entrepreneur must acquire the requisite skills and knowledge appropriate to the developmental tasks.

G. Socio Economic Environment. The venture must take into account both it's macro and microenvironments.

The theory goes on to suggest that, as shown in Figure 2, the entrepreneur is faced with ten organization building strategic challenges as the venture evolves from (A) vision, through (B) elaboration, to (C) a living system. These challenges are sorted into three broad groups (1) preparing the venture, (2) launching the venture and (3) growing the venture.

Figure 2: Evolving organizational challenges

GROUPING	STRAGEGIC CHALLENGES
Preparing	1. What business will we be in 2. What products/services will we manufacture and sell 3. What is our operating strategy
Launching	4. What resources will we employ 5. How will we produce 6. How will we sell and distribute our products
Growing	7. How will operating efficiencies be improved 8. How will we expand 9. How and when will we professionalize management 10. How will we continue to innovate

Adapted from McMullan and Long (1990: Chapters 5 & 7)

Of importance to the IS researcher, is to recognize the context of the subject business. Our suggestion is to undertake an IS research program using the aforementioned theory of entrepreneurship as a contextual model. The first focus of the research will examine a group of small businesses that are in the, growing the venture phase, as discussed below.

Figure 3 presents the challenges and developmental groupings in a slightly different and more detailed context. The component of this figure that applies most appropriately to the discussion presented in this document relates to the grouping titled, "Growing the Venture". The other two groupings are not pursued further in this document. These two groupings relate to planning and starting a venture, while the third grouping relates to on-going developmental components of the business. These latter stages represent the nearing of the ultimate goal of the entrepreneur and the necessity to adopt approaches more appropriately associated with activities of small business managers.

The growing the Venture grouping consists of four entrepreneurial challenges. The McMullan and Long (1990) Theory of Entrepreneurship number these challenges 7 through 10.

Challenge Seven, titled, "Standard operating Performance" relates to the development and implementation of operating efficiencies. With regards to IS, these efficiencies could be garnered through the automation of procedures, which support daily activities. Examples would include accounting and financial IS, as well as production management and inventory control systems. Earlier in this document, research projects were presented which determined that small business was indeed attempting to gain efficiencies by installing automated IS. The major concern, in this context, remains the consideration, by IS researchers, of the uniqueness of small businesses.

Challenge Eight is titled, "Expanding Strategically and Opportunistically". McMullan and Long (1990) suggest that the entrepreneur will continually engage in activities, which will contribute to the growth of the venture. However, within the context of the small business manager, expansion may not necessarily be a priority. Indeed, the small business manager, because of such concepts as resource poverty, may be solely concerned with the viable maintenance of current ongoing operations. Whether the goal is entrepreneurial expansion or managerial maintenance, it is important to be able to appropriately respond to the changing environment. Thus, IS relating to environmental reconnaissance should be considered. These systems could include investigations of financing alternatives or marketing IS. In general, systems should be considered that support a homeostatic balance within the business and allow it to evolve in response to environmental changes.

The Ninth Challenge, "Professionalizing Middle Management" relates to the necessity, on the part of the small business manager, to

Figure 3: Stages in developing an entrepreneurial venture

Entrepreneurial Challenge	Corresponding Attribute of Living System	Broad-Range Groupings
1. Identifying realizable Opportunities	All living systems have identifiable environments	
2. Designing feasible Products	All living systems have boundaries, which distinguish Them from their environment	Preparing the Venture
3. Planning resource Requirements	All living systems are composed of interacting parts involving Some functional differentiation And specialization	
4. Negotiating resource And client contracts	All living systems must take in energy and information	
5. Engineering efficient Production	All living systems transform energy and information from One state to another	Launching the Venture
6. Regularizing sales Revenue	All living system export outputs into their environments	
7. Standardizing Operating performance	All living systems have cyclical patterns of exchange activities Within the system and within The environment	
8. Expanding strategically And opportunistically	All living systems are characterized by homeostatic balance and Governance mechanisms, evolving Systematically to better fit their Environment	Growing the Venture
9. Professionalizing Middle management	All living systems become differentiated over time into more And more independent roles	
10. Institutionalizing Innovative capacity	All living systems are characterized by negative entropy	

Adapted from McMullan and Long (1990:267)

delegate some duties. Thus, it is necessary to implement a more formal approach to conducting operations. This requires the development of standardized operating procedures and planning for the acquisition of appropriate skills. The IS related activities of this Challenge are concerned with consolidation. That is, the small business manager must take action to ensure there is co-ordinated employment of IS that promote a standardized approach to conducting business. Consequently, it the small business manager must also ensure that the necessary skills are available to support the operation of the above IS. In this instance, the IS researcher will investigate the interaction effects of skills and standardization of processes. Again, it is incumbent upon the researcher to recognize the uniqueness of the small business environment in which these factors exist.

The Tenth, and last Challenge is titled, "Institutionalizing Innovative Capacity". Here the small business manager must remain cognizant of striving for continual innovation. The establishment of IS to support Research and Development and environmental intelligence would be appropriate initiatives.

CONCLUSION

This document has presented the suggestion that IS researchers consider the Theory of Entrepreneurship as a framework to adopt when investigating small business. Much of the existing research into the use of IS by small business adopts a perspective more appropriate, and in some cases based upon, large business. There is not sufficient consideration for the uniqueness of small business. Where these unique factors are considered, the investigation is conducted as a snap shot of a static situation. The contention of the proposal described in this document is that small business is both unique and continually evolving. The proposed framework responds to this situation. The challenge, then, is for researchers to adopt this framework and initiate projects which will further elucidate the understanding of how IS may be employed to support small business.

REFERENCES

Belich, T. J. and A. J. Dubinsky. "Information Processing Among Exporters: An Empirical Examination of Small Firms", *Journal of Marketing Theory and Practice*, Vol. 7, No. 4, Fall 1999, pp. 45-58.

Bridge, J. and M. J. Peel. "A Study of Computer Usage and Strategic Planning in the SME Sector", *International Small Business journal*, Vol. 17, No. 4, July – September, 1999, pp. 82-87.

Coghlan, D. "An Intervals Perspective of OD in IT Enabled Change", *Organizational Development Journal*, Vol. 19, No. 1, Spring 2001, pp. 49-56.

Cragg, P. & King, M. "Small-firm Computing: Motivators and Inhibitors, *MIS Quarterly*, 1993, pp. 47-60.

Dandrige, T. and N. M. Levenburg. "High-tech Potential? An Exploratory Study of Very Small Firms' Usage of the Internet", *International Small Business journal*, Vol. 18, No. 2, January – March 2000, pp. 81-91.

Hunter, M. Gordon, M. Diochon, D. Pugsley, and B. Wright. "Unique Challenges for Small Business Adoption of information Technology: The case of the Nova Scotia Ten", chapter in Burgess, S. (Ed.), **Managing Information Technology in small Business: Challenges and Solutions**, Idea Group Publishing, Hershey, PA.

Industry Canada. **Your Guide to Government of Canada Services and Support for Small Business: Trends and Statistics**, (Catalogue No. C1-10/1997E), Ottawa, Canadian Government Publishing Centre, 1997.

Long, W. A. "The Meaning of Entrepreneurship", *American Journal of Small Business*, Vol. 8, No. 2, Fall 1983, pp. 47-56.

Long, W. A. and W. E. McMullan. "Mapping the Opportunity Identification Process", in Hornaday, J. A. et al (Eds.), **Frontiers of Entrepreneurship Research**, Babson College, Wellesley, MA., 1984.

Longnecker, J., Moore, C., & Petty, J. **Small Business Management**, Cincinnati, South-Western College Printing, 1997.

McMullan, W. E. and W. A. Long. **Developing New Ventures: The Entrepreneurial Option**, Harcourt Brace Jovanovich, Publishers, San Diego, USA, 1990.

McMullan, W. E. and W. A. Long. "Entrepreneurship Education in the Nineties", *Journal of Business Venturing*, Summer 1987, pp. 261-275.

Pollard, C. and S. Hayne. "The Changing Faces of Information Systems Issues in Small Firms, *International Small Business Journal*, Vol. 16, No. 3, 1998, pp.70-87.

Stevenson, H. H. "A Perspective of Entrepreneurship", in Stevenson, H. H., H. I. Grousebeck, M. J. Roberts and A. Bhide (Eds.). **New Business Ventures and the Entrepreneur**, pp. 3-17, Boston: Irwin McGraw-Hill, 1999.

Stevenson, H. H. "A New Paradigm for Entrepreneurial Management", in *Proceedings from the 7th Anniversary Symposium on Entrepreneurship*, Boston, Harvard Business School, 1984.

Storey, D. J. **Understanding the Small Business Sector**, Routledge, London, 1994.

Taylor, J. "Fitting Enterprise Software in smaller Companies", *Management Accounting*, Vol. 80, No. 8, 1999, pp. 36-39.

Thong, J., C. Yap, and K. Raman. "Engagement of External Expertise in Information Systems Implementation", *Journal of Management Information Systems*, Vol. 11, No. 2, 1994, pp.209-223.

A Methodology for On-line Case Discussion: An Experiment in an Executive MBA Program

Henri Isaac
Assistant Professor, Paris Duaphine University, France
Tel: 3 (314) 405-4308, Fax: 3 (314) 405-4084, isaac@dauphine.fr

ABSTRACT

This paper presents the results of an experiment conducted in an executive MBA program to investigate the use of on-line case discussion. The paper gives the pedagogical context for the experiment and describes the experimental method. Finally, it discusses the results of a satisfaction questionnaire completed by the participants of the experiment.

INTRODUCTION

The Dauphine-UQAM Executive MBA program was created in 1999 by the University of Paris Dauphine and the University of Quebec at Montreal (UQAM). It is offered in various countries in Europe including France, Lebanon, and Turkey, as well as in Canada. It is a part-time MBA program that is taught three days per month (Friday, Saturday, and Sunday) for 24 months. Thirty-eight students enrolled in the program in September 2001. In order to create a competitive advantage over other executive MBA programs in Europe, the program sponsors chose to rely extensively on information technologies in the program's courses. An intranet system was established for the courses based on WebCT tools. Training on the use of the different WebCT tools (on-line documents, newsgroup, chat, electronic blackboard) was provided to all professors and students participating in the program.

In one of the courses in the program, "Information and Information Technologies", an experiment was conducted using WebCT tools to facilitate on-line case discussion. The purpose of the experiment was to determine if case discussion can be conducted effectively on-line. Case discussion is a key pedagogical method used in MBA programs, and thus we were interested in determining if technology-based tools can be used to create interactivity that is similar to that found in classroom. This paper presents the results of that experiment.

EXPERIMENTAL METHOD

The population participating in the experiment where the students enrolled in the Executive MBA in Fall 2001, consisting of 38 executives. A case was made available on the program's intranet at the beginning of the "Information and Information Technologies" course in September. The course, which ended in December, was divided into ten classroom sessions (two sessions per month). The case chosen illustrated the themes of the last two sessions of the course in December. The case presents a traditional French company going into e-business. Its conceptual themes are linked to e-business and include value migration, business process reengineering, IT infrastructure, extranets, and IT project management. The case examines the problem of going digital and using electronic relations to conduct business.

Most of the students did not have experience in on-line discussion before entering the Executive MBA program. Therefore, we trained the students in on-line discussion before starting the case discussion by conducting four on-line sessions on specific subjects related to the course.

During the course, we scheduled different milestones related to the case in order to enable all students to have time to read the case, prepare it, and participate to the discussions on the intranet. As the case discussion would be difficult without questions to help students prepare their contributions, we prepared four such questions. Then we divided the case discussion into four sessions of 45 minutes each with each session dedicated to one question. For example, the first question of the case was to establish a strategic analysis of the company based on a classical SWOT analysis.

To manage the case discussions, we used different electronic communication tools in WebCT to build an on-line case discussion system. These tools and their use in the experiment were:

- Calendar: Each on-line session was scheduled using this tool. The tool generating an electronic reminder to the students each time a new session was scheduled.
- Chat: This tools was used for on-line case discussion. For four weeks prior to the classroom session on the case, we scheduled a 45 minute discussion on one question on Wednesday at 9 :00 p.m. Each student was supposed to log in and participate to the discussion. Because the students were executives, only about 20 students were on-line each Wednesday. The total discussion was recorded and made available soon afterward on a dedicated newsgroup so that missing students could read the discussion.
- Newsgroup: We created a dedicated newsgroup for the case discussion. The newsgroup was divided into five discussion areas, one for each question about the case, and one for the recorded on-line discussions. Students were expected to post for each question a short assignment consisting in a one page Wordä document.

The evaluation of the participation was based on the tracking tool in WebCT and on the analysis of individual contributions to the debate.

EVALUATION OF SYSTEM SATISFACTION

After all case discussions were finished, a questionnaire was completed by the students. The questionnaire asks for a subjective evaluation of the efficiency of the system and the satisfaction of the students with the system by collecting opinions on specific aspects of the system using a 1 to 5 Likert scale. Two open-ended questions were included asking for the three main positive and three main negative aspects of the system in order to collect qualitative evaluations of the system. Because of space limitations, the questionnaire is not included in this paper; it is available upon request from the author. We received 29 usable questionnaires from the 38 students (76%). The responses to the relevant questions are shown in Table 1.

Participation

Several dimensions of participation were evaluated in the questionnaire. We asked whether the on-line system facilitated personal participation in the debate. We also asked if it was easy for the student to give his/her personal opinion in the debate. Finally we asked students whether their participation was higher than in classroom case discussion.

The average rate of participation was 70%. Non-participation might be explained by the nature of the students (executive) and the scheduled time of the discussions (9 :00 p.m.). The length of the session (45 minutes) was enough for most of the participants (Q6).

Students said that they were active in discussion (Q7). This response is consistent with what we observed during the on-line sessions and with the fact that students prepared the session (Q8). The ability to handle on-line discussion is a critical point in participation. Stu-

Table 1: Results of the satisfaction questionnaire

	Mean
Q4- The technical system is satisfactory.	**3.96**
Q5- The objective of each discussion session is known in advance.	**4.36**
Q6- The duration of the on-line sessions is sufficient.	**4.36**
Q7- During the sessions I actively participated in discussion.	**3.39**
Q8- I prepared the sessions.	**4.07**
Q9- I used the newsgroup before and after discussions	**2.89**
Q10- Overall, on-line discussions were as thorough as classical sessions.	**2.75**
Q11- It is easy to follow conversation during chat.	**2.68**
Q12- It is easy to express myself during debates.	**3.43**
Q13- I express myself better during chat than during class sessions	**2.32**
Q14- It is easy for me to express myself in a concise fashion during debates.	**3.50**
Q15- I am capable of handling on-line discussion.	**4.54**
Q16- The division of cases into four sessions facilitated discussion.	**3.89**
Q17- The case debates were longer than during a classical session.	**3.68**
Q18- Each question was treated in more depth than during a classical sessions.	**3.00**
Q19- I can more easily express myself than during classical sessions.	**2.65**
Q20- I give my own opinion more easily.	**2.67**
Q21- The exchanges are more direct.	**3.32**
Q22- The debates focus rapidly on essentials.	**2.93**
Q23- There was less digression than during debate in a classical session.	**2.54**
Q24- The interventions of the professor permitted a more animated debate.	**4.39**
Q25- The interventions of the professor refocused the debate.	**4.36**
Q26- There were more exchanges between students than between students and the professor.	**3.64**
Q27- Overall I appreciate on-line case discussion.	**3.93**
Q28- On-line case discussion is more efficient than classical session.	**2.54**
Q29- I get more from on-line discussion than from classical sessions.	**2.54**

dents felt that they had the ability to handle on-line case discussion after the training period (Q15). Students also felt comfortable with technical aspects of the discussion (Q4). However, they say it not easy to follow the discussions (Q11). This might be explained by the fact that during this experiment, the average number of participants was about 20 students.

Handling 20 students in an on-line debate is difficult; it is the role of the professor to encourage debate and make sure all students participate. Most students agreed that the professor in the course intervened appropriately during the on-line debate (Q24). On-line discussion is not as easy to control, however. We observed some students who logged-in but just "listened" to the on-line discussion and did not participate. The number of participants is an obstacle to focused debate even though we divided the case discussion into four main questions.

Nature of On-line Discussion

The case discussion lasted four sessions of 45 minutes each for a total of three hours. This duration enables more time than we usually have in a classroom. Three hours of discussion enables the students to discuss details and to go into deep analysis of problems embedded in the case. The students felt that the discussion was more in-depth on-line and that many more aspects of the case were debated (Q18). We also asked if the on-line interface made it easier for the student to give a personal opinion without the presence of group pressure. Students felt that there was little change from classroom discussion in this regard (Q20). Students did feel, however, that the direction of the discussion changed; they had more exchange between participants on-line than in a traditional classroom discussion (Q26) and these exchanges were more direct (Q21). We also evaluated if on-line discussion was more focused than in a classroom where sometimes students forget the initial question. Participants did not think on-line discussion was more focused than in traditional classroom discussion (Q23). In addition, students did not think they got more from the on-line discussion than from a classroom discussion (Q29).

Student Satisfaction

The overall satisfaction of the students was high (average 7.14 on a 1 to 10 scale). This satisfaction may be related to the learning of a new way of interacting rather than to the efficiency of the system. Students were asked about whether on-line case discussion is more efficient than traditional discussion and their response was neutral (Q28). Asked if they participated more on-line than in a traditional case discussion, students answered negatively (Q13). What is also a noticeable is the fact that few students use the newsgroup before or after the on-line discussion (Q9). The qualitative answers provided additional confirmation of the answers to the questions in the questionnaire.

CONCLUSION

This experiment tested a system for on-line case discussion in an executive MBA program. The system was successful with a good student participation and a good level of satisfaction for the students. In this experiment, we were concerned about whether we would get the same interactions as we get in traditional classroom case discussion. The experiment suggests that students do not see much difference between on-line and classroom discussions. It also suggests that students do not change their attitude when chatting, which implies that the on-line interface is neutral for this type of executive student. What is identified as an obstacle is the number of participants. Our group was too large, making it difficult for some students to express themselves and to follow the debate. Another finding of this experiment, which is consistent with the literature (Asensio and al., 2000 ; Salmon 2000), is the key role of the moderator in animating the participation.

REFERENCES

Asensio, M., Hodgson, V. & Trehan, K. (2000), *Is there a difference: Contrasting experiences of face to face and online learning*, in: M. Asensio, J. Foster, V. Hodgson & D. McConnell (Eds) *Networked Learning 2000* (Lancaster, Lancaster University & University of Sheffield).

Salmon, G. (2000). *E-moderating: the key to teaching and learning online*. London: Kogan Page.

Success of Outsourcing Customer Relationship Management Functions: An Empirical Study

Babita Gupta, PhD
Management Information Systems, California State University
Tel: (831) 582-4186, Fax: (831) 582-4251, babita_gupta@csumb.edu

Lakshmi S. Iyer, PhD
Information Systems and Operations Management, Bryan School of Business and Economics
The University of North Carolina at Greensboro, Tel: (336) 334-4984, Fax: (336) 334-4083, lsiyer@uncg.edu

INTRODUCTION

Explosive growth of the Internet is changing the nature of competition among companies and customer service is emerging as a key differentiator among competitors. This has changed the customer-related business requirements for all types of companies. With firms increasing their web operations, customers now have the ability to contact the organizations they do business with through various means (such as email, fax, call centers, and web based forms). This has lead companies to consider Customer Relationship Management (CRM) as an important part of its competitive strategy.

CRM is generally stated as a strategy that companies use to identify, manage and improve relationships with their customers. Thomspon (2001) defines CRM as a company's activities related to developing and retaining customers through increased satisfaction and loyalty. eCRM is a term generally used when a company's customer service operations are on the web. According to Cahners In-Stat Group (2001), worldwide revenues from CRM software application will increase from $9.4 billion in 2001 to approximately $30.6 billion in 2005. According to Tom Kaneshige of CIO Enterprise Magazine, CRM investments are expected to exceed $90 billion by 2003 (Kos 2001).

For effective CRM, companies must generally adopt a customer-centric philosophy to achieve goals such as increase in sales, customer loyalty, customer service and support, and better and effective distribution of products. CRM applications must be designed to integrate all the customer communication points across various functional areas of a company. CRM products are categorized as: operational (improving sales, marketing or customer service efficiency), analytical (collect better customer data and mining this data to formulate customer centric strategies), and collaborative (for eCRM, one-to-one marketing etc.) (Walter et al. 2001).

As companies engage in outsourcing, information systems functions of increasingly high asset specificity are being outsourced. CRM functions are one major IS area where companies are outsourcing. While there are many off-the-shelf CRM software packages, it is generally very difficult to integrate these into company wide CRM initiatives and also into other existing application like Enterprise Resource Planning (ERP).

While there are a number of studies for evaluating outsourcing of IS functions (Grover et al. 1996, Lee and Kim 1999, Maltz and Ellram 1999, King 2000, Kini 2000, Yang and Huang 2000), there is little literature on outsourcing CRM functions. This study hopes to contribute to the IS field by studying CRM outsourcing partnerships through an integrated framework of resource dependence and transaction cost economics. This study focuses on the CRM vendor-company relationship by extending the work of Grover et al. (1996). We plan to conduct a survey of companies that are either planning CRM initiatives or that already have an active CRM implementation and are outsourcing these functions. We plan to develop a framework to evaluate how these companies select a CRM vendor, how they adopt and integrate CRM technologies into their existing infrastructure and what factors affect CRM outsourcing success. We hope to develop a framework to answer questions such as:

1. How do the tangible characteristics of a CRM vendor like the length of operation, market reputation, geographic proximity, product features, and other tangible components influence CRM outsourcing success?
2. How do the CRM product components provided by the CRM vendor like reliability, security, compatibility, database quality and centralization, data warehousing capabilities, accuracy, maintenance requirements influence CRM outsourcing success?
3. Is there any relationship between partnership (between the company and CRM vendor) quality and CRM outsourcing success?

THE PROPOSED STUDY MODEL AND CONSTRUCTS

Quality of service provided by CRM vendor is an important consideration in the outsourcing decision. This study adopts and adapts the two dimensions of SERVQUAL instrument construct used in Grover et al. (1996) study, tangibles and reliability and adds a new one, CRM technology.

We also use the flip side of this concept by considering the internal management issues of the outsourcing company and if those issues affect the partnership quality and the success of CRM outsourcing.

Generally, relationship between organizations is categorized as being either transactional or partnership style. A transactional style relationship is well specified in its contractual obligations. In contrast, the partnership style relationships include risk and benefit sharing with a view to establish long-term commitment (Henderson 1990). Since CRM initiatives are not confined to a particular function but rather cut across various functions of an organization, it complicates the nature CRM implementation through outsourcing. To evaluate the company-CRM vendor relationship, we use four dimensions of communication, trust, cooperation and satisfaction.

Constructs:

1. Quality of service provided by CRM vendor
   - Tangibles of CRM vendor (e.g. physical space, geographic proximity, number of employees, number of other customers etc.)
   - Reliability of CRM vendor
   - CRM Technology (product features, does one vendor provide better fit with the outsourcing company's existing technology that others, etc.)
2. Partnership
3. Management Issues of Outsourcing Company
4. Outsourcing Success

The dependent variable is the success of CRM outsourcing measured by using the widely used concept of satisfaction with benefits from CRM outsourcing gained by a company (Grover et al. 1996).

RESEARCH METHODOLOGY

Data will be collected using a pilot tested survey based on above constructs. Both mail as well as web based survey will be conducted to increase the number of responses. The survey will be aimed at senior level executives in sales/marketing/Customer support functions of the

Figure 1

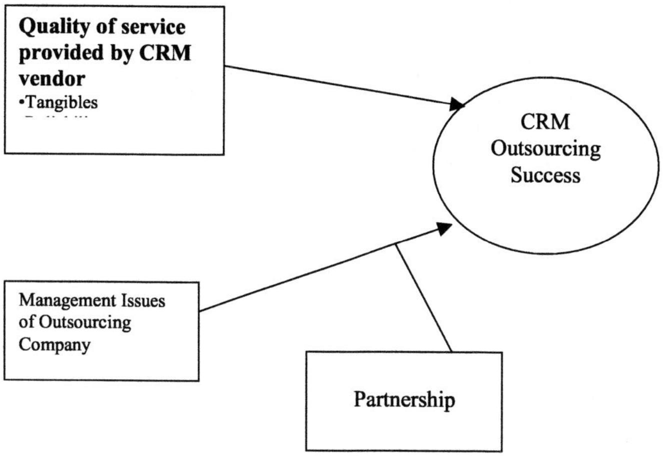

CRM and/or e-CRM outsourcing companies. The data will be analyzed and reported in future presentations.

SUMMARY

This is a research in progress in which we plan to develop a framework to evaluate how companies select CRM vendors, how they adopt and integrate CRM technologies into their existing infrastructure and what factors affect CRM outsourcing success. To validate the model we plan to conduct a survey of companies that are either planning CRM initiatives or those that already have an active CRM implementation and are outsourcing these functions.

REFERENCES

Cahners In-Stat Group (2001), http://www.instat.com/pr/2001/ec0105st_pr.htm

Grover, V, M. J. Cheon and J. T. C. Teng (1996). The effect of service quality and partnership on the outsourcing of information systems function. *Journal of Management Information Systems*, 12 (4), 89-116.

Henderson, J.C. (1990). Plugging into strategic partnerships: the critical IS connection. *Sloan Management Review*, 30, 37-18.

King, W. R. (2000). Developing a framework for analyzing IS sourcing, *Information & Management*, 37 (6).

Kini, R. B. (2000). Information systems outsourcing evaluation strategy: A precursor for outsourcing. *International Journal of Management*, 17 (1).

Kos, A. J., Sockel, H. H. And Louis K. Falk (2001). Customer relationship management opportunities. *Ohio CPA Journal*,60 (1) .

Lee, J. and Y. Kim (1999). Effect of partnership quality on IS outsourcing: Conceptual framework and empirical validation. *Journal of Management Information Systems,* 15 (4), 29-61.

Maltz A. and L. Ellram (1999). Outsourcing supply management. *Journal of Supply Chain Management*, 35 (2).

Thompson, B. (2001) "What is CRM", retrieved from the web at http://www.CRMguru.com, January 2001.

Walter, A., T. Ritter and H. G. Gemunden (2001). Value creation in buyer-seller relationships: Theoretical considerations and empirical results from a supplier's perspective. *Industrial Marketing Management*, 30 (4).

Yang C. and J. Huang (2000). A decision model for IS outsourcing. *International Journal of Information Management,* 20 (3).

Is It Cool To Be a Geek? Have Students' Perceptions of the IS Profession Changed in the Last Decade?

Morgan M. Jennings, Charles H. Mawhinney and Janos Fustos
CIS Department, Metropolitan State College of Denver, Colorado
Tel: (303) 556-8491, Fax: (303) 556-8044

ABSTRACT

Despite the recent downturn in the Information Technology (IT) economy and the seemingly widespread layoffs, there is still a shortage of qualified personnel that is predicted to continue into the foreseeable future. Previous researchers felt that part of the shortage is attributable to misperceptions of the work-style of Information Systems (IS) graduates. This paper repeats a study of undergraduate business majors that was performed in 1989, and compares the perceptions of contemporary students with those previously reported. We found that contemporary students do indeed have similar perceptions of the background and work-styles of IS graduates.

INTRODUCTION

More than a decade ago, Mawhinney, et al, [4][5] looked at undergraduate business students' perceptions of the Information Systems (IS) profession and found that their perceptions were inaccurate and narrowly focused. Have such perceptions changed over the intervening years? Have, for example, the World Wide Web and publicity about dot.com companies and millionaires influenced the perception of IS careers?

The motivation for the original study was a national decline in IS enrollments in the late 1980s that was adversely affecting staffing in the information systems industry. There is still a need to explore this topic because a decade plus later there is a demonstrated lack of qualified workers. According to the Information Technology Association of America (ITAA) over three-quarters of a million skilled workers are currently needed [1].

Mawhinney, et al, [4][5] believed that the decline in enrollments was due to misperceptions about IS on the part of high school students. The popular understanding was that information systems professionals worked in isolation writing computer programs. This perception is partly true if you look at the majority of the entry-level positions for an IS person.

Another reason for a low number of people entering the field may be that this career opportunity is simply not heavily promoted in high schools. A study out of Australia [8] notes that engineering, mathematics, and science receive more press from high schools than IS. They also report, (a.) "overall perceptions by both male and female students of the IT degree as difficult and demanding" [p.46] and (b.) perceptions from solely female study participants are that IT people work alone, have little contact with other people and the profession is strongly associated with high math skills [8]. The findings of [4] were similar. Both [4] and [8] studies were conducted in the mid to late 1980s, though the later study had collected data through 2000. Statistical data comparing any differences-over-time were not included in the article so it is not clear if perceptions have changed.

There are high school programs that encourage young people to explore information systems careers. For example, Wings 21 [3] located in Omaha, NE provides long-term exposure to technology and careers. This kind of long-term positive exposure to computer technology may be a means to promote accurate information regarding IS jobs as well as alleviate anxiety related to use of technology.

In addition to a lack of understanding related to what an IS worker does in his/her job, the dropout rate within entry-level college IS courses is a problem [6]. Many students feel they are computer literate until they enter an IS program. The skills that they possess and the skills needed within an IS degree are likely to be disparate. Rather than a sink or swim attitude on the part of colleges and universities, time spent coaching and encouraging students on relevant skills for the IS degree may help them complete the program [2]. This requires providing meaningful situations in which to use technology [7].

This current study revisits the original study [4] and looks at perceptions held by current undergraduate business students. It will compare their perceptions of IS characteristics against those of their own desired position. It will also compare the responses of the current students against the responses in the original study.

METHODOLOGY

Subjects

Five-hundred and nineteen usable responses were received from 15 sections of our entry-level computing course. Like the original study, our sample came from a course that is taught from a common syllabus and is a combination of hands-on computing labs and hardware, software and personal computing concepts. This course is required of all business majors and is often the first exposure they have to IS.

Some institutional differences between the two groups of students should be noted. The original study took place in a private college with traditional full-time residential students who were required to take the course as first semester freshmen. The current study took place in a public college with non-traditional commuter students who had some flexibility concerning when they took the course.

Instrument and Procedure

We utilized the original 18-item Likert scale questionnaire [4] (see appendix) with some minor adaptations. The first 9 items assessed perceptions of the work-styles of graduates of the IS program. The second 9 items assessed the respondent's own background and job work-style-preferences. The responses were converted to a numeric scale (SD=1, SA=5).

The original study used a factor analysis and subscale reliability analysis to determine if any subscales existed in the instrument. There were no sufficiently interpretable and reliable subscales, so the perception measures were treated as separate items. We used the separate items for comparison purposes.

Our data was collected during the first week of the semester. The only demographic collected was the student's major. [4][5] used a PRE and POST procedure. The first nine questions were included in both the original survey (PRE) and a follow-up mail survey (POST) eight months later. The remaining nine questions of the 18-item questionnaire were included in the mail survey only. Four-hundred and six responses were collected from the classrooms and 115 through the mail.

RESULTS

Two null hypotheses were tested. The first hypothesis was the same as the original study.

H_1: *Students perceive no difference between the work-style of the typical IS graduate and their own expected starting position's work-style.*

The second two-part hypothesis compares the responses from the current students against the responses from the original study:

H_{2a}: *The two groups of students had the same expectations for the work-style of their own starting positions.*

H_{2b}: *The two groups of students had the same perceptions of the work-style of the typical IS graduate.*

H_1

Table 1 shows the analysis (t-tests for paired comparisons of the corresponding means) for H_1: IS graduates perceived work-style (IS) and for their own expected starting positions (SELF).

Table 1: Perceptions of MSCD self versus IS graduate work styles

n = 519			Mean			Standard Deviation		
Item #	I S	S E L F	t-value	Signif	I S	S E L F	f-value	Signif
1	2.83	2.71	2.43	*	0.92	1.03	17.59	***
2	2.79	2.99	-3.67	***	1.02	1.17	18.32	***
3	2.78	2.24	10.94	***	0.93	1.00	0.02	
4	3.58	4.19	-5.81	***	0.88	2.32	0.60	
5	2.83	2.45	7.61	***	0.95	0.98	1.65	
6	2.68	2.12	11.73	***	0.94	0.94	4.13	*
7	3.17	2.63	10.02	***	1.03	1.15	14.07	***
8	3.26	3.49	-4.82	***	0.88	1.01	9.93	**
9	3.33	2.89	8.30	***	0.92	1.15	32.61	***
(2-tailed) * $p \leq 0.05$ ** $p \leq 0.01$ *** $p \leq 0.001$								

H_{2a} (Table 2) and H_{2b} (Table 3)

The responses from the current students are compared against the responses from the original study concerning, first (Table 1) their own background and preferred work-style and second (Table 2) the background and work-styles of IS graduates. The summary values provided by [4] from the original study were used to perform the analysis (t-tests for independent samples) for the comparisons.

Overall, the average perceptions of the IS graduate's work-style were different from the average expectations of the students' own starting positions for all 9 items (H1, Table1). This is consistent with the findings of [4], except they did not find differences for the first two items. Six of the 9 items showed differences related to H_{2a} (Table2) and four of the 9 items showed differences for H_{2b} (Table 3).

Table 4 summarizes the analysis of student's perceptions.

Table 2: Perceptions of self: MSCD versus Bently students

			Mean			Standard Deviation		
Item #	MSCD	Bentley	t-value	Signif	MSCD	Bentley	f-value	Signif
1	2.71	2.59	1.14		1.03	1.04	0.99	
2	2.99	2.52	4.07	***	1.17	1.11	1.11	
3	2.24	1.77	4.76	***	1.00	0.72	1.93	*
4	4.19	4.10	0.41		2.32	0.65	12.69	*
5	2.45	2.21	2.45	*	0.98	0.84	1.37	*
6	2.12	1.67	4.80	***	0.94	0.72	1.69	*
7	2.63	2.21	3.71	***	1.15	0.85	1.83	*
8	3.49	3.41	0.89		1.01	0.90	1.25	
9	2.89	2.58	2.65	**	1.15	0.98	1.38	*
(2-tailed) * $p \leq 0.05$ ** $p \leq 0.01$ *** $p \leq 0.001$								

Table 3: Perceptions of IS graduates: MSCD versus Bentley students

			Mean			Standard Deviation		
Item #	MSCD	Bentley	t-value	Signif	MSCD	Bentley	f-value	Signif
1	2.83	2.61	2.18	*	0.92	1.01	0.82	
2	2.79	2.72	0.66		1.02	1.08	0.88	
3	2.78	2.90	-1.34		0.93	0.90	1.07	
4	3.58	3.39	2.05	*	0.88	0.89	0.97	
5	2.83	2.72	1.22		0.95	0.86	1.21	
6	2.68	2.65	0.34		0.94	0.89	1.11	
7	3.17	3.28	-1.12		1.03	0.94	1.20	
8	3.26	3.09	2.00	*	0.88	0.79	1.25	
9	3.33	3.52	-2.07	*	0.92	0.73	1.58	*
(2-tailed) * $p \leq 0.05$ ** $p \leq 0.01$ *** $p \leq 0.001$								

Table 4: Summary of analysis

Questions	H_1: MSCD self relative to an IS grad	H_{2a}: MSCD self relative to Bentley self	H_{2b}: MSCD IS grad relative to Bentley IS grad
1. Math background	weaker		stronger
2. Computer background	stronger	stronger	
3. Time writing programs	less	more	
4. Time with others	more		more
5. Time working alone	less	more	
6. Involved in HW design	less	more	
7. Computer people interact	less	more	
8. Starting salary	higher		higher
9. Help select systems	less	more	less

SUMMARY AND CONCLUSIONS

From these results, H_1 can be rejected and it can be concluded that our students do perceive numerous differences between the work-style of the typical IS graduate and their own expected starting position's work-style. This seems to indicate that like the students 12 years ago, current students prefer more interaction with other people than they perceive an IS career to provide.

H_{2a} is also rejected. It should be expected that students would have a stronger computer background than students of twelve years prior. The MSCD students also exhibit differences in their preferred work-style, more in keeping with their perception of the work-style of IS graduates. This difference may be attributable to a higher number of IS majors. We do not have data from the original study to make a comparison. Another possibility is that business students in general perceive themselves and jobs as more technically-oriented.

It seems that the perceptions of the two groups of students regarding the background and work-style of IS graduates are more alike than different and we would therefore not reject H_{2b}. While 4 of the 9 items were different, 5 were not. The differences were not strong statistically nor strongly related to the questions concerning the work-style differences between programmers and system analysts (Please see the original study for a description of the questionnaire development).

Our hope was that we would find that students' perceptions of an IS career are more accurate. If so, then the issue would seem to be one of reducing the drop out rate by helping them succeed through coaching or other means of encouragement. We found, however, that inaccurate perceptions seem to persist. We will need to allocate resources for long-term solutions. Within high schools seems a likely choice, where a combination of accurate and persistent promotion of IS careers and opportunities to experience realistic use of information technology could be provided.

APPENDIX: THE QUESTIONNAIRE

My major is: ______________________________

The following questions deal with your perception of the undergraduate Computer Information Systems program at Metropolitan State College of Denver. Please indicate the strength of your agreement/ disagreement with each statement by circling the letter(s) that best describe your feeling about or reaction to each statement.

Legend: Strongly Agree Agree Undecided Disagree Strongly Disagree

The typical graduate of this program:	SA	A	U	D	DS
1. Is a whiz at mathematics.	SA	A	U	D	DS
2. Entered Metro with a strong prior background in computers.	SA	A	U	D	DS
During his/her first job after graduation, the typical graduate of this program:					
3. Spends most of his/her working time writing computer programs.	SA	A	U	D	DS
4. Spends most of his/her working time interacting with other persons.	SA	A	U	D	DS
5. Spends most of his/her time working alone.	SA	A	U	D	DS
6. Designs new computer hardware.	SA	A	U	D	DS
7. Interacts mostly with other computer people.	SA	A	U	D	DS
8. Has a starting salary above the average Metro graduate.	SA	A	U	D	DS
9. Helps managers select new computer systems.	SA	A	U	D	DS
The following questions deal with your assessment of your own background and job preferences					
I believe that I:	SA	A	U	D	DS
10. I am a whiz at mathematics.	SA	A	U	D	DS
11. Entered Metro with a strong prior background in computers.	SA	A	U	D	DS
During my first job after graduation, I expect to:					
12. Spend most of my working time writing computer programs.	SA	A	U	D	DS
13. Spend most of my working time interacting with other persons.	SA	A	U	D	DS
14. Spend most of my time working alone.	SA	A	U	D	DS
15. Design new computer hardware.	SA	A	U	D	DS
16. Interact mostly with other computer people.	SA	A	U	D	DS
17. Have a starting salary above the average Metro graduate.	SA	A	U	D	DS
18. Help managers select new computer systems.	SA	A	U	D	DS

REFERENCES

[1] Bredin, S., & Malyan-Smith, J. "On the fast track," *Techniques (Association for Career and Technical Education)*, 2000, 38-40. (online database:Wilson Select, accessed Sept, 2001).

[2] Compeau, D.H., C.A. & Huff, S. "Social cognitive theory and individual reactions to computing technology: A longitudinal study," *MIS Quarterly*, *23* (2), 1999, 145-158. (online database: WilsonSelect, accessed Sept., 2001).

[3] Greensberg, R. "Filling the gap," *Techniques (Association for Career and Technical Education)*, 2000, 2-27. (online database: First Search, accessed Sept., 2001).

[4] Mawhinney, C.H., Cale, E.G., jr., & Callaghan, D.R. "Freshman expectations of information systems careers versus their own careers," *CIS Educator Forum*, *2* (3), Spring 1990, 2-8.

[5] Mawhinney, C.H., Callaghan, D.R., & Cale, E.G., jr. "Freshman perceptions of the CIS graduate's workstyle," in *SIGCSE Bulletin*, *21* (1), February 1989, 78-82.

[6] Myers, M.E., & Beise, C.M. "Nerd work: Attractors and barriers perceived by students entering the IT field," in *Proceedings of the ACM SICCPR Conference* (San Diego, CA), 2001, 201-204.

[7] Venkatesh, V. "Creation of favorable user perceptions: Exploring the role of intrinsic motivation," *MIS Quarterly*, *23* (2), 1999, 239-260.

[8] von Hellens, L., & Nielson, S. "Australian women in IT," *Communications of the ACM*, 2001, 46-56.

The University of Colorado at Boulder's Development Center: Technology for the Community

E. R. Jessup
Department of Computer Science, University of Colorado
Tel: (303) 492-0211, Fax: (303) 492-2844, jessup@cs.colorado.edu

INTRODUCTION

Technology for the Community is an undergraduate long-term projects course offered by the Department of Computer Science at the University of Colorado at Boulder (UCB). In it, students develop computational products designed to serve the needs of local non-profit organizations.

BACKGROUND

During the summer of 2000, UCB's Department of Computer Science was selected to participate in the Institute for Women and Technology's (IWT) Virtual Development Center (VDC) [IWT]. The VDC is a network of collaborative college-based educational centers, termed Development Centers, that share the dual goals of stimulating the participation of women in technology and increasing the positive impact of technology on the lives of women. Through the Development Centers' educational activities, a diverse community of women are encouraged to participate in the development of technology. The Development Centers are at Purdue, Santa Clara University, Smith College, Texas A&M, the University of Arizona, the University of California at Berkeley, UCB, and the University of Washington. UCB's Center is unique in its emphasis on computer science; the others all focus on traditional engineering disciplines.

The primary activity of UCB's center is the Technology for the Community course. Project ideas for the course are generated in community brainstorming workshops, held annually and facilitated by IWT staff members. Participants in the workshops include technical and non-technical women from the Boulder community at large, representatives of local community service agencies, a few interested academics, and the students enrolled in the course. At the workshop, we identify problems confronting the agencies that can be solved computationally. Over the course of one or more semesters, the students work in groups to bring the solution ideas to product form with technical and non-technical faculty members and interested community members all serving as advisors.

The course has been offered each semester, beginning in Spring 2001. Its pilot offering will extend for four semesters, but we hope that it will become a permanent part of our curriculum.

CONTENT

In the course, students learn to use software tools for such computational tasks as composing and editing websites, maintaining and manipulating databases, and creating CD-ROMs. Future offerings of the course may also provide an introduction to film editing. We study the process of turning an idea into a useful software product. As all of the projects have a significant web component, students learn and use the process of task-centered user interface design [TCD]. As time permits, we also discuss the impact of technology on the community at large.

In the first three weeks of the semester, students put their new computational skills to work by creating a "guest book." A guest book is a dynamic website where users can enter or retrieve information. That information is stored in a database. The guest book may have any purpose and design that the student chooses.

The remaining weeks then are devoted to completing a computational project in collaboration with a local non-profit agency. Representatives of the agencies meet with the students in order to articulate their needs, and they later work with the students to test and evaluate prototypes.

While representatives of many agencies have played some role in the course, our primary clients in the first two semesters have been

- Boulder Community Foundation for an on-line events scheduling calendar for use by local non-profit agencies
- Boulder Senior Center for an on-line, self-paced introduction to computers
- Sojourner Charter Middle School for a variety of educational products
- Build Boulder for an on-line, in-kind donation and resource exchange site for the benefit of local non-profits

ENROLLMENT

The course is open to all undergraduate students. The first two offerings have seen a fairly even split between students with majors in Engineering and with majors in Arts and Sciences. Freshmen and sophomores have enrolled, but most of the students have been juniors or seniors.

The diverse student body is suitable. Students work in small, interdisciplinary teams to complete the projects. Students with capabilities in such areas as design, art, writing, and social science find natural roles, as do students with strong computational skills. There is particular need for students with expertise in databases, website development, and the writing of educational materials.

There are no formal prerequisites for the course, but, for maximal comfort, participants should be able at least to write a simple program, compose a web page, or have some familiarity with at least one commercial software package. Students with more advanced computing knowledge are invited to help with computational instruction.

Nine students completed the first offering of the course. Fifteen will finish the second offering. At the time of this writing, 18 are enrolled in the Spring 2002 course. Forty six percent of the students who have enrolled are female. That is a remarkable percentage in the Department of Computer Science where females have totaled between 11 and 16% of undergraduate majors in the last 14 years.

PHILOSOPHY

The course is a long-term projects course, meaning that projects may be larger than can be completed in a single semester. Students who do not deliver a finished product at the end of the semester are asked to write a continuation plan to guide student teams who take up the project in subsequent semesters. Students may also repeat the course any number of times for credit. Indeed, students are strongly encouraged to participate in the long term. We hope that future years should find a diverse group of collaborating students enrolled, from beginners to experienced technical leaders.

Because the course is based on new and developing concepts in technology education, we encourage students to help to drive its direction and content. Students in the course also need to be independent learners, willing to take responsibility for learning new material from sources other than textbooks. Students completing our first two offerings of the course all remarked at how much they'd benefitted from working with students of various majors and with the technical and nontechnical community participants. Indeed, the technical content of the course is not complex, but the people issues are.

ASSESSMENT

Given the experimental nature of the course and the large time commitment of setting it up, assessment of the students' work to date has been quite informal. Grades are assigned as about 85% work on the project and 15% on preliminary assignments (mainly the guest book). The project grade is determined in part by the instructor (30% of total), in part by the client (10%), but mainly by the project group members themselves (45%). By means of an evaluation form that poses several questions, group members are asked to evaluate themselves and their teammates with respect to both effort and results. In reality, a well-functioning group with an ecstatically happy client can expect high grades regardless of the other factors. It has not proven necessary to distinguish students according to major, but freshmen and sophomores are graded on a somewhat easier scale.

We expect to include more formal evaluation of learning gains and outcomes in future semesters. We are presently working with the authors of the Student Assessment of Learning Gains instrument [SLAG] to understand how that and other tools and techniques might be applied to our course.

REFERENCES

[IWT] Institute for Women and Technology, http://www.iwt.org/, October 11, 2001.

[SLAG] Student Assessment of Learning Gains, http://www.wcer.wisc.edu/nise/cl1, January 8, 2002.

[TCD] Clayton Lewis and John Rieman, Task-Centered User Interface Design: A Practical Introduction, University of Colorado, http://www.acm.org/~perlman/uidesign.html, October 11, 2001.

Standardization of Software Development In Contract Research Organizations in Pharmaceutical Data Management

Mustafa Kamal and James Spruell
Central Missouri State University, USA, Tel: (660) 543-8642, Fax: (660) 543-8465

Quality of software development is still plagued by a low degree of reusability, inconsistency in data definitions, lack of comprehensive standardization of processes, and sometimes, insufficient integration of technologies. Organizations that actually improve software quality will, however, also improve productivity. Delivering quality in systems eliminates rework, the major cause of lack of productivity. Application bugs and defects are responsible for $85 billion per year in lost revenue due to system downtime. Reliability requires more than just testing an application after it is built. Reliability has to be integrated into the application development process and built into the business plan[1-5]

Many traditional engineering disciplines have scientifically mastered its methods and approaches including modular reusability, deriving the creativity of new designs from existing knowledge repositories. Chemical engineering is an example of a field where standardization and scientific models set the pace for new development. Typically weaknesses and shortcomings that slow down development speed, lower the quality of software products, and increase cost of maintenance are usually results of small knowledge domain[6].

In particular, this can be noticed in Drug Research and Development Business Units and, more specifically, in Data Management (DM) areas where the most intensive software development takes place. However, many pharmaceutical Contract Research Organizations (CRO), are still lagging behind. DM's primary responsibility is to support data management for clinical trials conducted during drug research. DM is also delegated with the responsibility to prepare the largest portion of documentation being furnished to the FDA. There may be several groups in a DM department such as Data Coordination (DC), Database Programmers (DBP), Data Entry (DE), Statistical Programmers (SP), Remote Study Management team (RSM) and so on. Therefore, all groups have to work in close cooperation in order to achieve the ultimate deliverables. However, there has been little done to standardize DM development processes in many pharmaceutical CROs.

Using the experience and knowledge accumulated by DM, such companies' DMs can evolve in the direction of totalitarian standardization of their internal processes. Enhancements in their current approaches to data management support for clinical trials should ultimately establish leading software development practices and result in greater effectiveness.

We looked at two industry standard packages that consists of several highly integrated modules[6-9]. There are logical and physical objets used to implement and manage a clinical study database. Logical levels of granularity are an item, a panel, a protocol (owner), a page section, page template, and the study book. The physical objects are an item and table. The logical objects are needed in order to design the software interface used during entering of clinical data. But all logical objects are created only after the database physical objects are implemented. However, these did not have a central repository or global library. All data definitions are owned by a protocol resulting in data redundancy and inconsistencies. The Global Integrated DataBase (GIDB) methodology could reduce or eliminate problems of data definition discrepancies. Some clients require total compliance with their internal data management standards, and dictate which development strategies should be used. This may cause tremendous overhead of the same or similar data definitions.

A Global Librarian has to identify the first core library objects. Designs need to be standardized and a naming convention schema should be established. Once the work on the front-end is streamlined and structured, the back-end will follow. Various methods of standardizing DM support can be used as well. The speed and quality of the overall software development will increase. Pharmaceutical CROs that have more than one set of internal DM practices, can benefit from redesigning their current approaches. They will succeed in identifying standard system development requirements and implementing the software engineering orientation established for the global data management.

REFERENCES

1. "In Search Of Reliable Software": Desmond, Paul H.; Harding, Elizabeth U.; Waters, John K., Software Magazine, Vol. 20, 2000.
2. "Deming and the quality of software development", Yilmaz, M. R., Business Horizons, Nov/Dec. 1997.
3. "Software quality management strategies", Phan, Dien D.Information Systems management, Spring 1998
4. "Killer Apps and Dead Bodies", Kappelman, Leon A., Information Week, June 2000.
5. A Guide to Information Engineering Using the IEF: Computer Aided Planning, Analysis, and Design, Second Edition, Texas Instruments.
6. Clintrial 4 developer handbook,1998
7. Oracle Clinical 3.1, Oracle, 1999
8. SOP 3.1.a Database Design
9. Medica's Designer's Guide, Medica, 2000

Information Technology Utilization and Success Factors in Public Enterprises in Papua New Guinea

Limbie Kelegai
School of Information Systems, Queensland University of Technology, Australia
Tel: +6 (173) 864-2957, Fax: +6 (173) 964-1969, l.kelegai@student.qut.edu.au

ABSTRACT

The rapid advancement and diffusion of Information and Communication Technologies are having a profound effect on many organizations. Enterprises are increasingly investing in Information Technology(IT) for varying reasons. The underlying believe is that knowledge workers will utilize IT to enhance business process, efficiency and productivity. However these investments do not guarantee success. Despite these assumptions, Least Developed Countries(LDC) are beginning to realize the significance of IT as a strategic tool resulting in the increase in IT proliferation in all sectors in those countries. Numerous IT implementation and success studies have been conducted over the last decade. The majority of these studies were conducted in developed countries(DC). DCs and LDCs differ in a number of areas including cultural, social and economical factors. Due to the inherent differences, results from success factor studies conducted in DCs may be inappropriate for LDCs. A study is underway to investigate and determine factors influencing IT utilization and success in public enterprises in LDCs, in particular Papua New Guinea(PNG).

INTRODUCTION

Recently there has been an increase in the number of computers deployed into many least developed countries. The underlying belief is that employees will use computers to enhance their skills and improve efficiency and productivity in organizations. However there is no guarantee of IS/IT success and returns. The rate of failure in IT is high in many LDCs. There is also growing recognition that the full benefit of IT investments are not being realized, (Roberts & Henderson, 2000). Despite these concerns, LDCs are beginning to realize the significance of IS/IT in organizations and increasingly deploying IT to solve developmental problems (Harris & Davison, 1999). The intensity for IT deployment in LDC is characterized by the high (90%) World Bank lending for IT, six times the growth rate of total Bank lending (Harris & Davison, 1999). In an attempt to narrow the IT gap or digital divide, developed countries and other world organizations continue to promote, support and encourage LDCs to utilize IS/IT as a strategic tool. For example, in 1997, Japanese International Cooperation Agency (JICA) donated well over PNGK15million in IT equipment to the University of Technology (PNG) for educational use.

Although the proliferation of IT in LDCs has been increasing in recent years, Harris & Davison (1999) state that the level of utilization is far lower than developed countries. Compounded with economical, social and political difficulties there is growing concern regarding the implementation, utilization and success of IS/IT in these countries. Similarly there is limited research and literature in relation to determining IS/IT success or failure in LDCs in their various social, organizational, economical, cultural and political settings. The majority of IT utilization and success studies have concentrated on developed countries, especially in North America and Europe(Anakwe et al., 1999) compared to the relatively few studies conducted in LDCs. In addition a large part of these studies are based on the experiences from the private sector(Jain, 1997). IS/IT are implemented within a social context consisting of economy, political, cultural and behavioural factors differing from country and societies (Harris & Davison, 1999). The two significant differences between DCs and LDCs include cultural and developmental dimensions (Hofstede, 1983; Triandis, 1980; Anakwe *et al.*, 1999).

The study and measure of IS/IT effectiveness is difficult because of the multidimensional constructs and is subjective to varying perceptions of stakeholders and evaluators (Bajwa, Rai, & Brennan, 1998; Larsen & Myers, 1999). Similarly Delone & Mclean (1992) state that IS can be viewed from many perspectives resulting in varying success factors. Furthermore these factors may be differentiated between DCs and LDCs within their social/organizational and cultural settings. Failure to take into account these factors may inhibit adoption, utilization and success of IT and increase the chances of failure.

This study seeks to investigate IS/IT utilization and determine the factors that influence IS/IT success in the public sector enterprises (Public and Higher Education) in Papua New Guinea.

RELEVANCE OF THIS STUDY

Numerous IS/IT success studies have been conducted over the years using a number of approaches including the success factor approach. The success factors approach attempts to model user and organizational features to predict IS implementation outcomes. The majority of these investigations were conducted in differing social, economical, cultural and organizational settings in DCs. IT is imbedded in the social, cultural and economical dimensions of a nation. DC's and LDCs vary in national culture, social and economical factors. The notion of national culture and social settings can be further elaborated with Hofstedes (1983) four cultural dimensions. Hofstede, (1983) classifies nations by four categories, individual/collectivism, low or high uncertainty avoidance, power distance and masculine/feminine societies. In general LDCs identify close to collectivist societies while DCs are individualist societies. Due to the inherent differences between DC and LDCs, results from IS success studies in DCs cannot be generalized with LDCs.

In addition IS utilization and success studies have been criticized for the lack of uniformity and theoretical base. In an attempt to address these issues, IS researchers have turned to other disciplines for the underlying reference and theoretical base. For example, the social psychology discipline is often referenced for attitude and behavioural factors in IS utilization and success measures at the individual level.

With the rapid advances in IT and evolving business structure and process, assessing the success of computer-based information systems face a myriad of issues including skilled workforce and IS/IT implementation. This study attempts to address some of these issues. Furthermore the study is motivated by the numerous calls for more research to explore and identify factors that influence IS success in organizations in their varying social/organizational settings in the context of IT utilization and success in LDCs. Because of the differences between DCs and LDCs, generalization of studies conducted in DC's may be inappropriate for LDCs.

PNG is a LDC with a small but slowly developing IT industry and relies on technology imported from other countries. PNG has cultural norms that are different to other nations The aim of this study is to investigate and determine the factors that influence IT utilization and success in public enterprises within the social, cultural and economic settings in Papua New Guinea.

THEORETICAL FRAMEWORK

The theoretical basis of the proposed study is based in the social psychology discipline. The Theory of Reasoned Action(TRA) (Fishbein & Ajzen, 1975), and work by Triandis (1980) on behaviour state that beliefs and norms influence a persons attitude which lead to their behaviour towards the attitude object. The experience and other independent variables influence the individual's attitude in a loop back. TRA and Triandis(1980) provide the theoretical basis for concluding that an individual's perception of the computer system and related activities are predictive of success of the computer system (Doll & Torkzadeh, 1988, Delone & McLean, 1992). For example users belief that IT increases productivity (belief), therefore users are satisfied (attitude) with IT and users use(behaviour) the computer system as illustrated in Figure 1. Other dimensions in the Triandis model include, cultural, social situation and biological factors that can influence IT utilization.

Figure 1: Attitude-behaviour loop back

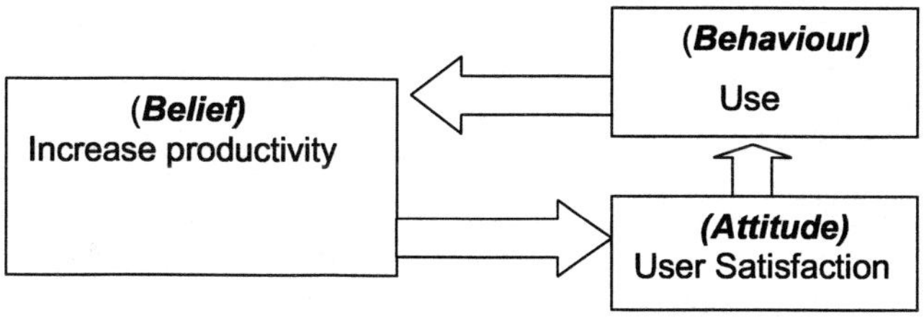

Since the theoretical base of this study relates to attitude and behaviour (cognitive psychology) it is important to clarify the concept of attitude. Delone & Mclean (1992) state that use/utilization impacts individuals who than collectively have an impact on organizational IT success. IS/IT success can be measured at the individual level, systems/process level or organization level. This study will attempt to investigate IS/IT success at the individual and organizational levels. It will also seek to determine influencing factors external to the enterprise. For example, factors such as the availability of skilled IS/IT professionals. The identified independent factors are categorized in the 3 dimensions, individual, organizational, and external. A research model depicting the research interest was developed (Figure 2.) for this study. The model posits that organizational, individual and external factors influence IT use/utilization and ultimately influence IT success or failure.

METHODOLOGY

Case Study

The research design includes multiple case studies comprising of 10 public organizations. The 10 organizations include 2 government run universities and 8 public statutory enterprises. Data collection will include document analysis and interviews with relevant authorities and IT managers.

Survey

A questionnaire will be developed and distributed to individuals employed in the public enterprises identified for the study. The questionnaire will attempt to determine the computer user perceptions of the identified factors that influence IT utilization and success in PNG.

CONCLUSION

IT utilization and success in public enterprises in LDCs may be attributed to a number of factors. For the purpose of this study, these factors are categorized into three dimensions, individual, organizational and external. Attitude and behavioural models by Triandis (1980) and Fishbein & Ajzen (1975) provide the theoretical basis for identifying the factors that influence IT utilization and success in public enterprises. LDCs and DC's differ in their social/organizational, economical and political settings. Therefore results from success factor studies in DCs may be inappropriate for LDCs. In LDCs, the particular circumstances of culture, economical and political context, and developing industry requirements, have a distinctive influence on IS/IT success. The study attempts to investigate factors that influence IS/IT utilization and success in public enterprises within Papua New Guinea's distinct social, economical, cultural and political settings.

The study is useful to researchers, academics, IT managers in organizations in LDCs, and will contribute to cross cultural issues for multinational organizations. Results of the investigation will be available upon completion of the study.

Figure 2: Research framework

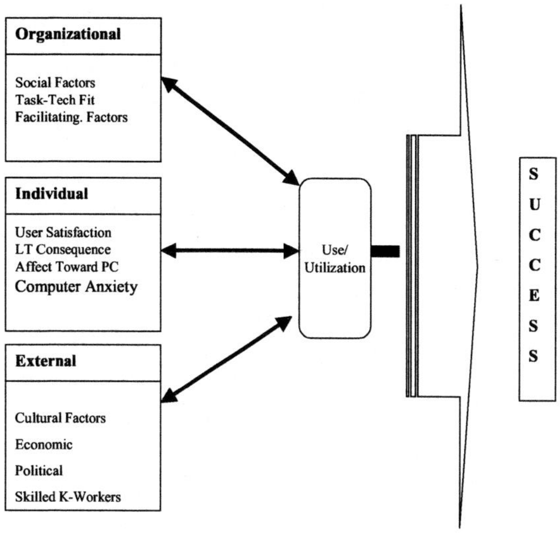

REFERENCES

Anakwe, U. P., Anandarajan, M., & Igbaria, M. (1999). Information Technology Usage Dynamics in Nigeria: An Empirical Study. *Journal of Global Information Management, Vol. 7*(No. 2), pp, 13-21.

Bajwa, D., Rai, A., & Brennan, I. (1998). Key antecedents of Executive Information Systems success: a path analytic approach. *Decision Support Systems, Vol. 22*, pp. 31-43.

Delone, W. H., & McLean, E. R. (1992). Information Systems Success: The quest for dependent variable. *Information Systems Research,* 1, pp. 60-95.

Doll, W., & Torkzadeh, G. (1988). The Measurement of End-User Computing Satisfaction. *MIS Quarterly*, pp. 258-274.

Fishbein, M., & Ajzen, I. (1975). *Belief, Attitude, Intention and Behavior: An Introduction to Theory and Research.* California: Addison-Wesley Publishing Company.

Harris, H., & Davison, R. (1999). Anxiety and Involvement: Cultural Dimensions Toward Computers in Developing Societies. *Journal of Global Information Management, Vol. 7*, 1, pp. 26-38.

Hofstede, G. (1983). *Culture and Management Development.* Geneva: UNDP/ILO.

Jain, R. (1997). A Diffusion Model for Public Information Systems in Developing Countries. *Journal of Global Information Management, Vol. 5*(No. 1), pp. 4-15.

Larsen, M. A., & Myers, B. L. (1999). When success turns into failure: a package-driven business process re-engineering project n the financial services industry. *Journal of Strategic Information Systems, Vol. 8*, pp. 395-417.

Roberts, P., & Henderson. (2000). Information Technology Acceptance in a Sample of Government Employees: A test of the Technology acceptance Model. *Interaction With Computers, Vol. 12*, pp. 427-433.

Triandis (1980).Values, Attitude and Interpersonal behavior, In Thompson et al. (1994), *Journal of Management Information Systems*, Vol. 11, 4, pp. 167-187

Challenges for Knowledge Management: Communities of Practice in Aerospace Design

Dr. Micky Kerr and Dr. Patrick Waterson
Institute of Work Psychology, University of Sheffield, UK
Tel: +44 (0144) 222-3269, Fax: +44 (0144) 272-7206, m. p.kerr@sheffield.ac.uk

INTRODUCTION

The management of knowledge has become a major issue in the drive for more efficiency in many work contexts. Knowledge is promoted as a resource that can be successfully managed to help increase organisational effectiveness and gain some competitive advantage (Newell & Swan, 1999). Codification approaches to knowledge management emphasise knowledge objects, which can be indexed and handled in explicit formats by information systems. Typical endeavours aim to stop re-inventing the wheel through technology-led implementations such as: corporate yellow pages and best practice databases. Alternative strategies focus on more tacit knowledge processes and dynamics, which rely on subjective insights and know-how. Efforts here include encouraging innovation and creativity, building knowledge sharing environments and fostering learning cultures.

Given the globalisation of operations, dispersed working and digitisation of business environments, the need for synergy between information technology and human creativity to meet the challenges of acquiring, storing and utilising knowledge is increasingly recognised. This paper focuses on communities of practice (CoPs) as an area of knowledge management, which confronts these challenges (Lave & Wenger, 1991).

Communities of Practice

The seminal work can be attributed to Etienne Wenger, Jean Lave and their colleagues at Xerox PARC in the mid-1980's, who developed the CoPs concept (Brown & Duguid, 1991; Lave & Wenger, 1991). CoPs are not formal teams, nor task forces, rather they are informal groups that can emerge around a work-related process/function or be focused on a discipline, topic or problem. CoPs are defined by the subject of engagement, setting their own goals and deciding their own membership. Several writers have characterised different types of CoPs, depending on their degree of self-organisation, formality and level of control by management (McDermott, 1999; Wenger, 1998).

What holds CoPs together is a common sense of purpose, which can be manifested in the common pursuit of solutions, goals and interests. Furthermore, CoPs may employ common practices, share a common language, and espouse similar beliefs and values. They are concerned with both tacit and explicit knowledge in practice e.g. what is represented in roles, procedures and regulations, and what is assumed in subtle cues, rules of thumb and assumptions. Along with this common and shared repertoire (Wenger, 1998), CoPs tend to exhibit a proactive stance in dealing with future events. For instance, conversations and war stories exchanged between photocopier service representatives about difficult repair problems and tough customers are seen as opportunities for learning which go well beyond formal training and as repositories of accumulated wisdom (Brown & Duguid, 1991; Orr, 1990). Furthermore, Wenger & Snyder (2000) propose that knowledge developed in CoPs can be used in business units to shape the organisation, in teams to take care of projects and in informal networks to form relationships.

Rationale

The knowledge management challenges outlined earlier are true for engineering design and these formed the background to the longer-term project, of which this study is part. Earlier work by Kerr et al (2001) had identified key social and technical requirements for the overall system of knowledge capture, sharing and reuse in aerospace design. One suggested implementation strategy was to exploit CoPs as a means to promote and develop a knowledge sharing culture. Wenger (1998) sees CoPs as natural organisational units which can facilitate a range of activities, including: knowledge transfer of best practice; tacit knowledge preservation; keeping competencies up-to-date; developing expertise and fostering a sense of identity. The role of technology to support conversation, discourse and correspondence within CoPs has also been recognised as worthy of research. Therefore, a coherent rationale for a study on the CoP initiative within the company can be argued.

Objectives

The study's objectives are:

- to characterise the nature of the communities under investigation,
- to highlight problems encountered,
- to identify examples of 'successes', and
- to suggest some interim recommendations, plus ways forward for future research.

METHODOLOGY

Organisational Context

The research was carried out within a leading international aerospace company. It is a market leader in the core business areas of civil and defense aerospace as well as industrial and marine power. This study focused on the aero engine engineering design enterprise, at the company's two main UK sites. The nature of the initiative meant that membership of the CoPs was international, including the US and Germany. The following design-related CoPs were selected as pilot groups and sampled in this study: Automatic Analysis; Bearings; Business Intelligence; Combustion Cost Reduction; Computer Aided Design; and Whole Engine Modeling.

Methods

The facilitators of each community were selected as key stakeholders and interviewed. In total, 10 interviews were audio-recorded and fully transcribed by the researcher. A preliminary inductive analysis of the data was undertaken. This approach allowed key features of the communities to be described and some tentative results concerning barriers and successes to be forwarded.

RESULTS AND DISCUSSION

The preliminary findings are summarised under a set of inter-related issues concerned with the defining characteristics of the CoPs under investigation.

Origins and Development

All the CoPs chosen by the company as pilot sites share the fact that they existed as informal groups. For example, the Computer Aided Design (CAD) CoP evolved from an interest group who met face-to-face every 6 months, but that wanted to facilitate more regular discussion across their distributed network. Indeed, the evolutionary nature of several CoPs has already been witnessed within the pilot study. There was a sharp decline in activity within the Bearings CoP after 3 months, while the CAD CoP has seen a diversification into several sub-CoPs. The findings support the idea that CoPs have life-cycles, with stages including: infancy, coalescing and regeneration (Wenger, 1998).

Objectives and Goals

A common view expressed by the interviewees is that the objective or goal of the CoP needs to be clearly specified. An initiation mechanism to agree a set of shared goals for the CoPs was often used. For instance, members of the Whole Engine Modelling (WEM) CoP collaborated to draw up a communal document to summarise the modelling issues they wanted to concentrate on. This study proposes that CoP goals can be classified as:

- focussed on problem solving and meeting clearly defined needs,
- the co-ordination activities of sharing and promoting best practice good / bad experiences to increase visibility and awareness within the CoP or,
- identifying experts and linking those with common interests in an attempt to disseminate experience (which may be concentrated in different places) to a wider audience.

CoPs can have multiple goals that cut across this differentiation and change over time.

Communication Practices

The CoPs employ a range of communication strategies, media and artifacts. The company intranet and discussion lists were not widely utilised, however some shared documents have been successful in co-ordinating the actions of the WEM CoP. Face-to-face meetings and workshops are widely promoted as vital for CoP survival, even if they happen infrequently. For instance, a dedicated focus group to take issues forward from the discussion list is planned by the Business Intelligence (BI) CoP. Wenger (1998) recognises that such multiple contact mechanisms are critical in creating value for members and providing a sense of history and progress to any CoP.

Problems and Barriers

At an early stage of the pilot, several barriers centred on the technology used to facilitate the discussion list. The system capability of the discussion list was less than what was expected, resulting in user-frustration and a low rate of participation within several CoPs. Another reason for a reluctance to use the list is that inexperienced members may not want to show a lack of knowledge in front of experts. Electronic discussion also raises confidentiality and security concerns about the consequences of sensitive knowledge breaching the boundaries of the CoP. Important cultural and organisational factors are the lack of priority given to CoP activity, especially in terms of reward and recognition.

Successes

Successes include the technological capability to cope with the high memory demands of pictorial information and to allow a record of discussions to be traced back. As a direct result of the initiative, boundary spanning was facilitated in the WEM CoP, with an individual travelling to meet experts who were located elsewhere. This CoP also demonstrated knowledge sharing, when the local practice was advanced as the corporate strategy, as well as knowledge re-use, when the UK-based members utilised the previous testing carried out by their US-based colleagues. It was also felt that CoPs were useful in allowing non-official opinions to be publicised.

CONCLUSIONS

This preliminary study highlights the importance of the social, organisational and cultural contexts within which a CoP initiative is situated, as well as the information and communication technology being used to support such a knowledge management strategy. In terms of promoting a knowledge sharing culture, the company's use of CoPs terminology can be seen as a start of this process. The findings outlined above can be translated into recommendations.

Interim Recommendations

Support and resources are critical for the facilitator role, while those supplying knowledge need to have their intellectual property protected. The ownership and control of knowledge within the CoP may therefore need a code of trust and privacy to be established. Feedback, rewards, recognition and other incentives for time and effort in contributing to a CoP are also vital facilitating factors, especially for CoPs with any electronic support. This nurturing of CoPs requires a careful balance between design and emergence.

Future Work

The research plans to examine the nature of activity within the CoPs through further interviews with members and tracking discussion list and other interactions. A comparative case study of selected CoPs over phases of their life-cycle is envisaged which will take forward issues such as:

- the impact of dispersed membership;
- media richness and technological support;
- emergent and new on-line communities of practice/discourse;
- the setting and achievement of goals; and
- the use of the Distributed Cognition to analyse activity (Hutchins, 1990)

ACKNOWLEDGEMENTS

This research is partly funded by the EPSRC, through the Rolls-Royce University Technology Partnership (UTP) for Design. The interview participants are also thanked for their time.

REFERENCES

Brown, J. S. & Duguid, P. (1991) Organizational learning and communities of practice: toward a unified view of working, learning and innovation. *Organization Science*, 2,1, 40-57.

Hutchins, E. (1990) The technology of team navigation. In J. Galegher, R. Kraut & C. Edigo (Eds.) *Intellectual Teamwork: Social and Technological Foundations of Cooperative Work.* NJ: Lawrence Erlbaum Associates.

Kerr, M. P., Waterson, P. E. & Clegg, C. W. (2001) A socio-technical approach to knowledge capture, sharing and reuse in aerospace design. *Paper presented at ASME 2001 Design Engineering Technical Conferences & Computers and Information in Engineering Conference.* Pittsburgh, Pennsylvania, Sept. 9-12, 2001.

Lave, J. & Wenger, E. (1991) *Situated learning: legitimate peripheral participation.* New York: Cambridge University Press.

McDermott, R. (1999). Why information technology inspired but cannot deliver knowledge management. *California Management Review*, 41(4), 103-117.

Newell, S. & Swan, J. (1999). Knowledge Management: what it is currently about versus what is currently about, *Journal of HRM*, 16, 10-16.

Orr, J.E. (1990). Sharing knowledge, celebrating identity: community memory in a service culture. In D. Middleton & D. Edwards (Eds). *Collective Remembering* (pp.169-189). London: Sage.

Wenger, E. (1998) *Communities of Practice. Learning, Meaning and Identity.* New York: Cambridge University Press.

Wenger, E. & Snyder. W. M. (2000) Communities of Practice: The Organizational Frontier. *Harvard Business Review*, Jan-Feb, pp 139-145.

A Framework for Selecting Corporate Network Security

Someswar Kesh and Sridhar Nerur
Department of Computer and Office Information Systems, Central Missouri State University
Tel: (660) 543-4767, kesh@cmsu1@cmsu.edu

ABSTRACT

This paper discusses research being done for developing a framework for selecting corporate network security. To develop the framework, selecting network security has been considered as a risk management process in which the cost of providing network security will have to be balanced against the threats and the assets protected.

INTRODUCTION

There is an ever-increasing dependence on networks today. Electronic transactions, business-to-business transactions carry confidential corporate and individual information. Along with that, threats to corporate network security have increased. The combination of these factors has made corporate network security extremely important. Yet, security is expensive. Moreover, users not only demand security, they also demand performance from the network. Having too much security not only becomes expensive, it also slows down network performance. The network administrator then has to decide on an optimum amount of security that balances the need for a secure network on one hand and cost and performance on the other. Because of this, the focus of this research is:

- To develop a framework for network security that will assist the network administrator in selecting a level of security that will balance these conflicting needs
- To apply the framework to corporate security scenarios

DEVELOPMENT OF THE FRAMEWORK

Because of the balancing act between security needs on one side with cost and performance issues on the other, we consider security management as a form of risk management. Therefore to develop the framework, we are using the framework developed for software engineering risk analysis by Barry Boehm. Each component in this framework is being critically evaluated for its applicability to security management. If a component is considered applicable, then that component is being retained. In some cases, a component of the model may be applicable, however, the definition of that component will change because of the new domain being considered. For example, checklists in this framework refer to the list of factors that contribute to risks in a software engineering project while in our case it refers to the factors that cause security risks. Components that are deemed not applicable to this domain are being dropped. Newer components are being added to take into account factors that the software engineering model has not considered.

The risk management framework provides two components for managing risk; risk assessment and risk control. While both these components are equally valid for both software development and developing network security, risk assessment in software development projects is concerned with whether the project will be completed on time and on budget, while in network security the concern is whether there is a risk of a security failure. The first step in risk assessment is risk identification. In this case, we consider both generic risks and risks specific to the organization. An example of a generic risk is a virus on the internet. An example of specific risk is the prominence of the organization in the marketplace that adds to the risk. Another example of a specific risk is the design of a corporate network that adds to the vulnerability of the network to security breaches. To properly identify the risks, checklists are used. Based on a survey of software development managers, the top ten risk items in software development projects include, personnel shortfalls, unrealistic schedules and budgets etc. A survey is being developed by us to identify the top ten risk items in network security. Viruses, for example, may be one of the top ten risk items. Examples of other components for risk identification that are being evaluated are assumption analysis, in which risks are identified based on experience.

Not all security risks are of equal importance. Therefore the next step of risk assessment is to use models (for example decision theoretic and cost models) to analyze the risks and the damage it can do. A critical issue in the development of and use of risk analysis models is to be able to identify the probabilities associated with an event and the damage that it is capable of doing. For example, the probability of a virus hit and the damage that it can do can be extremely high. At the same time, depending on the organization, the probability of a break-in can be very low. If however such a break-in does occur, it can do significant damage to the organization. Various subjective probability assessment techniques can be used to develop the probability of a security breach in an organization. Once the probability estimates and the possible damage estimates are done, the risk exposure factors can be calculated. Items with high-risk exposure will have higher priority than other items.

Once risks have been properly assessed, these risks will have to be controlled and managed. Boehm that can be directly used has identified three components of risk control. The first involves risk management planning, the second risk resolution and the third, risk monitoring. Various components of risk management planning have been identified. The first is to buy or collect information regarding the risks and how to manage it. In a network security scenario, this could be monitoring and collecting information about viruses and denial of service attacks and other possible security breaches identified in the checklist. Risk avoidance is also part of risk management planning. Developing policies that avoid virus infections can be an example of risk avoidance. Risks can also be transferred. Proxy servers as well as dummy servers are examples where risks are transferred. Finally, design of networks can be done so that risks are reduced. An essential element of risk management planning is to integrate entire risk management plans.

Risk resolution and monitoring involves developing prototypes etc. to test the steps outlined in risk management. In software development, the process involves development of software prototypes. In network security, development of a prototype network can be extremely useful in studying security concerns and implementing the fixes. Simulating a wide variety of security scenarios and testing the response of the security system can be used to assess potential weaknesses in the system. Currently, various network simulation software are available, however, they can only be used for monitoring the performance of the network under various traffic loads and security scenarios cannot be simulated using these software. Some what-if analysis can be performed by assuming certain servers or components of the network will go down if a security breach takes place.

Network security is a dynamic entity. Therefore, risks should be continuously monitored. Risks that did not exist few years back are now major problems for organizations. For example, with the proliferation of web sites corporations are now faced with the possibility of individuals or groups tampering with web site content. As organizations change, these issues will assume greater importance.

APPLICATION OF THE FRAMEWORK

The framework is being applied to various corporate security scenarios. These scenarios are being developed by interviewing network and systems administrators. After the security scenarios are developed, the different components of the framework will be applied for risk assessment. Then possible risk control mechanisms will be applied and recommended to each of the scenarios to develop a solution. Based on the results of the application of the framework, further recommendations will be made for improving the framework as well as for future research.

REFERENCES

Available upon request

Human Issues in Strategic Alliance

Chong Kim and Purnendu Mandal
Lewis College of Business, Marshall University, West Virginia, {kim, mandal}@marshall.edu

ABSTRACT

Human behavior plays a major role in success/failure of a strategic alliance between partners, but many managers pay little attention to this aspect while in the process of negotiations. This paper highlights a number of human and organizational cultural issues, which played a major role in the process of developing a strategic alliance between a telecommunications organization (TEL) and other retail electricity organizations. A framework for strategic alliance was developed for the new market situation, which helped in understanding the future informational requirements and dependence of partners on each other.

INTRODUCTION

A successful alliance should not imply an imposition of one organization's culture over another. Rather, it should create a new culture that brings together the best elements of each. Unfortunately, it is rarely practiced as alliances are often viewed solely from a financial perspective, leaving the human resource issues as something to be dealt with later and without a great deal of effort (Adler, 2001). The creation of a new culture involves operations, sales, human resources management, technology, and structure among other issues. It is undoubtedly expensive and time consuming to create a new culture, but, in the end, employees become contented and productive.

For an organization, to exploit the benefits of alliance both human aspects and information technology aspects form the core requirement. The case of a telecommunication company is presented here to highlight the major considerations in human and IT issues which resulted from strategic alliances with new business partners. The telecommunication company identified a new market opportunity as a result of changed market conditions. The company is in the traditional business of telecommunications and information services, but identified a new market opportunity in retail electricity distribution business that became apparent as a result of market deregulation in electricity industry. The firm's own strength in IT areas, strong market position and opportunities in forming alliances with other business partners in electricity industry were the main considerations for this strategic move. The company, however, inadvertently neglected the business-cultural differences that existed between TEL and potential partners in electricity business.

CULTURAL (BEHAVIORAL AND STRUCTURAL) ASPECTS IN ALLIANCE

Alliance among firms naturally would result many organizational changes. Leavitt (1965) viewed that there are four types of interacting variables looming especially in large industrial organizations: task variables, structural variables, technological variables, and human variables. He proposed structural, technological, and people approaches to organizational changes, which derive from interactions among the four types of variable mentioned above.

One should realize that the above-mentioned four variables are highly interdependent so that change in any one usually results in compensatory change in others. The introduction of new technological tools - computers, for example, may cause changes in structure (communication system) and changes in people (their skills and attitudes), and changes in performance and task. Therefore, it is imperative to consider all areas that might be affected when a company plans to introduce any one applied changing approach.

Pre-existing people related problems at a target company often cause many alliances fail to reach their full financial and strategic potential. Numerous case studies report failure of alliances due to lack of consideration for the potential impact of behavioral and structural aspects (Burrows, 2000; Numerof & Abrams, 2000). To build effective alliance, institutions must pay close attention to cultural, personality and structural incompatibilities. Leaders from alliance institutions need to recognize the personality differences in their managers as well as the demands required by the life cycle stage of their organizations (Segil, 2000). Understanding potential incompatibilities gives institutions contemplating alliances a solid foundation on which to explore the feasibility of joint projects.

Successful alliances are impeded when the culture of one or both associations highly differ in value. High control value is inconsistent with the toleration for ambiguity and the willingness to compromise often required for strategic alliances. Maron & VanBremen (1999) suggests the use of William Bridges' Organizational Character Index, which can be a useful tool for analyzing the cultural differences between two associations. It promotes better understanding between two associations; fosters an appreciation for what both partners could bring to an alliance; and identifies underdeveloped qualities in both associations that could inhibit the success of an alliance.

IT ISSUES IN ALLIANCE

Long term IT considerations, such as IT architecture, is a major consideration. A strategic consideration, such as new alliances, would require visioning of a different IT architecture. Applegate , McFarlan and McKenney (1999) view IT architecture as an overall picture of the range of technical options as well as business options. "Just as the blueprint of a building's architecture indicates not only the structure's design but how everything – from plumbing and heating systems to the flow of traffic within the building – fits and works together, the blueprint of a firm's IT architecture defines the technical computing, information management and communications platform" (p. 209).

Figure 1 brings out the dynamic nature of IT architecture development process. The technology part, shown by dotted oval, is concerned with design, deployment and its use. This part is the core of IT architecture and a huge proportion of IT professionals' time is devoted to these activities. Considerations of business options, which feed to various technology options, are higher level activities in IT architecture development process. Business options, such as strategic alliances, outsourcing, diversification, etc., are influenced by major internal as well as external factors, for example, current business practices, business opportunities, and organizational strategy. There is a direct link between technology and organizational strategy. The technology (with its operational and technical settings) exerts a strong influence on to organization's future strategic direction. Thus, one can observe (as shown in Figure 1 through connecting lines) a close link between technical and other business factors, and like ever changing business the IT architecture is a dynamically evolving phenomena.

Strategic alliances are a mutual agreement between two or more independent firms to serve a common strategic (business) objective (Bronder and Pritzel, 1992). A strategic alliance exists when the value chain between at least two organisations (with compatible goals) are combined for the purpose of sustaining and / or achieving significant competitive advantage (Bronder and Pritzel, 1992). An alliance can exist between any number of organisations. For example, telecommunication organisations could form an alliance for international joint

Figure 1: Forces affecting overall IT architecture

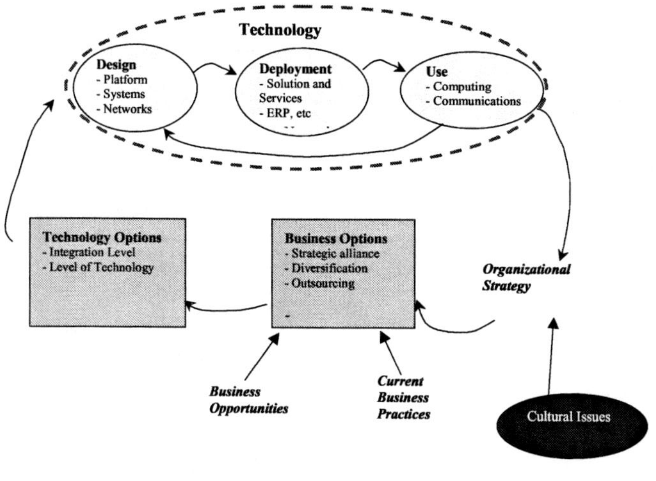

ventures, or an alliance can be established between a banking organisation and IT supplier. The notion of developing a strategic alliance suggests an organization's performance can be significantly improved through joint, mutually dependent action. For a strategic alliance to be successful business partners must follow a structured approach to developing their alliances, which may include strategic planning, communication, efficient and effective decision making, performance evaluation, relationship structure, and education and training.

Strategists have often suggested that organizations should consider entering into similar, or somewhat related markets sectors to broaden their product/service portfolios (Markides and Williamson, 1997; Henderson and Clark, 1990). Both the dimensions of market (customer and product as per Ansoff (1986)) in a related market can easily be identified and strategies formulated for deployment. The main advantage of adopting such a strategy is that an organization can easily use its competencies and strategic assets in generating a strategic competitive advantage (Markides and Williamson, 1997). Determining the design and the requirements of a new IS is a relatively simple task. In contrast, diversification into a significantly different market for an IT/IS organization is a very challenging task, which needs considerable evaluation of IT infrastructure and human relations.

THE NEW ENVIRONMENT – WITH ALLIANCE

The telecommunication organization (TEL) provides services to its customers through its own telecom network and would like to improve its customer base by forming a strategic alliance with retail electricity distribution organizations. As large telecommunication organizations exhibit structural inertia, generating a competitive advantage in a new market poses an enormous challenge (Henderson and Clark, 1990). Noteworthy, an organization must make a distinction between a new product and the means to achieve that new product. The recent merger between American On-line and Warner Publishing clearly demonstrates that it is not too difficult for an IT organization to offer new products in an existing market. Considering this point, strategic alliances and partnership could be a way out for an IT organization to enter into a completely new product market. From a systems development perspective, alliances may result in the development of interfaces to the existing ISs or alternatively a new integrated IS.

As per the deregulation rules a retail distributor must make financial settlement with other suppliers of the electricity industry supply chain. This needs to cover the cost of electricity from the wholesale electricity market, tariffs for distribution of the same by the transmission and distribution service providers, and meter data from Meter Providers and Meter Data Agents. The processes and systems therein must be able to interface with retail energy distributors accounting and billing, service activation and service assurance processes and systems.

To conduct business as a market participant TEL must purchase wholesale electricity and services for the physical delivery and metering to customer. There are two clear options available to TEL to purchase electricity:

- by *direct participation* and trading in the national electricity market (NEM). This means that TEL would perform all electricity trader functions, act to bid and settle wholesale purchases in the national electricity market from its own resources and carry all market and prudential risks and responsibilities:
- by *engaging an existing specialist energy trader*. This means that TEL form a close and long-term relationship with one (or more) existing trader(s) who would operate all market trader functions and processes on TEL's behalf. This would be an outsourced supply arrangement. The sharing of risk and responsibilities is a matter for specific agreement with the trader.

Figure 2 and Table 1 identify the risks associated with the Energy Trader functions for various participants in the national electricity market.

COMPLEXITY IN NEW INFORMATION SYSTEMS DEVELOPMENT

The management of TEL must realize the complexity and limitations of IT infrastructure before they venture into the new business.

Figure 2: Energy trading risks

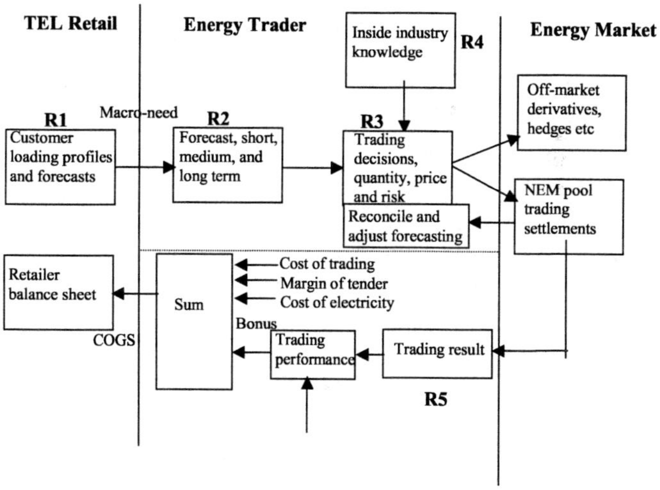

Table 1: Risk allocation for energy trading

Risk	Description	Risk Allocated to
R1	Customer numbers/market share not achieved.	Retailer
	Mix of customer profile types is not as expected	Retailer/Trader
R2	Load/Purchasing forecasts are not accurate	Trader
R3	Trading decisions are flawed	Trader
	Market price risk	Retailer/Trader
R4	Industry development expectations are incorrect	Trader
R5	Incorrect or unrealistic performance expectations are set	Joint Retailer/Trader

TEL follows a standard procedure called PDOM (Product Development Operational Model) for any IT product development and this procedure was also applied in IT architecture design. PDOM is very similar to standard SDLC (Systems Development Life Cycle) (Kendall and Kendall, 1995).

Figure 3 below shows the relationship between TEL and third parties that it must reconcile.

Figure 3: Relationships between TEL and third parties

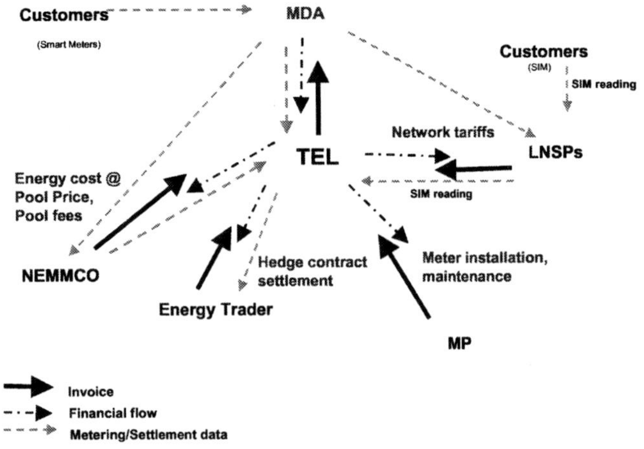

Reconciliation with these third parties is critical to ensure that charges are for correct customers, correct dates (i.e. customer's start and end dates), correct rates, services received, correct usage and correct loss factors. Reconciliation is also necessary to ensure that payments are settled for the correct dollar amount, and are on time. The third parties with whom TEL will be required to settle with are NEMMCO, LNSPs, Metering Data Agents, Meter Providers, Energy Traders, and Other Retailers.

For the proposed alliance become effective, TEL will be required to determine a number of third party relations with electricity retailers:

- *Electricity sourcing* - TEL will need to contract energy traders to purchase electricity in the national electricity market. TEL will be required to settle periodically with these organizations for services rendered;
- *NEMMCO* - TEL will be required to settle periodically with NEMMCO for wholesale electricity purchases. NEMMCO will provide billing reconciliation data;
- *MDA* - TEL will contract with NEMMCO accredited MDAs for the collection and provision of customer electricity usage data for billing purposes. TEL will be required to settle periodically with MDAs for services rendered;
- *MP* - TEL as an RP, will have a relationship with MPs in the provision and maintenance of meter installations and TEL will be required to settle periodically for services rendered;
- *LNSP* - TEL will enter into service agreements with each LNSP for the use of their distribution network and for the connection and supply of electricity. TEL will be required to settle periodically with LNSPs in terms of distribution fees for network use.
- *NEMMCO and State Regulators* - TEL will pay fees to NEMMCO and state regulators for operating licences and other regulatory charges;
- *Generators* - TEL may contract with generators (outside of the spot market) for long term energy requirements; and
- *TEL Partner sales commissions* - TEL could potentially enter into sales partnerships and pay appropriate commissions.

Table 2 shows that there are significant differences between TEL and other partners with respect to operational and behavioral issues.

Table 2: Structural and behavioral differences

Factors	TEL	Partners
Company organizational structure/ size	Very complex and large in sales volume	Small to medium size, relatively simple structure
Employee Work habit	Flexible work hours	Relatively rigid work hours
Customer relations	Good relations with existing customers – excellent customer services	Indifferent to customer complaints
Employee Training	Good opportunity for skill upgrading	Reasonable opportunity to technical skill development
IT system compatibility	Highly developed IT system	Manual or primitive IT systems
Employee Satisfaction	Highly motivated, well paid work force.	Competent, but low paid work force.
Employee turn over	High turn over	Relatively low employee turnover.

Strategic alliance in this situation requires careful evaluation of strengths and weaknesses of each firms, and detail planning of how the reorganized alliance would look like. The IT architectural planning will not only present the overview of future challenges, but will also provide chief information officers (CIO) the nature of human related activities they would be faced with once the alliance becomes a reality.

To forge a meaningful alliance TEL would be required to make a number of major business decisions, which would influenced the overall IT architecture. These decisions would form the core of the IT system and partnership relations:

- TEL will require a customer signed application form before the Retail Transfer process can commence.
- TEL will not enter into and conduct a customer transfer under the BETS process.
- The company will negotiate contracts with a LNSP, which will ensure that LNSPs will connect customers to their network at a customer nominated date and time or within a reasonable time. Noteworthy each LNSP will perform service location work for the electricity connection.
- TEL will appoint only registered Metering Data Agents (MDAs) to read meters at agreed customer start date and times.
- A Meter Provider will install and remove electricity meters only with company's written instructions.
- Each LNSP is responsible for fault rectification and maintenance of their electricity distribution network in their local area. TEL will hand off to the appropriate LNSP for fault calls made to TEL. TEL will pay the relevant service fee, but if the customer is culpable for the fault, the onus will be on the LNSP to recover costs.
- Meter Data Agents are to provide all customer electricity usage to the Retailer for billing purposes, typically daily overnight for smart meters. MDAs will employ manual meter readers to read SIMs at a minimum interval of monthly regardless of the billing cycle.
- TEL will settle with MDAs, LNSPs, MPs, energy traders and the Pool for electricity energy cost of goods sold.
- TEL must provide energy forecasts to energy traders so they can determine the amount of energy to hedge.

If these alliances are to eventuate the existing processes and systems will be used to generate reports to partner sales and commissions. TEL would be required to provide a lot of technical support to potential strategic partners. Partners in electricity retail business in general do not have well developed information systems, which could be a limitation to full-scale system integration. Electricity retailers currently have manual settlement systems.

DISCUSSIONS

In today's competitive business environment new methods of evolution from independence to interdependence are continuing to unfold - strategic alliance is one of those methods to achieve competitive advantage. In the process of strategic alliance, IT architecture and human factors play important roles. In addition to projecting the overview of information systems in the organization, information officers should focus on human aspects to make an alliance effective. IT planning highlights major weaknesses and incompatibilities with information systems of various parties. Those incompatibilities, however, can intensify further due to operational and work practices in partner organizations.

Though the case study pertains to a telecommunication company, the concepts can be applied to any business which contemplating to diversifying its operation. The development of IT system and focus to human issues would lead to practical improvement.

REFERENCES

Adler, L.(2001) Merger Mess. *Business Mexico.* Vol. 11, No. 7, pp.24 - 25.

Ansoff, I.H. (1986) '*Corporate Strategy*', Sidwick and Jackson, London.

Applegate, L. M., McFarlan, F.W., and McKenney, J.L (1999) Corporate Information Systems Management: Text and Cases, Irwin McGraw-Hill.

Bronder, C. and Pritzl, R. (1992) Developing strategic alliances: A successful framework for co-operation. *European Management Journal*, **10**(4), pp. 412-420.

Burrows, D. M.. (2000) How People Problems Can Sap Value From a Deal. *Merger and Acquisitions.* Vol. 35, No. 9, pp. 36-39.

Henderson, R and Clark, K (1990) 'Architectural innovation: the reconfiguration of existing product technologies and the failure of established firms', *Administrative Science Quarterly*, 35, pp.9-30.

Kendall, K.E and Kendall, J.E. (1995). '*Systems Analysis and Design*' 3rd Edition, Prentice-Hall International, New Jersey.

Leavitt, H. J. (1965) Applied Organizational Change in Industry: Structural, Technological and Humanistic Approaches. *Handbook of Organizations,* Edited by James March, Randy McNally & Company, pp. 1144 - 1170.

Markides, C.C and Williamson, P.J. (1997) 'Related Diversification, Core Competencies and Corporate Performance'. In: Cambell, A and Sommer Luchs, K., (Eds.) *Core Competency-Based Strategy*, pp. 96-122. International Thomson Business Press, London.

Maron, R. M. & VanBremen, L. (1999) The influence of Organizational Culture on Strategic Alliances. *Association Management.* Vol. 51, No.4, pp.86-92.

Numerof, R. E. & Abrams, M. N. (2000) Subtle Conflicts That Wreck Merger Visions. *Mergers and Acquisitions*, Vol. 35. No. 3, pp. 28-30.

Segil, L. (2000) Understanding Life Cycle Differences. *Association Management*, Vol. 52, No.8, pp.32-33.

The Internet's Potential to Provide Feedback to International Aid Organisations on Projects in Developing Countries

David King
PhD Candidate, Information Systems, Doctoral School, University of South Australia
Tel: 6 (108) 8302-0217, Fax: 6 (108)830-20992, David.King@unisa.edu.au

ABSTRACT

The purpose of this study is to highlight the use of the Internet to improve the reliability of information supplied to Aid organisations [IMF/ World Bank; UN] from official sources in developing countries. I argue that local people's confidential feedback on projects via the Internet would improve the effective utilisation of Aid from the Western world. Developing countries need good two-way flow of public information on project progress. The use of the Internet's potential(s) in a way that will benefit society at large and in particular vulnerable groups will be examined within a wider framework of the actual needs and existing facilities of these communities. How useful and in what areas the Internet will be applied to benefit social development will be explored. This research should highlight the pragmatics of giving local people an international voice.

INTRODUCTION

The researcher's concern is that Developing Countries (DCs) need good two-way flow of public information. This derives from a deeper concern about the lack of effective use of Aid monies on projects in developing countries. This problem has also been identified in the UNDP Human Development Report [1998,1999] and also announced in the World Bank [1987, 1999] World Development Report. The possibilities of using the Internet to improve communication openness need examination. In today's Information Systems Revolution, I argue that the Internet can be used to provide broader-based feedback essential for the effective allocation of aid provided to aid agencies in developing countries.

THE INTERNET'S POTENTIAL IN DEVELOPING COUNTRIES

Wilson, [1996] points out that the Internet has the potential for intelligence gathering, including public comment on social programs. Kaye and Little [1996] have also emphasized that in this way the Internet can become a tool for social development. However, the control of information flow by official government sources in Africa is seen as a gatekeeper mechanism that has the potential to distort the decision making within international aid organisations such as United Nations and the World Bank [Pettigrew, 1972; Bloomfield and Coombs, 1992]. The Internet has the potential to be used by international aid organisations and the public to ensure other sources of information are available. Exactly how this might be undertaken needs to be researched in the context of the problem.

Jones, [1995]; Montealegre, [1996,1998] and Simon, [1996] assert that the Internet serves as a medium for sharing knowledge, communicating knowledge, acquiring useful information and knowledge transfer to allow communities to grow. This however downplays the power issues. In developing countries those with the resources can ensure an unequal flow of information especially given the large investment costs of the technology [Uimonen, 1997]. This has particular application in developing countries that are constantly seeking aid [World Bank, 1987].

In response to obvious failures in current development investments, where monies are not reaching the intended projects, the international community has begun to demand more accountability and openness of information flows [UNRISD, 1995]. Seeking to promote improved information management and the increased efficiency and effectiveness of Aid programs, Graeme and Weitzner, [1996] recommended a government-wide requirement for agencies to set goals and report annually on the performance of projects program. The author believes these reports could include local people's confidential feedback.

It is important that the reliability of the source and the accuracy of the information as judged by data available at, or close to, their operational levels are re-examined. Beacham, [1997] argues that the Internet technology can allow for participatory democracy in developing countries (Africa in particular) to enhance decision-making. Of particular interest is whether aid organizations are correctly informed about application of their contributions. The feedback from governments to international aid organizations is often unreliable. This feedback needs to be evaluated, and it is believed that the best people to this are the locals. Decision-making on project funding has often been hampered by the lack of accurate information on the results of international aid organizations program efforts.

Kenney, [1995], Mansell and Wehn, [1998] asserted that the importance of expanding the access of developing countries to the Internet has been recognised by governments and international agencies with increasing consensus that the internet and related telecommunications technology should be regarded as strategic national infrastructure. However Goodman et al, [1994] claim that the ways in which different developing countries are adopting these new technologies and supporting business strategic and entrepreneur initiatives have received little critical attention.

The Internet can be used to provide continuous feedback on project implementation, and to identify actual or potential successes and problems as early as possible to facilitate timely adjustments to project operations. The creation or strengthening of monitoring activities under a project is not a temporary requirement to meet aid organisations information needs, but an institution-building component which should permanently improve overall management practice within borrower agencies [Dambia 1991].

The Internet is infrastructure independent, open, decentralized, abundant, interactive, user-controlled, and global in its reach, and can be used by the public. The World Bank [1999] experience on projects aimed at developing governance and policy-forming capacity in Africa, for example, finds that government failures in Sub Sahara Africa are often attributable in whole or in part to governments' unwillingness to make themselves accountable to the citizens they are supposed to serve. The Internet has tremendous potential for fostering democratic participation, giving voice to the voiceless [Bimber 1997]. Fig 1 shows that the Internet could allow the public to communicate with aid organisations about the progress of a project. The researcher sees the Internet as multi-directional.

Figure 1: The Internet is an intelligence gathering tool

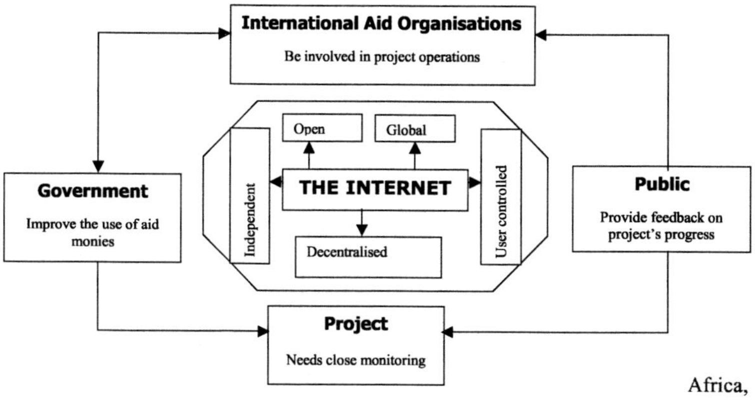

UNRISD, [1996] has already suggested that both the international aid organisations and the developing countries' governments need carefully evaluated information to help them make useful decisions about the programs they oversee. Also they need to implement Information and Communication Technology (ICT) tools that tell them whether, and in what important ways, an aid project is working well or poorly, and why. Madon, [1999] stated that, in the past, the tools for information evaluation have not proven to be reliable. This is supported by the uncountable number of project failures in most parts of the developing world. Rice and McDaniel (1987) also suggest that the Internet can allow developing countries' public to send and receive information on ongoing projects. This should help with their personal development through feeling of self worth and less feeling of helplessness.

Professor K. Griffin, a former Chairman of the UNRISD Board discusses the intrinsic value of human development and cultural diversity, and also their instrumental value in promoting growth [Griffin, 1997]. In discussing the ties that bind human development and economic growth, Griffin places emphasis on investing in human capacities, pointing out the positive economic repercussions of keeping such investments high and well distributed across society as a whole. He argues that creativity — new knowledge, new technology and new institutional arrangements are the fountainhead of economic growth, and contribute to creativity in all fields of endeavour. United Nations and other aid organisations are in a strong position to achieve economic growth and higher rate of project success by encouraging public involvement and the use of the Internet.

Information systems revolution could help level the international playing field in terms of opportunities for social and economic development. However, if appropriate care is not taken, the same revolution instead could lead to increasing inequality in incomes and information access across regions, countries, areas within countries, income groups, communities and individuals.

The Internet is today's electronic media that can profoundly influence economic and political development in developing countries. To what extent this influence will be, and its positive and sustainable effects will depend on a myriad of factors, some predictable and others not. The potential contribution of electronic media to political outcomes in developing countries, such as its impact on effective use of aid for socio-economic development, needs critical attention.

THE OLD MEDIA TECHNOLOGY AND INFORMATION OPENNESS

Beacham, [1997] and Ronning, [1994] claim that, at present, there is no empirical evidence that electronic media have contributed to "democracy" in Africa. Despite the long-standing presence of both radio and television in some African countries, there appears to be little linkage between access to these forms of media and political democracy. This may be the result of the state control of radio and television for much of the period for which data is available. It is only in the last five years that private radio and television has been allowed to exist in many African countries, and some lag time may be required for effects to become noticeable. In addition, the impact of electronic media on political activity is difficult to measure quantitatively across the continent.

As Ronning (1994) noted, one of the democratic mediums such as radio, when used in a decentralized manner may give local people and communities an opportunity to express their grievances in representative discussions. This, however assumes the establishment of decentralized structures and local and community radio stations as well as radio stations representing the views of "voiceless groups" in civil society such as minorities. For much of Africa, efforts to decentralize power and to establish community radio are in a preliminary state, which limits the ability of this analysis to capture their impact. Further, expansion of television is much more problematic for Africa, requiring a substantially greater outlay of capital resources and is therefore less likely to become a means for distribution of independent sources of information. Internet capabilities far outweigh any of the old communication media in terms of costs, efficiency and reliability. The Internet is the 'now' and 'coming' generation's educational communication medium .The Internet appears to hold great potential to improve access to information in Africa [Jensen, 1997].

CONCLUSION

Unique features of this new technology, if properly supported, can foster public freedom of expression essential to the effective use of aid monies on projects in developing countries. Moreover, World Bank, [1999] reported that the Internet could allow civil societies to participate in the progress of aid projects in developing countries in ways previously impossible. It is believed that the Internet can be useful, especially if integrated into the aid organisations' conditions of investment. This research will help clarify one appropriate role of the Internet in assisting in sustainable and equitable development in developing countries. Developing countries need a good independent non-corruptible monitoring system especially in complex projects with several agencies involved.

REFERENCES

Beacham, F. [1997] "The Internet: Will it Become the Next Mass Media?" In: Media and Democracy: A Collection of Readings and Resources. Washington D. C.: Institute for Alternative Journalism, at http://www.igc.apc.org/an/bo ok/beacham7.html

Bimber, B. [1997] "The Internet and Political Participation: The 1996 Election Season", paper prepared for delivery at the 1997 Annual Meeting of the American Political Science Association, Washington D. C., August 28-31.

Bloomfield, B.P. and Coombs, R. [1992] Information Technology, Control and Power: The Centralization and Decentralization Debate, Manchester School of Management, UMIST.

Dambia, P-C, [1991] Governance and economic development. - pp.17-19 In: AFRICAFORUM : a journal of leadership and development. - Vol 1, no 1.

Graeme, B. and Weitzner, D. J. [1996] Electronic Democracy : Using the Internet to Influence American Politics. Wilton, Conn.: Online.

Griffin, K. [1997] Culture, Human Development and Economic Growth.

Jensen, M. [1997] "Internet Connectivity for Africa", September, at http://demiurge.wn.apc.org/africa/afstat.htm

Jones, S. [1995] Cyber Society, Sage, California.

Kaye, R. and Little, S.E. [1996] Global Business and Cross-Cultural Information Systems, Technical and Institutional Dimensions of Diffusion. Information Technology & People, vol.9 No.3 1996 pp.30-50.

Kenney, G. [1995] The Missing Link – Information, Information Technology for Development, Vol. 6, pp. 33-38.

Madon, S. [1999] The Internet and Socio-economic Development: Exploring the Interaction. London school of economics.

Mansell, R. and Wenn, U. [1998] Knowledge Societies: Information Technology for Sustainable Development, Oxford University Press

Montealegre, R. [1996] Implications of Electronic Commerce for Managers in Less-Developed Countries, Information Technology Development, vol. 7 pp. 145-152.

Montealegre, R. [1998] Waves of Change in Adopting The Internet : Lessons from Four Latin American countries. University of Colorado, Boulder, College of Business and Administration, Boulder, Colorado USA.

Pettigrew, A. M. [1972] Information Control As a Power Resource. An article discussed in the IS doctoral School. UNISA.

Rice, R.E., & McDaniel, B. [1987] Managing organizational innovation: The evolution from work processing to office information systems. New York: Columbia University Press.

Ronning, H. [1994] Media and Democracy: Theories and Principles with Reference to the African Context. Harare: Sapes Books, pp. 16-19.

Simon, H. [1996] A computer for everyman, The American scholar. New York.

Uimonen, P. [1997] United Nations Research Institute for Social Development (UNRISD), Geneva.

UNDP, [1998] Human Development Report 1998. New York: Oxford University Press.

UNDP, [1999] Monitoring human development: Enlarging people's choices... UNDP, Washington, 1999, p 262.

UNRISD, [1995] States of Disarray: The Social Effects of Globalization, report prepared for the World Summit for Social Development, 1995.

UNRISD, [1996] Social Futures, Global Visions Social Development (News) No. 14, Spring/Summer 1996 also in Volume 27, Number 2, April 1996).

Wilson, M. [1996] Considering the Net as an Intelligence Tool.

World Bank, [1987] World Development Report, Oxford University Press, Washington, DC

World Bank, [1999] World Development Report 1999/2000, World Bank,Washington, 1999.

The ASP Paradigm for Strategic IT Governance: Reducing Know-What Uncertainties for Successful Implementation

Rajiv Kishore, PhD
The State University of New York at Buffalo, School of Management
Tel: (716) 645-3507, Fax: (716) 645-6117, rkishore@buffalo.edu

BACKGROUND

Fundamental changes in the way Information Technology (IT) and related business applications are owned, operated, and managed are being brought about by a rapidly emerging class of IT service providers, termed "Application Service Providers" (ASPs). ASPs, enabled by Internet technologies, are redefining the notion of "IT outsourcing" by altering the IT assets ownership and control equation. In this IT governance paradigm, business applications are rented/leased from ASPs on a recurring fee basis, and are run by individual and corporate users in a browser window on their desktops. The software application and the client data reside on ASP platforms and are accessed by customers through public and private computer networks, quite often the Internet.

The ASP governance model has been touted to provide several strategic advantages to the IT function, and thereby to the overall enterprise. Some of the potential advantages from the ASP paradigm that can accrue to the IT function of an enterprise include an accelerated speed of deployment of IT applications, seamless connectivity and integration among diverse business partners through shared web-based applications, scalability of IT infrastructure, and a lower and predictable total cost of ownership (2000). These advantages indeed have the potential to allow an enterprise to refocus on firm competencies and to provide flexibility in acquiring new business capabilities (1999).

However, the ASP governance model does not come without its share of challenges and risks. The fact that client data reside on ASP-owned servers poses new threats pertaining to data security and privacy. Software applications are operated and managed by ASP vendors generally as "packaged solutions" for multiple clients, because that is precisely what the ASP model provides for – a one-to-many relationship. However, in such a scenario there are risks of getting "locked in" with older versions of "vanilla" applications. Because the "value network" in the ASP model is quite complex, aggregating products and services from a number of vendors, including telecommunications and network providers, hardware vendors, application vendors, software tools vendors, service firms, and distributors and resellers (Gillan, et al., 1999), the overall quality of service to clients may be an important concern that needs to be fully addressed prior to adoption of this governance model. Finally, the financial viability of specific ASP vendors in the current financial climate, especially after the dot.com bust that started last year, is a matter of immense concern to potential adopters.

RESEARCH MOTIVATION AND GOALS

The goal of this research is to develop a better understanding about the comparatively nascent ASP phenomenon – it has just been around for nearly three years – in the context of its potential adoption as a governance choice. In its current state, the ASP model poses a number of "know-what," "know-why," and "know-how" uncertainties and barriers for potential adopters of this IT governance choice. Know-what "represents an appreciation of the kinds of phenomenon worth pursuing," know-why "represents an understanding of the principles underlying phenomenon," and know-how "represents an understanding of the generative processes that constitute phenomenon" (Garud, 1997). In the context of implementation of the ASP paradigm, know-what represents an appreciation and understanding about the promises and perils of the ASP paradigm, know-why represents an understanding about why this phenomenon will provide the benefits it promises, and know-how represents specific methods and techniques required to utilize this phenomenon, both in terms of managing the contractual relationship and in terms of using the IT services provided through this model. Overcoming "know-what" uncertainties is essential for potential adopters so that they are not only able to adequately discriminate the substance from the hype, and make informed choices during the adoption process, but also to negotiate "win-win" contracts and service level agreements with ASP vendors.

The IS literature has developed a considerable body of literature in the area of systems implementation over the last nearly two decades. IS literature has also devoted much attention during the last decade to the phenomenon of IS outsourcing, of which the ASP paradigm is a specific incarnation. However, there is a paucity of literature in both these streams that focuses on the issue of how know-what uncertainties can be overcome in the context of adoption of strategic information technologies or IT governance mechanisms. This research is an attempt to fill that void. It focuses on two broad mechanisms that can help organizations reduce know-what uncertainties as they evaluate the ASP option, the first being the notion of "organizing vision" (Swanson and Ramiller, 1997) and the second being the notion of "trust" (Rousseau, et al., 1998).

THEORY DEVELOPMENT

An overview of the proposed research is shown in figure 1 and the key concepts, constructs, and relationships shown in this diagram are briefly discussed in the following paragraphs. The actual research model with testable hypotheses will be included in the full research paper.

Organizing Vision

An organizing vision is a focal community idea for the application of information technology in organizations" (Swanson and Ramiller, 1997, p. 460). These visions are created by the larger IS community, comprising of IT vendors, IT consultants, potential adopters, research and advisory firms, etc., to facilitate the development and deployment of IT innovations. Organizing visions are crafted in a commu-

FIgure 1: An overview of the proposed research

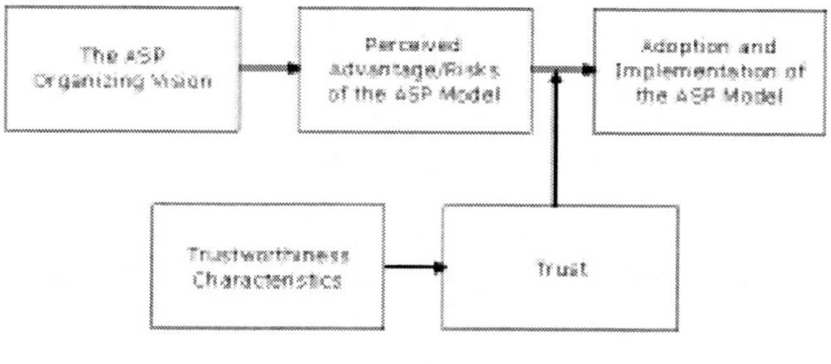

nity discursive domain through such means and channels as trade shows, professional meetings, trade magazines, virtual communities, etc.

Participating in the organizing vision discourse provides potential adopters with an opportunity to know more comprehensively the context and content of the focal innovation – ASP paradigm in our case – and its advantages and attendant risks, thereby reducing their know-what uncertainty pertaining to the ASP phenomenon. This participation not only provides potential adopters with knowledge about "... the existence and potential gains of a new innovation" (Attewell, 1992), or "signaling" information, it also provides the potential adopter with the opportunity to actually engage in richer two-way interactions with the various players in the ASP arena. Therefore, the ASP organizing vision is a much larger mechanism than signaling for helping reduce the know-what uncertainties, and it is expected to affect a potential adopter's perceptions about the advantages of and risks inherent in the ASP paradigm.

Trust

Trust is a psychological state comprising the intention to accept vulnerability based upon positive expectations of the intentions or behavior of another" (Rousseau, et al., 1998). While a heightened awareness about the relative advantages and risks of the ASP paradigm will result from a higher degree of participation in the organizing vision discourse, a potential adopter may still be uncertain about the "truthfulness" of the claims made and the likelihood of successful implementation. Trust – both an institutional trust in the ASP paradigm and calculative trust between the vendor and the client organizations – provides yet another mechanism for reducing know-what uncertainties pertaining to the fruition of benefits and the occurrence of risky and undesirable outcomes (Rousseau, et al., 1998). Trust is expected to moderate the relationship between the drivers of adoption – perceived relative advantage and risks of the ASP paradigm – and the adoption/implementation of the ASP model. Trustworthiness characteristics (Sheppard and Sherman, 1998) also act as mitigators for the various kinds of risks that are inherent in the ASP paradigm, and not only alleviate adopter concerns during initial adoption decisions but also provide mechanisms to manage inherently "incomplete" ASP outsourcing contracts through a judicious combination of control and trust (Das and Teng, 1998).

Perceived Advantages and Risks

The notion that perceived relative advantage is a key predictor of adoption of innovations is quite well-established in the innovation theory literature in various disciplines (Rogers, 1995). However, the innovation literature has not specifically focused on the disadvantages, or risks, from the focal innovation that may dissuade a potential adopter from adopting the innovation. This may perhaps be because of the "pro-innovation bias" that, according to Rogers (Rogers, 1995), pervades the innovation theory field, and leads "... diffusion researchers to ignore the study of ignorance about innovations ..." However, as mentioned earlier, the ASP phenomenon is not only in a nascent state, the last two years have been very turbulent for the ASP vendors many of which have gone into bankruptcy and several others have gone out of business completely. It is quite understandable that potential adopters may be shying away from adopting the ASP paradigm as a governance model in the current environment due to the high degree of risk inherent in such a decision. Any study of adoption and implementation of ASPs will be at best incomplete and at worst misleading, if it does not consider the risks inherent in the ASP paradigm as a key driver of the ASP adoption phenomenon. The "perceived risk" construct that we consider in this research is similar to the notion of "risk perception" in the organizational literature (Sitkin and Pablo, 1992; Sitkin and Weingart, 1995) and in the MIS literature (Keil, et al., 2000).

RESEARCH METHODOLOGY

The proposed research is planned to be conducted using the survey research methodology. The survey is planned to be administered as a web-based survey to a national sample of senior IT executives. Follow-up telephone interviews with survey participants, who agree for such interviews, may be conducted to elicit further insights pertaining to their quantitative and qualitative responses, and to seek clarifications, wherever necessary.

ACKNOWLEDGEMENTS

This material is based upon work supported by the National Science Foundation under Grant No. 9907325. Any opinions, findings, and conclusions or recommendations expressed in this material are those of the author and do not necessarily reflect the views of the National Science Foundation.

REFERENCES

"Application Service Providers (ASP)," Spotlight Report Cherry Tree & Co., October 1999.

"e-Sourcing the corporation: Harnessing the power of web-based application service providers," Fortune, *(2000:March 6), March 6 2000, pp. S1-S27.*

Attewell, P. "Technology diffusion and organizational learning: The case of business computing," Organization Science *(3), 1992, pp. 1-19.*

Das, T.K. and Teng, B.-S. "Between trust and control: Developing confidence in partner cooperation in alliances," Academy of Management Review *(23:3), 1998, pp. 491-512.*

Garud, R. "On the distinction between know-how, know-what and know-why," In Advances in Strategic Management, *A. Huff and J. Walsh (Ed.), JAI Press, 1997, pp. 81-101.*

Gillan, C., Graham, S., Levitt, M., McArthur, J., Murray, S., Turner, V., Villars, R. and Whalen, M.M. "The ASPs' Impact on the IT Industry: An IDC-Wide Opinion," Bulletin International Data Corporation, 1999.

Keil, M., Tan, B.C.Y., Wei, K.-K., Saarinen, T., Tuunainen, V. and Wassenaar, A. "A cross-cultural study on escalation of commitment behavior in software projects," MIS Quarterly *(24:2), 2000, pp. 299-325.*

Rogers, E.M. Diffusion of Innovations, *The Free Press, New York, NY, 1995.*

Rousseau, D.M., Sitkin, S.B., Burt, R.S. and Camerer, C. "Not so different after all: A cross-discipline view of trust," Academy of Management Review *(23:3), 1998, pp. 393-404.*

Sheppard, B.H. and Sherman, D.M. "The grammars of trust: A model and general implications," Academy of Management Review *(23:3), 1998, pp. 422-437.*

Sitkin, S.B. and Pablo, A.L. "Reconceptualizing the determinants of risk behavior," Academy of Management Review *(17:1), 1992, pp. 9-38.*

Sitkin, S.B. and Weingart, L.R. "Determinants of risky decision-making behavior: A test of the mediating role of risk perceptions and propensity," Academy of Management Journal *(38:6), 1995, pp. 1573-1592.*

Swanson, E.B. and Ramiller, N.C. "The organizing vision in information systems innovation," Organization Science *(8:5), 1997, pp. 458-474.*

Virtualisation and Its Role in Society—Diagnosis Attempt

Jerzy Kisielnicki, PhD
Warsaw University, Faculty of Management, Tel: 4 (822) 644-8233, jkis@wspiz.edu.pl

INTRODUCTION

Virtualisation, which is a subject of this thesis, could not exist without Information Technology. Most authors who write about the problem of virtualisation apply an object-centred approach. Within this approach, the analysis is based on organisations and their structure. It is believed this approach should be supplemented by a process-centred approach which allows to present both a complex nature of the virtualisation process and the analysis of its impact on society. According to L.Percival-Straunik [12], virtualisation triggers off the process of integration and creation of global organisations. It is the basis of new business quality measures such as E-business and E-Commerce.

The hypothesis which I would like to prove in this thesis is as follows:

In today's world, a controlled virtualisation process creates enormous opportunity for economic growth of those countries and organisations which so far, due to various restrictions, have had no chance to establish themselves on the global market and become competitive.

In practice, the restrictions on development are of varied nature. They might be economic, legal, psychological and organisational. The hypothesis presented earlier may be developed further; in the modern world, only those people and organisations who know how to make use of the possibilities presented by virtualisation may become competitive on the global market. Moreover, virtualisation creates best options for intellectual enterprise development. I fully agree with M.Barrenechea [2] that " E- business or out of business".

The reason for which the virtualisation process has to be controlled is the fact that it brings advantages as well as new unknown dangers. Some of these dangers have been described by N. Chenoweth [3] in "Reality war on the information's highway". In most cases, virtualisation, according to M.Breier [3], G.Gates [6], J. Maitland [11], is a chance for a significant improvement of one's life situation or development of an organisation.

The term virtualisation describes the processes connected with IT application. It is facilitated in the following areas of activity:

- In traditional organisations which want to expand their range of activities and have access to IT and global computer network. Such organisations develop through creating new subservient organisational units such as internet kiosks or shops. Other steps leading to further development include expanding, through the IT, the already existing sphere of activity, for example marketing or human resources.
- Creating a virtual organisation, i.e. an organisation established in order to achieve common goal or goals. In such an organisation, the participants enter various types of relationships. The duration of a relationship is determined by each of the participants of the virtual organisation. A decision to terminate or reconstruct may be taken by any participant who decides that the relationship is no longer beneficial for him/her. A virtual organisation operates in the so-called cyber-space. The duration of any relationship may be extremely short. A virtual organisation does not have one boss. It begins to exist precisely at the moment when the manager of any given organisation comes to a conclusion that he is unable to fulfil the task on his own and he needs to co-operate with other organisations.
- Supporting teaching in various areas including distant learning and application of computer simulation models for teaching such subjects as decision-making processes or complex process analysis.

The influence of virtualisation on the society is both varied and significant.

In this thesis, I present the results of my own research on this problem and the analysis of the literature on application of virtualisation in practice. The thesis also focuses on the problem of virtualisation as a chance for small and medium-size organisations and also on the role of virtualisation in stimulating professional activation.

VIRTUALISATION IN TRADITIONAL ORGANISATIONS

Virtualisation allows for development of any organisation at much lower cost than in the traditional way. The virtual elements established within the virtualisation process are very flexible. Thus the organisation may quickly adjust to the changing environment.

The development through virtualisation may be facilitated as follows:

- The organisation creates virtual kiosks or shops. For that a specialist software is required. Thus, the organisation which sells furniture, using computer graphics, may present its products on a computer screen. It may also receive orders in places located outside their traditional locations. In exactly the same way, other organisations, e.g. tourist, real estate, bookshops, stock exchange etc. may operate.
- An organisation places information about its activity on the appropriate internet pages. Through the monitoring programmes it is available to its potential clients 24 hours a day. This way, the operations of the organisation are not limited to office hours only.
- Organisation creates a possibility of working from home, the so-called Tele-work. In this way, the organisation may develop or restrict its activities depending on its needs. It is a very good way of increasing professional activity in those regions in which it is difficult to find employment in a traditional way. It should also be remembered that through Tele-work, a local organisation may become a global one.

Virtualisation allows traditional organisations to have a wider range of influence. A society is better informed on the organisation's activities both by the organisation itself and by its clients. The restrictions on the development are varied. The most common include: available financial resources to purchase the IT, language of presentation and a necessity to have access to global, reliable computer networks. It should also be stressed that unfortunately, virtualisation enables organisations which are not socially accepted (pornography, terrorism) to operate freely.

On the basis of the analysis of those organisations which utilise virtualisation in their activities, it can be assumed that their development requires five times lower investment outlays and cost connected with operational activities. Only in separated cases, the proportions were less favourable. Minimum savings obtained in result of virtualisation exceeded 60% of the financial resources which would otherwise be spent on comparable development of the same organisation.

In the organisations where the development is achieved through Tele-work, the proportions are difficult to calculate. The analysis of a situation in the organisations in which Tele-work is connected with group work (workflow management) or in those which obtain employees from the countries where salaries are low - confirms high effectiveness of virtualisation. Such a situation can be observed in software development. The companies from highly developed countries, such as for example USA, Great Britain or Germany employ programmers from India, China or Pakistan. This situation is beneficial for both the company and the countries the programmers come from. Whether it is beneficial for the tax system of the countries which buy such labour is another story.

It is a totally different situation when Tele-work is connected with professional activation of the disabled or the unemployed. Direct costs are higher as we deal with the poorer part of the society. Thus additional costs have to be incurred for training, hardware and software. Unfortunately, there is no data available to make a precise calculation. It is extremely difficult to establish how much money has been spent. In many countries, the cost of training and purchase of the equipment is covered by special social programmes. It is also difficult to estimate advantages. It may be said, that social effect which decreases the unemployment figures and, in the case of the disabled, enables them to live a normal life in the society is the most important one. It is a very significant advantage possible only through virtualisation. Tele-work ensures: reducing the necessity to directly invest in the development of an organisation, reducing overloading of communication systems, savings in the time spent on travelling to work, savings in expenses connected with creating new parking spaces.

The issue of outlays and effects connected with virtualisation of work places will be analysed in further research. The analyses which aim at more precise estimation of profitability of the decisions to develop an organisation through virtualisation are the most significant.

VIRTUAL ORGANISATION AS A CHANCE FOR SMALL AND MEDIUM ORGANISATIONS

Virtualisation which leads to creating a virtual organisation forms a separate category. The term virtual organisation was used previously. In the literature on this subject, there are many terms used to define such organisation. See among others: P.Drucker [4] ,M.Hammmer J.Champy [7].

The analysis of the existing virtual organisations confirms the fact that they are not created by big companies. Their development is made through previously stated directions of activity such as kiosks and internet shops and Tele-work. The reason for this situation might be fear of unethical conduct of other organisations who might destroy their reputation on the market [9].

Small and medium organisations, in order to establish themselves on the market and increase their competitiveness, create virtual organisations.

A questionnaire distributed by myself during the course on application of the Information Technology, provided the following result. (The questionnaire was completed by 65 owners and managers of small and medium organisations).

And thus given answers to the question:

Do you think that virtualisation may be a good direction of development for your organisation? – 48 positive answers.

There were also many reservations as to the development through virtualisation. They were mainly connected with the fear of:

- Unethical behaviour of the co-operating organisations, for example not fulfilling their obligations, offering low quality products and also dishonest competition (the so-called economic sabotage),
- Operating in the conditions of total transparency which may lead to the theft of an idea or new technology, especially by big organisations as they have the appropriate economic potential and staff and are able to perform the task independently.

The questionnaire as such has a limited cognitive value but show the problem. It was conducted once only, in one country, in a big industrial centre. The people who participate in professional skill development training are always those who search for new solutions. Their opinions may not always be the same as the opinions of the so-called average owners and managers.

Virtualisation is a chance for transformation of small and medium organisations into fully competitive organisations even for the big and well known companies. Virtual organisations perform the role of an incubator. And this is their positive influence on the society.

VIRTUALISATION OF TEACHING

The research conducted by me and published previously suggests that a significant number of students both in day studies and those working feel the need to learn how to manage an organisation [10]. The learning should be organised in circumstances as close to the reality as possible. Virtualisation is the discipline of studies which may cause the distance between the theory and practice to diminish. One may even risk a statement that it is the exact direction of the virtualisation which, in the nearest future, shall have the most significant impact on the society. Virtualisation has the influence on the increase of the effectiveness of the teaching process in the widest possible sense. It is virtualisation which allows for simulation of both the decision-making process and the analysis of complex technical or sociological processes. In virtualisation of teaching, two basic direction in which it develops can be identified.

The first one is the direction of common education in which everybody can, using the tools of Information Technology, possess a given knowledge. A classic example is a virtual stock exchange. This direction allows to educate societies. There are also numerous games available through internet.

Another direction is dedicated teaching. There are the following activities to be identified:

- Self-control, i.e. your own evaluation of the possessed knowledge.
- Help in learning specific subjects. This includes, amongst others, enterprise laboratories, business games.
- Distant learning.

Nowadays, all the decision-makers seem to appreciate the significant role of the virtualisation in the process of education, although they do not always realise how complex it is.

FINAL COMMENTS

Virtualisation is a very complex process. Nevertheless, it will certainly develop and be applied to an ever expanding range of activities. It carries a lot of positive impact on the societies, but also some dangers, I would not like the reader to get an impression that I treat virtualisation as a way to success. It should be remembered that, according to Thomson Financial Securities Data, for 20 internet companies introduced at the stock exchange by Merrill Lynch bank in 1997, the quotes of 15 of them dropped below the nominal value and two of them went bankrupt. The rates of eight companies, amongst the others of Buy.com- virtual computer shop and 24/7 Media- an internet advertising agency dropped below 10% of the nominal value [6]. The analysis of the reasons for this situation conducted by me shows that very often the reason lies within the management errors. The most apparent example is Pets.com- an internet animal food shop, which incurred a vast financial loss. The reason for this loss was the fact that the IT staff of the company could not solve the problem of defective codes. That was the reason for multi-million losses.

Despite these negative experiences with virtualisation – I remain an optimist and I would love to conduct research on this issue in various countries. The process of virtualisation has its features independent of the type of application. It also has its own character. Thus I welcome the opportunity to be able to discuss this issue on the forum of a global organisation such as IRMA which associates both practitioners and scientists.

REFERENCES

1. Barrenchea M, E-business, Mc Graw Hill, N-Y,2001.
2. Breier M, Internet Man@ger, Piatkus, London ,2000.

3. Chenoweth N.,Virtual Murdoch- Reality War on the Information Highway, Secker- Warburg, London ,2001.
4. Drucker P., The New Organisation, HBR, no 1-2.1998
5. Elstrom P, E-money, Business Week, July,2001, p.63.
6. Gates B.; Business @ the Speed of Thought, Pingwin, 2000.
7. Hammer M, Champy J.; Reengineering the Corporation, Harper Business,1994
8. Kisielnicki J.; Virtual Organisation as a Product of Information Society, Informatics 22/1998 p. 3
9. Kisielnicki J.; Management Ethics in Virtual Organisation, 10-th International Conference of the Information Resources Management Association, Hershey, Pennsylvania, 1999.
10. Kisielnicki J.; Virtual Organization as a Chance for Enterprise Development, in: Managing Information Technology in a Global Economy red. M. Khosrowpour, IDEA Group Pub. Hershey – London ,2001 p. 349
11. Maitland J. How to make your million from the Internet, Hodder&Stoughton, London, 2001.
12. Percival-Straunik L. E-commerce, The Economist Book, London, 2001

Five Dimensions of IT Strategy: A Framework for Minimizing Risk and Extending Strategic Impact

Linda V. Knight[1], James D. White[2] and Theresa A. Steinbach[3]
DePaul University, School of Computer Science, Telecommunications and Information, Illinois
[1]Tel: (312) 362-5165, [2]Tel: (312) 362-5777, [3]Tel: (312) 362-5064, [1,2,3]Fax: (312) 362-6116, {lknight, jwhite, tsteinbach}@cti.depaul.edu

ABSTRACT

This research proposes that, in addition to balancing risk in the total IT project portfolio as McFarlan suggested in 1981, organizations should also balance risk in their strategic IT portfolios. A framework is detailed that will both minimize the total risk of an organization's strategic project portfolio, and identify opportunities to extend the strategic life of its information systems. This framework incorporates five strategic dimensions distilled from the literature. These dimensions are (1) Primary Strategic Resource, (2) Competitive Strategy, (3) Strategic Target, (4) Strategic Mode, and (5) Competitive IT Orientation. To assess the framework's validity, a classic case in the strategic use of technology, American Airlines' SABRE reservation system, is used. Results indicate that overall strategic IT risk can be reduced by evaluating an organization's strategic IT portfolio against the five dimensions of the framework, and then seeking strategic IT projects and opportunities that would bring greater balance to the organization's efforts. In addition, by moving across boundaries in each of the five dimensions, strategic systems can adapt to competitive marketplace or technology changes, and thus maintain their strategic potency over extended time periods.

BACKGROUND

In 1981, McFarlan proposed that organizations develop aggregate risk profiles for their IT project portfolios. This research builds upon that idea by suggesting that organizations construct and analyze a risk profile specific to their strategic IT initiative portfolio. As Clemons (1999) noted, risks are rising as traditional technical, financial, and project risks are being supplemented or replaced by new kinds of strategic project risk, including functionality risk and political risk. Despite such increased risks to strategic IT projects, little research has been directed at better managing risk in strategic IT initiatives. This paper addresses that void. It also builds upon the work of those who have noted the difficulties involved in sustaining competitive advantage, including Leininger (1992) and Mata et al. (1995), by providing a framework that organizations can use to identify methods of extending the potency of their strategic systems.

METHODOLOGY

This research proposes a five-dimensional framework that can be used to evaluate and balance risk in the strategic IT project portfolio. A classic case in the strategic use of IT is then used to assess the framework.

DESCRIPTION OF THE FRAMEWORK

The Five Dimensions of IT Strategy (White, 2000) are summarized in Figure 1.

The five framework dimensions are based upon the literature, as summarized below:

Dimension 1, Primary Strategic Resource

An organization may strategically leverage either technology itself, or the information that IT systems track and analyze (King, Grover and Hufnagel, 1989).

Dimension 2, Competitive Strategy

Rackoff, Wiseman, and Ullrich (1985), building on the work of Porter (1980), identified five strategic thrusts: differentiation, cost, innovation, growth, and alliances.

Figure 1: Five dimensions of IT strategy

5	**COMPETITIVE IT ORIENTATION** (where?)	External		Internal		
4	**STRATEGIC MODE** (why?)	Offensive		Defensive		
3	**STRATEGIC TARGET** (who?)	Supplier		Customer		Competitor
2	**COMPETITIVE STRATEGY** (how?)	Differentiation	Cost	Innovation	Growth	Alliances
1	**PRIMARY STRATEGIC RESOURCE** (what?)	Technology		Information		

Dimension 3, Strategic Targets

A strategic initiative may be aimed at relationships with suppliers, customers, or competitors (Wiseman and McMillan, 1984; Rackoff, Wiseman and Ullrich, 1985).

Dimension 4, Strategic Mode

An offensive strategic mode is designed to achieve competitive advantage, while a defensive strategic mode is designed to mitigate competitors' real or potential strategic advantages (Wiseman and McMillan, 1984; Rackoff, Wiseman and Ullrich, 1985).

Dimension 5, Competitive IT Orientation

Just as Porter (1985) offered both his view of the external competitive marketplace and his concept of the value chain, Benjamin et al. (1984) noted that IT could be used either externally in the competitive marketplace or internally to improve efficiency and effectiveness. Bakos and Treacy (1986) also addressed the internal vs. external orientation in their causal framework of competitive advantage.

APPLICATION OF THE FRAMEWORK

The SABRE airline reservation system (Hopper, 1990; Fryxell, 1996) was evaluated against the Five Dimensional Framework of IT

Strategy. In its original strategic implementation, American Airlines' SABRE system allowed travel agents direct access to flight booking information, without having to phone airline reservation centers. The system has since evolved to include travelocity.com, serving individual customers on the Web. It is now tied into a broad spectrum of other services and marketing programs, including hotels, car rentals, and frequent flier programs.

Primary Strategic Resource

In terms of the first level of the Five Dimensions Framework, SABRE began by primarily leveraging technology. Initially, the same information was made available to travel agents as had been made available previously over the telephone, but online computer technology improved the way in which the information was distributed. Over time, as the marketing of complementary products and personal information was added, the system moved from primarily leveraging technology to primarily leveraging information, thus demonstrating how organizations can move systems across boundaries within one dimension of the framework to achieve greater strategic advantage.

Competitive Strategy

Initially, SABRE's competitive strategy was primarily one of differentiation and innovation. This innovation triggered a process change for the airline industry. As online reservations became the industry norm, SABRE's strategy evolved into one of growth through alliances with other travel industry providers.

Strategic Target

SABRE's strategic target has always been the customer, although as the industry has evolved over time, the concept of the customer has changed focus, moving from travel agents to include individual travelers.

Strategic Mode

SABRE was originally in part a defensive measure against the power of travel agencies, and the possibility that they might develop their own computerized system. As online reservations systems expanded, the power of travel agents within the industry declined precipitously, and SABRE evolved into an offensive competitive weapon.

Competitive IT Orientation

SABRE's strategic life has always been centered externally, on the competitive marketplace.

ANALYSIS

SABRE represents an externally oriented strategic system, whose focus is on the customer. However, SABRE's concept of the customer has evolved as individuals began making travel arrangements via the Internet, and the power of travel agents declined. Further, as SABRE's original innovation became the industry norm, the system's competitive strategy evolved into one of growth through alliances. At the same time, SABRE's defensive leveraging of technology became an offensive leveraging of information. Thus, the system was able to maintain its strategic value because as its external environment, including both the travel industry and supporting technologies, changed, the system itself also continued to adapt. The SABRE example demonstrates that such an ability to move fluidly, if not nimbly, across boundaries of the Five Dimensions of IT Strategy can keep strategic systems strategic over extended time periods.

Most significantly, the American Airlines case analysis supports the hypothesis that the framework proposed here could be used by organizations to balance risk in their strategic IT portfolios. Such a balanced portfolio would have a broad spread of strategic projects. Some strategic projects would leverage technology, while others would leverage information. Some would be aimed at relationships with customers, while others would be aimed at relationships with suppliers or competitors. Some would be aimed at achieving competitive advantage, while others would be aimed at reducing competitors' real or potential strategic advantages. Some would be aimed at the external marketplace, while others would be aimed at improving internal processing efficiency. Finally, some might rely on differentiation, and others on cost, innovation, growth, or alliances. When an organization's total strategic portfolio is balanced with respect to these five dimensions, its marketplace position would be less vulnerable to strategic project risk.

Limitations / Future Research

The primary limitation of this research is the fact that only one case has thus far been evaluated against the framework. Analysis of additional classic cases, including American Hospital Supply's order entry system, Federal Express' package tracking system, and Cisco Systems electronic commerce system, is now in progress. In addition, plans are underway to apply the framework to several organizations' strategic IT project portfolios, with the goal of helping each organization develop its own strategic IT risk profile.

Practical Significance

Strategic systems face inevitable changes in their external environment. They are affected by both changes in their competitive marketplace and advances in technology. To maintain their competitive advantage, strategic systems must morph, significantly changing in at least one of their five strategic dimensions. The classic airline reservation system analyzed here demonstrates that organizations can maintain strategic advantage over extended periods of time, by moving across boundaries within the framework of the Five Dimensions of IT Strategy. Thus the five dimensional framework proposed here can help organizations identify opportunities to develop existing strategic systems in new directions, to better address changes in the competitive marketplace and/or technology and extend the period of strategic benefit. In addition, the framework provides organizations with the opportunity to recognize potentially under-tapped strategic opportunities, and to identify and balance the risk in its overall strategic IT portfolio. In particular, the framework enables organizations to identify areas where they are most open to an aggressive competitor's move. Further, it reveals the vulnerabilities that come from clustering strategic initiatives, emphasizing one or two approaches, while ignoring others.

CONCLUSION

This research integrates prior research on strategic initiatives into a single comprehensive framework for use in identifying strategic opportunities. Further, this research proposes that this framework can be used to extend systems' strategic potency. Most significantly, this research suggests that balancing risk in the IT project portfolio (McFarlan, 1981), while important, is insufficient, and that organizations should also balance the risk in their strategic IT portfolios. In addition to identifying opportunities to extend the strategic lifespan of IT systems, the framework specified by this research can also be used to identify and control exposure to strategic IT risk.

REFERENCES

Bakos, J. Y., and Treacy, M. E. (1986). Information Technology and Corporate Strategy: A Research Perspective. *MIS Quarterly* 10(2), 107-119.

Benjamin, R. I., Rockart, J. R., Scott Morton, M. S. and Wyman, J. (1984). Information Technology: A Strategic Opportunity. *Sloan Management Review* 25(5), 3-10.

Clemons, E. K. (1999). Risk Watch. *CIO Magazine* 12(21), 38-43. http://www.cio.com/archive/081599/expert_content.html accessed October 5, 2001.

Fryxell, D. A. (1996). eaasySABRE. *Link-Up* 13(3), 10-11.

Hopper, M. D. (1990). Rattling SABRE - New Ways to Compete on Information. *Harvard Business Review* 68(3), 118-125.

King, W. R., Grover, V., and Hofnagel, E. H. (1989). Using Information and Information Technology for Sustainable Competitive Advantage: Some Empirical Evidence. *Information & Management* 17(2), 87-93.

Leininger, K. E. (1992). Open Systems Slam the Door on the Days of Competitive Advantage by IT Alone. *Chief Information Officer Journal* 5(1), 47-50.

Mata, F. J., Fuerst, W. L., and Barney, J. B. (1995). Information Technology and Sustained Competitive Advantage: A Resource-based Analysis. *MIS Quarterly* 19(4), 487-504.

McFarlan, F. W. (1981). Portfolio Approach to Information Systems. *Harvard Business Review* 59(5), 142-150.

Porter, M. E. *Competitive Strategy.* New York: Free Press, 1980.

Porter, M. E., and Millar, V. E. (1985). How Information Gives You Competitive Advantage. *Harvard Business Review* 63(4), 149-160.

Rackoff, N., Wiseman, C., and Ullrich, W. A. (1985). Information Systems for Competitive Advantage: Implementation of a Planning Process. *MIS Quarterly* 9(4), 285-294.

White, James D. (2000). Dissertation proposal: *Why bad things happen to good systems; Proposal for research into key elements responsible for accidents during the maintenance and operation phases of strategic information systems.* DePaul University School of Computer Science, Telecommunications and Information Systems.

Wiseman, C., and MacMillan, I. C. (1984). Creating Competitive Weapons from Information Systems. *Journal of Business Strategy* 5(2), 42-49.

Global Management and Software Confederations

Jaroslav Král and Michal Zemlicka
Faculty of Mathematics and Physics, Charles University, Czech Republic
Tel: +42 (022) 191-4263, Fax: +42 (022) 191-4323, {kral,zemlicka}@ksi.mff.cuni.cz

ABSTRACT

Many human organizations like global worldwide enterprises, state administration systems, heath service systems, and many others have often the structure of a network of autonomous subunits. The structure of the information systems of such organizations should reflect this fact. They should be peer-to-peer networks of autonomous components. The components are often autonomous applications, information systems inclusive. We call such software systems software confederations (SWC). SW confederations have many SW engineering advantages and substantially simplify the executive management of global organizations as well as the management of their information systems. It, however, require specific tool and attitudes. Some typical cases (e.g. message format agreements, the decisions if buy/ purchase a component, etc.) are discussed. The SWC supports modern decentralized structure of enterprises.

INTRODUCTION

Many human organizations have the structure of a varying network of autonomous organizational subunits. It is typical for worldwide (global) enterprises, but it is quite common. Examples are international enterprises (it is a network local enterprises/factories), state administrations (a network of offices), health care (a network of health care units), financial systems, etc. The information system of such organizations should be peer-to-peer networks of autonomous components (information or legacy systems, third party products) due to the following reasons:

i. If an organizational subunit is to be sold, it should be sold with its information system(s). It is easier if the subunits have their autonomous information systems loosely coupled with the information system of the network of the whole organization.
ii. The use of legacy systems and/or third party products simplifies the development, maintenance, and the use of the system. It is not only due to the fact that some products need not be developed. If people from a subunit use their legacy system and/or their local information subsystems then they are interested to develop and use it properly (see e.g. [Král98, Král99]).
iii. Autonomous components offer better chances to meet security requirements (e.g. application-to-application encryption).
iv. The people in the organizational subunits may not want to loss their positions and/or political power so they want to have their local information system as autonomous as possible.
v. Critical functions of components should be used even in the situation when the whole system does not work (a special requirement of autonomy).

We call such software systems software confederations (SWC). We shall show that the use of software confederations is not only the necessity but also a big management challenge and promise.

REQUIREMENTS ON GLOBAL INFORMATION SYSTEMS

Design Rationale of global information systems is following:

a) The size of the organization (enterprise) is so great that it is practically impossible to manage it and its information systems in a centralized way. So it is good to have a system allowing to make decisions and to evaluate information at the lowest possible organizational level. The information system (IS) should support the locality of local decisions/changes. There is a large varying collection of the roles of the people working with the system (employees, public, business partners, etc.).
b) There are different user groups having different, sometimes contradictory and usually changing needs. It is difficult to satisfy all the different needs via a universal fixed user interface.
c) Global information systems should easily communicate with other information systems (global or local ones). Typical case is the formation of loosely coupled coalitions of international enterprises as we can see now in the car industry. IS of a state administration must be able to communicate with IS of the enterprises residing on the territory of the state. The collection of partner information systems therefore varies.

SW confederation (SWC) is the proper architecture to fulfill the requirements. We show that global management must not only live with the software confederation but that software confederation simplifies many management tasks in the case of global management of global organizations but also of the management of software confederation itself. Some new managerial problems must be however solved.

It is often supposed that SWC is a temporary solution that should be replaced by a more uniform monolithic architecture. The autonomous IS of an organizational (sub)unit of an international enterprise is a counterexample of such a belief. Another example is the user interface of confederations.

The user interface should hide the internal structure of the confederation. It follows that a user can command several autonomous components by one message (fig. 1). And vice versa a tuple of messages from components should be transformed into one user interface message. The user interface can be implemented on the way shown in fig. 1c. UC is an application providing the message transformations. IT can be written in XSLT The system is more flexible if UC is an autonomous component. Confederations then have the structure from fig. 1a. Log database contains the history of the communication in the confederation. Due to many reasons partly discussed below the format of messages between UC and AC should be XML based. SWC then have the structure shown in fig.2.

SWC AND GLOBAL INFORMATION MANAGEMENT

The development of SWC consists of the autonomous development of some constituent components, whereas other components are purchased or used as legacy systems the design of the format and semantics of messages between the components, the design and development of the confederation user interface (UC in fig. 1).

- Reduction of the amount of information that should be handled by global management (actions that may be done locally should be hidden in components). A management problem is the optimal balance between the centralized and decentralized activities. A specific problem is the politics of the messages formats standardization/ agreements.
- The management of the confederation handles only the rules of the component cooperation, especially the rules for autonomous groups

Figure 1a: Architecture of a software confederation component view

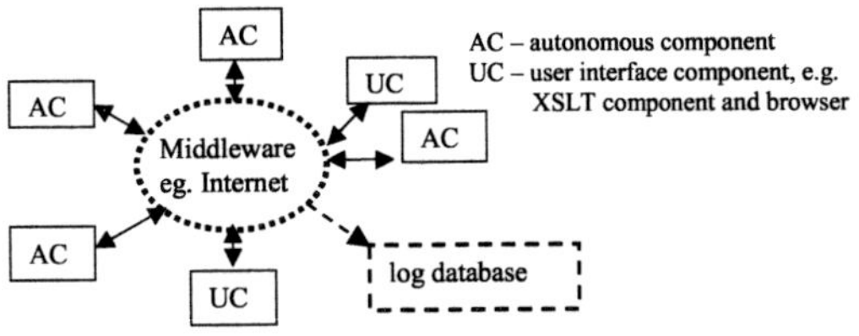

Figure 1b: Architecture of a software confederation user view

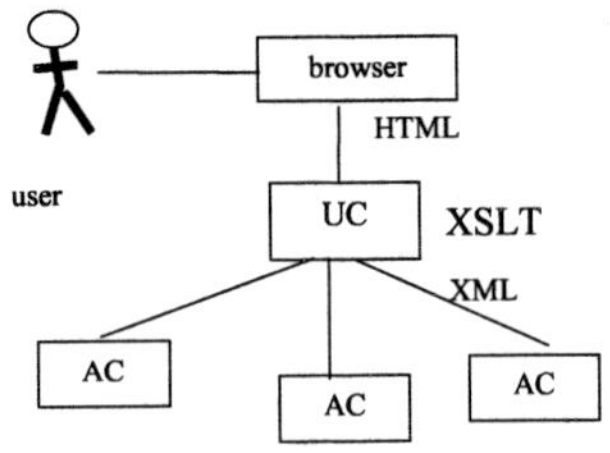

how to come to an agreement; it supports creation and setting of public standards, and formulates what should be done by particular subsystems.

- **The management should found an optimal balance between purchased and written components.**

The IT management may use some tools (e.g. message monitors, see log database in fig.1a) for the detection of problems in the system. Confederations are usually implemented as a set of components communicating via Internet based middleware. The components can be legacy systems (L - often three tier information systems), purchased applications (P), newly developed applications (D), and semiapplications (S) providing interface for particular group of users (Fig. 2). The users are connected to S-components via browsers. The · system has, therefore, a peer-to-peer architecture. The components must be equipped by gates implementing the interaction between the middleware and the particular component.

The components behave like Internet servers. The consequence is that the integration of "new" components is technically quite simple. From technical point of view it is irrelevant whether the newly "integrated" component is "own" or whether it is an IS of a partner organization or a purchased application. So the requirements *a) c)* and *b)* are fulfilled. Note, however, that it is a quite difficult business/management problem. The management must find a commercially feasible solution (e.g. the possibility to use above mentioned gates in purchased software). Large software vendors need not be happy with it as it can cause a greater independence of customers on their products. The

Figure 2: The structure of software confederation, three tier view

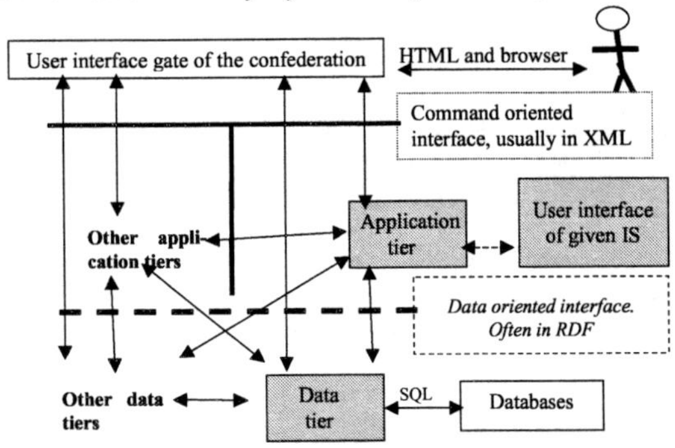

situation is changing now. Global management needs more and more data analysis, knowledge management and decision support tools. Such tools must usually be purchased from various vendors and integrated anyway.

As the components are often local information systems enhanced by interface gates, the local decisions ;;can be hidden. A new user group can be served by a newly developed S-component. The flexibility of interface required by b) is achieved if S-components are written as XSLT applications. As the number of clients of Internet can vary, the whole requirement b) is satisfied. The use of XSLT implies the use of XML message formats and the textual character of the messages.

It is not difficult to modify the middleware such that it stores the messages communicated over the network into a log database. The database allows the analysis of communication. This feature can be used by developers [K•01b], IT managers (monitoring the progress of the development, the detection whether some components should be rewritten due to instability caused by the long term maintenance), and executive managers (independent analysis of the business processes in the organizations). We can substantially reduce the maintenance, if we use SWC properly [K•01b]. It is an important observation. A great maintenance effort can imply the dissatisfaction with the system due its instability and due the frustration caused by frequent changes influencing users.

The philosophy of software confederations is a sound and powerful paradigm. There are, however, open problems.

1. The new paradigm requires a new way of thinking of developers and managers and sometimes of user as well. It is a quite difficult task.
2. The use of autonomous components must be based on knowledge domains forming the background of their functionalities. The developers should be able to understand various knowledge domains. A sound knowledge of mathematical skills and mastering of natural (mother) language is implicitly needed but missing.
3. The decentralization is a good strategy for software systems. There is not, however, enough know-how what is the optimal balance between centralized and decentralized activities and responsibilities.
4. It is not clear from what system size the concept of SWC should be used.
5. The components can be cloned and moved over the network. There are no sound principles how to use this option to optimize the system behavior.
6. Some security problems have not been solved yet.
7. There can be a problem with the effectiveness.
8. The confederation attitude is not supported by relevant modeling (CASE) tools.

CONCLUSIONS

The software confederations are the only known software architecture able to effectively fulfill requirements on the information systems of global organizations. A problem is that big software vendors need not feel software confederations to comply with their marketing policy. For example they need not will to offer their customer the opportunity to integrate third party products and the opportunity to realize a seamless change of main software supplier.

The philosophy of software confederation is not generally accepted by software experts (see [ThDo97, Press00]). The software confederation is a quite new technology for software public. The use of autonomous components and confederations is typical and unavoidable for very large systems. The large systems can be developed by large software vendors only. So the necessary knowledge and skills are difficult to achieve in academia.

REFERENCES

[Gold2] Goldratt, E.M.: *Critical Chain*, North River Press, Great Barrington, MA.

[Jac95] Jacobson, I., et al, Object Oriented Software Engineering: A Use Case Driven Approach, second printing, Addison Wesley, 1995

[Král99] Král, J.: *Architecture of Open Information Systems*, Proceedings of the ISD98 Conference, Bled, Slovenia, Sept. 1998, 8pp., in Plenum Press in 1999.

[K•01a] Král J., Zemlicka, M.: *Necessity, Challenges, and Promises of Peer-to-Peer Architecture of Information Systems*. Presented at the conference ISD 2001, September 2001, to be published by Kluwer Press.

[K•01b] Král, J., •emlièka, M.: *Software Confederations and the Maintenance of Global Software Systems*. To appear.

[Nie93] Nielsen, J.: Usability Engineering. Academic press, 1993.

[Press00] Pressman, R. S.: Software Engineering. A Practitioner's Approach. 5th Edition. McGraw-Hill, 2000.

[RDF] *RDF, Resource Definition Framework*. http://www.w3.org/RDF.

[ThDo97] Thayer, R. H., Dorfman, M. (Eds.): *Software Requirements Engineering, 2nd edition*. IEEE Computer Society Press, 1997.

[UML] *UML*, http://uml.systemhouse.mci.com/artifacts. Home page containing links to the proposed standard of UML, 1999.

[XML] XML: *Extensible Markup Language (XML)*. http://www.w3.org/XML.

[XSLT] *XSL Transformations (XSLT)*. http://www.w3.org/TR/xslt. W3C Recommendation, 16 November 1999.

Development of a Global IT Transition Framework

Yi-chen Lan
School of Computing and IT, University of Western Sydney, Australia
Tel: +6 (129) 685-9283, Fax: +6 (129) 685-9245, yichen@cit.uws.edu.au

INTRODUCTION

Rapid development of information technology (IT) has enabled the multinational corporations (MNCs) to conduct their global business operations extremely efficiently. Undoubtedly, a well-designed global information system is a critical success factor of managing and operating the MNC smoothly and effectively. In the past decade, researchers have identified a number of IT transfer issues that related to the organisations' global transition (Burn et. al, 1993; Edberg et. al, 2001; Nelson, 1996; Palvia et. al, 1992; Sankar & Prabhakar, 1992; Watson et. al, 1997). However, global IT transition challenges are not just identifying the IT transfer issues but consolidating and resolving these issues to support the organisations towards globalisation. The intent of this research is to categorise the IT transfer issues into various IT management classes, and develop a global transition framework that is mainly based on the IT transfer issues, while also taking into account the impact of the issues from intra- and inter-organisational perspectives.

LITERATURE REVIEW

The implementation of global information systems is based on the coordination and inter-communication of software applications, hardware components, telecommunications, networks infrastructure, and network management in a cross-border business environment (Sankar & Prabhakar, 1992). The management of these IT components is critical in terms of the successful operation of global information systems. Organisations need to realise and understand the global IT management issues (Figure 1) in order to adopt the most suitable technologies for global information systems. Furthermore, an organisation's IT architecture needs to be formally defined in term of the relationships between the system components and how the components integrate. Knowles (1996) and Passmore (1997) have precisely described the IT architecture as the underlying technology platform that supports all data and applications, including hardware, systems software and communication; accordingly, the fundamental properties of an organisation's IT architecture are essentially related to hardware, software, network, and data/information.

On the other hand, a need of clear organisational transition scope provides an overview of the level and category of IT requirement in both internal - within a single organisation and external - across two or more organisations (Fagan, 2001). The rest of this paper categorises the global IT management issues into four classes and develops the global transition framework for the conceptual direction of global IT transition.

GLOBAL TRANSITION FRAMEWORK

It is proposed that the development of the global transition framework involves the following two steps:

Step 1: categorising the global IT management issues into four major classes; and

Step 2: identifying the IT requirements based on the intersection of the IT management class and the organisational transition scope.

The review of the global IT literature and issues (Figure 1) suggests that an organisation's IT architecture can be divided into four classes. This is based on the fundamental properties of an enterprise IT environment as outlined in the above literature review, and they are namely global IT infrastructure (refers to hardware), global information systems (refers to systems software), global telecommunication network (refers to communication), and data/information systems improvement (refers to data and applications). Figure 2 shows these four classes with their correlated global IT management issues. The global IT management classes are labelled as global IT infrastructure, global information systems, global telecommunication network, and data and information improvement. The criteria of correlated issues of each class are outlined as follows.

Global IT infrastructure – this class covers the development, implementation and maintenance of global information architecture components such as hardware, equipment, technology platform, and supports.

Global information systems – this refers to all the development, management, implementation, maintenance, integration, and improvement of global business application softwares.

Global telecommunication network – this class includes all the network communication structures, facilities, supports, and management to provide the business data flowing within and between organisations.

Data and information systems improvement – this applies to the data or information amelioration in terms of quality assurance, integration, security, contingency plan, and effective utilisation.

Figure 1: Global IT management issues

Global IT Management Issues	Sources
Integration of DP, OA and telecommunications	Burn et. al, 1993
Telecommunication technology	Burn et. al, 1993
Configuration of user interfaces	Edberg et. al, 2001
Development methodology	Edberg et. al, 2001
General security	Edberg et. al, 2001
Hardware and software support	Edberg et. al, 2001
Knowledge of technology	Edberg et. al, 2001
Software availability	Edberg et. al, 2001
Support for telecommunications	Edberg et. al, 2001
Systems development standards	Edberg et. al, 2001
Telecommunications and utilities availability	Edberg et. al, 2001
Information technology quality	Nelson, 1996
Improving software development	Palvia et. al, 1992
Using IS to integrate across business functions	Palvia et. al, 1992
Global information systems equipment	Sankar & Prabhakar, 1992
Network management systems	Sankar & Prabhakar, 1992
Network standards/protocols	Sankar & Prabhakar, 1992
Transmission networks	Sankar & Prabhakar, 1992
Building a responsive IT infrastructure	Watson et. al, 1997
Changing technology platforms	Watson et. al, 1997
Determining appropriate IS funding level	Watson et. al, 1997
Developing and managing distributed systems	Watson et. al, 1997
Implementing decision and executive support systems	Watson et. al, 1997
Improving data integrity and quality assurance	Watson et. al, 1997
Improving disaster recovery capabilities	Watson et. al, 1997
Improving information security and control	Watson et. al, 1997
Improving the effectiveness of software development	Watson et. al, 1997
Instituting cross-functional IS	Watson et. al, 1997
Making effective use of the data resource	Watson et. al, 1997
Managing the existing applications portfolio	Watson et. al, 1997
Moving to open systems/standards	Watson et. al, 1997
National communication infrastructure	Watson et. al, 1997
Planning and managing telecommunications	Watson et. al, 1997
Developing and implementing an information architecture	Watson et. al, 1997, Palvia et. al, 1992

Figure 2: Global IT management classes and issues

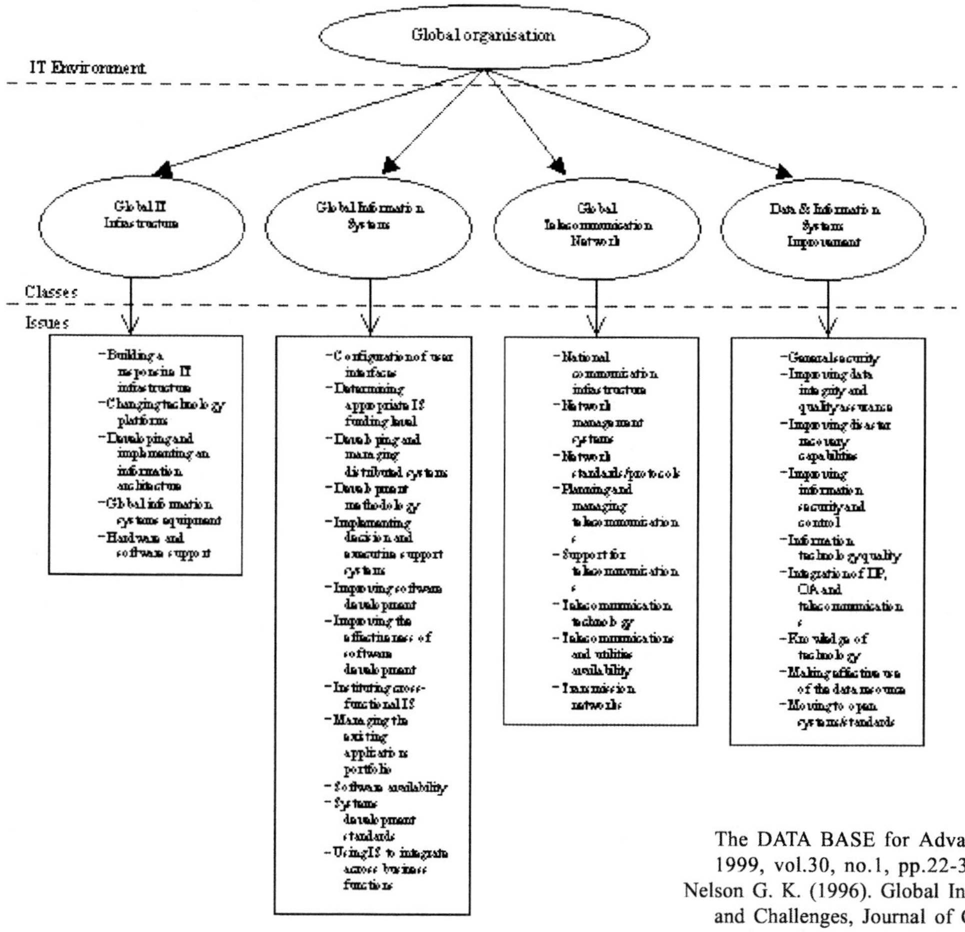

The key process of step 2 is the mapping of global IT management classes with the two organisational transition scope (intra-organisational and inter-organisational) and identifying the essential requirements of each cross-referenced cell in order to accomplish the complete global transition framework (Figure 3). The following section is still in progress and will delineate the investigation of eight cross-referenced cells. It will draw an overall picture to accommodate the senior executives and IT planners with comprehensive information of global IT transition processes.

- Global IT Infrastructure x Intra-organisational
- Global IT Infrastructure x Inter-organisational
- Global Information Systems x Intra-organisational
- Global Information Systems x Inter-organisational
- Global Telecommunication Network x Intra-organisational
- Global Telecommunication Network x Inter-organisational
- Data and Information Systems Improvement x Intra-organisational
- Data and Information Systems Improvement x Inter-organisational

Figure 3: Global transition framework

IT Management		Organisational Transition Scope: Intra-organisational	Organisational Transition Scope: Inter-organisational
	Global IT Infrastructure	Requirement/ Components	Requirement/ Components
	Global Information Systems	Requirement/ Components	Requirement/ Components
	Global Telecommunication Network	Requirement/ Components	Requirement/ Components
	Data & Information Systems Improvement	Requirement/ Components	Requirement/ Components

REFERENCES

Burn J. et. al. (1993). Critical Issues of IS Management in Hong Kong: A Cultural Comparison, Journal of Global Information Management, vol.1, no.4, pp.28-37.

Edberg D., Grupe F. H. and Kuechler W. (2001). Practical Issues in Global IT Management, Information Systems Management, vol.18, no.1, pp.34-46.

Fagan, M. (2001). Global Information Technology Transfer: A Framework For Analysis. Proceedings of the Second Annual Global Information Technology Management World Conference, June 2001.

Knowles J. H. (1996). Build an IT architecture on a business foundation. Datamation, July, p.25.

Kumar R. L. and Crook C. W. (1999). A Multi-Disciplinary Framework for the Management of Interorganizational Systems. The DATA BASE for Advances in Information Systems – Winter 1999, vol.30, no.1, pp.22-37.

Nelson G. K. (1996). Global Information Systems Quality: Key Issues and Challenges, Journal of Global Information Management, vol.4, no.4, pp.4-14.

Passmore, D. (1997). The Need for Architecture. Business Communications Review, Feb. pp.18-19.

Palvia S., Palvia P. C. and Zigli R. M. (1992). The Global Issues of Information Technology Management. Chapter 1: Palvia Shailendra, Palvia Prashant and Zigli Ronald M. (Eds.) Global Information Technology Environment: Key MIS Issues in Advanced and Less-Developed Nations, Idea Group Publishing. PA U.S.A.

Sankar C. S. and Prabhakar P. K. (1992). The Global Issues of Information Technology Management. Chapter 11: Palvia Shailendra, Palvia Prashant and Zigli Ronald M. (Eds.) Key Technological Components and Issues of Global Information Systems, Idea Group Publishing, PA U.S.A.

Watson R. T. et. al. (1997). Key Issues in Information Systems Management: An International Perspective, Journal of Management Information Systems, vol.13, no.4, pp.91-115.

A GISM Issues Model for Successful Management of the Globalisation Process

Yi-chen Lan
School of Computing and IT, University of Western Sydney, Australia
Tel: +6 (129) 685-9283, Fax: +6 (129) 685-9245, yichen@cit.uws.edu.au

INTRODUCTION

The rapid growth of information technology is one of the key drivers forcing organisations toward globalisation. The meaning of "globalisation" to an organisation seems no longer to be a business vision but a crucial strategy as the global market becomes a single entity. Nevertheless, without a clear understanding of multinational corporation (MNC) categories and the issues in global information systems management (GISM), organisations are most likely to fail in this transition. The objectives of this study are to a) review the MNC categories and outline the characteristics of each; b) construct a comprehensive collation of key GISM issues in the areas of culture, human resources management, individual country and region, business strategic planning, technology, and quality; c) classify these GISM issues in appropriate classes; d) develop a GISM issues model to help enterprise executives successfully manage their globalisation process and; e) validate the GISM issues model using empirical data. Figure 1 shows the framework of this study.

AN MNC CLASSIFICATION

In their seminal work Bartlett and Ghoshal (1989) defined four MNC categories, namely multinational, international, global and transnational. The organisational characteristics of each MNC category are shown in Table1.

These four categories of MNC are not radically new in concept. However, mapping the four varieties of corporations in terms of the GISM issues provides the senior executives a clear overview of the global information systems and assists them in making definitive decisions in the process of globalisation.

Figure 1: Framework of the GISM issues model development

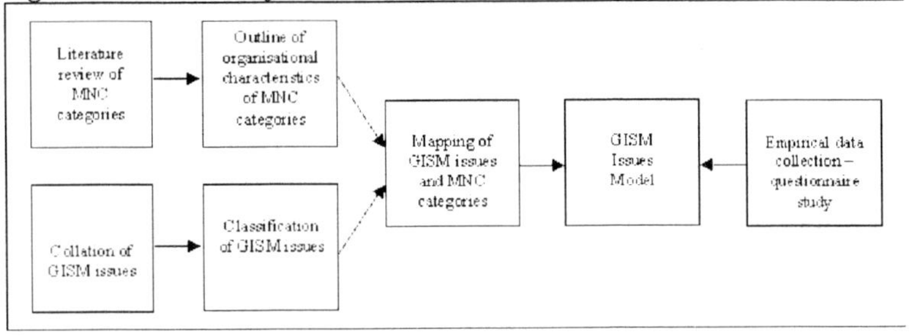

Table 1: Organisational characteristics of the four MNC categories (Bartlett & Ghoshal, 1989)

Characteristics	Multinational	International	Global	Transnational
Configuration of assets/resources and capabilities	Decentralised and nationally self-sufficient	Sources of core competencies centralised, others decentralised	Centralised and globally scaled	Dispersed, interdependent, and specialised
Overseas operations	Sensing and exploiting local opportunities	Adapting and leveraging parent company competencies	Implementing parent company strategies	Differentiated contributions by national units to integrated worldwide operations
Knowledge development and fusion	Knowledge developed and retained within each unit	Knowledge developed at the centre and transferred to overseas units	Knowledge developed and retained at centre	Knowledge developed jointly and shared worldwide

GISM ISSUES AND CLASSES

During the global transition, organisations often face many explicit or hidden factors that could delay or even terminate the globalisation process. In order to eliminate these unnecessary incidents, enterprises need to identify the possible issues before the process of globalisation has taken place. In the past decade, researchers have put in significant efforts into identifying these global MIS issues in the following areas: culture (Burn et al, 1993; Ein-Dor et al, 1993; Sauter, 1992; Yellen, 1997), human resource management (Agocs & Suttie, 1994; Boudreau et al, 1994; Harrison & Deans, 1994; Niederman, 1994; O'Connell, 1997; Pucik & Katz, 1986), individual country and region (Palvia et al, 1992; Watson et al. 1997), business strategic planning (Cheung & Burn, 1994; Ives et al, 1993; Gibson & McGuire, 1997; Kesner & Palmisano, 1996; Minor & Larkin, 1994; Neo, 1991; Palvia & Saraswat, 1992; Sethi & Olson, 1992), practical issues (Edberg et al, 2001), and the technology (Klein, 1999; Passino & Severance, 1990; Sankar et al, 1992; Waples & Norris, 1992).

Five classes of issues have been identified to cover the collated GISM issues. They are labelled as culture, business IS management (BISM), end-user management (EUM), people management (PM) and technology management (TM). Four of them (BISM, EUM, PM, and TM) are based on the management emphasis of the IT issues (Khandelwal & Warrington, 1999). Because of the main focus of cross-border and global information systems distribution and management, the culture class is also identified. In fact, a quality assurance class has been defined as a fundamental platform to incorporate the quality issues inherent in a number of issues identified.

GISM ISSUES MODEL DEVELOPMENT

The process of mapping of GISM issues and MNC categories requires two sub-processes to determine the components of the GISM issues model. The first sub-process is the determination of the GISM issues classes in terms of the globalisation stage. The GISM issues model is partitioned in three stages – pre-globalisation, the globalisation process itself, and post-globalisation. The pre-globalisation stage refers to the stage when the enterprise is preparing to expand its business operations internationally; the globalisation process refers to when the enterprise is in the global development stage; and the post-globalisation is reached when the enterprise has accomplished the process of globalisation. The GISM issues classes are placed in the appropriate partitions in accordance with their fundamental characteristics.

The second sub-process deals with the actual mapping operation. Firstly, a table consists of the organisational characteristics of each MNC category obtained from Table 1, plotted against the GISM issues classes, showing the level of importance of the issue to the characteristic, namely, "low", "medium", and "high". Each priority is given a numerical weighting. That is, 3 for high priority status, 2 for medium priority status, and 1 for low priority status. The total score of each GISM issues class is thus an indicator of positioning of the class in the GISM issues model.

After the completion of the above score matrix, each issue class is plotted in the global IS management model according to its total score. The higher the total score, the higher the priority of the issues class.

CONCLUSION

Enterprise globalisation has become the essential business strategy in the modern global market environment. In order to lead the enterprise towards globalisation, senior executives need to understand their organisational characteristics and realise the impact of GISM issues on the globalisation process. To provide a clear overview of the organisational structures, this paper presents the different MNC categories, and summarises the characteristics of each. Furthermore, this paper outlines a number of issues identified by previous researchers and defines the GISM issues classes in cultural, human resource management, business strategic planning, quality assurance, systems development, and technological areas. Finally, a GISM issues model is developed that will help executives successfully manage their globalisation process. A questionnaire study has been designed and will be conducted shortly to collect empirical data from enterprises for validating the appropriateness of the GISM issues model.

REFERENCES

Agocs C. and Suttie P. (1994). Global Information Systems and Technology: Focus on the Organization and Its Functional Areas. Chapter 20: Deans Candace P and Karwan Kirk R. (Eds.) Just Doing Business: Managing Human Resource Information in the learning Organization: Strategic Responses to the Global Environment, Idea Group Publishing, PA U.S.A.

Bartlett C. A. and Ghoshal S. (1989). Managing across borders: the transnational solution, Harvard Business School Press, Boston, Mass, U.S.A.

Boudreau J. W., Broderick R. and Pucik V. (1994). Global Information Systems and Technology: Focus on the Organization and Its Functional Areas. Chapter 21: Deans Candace P and Karwan Kirk R. (Eds.) Just Doing Business: Human Resource Information Systems in the Global Organization, Idea Group Publishing, PA U.S.A.

Burn J. et. al. (1993). Critical Issues of IS Management in Hong Kong: A Cultural Comparison, Journal of Global Information Management, vol.1, no.4, pp.28-37.

Cheung H. K. and Burn J.M. (1994). Distributing Global Information Systems Resources in Multinational Companies – A Contingency Model. Journal of Global Information Management, vol.2, no.3, pp.14-27.

Edberg D., Grupe F. H. and Kuechler W. (2001). Practical Issues in Global IT Management, Information Systems Management, vol.18, no.1, pp.34-46.

Ein-Dor P., Segev E. and Orgad M. (1993). The Effect of National Culture on IS: Implications for International Information Systems, Journal of Global Information Management, vol.1, no.1, pp33-44.

Gibson R. and McGuire E. G. (1996). Quality Control for Global Software Development. Journal of Global Information Management, vol.4, no.4, pp.16-22.

Harrison J. K. and Deans P. C. (1994). Global Information Systems and Technology: Focus on the Organization and Its Functional Areas. Chapter 22: Deans Candace P and Karwan Kirk R. (Eds.) The Design and Development of Modules for an International Human Resource Information System (HRIS), Idea Group Publishing, PA U.S.A.

Ives B., Jarvenppa S. L. and Mason R. O. (1993). Global Business Drivers: Aligning Information Technology to Global Business Strategy, IBM Journal, vol.32, no.1, pp.143-161.

Kesner R. M. and Palmisano P. F. (1996). Transforming the Global Organization: Integrating the Business, People, and Information Technology at Camp Dresser & McKee, Inc. Information Strategy, vol.12, no.2, pp.6-15.

Khandelwal V. & Warrington J. (1999). Management of Information Technology in Australian Enterprises: Critical Success Factors of CEOs, University of Western Sydney, Nepean, Australia.

Klein B. D. (1999). A Spreadsheet Project for Integrating Global Issues in the Software Tool Kit Course. Journal of Computer Information Systems, vol.40, no.1, pp.64-68.

Minor III, E. D. and Larkin, M. (1994). Global Information Systems and Technology: Focus on the Organization and Its Functional Areas. Chapter 12: Deans Candace P and Karwan Kirk R. (Eds.) Information Technology and Global Operations Integration, Planning, and Control, Idea Group Publishing, PA U.S.A.

Nelson G. K. (1996). Global Information Systems Quality: Key Issues and Challenges, Journal of Global Information Management, vol.4, no.4, pp.4-14.

Neo B. S. (1991). Information Technology and Global Competition: A Framework for Analysis. Information and Management, vol.20, no.3, pp.151-160.

Niederman F. (1994). Global Information Systems and Technology: Focus on the Organization and Its Functional Areas. Chapter 23: Deans Candace P and Karwan Kirk R. (Eds.) Information Systems Personnel, Human Resource Management and the Global Organization, Idea Group Publishing, PA U.S.A.

O'Connell S. (1997). Systems Issues for International Business. HRMagazine, March 1997, pp.36-41.

Palvia S. and Saraswat S. (1992). The Global Issues of Information Technology Management. Chapter 24: Palvia Shailendra, Palvia Prashant and Zigli Ronald M. (Eds.) Information Technology and the Transnational Corporation: The Emerging Multinational Issues, Idea Group Publishing. PA U.S.A.

Palvia S., Palvia P. C. and Zigli R. M. (1992). The Global Issues of Information Technology Management. Chapter 1: Palvia Shailendra, Palvia Prashant and Zigli Ronald M. (Eds.) Global Information Technology Environment: Key MIS Issues in Advanced and Less-Developed Nations, Idea Group Publishing. PA U.S.A.

Passino Jr. J. H. and Severance D. G. (1990). Harnessing the Potential of Information Technology for Support of the New Global Organization. Human Resource Management, vol.29, pp.69-76.

Pucik V. and Katz J. H. (1986). Information , Control, and Human Resource Management in Multinational Firms. Human Resource Management, vol.25, no.1, pp121-132.

Sankar C. S. and Prabhakar P. K. (1992). The Global Issues of Information Technology Management. Chapter 11: Palvia Shailendra, Palvia Prashant and Zigli Ronald M. (Eds.) Key Technological Components and Issues of Global Information Systems, Idea Group Publishing, PA U.S.A.

Sauter V. L. (1992). The Global Issues of Information Technology Management. Chapter 14: Palvia Shailendra, Palvia Prashant and Zigli Ronald M. (Eds.) Cross-Cultural Aspects of Model Management Needs in a Transnational Decision Support System, Idea Group Publishing. PA U.S.A.

Sethi V. and Olson J. E. (1992). The Global Issues of Information Technology Management. Chapter 23: Palvia Shailendra, Palvia Prashant and Zigli Ronald M. (Eds.) An Integrating Framework for Information Technology Issues in a Transnational Environment, Idea Group Publishing. PA U.S.A.

Waples E. and Norris D. M. (1992). Information Systems and Transborder Data Flow. Journal of Systems Management, vol.43, no.1, pp.28-30.

Watson R. T. et. al. (1997). Key Issues in Information Systems Management: An International Perspective, Journal of Management Information Systems, vol.13, no.4, pp.91-115.

Yellen R. E. (1997). End User Computing in a Global Environment, Journal of End User Computing, vol.9, no.2, pp.33-34.

Effects of Point-Based Incentives on the Use of Knowledge Sharing Technology

Jintae Lee
University of Colorado, Boulder, Tel: (303) 492-4149, Fax: (303) 492-5962, jintae@colorado.edu

Understanding the role of incentives in the use of knowledge sharing technology is critical for both students and teachers of Information Technology (IT) education. On one hand, it is an important subject matter to be taught in IT education. Students of information technology should know what motivates the use of IT and how. On the other hand, it is important for any teacher using an educational technology to understand the effects that different types of incentives have on the students' use of the technology.

Recently, web-based knowledge-sharing systems, such as experts-exchange.com, have emerged that adopt point-based incentive schemes to promote participation among its members. In a typical point-based system, each member would start with a set amount of points and then uses a certain number of points each time he or she asks a question. These points would then be awarded to the person who answers the question. There are variations on the ways in which the points are initially acquired, earned or awarded to the information provider. For example, some systems may give a fixed number of points to their members initially while others require them to purchase the points. Members may earn points through purchase, through answering questions, or through any form of participation. The answerer of a question may earn full or part of the points assigned to the question depending on how satisfied the questioner is with the answer. In addition, users can use their earned points in different ways. For example, in some systems, the highest scorer may be given a formal recognition as the expert of the week while in other systems one can exchange their points for material goods or for chances for sweepstake prizes.

The point-based incentive schemes in a technology-enabled knowledge sharing community raises a number of interesting research issues for those interested in IT education. Under what circumstances do they work, if at all? For example, the expert-exchange.com seems to be very successful with its half-million registered users. They currently have 2.6 million postings and a heavy volume of daily message traffic. Would such a point-based system work for knowledge sharing within the IT education community? What would be its effect on the relationship among the community members? Would it work for a communal-based community, where "unspecified obligation" is the norm rather than tit-for-tat exchange (Blau 1964,Clark and Waddell 1985, Clark and Mills 1986). What can we learn from, or contribute to, motivation research (Deci 1992, Vallerand 1997) regarding such point-based incentive schemes?

The goal of this study is to investigate some of these questions. In particular, it proposes to examine the relationship between a point-based incentive and what the motivation research has found out about the intrinsic vs. extrinsic motivations. Does a point-based scheme promote intrinsic or extrinsic motivation? To the extent that it promotes the feeling of challenge and recognition, it seems to be based on intrinsic motivation. On the other hand, to the extent it provides external rewards such as prizes associated with the points or even the points themselves, it seems to be based on extrinsic motivation. If a point-based scheme promotes extrinsic motivation, would it undermine the intrinsic motivation that students might have in learning and sharing knowledge (Deci 1971, Eisenberg et al. 1999, Lepper et al. 1999, Deci et al. 1999)?

To answer these questions, the following set of hypotheses are formulated in the context of educational technology use:

H1a. A point-based scheme with no associated rewards is intrinsically motivating.

H1b. The usage of a knowledge sharing technology will be higher with the introduction of a point-based scheme even when the points are not associated with any reward.

H2a. A point-based scheme associated with intrinsic rewards (e.g., best expert of the week) is intrinsically motivating

H2b. The usage of a knowledge sharing technology with a point-based scheme will be higher when the points are associated with intrinsic rewards than when they are not associated with any reward.

H2a. A point-based scheme with extrinsic rewards (e.g., prizes for the highest scorer) is extrinsically motivating.

H2b. The usage of a knowledge sharing technology with a point-based scheme will be higher when the points are associated with extrinsic rewards than when they are associated with intrinsic rewards.

H3a. Introduction of a point system with extrinsic rewards will undermine the intrinsic motivation that the user may have.

H3b. The usage of a knowledge sharing technology with a point-based scheme will be lower when the association of the points with extrinsic rewards stops than when the points were associated with intrinsic rewards before the introduction of extrinsic rewards.

METHOD

For the test of these hypotheses, the following research design is used to gather the data . Students in two sections of the same course are introduced to an online threaded discussion board where they could ask questions and post answers asynchronously. This system has been customized so that any time a student accesses a new posting on the discussion board, an email message is sent to the administrator of the system. This way, one can keep track of who accessed which posting how many times and use the number of page access as the measure of motivation to use the system. The nature of the motivation, i.e., whether intrinsic or extrinsic, is assessed by using the self-determination scale developed by Vallerand (1997).

Table 1 shows the schedules for the experimental group and the control group side-by-side:. In the experimental group, the system is used without the point scheme for the first three weeks. Then a point system is introduced where the user is initially allocated a certain number of points, and then uses them to ask questions or earn points by answering them. The system is used with the point system for the following three weeks, but without any rewards for the points earned. At Week 7, the point system is associated with intrinsic rewards by announcing that the top ten highest scorers will be recognized in the Hall of Fame at the end of the next three weeks. At Week 10, the point system is associated with extrinsic rewards by announcing that the top five highest scorers can exchange their points with prizes such as gift certificates of corresponding value. At the end of each of these periods, a survey will be taken that measures the level of intrinsic and extrinsic motivation, as well as other intentions to use the technology.

The same sequence is followed for the control group except that the introduction of the point system and the different types of rewards are lagging three weeks behind the corresponding introduction in the experimental group. The objective of this design is to ensure that the effect of a manipulation is not simply due to lapsed time or longer experience by comparing each of the post-manipulation state (of the experimental group) with the pre-manipulation state (of the control group).

Table 1: Research design

Week	Experimental Group	Control Group
1	Introduction of the online threaded discussion board. A survey t at the end of the period to assess the perception of the system without any point-based scheme.	Introduction of the online threaded discussion board. A survey at the end of the period assesses the perception of the system without any point-based scheme. A survey at the end of the period to assess the perception of the system without any point-based scheme
2		
3		
4	Introduction of the intrinsic rewards for the point-based scheme, e.g., expert of the week recognizing the highest scorer. A survey at the end of the period.	
5		
6		
7	Introduction of the extrinsic rewards for the point-based scheme, e.g., prizes for the highest scorer. A survey at the end of the period.	Introduction of the intrinsic rewards for the point-based scheme, e.g., expert of the week recognizing the highest scorer. A survey at the end of the period.
8		
9		
10	Stop the association of the extrinsic rewards and re-association of intrinsic rewards with the point-based scheme. A survey at the end of the period.	Introduction of the extrinsic rewards for the point-based scheme, e.g., prizes for the highest scorer. A survey at the end of the period.
11		
12		
13		Stopped the association of the extrinsic rewards and began the re-association of intrinsic rewards with the point-based scheme. A survey at the end of the period.
14		
15		

STATUS

I plan to recollect the data because of some difficulties experienced in gathering the data. In particular, there was a difficulty setting up the two groups in such a way that they balance in size and in their demographic composition. Because it is a longitudinal study that expands the period of fifteen weeks, the data collection has to wait for the beginning of a new semester with the right set of conditions. In the meantime, the schedule for the control group in the original research design had to be redesigned to prevent possible confounding effects of time or experience on any change on the motivation.

CONCLUSION AND FUTURE RESEARCH

As the implementations of a point-based scheme in today's knowledge sharing contexts have become not only facile but also common, it is important to have a good understanding of what effects that such a scheme has on the use of knowledge sharing technologies. The immediate motivation for this study is to examine such effects on the use of a Web-based discussion forum in an educational context. In particular, its goal is to articulate in what way, if at all, the use of a point-based scheme would motivate the students in sharing their knowledge. But the relevance of this knowledge extends beyond the educational context to other knowledge sharing contexts where point-based incentives may be used, including many currently popular existing websites that provide knowledge sharing forums.

The current study has formulated a set of hypotheses that examines the effects of point-based schemes from the motivational theory perspective. When the data becomes available for testing these hypotheses, I expect that they will yield both practical and theoretical insights. Practically, they could help us better understand the situations for which a point-based incentives approach would be effective and why. In particular, they might tell us when associating external rewards with points might diminish knowledge sharing. Theoretically, the study will provide a research framework, based on motivation theory, with which to explain the findings and generate further hypotheses to test in knowledge sharing contexts.

However, the difficulty in gathering the data as evidenced by our attempts to date also point to the challenges that lie ahead—such as the need for longitudinal studies and the difficulty of finding an appropriate set of experimental conditions that will minimize potentially confounding effects. Nevertheless, I believe that the study opens a door to a rich mine of theoretical and practical insights into some of the factors influencing the use of knowledge sharing technologies.

REFERENCES

Blau, P. (1964). Exchange and Power in Social Life. New York, John Wiley.

Clark, M. S. and B. Waddell (1985). "Perceptions of exploration in communal and exchange relationships." J. of Social and Personal Relationships 2: 403-418.

Clark, M. S., J. Mills, et al. (1986). "Keeping track of needs in communal and exchange relationships." JPSP 51: 333-338.

Deci, E. L. (1971). "Effects of externally mediated rewards on intrinsic motivation." J. Personality and Social Psychology 18: 105-115.

Deci, E. (1992). "On the nature and functions of motivation theories." Psychological Science 3: 167-171.

Deci, E. and R. M. Ryan (1985). Intrinsic motivation and self-determination in human behavior. New York, Plenum.

Deci, E. L., R. Koestner, et al. (1999). "A meta-analytic reviewer of experiments examining the effects of extrinsic rewards on intrinsic motivation." Psychological Bulletin 125(6).

Eisenberger, R., W. D. Pierce, et al. (1999). "Effects of reward on intrinsic motivation - negative, neutral, and positive: comment on Deci, Koestner, and Ryan." Pscyhological Bulletin 125(6).

Lepper, M. R., J. Henderlong, et al. (1999). "Understanding the effects of extrinsic rewards on intrinsic motivation - uses and abuses of meta-analysis: comment on Deci, Koestner, and Ryan." Psychological Bulletin 125(6).

Vallerand, R. J. (1997). Toward a hierarchical model of intrinsic and extrinsic motivation. Advances in Experimental Social Psychology. San Diego, CA, Academic Press.

Developing a Channel Management Framework for Hybrid E-Commerce Organizations

In Lee and Tej Kaul
Department of Information Management and Decision Sciences, College of Business and Technology
Western Illinois University, I-Lee@wiu.edu

ABSTRACT

This research investigates the impact of e-commerce marketing and coordination strategies on organizational performance. Based on e-commerce marketing and organization theories, we present a computational business framework that models multiple channels, customers, and organizational performance. Based on the framework, we develop a computational system used to study e-commerce marketing and coordination strategies for a variety of business environments. Through extensive simulations of a hypothetical retail organization and empirical data, we expect to show how organizational structure and coordination strategies affect organizational performance.

INTRODUCTION

There are broadly two types of e-retailers in the B2C e-commerce environment: (1) standalone e-retailers and (2) traditional retailers with e-retail business (hybrid e-retailers). Advantages for standalone e-retailers include little or no organizational and cultural barriers to e-commerce adoption, fast decision-making cycle, and rapid introduction of new products to customers. However, standalone e-retailers suffer from weak complementary assets such as logistics, customer service infrastructure, and low brand recognition. They also suffer from low product differentiation and high competition. These weaknesses have made e-retailers most vulnerable to the recent e-commerce shakeup. On the other hand, while traditional retailers suffer from inflexible organizational structure, slow decision-making process, and cannibalization of existing channels, they can capitalize on the existing customer base, distribution networks, and brand images in the e-retail expansion.

In this paper we develop a framework used to develop e-commerce channel strategies for hybrid e-retailers to maximize the organizational performance of a firm. According to a recent survey (Melyamuka [2000]), managing the e-commerce channel is one of the most important tasks for marketing managers. However, key managers in most large companies are still unclear about e-commerce strategy, and their people lack e-commerce skills. When traditional retailers add e-commerce channels, they need to investigate how the e-commerce channel affects the existing channels and develop a company-wide channel integration program. While the marketing strategies and coordination among multiple channels affect organizational performance, there has been little theoretical and empirical study on e-commerce channel management in a multi-channel environment. Our research addresses the following questions: (1) What will be the benefits of offering on-line stores? (2) If on-line stores are offered, should they create on-line division or spin-off? (3) Which market segments should the e-commerce try to reach? (4) What products should be offered at what price on the web site? (5) What will be the impacts of the e-commerce channel on other marketing channels?

The rest of the paper is organized as follows. In Section 2, a brief review of e- multi-channel management issues is presented. In Section 3, the context and components of the e-commerce computational model and simulation experimental design are discussed.

REVIEW OF E-COMMERCE MULTI-CHANNEL MANAGEMENT ISSUES

While the e-commerce customer base has been growing rapidly, many e-business models have failed to generate sustainable long-term profits. Standalone e-retailers of commodity products are among the hardest hit due to rising customer acquisition cost, low product differentiation, and lack of financial support of investors. Some e-retailers such as Garden.com are consolidating with brick and mortar companies to achieve synergy effects. A few surviving companies from the e-commerce shakeout will have much stronger presence in the market, building high technological barrier and profitable business models.

While existing e-commerce start-ups currently face increasingly high entry barriers, many traditional retailers implement the click and mortar business model, leveraging extensive distribution networks, brand images, and financial resources. Traditional retailers also leverage existing channels such as physical stores, call centers, and catalogues for their e-commerce channel to achieve competitive advantages over the standalone e-retailers. For example, customers place an order through the web site. Instead of receiving products through regular mail, customers can choose to pick up products at the nearest physical store. Customers can also be allowed to return products and get a refund at the physical store. This kind of multi-channel collaboration increases customer satisfaction and helps multiple channels keep their own loyal customers as well as expand new customer bases. The challenge to retailers operating multiple channels is how to manage the product offerings and prices across multiple channels.

One of the major reasons that people prefer a specific channel to buy products or services is that it provides more surplus (i.e., utility minus price) than other channels. E-commerce affects the perceived surplus of customers by changing the utility and price levels. Utility is idiosyncratic to individual customers and can be broadly categorized into two groups: product-specific and channel-specific. Product-specific utilities such as functionality, color, and size are typically independent of channel types. For many people, time and convenience are positive channel-specific utilities that are added to the total product or service utilities. On the other hand, lack of touch and feel, difficulty in product returns, and lack of transaction security are channel-specific negative utilities subtracted from the total product and service utilities. Certain commodity type products and services are likely to have less negative utility in touch and feel than specialized products or services and are therefore more suitable for e-commerce. E-commerce influences the price side as well as the utility side. Severe competition in the B2C e-commerce market has driven down prices of products and services traded online. Customers can experience increased surplus from the competition-driven e-retailers' margin shrinkage. In addition, e-commerce creates an opportunity for removing intermediaries in some industries, thereby saving commissions. In the travel industry, the direct web-based marketing of major airlines has accelerated the disintermediation of travel agencies. These savings can be translated into reduced cost of airlines, and thereby contribute to the increase of surplus for customers.

Traditional brick and mortar companies pursue two kinds of click and mortar models: on-line division and spin-off. Some arguments for creating an on-line division include use of complementary assets, sharing of technological resources, and ease of channel coordination. Office Depot, an office product supplier, pursued the on-line division strategy and achieved the largest on-line sales among three major office product suppliers. Office Depot developed a specialized web-based ordering system for major business customers and later opened a web site for consumers. To counter the e-commerce initiative of Office Depot, Staples launched Staples.com as a spin-off company. Advantages of spin-off strategies include new culture, flexible organizational structure, and reward systems that are suitable to e-commerce environment. Staples believes that the spin-off will create a managerial responsibility and culture that is suitable to the e-commerce.

MODELING E-COMMERCE ORGANIZATIONS FOR MULTI-CHANNEL COORDINATION STRATEGIES AND EXPERIMENTAL DESIGN

We develop a computational model for a traditional retailer operating an e-commerce business and multiple physical stores located in different regions. Our model tries to answer some commonly shared questions of many brick and mortar retailers that offer on-line stores. Our computational model consists of four components: channel, customer, environment, and performance measure. This model is used to test the effects of changes in model parameters on organizational performance. Based on the model and parameters, we develop a computational system and simulate a hypothetical retail organization by changing parameter values.

The channel component consists of six dimensions: the channel type, the number of operating business units, target markets, product offerings and prices in each channel, decision making procedure, and coordination mechanism. Two types of channels are considered: physical store and on-line. Each channel makes decisions about what to sell and how much to charge. Physically distributed stores serve regional customers. On-line stores do not have space and time barriers. Physical stores offer a limited line of products due to limited shelf space. A coordination mechanism is concerned with coordinating the product offerings and pricing decisions among multiple channels. Channel coordination initiated by physical stores may result in a different organizational performance from coordination initiated by on-line divisions.

The customer component consists of three dimensions: customer profile, channel preferences, and market heterogeneity. Each customer has a unique utility for each product. Idiosyncratic customers' utilities can be measured with conjoint analysis. Customers' choices of products/services are based on the surplus provided by products/services. Two types of customers are considered: traditional customers and e-commerce customers. E-commerce brings about two effects: cannibalization and addition. The cannibalization effect occurs when on-line customers find that the surplus of the products/services offered in the e-commerce channel is greater than any of the same or substitutable products/services in the existing channels. The addition effect occurs when customers can buy products/services from e-commerce channels that would otherwise not be available. Market heterogeneity is defined as the difference of customers' utilities between market segments. Market heterogeneity causes market segments to offer different products and prices from each other.

Competitors offer products and prices. A competitors' market presence is modeled in terms of product line, the number of products in a product line, and price offered by them. Competitors' channels are also modeled with both on-line and physical stores. We chose profit as a performance measure.

We address the following research hypotheses through extensive organizational simulation. Base data for simulation is collected from Office Depot and Staples stores and web sites.

1. As the proportion of e-commerce shoppers increases, the decentralized e-commerce organization performs better than the centralized e-commerce organization.
2. As the proportion of the e-commerce shoppers increases, fewer on-line product offerings are beneficial.
3. As the market segments are more heterogeneous, higher on-line product price is beneficial.

To test these hypotheses, three decision variables are considered: e-channel organizational structure (2); proportion of e-commerce shoppers (5); market heterogeneity (5). Data generation is based on a full-factorial design. For each parameter value combination, 30 replications are run. All together 1,500 simulation runs (i.e., 2*5*5*30) will be performed. Simulation and data generation are currently under way and the results will be presented at the IRMA 2002.

ACKNOWLEDGMENTS

This research was supported in part by a faculty development summer stipend grant from WIU Foundation at Western Illinois University.

REFERENCES

Anders, G., "Click and Buy: Why and Where Internet Commerce Is Succeeding," *The Wall Street Journal*, December 7, 1998, p. R4.

Fusaro, R., "Computerworld Online, Feb. 8, 1999, www.computerworld.com.

Melymuka, K., "Survey Finds Companies Lack E-commerce Blueprint," *Computerworld*, Vol. 34, No. 16, p. 38.

Modeling Trader Reputation Distribution in an Online Customer-to-Customer Auction Market

Zhangxi Lin[1] and Dahui Li[2]
The Rawls College of Business Administration, Texas Tech University
[1]Tel: (806) 742-1926, [2]Tel: (806) 742-2397, [1,2]Fax: (806) 742-3193, zlin@ba.ttu.edu, dali@ttacs.ttu.edu

Wayne Huang
Department of MIS, College of Business, Ohio University
Tel: (740) 593-1801, Fax: (740) 593-9342, huangw@ohio.edu

INTRODUCTION

In the era of e-commerce, reputation becomes an important organization asset that is sensitive to the organization's online performance due to worldwide exposures (Tadelis 1999). In an online Customer-to-Customer (C2C) auction market, while an honest trader may turn its name (reputation bearer) into valuable assets after many transactions, a guileful trader may easily defraud his trading partner to exploit more benefit and then changes his identity. As Internet frauds have been prevailing, more Internet users have been deterred from online trades because of their increased risk perception (Selis, Ramasastry and Wright 2001). In this situation a trading partner's reputation becomes a critical signal to a trader in his decision-making. To promote safer online trades, major auction market providers like eBay have offered the service of reputation feedback for their traders. While study has shown that such reputation mechanisms have facilitated buyer-seller transactions (Resnick and Zeckhauser 2001), several potential problems with these mechanisms deserve further investigations (Zacharia et al. 2000). On the other hand, a substantial amount of research work has been done on eBay's reputation feedback system since 1999. Lee, Im and Lee (2000) investigate the effect of negative buyer feedback on auction price. Ba and Pavlou (2001) conduct an empirical study on how trust can be induced by proper feedback mechanism based eBay's reputation scoring system. Dellarocas (2001) studies the efficiency of reputation reporting mechanisms from the viewpoint of economics. However, as the fundamental issues, what the nature of reputation score distribution is and how the distribution affects online traders' risk decisions remain open questions. Based on the above prior studies, this paper reports some preliminary research outcomes in this direction. The main objective of the research is to further examine the nature of reputation, including its measure, model building, and relationship with perceived risk and trust.

REPUTATION SCORE DISTRIBUTION OF SELLERS ON EBAY.COM

Resnick and Zeckhauser (2001) have a thorough examination of eBay's trading data, in which two histograms of the logarithm of scores, for buyers and sellers respectively, are presented. Both curves have a decreasing trend with an up-and-down section before declining totally. We randomly collected two sets of trader reputation scores, 200 sellers and 200 buyers respectively, from the eBay.com to study the distribution. About a half of the traders have obtained the scores less than 150. About 90% of them fall in the scores ranging 0-950. Reputation scores of 95% traders are less than 1850. Using a two-step moving average on the subset of samples that have reputation scores less than 1100, these reputation scores can be approximated to the exponential distribution ae^{-bx} with b as -0.0029 ($R^2 = 0.9218$) and -0.0035 ($R^2 = 0.9159$) respectively for seller and buyer. Figure 1 is the histograms of 6-month positive reputation scores from a full set of sellers.

Figure 1: A histogram of reputation scores in a 6-month period with two-step moving average (Data samples: 200 sellers, Source: eBay.com, Access Date: October 12, 2001)

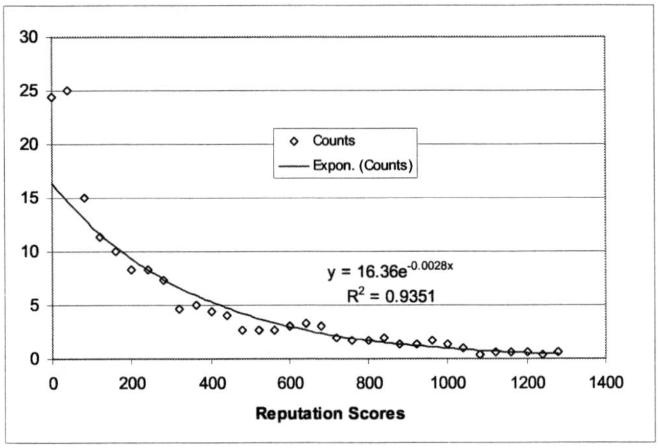

A STOCHASTIC PROCESS BASED REPUTATION SCORING MODEL

In this section we propose a reputation-scoring model to investigate the formation of positive reputation score distribution. Consider a simplified reputation scoring system with only positive feedback record for a trader:

1) When a trader initially participates an online auction market his score is 0;
2) The trader's score increments one after each honest trading;
3) The trader's score is reset to 0 if either he naturally quits from the market or he cheated; and
4) Assume that all traders have the same probability to abort their account because of cheating or quitting if they have the same reputation score.

This reputation scoring system can be modeled as a discrete-time Markov chain (Ross 1993). Define a stochastic process $\{X_n, n = 0, 1, 2, ...\}$ that takes on a countable number of possible values. Denote $\{0, 1, 2, 3, ...\}$ the score state set, $\{p_0, p_1, p_2, ...\}$ the distribution of the score, and $q_i = P\{X_n = i | X_{n-1} = i-1\}$ the probability the reputation score increments one, where $i > 0$ and $0 < q_i < 1$.[(1)] Then:

$$p_0 = \frac{1}{1+\sum_{i=1}^{\infty}\left(\prod_{j=1}^{i} q_j\right)} \text{ and } p_i = p_0 \prod_{j=1}^{i} q_j, \quad i = 1, 2, ...$$

If $q_i = q$ " i, i.e., the probability that a trader abort his current account is irrelevant to the reputation score, when $n \to \infty$

$$p_0 = 1 - q \text{ and } p_i = q^i(1-q), \ i = 1, 2, ...$$

It clearly shows that $X = lim_{n \to \infty} X_n$ has a geometric distribution, the discrete form of exponential distribution.

The above reputation model has been tested in a C2C auction simulation system. A computer-based system has been developed to simulate a whole process of C2C transaction. Frauds are randomly generated and traders are scored after each transaction according to their honest behaviors. Figure 2 is a histogram of reputation scores from 320 traders after running 200,000 trades using this system. (2) Obviously, it is a geometric distribution curve. An adjusted logarithm of reputation scores having a linear-like decreasing curve further supports the distribution. (3) The trend curve in Figure 2 is consistent to the one in Figure 1. Although in Figure 2 $a = 78.784$, $b = 0.0111$, they are adjustable by changing a few parameters.

Figure 2: Histogram of reputation scores after 200,000 transactions (Trader samples: 320 traders including buyers and sellers)

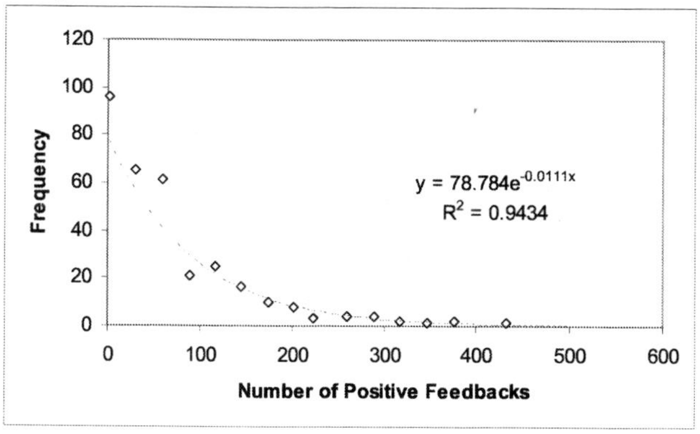

REPUTATION SCORE DISTRIBUTION AND PERCEIVED RISK

As a research-in-progress paper, we just raise the discussion on the relationship between reputation distribution and perceived risk. The finding in the formation of the reputation score distribution will lead to further study in the game between honest traders and cheaters. Hu et al (2001) present decision-making models for honest trader and cheater in a C2C auction market with escrow services. An honest trader's escrow service adoption decision making is based on the perceived risk that becomes a function of the trading partner's reputation scores. Surely, the relationship between the reputation score and perceived risk is: the higher a trading partner's reputation score is, the safer the trade is. By intuition, the potential cheater must have a reputation score distribution that "shrunk" to left-hand side. That is, the reputation score distribution of a potential cheater decreases more sharply than the overall reputation score distribution. This can be converted to a decreasing perceived risk curve with regard to reputation scores. Since this distribution is unobservable, the estimated risk that an honest trader perceives will not exactly match the real one. Then the new question from this analysis is how we justify the fitness of the perceived risk curve with the real risk curve.

DISCUSSION AND FURTHER RESEARCH

The limitation of this research is that the study of reputation score distribution is only focused on positive feedback scores. EBay provides three types of reputation scores for every traders: positive, negative and neutral. Also the length of observation window also affects the reputation scoring outcomes as eBay has windows in both week and 6-month sizes.

Our further research will focus on two aspects. First, a game-theory-based model will be proposed for traders with the reputation effect to study the relationship between the distribution of fraud rate and reputation distribution. Second, empirical studies will be conducted to further validate the research findings from consumer behavior perspectives, which may provide some additional insights into the important issue of trader reputation in online customer-to-customer auction market.

ENDNOTE

1 Derived from Friedman and Resnick (2001), the higher the reputation score, the higher the cheating cost, and the lower the probability a trader will cheat.

2 The number of traders is configurable and the outcomes are consistent to the example.

3 The conversion formula is $x' = ln(x+1)$.

REFERENCES

Ba, S., and Pavlou, P. A. "Evidence of the Effect of Trust Building Technology in Electronic Markets: Price Premiums and Buyer Behavior," Forthcoming in *MIS Quarterly*, 2001.

Dellarocas, C. "Analyzing the Economic Efficiency of eBay-like online Reputation Reporting Mechanisms," *Proceedings of the 3nd ACM Conference on Electronic Commerce*, October 14-17, 2001, Tampa, Florida.

Friedman, E., and Resnick, P. "The Social Cost of Cheap Pseudonyms," Forthcoming in *Journal of Economics and Management Strategy*, 2001.

Herbig, P., Milewicz, J., and Golden, J. "A Model of Reputation Building and Destruction," *Journal of Business Research*, 31, pp.23-31, 1994.

Hu, X., Lin, Z., Whinston, A. B., and Zhang, H. "Perceived Risk and Escrow Adoption: An Economic Analysis in Online Consumer-to-Consumer Auction Markets." *The Proceedings of ICIS 2001*, December 16-19, 2001.

Lee, Z., Im, I., and Lee, S. J. "The Effect of Negative Buyer Feedback on Prices in Internet Auction Market," *The Proceedings of ICIS 2000* (Brisbane, Australia, Dec. 10-13, 2000), pp.286-287.

Resnick, P., and Zeckhauser, R. "Trust Among Strangers in Internet Transactions: Empirical Analysis of eBay's Reputation System," Working paper, February 5, 2001.

Ross, S. M., *Introduction to Probability Models*, 6th Edition, Academic Press, 1997.

Selis, P., Ramasastry, A., and Wright, C. S. "BIDDER BEWARE: Toward a Fraud-Free Marketplace – Best Practices for the Online Auction Industry," *2001 Annual LCT Conference*, April, 2001, http://www.law.washington.edu/lct/publications.html#Online

Tadelis, S. "What's in a name? Reputation as a Tradeable Asset," *American Economic Review*, 89(3), pp.548-563, June 1999.

Zacharia, G., Moukas, A., and Maes, P. "Collaborative Reputation Mechanisms for Electronic Marketplaces," *Decision Support Systems*, 29(4), pp. 371-388, Dec. 2000.

The Use of XBRL in Managerial Accounting

Cornelia Lind
University of Texas at Dallas, School of Management, clind@utdallas.edu

ABSTRACT

Accounting professionals recognized the potential of XML as a way to share accounting information using the internet. For this purpose the standard XBRL is being developed based on XML. So far the definition of XBRL has focused on external accounting. Managerial accounting could, however, benefit in similar ways from the use of XML. It could for example ease the information sharing for global companies with different information system standards. It could also enhance reporting by integrating external data in a convenient way. XBRL will open ways for a new reporting using the functionality of the internet. For that purpose however a similar framework for managerial accounting as for financial reporting is needed, and some design support tools as well.

INTRODUCTION

Communication in the world wide web is increasingly being based on XML, the eXtensible Mark up Language. Major software providers like Microsoft and SAP are integrating XML into their products. XML is not another programming language, it is independent of hardware, operating system or application. XML is primarily a way of syntactically, and semantically formatting data and therefore of wide use. Accounting is only in the beginning of using XML for its purposes. One initiative to promote the use of XML for accounting is under way let by the XBRL Specification Working Group[1]. Based on XML this group is developing a standard for business reporting. The name of this standard has changed from eXtensible Financial Reporting Markup Language (XFRML) to eXtensible Business Reporting Language (XBRL) to signal the broader potential use of the standard. In XBRL jargon such a standard specification is called a taxonomy. A taxonomy defines data elements, and additional characteristics, like attributes, value definitions, style formats, constraints, etc. Each definition is represented by a tag adhered to the individual data value in the XML data document. Reports based on taxonomies are simple to define but powerful, workable and flexible.

So far the work on XBRL has been focused on financial reporting. Up to this day there are several officially accepted and published taxonomies for the financial reporting of balance sheets, profit and loss statements, and cash flow statements according to different regulations like US-GAAP, and IAS. More definitions are under way.

In addition to the taxonomy definitions applications that create, and use documents based on XBRL are already available. Other than publishing financial reports in an XBRL format, the applications are used as a way of "interfacing" diverse accounting systems within one company. XBRL is much more than just E-reporting.

The benefits for a company adopting the standard are multiple, that is of course if the standard is widely being accepted as such, which is to be expected. XBRL will make the distribution, translation, and processing of accounting data, and other relevant information easier, and therefore more economical as the following examples will show [Strand, 2001]:

- *Consolidation of subsidiaries*: subsidiaries with different accounting systems can be consolidated with the help of XBRL files. These files would be validated with an "internal" taxonomy, which would represent the least common denominator for the consolidated accounting/reporting system. Further on the XBRL files can be used for easy SEC filings.
- *Issue of financial statements*: the creation of financial statements can be automated with XBRL, and the distribution can take place electronically. This will save time and costs to the issuing company. The XBRL instance file is independent from the future presentation format, thus it is available to be printed, to create a web-page, or to be analyzed by other applications.
- *Analysis of financial information*: in December 2000 the Security & Exchange Commission of the United States announced a project to transfer the data available in the EDGAR Online database into an XBRL repository for easier access, and analysis.
- *Collaborative Planning, Forecasting, and Replenishment*: describes an approach of integrating business partners, such as customers and vendors, in the planning process. XBRL can be the means to approach this integration.
- *Electronic filing*: electronic filing based on XBRL will ease, and shorten the filing process substantially for all involved parties. This applies for filings required by the government, as well as filings by private institutions, like financial institutions receiving credit application data, etc.

With XBRL accounting benefits in two ways. On one hand it gains all the advantages that come with the introduction of a standard, and on the other hand it enables accounting to use some of the power of the internet for its purposes. So far both gains have been exploited to some extend for external purposes but it is on the inside companies still have a high potential for lowering costs, and implementing new functions using the internet technology. Managerial accounting has yet to find ways to benefit from this approach.

XBRL FOR MANAGERIAL ACCOUNTING

The purpose of managerial accounting information is to provide meaningful data to the company's management to control and run the operational business activities and to ensure future efficiency. Primarily the timeliness of the data and the data allocation to the corresponding cost or profit objects present key issues for managerial accounting. For instance may cost associated with a research and development project in managerial accounting not be expensed out completely at the time of occurrence but rather "capitalized" and "depreciated" and therefore of-set with future revenues that can be linked to the project. Secondly managerial purposes can be improved significantly with the incorporation of non-financial data. The nature of XBRL allows the combination of any data sources, while adding semantics to the structure so that it will support meaningful managerial accounting reports for managers, and other applications. One of the most popular approaches of integrating financial and non-financial data is the balanced scorecard technique [Kaplan, Norton, 1996]. Again XBRL could be used as the electronic technique to create, and communicate these special reports.

In order to be able to use XBRL for managerial accounting two basic questions need to be addressed:

1. Can a taxonomy be defined for managerial accounting?
2. How can the definition of "managerial" XBRL-reports be supported by design tools?

Ad 1: Because managerial accounting information is - in contrast to financial accounting information - not regulated it is harder to standardize. Since the existing XBRL framework is, however, extremely flexible, and general, a similar approach for managerial accounting reporting is possible. The new definition should include the following characteristics:

(1) The definition of a general XML framework on which different taxonomies for managerial accounting can be based on.

(2) The consideration of accounting data, as well as non-financial information for the reports.

Ad 2: The development of such a design tool would certainly help to spread the use of XBRL. For managerial accounting such a tool would be almost essential since managerial accounting reports are subject to more changes than financial reporting, and are also often ad-hoc reports. With a graphical design tool users could easier define their reporting needs, and use it as a basis for discussion, and communication. Based on the framework for the taxonomies XML data elements, their attributes, and their relationships will make up the elements of a graphic modeling tool.

The w3 consortium responsible for the suggestion of XML standards has created a specification that standardizes application programming interfaces for XML applications. This specification is called "The XML Document Object Model (DOM)". An XBRL tool to support the creation of XBRL documents/taxonomies will have to based on these suggestions.

ELEMENTS OF A TAXONOMY FOR MANAGERIAL ACCOUNTING

Taxonomies are XML documents[2] that define elements and attributes, as well as their relationships and constraints. The created XBRL instance document has to apply to XML rules, and to the definitions specified in the taxonomy. The outline of a taxonomy for managerial accounting is based on the Extensible Business Reporting Language (XBRL) Specification 2000-07-31 [XBRL, 2000]. It includes anon normative examples of XML elements and attributes that can be used to express information used in managerial accounting.

According to the XBRL framework [XBRL, 2000] a XBRL instance document is made of items, labels, and groups. The *item* is the most basic concept. An *item* represents a fact, a numerical or a non numerical information. A *group* is a set of related items that can appear in any order and in any other XML document as well. The *label* of an element names the element. It is defined as a separate type because the label element allows applications to override the label within an instance document. Based on these components and their attributes a taxonomy defines the individual elements, and their relationship.

The most basic relationship is the parent-child relationship. In XBRL this relationship is defined through a *rollup* element, which specifies the direct parent of the element.

Managerial accounting uses many different reports concerning reporting subjects, level of detail, and time periods. As a consequence multiple taxonomies for the different subjects like cost center reports, profit center reports, balance score cards, profitability reports, sales center reports, etc. will be necessary. Since an XBRL instance document can be based on multiple taxonomies one general taxonomy can define the document, the entity, and the supplemental information structure. These sections have been identified in the taxonomy for Financial Reporting for Commercial and Industrial Companies [Taxonomy, 2000]. The document section describes the document itself: its date of creation, the author, the addressees, the title, and so on. The entity contains information about the entity that issued the report (for example a company, a profit center, a business line).

Basic elements to be defined are:

- Cost centers
- Profit centers
- Projects
- Other organizational units
- Profitability objects
- Actual costs and revenues
- Planned costs and revenues (future costs and revenues)
- Variances
- Statistical information, and
- Key figures

Of great importance for managerial accounting is the time aspect. The use of the time period, as in financial accounting reporting, will not prove to be sufficient. Data must be marked as planned, forecasted or budgeted data. That is the reason for having special elements for the "future" data.

Groupings will prove to be a major structuring element in the managerial accounting taxonomies, since an additional "allocation" information has to be included into the taxonomy. Allocation refers to the link between elements as for example the number of employees of a particular profit center, or the costs of a collection of cost centers. Combined with the *rollup* relationship complex hierarchical structures can be modeled.

FUTURE RESEARCH

The present document gives only an outline of the possibilities of an XBRL taxonomy for managerial accounting. A sample taxonomy for cost center reporting is currently under development. Modeling support, probably in a graphical way, is also needed in practice, and can be supported by academics.

XBRL will proof to be one of the research areas where practitioners, and researchers alike will find many issues of further interest. The impact of XBRL on electronic business will have to be investigated in order to identify risks, and ways of improvements.

A less academic question might possibly be the translation of a graphical XBRL model into XBRL code.

Research on how XBRL will change the importance, and the impact of reporting will surely be a future research topic, externally as well as internally.

ENDNOTES

1 for a list of members please consult the web page at www.xbrl.org
2 XML Schema Documents

REFERENCES

[Kaplan, Norton, 1996] Kaplan, R.S. and D.P. Norton: using the balanced scorecard as a strategic management system. California Management Review, 1996

[Strand, 2001] Strand, C.A., B.L. McGuir, L.A. Watson and C. Hoffman: The XBRL Potential. Strategic finance, June 2001

[Taxonomy, 2000] XBRL Taxonomy, Financial Reporting for Commercial and Industrial Companies, US GAAP. Editors: Sergio de la Fe, Charles Hoffman and Elmer Huh. http://www.xbrl.org/us/gaap/ci/2000-07-31.doc

[XBRL, 2000] Extensible Business Reporting Language (XBRL) Specification. Editors: Walter Hamscher and David Vun Kannon. http://www.xbrl.org/tr/2000-07-31/xbrl-2000-07-31.doc

The Integration of Material Flow, Cash Flow and Information Flow in E-Commerce

Zhang Liyang[1] and Lai Maosheng[2]
Peking University, China, [1]Tel: 86 (106) 276-1743, [2]Tel: 86 (106) 275-6907
[1,2]Fax: 86 (106) 275-1681, liyangzhang@263.net, lms@im.pku.edu.cn

ABSTRACT

This research focuses on the issue of the integration of material flow, cash flow, and information flow in E-Commerce and tries to solve the relevant problems in theory and practice. Based on the analysis of the roles and characteristics of material flow, cash flow, and information flow in management information systems, the authors propose a new administrative idea in E-Commerce, which puts stress on the organic integration of the three kinds of flows and meanwhile highlights the role of information flow. In practice, this idea will be carried out through the design and implementation of new management information systems, which will develop from current ERP systems and reinforce the integrated function.

INTRODUCTION

According to the investigation of approximately ten existing management information systems, the lack of integration of material flow, cash flow and information flow exists in most of the systems and has influenced the systems' value. Some earlier studies point out this situation, but few of them try to figure it out. How to unify these three kinds of flows, how to improve the system, and how to implement in the design of new management information systems, especially in E-Commerce, have become the vital problems businesses faced. This research will focus on these problems and solve them in theory and practice.

Material flow, cash flow and information flow act different roles in management information systems, respectively like three kinds of human circulatory systems, that is, digestive system, blood circulation system, and nervous system. In human body, these systems have their particular functions, however, they can operate effectively only on the condition that they are unified as an organic whole. Analogously, when the three kinds of flows are integrated harmoniously, they could bring out the best result as a whole, while each value of the three flows is also increased.

In the management information system, material flow, cash flow, and information flow have three general characteristics, which become the main basis of integration.

- Material flow and cash flow are unidirectional, while information flow is bi-directional.
- The information of material and the information of finance compose the important part of information flow.
- Information flow reflects the status of material and finance, operational situation of material flow and cash flow, and meanwhile plays the role of control and coordination.

The research carries out from two levels: one is the theoretical level, and the other is the practical level.

In the first place, the study attempts to answer the questions, in theory, why material flow, cash flow and information flow should be integrated, what new benefit will be brought after the organic integration and how to achieve this integration. It will help decision-makers realize the issue's significance and put into effect execution.

In the second place, the study concentrates on the integration methods, procedures, possible questions and solutions in detail. Management information systems develop from CAD(Computer Aided Design), MIS(Management Information System), MPR(Material Requirements Planning), MPRa!(Manufacturing Resource Planning) to ERP (Enterprise Resource Planning). Based on the analysis of this developmental history, the trend of integration got attention gradually. The original systems just completed the transition from manual operation to electronic data processing with great efficiency and speed. Then MRP systems began to automatically assemble the entire material flow in the process of manufacture and control it at the same time. The subsequent systems, MRPa!, whose core is MRP, tried to unify the material flow and cash flow to gain the enterprise entire profit. However the lack of flexibility greatly impacted their high-performance. With the appearance of ERP, whose important part is MRPa!, system designers made an attempt to add information flow to the entire process. And with the addition of DRP (Distribution Resource Planning) and CRM (Customer Relationship Management), ERP systems partially fulfilled the integration of material flow, cash flow and information flow. In spite of that, the role of each flow, especially the information flow, has still not reached the best performance level and meanwhile the whole efficiency of the ERP systems got negative influence. To improve this situation, the integration of three kinds of flows becomes essential and significant, particularly in current E-Commerce business environment. Nevertheless, at the same time the progress of management information systems also shows the trend of integration. From this point of view, the expansion and extension of the existing system functions will contribute to the successful and organic unification of material flow, cash flow and information flow.

Furthermore the study will emphasize the control and coordination role of information flow in the whole systems. In E-Commerce, the information flow is a clue that connects the material flow and cash flow. Its position is non-fungible and decisive. The information flow not only records the current situation of material flow and cash flow, but also provides the previous data on the material and finance, which help people to obtain the valuable performance information and then make scientific prediction. Through the exchange of information, different divisions of the company are connected to communicate and share information easily and smoothly. This study will address the issues about the way in which information flow plays the important role among all the flows and organizes the entire business process.

In this research, there are certain arduous problems to resolve, such as the design and implementation of actual information systems, the evaluation of new systems, and so on.

Various methods are made use of in the study. They are listed as follows.

- **Literature Overview**: occupy the complete theses and research reports in this field to make a clear framework about the current research status.
- **Theory Analysis**
- **Case Study**: choose typical cases in different lines of business and study their system operation, performance, existent problems, etc. The cases being chosen include management information systems of Wal-Mart Stores, Inc., distribution systems of Dell Computer Corporation, research and development systems of The Boeing Company, and information systems of Legend Group.

In conclusion, the research will propose a new administrative idea in E-Commerce, which puts stress on the organic integration of material flow, cash flow and information flow and meanwhile highlights the role of information flow. In practice, this idea will be carried out through the design and implementation of new management information systems, which will develop from current ERP systems and reinforce the integrated function.

REFERENCES

1. Gao Yuesheng. The logistics mode in E-business. Commercial Research, 2001 (1): 65-67.
2. Chen Zhijie. The analysis and design of material flow in E-commerce. Market Modernization, 2000 (8): 16-18.
3. Song Hua. The innovation and development of material flow strategy in modern enterprises. Economic Theory and Business Management, 2000 (1): 41-44.
4. Dou Yihong. Information flow in E-Commerce. Information Science, 2000 (6): 485-487, 501.
5. Wang Yingjun, Guo Yajun. Information flow in a supply chain. Industrial Engineering and Management, 2000 (3): 37-40.
6. Lei Hongzhen, Ding Jutao. The new thought of management in the enterprises' informationalization. Journal of Institute of Economics and Management of Northwestern University, 2000 (6): 23-26.
7. Wang Wei. The current problems in the Business Process Reengineering of state enterprises in China. Economic Herald, 2000 (5): 63-66.
8. Tong Lijuan. The business process in E-commerce. Modern Information, 2000 (5): 41-42.
9. Chen Zhaohui. The new concept of information management: EVP (Enterprise Value Planning). Commercial Research, 2001 (2): 42-44.
10. Zhou Peng. The network management solution to information flow, material flow, and cash flow in enterprises. http://www.wtcyber.com/gb/match/jinshida/article7.htm
11. Li Xiuhong. Material flow, cash flow, and information flow in E-Commerce. Commercial Research, 2000 (10): 53-54.
12. Sun Qunli. The relationship between E-commerce and material flow, information flow, and cash flow. Journal of Zhongnan University of Finance and Economics. 2001 (2): 65-68.
13. Gao Jianmin, Chen Fumin, Luo Guangxiong. The integration of material flow and cash flow in MRPII systems. Journal of Computer-Aided Design & Computer Graphics, 1999 (3): 238-240.
14. The Origin of Distribution (Jan. 4th, 2002) http://www.chinabig.com/zhs/business/distribution/knowledge/distribution/w_general/origin.htm
15. Yang Yuanqing. The establishment and enhancement of management information system for large Chinese enterprises to improve operational efficiency and enhance customer satisfaction. (Nov. 25th, 2001) http://www.legend.com.cn/huodong/xinxihua/yangyq.asp
16. C. Forza, F. Salvador. Information flows for high-performance manufacturing. International Journal of Production Economics, 2001 (70): 21-36.
17. R. Garcia-Flores, X.Z. Wang, G.E. Goltz. Agent-based information flow for process industries' supply chain modeling. Computers and Chemical Engineering, 2000 (24): 1135-1141.
18. Wil M.P. Vander Aalst. Process-oriented architectures for Electronic commerce and interorganizational workflow. Information Systems, 1999 vol.24 (8): 639-671.
19. Liwen Qiu Vaughan. The contribution of information to business success: a LISREL model analysis of manufacturers in Shanghai. Information Processing and Management, 1999 (35): 193-208.
20. Don Tapscott, Alex Lowy, David Ticoll. Blueprint to the Digital Economy: Creating Wealth in the Era of E-Business. Dalian: Dongbei University of Finance and Economics Press, The McGraw-Hill Companies, Inc., 1999.
21. Don Tapscott, Art Caston. Paradigm Shift: The New Promise of Information Technology. Dalian: Dongbei University of Finance and Economics Press, The McGraw-Hill Companies, Inc., 1999.
22. James A. O'Brien. Introduction to Information Systems: An Internetworked Enterprise Perspective. Irwin/McGraw-Hill, 1998.
23. Jack D. Callon. Competitive Advantage through Information Technology. Beijing: China Machine Press, The McGraw-Hill Companies, Inc., 1998.
24. David Simchi-Levi, Philip Kaminsky, Edith Simchi-Levi. Designing and Managing the Supply Chain: Concepts, Strategies and Case Studies. The McGraw-Hill Companies, Inc. 2000.
25. Stephen Haag, Maeve Cummings, James Dawkins. Management Information Systems for the Information Age. Beijing: China Machine Press, The McGraw-Hill Companies, Inc., 2000.
26. David G. Schwartz, Monica Divitini, Terje Brasethvik. Internet-based Organizational Memory and Knowledge Management. Idea Group Publishing, Hershey USA, 2000.
27. Lynda M. Applegate, F. Warren McFarlan, James L. McKenney. Corporate Information Systems Management: The Challenges of Managing in An Information Age. Dalian: Dongbei University of Finance and Economics Press, The McGraw-Hill Companies, Inc., 2000.
28. Lynda M. Applegate, F. Warren McFarlan, James L. McKenney. Corporate Information Systems Management: Text and Cases. The McGraw-Hill Companies, Inc., 1996.
29. Lynda M. Applegate, F. Warren McFarlan, James L. McKenney. Corporate Information Systems Management: The Issues Facing Senior Executives. The McGraw-Hill Companies, Inc., 1996.
30. Zhang Duo. E-Commerce and Physical Distribution. Beijing: Tsinghua University Press, 2000.
31. Qi Ershi, Zhou Gang. Logistics Engineering. Tianjin: Tianjin University Press, 2001.
32. Larry M. Singer. McGraw-Hill Guide to Effective Communications for MIS Professionals. McGraw-Hill, Inc., 1992.
33. Alan Burton-Jones. Knowledge Capitalism: Business, Work, and Learning in the New Economy. Oxford University Press, New York, 1999.
34. Jeffrey L. Whitten, Lonnie D. Bentley, Kevin C. Dittman. System Analysis and Design Methods. Beijing: Higher Education Press, The McGraw-Hill Companies, Inc., 2001.
35. Bob Ortega. In Sam We Trust. Beijing: Hua Xia Press, 2001.
36. The Council of Logistics Management (CLM) http://www.clm1.org/
37. Wal-Mart Stores, Inc. http://www.walmart.com/, http://www.walmartstores.com/wmstore/wmstores/HomePage.jsp
38. Dell Computer Corporation http://www.dell.com/
39. The Boeing Company http://www.boeing.com/
40. Legend Group http://www.legend.com.cn/

Transition to Java in the IT Curriculum

Wendy Lucas
Assistant Professor, Computer Information Systems Department, Bentley College
Tel: (781) 891-4705, Fax: (781) 891-2949, wlucas@bentley.edu

ABSTRACT

The object-oriented (OO) programming paradigm has gained popularity in both industry and academia, and Java is becoming the language of choice. Yet it can be a difficult language to learn, with many hurdles for novice programmers. This paper describes our experiences transitioning to Java as the first programming language in an IT master's program. Careful consideration was given to a variety of factors, including when to introduce OO concepts, which integrated development environment (IDE) to use, and how to support students with minimal prior experience. The impact of these choices on the learning experience is presented, and is followed by a discussion of success factors for introducing Java as the first language.

INTRODUCTION

Object-oriented technology (OOT) is becoming increasingly prevalent throughout the system development process (Jordan, Smilan, & Wilkinson, 1994). Students must be knowledgeable in OOT in order to be adequately prepared for their future careers. The ACM/AIS 2000 model curriculum includes OO concepts within several courses, including analysis and design, software engineering methodologies, databases, and programming (Gorgone & Gray, 2000). The Java programming language, which became generally available in 1995, has achieved a high level of adoption in both industry and the classroom. Information system programs have also begun to integrate OOT in general, and Java in particular, into their course offerings (Lim, 1998).

The Master of Science in Information Technology (MSIT) at Bentley College, which was introduced in the fall of 2001, is built upon the OO paradigm, with Sun's Java™platform providing the technical foundation. Formerly, the programming course was taught in Microsoft® Visual Basic® 6.0, an object-based language. This paper focuses on the transition to teaching the first programming course in Java.

Many of our students have little or no programming experience. Java is a difficult first language to learn for several reasons, including the complexity of its extensive class libraries; the instability of the Java platform, which is updated on a regular basis, often with significant changes to the language itself; the lack of standard methods for reading keyboard input; and a hard-to-use graphics model (Roberts, 2001). On the positive side, Java is in many ways less complex than C and C++, to which it bears a strong surface resemblance. This is largely due to the lack of pointers, which are a major stumbling block for students (Mehic & Hasan, 2001). In addition, Java was designed from the start as an OO language and has all of the advantages inherent to this paradigm, including the reusability of objects, flexibility and extensibility from inheritance and polymorphism, and enhanced reliability and modifiability from encapsulation.

Proactive ways were sought to combat the anticipated high level of frustration for novice programmers with this course. A key component was web-based access to lecture notes, assignments, source code, and links to relevant Java sites. Faculty offered extended office hours, and student assistants were available daily in the computer lab.

The next section of this paper describes the OO programming course and presents selected results from a survey (available upon request) filled out mid-way through the course by the students. This paper concludes with a discussion of success factors for delivering a first course in OO programming to IT graduate students.

OBJECT-ORIENTED PROGRAMMING COURSE

This course was taught for the first time in the fall of 2001 to fifty-eight graduate students in three sections. Students first gain a solid understanding of the fundamentals of structured programming, which is an essential prerequisite to the understanding of the more complex OO concepts that follow. Advanced topics, including servlets, JDBC, and Java Beans, are covered in a later course.

There are no prerequisites, as this is one of three foundation courses that all incoming MSIT students must take. Most students do not have significant prior programming experience. On a scale from one (*novice/beginner*) to seven (*expert*), students averaged 3.14 ± 1.78. Figure 1 shows the distribution of these self-rankings.

Figure 1: Self-ranking of prior programming experience

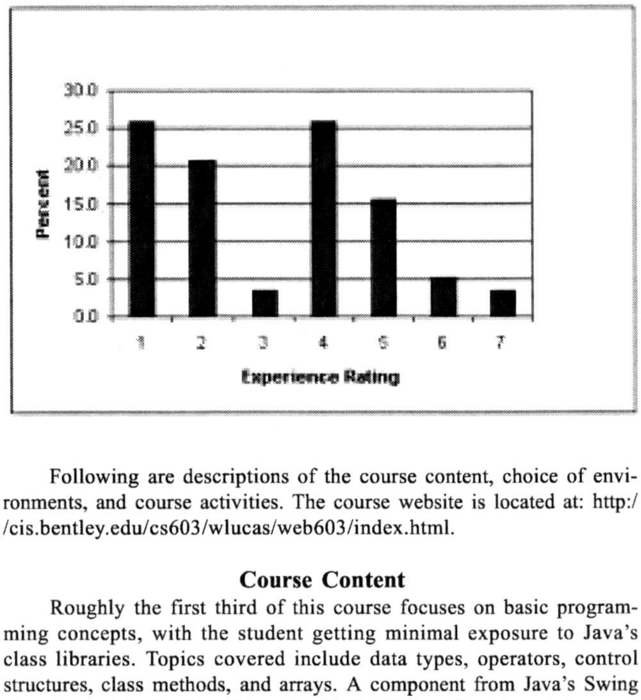

Following are descriptions of the course content, choice of environments, and course activities. The course website is located at: http://cis.bentley.edu/cs603/wlucas/web603/index.html.

Course Content

Roughly the first third of this course focuses on basic programming concepts, with the student getting minimal exposure to Java's class libraries. Topics covered include data types, operators, control structures, class methods, and arrays. A component from Java's Swing class is used for keyboard input, with detailed explanation of the component and the package containing it held off until later in the course.

The next third of the course focuses on the OO concepts of classes and instance methods, encapsulation, inheritance, polymorphism, and abstract and interface classes. Additional topics include dynamic data structures, exception handling, and file I/O. Students are guided through Java's class libraries to a greater degree in this segment, and, toward the latter part, are encouraged to explore the libraries themselves.

Up until this point, only Java applications, which run on the server side and require only one method, are developed. In the final third of the course, graphics and event handling are taught using client-side applets. Applets, which are embedded in a web page and are most frequently run from a browser, have inherent complexities that make postponing their introduction worthwhile. Each browser has its own Java interpreter, which may or may not support the latest version of the Java platform. To truly understand the code required by the most basic of applets requires knowledge about a predefined startup sequence of method calls, system-defined and -passed arguments, and inheritance.

Students read weekly assignments from an introductory Java text by Gittleman(2001). On a scale from one (*no value*) to seven (*high value*), the average rating of the text was 4.59 ± 1.57. Lecture notes used in class are also posted on the web. These notes augment the text and include several programming examples, with corresponding Java files posted on the web. Students judged the overall helpfulness of the web site as 6.02 ± 0.98 based on the same seven-point scale.

The average difficulty of the course at approximately the midway point was rated on a seven-point scale as 4.79 ± 1.14, where *one* represents *not challenging*, and *seven* represents *very demanding.* Figure 2 contrasts the difficulty ratings to those for the prior programming course taught in Visual Basic (VB). A total of 143 students over six semesters filled out questionnaires on that course. Their average difficulty rating for the VB course was 4.69 ± 1.15. The mean difference between the two groups is not significant.

Figure 2: Comparison of VB course difficulty to java course difficulty

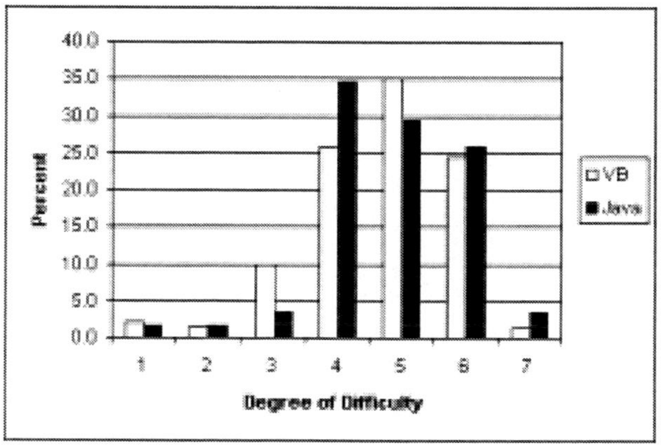

The mean difference in perceived difficulty for students in the Java course with prior programming experience versus those without is significant. Figure 3 shows this relationship, where *little* experience refers to those who rated their experience as either a one or a two, *somewhat* refers to those in the three to five range, and *very* includes those with a rating of six or seven.

Figure 3: Java course difficulty as a function of prior experience

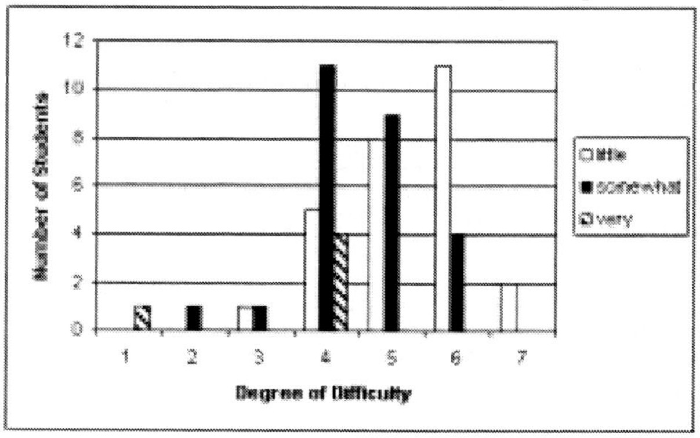

These self-assigned ratings were collected after objects had been introduced but more advanced OO concepts had yet to be covered. As the course proceeded, even those students with prior procedural programming experience had difficulty with these concepts, based on assignment and exam performance. This agrees with Mehic and Hasan (2001), who found that prior procedural language experience could actually create an obstacle for students learning OO design. The timing of when the survey was conducted is also believed to have contributed to the similarity in difficulty ratings for the VB and Java courses.

Programming Environments

Students completed their first assignment using Sun's Java™2 SDK software from a DOS shell program along with a text editor of their choice. This exposed the students to the concepts of compilers, byte code, and the Java Virtual Machine (JVM). Help facilities within this environment are very limited, and compiler and runtime errors are often difficult to interpret. Students were then required to complete the second assignment using the Borland® JBuilder IDE. Subsequent assignments could be completed using the environment of their choice.

The majority of students (86%) continued using JBuilder. Among its advantages are built-in help facilities and an excellent debugging tool. It also supports the full implementation of Java and its extensive class libraries. Students were shown how to use the debugger in the classroom, and lab assistants were able to help them with the environment outside of class. The average rating of the JBuilder IDE by students using it was 5.57 ± 1.25. Figure 4 shows the distribution on a helpfulness scale ranging from one (*no value*) to seven (*high value*).

Figure 4: Student ranking of JBuilder

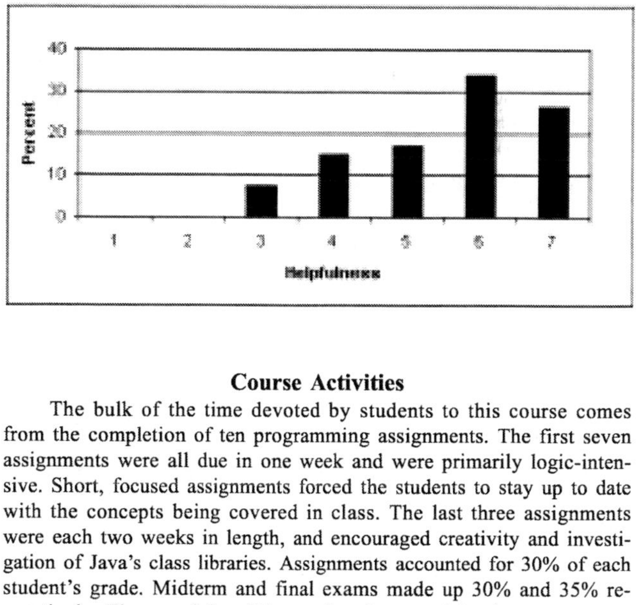

Course Activities

The bulk of the time devoted by students to this course comes from the completion of ten programming assignments. The first seven assignments were all due in one week and were primarily logic-intensive. Short, focused assignments forced the students to stay up to date with the concepts being covered in class. The last three assignments were each two weeks in length, and encouraged creativity and investigation of Java's class libraries. Assignments accounted for 30% of each student's grade. Midterm and final exams made up 30% and 35% respectively. The remaining 5% was for class participation.

The average number of hours worked per week was 8.24 ± 4.62, while the average for the VB course had been 6.59 ± 4.35. The mean difference between the two is significant at the .05 level. There was also a significant difference between means for those students with prior experience versus those without. Figure 5 illustrates these differences, using the same categorizations as in Figure 3.

CONCLUSIONS

There are several factors that led to the successful implementation of this Java course. Students particularly liked the frequent programming assignments, which reinforced their understanding of course

Figure 5: Hours worked in java course as a function of prior experience

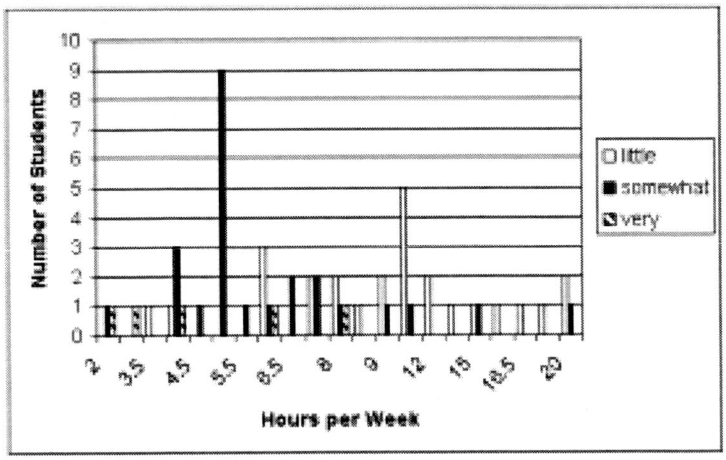

material. Earlier assignments covering the fundamentals of programming boosted confidence in their ability to write functioning code. Those successes helped students maintain a positive attitude when the level of complexity increased, primarily from the introduction of OO concepts. The incremental dependence upon Java's class libraries helped students learn to navigate the overwhelming documentation.

Holding off on introducing applets until after covering OO concepts enhanced the students' ability to understand the code. In addition, they were able to differentiate logical errors from environmental ones, which would have stymied them earlier in the course. Working with applets and visual programs is very rewarding, and the course unfortunately came to an end when student interest was at its peak.

Lab assistants were critical to the success of this course, from student and instructor perspectives. While they were not allowed to give solutions, their help in debugging code and deciphering error messages was greatly valued.

One negative aspect to this course from the instructors' perspective is the tremendous amount of grading. For this reason, we are currently working on an automated grading system to which students will be able to submit their assignments.

REFERENCES

Gittleman, A. (2001). *Computing with Java: Programs, Objects, Graphics* (Second Edition ed.). El Granada, California: Scott/Jones, Inc.

Gorgone, J. T., & Gray, P. (Eds.). (2000). *Model Curriculum and Guidelines for Graduate Degree Programs in Information Systems*: Joint ACM/AIS Task Force on Graduate IS Curriculum.

Jordan, R., Smilan, R., & Wilkinson, A. (1994). *Streamlining the project cycle with object-oriented requirements*. Paper presented at the Ninth Annual Conference on Object-Oriented Programming Systems, Language, and Applications, Portland, Oregon.

Lim, B. B. L. (1998). *Teaching Web Development Technologies in CS/IS Curricula*. Paper presented at the 29th SIGCSE Technical Symposium on Computer Science Education.

Mehic, N., & Hasan, Y. (2001). *Challenges in Teaching Java Technology*. Paper presented at the Informing Science, Krakow, Poland.

Roberts, E. (2001). *An Overview of MiniJava*. Paper presented at the 32th SIGCSE Technical Symposium on Computer Science Education, Charlotte, NC.

Software Proficiency Testing in a General Education Computer Course at a Moderately-Selective Midwestern State University

Linda Lynam
Instructor, Computer and Office Information Systems, Central Missouri State University
Tel: (660) 543-8645, Fax: (660) 543-8465, llynam@cmsu1.cmsu.edu

ABSTRACT

Approximately 600 students in a general education computer course at a Midwestern state university with a technology focus were required to demonstrate proficiency in Microsoft Word, Excel and PowerPoint for the first time during the Fall 2001 semester. The entrance requirement at the university requires a minimum of an ACT score of 20 or in the upper two-thirds of their high school graduating class. Many students are in the 20-23 range of ACT scores. A large portion of the students lack high school experience in independent study and individual responsibility. Results of the project indicate that students with little experience in self-responsibility can achieve at the university level when required.

BACKGROUND

Three full-time faculty members teach most of the general education computer literacy courses in the College of Business and have had a long-term goal of requiring all students to demonstrate a basic proficiency in the major business software applications: word processing, spreadsheet and presentation software. These instructors have long known that students think they know more about the computer than they really do. Professors in other courses assume students know basic computer use and employers expect graduates to possess basic computer skills.

A pilot project was performed in 1999 with a small group of approximately 35 students in the College of Applied Science and Technology. Software tests were created specifically for this purpose and individually graded. Students self-evaluated their skill level before taking the exams. The results indicated that students generally overestimated their knowledge of the various software programs.

The result of this small study encouraged the campus director of assessment, the director of educational development and the computer faculty to talk to the university administration about implementing an institutional requirement that all students graduating from the university must show a basic proficiency in the most common business software programs. The most logical time to test the students is as they enter the university. If they have the necessary skill level, the requirement would be satisfied. If they do not, they immediately are aware of deficiencies and can enroll in remedial courses to prepare for retaking proficiency exams. The most common reason given not to implement a software proficiency requirement was the logistic problem of adding more to the freshman/new student orientation. The current program is a one-day on-campus visit the summer before the student first attends the university. Software testing would add approximately 90 minutes to the schedule. Another reason given is that not all students are majoring in computers. To counter this objection, it was pointed out that most employers expect college graduates to know basic computer skills, enough to write a report, keep a budget and make a simple presentation. The third objection is that it would not be fair to allow one department to get all the credit hours that would be generated as a result of the necessary remedial classes that would be taken.

IMPLEMENTATION

Because the instructors of the general education computer course believed the students needed the software skills now and not when the political battles were settled, a software proficiency requirement was implemented in all sections of the general education course. In the fall 2001 semester, approximately 600 students enrolled in the course were required to achieve at least 80% on each of the exams in Microsoft Excel, PowerPoint and Word. When a minimum of 80% was achieved, a pass was recorded for that exam. No points were awarded for the proficiency exams. Students who did not master the three exams could not receive a grade higher than a D in the course, even if grades for other course work was higher than a D. The proficiency exams were only a portion of the course. Regular class periods included lecture and videos over computer hardware, online research and Internet use. Course work included three multiple-choice exams over lectures, several homework exercises to apply lecture material and a software project applying class material incorporating into Word, PowerPoint and Excel.

Very basic software skills were required. For example, in all program, students had to know how to open a file, save a file, insert graphics, change fonts, etc. Additional Word skills were setting margins, headers, footers, and page numbers. Excel required ability to enter formulas and create a simple graph. PowerPoint included automating bullet entry, changing backgrounds and slide transitions.

To automate testing, give immediate feedback and allow full use of the software programs including help files, Software Assessment Manager (SAM), a product of Course Technology/Thomson Learning, was used. Students had many chances to take the exams: eight class periods were reserved for testing, every Friday afternoon and the final exam time. The same exams were given every time. To ensure the correct student was taking the exam, every student had to check into the testing session with a photo ID and was required to show the proctor their passing score.

Remediation was keyed to another Course Technology/Thomson Learning product: Course CBT, a CD-based computer-based-training tool. The SAM program created a study guide for each exam. Students could look at the study guide; see exactly what they missed and where on the Course CBT the skill was covered.

Students were not given in-class instruction in the software. In fact, the class is taught in a large lecture hall with only one computer for the instructor. At no time were the students in a lab setting with the instructor to learn the software.

STUDENT DEMOGRAPHICS

Our students have ACT scores in the 20-23 ranges. In high school, many of the students were not required to be responsible. Many are accustomed to having class time to do all homework, to having leniency on due dates, and having opportunities for extra-credit. Our students had little experience in being responsible for learning required material on their own.

Students were surveyed as to their previous software training. 11% indicated they had no software training, 56% had taken a high school class, 8% had taken a college class and 67% were self-taught. The numbers do not add up to 100% due to more than one method selected.

METHODOLOGY

Results were gathered by student surveys. The first survey was completed at mid-semester after the students had two weeks of in-class opportunities (eight class days) to take the proficiency exams. The first round of testing was completed immediately after class rosters were finalized in the third week of the semester. The second round was completed at the semester mid-point. Students had the opportunity to take the exams on Friday afternoons, however by mid-semester, few students had taken advantage of the Friday afternoon testing.

The Blackboard program was used for the mid-semester survey. Blackboard includes a survey function in the program, makes it very easy to create and take a survey, but does not provide a way to get the data out of the program to manipulate. Only the numbers of students taken the survey and summary percentages by section are shown with no provision to obtain the data in a raw form to use. The Blackboard administrators at the university were unable to determine how to extract the data. Excel was used to attempt to determine the totals overall, but the method was imprecise and clumsy.

A second survey was completed at the end of the semester. Students were asked not to complete the survey until they had completed the course, that is, either passed all three exams or had taken advantage of every opportunity to take the exams. The second survey was also web-based, but Access was used to collect the data, which made the data greatly more accurate and easy to manipulate.

Students received points for completing both surveys. The Blackboard program reported which students had taken the survey, but does not allow survey responses to be matched to student name. The last question of the second survey required students to go to the Blackboard program to indicate they had completed the survey. Again, responses were not tied to student name.

RESULTS

The overall results of the proficiency testing were much better than anticipated. At the end of the semester, 81% of students had passed all three exams; 11% had passed two exams, 5% had passed one exam and 3% had passed no exams. It is important to remember that all three exams had to be passed to get better than a D in the course. Of the students who did not pass all three exams, 2% of the 600 students would have received a grade higher than D had they passed the exams; the remainder of the 19% who did not pass all three would have received a D or F in the course even if they had passed all three exams.

More important than merely passing exams is the ability to apply the skills in other situations. Students were asked on the second survey if they felt prepared to use Word, Excel, and PowerPoint to complete assignments in other classes. 92% of students responding indicated that they felt they knew enough to use the software.

During the semester, students frequently complained that no points were assigned to the proficiency exams. However, when asked at the end of the semester, 76% advocated keeping the pass/fail scoring and only 14% recommended assigning a point value to the exams.

Method of studying for the exams was disappointing. When asked how they studied, the students responded: 60% already knew the skills, 40% used trial and error on the exams. However, in another question, they were asked if they used the Course CBT to study and 54% indicated they had used it at least once. Based on the number of times most students took the exams, trial and error was probably the most common method.

The Friday afternoon testing sessions, held in a 30-station lab, were not heavily used until the end of the semester. Until mid-semester, the greatest number attending was ten. Several weeks no students came to the session. Until mid-semester, the graduate assistant proctor was also available to provide tutoring on the software during the sessions. Only one person took advantage of tutoring. Toward the end of the semester, attendance greatly increased at the Friday sessions. The last three weeks saw lines at the sessions, with a minimum of 50 students per week taking exams and many others being turned away. No time limit was enforced on Friday tests. If a student got on a computer at the beginning of the session, they were not forced to leave after a specific period even if there was a line.

By the week of finals, most students had passed the exams. A maximum of ten to fifteen students per section took exams during the final week. Sixty students were enrolled in each section. Several students did not take the proficiency exams at the final week because they had determined they wouldn't get better than a D in the course based on other course work.

84% of the students indicated that felt proud when they had successfully completed an exam.

CONCLUSION

Students who were not prepared in high school to be self-motivated learners were able to accomplish the goal of achieving at least 80% on each of three software proficiency exams. Students did learn the skills, maybe not using the method expected, but the end result was successful completion of the exams. The proficiency requirement will stay in the general education computer course with a difference of including about four class days to teach the software as requested by 75% of the students.

Wireless Technology Standards and Protocols

Benjamin R. Pobanz and Julie R. Mariga[1]
Department of Computer Information Systems and Technology, Purdue University, Indiana
[1]Tel: (765) 494-0879, [1]Fax: (765) 496-1212, {brpobanz, jrmariga}@tech.purdue.edu

ABSTRACT

In much of the modern world today, mobile devices are becoming ubiquitous. From cell phones to wireless PDA's, pagers and smart phones, the wave of mobile devices has exploded over recent years. Information in today's business world never stops. From mobile calls, pages, emails, business documents, faxes, pictures, text messages, voice messages and stock quotes all total in the billions daily. Businesses are continually faced with the challenge of meeting ever-changing information technology. This paper will discuss several wireless standards, specifically 802.11, 802.11b(Wi-Fi), 802.11a, 802.11g and how they support wireless communications technologies. This paper will also discuss Bluetooth and Wireless Application Protocol (WAP) and their significance in current wireless communications.

INTRODUCTION

Not all wireless devices are identical; fortunately wireless protocols and IEEE standards assist with the transaction of data back and forth, mediating between software and hardware. Today's consumers demand reliable mobile service. To ensure successful and reliable mobile communication, selecting the proper wireless devices, applications and network protocols is crucial. Which wireless standard should companies or individuals implement generally boils down to supporting and adding values to the strategic business plan, or value individual needs. With variations in '802.11' standards issues regarding overcrowding may come into question with 2.4 GHz frequency. The significance of these standards will drive industry and technology in the future. Affecting business and consumer communication habits, opening up new business opportunities not yet imagined.

Introduction: Wireless Standards and Protocols

802.11 is the Institute of Electrical and Electronics Engineers (IEEE) standard for wireless networking. This standard allows for wireless integration with wired Ethernet networks, sending Ethernet data through the air at a maximum of 2 Mbps. This standard supports all standard Ethernet network protocols including TCP/IP, NetBEUI, Novell's IPX/SPX and Apple talk, and has two frameworks for sending wireless network communications. The two frameworks are frequency hopping spread spectrum (FHSS). Frequency Hopping Spread Spectrum uses 79 distinct frequency channels, where direct sequence spread spectrum (DSSS) has 14 different fixed frequency channels in its spectrum at its physical layer to communicate. The variations of fixed channels (DSSS) and channel hopping (FHSS) set off challenges with equipment compatibility. To remedy the compatibility issues, IEEE standardized DSSS and created 802.11b.With FHSS's frequency channels removed, 802.11b's throughput was increased to a maximum of 11 Mbps.

Wireless Standard 802.11b

802.11b is the DSSS intermediate range wireless frequency standard that runs at speeds comparable to hard wired Ethernet. Speeds range between 2 Mbps and 11 Mbps at distances of 50 to 110 meters. Lowering the transmission speed can help expand the wireless operating range. However, the number of users on the network, geographic obstructions, and processor speed as well as application requirements can affect transmission speeds. Typically anywhere from 10 to 50 simultaneous users may be sufficiently supported without any significant loss in data transmission. Standard Ethernet network protocols are supported by 802.11b. These protocols include TCP/IP, AppleTalk, NetBEUI and IPX/SPX. Support from Apple Computer, 3COM, Lucent Technologies, Nokia and Nortel adds value to 802.11b as the industry standard. In a survey done by COMDEX, 22% of the 561 companies surveyed said they were more likely to say that improving internal productivity was the most important driver of wireless technologies, and 90% of the responding companies either currently support or plan to support 802.11b and Bluetooth wireless data technologies over the next 12 months.

Deploying 802.11b wireless LAN standard requires an 802.11b access point to be connected to your wired Ethernet LAN and the use of 802.11b equipped wireless PC's. Today's wireless technology can be configured to automatically connect and transition the connection between access points within transmission range. The advantages offered by 802.11b standout when used with wireless access on college campuses. Iowa's Buena Vista University, Carnegie Mellon University and University of Southern Mississippi are three examples of wireless campus networks. That said, there are limitations to 802.11b's capabilities, like requiring wireless access points and wireless PC's to use the same wireless standard on the same network. Also, the 2.4GHz frequency used by 802.11b is home to microwaves and cordless telephones raising an interference issue when these devices are placed within close proximity. The future of 802.11b is uncertain, however as the current choice for data connectivity and its backward compatibility, 802.11b may reach critical mass in mobile devices and be around for some time to come.

Wireless Application Protocol

WAP (Wireless Application Protocol) is an open specifications based on IP and XML. This application protocol supports standard data formatting and transmission of wireless devices and provides Internet communications and telephony service for wireless devices. Designed to work with most wireless networks, WAP has a self-governing ability, making it aware of its own scalability and range limitations. This ability is rooted in its protocol stack. The protocol stack establishes communication, transports applications and handles encryption at different layers. Figure 1 shows the WAP Wireless Protocol Stack and how it relates to the OSI Model.

At the top of the wireless protocol stack table is the *wireless application protocol* interfacing between the device and user similar to the application layer in the OSI model. Next is the *wireless sessions protocol*, a connection oriented or connectionless protocol, spanning the presentation and session layers of the OSI, this protocol supports the application layer and has the ability to suspended or resume at will. The *wireless transaction protocol* is the workhorse of the protocol stack and is located between the session and security protocols and similar to OSI's transport layer it too handles packet sequencing and tracks packets. *Wireless transport layer protocol* is the dump truck of wireless protocols handling all the network connections and delivery of information packets. At the MAC Layer / Data Link Layer which is made up of digital hardware and software the data rate is determined. According to Gartner, as mobile devices and wireless networks continue to improve, WAP will become increasingly irrelevant making applications created with WAP technology obsolete in the long term. (Gartner 2001)

Wireless Standards 802.11a and 802.11g

The IEEE 802.11a wireless Ethernet frequency operates at the 5.4 GHz range transmitting upwards of 54 Mbps. At this frequency, 802.11a avoids the possible "wave" congestion predicted to envelop devices using 802.11b. 802.11a has been described as a more secure

Figure 1: WAP wireless protocol stack and the OSI model

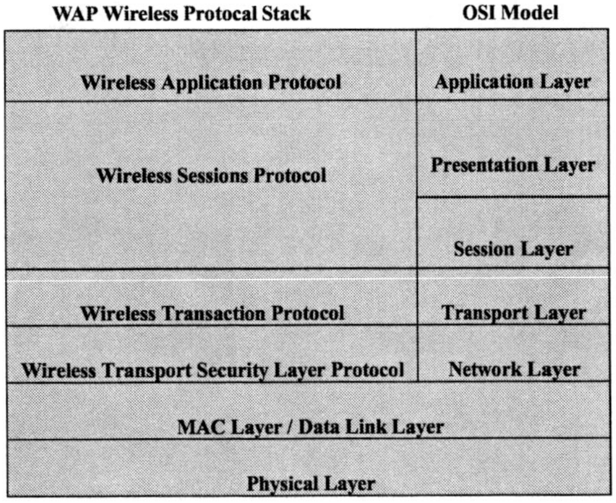

standard than 802.11b. From a tactical standpoint, 802.11a is industries answer to multimedia, streaming video and telephony demands with its 54 Mbps throughput. The current playbook out on 802.11g is that it claims to offer transfer rates nearing 50Mbps in the 2.4 GHz frequency. This would greatly reduce additional hardware expenses for businesses since current 802.11b devices could be used.

Bluetooth

Figure 2 shows an architectural overview of Bluetooth's communication standards and protocols, and a description of each layer. At the radio *frequency layer* Bluetooth combines frequencies converting data from bits into transmittable symbols. The *baseband layer* handles the coding /decoding of data packets and manages frequency hopping. The *link manager layer* manages connections to devices that are either established or released depending on the nature of the connection and the device.

Originally created by the Ericsson company, this a very short-range wireless technology much like the 802.11's. With the demand of portable PC's and WLAN's greatly increasing over the past two years, demand for cordless connections is needed. Mobile computing equals desktop computing. Bluetooth is designed to link devices for automatic data exchange within a range of 30-35 feet, delivering transparent wireless solutions across a broad range of devices. The term "location independent" or ad-hoc networks, will be the real exploiters of Bluetooth. An example of this would be receiving PDA updates in airports and other public areas. Another strength of Bluetooth is that it performs authentication, payload encryption and key handling. It is also able to switch between synchronous connection-oriented and asynchronous connection-less links, which allows Bluetooth to select the appropriate switching method, circuit or packet. With the multitude of compatibility options associated with Bluetooth, and with the increase of devices being manufactured with Bluetooth capabilities, Bluetooth will likely surpass 802.11b in the arena of wireless communication within the next two years (Gartner 2001).

CONCLUSION

These wireless protocols and IEEE wireless standard are the catalysts through which mobile computing will continue to grow. That said, these standards will change over the next two to five years due to market demand for faster transmission speed and the necessity to integrate mobile devices. Figure 3 shows a breakdown by percentage of the wireless data technologies that organizations plan to support over the next 12 months. COMDEX (2001)

REFERENCES

Bennett, W; Stanley, J. (2001). *Comdex wireless technology: The big picture.* Retrieved November 20, 2001, http://www.key3media.com/comdex/

Figure 2: Bluetooth layer model

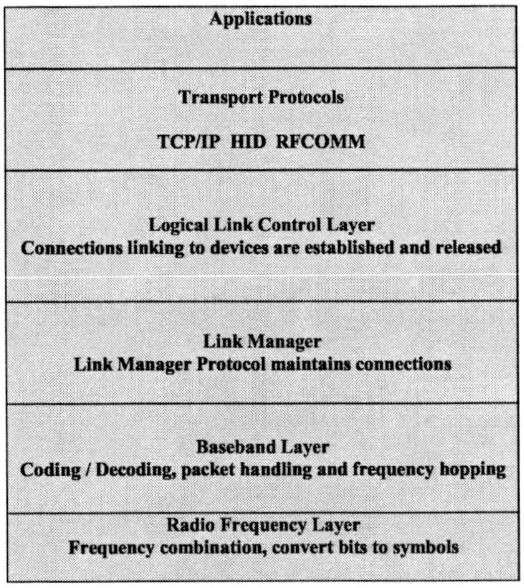

Figure 3: Wireless technologies supported over the next 12 months

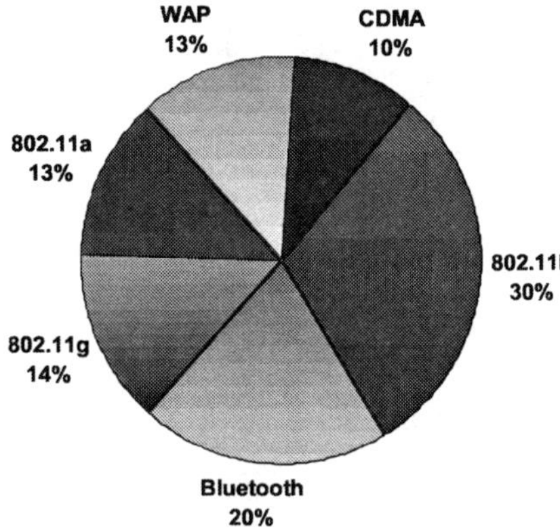

Conover J, (2001). *Anatomy of IEEE 802.11b wireless.* Retrieved, October 17, 2001, http://www.networkcomputing.com/1115/1115ws2.html

Davis, H (2001). *Understanding 802.11b and Bluetooth*, Retrieved, November 4, 2001. http://www.mightywords.com/browse/details_bc05

Dornan, A (2000). *Product focus: Pulling the Internet's plug.* Retrieved, September 10, 2001, http://www.networkmagazine.com/article/NMG20000710S0007

Egan, B. (2001). *Mobile and wireless computing: The next user revolution.* Gartner Group Symposium 2001.

Freise, K. (2001), *Wireless revolutionizing campuses*, Retrieved, September 19, 2001 http://thesource.micronpc.com/articles/050201.html

Gleick, J (2001). *The Wireless age: Theories of connectivity.* Retrieved, April 22, 2001, http://nytimes.com/search/abstract?res=F20B1EF934550C718EDDAD0894D9404482

Goldman, J and Rawles, P. (2000). *Local area networks: A business-oriented approach*, pg 658-662, New York, Wiley & Sons.

Jones, N. (2001). *Mobile commerce business scenario.* Gartner Group Symposium 2001.

Lanowitz, T. (2001). *Software quality: Necessity for mobile computing.* Gartner Group Symposium 2001.

Trivedi A, (2001). *Wireless local area network IEEE 802.11.* Retrieved, October 12,2001, http://grouper.ieee.org/groups/802/11/main

Mobile Computing Platforms

Julie R. Mariga
Assistant Professor, Telecommunications and Networking Technology
Department of Computer Information Systems and Technology, Purdue University, Indiana
Tel: (765) 494-0879, Fax: (765) 496-1212, jrmariga@tech.purdue.edu

ABSTRACT

Mobile computing is having an enormous impact on both companies and individuals. Companies have to face many issues related to mobile computing. For example, which devices will be supported, which devices will fulfill business objectives, which form factor will win, which features and networks will future devices offer, which operating systems will they run, what will all this cost, what are the security issues involved, what are the business drivers? This paper will discuss the major business drivers in the mobile computing field and provide an analysis of the top two platforms that are currently running the majority of mobile devices. These platforms are the 1) Palm operating system 2) Microsoft Pocket PC operating system. The paper will analyze the strengths and weaknesses of each platform, discuss market share and, future growth.

INTRODUCTION

Mobile computing defined as a generalization of all mobile computing devices including Personal Digital Assistants (PDAs, e.g. Palm Pilots, Pocket PCs), smart phones, and other wireless communication devices will continue with dramatic changes in the next two to five years. There are a number of reasons for change but two main factors are the convergence of next-generation handhelds and high-speed wireless technology. The operating systems found in today's handhelds will provide the foundation for future devices and applications. The two main platforms for PDA's are Palm and Pocket PC. Which operating system should companies or individuals implement? It depends on a number of items. One important issue to consider is what application(s) need to be used by the user(s). Once this question is answered it may help eliminate some operating systems and devices. Another important item to consider is portability. Portability of applications is important since devices change rapidly and if applications are portable then they can be reused on new devices without having to be rewritten. If applications are developed in a language that allows for portability, such as Java, then these can be deployed to a wide range of devices, including handhelds that support various operating systems, embedded Linux devices, and pure Java devices. Another important issue to consider in selecting an OS is what type of development tools is available as well as the number and strength of the programmers so they can create and maintain applications. Currently, the Palm OS supports the largest number of packaged applications. Many of these applications however are better suited for individual use rather than business use.

BUSINESS DRIVERS

According to Jones, there are four main factors driving the mobile business phenomenon and they are 1) Economics, 2) Business Need, 3) Social Trends, and 4) Technology. The economics include the falling prices of mobile air time and the inexpensive cost of devices. Jones states that over the next five years costs will continue to decrease which will allow for new mobile applications to be developed and Bluetooth chip sets to cost under $5 which will enable electronic devices to be networked together. The business needs include organizations needing new types of mobile applications to increase customer service and allow for better supply chain management. In many countries, mobile devices have become a lifestyle accessory, mainly among younger adults. As young adults continue to want more functionality from their devices and applications there will be a mix between the mobile technology and entertainment and fashion. New core technologies, such as, WAP, i-mode, Bluetooth and 3G networks are enabling a new generation of mobile applications. As these four factors continue to evolve they will continue to push the growth of the mobile business arena.

The main differences between the Palm OS and the Pocket PC OS are discussed in the next section of the paper.

PLATFORMS

Palm Operating System

The Palm operating system was developed specifically for use with Palm Pilots. As these devices began to proliferate, 3Com (who has since then spun off its Palm division as a separate company) licensed the Palm OS to other handheld device manufactures and developers. As a result, the Palm OS currently maintains a large market share in the handheld device market. Though the use of the Palm OS, software developers can build data applications for use with Palm devices, which can be implemented via wireless or synchronized data access to corporate data. According to Dulaney, for IS organizations, setting standards for PDAs, Palm OS devices will have the broadest appeal and application support. The Palm OS has the following strengths:

1) The number of partners working with Palm is extremely large
2) The number of applications available to run on top of the Palm OS
3) The current amount of market share owned by Palm

There are weaknesses with Palm and the Palm OS and some of them are:

1) The core OS functionality is limited (as compared to Pocket PC).
2) Palm as a company is undergoing major changes and some question their leadership and future business directions

There is a ongoing debate in the industry about the future of Palm and Microsoft. Palm supporters are becoming concerned that the Palm market share is stagnating while Pocket PC market share is increasing. "The conventional wisdom is that Microsoft is gaining a lot of momentum. But Palm is still the market leader," said Alexander Hinds, the president and CEO of Blue Nomad, makers of the Wordsmith word processing application for the Palm OS. (Costello). According to Costello, one of the reasons for the sense of impending doom ascribed to Palm by many is Microsoft's push into the enterprise market, an area Microsoft has traditionally dominated. Many industry experts believe that the Pocket PC will post large gains in the market in the next year and that Palm will need to work more closely with third-party developers who are already strong in the enterprise in order to counter that move. However, many of the vendors supporting the Palm OS are still confident in the future and believe that the release of Palm 5.0 will be a key in sustaining the Palm market share. Many observers tout the functionality of the Pocket PC platform, with its native support for full-motion video, digital music and high-resolution color screens as major selling points for corporate customers. This situation hasn't been helped any by the length of time Palm has let go by between major upgrades to its operating system. Palm OS 5.0, a major upgrade that will mark the platform's transition to the more powerful StrongARM processor, is set for sometime in 2002.

Pocket PC Operating System

The Microsoft operating system, Windows CE, has been renamed and the new name is Pocket PC. The latest release is Pocket PC 2002. The new version comes with bundled software but most industry analyst see the new release as an evolutionary upgrade and not a major change. The OS now looks very similar to the Windows XP operating system. With Pocket PC 2002, memory management is handled much more effectively. This is an important improvement since most of the applications that run on top of the OS require extensive hardware requirements, as compared to applications that run on the Palm OS. Both Pocket Word and Excel come bundled with the OS but it still does not include Pocket PowerPoint. Another application that comes bundled is MSN Messenger which works just like the desktop version. Many users will enjoy this since messaging is a popular application on PDAs. Another bundled application is Windows Media Player 8, which supports streaming video. Other important features include a new terminal client which provides access to Windows NT and other servers. It also includes virtual private network (VPN) access support for connecting to an intranet. The new version also supports Windows 2000 level password security. This is an important feature because if the handheld device is lost or stolen the data stays protected. Pocket PC 2002 also improves as a personal organizer. A few problems still exist like Pocket Internet Explorer does not handle frames and pop-up windows correctly. Another problem occurs when transferring between Pocket Word and the desktop version of Word. Some of the formatting in the document can be lost. The Pocket PC OS has the following strengths:

1) Utilizes the Microsoft infrastructure
2) Overall performance of the OS
3) Many developers are familiar with the Microsoft development environment

There are weaknesses with Pocket PC OS and some of them are:

1) The anti-Microsoft sentiment
2) The inability of the OS to work with Java applications. This must be done through the use of third party tools.

MARKET OVERVIEW

The market for mobile devices and applications will continue to grow over the next ten years. There is still a lot of speculation as to what companies will be the leaders but according to data from Stanley the breakdown for PDA sales both worldwide and in the United States is as follows.

CONCLUSION

Mobile computing platforms are going to continue to evolve over the next five to ten years but companies must start making decisions and putting together business plans now. Below are list of recommendations that both individuals and organizations should start implementing.

Figures from Stanley article (December 17, 2001)

Worldwide PDA Unit Sales (in millions):	**2001**	**2005**	**2007**
Pocket PC	4,205	15,960	24,355
Palm OS	7,595	14,035	16,395
Other OS	4,575	13,530	20,620
Worldwide PDAs Total	16,375	43,525	61,370

USA PDA Unit Sales (in millions):	**2001**	**2005**	**2007**
Pocket PC	1,430	5,565	8,445
Palm OS	4,780	8,390	9,710
Other OS	430	1,725	2,955
USA PDAs Total	6,640	15,680	21,110

Recommendations

- Organizations should select mobile technologies that match their business goals.
- IT leaders should plan to manage the purchase and deployment of handheld devices in the same manner that PCs are purchased and deployed.
- Organizations should support personal devices for business purposes.
- Companies need to build flexible and extendible architectures that can support multiple devices and applications.
- Create policies in the types of devices, operating systems and applications that will be supported. Adopt standardized synchronization and development tools.
- Technology, mobile economics, social trends and business needs will combine to drive the evolution of mobile e-commerce.
- Currently there are not any “killer” mobile applications. Users have different needs and value applications differently.
- Companies developing and operating mobile applications will see risks and it will require a new skill set as well as new attitudes in management.
- Pocket PC should be strongly considered for vertical market applications.

REFERENCES

Biggs, M. (2001). *Analysis: It's time for a handheld strategy.* Retrieved November 16, 2001, http://www.mbizcentral.com/story/MBZ20011115S0009.

Costello, S. (2001). Comdex - despite Microsoft, developers stick with Palm - for now.

Retrieved November 16, 2001, http://www.nwfusion.com/news/2001/1116palmms.html

Dulaney, K. (2001). *Outfitting the frontline: Phones, PDAs, and strategies for use.* Gartner Group Symposium 2001.

Duwe, C. (2001). *Microsoft Pocket PC 2002.* Retrieved September 6, 2001, http://www.zdnet.com/filters/printerfriendly/0,6061,2810757-3,00.html

Egan, B. (2001). *Mobile and wireless computing: The next user revolution.* Gartner Group Symposium 2001.

Jones, N. (2001). *Mobile commerce business scenario.* Gartner Group Symposium 2001.

Microsoft muscles in on global PDA shipments. (November 2001). mbusiness. 16.

Schwartz, E. (2001). *Opinion: The Pocket PC steamroller.* Retrieved September 21, 2001, http://www.mbizcentral.com/story/MBZ20010921S0011.

Shaw, K. (2002). Looking into Palm's future. Retrieved January 3, 2002, http://www.nwfusion.com/newsletters/mobile/2001/01142706.html

Stanley, D. (2001). *Palm's Up? Palm's Out?* Retrieved December 17, 2001, http://www.unstrung.com/server/display.php3?id=725&cat_id=2

The U.S. Paging Industry—The Impact of Mergers and Acquisition

Luvai F. Motiwalla, Stuart Freedman and David Duclos
University of Massachusetts Lowell, Tel: (978) 934-2754, luvai_motiwalla@uml.edu

ABSTRACT

The rapid growth of wireless industry has created an opportunity for competing business models and agile strategic planning approaches from management in wireless corporations. This paper focuses on the Mergers and Acquisition (M&A) strategy of positioning the traditional one-way paging carriers into leading providers of interactive wireless services adopted by several US Corporations such as Arch Wireless, Weblink Wireless, and others. Competing in this Wireless Mobile Data industry has required that once fierce competitors join together via M&A so that the strength of the combined companies places the organisation in a better competitive position. A field study with 50 employees from 10 Wireless companies was conducted to identify the strategic issues and problems associated with the M&A strategy in the Wireless industry as it tries to merge its various technologies, standards, systems and people into a successful business model to provide the next generation of m—commerce applications.

INTRODUCTION

Advances in both wireless communications and computer technologies that, combined with surging demand for instant information by both businesses and individuals, have created a revolution in the way information is conveyed. A Dataquest Inc. forecast predicts that wireless data subscribers will blossom in the coming years to a whopping 137.5 million by 2005. But as demand for wireless data grows - at a rate now projected to nearly double that of voice minutes of use by 2007 - many wireless carriers need a new strategy to satisfy this demand quickly or loose this opportunity.

Some industry analysts project that revenue for the wireless data industry will grow at rates in excess of 30% over the next five years. If true, this growth translates into an industry with revenues of nearly $32 billion, compared to total messaging sector revenues today of around $6 billion. If the one-way paging industry is to garner even a small share of that burgeoning market, they will need to adopt a fast-growth strategy of Mergers & Acquisition (M&A) to participate in the growth of interactive messaging and wireless mobile data! Communications mergers in the U.S. alone totalled 141 in one recent quarter with a total announced transaction value of 19 billion dollars - a serious indicator of the importance of M&A strategy for companies to compete successfully.

The primary objective of this research was to investigate the issues, problems and impact M&A have on the 'new' wireless organisation. Assets need to be integrated, decisions need to be made about whether to invest in or rationalise various aspects of the merged entity. 'How can the Paging & Wireless industry survive in this environment?' In short, the answer is: 'Strategic acquisitions of competitors and successful merging/integration of the wireless networking standards, systems, and employees from differing cultures. This paper provides opinions on how to integrate these three areas successfully. The next section presents the Integration issues; followed by our research Methodology, Key findings, and Conclusions.

INTEGRATION ISSUES

Paging companies are going through a convulsive period in their history, as a result of changing customer preferences for cellular telephones and other wireless devices. Recently, the industry has suffered through a massive decrease in the number of one-way paging subscribers. Between March and June 2001, one of the Industry leaders lost almost one million one-way subscribers alone. Additionally, excess competition over the years has created poor business deals that drove revenues down at a time when paging providers were valued by units in service. Today, the focus has shifted, as they are now valued on financial performance, this has had a significant impact on the industry leading to plummeting stock prices. The last straw for this already suffering industry was the huge cost burden to carriers during the recent FCC RF spectrum auctions. This was a huge cost burden as carriers spent billions of dollars for spectrum, which has significantly contributed to many bankruptcies filings in the paging sector. Another area of concern in the Paging sector is that the race to be number one has led to overpayment for companies due to 'bidding wars', as companies scramble looking for additional RF spectrum/systems - yet another example of why this industry is suffering. During the next five years, wireless data providers will face dwindling coffers and many could even be forced to sell their assets, according to Mercer Management Consulting.

Wireless Operations

Although there are many operational areas to consider during an M&A, our focus is on the problems and issues related to the wireless industry. Certainly, the Telecom Act of 1996 has exposed regulatory changes impacting the way that carriers manage and maintain the millions of telephones numbers they own. The Federal Communications Commission (FCC) now requires both Federal and State number reporting which potentially becomes a complex problem during M&A. Another challenge is how to properly integrate proprietary wireless platforms and billing systems, which were typically customised to the specific carriers needs. Lastly, cutting expenses becomes a major concern.

METHODOLOGY

Data was collected for this research by interviewing 50 executives and employees in the paging and mobile data industry. Selection criteria favoured organisations, like Arch Wireless, PageNet, MobileComm, Weblink Wireless, Airtouch, Motorola, Glenayre, and Metrocall, involved in M&A over the last three years. The goals of our survey were to get an understanding of how M&A activity impacted their organisations and what strategies their companies put in place to minimise the impact of such an event. The goals of our focus group were to generate open discussion on topics ranging from the 'state of the industry' to how M&A activity has impacted each of their respective companies. To fully analyse the impact, employees from different functional areas, such as Sales, Engineering, Operations, IT and HR, were either interviewed or participated in focus groups. Primary objective was to determine the lessons learned from the big M&A; therefore; large companies were targeted with primary focus on the acquirer. Each interview lasted no longer than 30 minutes using a semi-structured interview format. The following types of survey formats were utilised:

Personal one-on-one interviews were conducted with 30 past and present employees. Phone interviews with 20 employees from the same companies were incorporated in order to reach additional employees outside of our 'geographic reach'. Three *focus groups*, about an hour each, were conducted in the Dallas, Texas with 15 employees from the same companies. Each group of five focused on a specific interest area such as H.R., Wireless Standards, Operational Efficiency and Common Systems. Most of our survey participants (55%) were non-management professional workers, followed by executives (25%), and middle management (20%). An overwhelming (79%) percent of our participants had participated in one to three M&A event; ten percent had participated in more than four M&A events, while ten percent had no M&A experience. The data were transcribed by the interviewer and are summarized below.

KEY FINDINGS

Results from our survey indicate that half of all the M&A failed to meet expectations, or were outright failures. Nonetheless, they learned important lessons from these failures. For example, the paging companies are referring to themselves as providers of 'advanced messaging services'. The term is intended to better reflect services such as wireless e-mail, Internet information and two-way paging. Discussed below are a summary of our findings.

Human Resource Concerns: Skilled employees in the wireless sector are in big demand and often times the inadequate emphasis on rapid completion of integration of the acquired organisation has lead to the loss of quality team members. Human Resource personnel reported that employee morale, as well as financial concerns when acquiring wireless companies that have filed for chapter 11 bankruptcy protection have created major clashes in organisational cultures due to a lack of emphasis on people and cultural issues. In general, our participants overwhelmingly said that M&A strategy usually is not properly communicated to, or accepted, by employees often leading to staff retention/morale problems. Management should be aware of three common psychological shockwaves that hits the organisation – 1) uncertainty and ambiguity; 2) mistrust; and 3) self-preservation. Lastly, the merger must be a top priority for the company.

Need for Open Wireless Standards: Although Reflex is a closed proprietary standard, a key feature of the Reflex protocol is that it supports wireless application protocol (WAP) extensions. This is important for North American cellular and wideband PCS service providers who lack a common air interface protocol that will seamlessly support the basic function of receiving a data message from an application on one mobile unit and delivering it intact to another. Instead, what one sees is a set of isolated wireless domains with incompatible protocols that can only reach one another through Internet SMTP e-mail as a backbone.

Need for common Wireless/Business Systems + Operational Efficiency: The industry is experiencing many operational integration failures. Cost savings are not easy to achieve by quickly collapsing legacy wireless systems. Inadequate due diligence has impacted several wireless M&A as cost savings that initially looked good on paper were not easily realised. A Senior VP & CTO for Arch Wireless, Mark Witsaman, states that cost savings achieved by collapsing and integrating wireless systems often times are difficult to obtain. Many times paging customers have to be moved to other systems (both on the direct and indirect side of the business) which is time consuming and requires costly wireless device inventory. How should the industry react to this? Readiness and stability are important. Overall, develop a transition plan so the company can quickly converge to a single environment.

Standardization of Government Regulations: FCC spectrum auctions, which wireless companies paid billions of dollars for, have created a huge financial burden for wireless carriers prematurely forcing many companies into bankruptcy. Once the courts become involved, M&A activity becomes a long drawn out process. Recent acquisitions by Arch Wireless of Mobile and Paging Network were significantly delayed as both companies filed for bankruptcy during the M&A process, this action significantly impacted the strength that the combined companies would have had if the M&A had taken place on time. Customers were lost, vendor relationships were strained and valuable employees looked for other employment not knowing if their jobs would be secure!

Federal and State telephone number reporting is now a mandatory and appears to create many challenges during M&A as most wireless companies have Telco groups located in different areas of the country using non-standard databases and reporting tools. Additionally, inconsistent provisioning processes and lack of knowledge almost always are uncovered. To fight this challenge, companies must quickly move to centralise Telco operations consolidating to a single database, as well as common work procedures. This will allow them to quickly gain economies of scale and reduce expense by renegotiating expensive Telco contracts and eliminating duplicate expenses.

CONCLUSION

Move quickly and communicate clearly: If you wait a month to start building a single team, it will be too late. The new management team should be in place on day one and reporting structures should be established in the first few weeks. Manage the expectations of key internal and external audiences. The first step in doing this is to communicate objectives clearly, in language that is unambiguous and direct. Internal communication plans are as important as the external and should be prepared and launched simultaneously.

Empower a transition team: Integration teams during wireless M&A were generally non-existent or not properly supported often resulting in leadership clashes. A major theme that was uncovered is that the industry could do a much better job during the M&A if integration teams reporting to the CEO were in place. This certainly would ensure that all voices are heard and would allow the new company to react quickly when needed. It is essential that everyone know who is in charge and to give these people the power and the obligation to make the tough decisions. Also consider bringing in a third party that has no vested interest in either infrastructure.

Manage attitudes and expectations: Leaders have a significant role in creating the state of mind that is the society. They can serve as symbols of the moral unity of the society. They can express the values that hold the society together. Most important, they can conceive and articulate goals that lift people out of their petty preoccupations carry them above the conflicts that tear a society apart, and unite them in the pursuit of objectives worthy of their best efforts.

In summary, the 'Handwriting on the Wall' is that everyone involved in M&A must realise that change happens, therefore, they must anticipate change, monitor change, adapt to change quickly, and ultimately 'enjoy change'.

REFERENCES

References available upon request.

Gender Influences in Choosing an Information Systems Program

Lisa Mullin[1] and Donna MacDonald[2]
[1]Dept. of Information Systems, St. Francis Xavier University, Canada, Tel: (902) 867-2438, Fax: (902) 867-3352, lmullin@stfx.ca
[2]Dept. of Sociology and Anthropology, St. Francis Xavier University, Canada, dmacdona@stfx.ca, Tel: (902) 867-5217, Fax: (902) 867-2448

ABSTRACT

While on a sabbatical replacement at St. Francis Xavier University during the 1997/98 school year, I taught a couple of sections of courses for information systems students. In my new teaching assignment, I was pleasantly surprised to see so many young women in my classes. My background is in computer science, and the female student presence in my information systems classes was much higher than in the computer science field. Witnessing this phenomenon, I began a thrust of research to study the emerging trend of having female students in the Information Systems program at St. Francis Xavier University.

INTRODUCTION

The primary research question I wanted to answer was why are the women choosing the Bachelor of Information Systems program? The work began by seeking some advice from Dr. Liisa von Hellens at the School of Computing and Information Technology, Griffith University, Brisbane, Australia who had used focus groups and a follow-up survey to study similar statistics in a different demographic (Nielsen , 1998).

Some of the initial questions that were to be answered included:

- Do the economic conditions of our region play a significant role?
- Since this university generally has about 55% female students, is it just a natural phenomenon to have a high percentage of women in Information Systems?
- Is the joint study of business and technology the draw, thus bringing the number of female students in our Business Administration program down?
- What role do the Department of Information Systems faculty play in encouraging young women to come to our program?
- Many courses in the Information Systems curriculum require group work. Do females prefer this interaction?
- Does the study of calculus in computer science programs and not in information systems play a role?

METHODOLOGY

Following a similar methodology to von Hellens (1998), two focus groups consisting of approximately 8 to 10 female Information System (IS) students at St. Francis Xavier University were held. The students in this focus group ranged from first year to fourth year. During the focus groups the students discussed their career paths and reasons for being in the IS program at St. Francis Xavier University. Broadly, these reasons included job prospects, flexibility, or the presence of friends or relatives in the program. These reasons were included in the questionnaire. The questionnaire also included questions related to areas that have found gender differences in the past and other areas we thought may reveal significant differences[1]. However, not all of our initial questions were included in the survey. The survey was limited to the questions that seemed most appropriate without making the survey so long as to deter respondents from completing it.

Based on the information received in these focus groups, and the sample survey provided by von Hellens, we constructed a new survey. This survey was used to gather the reasons our students had for choosing an IS program, and to see if the reasons differed between the males and females. The questions in our survey were divided into categories. These categories include demographics, career and economic issues, program specific issues, recruitment issues, and other traditional gender differing areas such as expected salaries. An online survey was distributed to the population of students in the program, both male and female. The response rate was 62% (n=147), with a minimum response rate of 34% from each of the four years of the IS program. The results were analyzed using chi-square tests in Statistical Package for the Social Science (SPSS).

RESULTS

As expected, the prospect of getting a job after graduation from IS was very influential in determining why all students, both male and female selected the IS program (only 1 respondent indicated otherwise). We also found no gender significance emerged when asked about whether mobility and flexibility in their career was an influential factor in choosing to study IS; both male and female students thought that this was an influential factor.

Although there was no overall statistical significance between males and females when asked what recruitment techniques influenced their decision to come into the IS program, hearing about the program from friends and relatives who were enrolled in the program was more likely to be influential for females. The survey found that 79.2% of the female respondents indicated that their decision to enter IS was influenced by a friend or relative, as compared to 63.7% for the males. There is also a greater tendency for the females to think that the IS field is prestigious and a significant finding that they estimate their expected salaries to be lower than their male counterparts.

Other areas of significance also demonstrated that the female students were less likely to own their own computer and had less access to computers outside of school. Surprisingly, however, an area that did not show significant gender differences was the perceived difficulty of high school mathematics. Both males and females found math relatively easy.

DISCUSSION AND CONCLUSION

The results of the survey have answered some of my questions - job prospects are important to all students, but when looking at particular influences for females, word of mouth from friends and relatives maybe more effective (Church, 2001). If this trend continues this could be particularly important for program recruiters. When recruiting new students it may be more effective for the females in the program to talk to potential female students, possibly through a mentoring program. The study also showed that the myth that math is the reason females do not take technical programs did not hold with our students and that you do not need to own a computer to choose a program in a computer related field.

ENDNOTE

1 p d•0.05

REFERENCES

Church, Elizabeth, "Women at Work", Globe and Mail, Thursday, March 15, 2001.

Nielsen, S.H., von Hellens, L.A, Greenhill, A. & Pringle, R. "Conceptualising the influence of cultural and gender factors on students' perceptions of IT studies and careers" (1998), by, Proceedings of the 1998 ACM SIGCPR Computer Personnel Research Conference, Boston, USA, March 1998: 86-95.

Using Forster's *A Passage to India* as a Case Study in Systems Analysis Courses

Athar Murtuza
Stillman School of Business, Seton Hall University, New Jersey, Tel: (973) 761-9233, murtuzat@shu.edu

A disconnect between what is provided by information systems (IS) and the need of the users often exists and has been for sometime. Dykman and Robbins pointed out the problem of "runaways." by noting how extensive and common were the failures: "75% of all large systems are either not used, not used as intended, or generate meaningless reports. Many of these problems can be attributed to ineffective or incomplete systems analysis efforts"(1991). More recently, Marchand, Kettinger, and Rollins (2000) have shown that similar problems still exist. Knowing how to analyze a system is very important if MIS resources are to be effectively used.

This paper argues that teaching MIS students skills that will allow them to grow into effective systems analysts ought to start first by teaching them about nature of information itself and its relationship with human behavior. Secondly, it would help if one could impress upon the students how prevalent are the unstructured decisions involving non-recurring and non-routine issues that cannot be subjected to models and conceptual frameworks. One way to improve their ability to deal with unstructured situations is by making sure they apply their skills as systems analyst to unfamiliar contexts. By doing this, one is teaching them critical thinking, recognized as a higher form of learning.

To help the MIS students understand the nature of information, it would help if they were taught the kind of ideas being argued by James March and Edward Boland some years ago. James G. March, noted Stanford professor said in his address given at the annual meeting of the American Accounting Association (AAA) in 1986, noted that literary works and theories can help decision making by assisting the users of information interpret the information provided. The same year, a paper written by Richard Boland, Jr. called upon its readers to be wary of the fantasies of information and to see information as intrinsically grounded in interpretation and human dialogue. Ideas expressed by March and Boland are not dealt with extensively in introductory textbooks for systems courses.

Even before his address to the AAA annual meeting, March had argued that the theories of art and criticism enable one to see information engineering not as a passive or a manipulative activity in a decision scheme, but as an instrument of interpretation (1976). The intended and actual users of accounting information, according to March, interpret reports they are provided by the accounting departments of their organization. Accordingly, he told his audience made up of accounting professors and professionals that the notion of treating an accounting report the way one does a poem is not "entirely ludicrous" even if appears to be a "strange vision." In asking accountants to treat accounting information with its "language of numbers, ledgers, ratios" as poetry, March sought to "extend our horizons and expand our comprehensions. Information for March meant something more than simply filling in "the unknowns on a decision tree." (1986, p. 44). Choices available to decision makers are not as clear-cut as decision theory would make them out to be. There is considerable semblance between managers and that Danish prince of indecision. Shakespeare's Hamlet would not have been all that better off by applying the decision tree technique to the question of "to be or not to be."

March's argument follows from his perception that the contemporary view of information engineering draws upon decision theory and links information to choice. For March, the information systems that are "closely articulated with choices in the way anticipated by the decision theory" are often "incomplete." The solution for such lack of completeness, according to March, rests in blending the theories of choice in decision theory with the traditions of history, culture, and literature (pp.31-32). The engineering of information would gain from such a synthesis.

Like March, Boland also wants greater attention paid to human factors. His exhortation to be wary of scientism is grounded in his belief that "the logic of an organization is a lived logic. The contradictions of an organization are lived contradictions. Any fantasies that divert an accountant from a search for the lived experience of organizational members must be rejected" (p. 64). For Boland, there exist five fantasies that are promoted by scientism, which ought to be rejected by those preparing information. For Boland, these fantasies mistakenly suggest:

- Information is structured data
- An organization is information
- Information is power
- Information is intelligence
- Information is perfectible

Even though these fantasies flatter the accountant's role in the organization and self-image, they are "erroneous" according to Boland, and must be rejected. They also "lead to organizations that are monotonous, unchallenging, white-collar sweat shops." In addition, Boland argues that these fantasies fail to "respect the dignity of the individual worker" and "they deny the fundamental importance of interpersonal dialogue and the search for meaning through language for a human community" (p. 63). One must acknowledge the important relationship existing between information and its communication within an organizational context as well as between potential investors and their interpretation of financial reports. There is more than numerical significance to accounting information. Human factors and socio-political concerns are as important as the purely economic ones, and they do impact the development, communication, and reception of accounting information as well as the decisions that are made with its help.

In addition to being shown that information is more than bits and bytes, MIS students should also be asked to apply the skills they are taught to unstructured situations, which still imitate real-life cases.

It is generally agreed that the experiential approach to teaching behavior can facilitate a greater student involvement, promote class discussion, and facilitate the understanding of complex behavioral concepts. Experiential learning stays with the students much longer. They tend to remember an experience much longer than they do parts of lectures or pages from a textbook. Games, business simulations, behavioral exercises in the classroom, and case studies seek to bridge the gap between abstract lectures and experiential learning. These approaches contrast with courses relying strictly on lectures, where human behavior is talked about rather than observed, felt, or experienced.

Culture, art, and literature can also help improve students' perceptions about human behavior. For thousands of years and in virtually every civilization, cultural artifacts such as music, paintings, novels, poems and plays have dramatized human behavior. The hold literature has on the human imagination can be attributed largely to its ability to evoke empathy in its readers. While reading a novel, reciting a poem or watching a play, readers and audiences are able to empathize with the characters and actions being portrayed and are able vicariously to experience it themselves. Literature may be seen both as a mirror that reflects human behavior and a lamp that helps illuminate it. Because literature evokes empathy and permits readers to experience life vicariously, it can serve as a resource for vicariously experiencing life and through it human behavior. Some will argue that not only the literary works capture life more effectively than do the narratives in case-studies, they happen to be more readable as well. One ought to be able to use literature as a surrogate for vicarious experiential learning pertaining to human perception, motivation, anxiety, conflict, attitude and attitude change as well as interpersonal communication. The incorporation of literature as a supplementary resource in business and management information systems curriculums would serve not only as a surrogate for experiential learning of behavior but it could also make students aware of the complex diversity of human behavior.

Games, case studies, simulation, and experiential exercises have often been used to supplement the teaching of courses in all areas of Business including accounting and management information systems (MIS); however the experiential potential of literary works remains largely untapped in courses involving information systems as well as accounting. Still, such a use of literary works in the context of accounting and systems courses seemingly fits the various definitions of creativity quoted by J. Daniel Cougar (1995). Among the definitions quoted by Cougar is the one by J. S. Bruner that sees "effective surprise" to be the essence of a creative approach. John Ciardi sees creativity to be imaginatively recombining known elements into something new, while the French mathematician Poincare equated the creative process with a fruitful combination that reveals an unsuspected relationship between facts, long known but wrongly believed to antithetical to each other. In order to merit classification as creative, an activity must be new or unique and it must have utility and/or value according to Cougar (Cougar, 1995, p. 14).

The novel, **A Passage to India** can serve as a surrogate for experiential learning in a systems analysis course by treating the subject of the novel, British India in the 1920's and the relationships between the ruling Anglo-Indian and the ruled South Asians, as a system and analyzing it by using the analytic tools of system analysis. One could see British India described in the book itself as comprising of three sub-systems: Anglo-Indians who ruled made up one sub-system, while South Asians Muslims and Hindus comprised the other two subsystems. The characters belonging to each of the three sub-systems are unable to transcend their cultural prisons and relate to each other in a positive manner. The interface among these sub-systems and the individuals belonging to them, their failure to communicate with each other, as well as the factors that make such communication dysfunctional lend itself to analysis and understanding through the lens of system analysis tools and concepts. Students can use the techniques associated with system analysis define each of the three sub-systems. They can also discuss how each sub-system perceives the other two as well as its own self-perception. They can then be asked to explain why the three sub-systems are unable to communicate well with each other. The focus on the dysfunctional communication between the three subsystems can best serve the use of the novel in a systems analysis course.

One could further strengthen the case study by drawing upon notions of cultural values such as those put forward by Geert Hofstede, since the characters in the novel act in accordance with their respective cultural values. Yet another lens to focus the analysis of the three sub-systems is through the notion of organizational sense making put forth by Karl Weick.

The novel written by E. M. Forster can be used to supplement the teaching of systems analysis. Doing so seems highly relevant to multinational corporations of the 21st Century, where managers and employees representing diverse cultures have to work together despite their cultural diversity. By using the novel as a case study, one can sensitize students to the cognitive, behavioral, linguistic, and cultural factors that can impact on the communication of information, the raison d'etre for an information system. It is true that for many MIS academics the idea of assigning a novel to their students would seem foreboding, yet the time it will take to read a classic novel is well worth the effort. Reading literature can be fun, it is food for critical thinking, it can improve communication skills, and it also happens to be a good teaching resource albeit under-utilized in MIS classes.

REFERENCES

Boland, R. "Fantasies of Information," Advances in Public Interest Accounting, v. 1 (1986), pp. 49-65.

Cougar, J. Daniel. Creative Problem Solving and Opportunity Founding (Danvers, MA, Boyd & Fraser, 1995).

Dykman, C. A. and R. Robbins, "Organizational Success through Effective Systems Analysis," in Journal of Systems Management (July 1991), pp. 6-8.

March, J. "Ambiguity and Accounting: The Elusive Link Between Information and Decision Making" in Accounting and Culture, ed. Barry Cushing (Sarasota, FL, AAA, 1987), pp. 31-49.

Marchand, D., W. Kettinger, & J. Rollins, "Information Orientation: People, Technology, and the Bottom Line," Sloan Management Review (Summer, 2000), pp. 69-80.

Modeling Inter-Organizational Behavior in IT Distance Education: Going Beyond Instructor-Student Interactions

Peter R. Newsted
Centre for Innovative Management, Athabasca University, British Columbia, Canada
Tel/Fax: (250) 890-3683 (Please call first if sending a fax), petern@athabascau.ca

Today's technology-enabled distance education (DE) has moved beyond simple interaction of a student and a tutor or instructor. Not only must these two primary components of DE be included in understanding behavior in this educational environment, but the organizational context in which they exist must also be considered. This context can include multiple organizations. Over time individual students and instructors may participate with many organizations. Increasingly there are networks of cooperation among related institutions. The Instructional Telecommunications Council (2001) already maintains a list of 50 such networks. In particular it behooves the academic community in information technology (IT) to determine if actually teaching and learning about the underpinning technology itself differentially facilitates or even hinders the IT community's actual *use* of IT for DE.

To study the complexity of these relations a comprehensive three-part model is proposed with potential behaviours among the individuals and organizations involved. The behaviours perceived so far (based on personal experience and an initial review of the literature) suggest testable hypotheses. Verifying or disconfirming these will further the understanding of the use of IT as an enabler of DE. The purpose of this paper is to present this model with suggested hypotheses to further research. Some issues involved in these relationships have already been considered in a fictional case study (Newsted, 2000) — albeit without any special attention to use by the IT community. Nonetheless this is still research in progress at the very early stages of model creation and refinement.

Figure 1: Interactions of Students, Instructors and Organizations

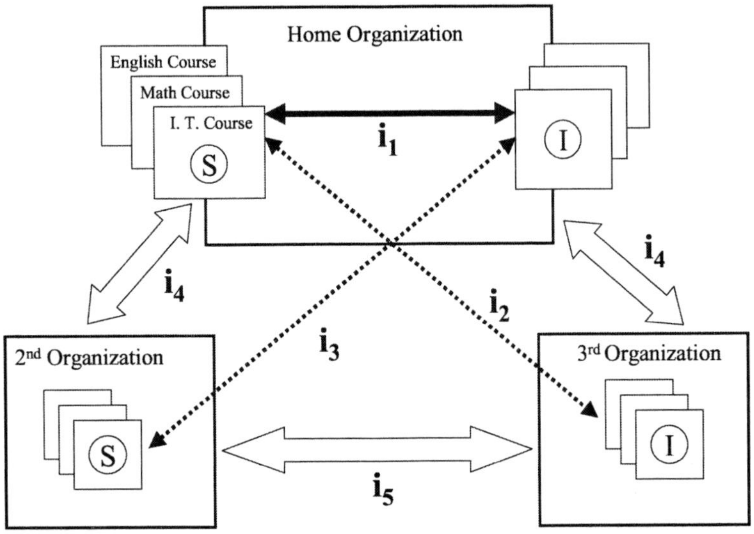

Three types or units of behaviours can be considered: student, instructor and organization. In each of these there are both positive and negative aspects of DE that will guide the behavior of these entities and especially influence their interaction. In particular it is useful to identify aspects that are or are not unique to information technology.

A graphical model can be used to explore the possibilities (see Figure 1 below). The bold solid line in this model (i_1) represents traditional and expected interactions of students (S), instructors (I) and an organization where both the students and instructors are part of the same organization or institution. (At this stage of model creation, this and the following interactions should just be considered as general relationships and not necessarily viewed as causal links — as would ultimately be required in a refined analysis using a tool such as structural equation modeling.)

In this model, students may either reside within the organization or take course at a distance. Similarly — though not as common — instructors may be physically present at the organization — or may teach from a distance (telecommuting). The dotted lines (i_2 and i_3) represent potential additional interactions when multiple organizations are considered. The general term "organization" is used to encompass both nonprofit institutions such as typical universities and colleges as well as profit-based universities (e.g. Phoenix University (www.phoenix.edu)) and consortiums (e.g. Universitas 21 (www.universitas.edu.au)). Organizations could also include both providers of content (e.g. UNext (www.unext.com)) and delivery mechanisms (e.g. Blackboard (www.blackboard.com)). The multiple "layers" of both students and instructors in Figure 1 recognizes the involvement in different courses and disciplines by the same and different individuals (e.g. the same student may take Introductory Information Systems, Systems Analysis, English, Mathematics.). More complex interactions between organizations are represented by thicker arrows (i_4 and i_5).

Based on these definitions and connections the following hypotheses are generated as to interactions and what their strength would be.

First, there are a number of simple hypotheses regarding the i_1 interactions:

Both students and instructors will pursue these connections:

- If it is convenient
- If it is flexible as to time and location
- More so if they have access to technology
- More so if they have readily accessible support
- Depending on past experience

Specifically students will pursue this based on:

- Need for specific courses
- Cost course
- Whether they feel they belong to the class (cf. Salisbury, Pearson, Miller, and Marett, 2002)

- Meeting their expectations about feedback (cf. Hara and Kling, 2001)
- How successful required group interactions can be using technology-based media (cf. Haggerty, Schneberger, and Carr, 2001)

Instructors will engage in this interaction if:

- They are rewarded
- They view DE as appropriate (vis-à-vis such things as their institution's mission and the performance of DE students) (cf. Ross and Klug, 1999)
- Their peers support them (both internally and across their discipline)
- Their professional identify is maintained or enhanced (cf. Jaffee, 1998)
- They see the value of various intrinsic rewards such as the ability to reach new students and generally be able to explore new ideas and technology (cf. Wolcott and Betts, 1999).

Next there are more complex links. The link of students to instructors outside their organization (i_2) will happen if:

- A desired course is not available at the home institution
- Their own institution accepts this course

The complimentary relationship of instructors to students at other organizations (i_3) will occur if instructors are allowed to do this by their home organization. Influencing this choice are the issues as to whether this is considered approved consulting or whether it is considered as competing with the home organization. Readily available and inter-organizational compatible technology paths will also facilitate this interaction, as will adequate channel bandwidth.

Links between organizations are more complicated. The i_4 link can be expected to flourish if:

- The involved organizations have complimentary needs.
- One needs a specific course on something like advanced object-oriented databases that is not offered at the other organization
- The programs mesh as to accreditation, credits and course content
- There exists an acceptance that courses can be bought and sold, or at least bartered
- The inter-organizational climate is supportive. This can occur when sharing is proposed within a defined system such as a single state (e.g. Colorado (Colorado Commission on Higher Education, 2000)), or a small country (e.g. Sweden (Bollags, 2001)).

Inter-organizational links such as i_5 may develop if this is seen as promoting a competitive advantage over the separate home organization. Such links would diminish the likelihood of i_2, i_3 and i_4 happening. In all inter-organizational linking it is also likely that this behavior will happen more frequently if it can be shown to have a positive impact on an institution's performance indicators. However, as Shale and Gomes (1998) have suggested this is more complex in the DE environment than in traditional instruction.

Regarding the impact of the IT discipline on these interactions it can be predicted that:

- IT students and instructors will only have a very slight initial edge given that a minimal level of technical skill is needed to pursue technology-based DE. This is a hygiene effect that will minimize any effects of knowledge of the IT discipline.
- It is also suggested that the IT discipline may in fact be slower to adopt such links given the amount of study that is given to the interactions of technology and people. Academics in this field are more aware and often more critical of this interaction and hence may not accept it as readily.
- Further, instructors in the IT area may also be slowed in their adoption of DE by waiting to find the "perfect" tool for this interaction. Rather than accepting an off the shelf product they will strive to invent their own solution. And given that such software creation typically goes through multiple versions, it can be expected that IT-based interactions may have less initial success that those in other disciplines using commercial products.

Testing the validity of all of the hypotheses suggested above is an ambitious endeavor. Fortunately it can be shortened by examining a number of existing studies that bear on the acceptance of DE. Some of these have already been cited above. Further reviewing additional studies is beyond the scope of this short paper — though it will be required in the full validation and development of this model. At this stage this model is presented as an attempt to provide a comprehensive view of factors influencing the use and acceptance of technology enabled distance education — especially considering the inevitability of organizational interaction and competition.

Lastly, potential methodologies need to be considered for testing hypotheses still unresolved after the literature search. Three possibilities have potential. First, an action research approach of immersing oneself in one or more of the interaction pathways will illuminate the importance of these various relationships. Second, cases can be written about the activities and interactions explored using the action research approach. As the relations and variables become clearer, specific constructs involved in interaction can be identified and developed into questionnaires to further triangulate the findings about interactions among students, instructors, and organizations.

REFERENCES

Bollags, B. (2001). Sweden Will Create a Virtual Institution by Compiling Universities' Online Offerings. *Chronicle of Higher Education*, September 20, 2001. Retrieved November 29, 2001 from the World Wide Web: http://www.chronicle.com/free/2001/09/2001092001u.htm

Colorado Commission on Higher Education (2000). Agenda Item VII, D, Attachment, Summary and Recommendations. Retrieved November 29, 2001 from the World Wide Web: http://www.state.co.us/cche/agenda/agenda00/novviid1.html

Instructional Telecommunications Council (2001). Statewide Virtual Networks. Retrieved December 7, 2001 from the World Wide Web: http://www.itcnetwork.org/virtualalliancelist.htm

Haggerty, N., Schneberger, S. & Carr, P. (2001). Exploring media influences on individual learning: Implications for organizational leaning. *Proceedings of the 22nd International Conference on Information Systems*. Retrieved December 7, 2001 from the World Wide Web: http://aisel.isworld.org/proceedings/ICIS/2001/ICIS2001.asp

Hara, N. & Kling, R. (2001). Students' distress with a web-based distance education course: An ethnographic study of participants' experiences. Retrieved December 7, 2001 from the World Wide Web http://www.slis.indiana.edu/CSI/Wp/wp00-01B.html

Newsted, P. R. (2000). Developing shared distance education at North Coast University: A case on the issues involved in using technology to enable syndicated distance education. *Journal of Distance Education*, 15(2), pp. 97-112.

Jaffee, D. (1998). Institutionalized Resistance To Asynchronous Learning Networks. *Journal of Asynchronous Learning*, 2(2). Retrieved December 4, 2001 from the World Wide Web: http://www.aln.org/alnweb/journal/vol2_issue2/jaffee.htm

Ross, G. J. & Klug, M. G. (1999). Attitudes of business college faculty and administrators toward distance education: A national survey. *Distance Education*, 20(1), pp. 109-128.

Salisbury, W. D., Pearson, R. A., Miller, D. W., & Marett, L. K. (2002). The limits of information: A cautionary tale about one course delivery experience in the distance education environment. Forthcoming, *eService Journal*.

Shale, D. & Gomes, J. (1998). Performance indicators and university distance providers. *Journal of Distance Education*, 13(1). Retrieved October 25, 2000 from the World Wide Web: http://cade.athabascau.ca/vol13.1/shale.html

Wolcott, L. & Betts, K. (1999). What's in it for me? Incentives for faculty participation in distance Education. *Journal of Distance Education*, 14(2). Retrieved November 29, 2001 from the World Wide Web: http://cade.athabascau.ca/vol14.2/wolcott_et_al.html

Changing a Business School Corporate Culture: Teaching in the 21st Century on a Different Blackboard

Jennifer Paige Nightingale
Visiting Instructgor of Information Technology, A.J. Palumbo School of Business Administration
John F. Donahue Graduate School of Business, Duquesne University, Pennsylvania
Tel: (412) 396-6257, Fax: (412) 396-4764, nightingale@duq.edu

ABSTRACT

This paper details a predictive model development and empirical validation of introducing information technology into the organizational structure. The model was developed from the results of implementing the Blackboard® Course Management System (CMS) at Duquesne University's School of Business. A user group of 1683 students, faculty, and staff, were surveyed, of which 186 respondents were used to test the model; a shift in the school's culture is largely determined by individuals' attitude toward improving school-wide communication and perceived software learning curves. The results add to a growing stream of Information Systems (IS) research into introducing information technology (IT) into the organizational structure and have significant implications for organizations and industry groups aiming to incorporate a sizeable technological change. A follow-up survey that the academic advisors will help enforce and advertise is also planned for after the spring registration period to see if the students are finding the information contained within to be helpful.

INTRODUCTION

Employing technology that students find enticing and will prepare them well for the future, may be easier than preparing the teachers who will integrate this technology into learning activities. Competition among educational institutions for students is increasing exponentially, which requires a greater sensitivity to student needs.[1] Course Management Systems (CMSs) can build a framework for using technology as a technique of providing this responsiveness to students, predominantly in the form of communication. The aim is to ultimately create an environment conducive to teaching and learning via a technological community where students, faculty, adjunct instructors, staff, and administration can work together to achieve a common goal – produce quality graduates.

The Duquesne University (DU) School of Business (SOBA) in Pittsburgh, Pennsylvania, is bridging the communication gap between students, faculty, and staff with an online community called **SOBA-Net** (School of Business Administration Network). Using the CMS, Blackboard®, as a portal, users find important information, communication, and resources for their programs. SOBA-Net is quickly becoming a tool on which students, faculty, and staff depend.

A portal is not a new concept to the IT industry; in fact, www.yahoo.com and www.msn.com are two of the many organizations that have used portals from the beginning. Building an online community in Blackboard® has made it convenient for students to find the tools and resources they need to be successful in their academic career. "In the Internet economy, people, process, and technology must be inextricably linked," explained Greg Baroni, national partner-in-charge of the KPMG higher education practice. "Portals are the latest iteration of enabling technology that universities can integrate to create strategic advantage."[2]

THE IMPACT OF TECHNOLOGY

Technology clearly has had, and will continue to have, a major impact on education. Many institution segments are moving transactions and shared information into online communication channels, such as the Internet. For example, the percentage of students using computers in colleges and universities has increased from 55.2% in 1994 to 64.7% in 1997; and has nearly doubled for students using computers at home for schoolwork from 23.1% to 40.8%.[3]

E-mail, the Internet, and websites are rapidly becoming core components of postsecondary instruction for students in the United States.[4] A fall 1998 survey reported on in *The Condition of Education 2001* showed that 97% of full-time faculty and staff had access to the Internet, 69% used e-mail to communicate with students, and 40% used a course-specific website.[5]

"Education is the fuel for the New Economy, and demand for online teaching and learning resources has already reached critical mass. Web-based and Web-enhanced courses are....already popular e-learning platforms in higher education today. According to *Student Monitor*, 90% of college students used the Internet last fall and 66% were connecting once a day or more often. According to *Campus Computing*, over 53% of college courses used e-mail last year, almost 39% used Internet resources, and almost 28% used Web pages for class materials and resources...."[6]

As education and technology continues to amalgamate and evolve at rapid speed, institutions will find an enormous array of effective solutions to enrich their educational offerings and build deeper relationships with current and prospective students, alumni, and administrators.[8] CMSs are modifying the way instructors disseminate information. A growing number of campuses identify CMSs as "very important" in their institutional IT planning and that approximately one-fifth (20.6%) of all college courses now use course management tools, up from 14.7% in 2000.[8] A leading e-Learning industry analyst firm projects that the higher education e-Learning market will grow from $4 billion today to $11 billion by 2003.[9]

THE HISTORY OF SOBA-NET

There is no doubt that technology has had a major impact on our daily lives. In summer 1999, DU adopted the Blackboard® CMS. This system traditionally allows for teaching online, where colleges and universities all over the world are diving into the online education arena. In an effort to meet student demands, this CMS was modified to build human relationships that allow students to: (1) take an active role in; and (2) be held accountable for their academic career. Ultimately, the creation of SOBA-Net has taken the foundation of a CMS and altered it to become a School Management System (SMS).

What is a School Management System? A management information system is "a computer-based system that supports managers and their subordinates in their daily work and strategic planning....managerial decisions and daily operations."[10] An SMS manages a school's key functional data including items such as staff and faculty data, class schedules, school guidelines, special programs, and other school information, and, depending upon the type of SMS implemented and the desired outcomes, the system can range from low-end to high-end capabilities. Many schools depend on integrated information systems to manage their data and provide detailed information that aids in the communication process.[11]

Why Blackboard®? Although DU supports both WebCT® and Blackboard® CMSs, Blackboard® was selected because of its low learning curve, visual appeal and secured environment as well as the ability to access information via the Internet. In addition, some of the school's faculty participated in training when Blackboard® was initially implemented campus-wide in summer 1999, bringing a familiarity component into play, and encouraging faculty involvement in implementation.

SOBA-Net reinforces both DU and SOBA's directive of integrating technology across the curriculum. For many faculty members, the shear thought of integration can be greatly intimidating. By using Blackboard®, faculty members can observe how a CMS is used to aid in disseminating materials and communicating with students; in moving from observing to participating, the intimidation can be significantly reduced.

What Were the Initial Objectives? The academic advisors were initially thought to be the staff that would benefit the most as they constantly searched for a better method of communicating with the students. Thus, they embraced and encouraged this improvement and rather than merely adding to the student's knowledge bank, the objective was to set students up for success by requiring them to take an active role in their education. This transforms the role of the student and requires them to interact in the activities in which they currently participate.[12] Students and advisors would be able to work smarter and more efficiently, help improve overall communication between faculty, staff and students, validate concepts taught throughout curriculum (i.e. teamwork), and greatly reduce the paper trail.

METHODOLOGY

A survey was posted on SOBA-Net and users were asked to respond. The correlating message explained the purpose of the survey, indicated that it would not take more than five minutes to complete, and offered several give-away items as an incentive. The resulting sample was 186 completed questionnaires, an 11.1% response rate.

The questionnaire consisted of both close-ended and open-ended questions. The close-ended questions asked about login instructions, awareness of tool, navigation, and academic career management. The open-ended questions allowed the respondents to indicate their answers in their own words and inquired about items that could be added to improve SOBA-Net. In addition, it included an area for additional thoughts if the respondent wished to express.

RESULTS

Table 1 illustrates the basic results of SOBA-Net users, average hits per day, and the percentage of users who have logged in as compared to the overall user base. The figures do not equal the *Current Total* because summer activity is not reflected in the table. The formal implementation was September 2001. In considering adoption of this initiative, statistics show that 1,035 users out of 1,683 potential users, or 83% of all potential users, have accessed SOBA-Net as of January 7, 2000. Of the potential users, 1470 are students, (81.5% of all potential student users), 46 are full-time faculty (85% of all potential full-time faculty users), 63 are adjunct instructors, 16 are administrators (100% of all potential administrator users), and 88 are staff (100% of all potential staff users).

Over 28,000 user logins have been recorded as of end December 2001, with an overall average of 222 hits per day. Of the potential respondents, 1,035 users (61.5%) have logged into SOBA-Net, and as documented in a recent survey, 54% of those student users cited "professor or instructor" in response to the question, "How did you learn about SOBA-Net?" Research is currently being pursued to determine characteristics of regular users, occasional users, and infrequent or non-users and occasional users, and infrequent or non-users will be surveyed for needs analysis and improvement of SOBA-Net.

SOBA-Net serves its main purpose as a means of school-wide communication medium through its ease of use, high percentage of users, and variety of user options. In terms of ease of use, 92% of respondents found login instructions easy to comprehend and follow, while 75% reported that navigating through SOBA-Net was simple.

Table 1: General SOBA-Net statistics

	Total Users	Total Logins	Unique Logins	Average Hits/Day	Ratio: Users vs. Potential Users
September 2001	1,364	5,943	523	198	38.3%
October 2001	1,439	10,797	670	348	46.6%
November 2001	1,678	3,992	380	133	22.6%
December 2001	1,680	3,435	356	111	21.2%
Current Total	1,683	28,217	1,035	222	61.5%

CONCLUSION

SOBA-Net provides connectivity via the Internet, maintaining SOBA's initiative for technology integration, and appeals to the students' desire for online resources. The data illustrates that many potential users are taking advantage of this communication medium from internal job postings to scholarships geared toward business students. While it may be too early to determine SOBA-Net's effectiveness in fostering academic success, it has encouraged students to become more self-sufficient and assume some responsibility and accountability for their educational outcomes. In addition, there has been a notable increase in faculty use of Blackboard® in their classes, and students are encouraging those who don't use it to adopt it.

REFERENCES

1. R. Heckman and A. Guskey, "The relationship between alumni and university: toward a theory of discretionary collaborative behavior," *Journal of Marketing Theory and Practice*, 6:2 (1998), 97-113.
2. G. Baroni, "Portal technology - into the looking glass," presented at 1999 Portal Technology Symposium in Baltimore, Maryland, October 1999.
3. U.S. Department of Education, National Center for Education Statistics, *Digest of Education Statistics 1999* (NCES 99-036), (Washington, DC: U.S. Government, 1999).
4. B. Greene, A. Cattagni, and E.F. Westat (2001), U.S. Department of Education, National Center for Education Statistics, *Internet access in U.S. public schools and classrooms: 1994 – 2000* (NCES 2000-071), (Washington, DC: U.S. Government, 2001).
5. U.S. Department of Education, National Center for Education Statistics, The context of postsecondary education, *The Condition of Education 2001* (NCES 99-036), (Washington, DC: U.S. Government, 1999).
6. Testimony of Carol Vallone, President and CEO, WebCT, On The Internet, Distance Learning & the Future of the Research University, Presented to the Subcommittee on Basic Research, Committee on Science, U.S. House of Representatives, May 9, 2000, [Online]. Available: http://www.house.gov/science/vallone_050900.htm
7. Blackboard Incorporated (2001), "Course and portal solutions: Blackboard 5," Available: http://products.blackboard.com/cp/bb5/index.cgi
8. K. Green, "2001 national survey of information technology in U.S. higher education," presented at Educause 2001 in Indianapolis, October 29, 2001.
9. P. Stokes, "E-Learning: Education Businesses Transform Schooling" (June 2000), Eduventures.com, [Online]. Available: https://www.eduventures.com/pdf/doe_elearning.pdf
10. E. Oz (2000), *Management information systems, 2nd edition.* Massachusetts: Course Technology, 21-22.
11. M. Bober, "School information systems and their effects on school operations and culture," *Journal of Research on Technology in Education,* 33:5 (2001).
12. B. Rogoff, "Developing understanding of the idea of communities of learners," *Mind, Culture, and Activity,* 1:4 (1994), 209- 229.

Support of Electronic Services within the Public Sector

Birgit J. Oberer
University of Klagenfurt, Austria, birgit.oberer@gmx.at

Dr. Alptekin Erkollar
Union Bank of Switzerland, alptekin.erkollar@gmxpro.de

ABSTRACT

Electronic Services, like inquiry possibilities which are made available to citizens by administration authorities, are the most apparent proof of changes in the public sector because of modern information and communication technologies. Electronic Government causes an improvement of the relationship between administration, citizens and business. It includes all governmental measures at administrational levels (union, states and local governments) for qualitative improvements in citizen's different spheres of life and for optimization of business processes within the administration.

INTRODUCTION

The use of information and communication technologies enables the development of Electronic Government and causes an improvement of the relationship between administration, citizens and business [9]. E-Government includes all administrational measures at all levels (union, states and local governments) to improve the requirement satisfaction for citizens and businesses and to optimize the business processes within the administration (structural changes). Possible interaction partners in the area of Electronic Government are Government, Citizens / Customers and Business. In Section 2 there will be shown two different methods for analyzing the weaknesses of electronic government approaches: critical conditions and classification portfolios. In section 3 there will be given a short overview about Electronic Government activities in the European Union (EU) followed by the description of E-Government incentives of Switzerland. In section 4 there will be done a strengths and weaknesses analysis for the different electronic government incentives [6]. Additionally, there will be done a comparative analysis of the E-Government approaches.

ANALYZE METHODS FOR WEAKNESSES OF ELECTRONIC GOVERNMENT APPROACHES

Critical Conditions for Electronic Government

For the successful implementation of Electronic Government systems there exist some critical general conditions [3]. Principles are public access, possibility to select whether the conventional method of contact or the electronic one, prevention of abuse, creation of trust in the service's quality on the part of the users, measurements for adjusting the administrational processes (redesign or optimization of processes) [3]. Areas for reaching a sufficient development of E-Government are demand orientation of the services, organizational, legal and technological conditions [3].

Demand orientation:

The main interests of citizens as users of governmental services are simple and fast information procurement and transactions to simplify the contact to the governmental authorities. [3].

Organizational conditions:

- Redesign of administrational processes and structures according to the New Public Management (NPM) approach: reform of tasks and structures as well as 'within' modernization for higher efficiency and better control of transactions.

Legal conditions:

- formulation of an information policy
- definition of rules for access and use of electronic services by citizens and businesses.
- Regulations about security infrastructure [3,4]

Technological conditions:

Use of modern information and communication technologies [5,3].

Classification Schemes and Portfolios

One method for evaluating E-Government incentives is to create classification schemes for these initiatives and strategies. In a classification scheme there are analyzed different characteristics of a e-government procedure for assigning the procedure to different classes. Table 1 shows the criteria for suitable classification schemes.

Table 1: Criteria for classification schemes

Transparent and simple assignment of e-government procedures to different classes
The classes should show the value-added utility for users of e-government (citizens and businesses)
The classes should differentiate the potential for increasing efficiency within administration authorities
The class assignment should show the degree of complexity for realization.

Targets of the classification are the evaluation of main features of procedures and the creation of comparable initiatives. There are two main views: the user-view and the IT-view; using these views there can be created a two-dimensional classification scheme which is shown in figure 1.

Each rectangle represents one class, orientated by the corresponding state of the two possible views. Within the user-view the following states are possible:

Information: public online access to administrational information

General service: public online access to administrational information with respect of special needs

Individual service: information provision to identified persons and legal entities

Within the IT-view the following states are possible:

Media break: information technology based service provision without continuous processing

No media break:

Automation: complete information technology based service provision and processing. The more to the right and the more upwards the

FIgure 1: Two-dimensional classification scheme

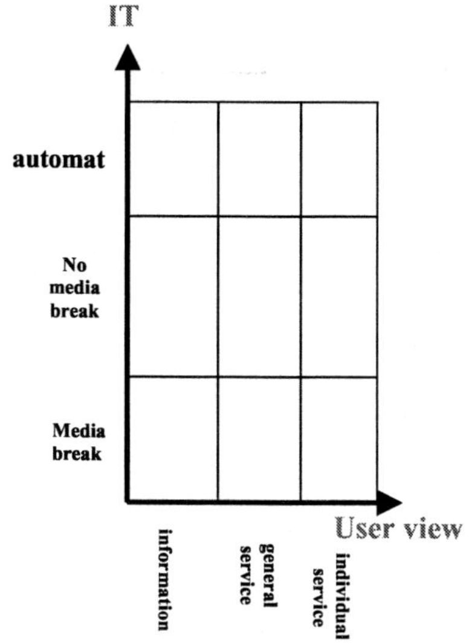

less weaknesses can be found within e-government processes[6]. In the two-dimensional classification scheme there is made no comment on how efficient for the administration the evaluated e-government incentives are. The classification scheme has to be enlarged with the dimension of the administration to a three-dimensional portfolio, which is shown in figure 2.

The portfolio considers the user-, IT- and the administration-view.

Within the administration view the following states are possible [6]:

Negative - efficiency: large - scale administrational work because of e-government incentives

Null-efficiency: no effect on administrational work because of e-government strategies and activities Effective - efficiency: decrease in administrational work because of e-government initiatives

Figure 3 shows possible efficiency levels and state combinations for e-government approaches.

INTERNATIONAL ELECTRONIC GOVERNMENT APPROACHES

Electronic Government in the European Union

Most countries have chosen different ways in developing their own national strategies [3]. There were founded national committees

Figure 2: Three-dimensional classification portfolio

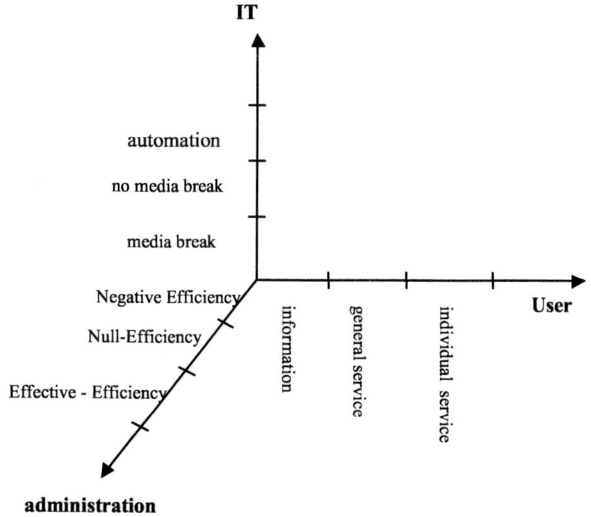

Figure 3: Efficiency levels

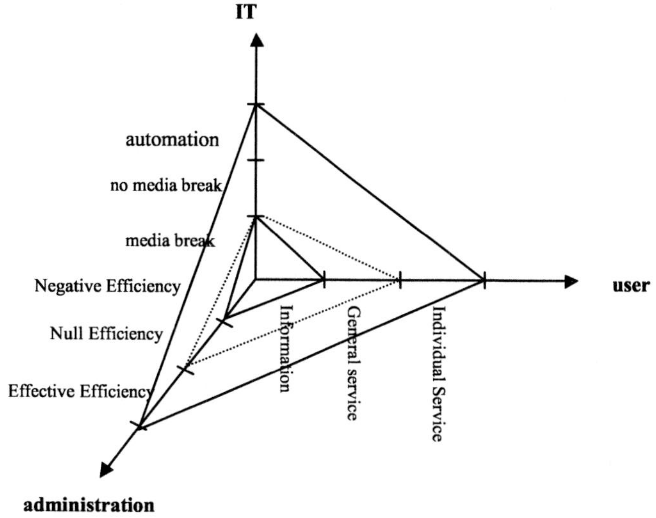

for information society (Belgium, Finland), consulting institutions (Sweden, Ireland), committees of ministers (France, Spain, Greek, Portugal), public control committees for information technologies, (Ireland, Italy), groups of experts (Austria, Spain, Denmark, Netherlands) [9,5,3,4].

There are three different supply models for doing Electronic Government: information, communication and transaction [7]. In most countries there is realized the first level: information. In some countries you an find approaches of the second level: communication. Most of the time this communication is limited to offering e-mail functions for users. The third level - transaction - is not at all or not sufficient realized in the countries of the European Union [3].

E-Government Strategies in Austria

In Austria there are realized services at level 1 (information) and level 2 (communication) in a sufficient way AND partly in level 3 (transaction):

- information provision to citizens from the administration (citizen information systems)
- access for users to relevant data from a coordination authority (mostly for business relevant data)
- creating of value-added products (mainly for geographic information systems)

For the first level (information) Austria offers a very sufficient citizen / business information system with components for level 2 (communication): the information system **help.gv** [1]:

- Creation of a Citizen Information System
- Creation of a Business Information System
- Combining the two created information systems within one unique portal

But there is still a media break in the chain of the processes of this Citizen Information System. Till now you can download the form, have to fill it out, give it to the corresponding authority which has to register your data separately. According to governmental strategies most mentioned media breaks should be eliminated till 2003. Having removed these media breaks the third sort of contact - the transaction - will be realized (planned for 2005). Additionally to the information procurement, you can contact administrational authorities via e-mail options (communication level). The Business Information System is organized in the same way as the Citizen Information System.

Electronic Government in Switzerland

The main idea of Electronic Government is networking all governmental offers digitally. Especially in federalistic structured countries, like Switzerland, citizens have to deal with heterogeneous cantons and local governments. In this case a networking of all governmental offers is necessary for the functioning of electronic administration [8,7]. One instrument for reaching the targets of the strategy is the Guichet virtuel. It is a web portal which will allow a customer oriented and service oriented access to the electronic administrational supply at all levels of government. One aim of the Guichet virtuel is to improve the relationship between administration and citizens in using a link system with references to already existing webpages of the union, single cantons or various local governments [2].

STRENGTHS AND WEAKNESS ANALYSIS

Analysis with Critical Conditions

Table 2: Critical conditions for Austria

Austria		
Critical conditions	**Positive (+)**	**Negative (-)**
Demand orientation	Information and communication levels realized, transactions planned Information System clearly arranged in two parts: citizens, business	
Organizational conditions	Partly realized organizational redesign Sufficient coordination when redesigning Concrete strategies for redesign of processes and structures	Poor coordination of technical organization decisions
Legal conditions	Most regulations are formulated by the European Union (EU) information policy available regulation for access to administrational services good security infrastructure	Too less legal adjustments in the legislation for required E-Government security issues
Technological conditions	effective use of information and communication technologies (regulations by the EU)	Partly insufficient effectivity in using information and communication technologies

Table 3: Critical conditions for Switzerland

Switzerland		
Critical conditions	**Positive (+)**	**Negative (-)**
Demand orientation	Good surveys about citizens/users needs; high degree of demand orientation	
Organizational conditions	Partly realized organizational redesign Sufficient coordination when redesigning	Web appearance of single local governments - national coordination too slow
Legal conditions	information policy available On average good legal adjustments to E-Government issues	
Technological conditions	effective use of information and communication technologies	No concrete web portal available (online start at the end of 2001)

Analysis with Classification Portfolios

The use of classification portfolios enables to evaluate the utility for the user, the degree of information technology use and the state of efficiency for the administration [6]. In this section there are shown classification portfolios for the above mentioned international Electronic Government approaches.

Austria

Figure 4 shows the classification portfolio for Austrian Electronic Government approaches with the highest realized state combination [6]. At the IT-view the highest reached state lies above media break; the tendency from the user's point of view can be stated between 'general service' and 'individual service'. The highest reached state at the administrational dimension lies near 'effective efficiency' [6].

Figure 4: Highest state combination of Austrian approaches

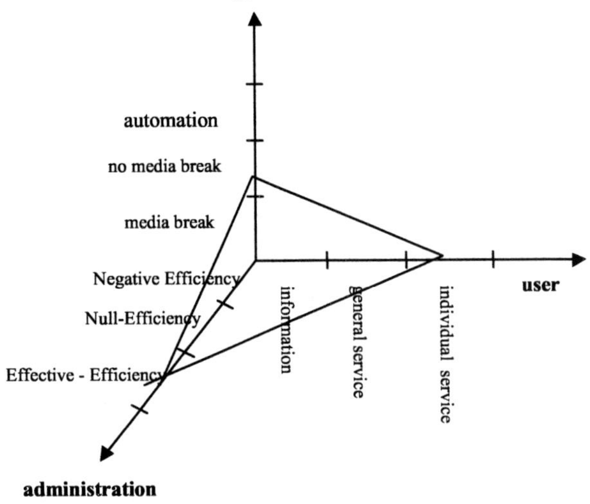

Switzerland

Figure 5 shows the classification portfolio for Swiss Electronic Government incentives with the highest realized state combination [6]. At the IT-view the highest reached state lies at media break; the tendency from the user's point of view can be stated between 'information' and 'general service'. The highest reached state at the administrational dimension lies between 'null-efficiency and 'effective efficiency' [6].

Comparative Classification Portfolio

Figure 6 shows a comparative classification portfolio with comparison of average state values. The larger the triangle between the

Figure 5: Highest state combination of Swiss approaches

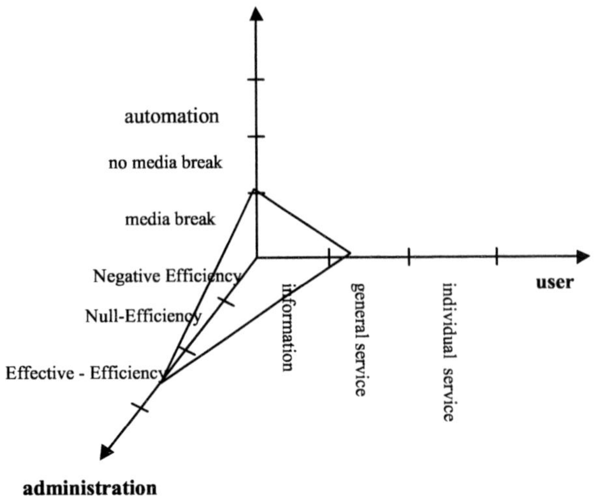

states of the three dimensions the higher the reached states (higher efficiency, higher user-utility and technological progress) and the higher the development which can be expected [6].

CONCLUSION

Within this work were analyzed the weaknesses and progress-levels of some international E-Government approaches with different methods, like critical conditions (demand orientation, organizational, legal and technological conditions) and classification portfolios. For further analysis it will be necessary to consider additional critical circumstances, for example ergonomic factors or information content, and to analyze Electronic government approaches according to these conditions.

REFERENCES

[1] Aichholzer G.; Schmutzer R.; E-Government - Elektronische Informationsdienste auf Bundesebene in Österreich,; Institut für Technikfolgen-Abschätzung der österreichischen Akademie der Wissenschaften; Wien 1999.

[2] Arbeitsgruppe e-government der Koordinationsgruppe Informationsgesellschaft; Guichet virtuel - Der elektronische Weg zu Verwaltung, Parlament und Gericht; Bern 1997

[3] Europäische Kommission; eine Informationsgesellschaft für alle, Brüssel 2000

[4] Gesellschaft für Informatik (GI); Informationstechnische Gesellschaft (ITG); Memorandum Electronic Government, Bonn/Frankfurt 2000

[5] Kommission der Europäischen Gemeinschaften; eEurope 2002; Tagung des Europäischen Rates 19./20.06.2000 Feira.

[6] Oberer; classification portfolio for Electronic Government approaches, Klagenfurt 2001, unpublished

[7] Weber Beat; Die öffentliche Verwaltung in der digitalen Gesellschaft, in Proceedings 1. Swiss eGovernment Symposium, 22.08.2000, Zurich, Switzerland

[8] Weiss Juri; Die Idee des Guichet virtuel, in Proceedings 1. Swiss eGovernment Symposium, 22.08.2000, Zurich, Switzerland

[9] Wraight Chatrie; Wraight Paul; Public Strategies for the Information Society in the Member States of the European Union; Information Society Activity Centre; 2000

Measuring the Potential for IT Convergence at Macro Level: A Definition Based on Platform Penetration and CRM Potential

Margherita Pagani
I-LAB Research Centre on Digital Economy, Bocconi University, Italy
Tel: +39 (025) 836-6920, Fax: +39 (025) 836-3714, margherita.pagani@uni-bocconi.it

ABSTRACT

This paper sets out to define what convergence is and to mesure it in Europe. It begins by proposing that the concept of digital convergence – as it is commonly expressed – is taken to refer to three possible axes of alignment: convergence of devices, convergence of networks and convergence of content. Although there is evidence in digital environments of limited alignment in some of these areas, there are considerable physical, technical, and consumer barriers in each case. In fact, rather than convergence, the transition from analogue to digital is often being accompanied by a process of fragmentation.

A better way of looking at convergence may lie in the degree to which two way digital networks facilitate cross platform management of customer relationships – regardless of the type of networks those customers inhabit or the kind of their consume.

The paper argues for a definition of convergence based on penetration of digital platforms and the potential for cross platform Customer Relationship Management (CRM) strategies, before going on to develop a convergence index according to which different European territories can be compared.

INTRODUCTION

As digital Tv, Internet and mobile telephony begin to converge, companies occupying any or all these platforms need to understand what the processes are, which are at work, and the pace at which these will develop. Without a clear grasp of what is happening in a confused and complicated area, they will be unable to implement coherent business plan, or minimise risk.

Some of the questions that arise for companies with respect to convergence include:

- whether they should cross from one platform to another, and if so, when;
- if it is possible to leverage assets in one sector into another;
- how to maintain or create customer relationships as they migrate to other platforms;
- what the size of these "converged" markets are going to be in different territories.

The problem is that the notion of "convergence" itself is generally taken to be a characteristic of digital media, suggesting a possible future in which there might just be one type of content distributed across one kind of network to one type of device. Convergence remains ill defined particularly in terms of what it might mean for businesses wishing to develop a new media strategy. This study argues for a definition of convergence based on penetration of digital platforms and the potential for cross platform Customer Relationship Management (CRM) strategies, before going on to develop a convergence index according to which different European territories can be compared.

CONVERGENCE DISCUSSED

In general the concept of digital convergence is used to refer to three possible axes of alignment: convergence of devices, convergence of networks, and convergence of content. Although there is evidence in digital environments of limited alignment in some of these areas, there are considerable physical, technical, and consumer barriers in each case.

Rather than convergence, the transition from analogue to digital is often being accompanied by a process of fragmentation.

This paragraph describes, what the limits are to convergence understood as a phenomenon that involves the bringing together, merging or hybridisation of different types of digital device, network or content.

In the *physical domain* the barriers to PC/TV convergence lie principally with respect to the size of the input device and its portability. Those to PC/mobile phone convergence are rather more acute and there is a divergence along every physical measure.

Table 1: Physical characteristics of consumer devices

Characteristic	TV	PC	Mobile phone
Size of display device	Large	Large	Small
Size of input device	Small	Large (keyboard)	Small (keypad)
Portability	Low	Medium	High

A comparison of the relevant *technical characteristics* of the three different types of consumer device (Table 2) shows that there is little evidence of TV/mobile phone convergence as yet, and in any case the technical constraints with respect to this particular combination are implicit in the consideration of the other instances.

Table 2: Technical characteristics of consumer devices

Characteristic	TV	PC	Mobile phone
Display type	Cathode ray tube	Cathode ray tube	Liquid crystal display
Display resolution	Medium	High	Low
Display scanning mode	Interlaced	Progressive	Progressive
Display refresh rate	Medium	High	High
Processing power	Low	High	Low
Storage	Low	High	Low
Power requirement	High	High	Low

Consumer attitudes to devices that inhabit the Tv environment as opposed to the PC and mobile telephony ones are also widely different. The diagram serves to differentiate some relevant characteristics.

The types of content that are carried over PC/Internet, broadcast and telephony networks, show some sharply differentiated characteristics and consumer usage and distribution differs across platforms (Tab. 4).

Table 3: Differing consumer expectations for different platforms

Consumer expectations in Tv space	Consumer expectations in PC space	Consumer expectations in the mobile phone space
Medium, stable pricing of goods	High, unstable pricing of goods	Low unstable pricing of goods
Infrequent purchase (once every 7-11 years)	Frequent purchase (every 18 months to 3 years)	Frequent purchase (every 18 months to 3 years)
Little requirement for software and peripheral upgrades	High requirement for software and peripheral upgrades	Medium requirement for software and peripheral upgrades
Works perfectly first time	Probably will not work perfectly first time	Probably will work first time
No boot-up time	Long boot-up time	No boot-up time
Low maintenance	High maintenance	Low maintenance
Low user intervention	High user intervention	High user intervention
Little or no technical support required	Substantial technical support required	Little technical support required

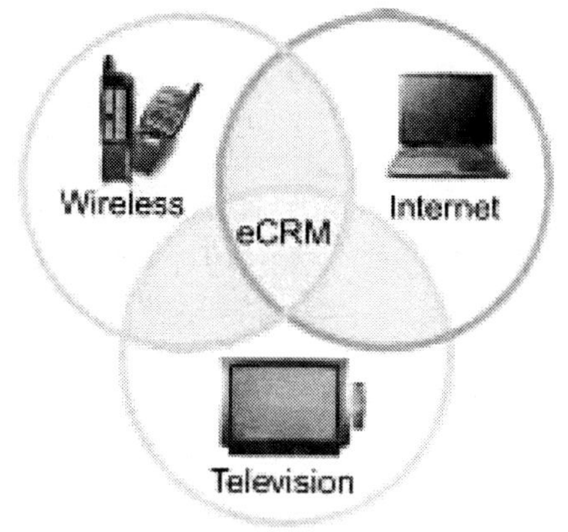

Table 4: Different content characteristics of the three major digital platforms

Tv/broadcast content attributes	PC/Internet content attributes	Mobile telephony content attributes
Video heavy (moving pictures lie at its core, rather than text)	Video light (text and graphics lie at its core, rather than video)	Voice based (audio lies at its core, rather than text, graphics or video)
Information medium (the factual information transmitted is not vey dens e)	Information heavy (the factual information transmitted is dense)	Where non voice based material is transmitted, it is information light (any textual information transmitted in an SMS message or on a WAP phone is sparse)
Entertainment based (to provide a leisure activity rather than learning environment)	Work based (to provide work related or educational information or to enhance productivity rather than to be entertained)	Both work based and socially based (to provide work related information or to enhance productivity rather than to be entertained).
Designed for social o family access	Designed to be accessed by solitary individuals	Designed to be accessed by two individuals
Centrally generated (by the service provider)	Both centrally generated (content on a CD-Rom or website) and user generated (email, chat, personalisation, etc)	Predominantly user generated
User unable to influence content flow which is passively received rather than interacted with and linear in form	User tipically interacts with the content producing a non linear experience	Where centrally generated content is provided, user tipically interacts with the content, producing a non linear experience
Long form (the typical programme unit is 25 minutes long)	Short form (video information tends to be in the form of clips or excerpts).	Short form (text and websites highly abbreviated, audio in form of clips or excerpts).

There are many network differences (up/down stream capacity and interactivity) and authoring differences (development platforms, security and standards) but consumer use multi-platform content/commerce.

The true economic advantage to be derived from the analogue to digital transition lies in the potential to facilitate cross-platform management of customer relationships – regardless of the type of networks those customers inhabit or the kind of content they consume.

The ability to merge data about consumer preferences and transactional profiles across platforms (eCRM) is critical for any interactive media business and this can be achieved through a process of cross platform tracking.

New killer applications are found by understanding the consumer and leveraging current consumer relationships.

The business potential in x-media commerce is in attracting, retaining and capitalising on customer relationships through interactive media channels.

This suggests a definition of convergence based not on the merging of digital devices, networks or content, but on the extent to which the transition to two way digital networks facilitates "consumer convergence" or cross platform customer relationship management (CRM).

A DEFINITION BASED ON PLATFORM PENETRATION AND CRM POTENTIAL

Customer relationship management (CRM) can be described as the process of attracting, retaining and capitalising on customers.

CRM defines the space where the company interacts with the customer. At the heart of CRM lies the objective to deliver a consistently differentiated and personalised customer experience, regardless of the interaction channel.

For companies looking at their digital investment strategy in Europe and seeking to maximise the benefit to them from this type of convergence, it is key to know which territories exhibit the best potential for its development so that those companies can decide where initially to trial or introduce interactive applications or how to assess the likely success of existing European projects in an eCRM context.

Purpose of this study is to propose a model that adresses the issue of how to measure convergence.

Three indicators in the measurement of convergence potential are considered:

- critical digital mass index
- convergence factor
- interactivity factor

The Concept of "Critical Digital Mass Index"

One cornerstone in the measurement of convergence potential is going to lie in the extent to which digital platforms (such as digital Tv, PC/Internet access and mobile telephony) are present in a given territory. This will obviously make it easier to reap the efficiencies and economies of scale that eCRM offers.

However, since eCRM strategies derive their greatest benefits across multiple channels, one needs to measure the penetration of such platforms in combination. This combined measure (penetration of platform A plus penetration of platform B plus penetration of platform C) indicates the "critical digital mass" of consumers in any given territory.

The *critical digital mass* index for a territory is created by adding together the digital TV penetration, mobile telephony penetration and PC Internet penetration in each territory from data at the end of 2001.

The Convergence Factor

The potential for eCRM is greatest where the same consumers are present across all three digital platforms: this would be the optimal

Figure 1: Critical digital mass in Europe 2001

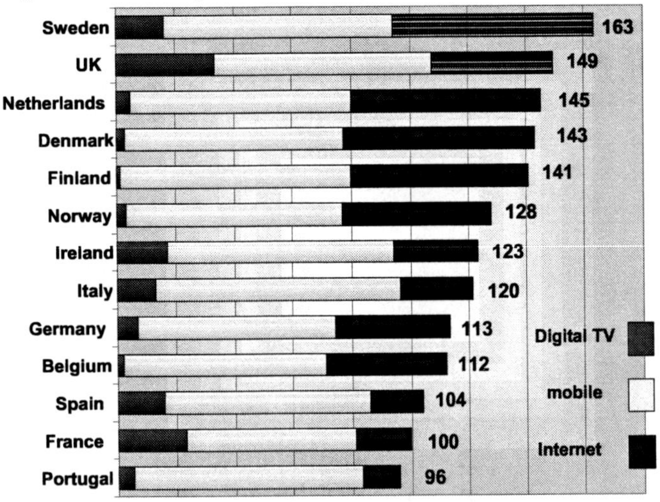

situation for an integrated multi-channel eCRM strategy. The degree of overlap tends to be much higher when overall digital penetration is higher (this is not a linear relationship). If penetration of digital TV, PC/Internet access and mobile telephony are all above 50 per cent, the number of consumers present across all three is likely to be much more than five times greater than is the case if penetration is at only around 10 per cent in each case. Fig. 2 illustrates this effect at work (the area within each triangle represents the boundaries of the total consumer universe).

Figure 2: Platform overlap increases faster than platform increases

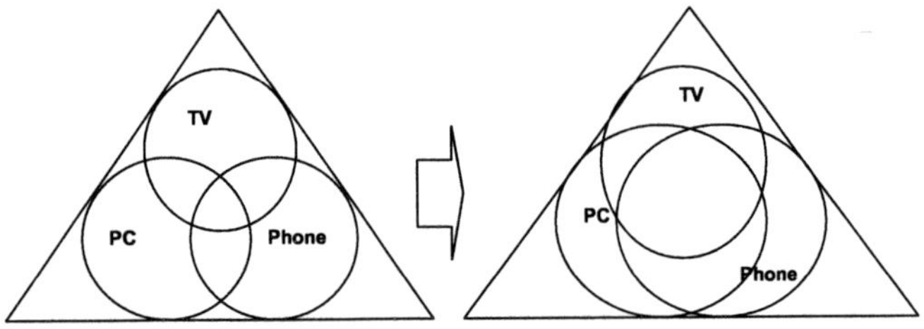

This means that the critical digital mass indicator needs to be adjusted upwards for higher overall penetration levels.

The study uses simple probably theory to give a way of measuring the rate at which cross-platform populations increase as penetration of those platforms increases.

The "convergence factor" is derived from the penetrations of the three platforms multiplied by each other.

The convergence factor for a territory is calculated according to the following formula:

D x M x I

Where D=digital TV penetration, M=mobile telephony penetration and I=PC Internet penetration

The Relevance of Interactivity

Another important element in assessing eCRM potential is the extent to which the digital networks facilitate customer tracking.

Four level of interactivity are considered:

- local,
- one-way,
- two-way (low)
- two-way (high).

Figure 3: Convergence factor in Europe 2001

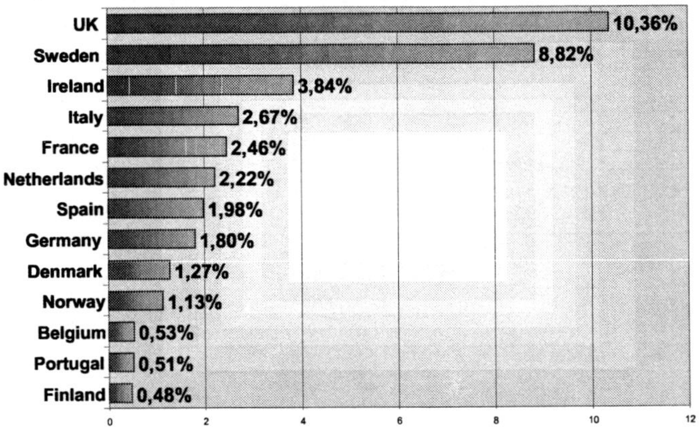

Networks exhibiting a high level of two way interactivity are obviously those where eCRM potential is greatest. In general digital TV networks offer a lower level of interactivity than mobile and PC/ Internet ones.

The interactivity factor for a territory is calculated according to the following formula:

D+(M*2)+(I*2)/5

Where D= digital TV penetration, M= mobile telephony penetration and I= PC Internet penetration

Figure 4: Interactivity factor in Europe 2001

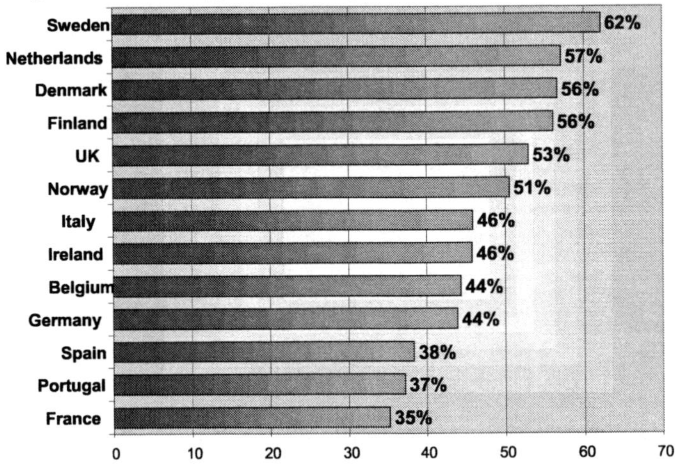

The Convergence Index

The convergence index is generated as follows:

[critical digital mass index * (1+ convergence factor) * (1+ interactivity factor)]

[(D+M+I)*(1+D*M*I)*(D+2M+2I)/5)]

Where D= digital TV penetration, M= mobile telephony penetration and I= PC Internet penetration

This index represents the "critical digital mass of consumers", it is possible to derive estimates of the number of consumers likely to be present across all three platforms by the simple expedient of taking the population of each territory and multiplying it by the triple platform penetration factor. It is also possible to give an indication of the number of consumers likely to be present across two platforms by doing a double-platform penetration calculation.

Sweden and UK emerge as the territories with the highest eCRM potential, Portugal and France the territories with the lowest.

Figure 5: Convergence index in Europe 2001

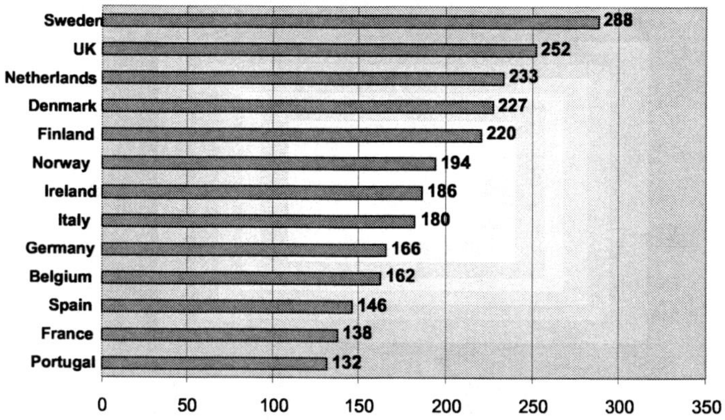

The countries at the top of the table owe their position largely to high penetrations of mobile telephony and Internet, rather than to digital TV. The UK is a notable exception.

CONCLUSION AND RESEARCH OUTLOOK

The conclusions that the model generates are designed to give companies guidance as to how the broad convergence picture will evolve over time in each of the European countries studied, so that they might fine-tune their investment strategies. The goal of the model is not to obtain the precise size of these cross platform populations. The model is also a good starting point to address other related questions and it allows further researches going on to profile some of the key players in each territory and channel, in order to assess which types of company are best placed to exploit this newly defined type of convergence.

For companies looking at their digital investment strategy in Europe and seeking to maximise the benefit to them from consumer convergence it is key to know which territories exhibit the best potential for its development.

Companies knowing this can decide where initially to trial or introduce eCRM systems, or how to assess the likely success of existing European projects in an eCRM context.

REFERENCES

Abell D. [1994], *Managing Dual Strategy*, New york Free Press

e-Economics [2000], *European Communication Council Report*, Springer

Flynn Barry [2001], *Digital Tv, Internet & Mobile Convergence*, Report Digiscope

Gilder G,. [2000], *Telecoms*, New York, Free Press

Moore J.F., [1996], *The Death of Competition*, John Wiley

Owen B.M., [1999], *The International Challenge to Television*, Boston, Harvard University Press.

Pine B.J., Gilmore J.M. [1999], *The experience Economy*, Boston, Harvard Business School Press

Yoffie D.B., [1997], *Competing in the Age of Digital Convergence*, Boston, Harvard Business School Press.

Valdani E., Busacca B., [1999], *Customer based view*, Finanza Marketing e Produzione, 3, 95-131

Making Sense of E-Supply Chain Landscape: An Implementation Framework

Somendra Pant* and Rajesh Sethi
Clarkson University School of Business Tel: (315) 268-7728, pants@clarkson.edu

EXECUTIVE ABSTRACT

Business firms are increasingly embracing integrated supply chains because they promise cost reduction, efficiency, and effective fulfillment of market demand (Fisher, 1997, Hutt and Speh, 2001, Margretta, J. Fast. (1998), Kalakota and Robinson, 1999). As business-to-business transactions are increasing on the Internet, it is becoming critical for firms to rely on Web-based supply chains (or e-supply chains) in order to provide almost real-time response to market conditions that e-commerce has come to signify.- However, not much is known about the issues and the challenges involved in creating and implementing integrated e-supply chain systems.

In recent times, the e-supply chain movement has received a boost from a variety of supply chain software packages that are now available in the market (for example, software from i2 Technologies and Manugistics and integrated suites like mySAP.com and Oraclelli). Suppliers of these packages make many claims about the effectiveness of their products in creating integrated supply chains and thus improving both efficiency and responsiveness to market needs. There is also a great deal of hype in the market about how these packages can fully integrate the supply chain of a company and bring manifold improvements in its competitiveness.

While software indeed has a role in improving integration and in enhancing the efficiency and effectiveness of a supply chain, it will be erroneous to assume that creating integrated e-supply chains is as simple as buying and installing a software package. Creation and implementation of highly integrated supply chains can require tremendous resources, a great deal of management time and energy, large organization-wide changes, huge commitment from suppliers/partners, and sophisticated technical infrastructure. In other words, while there are benefits of creating integrated supply chains with these software packages, there are numerous challenges and costs of undertaking such an endeavor. However, the enthusiasm in the marketplace about supply chain software packages seems to be ignoring the challenges involved in the implementation of e-supply chains.

The other impression in the marketplace that is being created about supply chain software is that e-supply chains basically refer to highly integrated supply chains implemented through the use of standard, off-the-shelf software packages. This impression has major problems as different firms have different supply chain requirements, i.e., not all supply chains are created equal. Thus, a standard solution cannot fit them all. Yet, very little effort has gone into understanding different approaches to creating supply chains that are suitable for different types of supply chain requirements. Therefore, the objective of this study is to develop a framework that captures different approaches to e-supply chain implementation.

Our work draws upon studies in areas such as supply chain, Web-based information systems and inter-organizational information systems. In addition, we conducted many discussions with professionals and consultants who are involved in planning, creating, and implementing e-supply chain systems in a variety of companies. In terms of actual implementation, we have completed a detailed study of a large US computer manufacturer that recently installed an integrated e-supply chain system.

INTEGRATED SUPPLY CHAIN SYSTEM OF A COMPUTER MANUFACTURER

The computer manufacturer has fairly complex internal manufacturing operations. They also have a fairly complex supply chain because of very high reliance on external partners who supply major components to them. The supply chain system implemented by the company is quite sophisticated and offers functionalities like: collaborative demand and fulfillment planning between the company and external partners like suppliers, distributors, and transporters, automated competitive bidding by suppliers, and automated and integrated response to customer query.

However, despite the good IT infrastructure, during the implementation of such an integrated supply chain, the computer manufacturer experienced numerous challenges concerning IT resources, systems integration, change management, process redesign, and in getting external partners integrated in to the supply chain. While studying such implementation challenges, we felt that not all organizations have the resources, technical infrastructure, management skills, and readiness of business partners required to implement an integrated e-supply chain system.

Yet, this does not imply that organizations that are not very resourceful will be deprived of all the benefits of e-supply chain systems. Not every organization has to aim for a fully integrated e-supply chain. However, there is very little literature that can help managers arrive at an approach for creating e-supply chain that is suitable for their context. In this study, we have developed a framework that goes beyond the simplistic *fully integrated* or *very low integration* scenario and shows how managers have multiple alternatives for creating and implementing e-supply chain systems.

E-SUPPLY CHAIN IMPLEMENTATION FRAMEWORK

During our study of various supply chains, we found that the issue of e-supply chain implementation can be studied along two important dimensions: complexity and criticality of a firm's operations, and the firm's ability to integrate their external business partners into their e-supply chain. By complexity and criticality of a firm's operations we mean that the operations are complex in nature (i.e., they involve numerous activities and transactions) and at the same time have a critical role in enhancing the firm's competitive position in the market. Such complexity and criticality can be a characteristic of a firm's internal operations, operations with its external partners, or both — its internal and external operations. If operations are not complex and critical, the need to integrate them through a sophisticated supply chain system is reduced. Such a determination of the suitable level of system integration has been considered a critical issue in the IS literature as well (Allen and Boyton, 1991; Yakhou and Rahali, 1992, King, 1984, Mukhopadhyay 1993; Premkumar, et al, 1995, Premkumar, et al, 1994).

A firm's ability to integrate its external partners into the supply chain refers to its ability to persuade the partners to agree to participate in the chain and create necessary infrastructure and redesign business processes to match the supply chain system being implemented by the firm. Two factors that will facilitate the integration of external partners in a firm's supply chain are: trust between the parties

* corresponding author

and the power the firm has over the partners. Obviously, some firms will be more successful than others in integrating external partners into their systems that will have an impact on the type of supply chain systems that firm will install with these partners. This ability to persuade business partners to integrate their information systems with those of a firm has been considered an important dimension in IS literature (Premkumar et al 1995, 1994).

Thus, we develop the supply chain implementation framework by taking into account the above dimensions. As discussed above, the first dimension, *the complexity and criticality of a firm's operations* can apply to the firm's internal operations, external operations, or both (i.e., it has three levels). Similarly, the second dimension, *the firm's ability to integrate partners into the supply chain* can either be high or low (i.e., it exist at two levels). Thus, we have a 3X2 scheme for classifying approaches to e-supply chain implementation. It is pertinent to note that in the situation where a firm's operations are complex and critical only internally, it is not important for the firm to integrate external partners into the supply chain. We, therefore, fold the two cells of our classification corresponding to the complexity and criticality of internal operations into one. This reduces the number of distinct e-supply chain implementation strategies to five, as shown in figure 1. We now discuss supply chain strategies that are suitable for various cells in the framework.

Figure 1: A framework for supply chain management

Ability to Integrate Partners	Internal	External	Internal and External
High	I Strategic Enterprise Systems	III Strategic External Systems	V Strategic Extended Enterprise Systems
Low		II Operational External Systems	IV Strategic Enterprise and Operational External Systems

IMPLEMENTATION FRAMEWORK

Suitable strategy for firms in Cell I (i.e., with complex and critical internal operations) will be to install strategic enterprise systems such as ERP systems. Since in this situation, external linkages are of minimal importance, an appropriate e-supply chain strategy for firms would be to share the output of the ERP system with external partners over a Web-based EDI linkage. Sophisticated off-the-shelf packages for supply chain planning, execution, and logistics packages for integration with external partners will not be cost effective for such firms. Firms in Cell II (i.e., with complex and critical external operations, but low ability to integrate external partners into the supply chain) need to use operational external systems (e.g., systems like Commerce One and Ariba for procurement and McHugh Software and EXE technologies for logistics management). Since the firm cannot effectively integrate external partners into a sophisticated supply chain arrangement, a limited arrangement in which they seek integration with partners in operational areas like procurement and logistics is more appropriate. On the other hand, firms in Cell III (i.e., with complex and critical external operations and with high ability to integrate external partners into supply chain) need to focus on strategic external systems like the ones available from suppliers like i2, Manugistic, etc. In other words, such firms should seek supply chain integration with external partners in strategic areas like collaborative planning, forecasting and replenishment, collaborative product design, and integrated customer relationship management (CRM). For firms falling in Cell IV (i.e., with complex and critical internal and external operations, but low ability to integrate external partners into the supply chain) an appropriate strategy will be to rely on operational external systems that are well integrated with strategic enterprise systems. Finally, companies that fall in Cell V (i.e., with complex and critical internal and external operations and high ability to integrate external partners into the supply chain) will benefit mostly from strategic extended enterprise systems. These systems include enterprise resource systems integrated with strategic external systems A strategic extended enterprise system will be the most challenging system to install, but it is most likely to be beneficial in terms of gaining competitive advantage.

CONCLUSION

In this study we have evolved a framework for different approaches to e-supply chain creation and implementation. This framework advises managers to assess their supply chain requirements and environment before jumping on the e-supply chain bandwagon. In particular, managers need to carefully evaluate their integration needs, resources at their disposal, and their ability to persuade business partners to be a part of their e-supply chain system and then select the systems strategy from our framework that is appropriate for their needs.

REFERENCES

Allen, B. R. and Boynton, A. C. , "Information Architecture: In Search of Efficient Flexibility," MIS Quarterly, Vol. 15, no. 4., 1991.

Arthur, L. J. , "Quick and Dirty," *Computerworld*, December 14, 1992.

Fisher, M. L., "What is the Right Supply Chain for Your Product?" *Harvard Business Review*, March-April, pp.105-16, 1997.

Hutt, M. D. and Speh, T.W., *Business Marketing Management*, New York: Dryden Press, 2001.

Kalakota, R. and Robinson. M. E., *Business: Roadmap for Success*, Addison-Wesley Information Technology Series, 1999.

Margretta, J. F., "Global, and Entrepreneurial: Supply Chain Management, Hong Kong Style," *Harvard Business Review*, September-October, pp. 103-14, 1998.

Mukhopadhyay, T. Assessing the economic impacts of data interchange technology. In: *Strategic Information Technology Management: Perspectives on Organizational growth and Competitive Advantage*, Banker, R.D., Kaufman, R.J. and Mahmood, M.A. (eds.), Harrisburg, PA: Idea group Publishing, 1993; 241-264.

Premkumar, G. and Ramamurthy, K. "The role of interorganizational and organizational factors on the decision mode for adoption of interorganizational systems," *Decision Sciences* 1995; 26 (3): 303-335.

Premkumar, G., Ramamurthy, K., and Nilakanta, S. (1994). "Implementation of Electronic Data Interchange: An Innovation Diffusion Perspective," Journal of Management Information Systems, Vol. 11, No. 2, pp. 157-176.

Yakhou, M. and Rahali, B. (1992). "Integration of Business Functions: Roles of Cross-Functional Information Systems," *APICS*, December.

A UML-Based Framework for Designing On-Line Business Model

*Yongtae Park, Yeongho Kim, Yongho Lee, and Seonwoo Kim
Department of Industrial Engineering, Seoul National University, Korea
Tel: (822) 880-8358, parkyt@cybernet.snu.ac.kr

INTRODUCTION

It is yet an unexplored attempt to design business model using UML. A notable exception is due to the seminal work by Eriksson[3]. He suggested a comprehensive guideline for UML-based business modeling. Although his work widened the applicability of UML to business modeling, its utility is still limited in that the framework is mainly for intra-firm business, not for inter-firm business. Furthermore, the possibility of expansion is open to on-line business model that has attracted increasing attention recently. In this research, we suggest a framework to design an intra-firm, on-line business model using UML. The framework includes such elements as business players and values and relationship among players. Specifically, business model is visualized by two forms of diagrams, value diagram and structure diagram. Finally, we adopt a real case to illustrate how the proposed framework is applied.

CONCEPTUAL ARCHITECTURE OF FRAMEWORK

The conceptual architecture of the framework is divided into two stages, as definition stage and design stage. In the definition stage, values and players are defined and the relationship between values and players are identified. In the design stage, value diagram and structure diagram are drawn to describe the overall nature of business model (see Figure 1).

Figure 1: Conceptual Architecture of Framework

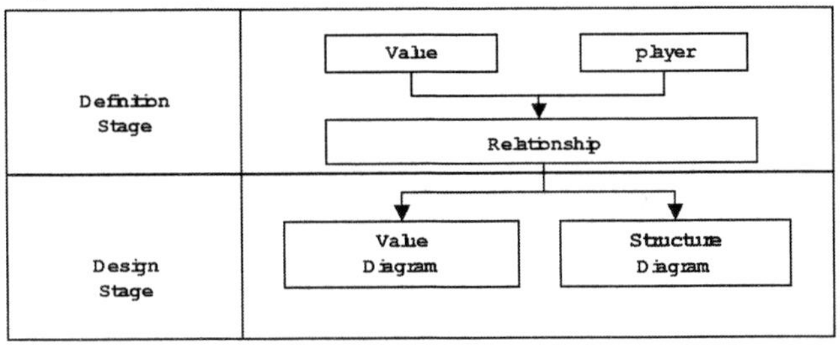

DESIGN OF BUSINESS MODEL

Definition of Elements

The major elements of business model are presented in Table 1.

(1) Value

The value of business is defined as either a service or a product. A service is materialized as value as it is used through real-time interaction between players. A product is changed to value as it is transferred to customers in packaged form. In case of on-line business, it is also critical whether a value is of physical form or of digital form because it determines the way of transaction, transfer, use, and etc. Value can be considered as an object that has its name, attributes, and functions. Hence, as shown in Table 2, we employ the same notation of object as used in UML [2], [3], [11].

Table 1: Elements of a business model

Elements	Description
Value	A product or service produced, transferred and used to achieve a specific goal
Player	A person or a group who participate in the business process
Relationship	Relationship between players

Table 2: Classification and notation of values

Value	Form of value	Notation	Examples
Service	Physical	PS	fedex.com (on-line order based delivery)
	Digital	DS	etrade.com (on-line financial service provider)
Product	Physical	PP	amazon.com (on-line book seller)
	Digital	DP	MP3.com (on-line contents provider)

(2) Player

In general, players in business model can be described by their names, roles, and numbers of players. The roles of players are classified into seven typical ones: supplier, main player, distributor, logistics, customer, indirect revenue source, agent (see Table 3). Obviously, it is not uncommon that only part of roles is required to form a business model.

Table 3: Typical roles of players

Roles	Description
Main player	A player who designs and constructs business model
Customer	A player who uses or buys the values provided by main player
Supplier	A player who provides (part of) values to main player
Distributor	A player who buys and resells values provided by main player
Logistics	A player who delivers values from one player to another
Agent	A player who facilitates the flow of values between players
Indirect Revenue Source	A player who utilizes additional values produced in interaction between other players and provides some revenue to main player

The number of players to undertake a specific role is important in business model. The number of players can be specified as single, multiple, and unspecific.

(3) Relationship

The relationship between players can be defined by the way to transfer values. Broadly, there are two ways to transfer values. One is to transfer the ownership of value to buyer or user. The other is merely to grant a right to use without ownership. In on-line business, it is also important whether value is transferred physically or electronically (see Table 4).

Figure 2: Notation of player in a business

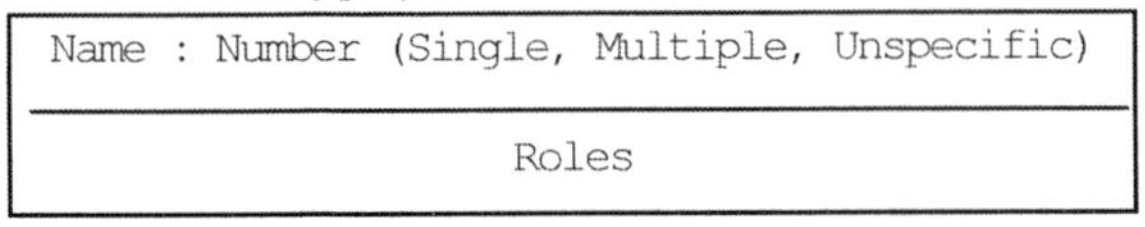

*corresponding author

Table 4: Relationship between players

Ownership	Transmission	Relationship	Notation
Ownership Transfer	Physically	Physical transfer of ownership	———▶
	Electronically	Electronic transfer of ownership	·········▶
Without Ownership transfer	Physically	Physical use	———●
	Electronically	Electronic use	·········●

Vaue Diagram

The value diagram encompasses values with their attributes and functions, players, benefits, and relationships between them. It shows how the value provides benefits to participating players and delineates the relationship between values and players. In this research, we adopt and revise to some extent the notation of use case diagram in UML to describe those [2] [3] [11]. Figure 3 portrays the typical form of value diagram.

Figure 3: Illustration of value diagram

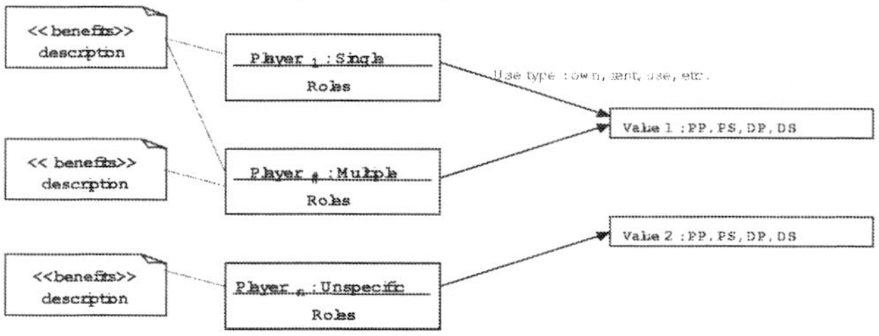

Structure Diagram

The structure diagram depicts the overall structure of business model. It comprises values, players, relationship, flow of revenue. In drawing structure diagram, the way of payment deserves attention. As summarized in Table 5, we propose four ways of payment. Note that double line is used to differentiate revenue-flow from value-flow. Figure 4 illustrates a typical form of structure diagram.

Table 5: Four typical ways of payment

Way of payment	Description	Notation
/product	Revenue is paid per product	⟹
/use number	Revenue is paid per number of use	⟹
/use time	Revenue is paid per use time	⟹
/license	Revenue is paid per license	⟹

Figure 4: Illustration of structure diagram

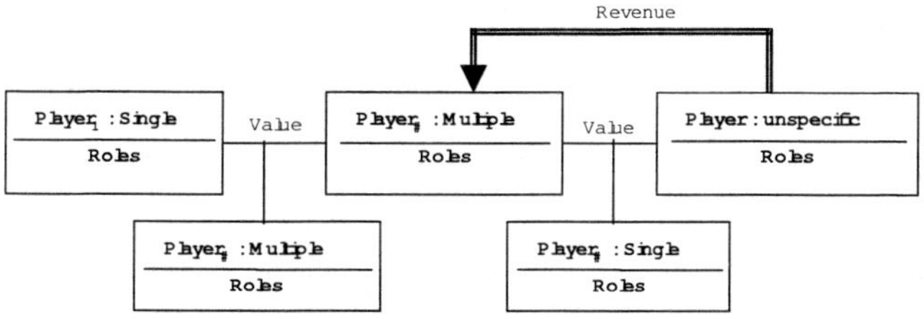

CASE STUDY

For the purpose of illustration, we adopt a real world example and explains how the proposed framework works. The on-line company buys physical comic books, digitalizes them, and sells to unspecific end-users through internet or several portal sites. It transfers ownership of its contents when it sells to portal sites. In case to unspecific end-users, however, it just grants a right to view their contents without downloading.

(1) Step 1: To Define Value

Value	Form of values	Description
Comics contents	PP, DP	Froms of value change
Payment system	DS	Agent for transaction

(2) Step 2: To Define Players

Player	Number	Role of player
Main player	Single	Main player
Customer	Unspecific	Customer
Comics production	Multiple	Supplier
Portal site	Multiple	Distributor
Credit card co.	Multiple	Agent
Advertiser	Multiple	Indirect Revenue source

(3) Step 3: To Define Relationship

Producers transfer ownership of comics contents to main player physically. The main player then changes value form, and transfers contents with ownership to portal sites. It also provides advertisers with advertising pages. Advertisers only use electronically. Credit card company owns payment system and customers and main player use the payment system without transferring ownership.

(4) Step 4: Value Diagram

Figure 5: Example of value diagram

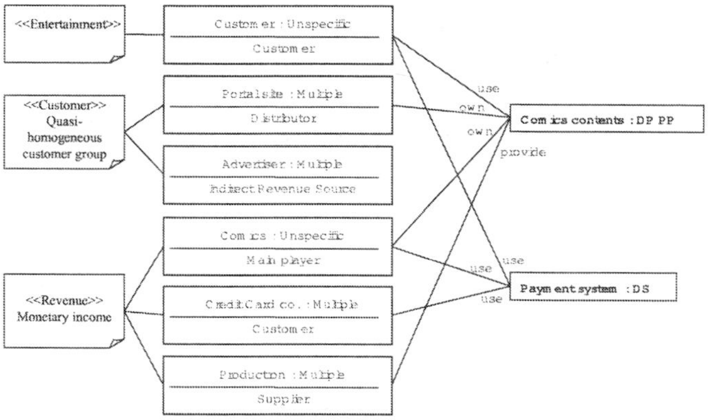

(5) Step 5: Structure Diagram

Figure 6: Example of structure diagram

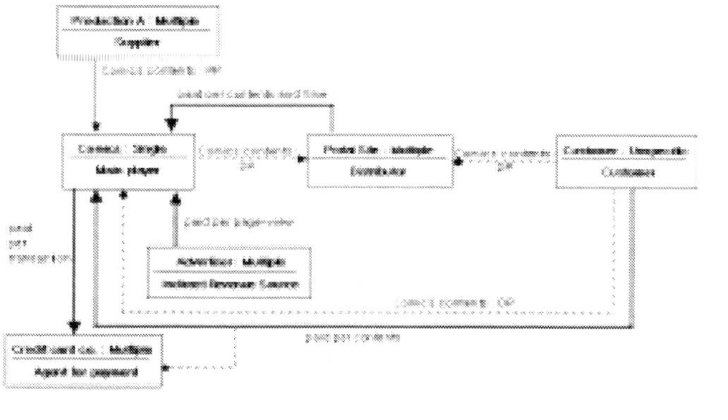

CONCLUSIONS

In this research, we searched for the possibility of applying UML to designing an inter-firm, on-line business model. It is expected that the proposed framework will be of help in designing complex on-line business and solving potential problems. In nature, the current research is exploratory and, for the purpose of illustration, it deals with a rather simple business form. In reality, there may exist more complexity and diversity in terms of roles of players and relationship between players. In that regard, extension and elaboration of the current research is required in the future.

REFERENCES

[1] Dawn Jutla, Peter Bodorik, Catherine Hajnal and Charles Davis, "Making Business Sense of Electronic Commerce", IEEE Computer, March 1999, Vol. 32, No. 3

[2] Desmond F. D'souza, "Objects, Components, and frameworks with UML", Addison Wesley, Massachusetts, 1999

[3] Hans-Erik Eriksson and Mangnus Penker, "Business Modeling with UML – Business Patterns at work", John Wiley & Sons, New York, 2000

[4] Mary Modahl, "Now or never : How companies must change today to win", Forrester Research Inc, New York, 2000

[5] Martin E. Modell, "A professional's Guide to Systems Ananlysis", McGraw-Hill, New York, 1988

[6] Michael Rappa, "Business Models on the Web", E-Commerce Learning Center @ NC State University [Online], Available : http://ecommerce.ncsu.edu/ business_models.html, 1999

[7] Paul Timmers, "Business Models for Electronic Markets", EM-Electronic Markets, Vol. 8, No. 2, 1998

[8] Paul Timmers, "Electronic Commerce – Strategies and models for Business-to-Business trading", John Wiley & Sons, New York, 2000

[9] Pete Martinez, "Models made "e ":What business are you in?", IBM [Online], Available : http://www.ibm.com, 2000

[10] Ravi Kalakota and Andrew B. Whinston, "Frontiers of Electronic Commerce", Addison-Wesley, Massachusetts, 1996

[11] Stefan Sigfried, "Understanding Object-oriented software engineering", IEEE press, New York, 1996

[12] Steven Kaplan and Mohanbir Sawhney, "B2B E-Commerce Hubs: Towards a Taxonomy of Business Models", E-Commerce Learning Center @ NC State University [Online], Available : http://ecommerce.ncsu.edu, 1999

On the Design of Workflow-based Knowledge Management System for R&D Organization

*Yeongho Kim, Yongtae Park, and Intae Kang
Department of Industrial Engineering, Seoul National University, Korea
Tel: (822) 880-8335, yeongho@snu.ac.kr

INTRODUCTION

R&D organization serves as primary actor of knowledge management (KM) since it is the major source of knowledge generation and dissemination. The main purpose of this research is to propose a framework for designing KM system (KMS) of R&D organization. Overall, the framework is composed of two major pillars, process management for R&D activity and contents management for R&D knowledge. Then, we propose two operational systems, workflow management system (WFMS) for R&D process and R&D knowledge management system (RKMS) for R&D contents. The overall architectures of WFMS and RKMS are briefly described and the procedure to integrate RKMS and WFMS is explained. The proposed system is web-based in that it is designed and developed on the web environment.

FRAMEWORK OF KMS FOR R&D ORGANIZATION

Matching WFMS and RKMS

KMS for R&D organization comprises two major components, R&D activities and knowledge contents. R&D activities are associated with processes to generate and utilize knowledge, and knowledge contents are related with input and output of knowledge activities. Therefore, the overall framework of KMS is constructed by matching *process management* to administer knowledge activities and *contents management* to deal with knowledge contents, as portrayed in Figure 1.

Figure 1: Overall framework of KM to integrate WFMS and RKMS

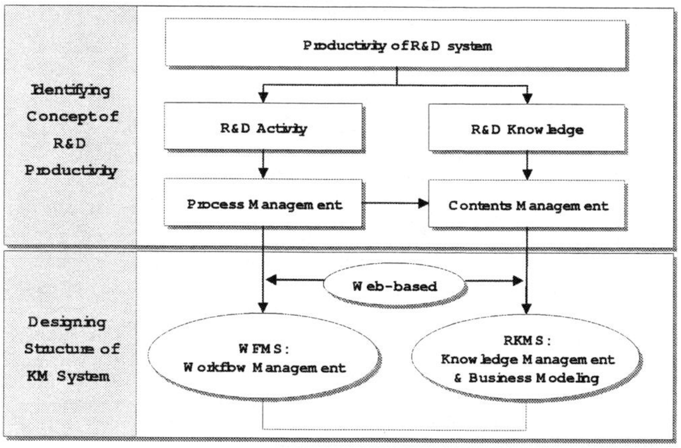

Matching R&D Organization Types and KMS Domains

KMS of R&D organization encompasses heterogeneous and multidisciplinary knowledge that is hard to formalize and R&D activities comprise complicated and unstable processes that are hard to standardize. Therefore, it is impossible to propose a general structure of KMS that is applicable to all the forms of R&D organizations. The design of KMS, thus, needs to be customized by matching characteristics of individual R&D units and characteristics of KMS domains. To this end, it is necessary to classify R&D units into several types and to identify the best-practice form of KMS for each type of R&D units. The conceptual scheme of customization is depicted in Figure 2.

Figure 2: Matching of R&D organization and KMS domain

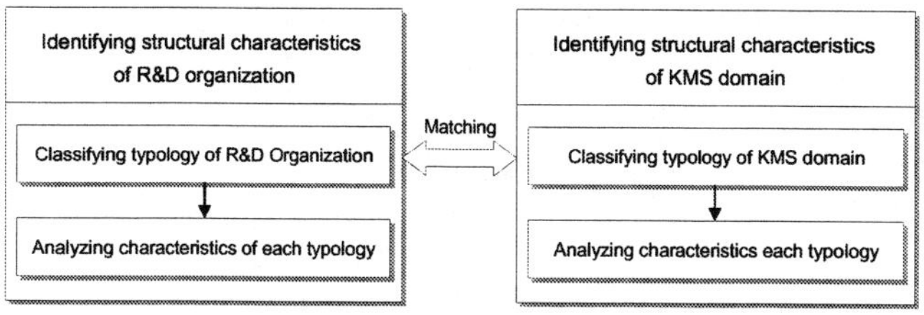

To illustrate, as presented in Table 1, it may be possible to classify R&D units into five types and develop customized KMS domains according to the characteristics of each type.

Table 1: Typology of R&D organization

Typology of R&D organizations	Description
Product-oriented Organization	R&D organization comprise separate units, each takes charge of development of individual product
Process-oriented Organization	R&D organization comprise separate units, each is related to different process of research and/or manufacturing
Technology-oriented Organization	R&D organization comprise separate units, each takes charge of development of component technology
Function-oriented Organization	R&D organization comprise separate units, each takes charge of management of different function
Matrix(hybrid) Organization	R&D organization comprise separate units, each is a combination of multiple features

DESIGN OF RKMS

RKMS is composed of main system and several supporting tools. The main system includes *management module* to create, store, secure, distribute and retrieve knowledge and *utilization module* to structure knowledge map, evaluate knowledge asset, and commercialize knowledge to business model. To support main system, several supportive tools such as classification, visualization, agent, navigation, and decision-making criteria are also included in the framework. Figure 3 describes the overall architecture of RKMS.

DESIGN OF WFMS

WFMS is composed of two main modules, *definition module* to identify and design R&D processes and *execution module* to monitor the progress of processes, control and carry out tasks, and manage application programs. These modules are basically developed and implemented on the workflow engine. The overall architecture of WFMS is exhibited in Figure 4.

*corresponding author

Figure 3: Overall architecture of RKMS

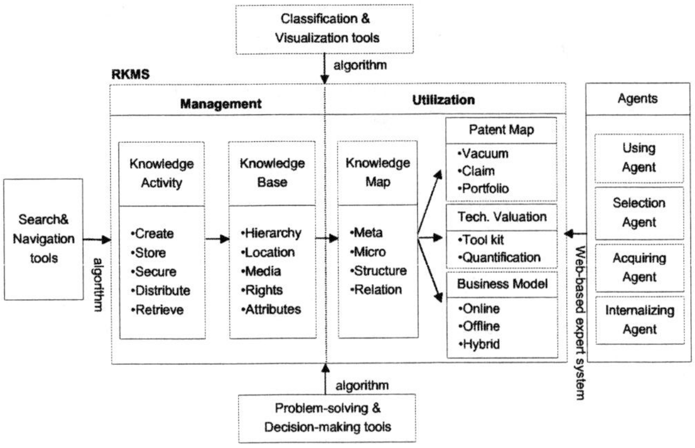

Figure 4: Overall architecture of WFMS

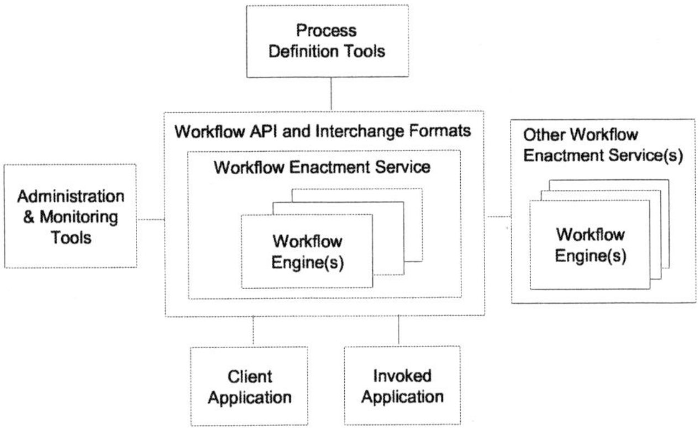

INTEGRATION OF WFMS AND RKMS

Finally, RKMS and WFMS need to be integrated. The integration of RKMS and WFMS is accomplished by developing workflow-based knowledge map. Basically, the construction of knowledge map of RKMS consists of two steps, *knowledge collection* and *knowledge structuring*. As depicted in Figure 5 and as explained below, these two steps of RKMS necessitate information from WFMS.

First, in the knowledge collection step, knowledge in the knowledge repository is filtered in accordance with knowledge users and related tasks. In building a knowledge map, it is critical to provide right knowledge to right user. For the relevancy in terms of knowledge contents and knowledge users, we need information on user and task attributes. This information is obtained from the process definition in WFMS. By doing so, the knowledge collection takes the relationship of user-task and task-knowledge into account.

In the second step, the filtered knowledge is structured and presented based on the *vertical relationship* and *horizontal relationship* of knowledge. The term vertical relationship means the hierarchical linkage of knowledge artifacts, whereas horizontal relationship indicates the input-output relationship of knowledge artifacts. The information on the vertical and horizontal relationship among knowledge artifacts is also obtained the workflow definition of WFMS.

The proposed system is web-based in that it is designed and developed on the web environment.

CONCLUSIONS

In this paper, we proposed a framework for designing workflow-based KMS of R&D organization. The framework consists of two major components, WFMS for process management and RKMS for contents management whereby RKMS derives necessary information from WFMS.

This research in nature is an exploratory proposal that suggests merely a conceptual scheme. Therefore, it is required to elaborate detailed procedure and materialize real system. We are now developing a full-scale KMS based on the framework proposed here. The research output will be presented later on.

Figure 5: Integration of WFMS and RKMS

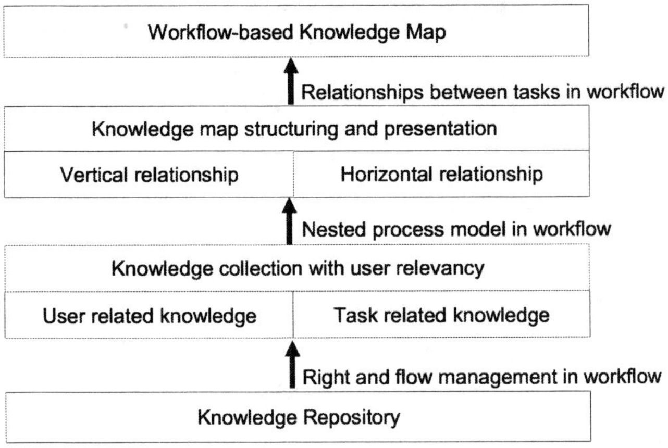

REFERENCES

Casati, F., Ceri, S., Pernici, B. and Pozzi, G. (1996) "Deriving Active Rules for Workflow Enactment", Proc. 7th Int'l Conf. Database and expert Systems Applications, Lecture Notes in Computer Science, Springer-Verlag, pp. 94-110.

Eppler, M. (2001) "Making Knowledge Visible through Intranet Knowledge Maps: Concepts, Elements, Cases", Proc. 34th Hawaii int'l Conf. System Sciences, IEEE, pp. 1530-1539.

Eriksson, H. and Penker, M. (2000) "Business Modeling with UML – Business Patterns at work", John Wiley & Sons, New York.

Gaines, B. and Shaw, M. (1995) "Collaboration through Concept Maps" Proc. CSCL95. Computer Supported Cooperative Learning, Mahwah, New Jersey: Lawrence Erlbaum, pp.135-138.

Gomez, A., Moreno, A., Pazos, J. and Sierra-Alonso, A. (2000) "Knowledge maps: An essential technique for conceptualization", Data and Knowledge Engineering, vol. 33, No 2, pp. 169-190.

Harvard Business School, (1998) "Harvard Business Review on Knowledge Management", Harvard Business School publishing, Boston.

Kakabadse, N., Kouzmin, A. and Kakabadse, A. (2001) "From Tacit Knowledge to Knowledge Management: Leveraging Invisible Assets", Knowledge and Process Management, vol. 8, No 3, pp137-154.

Kim, Y., Kang, S. and Kim, D. (2000) "WW-FLOW: Web-Based Workflow Management with Runtime Encapsulation", IEEE Internet Computing, vol.4, No 3, pp. 55-64.

Kumar, A. and Zhao, J. (1999) "Dynamic Routing and Operational Controls in Workflow Management Systems", Management Science, vol. 45, No 2, pp. 253-272.

Liebowitz, J. (1999) "Knowledge management Handbook", CRC press, New York.

Mineau, G., Missaoui, R. and Godinx, R. (2000) "Conceptual modeling for data and knowledge management", Data and Knowledge Engineering, vol. 33, No 2, pp. 137-168.

WFMC, (2001) "The workflow coalition specification – Interface 1: Process definition interchange process model", [Online], Available: http://www.wfms.org.

Setting up a Remote Access Unix Lab (RAUL)

Ludwig Slusky[1] and Parviz Partow-Navid[2]
Department of Information Systems, California State University, Los Angeles, USA,
[1]Tel: (323) 343-2922, [2]Tel: (323) 343-2927, {lslusky, ppartow} @calstatela.edu

INTRODUCTION

In January 2001, Department of Information Systems at California State University, Los Angeles received a $140,000 Workforce Enhancement grant from State of California for improving instructional facilities. This paper describes our experience in setting up a Unix Lab, and incorporating it in our curriculum.

BACKGROUND

A comprehensive university, California State University, Los Angeles (CSLA) offers a broad range of liberal arts and professional programs. The college of Business and Economics is nationally accredited, at both graduate and undergraduate levels, by AACSB . The College offers undergraduate programs leading to bachelor's degrees in Business Administration, Computer Information Systems (CIS), and Economics.

Traditionally, the information technology (IT) training and practices for students are based on the client technology of the client-server architecture [4]. As the Internet shifts the emphasis from clients to servers and as the clients are more frequently implemented as personal servers, it becomes apparent that there is a need to enlarge the scope of the CIS curriculum by providing more server-focused courses.

Technological support of such server-focused training is fairly complex as it goes to the core functions of the server operating system administration and to the core of the database server administration. Server-focused knowledge and skills are also at the center of e-business. This leads us to a new (and very much in demand) category of **server-focused courses** at CIS department.

MISSION

The Unix Lab, an innovative academic resource for CIS students and faculty, is designed to provide server-focused training for Unix/Linux Administrators and Oracle DBAs. It is committed to [3]:

- Supporting traditional and innovative curriculum content.
- Advancing the learning and teaching experience in Unix, Linux, and Oracle in a predictable atmosphere of competence, control, and satisfaction.
- Using information-based techniques with promising new capabilities for enhancing quality of IT education for CIS students, such as personal database servers, interactive learning, virtual classrooms, and distance learning.

To accomplish this, the CIS Department has established academic and business contact with similar labs at other universities and IT businesses from whom the experience, methodological materials and advisement have been secured. Certificate of knowledge is a current trend in corporate training. The CIS Department is seeking educational and IT resources for Unix Lab necessary to collaborate with recognized certificate programs such as Sun, Oracle, and Rational Software.

ARCHITECTURE

Unix Lab (UL) consists of two branches – the **main** walk-in UL branch – Direct Access Unix Lab (DAUL) facility and UL extension — **Remote Access Unix Lab (RAUL)** facility at Academic Technology Support (ATS) department. Both, DAUL and RAUL are built on Sun servers and Sun workstations (used as micro-servers) for server-centered and server-critical training as illustrated in Figure 1.

RAUL is a new solution to the need for the server-focused training such as Oracle DBAs or system administrators on individual basis: a dedicated micro-server is assigned to a student (or to a team of 2 students). Furthermore, these RAUL micro-servers are available to students remotely over the Internet. The department's ability to train students in performing server-critical Oracle DBA or system administrative functions on servers remotely over the Internet – is a very much in-demand resource for students and is also a very valuable asset for the Department and the College.

The main classroom facility UL includes:

- 1st server (Sun Enterprise 250 model) controls access to micro-servers, supports rebuilding software installation images on micro-servers, provides share ability for some optional software resources,

Figure 1: Unix Lab Architecture

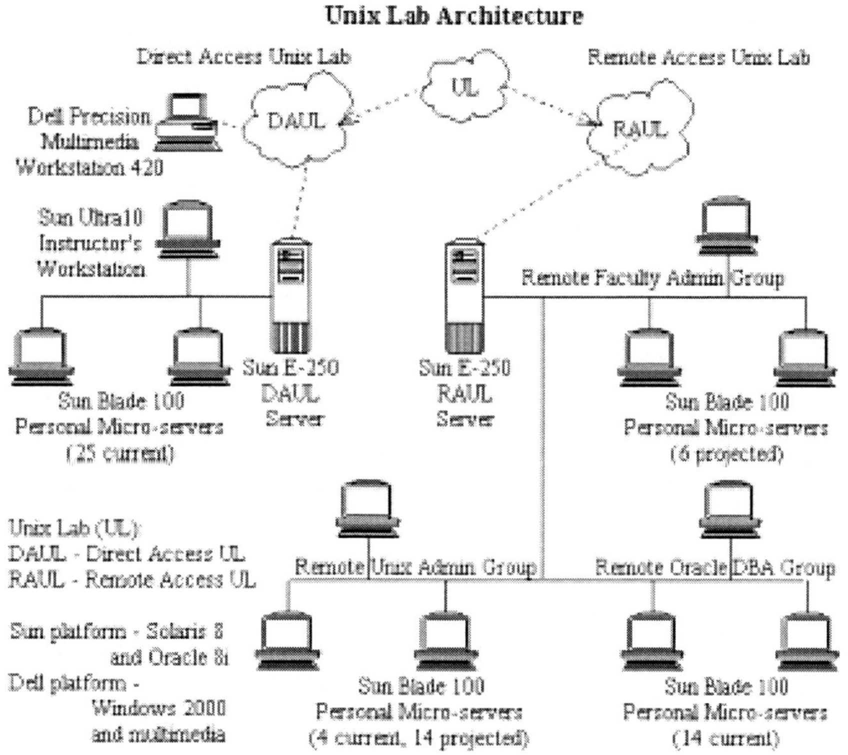

and to support regular UL operations

- 25 students' micro-servers are based on Sun Blade 100 workstations for Unix/Linux/Java and Oracle DBA training
- One instructor's micro-server is based on Sun Ultra 10 workstation
- One instructor's multimedia workstation (Dell Precision WorkStation 420) supports multimedia interactive and distance learning development and presentations

The Remote Access extension of the Unix Lab – RAUL – includes a server and three groups of micro-servers:

- 2nd server (Sun Enterprise 250 model) supports remote access to RAUL micro-servers for faculty experimental development, remote products evaluations and testing testing, students' server-based projects and exercises, etc.
- Student Oracle DBA group consists of 14 micro-servers (based on Sun Blade 100 workstations) for Oracle DBA training (located at ATS and accessed remotely)
- Student Unix Admin group consists of 4 micro-servers (based on one Sun Ultra5, one Sun Ultra10, and two Sun Blade 100); there is a plan to expand this group to 14 micro-servers.
- Faculty Admin group will be added over period of time to support faculty involved in Unix/Oracle distance learning curriculum development; here each participating faculty member will use an individual remotely accessed micro-server.

Distributed architecture of DAUL and RAUL with separate environments for Unix Admin and Oracle DBA supported by different groups and micro-servers is needed to de-couple Unix and Oracle administrative users who do development having full control of micro-servers.

Both servers store the default installation images for DAUL and RAUL micro-servers and use the Sun's JumpStart utility as a convenient way to rapidly rebuild these images on damaged machines.

CHALLENGES

Critical issues involved in server-focused courses are related to granting students powerful administrative privileges to work on Sun-based servers as Oracle DBAs or Solaris (Sun Unix-like operating system) Administrators.

- Oracle DBA (and Solaris Admin) privileges allow full administration of Oracle (and Solaris) installation, including operations on Oracle structures (databases, data dictionaries) and on files controlled by Solaris. Lack of this knowledge or improper use of it may result in **system (server) crashes, shutdowns, data destruction**, etc. Thus, mixing Oracle DBA training of one student with Unix Admin training of another student using the same micro-server must be avoided.
- RAUL is setup as a **training platform to provide technology necessary for building DBA and system administration skills**, and at the same time as a secure environment that limits the impact of personal errors on a micro-server to only one or two students assigned to that machine, so other students can continue their work unaffected.
- Training in DBA (and system administration) functions on servers requires much **higher level of support** (and entails a much greater risk of maintenance repairs) for the support personnel then it is on a client side (in client-server architecture). Therefore, **it is critical to have maintenance procedures and students' guides developed, tested, and implemented** — for proper and uninterrupted operations with remote servers without sacrificing the quality of self-paced practice for students.
- Security – students are assigned different levels of access security to Sun servers and to Oracle as they gain expertise and progress trough the courses. Thus, maintenance of students' access security is a time-consuming responsibility of ATS and an instructor.
- Predictably, limits of network access capacity for off-campus RAUL users became the most complex issue: distance learning shifts networks loads from in-campus to off-campus users. Information Resource Management's plan to expand network infrastructure at CSLA addresses exactly this issue.

ORGANIZATIONAL TASKS

Several tasks and measures have been accomplished for successful implementation of UL with RAUL extension:

- The Lab administration has been setup as follows:
  o Faculty Lab Administrator, a faculty member – responsible for overall planning and administrating of the Lab
  o Managing team consisting of two faculty members – responsible for the use of the Lab resources
  o ATS specialist – responsible for the hardware/software installation and access privileges control. As the Lab Administrator and the Managing Team gain more experience in the Lab supervision, they are becoming increasingly involved in sharing with ATS the responsibilities of assigning and managing students' access privileges (both, direct and remote) in accordance with the university network access policy.
- Lab hardware and software are purchased, installed, and implemented in courses.
- Administration of the Unix Lab has adopted and implemented a plan for periodical hands-on training workshops on using the lab resources for faculty and staff.
- The following courses have been modified to take advantage of the new lab facilities:
  o Java Programming
  o Database Design
  o Application Programs and Database Connectivity
  o Unix Operating System
- Two courses are added to the curriculum:
  o Linux Operating System
  o Oracle DBA with Solaris

Remote Access Unix Lab has already proved itself as an indispensable resource for distance learning courses that require a dedicated micro-server per each individual or collective user. The scope of RAUL can further be extended in the future to support such server-centered, "server administration" courses as Web Server Administration and Application Server Administration.

FUTURE WIRELESS SERVICES

Mobile access to data will bring significant changes to distance learning services. According to Sun Microsystems, "The number of wireless communications devices installed worldwide already exceeds the number of desktop PCs." This proliferation of mobile information technologies is creating new demand for educating IT managers.

For example, MBA High Technology Program at Arizona State University's (http://www.cob.asu.edu/mba/courses/tech_curriculum.cfm) offers Compaq iPAQ Pocket PCs pre-loaded with course materials to the students of the Program. The focus of the Program is on "continuous project in which teams develop a new product from beginning to end." (http://www.cob.asu.edu/mba/asu_mba_tech.cfm) The specific feature of the project is addressing "the issues of cross-team coordination, particularly when the teams are geographically dispersed."

Students of courses based on the Unix Lab use computers extensively and are expected to have access to personal computers off-campus. With wireless access planned for the Winter quarter of 2002, the RAUL will offer complete the learning solution for students who will be able to access RAUL resources (with firewall restrictions) from off-campus (and on-campus) using wireless mobile devices such as Pocket PCs, Handheld PCs.

Various vendors provide technical solutions for wireless learning environment. For example, Wireless University Solution from Compaq (http://www.compaq.com/education/higher-ed/wireless_university.html) addresses the wireless connectivity requirements for a learning environment without walls, in particular an environment of wireless handheld devices.

Sun identifies three components in mobile architecture: new services, utility-like quality/availability, and a flexible, future-oriented platform [1]. Enhanced RAUL server configuration will include

Oracle9*i*AS Wireless and Oracle9*i* Lite on students' Pocket PCs.Oracle9*i* Lite provides infrastructure and application services specifically for mobile devices. Oracle9*i* Lite is an add-on to Oracle9*i*AS Wireless, providing a simple mobile e-business environment [2].

Students will communicate with the RAUL resources using mobile devices like iPAQ pre-loaded with Windows CE and Oracle 9i Lite for mobile applications (other databases for iPAQ are available too).

CONCLUSION

Planning and setting up a Unix lab architecture has been progressing through several phases:

- Setting the direct access UL facility (DAUL)
- Setting the remote access UL facility (RAUL)
- Expanding RAUL resources for various functional groups of users (Solaris administrators, DBAs, Instructors of both, etc.)
- Expanding RAUL resources to wireless services for on-campus and off-campus users

The first two phases were completed without major setbacks. The third phase is in progress, and may never stop as new categories of functional users continue joining RAUL. The fourth phase of implementation will begin in Winter 2002.

REFERENCES

[1] Anonymous, "Enabling The Wireless Net Effect: How Sun Drives Wireless Architectures to 3G and Beyond," http://www.sun.com/sp/supplements/wireless_whitepaper.pdf, Sun Microsystems, October 2000, Revision 11

[2] Anonymous, "Oracle9i Lite: The Internet Platform for Mobile Computing," http://technet.oracle.com/products/lite/content.html, December 2001.

[3] Djoudi, Mahieddine, and Saad Harous, " Simplifying the Learning Over the Internet," *T.H.E. Journal*, November 2001.

[4] Watson, Ruth, " The Trumbull County Community Network Project," *T.H.E. Journal*, May 2001.

An Adaptive Neural Network for Understanding Website Usage Patterns

Victor Perotti and Raj Kiran
Rochester Institute of Technology College of Business, New York, USA, Tel: (716) 476-7753, Fax: (716) 475-7055, vic@mail.rit.edu

As the importance of the Internet rises, the need to create more adaptive and more usable web sites also grows. Most improvements to a web site require some knowledge of the site's users and how they are interacting with the pages. However, web professionals today have relatively few good options for capturing this information. Certainly, there are software and services to help summarize the basic information from the web site logs. This could mean keeping track of the frequency of visits for the individual web pages that make up a site, counting how many times the overall web site is visited from a specific web location, or other basic statistics.

At the IRMA 2001 conference, Perotti and Burke presented a technique and visualization that offers web developers an opportunity to easily see the pattern of usage at a website. Unlike earlier depictions, their Web Usage Plot emphasizes the relationship between the various pages at a web site by displaying them in a topographic organization: sites that are visited together frequently appear close together, while those that are seldom visited together in the same session appear far apart. Their process to create the Web Usage Plot visualization has several steps, as depicted below:

Table 1: A simple process for visualizing web usage (adapted from Perotti and Burke, 2000).

1. Cleaning and organizing the web server logs
2. Creating an aggregate representation of all users web page visits, the co-occurrence matrix
3. Visualizing this representation.

The final visualization step relies on a multivariate statistical technique called Multidimensional Scaling (MDS). This technique allows the reduction of the high dimensional data into lower dimensional coordinates that can be more easily visualized. The Web Usage Plot created with MDS does have many advantages over earlier representations of web site usage patterns.

Unfortunately, using MDS for web usage visualization can be tedious because the algorithms for reducing the data dimensionality are computationally expensive. For example, the authors used the SPSS software package, which limits the user to visualizing no more than 100 web pages. Clearly, many web sites have more web pages than this arbitrary limit. The present research explores an alternative and potentially superior approach using a Neural Network to capture the usage patterns at a web site. In this technique, a neural network would be trained with the patterns of usage at a web site, and then would automatically organize a low dimensional representation of these patterns.

KOHONEN SELF ORGANIZING MAP

Kohonen's Self Organizing Map (SOM) is a well-known neural network technique to do data dimensionality reduction. In this technique, a neural network is created in the desired low dimensionality, say two dimensions for the sake of explanation. This network is then trained with a set of input patterns that correspond to the high dimensional data to be reduced. As the network adapts, one of the network nodes becomes highly associated with each input pattern, so that when the correct input pattern is presented, it will be the most highly active node in the network. After training, the neural network represents a simple (two dimensional) map with nearby nodes representing similar input patterns in the multidimensional input data.

Self organizing maps have been already used for a great variety of problems, including browsing a picture database, data exploration, representing large text collections and classifying web documents based on their textual content (Kohonen et al, 2000).

The goal for the present research is to create and visualize a self-organizing map neural network representation of web site usage patterns. As in the Web Usage Plot, the self-organizing map visualization should be useful for web page developers to identify clusters of web pages that are visited together frequently. However, the new techniques go well beyond a simple substitution of the SOM for the Multidimensional scaling in the procedure outlined above.

One of the key issues in using a SOM is how the data is represented for training. We have found that the co-occurrence matrix (in Table 1 above) is not well suited for training a neural network. To understand why, consider the structure of the co-occurrence matrix. For every web page at the given web site, both a row and a column are created. So, if there were n total web pages at the web site, then the resulting co-occurrence matrix would be of size n^2. Inside a specific cell in the matrix is the number of times that the two pages (represented by the row and column) were visited together in the same session. So, for example, if webpage 16 were visited frequently with webpage 42, then we would see a high number in the cell for column 16 and row 42. Of course, only half of the matrix is really needed, since the usage of two pages in the same session is symmetrical.

To use the co-occurrence matrix as input to the SOM simply requires the treatment of each row in the matrix as an input pattern, since each row is a vector that describes the aggregate usage for one web page with all other web pages. The problem with this is that the goal for the SOM is to have pages that are visited together frequently map to nearby nodes in the two dimensional network. Unfortunately, the vectors representing two highly associated pages may be very different. Consider the example given above: the row for web page 16 will have a high number in column 42, while the row for web page 42 will have a high number in column 16. These two vectors are thus very different!

A potentially superior representation of the same information for input to the SOM could be called the **session membership matrix**. As before, each row corresponds to a specific web page. However, each column now corresponds to a particular user session that was recovered from the web log file. For a given row, each column will have a one (1) in it if the web page represented by the row is visited the session corresponding to the column, and a zero (0) otherwise. Thus, to continue the example above, because web pages 16 and 42 are visited together in the same sessions, they should have a similar pattern of ones and zeros along their corresponding rows. Because web pages that are visited together in the same session will have similar vectors, the session membership matrix is more appropriate to train the SOM than the earlier co-occurrence matrix.

VISUALIZATION OF THE SELF ORGANIZING MAP

Another unique contribution of the present research is in the visualization of the SOM. While there are several existing techniques to create a depiction from the self organizing map, the resulting pictures are often much more difficult to interpret than the simple map-like presentation in the Web Usage Plot. For example, a common SOM depiction requires the viewer to infer the presented relationships from a complex image of gray-scale or color levels. Since the goal of the research is to make an effective tool for web administrators and developers, a simpler image is desirable.

One existing way to visualize an SOM is to simply note which node in the matrix responds the most when presented with a given input pattern. The matrix can then be visualized by plotting a point at every grid location whose node responded the most during the presentation of the input. In our case, each web page would be represented by a point located at a grid location. However, this approach has two problems. For one, multiple pages frequently map to the same network node. So, the viewer would only see one point, when in fact several associated web pages may be represented there. A second problem is that the distance between points is somewhat arbitrary, since it simply corresponds to the regular distance between the SOM nodes in their grid.

Figure 1: A jittered grid depicting clusters of web pages

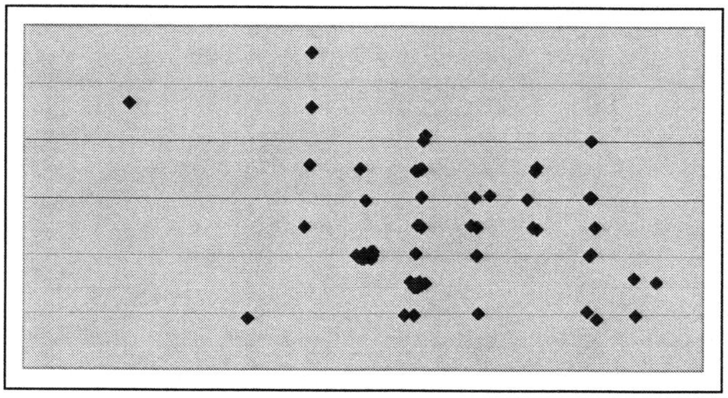

Figure 1 demonstrates a novel "jittered" visualization of the self organizing map neural network, which overcomes the two problems mentioned above. Using this procedure, the visualized location of each web page is jittered by a small amount to displace it from the regular grid location. The displacement of each point is proportional to the error reported by the SOM network when responding to the specific input pattern. Thus, multiple web pages can be visualized at the same node location, and the association between the two of them can be seen as a cluster by the viewer. Also, the distance of any point from the regular grid location is a measure of how well that grid location's node succeeded in distinguishing that input pattern from the rest. Such a depiction is easy to interpret, and a viewer can quickly get a sense for the primary usage patterns that are present at the web site.

DISCUSSION

The Self Organizing Map has great potential as a tool for creating useful visualizations of web sites. The present research has begun to develop the techniques necessary to get meaningful and useful results from the SOM neural network. In doing so, a visualization can be created that is as useful as the Web Usage Plot, but more robust in its computation. The SOM technique is relatively fast to compute, and has no restriction on the number of web pages that can be considered.

However, there is still much more research necessary to successfully use the SOM as part of a professional visualization system. One difficulty in using the SOM is a problem with dealing with sparse data sets. In a small web site sample, it is quite possible that most of the web pages are never visited, or are visited in one session. This means that of the hundreds of sessions available, a given web page will have only a single column active. The SOM network will frequently overlook the subtle difference between such pages, in considering the vast similarity in their pattern of not being accessed in so many sessions. Finding a set of parameters and appropriate training regimen for dealing with this problem can be quite time consuming. At present, a variety of different parameters must be experimented with using trial and error in order to find a useful visualization.

Perhaps even more important than the enabling of intuitive visualizations, capturing a web site's usage pattern in a neural network could provide a remarkably versatile component in new web-based applications. Recommendations could be made to the user on the fly, since when a user goes to a particular web page, it will be clear which other pages the other users have visited from there. Also, it would be possible to recreate some user behaviors from the network itself, so that novel web site structures can be readily evaluated or compared.

REFERENCES

Kohonen, T., Kaski, S., Lagus, K. Salojärvi, J., Paatero, V. and Saarela,A. (2000) *Self Organization of a Massive Document Collection.* IEEE Transactions on Neural Networks, Special Issue on Neural Networks for Data Mining and Knowledge Discovery, volume 11, number 3, pages 574-585. May 2000

Perotti, V. and Burke, A., (2000) *The Visualization of Usage Patterns for Web Customization*, presented at the IRMA conference, Toronto, CA

Engineering the Cognitive Processes in Software Projects: Machine Learning, Knowledge Integration and Scheduling

Valentina Plekhanova
University of Sunderland, School of Computing, Engineering and Technology, UK, valentina.plekhanova@sunderland.ac.uk

BACKGROUND

It is recognised that most software development tasks are cognitively driven and the focus on people quality and their management may provide considerable software process improvement [Curtis, 1981; Kellner, and Hansen, 1989; Kellner, and Rombach, 1991; Sommerville, and Rodden, 1996]. However, most existing process models and conventional project management approaches do not consider *cognitive processes* [Plekhanova, 1999] and *human resource quality* [Sommerville, and Rodden, 1996]. Instead they over emphasise the technical components. For this reason, their practical application is restricted to those projects where human resources are not a critical variable. Formal representation and incorporation of cognitive processes [Plekhanova, 1999] and human aspects in modelling frameworks is seen as very challenging for software engineering research [Kellner, and Hansen, 1989; Kellner, and Rombach, 1991; Rombach, 2001].

In our research *we consider human resources as a cognitive system*. We define models of cognitive (software development) tasks and models of human agents/systems that can be allocated to cognitive tasks. We analyse available knowledge and skills of human agents to define their critical, missing and potential capabilities with respect to the given cognitive tasks [Plekhanova and Offen, 1997]. These capabilities outline critical stages in software development process that have to be improved.

We are not interested in chaotic activities and interactions between cognitive agents, nor interested in detailed tasks descriptions, detailed steps of performance of the tasks and internal pathways of thoughts. Rather, we are *interested in how available knowledge/skills of cognitive agents satisfy required knowledge/skills for the performance of the cognitive tasks.*

We recognise that different initial knowledge capabilities of the cognitive system define different performance and require different learning methods. We study how human-cognitive agents use their knowledge and skills for learning the cognitive tasks. Learning methods lead the cognitive agent to the solution of cognitive problems/ tasks. We consider a learning method as a guider to the successful performance. That is, we correlate initial knowledge capabilities of human agents and learning methods that define cognitive processes. We analyse impact of cognitive processes on the performance (or behaviour) of human agents. To provide optimal level of learning processes we consider optimisation tasks within framework of the cognitive system/process modelling.

The **aims of the work** are to develop a formal method for the modelling and engineering of a cognitive system in order to support the required learning processes.

Our research brings together work in *systems engineering, knowledge engineering* and *machine learning* for modelling cognitive systems and cognitive processes. We consider *engineering the cognitive processes* as the application of mathematical techniques and rigorous engineering methods to cognitive processes. We believe that the establishment of engineering methods with a sound theoretical basis can lead to the improvement of cognitive processes in software projects. We also use a *synthesis of formal methods* and *heuristic approaches to engineering tasks* for the evaluation, comparison, analysis, evolution and improvement of processes.

In order to define learning processes we engineer *cognitive processes* via a study of knowledge capabilities of cognitive systems. We address the problem of cognitive system formation with respect to the given tasks and consider the cognitive agent's capabilities and compatibilities factors as critical variables, because these factors have an impact on the formation of cognitive systems, *the performance processes and different learning methods*. We provide support for a solution to resource-based problems in **knowledge integration** and **scheduling** of cognitive processes to form a capable cognitive system for learning the required cognitive tasks.

In a cognitive system we address the problem of *agent allocation* where we consider *not only* ***task scheduling*** *as in traditional approaches but also* ***scheduling machine learning methods*** *and* ***knowledge of cognitive agents***. Reinforcement tasks [Sutton and Barto, 1998] are built into framework of the cognitive system/process modelling to provide optimal level of learning processes.

In the proposed work we use the profile theory [Plekhanova, 1999; Plekhanova, 2000] for formalisation of cognitive systems and cognitive processes, and for the identification of critical areas in software development where improvement should be taken. In particular, we consider engineering the cognitive processes to provide improvement of software development by means of integrating adaptive machine learning into the profile theory. In order to model cognitive processes in software projects we combine the profile theory, which is used for knowledge engineering (analysis, integration, scheduling), and learning methods (e.g. supervised, unsupervised, Boosting, Lazy Learning, Neural Nets, Incremental Decision Tree Learning). Machine learning methods are applied to the initial available knowledge capabilities of the cognitive system to define learning methods for the tasks. (Note that different initial knowledge capabilities of the cognitive system require different hybrid learning methods.)

NOVELTY

The proposed work is particularly novel in its approach to cognitive (learning) processes that incorporate a synthesis of *systems engineering, knowledge engineering* and *machine learning methods*. The proposed method for the modelling and engineering of cognitive systems and cognitive processes can be used in software/systems engineering and machine learning for a formalisation of cognitive processes, cognitive systems, and capability and compatibility aspects.

Existing machine learning approaches do not address scheduling problems *in learning methods*. We develop a *new scheduling approach* where we consider scheduling machine learning methods and knowledge of cognitive agents vs task scheduling in traditional approaches. A *new machine learning method* has to be developed and incorporated into an engineering framework for cognitive processes.

BENEFICIARIES

Engineering the Complex Systems: Research in engineering of complex systems will provide insight into new methods and approaches to learning in cognitive systems. Research in machine learning will deliver adaptiveness to knowledge integration and scheduling of learning methods. Scientists in cognitive systems research will receive a formal method for modelling of cognitive processes.

Industry: The application of a new approach could provide *learning software and IT development organisations* with:

- superior management of resource capabilities and compatibilities;
- streamlining of process development through better management of project resources, tasks;
- increased opportunities for organisations to implement process improvement based on the constructive criticism derived from self analysis.

It is apparent that there is a world-wide interest in the application of this research. Since most modern processes are cognitively driven our method can be used for the formal modelling of cognitive systems. It is important for the future competitiveness of the software and IT industry to employ a scientific (vs heuristic) approach to the engineering of cognitive processes.

Technology: Formal modelling of the capability and compatibility of cognitive systems ensures the automation in cognitive system modelling. It leads to development of new technologies in system (or object) modelling. Some of the enhancements that we intend to offer through this method are to provide support for development and engineering of *new knowledge capabilities of cognitive systems*, i.e. innovative technologies.

REFERENCES

1. Curtis, B., (Eds), Human Factors in Software Development, IEEE Computer Society, Box 80452, Los Angeles, Calif. 90080, 1981.
2. Kellner, M.I. and Hansen, G.A., Software Process Modeling: A Case Study, in Proceedings of the 22nd Annual Hawaii International Conference on System Sciences, Vol. II, 1989, 175-188.
3. Kellner, M.I. and Rombach, H.D., Session Summary: Comparisons of software process descriptions, in Proceedings of the 6th International Software Process Workshop, IEEE Computer Society, Washington, DC, 1991, 7-18.
4. Plekhanova, V., Applications of the Profile Theory to Software Engineering and Knowledge Engineering, Proceedings of the Twelfth International Conference on Software Engineering and Knowledge Engineering, July 2000, Chicago, USA; pp. 133-141.
5. Plekhanova, V., A Capability- and Compatibility-based Approach to Software Process Modelling, PhD thesis– Macquarie University, Sydney, Australia and the Institute of Information Technologies and Applied Mathematics, Russian Academy of Sciences, July 1999
6. Plekhanova, V. and Offen, R., Managing the Human-Software Environment, Proceedings of the 8th International Workshop on Software Technology and Engineering Practice (STEP'97), *IEEE Computer Society Press*, pp. 422-432, 1997, London, UK.
7. Rombach, H. D. and Verlage, M., Directions in Software Process Research, in *Advantages in Computers*, Vol. 41, Academic Press, Inc., 1995.
8. Rombach, D., Experimental Software Engineering: Building a Research Community, Australian Software Engineering Conference, Canberra, Australia, 26-28 August, 2001
9. Sommerville, I. and Rodden, T., Human, social and organisational influences on the software processes, in *Software Process*, Vol. 4 of Trends in Software (A. Fuggetta and A. Wolf, eds.), J. Wiley, 1996.
10. Sutton, R.S. and Barto, A.G., Reinforcement Learning: an Introduction, MIT Press, Cambridge, MA, 1998

An Internet-Mediated Data Abstraction Course

Ronald E. Prather
Department of Computer Science, Trinity University, USA, Tel: (210) 999-7399, Fax: (210) 999-7477, rprather@trinity.edu

INTRODUCTION

Situated in San Antonio, Texas, Trinity University is a learning community committed to the highest standards of academic excellence. It has been ranked number one for ten consecutive years by *U.S. News and World Report* among universities in the Western United States. A recently implemented initiative, led by the Vice President for Information Technology, has set as its goal to enrich the education of Trinity students through the use of *Internet-mediated* learning technologies. As an experimental pilot study, testing the boundaries of the Internet-mediated learning environment, approval was granted to the author to offer his Computer Science course on the *Principles of Data Abstraction*, Fall Semester 2001, in the model of the *virtual university* (no formal classes; all learning taking place via the Internet). This paper describes the parameters of this study, outlining the specific course objectives and requirements, with emphasis on the unique pedagogical features of the course design. A comprehensive evaluation of the study is included.

COURSE REQUIREMENTS

The object of study is a modern, laboratory-supplemented course in the Principles of Data Abstraction, as implemented in the C++ programming language, with emphasis on the notion of an abstract data type (ADT). There are two texts [1,2], the latter consisting of nine experiments having titles as shown:

Experiment 1: Complex Arithmetic Package
Experiment 2: The Polynomial ADT
Experiment 3: The SortedList ADT
Experiment 4: The Stack ADT
Experiment 5: The Queue ADT
Experiment 6: The SearchTree ADT
Experiment 7: The PriorityQueue ADT
Experiment 8: The Graph ADT
Experiment 9: Minimum Spanning Trees

Accordingly, the course is divided into nine week-and-a-half periods, during which an individual experiment is discussed (and performed by the students), as a supplement to readings in the main text [1].

The course grade is determined by a student's performance on two *in class* examinations (one midway through, the other at the end of the semester), nine laboratory quizzes (submitted by email at the beginning of a laboratory period), six-of-nine laboratory reports (submitted hard-copy to the instructor's real-world mail box at the end of a laboratory period), and participation in the course *bulletin board* (See details below). The quizzes, routine questions on the laboratory experiment and related readings, are emailed to all students simultaneously as an addenda to the comprehensive *study guides* (Again, see details below). And as suggested above, each student is required to perform six experiments (of the nine that are studied), and to write formal reports on these six investigations.

Besides the previously stated requirements of a student, he or she is also expected to attend three scheduled *in class evaluations* of the Internet-mediated environment, where the instructor has the opportunity to determine the effectiveness of the unique pedagogical course design presented here, from a student perspective. Student responses to detailed questionnaires at these "get-togethers" constitute one focus of the end-of-semester evaluation that the instructor has prepared. Except for these meetings, all contact with the instructor is via the Internet (or at his scheduled office hours, when problems of understanding are so acute that they cannot be resolved any other way.)

THE BULLETIN BOARD

A critical component of the Internet-mediated environment designed here is the *bulletin board*, an email forum for discussion of the course material. Two or three days before the beginning of each of the nine laboratory experiment periods, the instructor broadcasts to all students simultaneously, a *study guide*, assigning, outlining, and commenting on the related readings (particularly as concerns the laboratory experiment at hand), pointing out "trouble spots," etc., and this email message serves as a focus for the discussions to follow. Students are encouraged to post questions, comments, etc., relating to the topic(s) under discussion, after which other students will post answers, further questions, comments, etc., in a continuing dialogue (the instructor will also participate, in the role of moderator and tutor). Each student posting is broadcast to the class as a whole, after perhaps some editing by the moderator, though he or she only communicates directly with the instructor. In this way, the bulletin board functions much like an Internet *moderated mailing list*.

As a major thrust of the recently implemented Trinity University Internet-mediated teaching environment, the *Blackboard 4 e-learning System* has been installed. It is of interest to compare the *blackboard* and the bulletin board methodologies in relation to the course at hand. With the blackboard, an ongoing dialogue can again be established, but as an informal, freely accessible media, open to any student who wishes to express himself or herself (hopefully in a manner that has some bearing on the course at hand). In it's functionality, the blackboard is more like an Internet *chat room*. The instructor looses all control over the discussion. Such a free-flowing medium may be "just the ticket" in certain seminar courses, where individual opinions are admitted, even welcomed. But in a technical course, such as that under consideration here, an unmoderated, unmodulated posting of a student might be confusing and misleading to those others in the class who are tuned in to the blackboard. With the bulletin board methodology, as described above, the instructor has ultimate control over the content of the discussion. Often students in computer science are not able to phrase their questions or comments in the proper terminology. With the bulletin board, student question can be rephrased by the instructor-moderator for technical accuracy, so as to ensure that the proper understanding is being conveyed to the rest of the class. Each technology undoubtedly has its place. But our experience thus far has provided overwhelming evidence that for the course under study, the right choice has been made between these two competing methodologies.

COURSE EVALUATION

By every measure that the instructor could apply to the performance of students in the experimental pilot course offering, as opposed to that of students of previous years in the more traditional classroom setting, results were seen as favorable. The median for the midterm exam was within a percentage point of that from previous years. The same held true for the final examination. And laboratory reports, if anything, were of a superior quality.

However, it is in the transcriptions from the bulletin board that the instructor draws his most favorable impressions. *These postings, some seventy pages of text, represent the most detailed and substantive interactions that this instructor has ever had with a group of students.* In the traditional classroom setting, many students are reluctant to ask a question or to participate in discussions, whereas with the online bulletin board, somehow these same students are motivated to become involved. And the instructor, rather than giving offhand and perhaps only half-correct answers to student questions, as we often find in the classroom setting, has the time and the motivation for giving the clearest and most precise responses. All in all, the idea of the bulletin board is seen as the most successful component of the Internet-mediated environment designed here. One could argue for its inclusion as a supplement to the course delivery system, whatever the teaching environment.

But the real test is to be found in the student evaluation of the course. In a questionnaire submitted to the students at the end of the semester, the following are representative of the responses:

> I was "more or less comfortable" with the Internet-mediated environment of this course.
>
> I have learned "about the same amount" in this course in comparison with others.
>
> I have had "hardly any" difficulty with the laboratory quizzes.
>
> The answers provided to questions on the bulletin board were "quite helpful" and they were "quite clear."
>
> "For the most part," the instructor was very helpful in my being able to perform the experiments successfully.
>
> They were "interesting, well -presented and challenging."
>
> They were "very well coordinated" with discussions in the text.
>
> The study guides were "quite helpful" in organizing my reading and experimental work.
>
> In my estimation, the instructor has devoted "considerably more time" to the organization of this course, compared to others.

Only 3 out of 20 students indicated that, knowing what they know now (at the end of the semester), they would "prefer to have taken the course in a traditional classroom setting." Even when an individual student may have been somewhat critical of the Internet-mediated environment, they were good-humored in their response:

> "I enjoyed the freedom, but (at first) had difficulty with the responsibility."
>
> "At first I had difficulty with the experiments. But after doing a few, I didn't find them so daunting."
>
> "I enjoyed the flexibility but it often lead to procrastination."
>
> "This course taught me to be self-motivated."
>
> "It added an extra wall between the professor and the students. Remember, it's data abstraction, not student abstraction."

But all in all, the student reaction to this experimental course offering has been most encouraging and supportive. The class was especially pleased to learn that a paper describing their experience had been accepted for presentation at this international conference. And it is my pleasure to report the results of this study in this forum.

REFERENCES

1. F.M. Carrano, *Data Abstraction and Problem Solving in C++*, Third Edition, Addison-Wesley, 2001.
2. R.E. Prather, *Laboratory Manual for Data Abstraction*, Trinity University (http://www.cs.trinity.edu/~rprather), 2001.

Strategies of Securities Electronic Commerce in China—Implications of Comparative Analyses Between China and Other Countries

Li Qi and Zhang Xianfeng
[1]EC Research Institute, Xi'an Jiaotong University
Tel: +86 (029) 522-2076, Fax: +86 (029) 522-2796, Liq@xjtu.edu.cn, xianfeng.zhang@263.net

Sun Chenjian and Wang Shufang
Shenzhen Securities Communication Company

ABSTRACT

This paper does a comparative analysis in SEC development between China and other countries from the aspect of economic environment, supervision & regulation systems and technology applications. Through the corresponding research, discretions of SEC development are dipped out. Accordingly relative strategies are proposed in the end so as to supply beneficial references for governments, brokers and technology suppliers of China and other developing countries similar to China.

RESEARCH BACKGROUNDS & COMPARISONS

When APARNET was firstly built, its originators and users had never expected that it might bring a complete reform to the whole society in the 21th century. In just a few years, the Internet had penetrated every industry and will further produce a deeper transformation.

America is always in the front line whatever in advanced technologies researching or economic activities modernizing. There are no exceptions in securities electronic commerce development in these several years. Take the investors' accounts for example, in 1997 there are over 3.7 million online investors and the number reaches 5.8 million in Dec. 1998. At the end of 2000, about 10 million investors have been executing online securities trading and it is further predicted that by 2002, more than 20 million people in the USA will trade stocks, bonds and mutual funds online (Electronic Commerce). On the other hand, online trading value has taken up 35% of the total value by June 2000 (Wall Street Journal 2000). Korea, with the fastest developing pace in the field has gained much bigger benefits. The electronic trading value of stocks surged to nearly 63.1% of the total trading value in Aug. 2000, excluding foreign investors and institutional investors, the electronic trading value of stocks reached a high of 74.9%. (KSDA, 2000) In addition, the electronic commerce development in Hongkong and European countries also contribute great efforts in the whole society growth.

When the tide of electronic commerce swept every corner of the world, it is the IT industry intellectuals that move first in China. They actively adopt electronic commerce in many fields and set up their own websites. The first non-broker website in China was homeway.com established at the end of 1996, which also represents the start of securities electronic commerce. Stockstar.com and yestock.com tightly followed the trend in 1997. By September of 2000, various non-brokers had established over 40 websites.

At the meanwhile, traditional brokers also took due actions. In Jan.1997, Huarong Trust & Investment Corporation, Zhanjiang Branch primarily applied its online stock trading system. The action clearly marked China's real beginning of electronic commerce in securities industry. About 200 brokers or entities dealing with brokerage had set up their own websites and developed online broking until 2000. The corresponding online stock trading value stands for about 3% of the total value in 2000. Due to the lack of online stock trading regulations and relative guarantee, brokers and other non-brokers had little idea of how to develop and consumers can hardly trust this new kind of operation process.

Since the issue of *Online Brokerage Administrative Regulation* by China Securities Regulation Commission in Feb. 2000, online brokering operations turned to be gradually standardized. By the end of Aug. 2001, among the 104 traditional brokers, 71 of them had opened online brokering businesses and 45 had gained the qualifications to execute their operations online. Accordingly China's securities electronic commerce begins its slow and steady developing process. Large progresses though China securities industry has achieved, as the Table 1 shows, there still exists great gaps. These backgrounds not only show the great lag of electronic commerce applications in securities industry between China and other countries like America and Korea, but more clearly state the fact that securities electronic commerce needs large enhancement and relative steps is proposed to be large.

Table 1: Online stock trading situation (six months)

Month	Customer accounts (thousand)	Ratio of the total	Monthly trading value (billion)	Ratio of the total	Total trading value (billion)	Ratio of the total
June	2710	8.5%	45.619	4.63%	202.298	4.07%
July	2890	8.93%	26.6	3.98%	226.2	3.82%
August	3010	9.22%	29.5	5.53%	255.7	3.96%
September	3100	9.46%	20.9	5.26%	276.6	4.03%
October	3190	9.7%	24.6	5.74%	301.2	4.13%
November	3290	9.94%	27.8	6.17%	329	4.25%

This is a large project in which government supervision, technologies applications and economic environment are all discussed. This project stands high and seeks into a wider sphere and with which the deep roots for stirring China's securities electronic commerce can be perceived. When the dissimilarities are reached, suitable advices in developing electronic commerce in securities industry are proposed not only for China but also for those developing countries that resemble China.

RESEARCH METHODOLOGIES

Since the project is divided into three subunits, each of which employs such methodologies as theoretical researching, data collecting and questionnaires, on-site visiting. After the independent analyses, their results are combined and comparatively balanced so as to understand the core troubles for securities electronic commerce development in China and respective problems of the three aspects. The project is more an empirical research than a wholly theoretical discussion. For we mainly focus on what government, brokers and customers are doing rather than what they should be. Through research in three aspects, it is optimistic that securities electronic commerce's growth trend is large and chances for due development is also valuable in China. Finally strategies and plans are respectively posed out.

RESEARCH PROCESSES & RESPECTIVE RESULTS

Based on the definition of electronic commerce, the connotation of securities electronic commerce is pointed out. In our project, securities electronic commerce is broadly defined as the recreating and broadening of securities operations through the use of electronic tools which include things from low communication networks like telephones, faxes to higher computer technologies. The securities operations not only include the traditional brokerages, IPOs, or investment banks, but also new emerging ones in the Internet environment. Throughout the project, it mainly focuses on the narrow connotation: online brokerages and other operations with the utilization of the Internet.

The project is then further divided into three aspects: supervision & regulation, economic environment and technological aspect. Relative analyses are done.

Research From Supervision & Regulation Aspect

From the supervision and regulation aspect, there are two problems. The advert of the Internet in itself represents many challenges to supervision systems in which information asymmetry is the essence. To some degree, it holds true that information asymmetry is even more severe in the new environment due to the many distinct traits. Thus the prevailing supervision systems of information, brokers and investors as well need reforms. On the other hand, regulations play an important role in securities electronic commerce development, especially in China who has a comparatively short history (from the establishment of Shanghai Stock Market in 1990 and Shenzhen Stock Market in 1991). Comparing with free commission and register system, China as well as brokers, companies and investors undoubtedly lack the appropriate economic motivation. Furthermore, in Feb. 2000, CSSR issued the *Online Brokerage Administrative Regulation* means only those authorized traditional brokers can execute online brokerage. Unable to fully use price sensitivity psychologies and better, creative services, online brokerages turn to be simply an alternative for other channels like telephone brokerages for the populace.

To reform the whole supervision and regulation system for China is not a simple question. It not only concerns the optimal models, it more focus on the situation and capability of China's market. Therefore we can only rely on the gradually opened capital market, established policies and regulations, then accordingly cite relative systems.

Research From Economic Environmental Level

In the economic environmental level, there shows many questions. Securities electronic commerce as a whole is more concerned with basic environment, participating entities and history factors.

Firstly, the basic environment composes economic, development and social ones. Comparatively speaking, the liquidity of the capital market in China is not as strong as other developed countries, and the size is not as big as others. Thus securities cannot work efficiently in the economy and basic economic environment for securities growth accordingly may seem to be poor. Besides, region growth disparities have long been the puzzle of the State. There is also no exception to securities. Online brokerage mainly focuses on southern and coastal cities, and inner-land cities lack the sense that it would be beneficial to develop online stock. Even employees of the various broker companies do not understand the significances, not to speak of numerous investors who only pay attention to how they can earn from price margin. Thus in order to complete the cited developing degree of the mother company, many branches "create" their online account and online trading volume through their employees' participation into the processes. As for social environment, it mainly talks about the average knowledge (on securities and electronic commerce as well) level. Though the network users have reached 26.5 million (as Table 2 shows), but most of them are young people who haven't go into the securities market.

Table 2: Internet development in China (from 1997-2001)

Indexes / Date	Connected Computers (Thousand)	Internet Users (Thousand)	Domain Name End with CN	www Websites	Total Banwidth (M)
1997? 11	299	620	4066	1500	25? 41
1998? 07	542	1175	9415	3700	84? 64
1999? 01	747	2100	18396	5300	143? 25
1999? 07	1460	4000	29045	9906	241
2000? 01	3500	8900	48695	15153	351
2000? 07	6500	16900	99734	27289	1234
2001? 01	8920	22500	122099	265405	2799
2001. 07	10020	26500	128362	242739	3257

Participating entities in sundry countries are dissimilar, thus a deep analyses in these also help. American investors mainly put their personal investment operations to companies so once the investment companies decide to go stock online, all problems are solved. As to Korea investors, though majority of them are individual ones, the wide use of Internet and communication equipments can greatly help. In China, those majority individual investors who live in large cities or developed areas and minority company investors who take only a few percentage of the whole constitute the participating investors' features.

Owning to the short developing history in capital markets as well as securities institutions, stock market of China in itself is still immature, not to speak of online stock. Therefore whatever in developing strategies or in penetrating degree, are lower than countries with developed market and long histories.

Clearly, securities electronic commerce is a long developing process, in which government, brokers and individual investors, public companies are all needed. As for government, the macro-regulations and regional development favorable policies should be set. Strategies for brokers are a complicated project, which ranges from initial website designing to internal managing, strategic planning and global marketing. For the latter two entities, to let them understand the benefits of securities electronic commerce and to actually use them is vital in the long process.

Research From Technological Aspect

Strictly speaking, technologies are far easier than business models. That is also why .com companies remain in deficit with the most powerful technologies and some even go bankrupt. This also holds true in China. The one problem of securities electronic commerce development in China stays in the existence of various operating standards. There is lack of mutual authentication third party and common standards like information-issuing format. Thus when each brokers establish their own website and seek their CAs, payment gateways and so on, investors undoubtedly have to be accustomed to certain brokers and comply their rules.

In China, though EC tides are firstly irritated by IT intellectuals, technologies eventually is also for business benefits. It is concluded that common platform, common standards and mutual authentication are needed.

IMPLICATIONS FROM THE RESEARCH

From the above analyses, it is clear that in China, the main problem of securities electronic commerce stays in supervision & regulation system that nevertheless can seldom step over the contemporary environment. It is originated from the immature securities market development and slow electronic commerce penetration processes. Besides, economic and technological growth is the two wings that can promote the whole development. Without due support of the two wings, securities electronic commerce in China can never grow.

ENDNOTE

This is a cooperated project of EC Research Institute of Xi'an Jiaotong University and Shenzhen Secuties Communication Company. The 150 thousand- word report consists of three large subunits and two small subunits

REFERENCES

1. Efraim Turban, J. Lee, D. King & H. Michael Chung: Electronic Commerce A Managerial Perspective, Prentice-Hall Incorporation, New Jersey 07458
2. Seongcheol Kim: "Factors Influencing Customers' Use of Electronic Commerce in Stock Trading: An Empirical Study in Korea", PACIS2001 Proceedings
3. Kongxiang: "Online Stock Transactions & Supervisions" Shenzhen Stock Exchange Integrated Research Report, 2000.6
4. Sang Hoon Lee: "Securities Transactions in Changing: Online Stock Transactions in Korea" Capital Market, 2000.11
6. Ruben Lee: "Securities Transactions in Changing: New Exchange Stock in the New Economic Environment" Capital Market, 2000.12
7. www. csrc.gov.cn
8. www. cnnic.net
9.www.set.gov

An Evaluation of Current Practices of Software Security in Custom Software Applications

Vijay V. Raghavan, PhD
Associate Professor of Information Systems, Northern Kentucky University, Tel: (859) 572-6358

INTRODUCTION

There has recently been a heightened awareness of Information Technology (IT) management on computer-related security issues (Hulme, 2001). Academic research as well as industry practice has long recognized the need for securing information systems and computer architectures. IT managers are increasingly concerned about possible attacks on computer facilities and software, especially for mission critical software. It is obvious there are indeed many dimensions to providing a secure computing environment in an organization -ranging from computer virus, trojan horses, unauthorized access, identity theft to infrastructure intrusions. This complexity requires that the problem of security be tacked at many fronts simultaneously. This study attempts to identify a comprehensive list of issues relating to providing security in the context of custom software applications. Custom Software Application (CSA) is defined as an application developed for use by an organization and its partners using tools typically provided by another vendor. Thus, an extranet application written in a programming language such as java server pages and implemented in a database environment would be a CSA but *Microsoft Word 2000* would not be one. Compared to the technical and financial resources available to developers of off-the-shelf software applications resources, CSA developers have fewer resources and greater developmental constraints. Hence, there is a significant need to understand the possible security concerns in the development of CSAs.

THEORETICAL MODELS OF SECURITY

One of the difficulties in specifying data security requirements for an application is its complexity. The characteristics of application dependent security policies and requirements have not been clearly understood. (Ting, 1993). There has been two distinct approaches to security research (Nelson, 1997): Formalist school that focuses on correctness and universality by attempting to ensure system independent methods (notably, access control) while pragmatist stream focuses on attacks on and countermeasures for real systems (notably intrusion detection). Nelson (1997) has argued for integration of these two schools of research. Nelson is also of the opinion that traditional research on security methods has been divorced from mainstream systems design, development and operation. The present study attempts to evaluate current practices of software security of Custom Software Applications. Security issues relating to the two major streams of security research will be identified and evaluated. The concept of Run-Time Security Evaluation (RTSE) proposed by Serban and McMillin (1996) highlights the need to provide for an ongoing security evaluation after the system is operational. They advocate RTSE in addition to securities implemented during developmental life cycles of a CSA.

Formalist Issues Of Software Security

In order for a software application to be secure it must first designate a group of valid users. The responsibility for maintaining this list of valid users must be accounted for the design of the system. It is also conceivable that the application must have distinct components, which are open to users with different level of security. These different modules must have distinct entry points that can be controlled. Multiple entry points for different modules must be clearly identified and checks must be performed before users are allowed to enter those modules. A matrix of list of valid users and the components that they are allowed to access must be integral part of the security model for the application. The location of this matrix whether it is part of a secure database that is accessed by the application or hard coded into the application may determine the security level of the application.

Pragmatist Issues Of Software Security

The set of issues under the pragmatist school focus on deliberate intrusion into the system after it is built. Even in cases where the application designers have exercised sufficient care in implementing a security model of the system, once the system is operational there is potential for security breaches through the infrastructure where the application is running. As an example, if a list of valid users and modules are maintained in a database, there is still a potential for security breaches if access to databases is not sufficiently controlled. Although, this is often outside the responsibility of application developers, it still presents a potential security problem for the system. The location of the application code and the physical security of the code are critical for the security level of the CSA. In addition, if the infrastructure (access to operating system, servers an database servers) in which the application is running is NOT secure, it will compromise on the security of the CSA as well.

Although formalism and pragmatism have been identified as two distinct streams of security research, the degree of security that a CSA enjoys is a function of formalist and pragmatist security concerns. It is imperative that they both are considered during SDLC (System Development Life Cycle) and security research must attempt to integrate them (Nelson, 1997).

CONCLUSION

The model proposed identifies the issues highlighted above. The research plan is first to understand all areas of a CSA's degree of security. Two focus groups consisting of eight software developers each will be used to first elicit additional security related areas that might have been overlooked and provide an ordinal ranking of all

Figure 1: An integrative model of software security

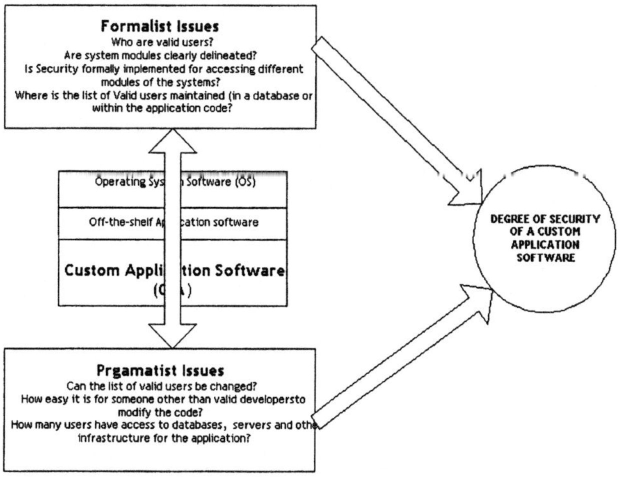

items that might compromise on security. A survey of software developers will be developed based on the focus group to understand current practices.

REFERENCES

Ting T.C. (1993). Modeling Security Requirements for Applications. Proceedings of the eighth annual conference on Object-oriented programming systems, languages, and applications, September 26 - October 1, 1993, Washington United States pp. 305.

Department of Defense Trusted Computer Security Evaluation Criteria (1985). DoD 5200-28-STD, National Computer Security Center, December 1985.

Hulme, V George (2001). Management Takes Notice, *Information Week*, pp.28-34.

Nelosn, Ruth (1997). Integration Formalism and Pragmatism: Architectural Security. New Security Paradigms workshop, Langdale, Cumbria, UK.

Serban Cristina and McMillin, Bruce (1996). Run-time Security Evaluation: Can We Afford It? ACM – New Security Paradigms Workshop, Lake Arrowhead, CA.

Impact of Legislation on Design of E-Commerce Systems—An Exploratory Study

Sam Ramanujan and Someswar Kesh
Central Missouri State University, Tel: (660) 543-8565, ramanujan@cmsu1.cmsu.edu

INTRODUCTION

The legislative environment of e-commerce, like in other businesses governs how business can be conducted in this new marketplace. The attention to e-commerce legislations by IT managers can make the difference between a confident, well-designed e-commerce effort and one that fails. In this research we propose to study:

1. the level of understanding of the e-commerce legislations in the Information Technology Management community, and
2. the impact of such legislations on the development of e-commerce software.

This research study will be conducted in three phases. In phase 1, we will review all the important aspects of e-commerce legislation adopted by the states. We are restricting this research to the U.S. currently. Most of Phase 1, has been completed and we are currently compiling the results in a easy to read format that can be shared with subjects in phase 2 of our research study.

In phase 2 of the study, we intend to adopt the case study method to address the two research questions. We will be interviewing senior and mid level IT development executives in firms that have e-commerce applications, in order to study their level of understanding of e-commerce laws. In addition, we will also be gathering any anecdotal evidence to show the impact of such laws in the design of e-commerce solutions.

In the final phase of the research study, we will be conducting a survey to study the two research issues presented earlier. The purpose of this phase is to triangulate the results from phase 2. Such an effort will lead to results that have both internal and external validity and thus can be readily used as guidance for future e-commerce development efforts.

In the following paragraphs we are providing a brief description of some of the e-commerce areas that will become the primary focus of this study. This focus was developed based on the literature review conducted in Phase 1 of this research.

Uniform Electronic Transactions Act in the U.S.

In 1999, the National Conference of Commissioners on Uniform State Laws approved and recommended the Uniform Electronic Transactions Act (UETA) for enactment in all the states. It provides for the legal basis for electronic transactions, particularly as they involve electronic signatures and records. It has increased the enforceability of the related regulations at a time of lack of standard methods of accountability. In e-commerce the responsibility for contents and transactions is not always as clear as in the traditional commercial world, where codes of conduct have consolidated over many generations of use.

Definitions of 'Electronic Signature' in Law

"Electronic signature" is a generic, technology-neutral term that refers to the universe of all of the various methods by which one can "sign" an electronic record. Although all electronic signatures are represented digitally, they can take many forms and can be created by many different technologies. Examples of electronic signatures include: a name typed at the end of an e-mail message by the sender; a digitized image of a handwritten signature that is attached to an electronic document, a secret code or PIN (such as that used with ATM cards and credit cards) to identify the sender to the recipient; a code or "handle" that the sender of a message uses to identify himself; a unique biometrics-based identifier, such as a fingerprint or a retinal scan; and a digital signature. Different states have slightly different definitions of related terms. In the following section, a sample of state definitions is provided.

Legal Regulation of Electronic Commerce Taxation

Globalization has some problematic consequences, one of which impacts on the collection of taxes. Electronic commerce itself poses a number of distinct problems for taxation authorities around the world. Electronic commerce is borderless and promotes disinter mediation, which makes tax collection complex. Where previously an undertaking from one state would export to an importer from another, which would then resell to local businesses, the local business are now faced with the opportunity to deal directly with the exporter. This results in a whole swathe of cross border transactions instead of only one.

Electronic Commerce is bringing about changes not only in the physical characteristics of products but also in the way in which they are delivered. A common example is software that can be downloaded over the Internet instead of being bought in a shop. This raises important questions as to the nature of the software. Few would argue that software bought in the shop is a product. The same software downloaded must also be a product. This is more than simply some irrelevant debate over definitions.

On 23 June 1998 the US House of Representatives passed the Internet Tax Freedom Act which creates a body designed to consider possible changes in the law of taxation on the Internet.. The Act includes provisions for a ban on new local and state taxes that discriminate against electronic commerce. It also calls for the US Administration to put pressure on other countries to refrain from taxation of the Internet. According to the Information Technology Association of America, there should be no discrimination between products on the basis of whether they were sold on-line or by conventional means. They single out the case of purchasing tangible goods over the Internet, which are later delivered. These, says the ITAA, should be treated in the same way as mail order purchases.

The taxation problems raised by electronic commerce problems are very real, especially if growth is as rapid as some have predicted. There is the possibility that a large percentage of government revenue may be removed from the system. If treated correctly, electronic commerce could be a major source of wealth creation. It must thus be given the opportunity to grow and create wealth.

CONCLUSION

Development of Internet and e-commerce has posed new challenges to the law in an unprecedented way. Both scholars and legislators are searching for ways to respond to this new e-commerce environment. One of main purposes of imposing regulations is to protect consumers. When legislative efforts are focused on things like electronic signatures, the regulation is for the benefit of all participating parties. Taxing policies, on the other hand, are meant to ensure the fair distribution of wealth. However, the changes in the business environment due to the emergence of e-commerce is going to have a significant impact on how we are going to design e-commerce systems in future. It is thus imperative to study the impact of the legal environment on e-commerce.

REFERENCES

The authors will provide references by request.

Federal Agency Intranets: Worksites for Management Problem Solving and Collaboration

Julianne G. Mahler and Priscilla M. Regan
Department of Public and International Affairs, George Mason University
Tel: (703) 993-1419 or (703) 993-1414, Fax: (703) 993-1399, {jmahler, pregan}@gmu.edu

While e-government initiatives have focused on effective linkages with citizens and businesses, there is growing interest in Intranets for linkages between government and its employees. Such linkages provide opportunities for agency actors to create professional work groups by initiating online collaboration. Agency intelligence and capacity can be enhanced by interactive agency management and increased communication among task group members. While promise is great, little data has been collected to determine the state of Intranet development. The purpose of our research is to describe Intranet development in the federal government; identify trends in use, sources of growth, and impediments to development; and analyze the conditions under which the potential of the Intranet for enhancing agency capacity and intelligence is likely to be realized.

The growing interest in Intranets is spurred by their usefulness as management tools to foster productive communication and coordination, manage information, and encourage self-organizing work teams. Business to employee (B2E) Intranets are developing rapidly because of their advantages in optimizing strategic communications. Allcorn (1997) identifies the "parallel virtual organization" composed of an Intranet and organizational databases as the information and knowledge management model for the future. Curry and Stancich (2000) identify the advantages of the Intranet for strategic decisionmaking. GAO cites Southwest Airlines as an exemplar of the uses of Intranets for informal communication among members at dispersed work sites to develop a culture of teamwork and pride (GAO/GGD-00-28).

Many have noted the use of Intranets for speeding and personalizing human resources functions in organizations (Holz, 1997). GAO reports uses of Intranets to foster human capital development in private firms that can serve as models for government (GAO/GGD-00-28). GAO reports an ideal use at Federal Express where senior managers apply an automated Intranet-based tool to assess leadership skills, potential and development needs of mid-level managers so that new assignments and promotions can be made quickly and effectively.

A number of federal agencies have reported plans to develop Intranets, but the extent of the content and the level of actual use in agencies vary widely.

For example, Intranets are central to the IRS reform efforts by providing a communications strategy for informing staff about changes in tax law, policy and procedures, and improving agency-wide communication (GAO/GGD-00-85). The National Resources Center, the IRS's Intranet web site, was created in 1998 to serve as a site for centralized guidance on policy and procedures, to provide a way to disseminate answers to employee questions so that all staff would have the same answers, and to provide training.

Other examples of Intranet uses for management are included in GAO's report on successful strategies by Chief Information Officers for enhancing agency information and knowledge management (GAO/GAO-01-376G). One example is the use of the agency Intranet to make press clippings available to staff, a significant improvement in speed and cost from traditional methods. In the Veterans Health Administration, Intranet access to performance information such as patient satisfaction data is used to encourage improvement (GAO/GAO-01-376G).

RESEARCH QUESTIONS AND HYPOTHESES

Based on the development of Intranets and e-government solutions in the federal government we expected to find a range of Intranet designs and purposes from simple newscasts to sophisticated portals linking members to sites for human resources needs, travel planning, training, and self-designed collaborative linkages. We found a narrower range of designs than expected. The reasons for this and other patterns in the development of the Intranets emerge from the individual case studies.

We interviewed several individuals in six departments. We began to identify these agencies and the offices and actors within them from leads provided by the Chief Information Officer's Council, its e-Government Committee, and its Intranet Roundtable. Additional contacts were recommended by these actors. Our rationale for case selection cases was that we wanted to optimize our chances of finding the most advanced examples rather than a representative sample of all stages of Intranet development. Case studies of agencies with little Intranet experience would not have as much to tell us about their potential or use. The emerging vision of Intranets as key management tools is more easily observed in agencies that are more advanced in their exploration of uses and limitations.

We posed questions about the current state of agency Intranets, their origins, and major changes to the site. In several cases we were able to document the design of sites at different stages of development. We questioned actors about the original purposes and motivations behind Intranet creation. We tried to determine what pressures within the federal setting might encourage Intranets. We also probed the sources and level of resources. The composition and mission definition of the Intranet development teams were investigated. We also became aware as research progressed of the need for agencies to encourage Intranet recognition and usage, and so we came to collect stories about how the Intranet was marketed to agency staff. Finally we investigated other factors that appear to have encouraged or impeded Intranet development.

CASE STUDIES

Department of Transportation

Existing Intranets in each of the agency's eleven operating divisions preceded efforts to establish a single, unifying Intranet. Management designers hoped to carve out a place for it by identifying cross-cutting features. Efforts to make the site attractive included using existing terminology rather than requiring users to learn a new vocabulary of work functions. Another feature is that each worker's home page can be personalized. A feature allowing interest-based groups to form and to collaborate on line has drawn many adherents.

Department of Housing and Urban Development

In contrast to Transportation, the HUD@work Intranet was the only internal net in the agency. It developed rapidly as a communications tool. It had a staff separate from the Internet team, which is unusual, and headed up by a manager who designed it to carry out management tasks. The Intranet had top level support from the HUD Secretary and was designated as the site to report downsizing decisions. These factors contributed to high use rates.

Environmental Protection Agency

The EPA Intranet was created by a team of information resource management professionals. The first version was composed of text-based links. Despite the capacity of the Intranet to support chat and collaborative work, respondents suggest the site is underused. Major marketing efforts are slowly getting underway.

General Services Administration

The GSA Intranet was created by a former private sector web designer. Travel and human resources links were first offered. Over two years the site grew in features and popularity. Now it is a work site as well as a document site. A simple bulletin board site increased in use when the Administrator began to monitor it and make comments. Rewards for good suggestions made on the site have further increased its worth.

Department of Commerce

This Intranet, like the one at Transportation, faces challenges because of seven pre-existing divisional intranets. Investigation of one of these intranets, in Commercial Service, indicates that it is a well-developed collection of work tools for identifying client matches and scheduling events. The site is a joint product of a few contractors and CS staff. The Intranet for the Department as a whole was built quickly in response to calls for "digital democracy." It has functioned as a document site with an information resources management design team. Visits to the site have not been as numerous as designers had hoped, and efforts are underway to improve its usefulness.

Department of Justice

Like Commerce and Transportation, Justice houses a number of units with separate identities and their own Intranets. Both the Internet and Intranet are maintained and designed by the same staff group, composed of computer technicians and library information resource specialists. The Intranet content is now a component of the DOJ library. The site is largely non-interactive at present. It offers links to the most recent Department policy files. The next generation of the Intranet is to be more interactive, but this will take a major change in architecture and represents a huge investment. The information resource staff will depend on the Internet builders in the Department for this advance.

TRENDS

The case studies reveal six overall trends in Intranet use and development.

- *Within federal agencies, more attention and energy is devoted to the agency's Internet than to its Intranet.* This is not remarkable given legislative and public support for online Government to Citizen interactions, the federal government's commitment to digital government, and the number of Internet champions. Despite this, all agencies are experimenting with transferring Internet technology and software, as well as the knowledge gained from developing and deploying Internet websites, to an internal agency Intranet.
- *Upper management active support for and interest in the agency's Intranet is especially critical in initial planning and launching.* In virtually all the agencies examined, support from the Secretary or Deputy Secretary level was essential.
- *Marketing of an agency Intranet is crucial in encouraging staff use.* In some agencies, actual advertising campaigns were developed. In other agencies, events were held to publicize and showcase the Intranet. Active promotion was regarded as critical by all agencies.
- *Agency-wide Intranets co-exist with bureau, program and field office Intranets.* This is evidence of the usefulness of an internal, closed website. It may be that there is an optimal size for Intranet utility and functionality. In most agencies examined, the agency-wide Intranet was eclipsed by sub-agency Intranets. It would appear that most of the work of the department occurs in the smaller units and those Intranets are more valuable to staff on a day-to-day basis.
- Cost constraints limit the ability of agencies to purchase the applications and the consultant work they would like.
- *To date, Intranet applications in some agencies are limited to providing one-way information on fairly mundane agency tasks such as room scheduling and cafeteria menus.* But many agencies are adding interactive services such as travel arrangements and personnel record changes. Only a few agencies are developing more interactive managerial uses such as online collaborative work groups and personalized Intranet home pages. Security concerns in some cases limit interconnectedness.

ANALYSIS

Preliminary analysis indicates that there may be several pathways for Intranet development. In some agencies Intranets were designed by information technology specialists with little guidance regarding potential management uses. In others mid-level managers controlled the early formation of Intranets. In a few agencies, top-level management supported an Intranet because they wanted to appear progressive but had little understanding of its potential or any particular expectations for its use. In still other agencies much of the design of an Intranet was in the hands of information resource managers. Each of these paths gave rise to different objectives, technologies, and results.

We found that Intranet development is most effectively directed by administrative staff and program managers, rather than by technical staff. This ensures that employee desires and organizational needs define intranet functions and applications. When decisions are driven by technical capacity, employees must readjust work habits to suit the new technology, discouraging use. The IRM model creates portal sites with potential for management use, but without the configuration that makes the site useful for coordination and performance feedback, core management concerns. To be utilized and functional, Intranet technology should support employee and organizational needs. If management and staff needs drive development, new technical features may be created. Managers can challenge technical people to find appropriate solutions that may spur new technological solutions.

REFERENCES

Allcorn, Seth. 1997. Parallel virtual organizations: managing and working in the virtual workplace. *Administration and Society* 29:412-39.

Curry, Adrienne and Lara Stancich. 2000. The Intranet—an intrinsic component of strategic information management? *International Journal of Information Management* 20:249-68 (August).

Holz, Shel. 1997. Strategizing a human resources presence on the Intranet.

Compensation and Benefits Management 13:31-7 (Autumn).

GAO Human Capital: Key Principles From Nine Private Sector Organizations

(Letter Report, 01/31/2000, GAO/GGD-00-28).

GAO Executive Guide: Maximizing the Success of Chief Information Officers:

Learning From Leading Organizations. (Guidance, 02/01/2001, GAO/GAO-01-376G).

GAO Tax Administration: IRS' Implementation of the Restructuring Act's

Taxpayer Protection and Rights Provisions (Letter Report, 04/21/2000, GAO/GGD-00-85).

MERLOT TWO—Teaching Well Online

Dr. Sorel Reisman
College of Business and Economics, California State University
Tel: (714) 278-3325, sreisman@fullerton.edu

Dr. Gerry Hanley
California State University, Office of the Chancellor
Tel: (562) 951-4000, ghanley@calstate.edu

ABSTRACT

This paper will describe the online electronic community MERLOT (Multimedia Educational Resource for Learning and Online Teaching), and the functionality of the recent extension, TWO (Teaching Well Online).

BACKGROUND

In 1997, the California State University (CSU) Center for Distributed Learning (CDL) developed and began providing free student and faculty access to a new online resource called MERLOT. Since that time MERLOT has become an open source collection of thousands of web-based learning materials, with over 2,000 individual members.

In 1999, the University of Georgia System, Oklahoma State Regents for Higher Education, University of North Carolina System, and the California State University System recognized the significant benefits of a cooperative initiative to expand the MERLOT collections, conduct peer reviews of the digital learning materials, and add student learning assignments. Each system contributed $20,000 to develop the MERLOT software and over $30,000 in in-kind support to advance the collaborative project. The CSU maintained its leadership of and responsibilities for the operation and improvement of processes and tools.

In January, 2000, the four systems sponsored 48 faculty from the disciplines of Biology, Physics, Business and Teacher Education (12 faculty from each of the four systems) to develop evaluation standards and peer review processes for on-line teaching-learning material. In April, 2000, other systems and institutions of higher education were invited to join the MERLOT cooperative. In July, 2000, twenty-three (23) systems and institutions of higher education had become Institutional Partners of MERLOT, each contributing $25,000 and support for eight faculty and a part-time project director to coordinate MERLOT activities.

Since that time, with a continually growing collection of learning materials, assignments and reviews, MERLOT has become a community of contributing individual members who strive to enrich teaching and learning. Individuals can become members by creating a profile that becomes public to users, but is not available to others. MERLOT member-faculty can add teaching-learning materials, comments, and assignments to the MERLOT collection. As well, MERLOT's discipline-set has expanded to include Biology, Business, Chemistry, Engineering, Health Sciences, History, Information Technology, Mathematics, Music, Psychology, Teacher Education, Physics, and World Languages.

MERLOT TWO

In 1999, the California State University System (CSU) and MERLOT's institutional partners identified as a priority, the need to develop and include in MERLOT, functionality to support the integration of technology in teaching and learning. As a result, the CSU Institute for Teaching and Learning (ITL) and the Academic Technology Services of the CSU Office of the Chancellor initiated a collaboration to support the development of an online community for "teaching and learning online" – MERLOT TWO (Teaching Well Online). The MERLOT TWO website would be a searchable database of materials that would provide college and university faculty, faculty development personnel, academic technology staff, and others interested in technology mediated instruction, with online resources for using technology to improve teaching and learning.

MERLOT TWO was designed to answer the following kinds of instructor questions?

- What are the benefits of teaching a Web-based course?
- Can I use technology to adapt instruction to different student learning styles?
- How can I find examples of good distance learning courses?
- What kinds of tools and technologies are available for TMI?
- How can a technological tool assist various methods of teaching and learning?
- Which course management system should I use?
- Are there guidelines or "best practices" for teaching online?
- How can I find supplemental and/or Web-based material for student activities in my own discipline?
- What are the pros and cons of online student collaboration?
- What tools and techniques are available to facilitate students-to-student, or student-to-instructor communication?
- How can I evaluate student "online performance?"
- Is there a scholarly discipline concerned with TMI, and are there conferences and publications that focus on this?
- Are there institutional or government policies concerning TMI of which I should be aware?

Ongoing Work

This presentation will present the status of MERLOT TWO, focusing on its continued evolution, and the functionality it provides to multidisciplinary online, teaching/learning electronic community members.

Knowledge Stickiness During Systems Development: The Role of Knowledge Characteristics, Systems Users, and System Developers

K. D. Joshi and Saonee Sarker*
Washington State University, Tel: (509) 335-5772, Fax: (509) 335-4275, {joshi, ssarker}@wsu.edu

ABSTRACT

Information systems development (ISD) remains a topic of great interest for IS researchers. Literature suggests that the lack of user-developer knowledge transfer is one of the possible causes of ISD failures, a phenomenon that has not been adequately studied. Therefore, the objective of this study is to examine the factors that impede the transfer of knowledge between users and systems developers during ISD. Currently, a pilot study is being conducted to gain an understanding of "knowledge stickiness" during ISD and to validate the newly developed instrument that measures its determinants.

INTRODUCTION

Knowledge transfer is one of the most important activities of knowledge management (Holsapple and Joshi, forthcoming). The literature suggests that knowledge transfer is an extremely important and complex process and often witness tremendous difficulties (Zander & Kogut, 1995; Szulanski, 1996, 2000). However, these studies examined the transfer of best practices and knowledge among organizational units, or between strategic alliances and partners. We are interested in extending their work by examining the knowledge transfer process in light of information systems development.

Information systems development process (ISD) remains a topic of great interest for IS researchers, especially due to the increase in the number of ISD failures (Guinana, Cooprider, and Faraj, 1998). Different factors such as the user's inability to specify the necessary systems requirements (Boland, 1978) and the developers' inability to elicit requirements from the users and follow those requirements in systems design and development (Davis, 1982), has been cited as possible cause of ISD failures. However, in spite of this realization, ISD research has not focused on the dimensions of knowledge transfer that may be impeding the successful transfer of knowledge between the users and the developers. Taking a knowledge management perspective, this study focuses on the specifics of the nature of knowledge, the characteristics of the users and the developers, and the characteristics of their relationship that affect the transfer of the system requirements knowledge during an ISD process, leading to the research question:

What are the determinants that constrain or facilitate the transfer of knowledge between users and systems developers during an information systems development process?

BRIEF LITERATURE REVIEW

Knowledge Transfer

Szulanski (1996) examined the impediments to the transfer of best practices in the firm and concluded that the major barriers to knowledge transfer are the lack of absorptive capacity of the knowledge recipient, the nature of the knowledge transferred (i.e., tacitness), and the relationship among the source and the recipient. From a study of the transfer of marketing know-how, Simonin (1999) concluded that knowledge tacitness has a significant impact on knowledge ambiguity, and thus, on the knowledge transfer process. Bresman et al (1999) conducted a study of knowledge transfer in international acquisitions and concluded that communication and frequency of the meetings were significant predictors of knowledge transfer.

Stickiness in Information Systems Development

In our study, knowledge transfer refers to the process where the source (i.e., the system users) communicates the system requirements (the task related knowledge required to build the system) to the recipient (i.e., system developers). Stickiness refers to the difficulty experienced in this process (Szulanski, 1996, 2000). Although, ISD research recognizes the existence of stickiness during the systems development process (Walz, et al, 1993), information systems researchers have paid little attention to the understanding of the origins of stickiness. The degree of stickiness in a transfer process is partially determined by the nature of knowledge (von Hippel, 1994), by the characteristics of the source and the recipient, and the nature of relationship cultivated by the source and the recipient over the system development process (Szulanski, 1996; Simonin, 1999).

THEORETICAL MODEL

Based on the literature, the model (see figure 1) posits that the *nature of knowledge*, the *characteristics of the source and the recipient*, and the *relationship and interaction between them* collectively conspire to cause stickiness during an ISD process. Each of these three constructs is briefly described in this section.

Knowledge Specific Determinants of Stickiness

The three knowledge specific properties that appear to be salient during systems development are knowledge tacitness, knowledge specificity, and knowledge complexity. Knowledge tacitness refers to that aspect of knowledge that cannot be easily and readily communicated and/or shared (Polanyi, 1967; Nonaka, 1994). Knowledge specificity is defined as specific skills and knowledge used in performing the task(s) that the system is going to support. Past research in the transfer of marketing knowledge has shown that knowledge specificity affects stickiness (Simonin, 1999). Complexity refers to the number of interdependent tasks, individuals, and resources linked to a particular knowledge asset that is being transferred (Simonin, 1999). In the context of systems development, knowledge is considered to be complex if the knowledge about the task(s) that the system will support is distributed across various individuals or departments.

Source and Recipient Specific Determinants of Stickiness

The source and the recipient specific determinants of stickiness refer to the attributes/characteristics of users and system developers, which can be potential causes of barriers to the process of knowledge

* corresponding author

transfer. Attributes include the domain experience of the source and the recipient (Zander and Kogut, 1995), the reliability of the source (Szulanski, 1996), a lack of motivation of the source/recipient (Szulanski, 1996), the degree of absorptive and retentive capacity of the recipient (Szulanski, 1996).

Source and Recipient Relationship and Interaction Specific Determinants of Stickiness

Drawing on the literature it can also be argued that the success of knowledge transfer between the users and the developers can also be measured by the extent of perceived collaboration between the users and the developers, the nature and frequency of communication between them, and the interpersonal and communication related skills of the users and the developers (Nonaka, 1994; Szulanski, 1996 ; Simonin, 1999).

Figure 1: The research model

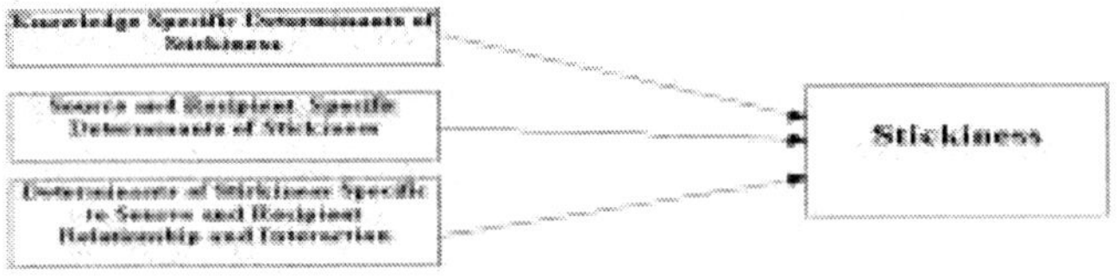

METHODOLOGY

An initial pilot study has been conducted to validate the newly developed instrument measuring the determinants of knowledge transfer, and also to gain an initial understanding of stickiness during an ISD process. Student teams in a large public U.S university played the role of systems developers and developed information systems for external clients. The systems development process was divided into three phases: outlining system requirements, creating system design, and building a system. Data was collected in all three phases and is yet to be analyzed. It is hoped that the three constructs in our study (i.e., the nature of knowledge, the characteristics of the user and the recipient, and the relationship between them) may show varying impacts on stickiness at each of these phases.

Measures

The research model consists of one dependent variable and eleven independent variables. The dependent variable is the stickiness of the knowledge. This was operationalized as the level of satisfaction of the product delivered and the quality of the information exchanged between the user and the developers. The dependent variable was measured using items such as: "The outcome of the initial phase (creation of project ID and proposal) of the project met my expectations." Another item measuring the dependent variable was "I am satisfied with the quality of the information/knowledge provided by the user." The items measuring the dependent variable were modified from the set of eight items used by Szulanski (1996). These items were initially drawn from Pinto and Mantel's (1990) technical success indicators of a project.

The three independent variables are knowledge specific determinants of stickiness, source/recipient specific determinants of stickiness, and determinants of stickiness specific to the source and the recipient relationship. The knowledge specific determinants of stickiness were operationalized as the perceived tacitness, knowledge specificity, and complexity. Perceived tacitness was measured by the codifiability and the causal ambiguity of the knowledge. Items measuring codifiability were drawn from Zander and Kogut (1995). For example, an item such as "The problem statement can be easily described in a written form," measured the codifiability of the knowledge. Similarly, items such as "it was difficult to understand at this point the problem scenario for which the system needs to be built," were drawn from Szulanski (1996) and were used to measure the causal ambiguity of the knowledge.

The study drew on the work of Simonin (1999) to develop the items for measuring complexity. A sample item is: "in order to fully understand the nature of the business process for which the system is going to be built, the system developer has to invest significant amount of time and resources." Finally, complexity was measured with items such as "this system will be one of the most complex systems among the currently existing systems within our organization."

The second independent variable, source and recipient specific determinants of stickiness was operationalized as the domain experience of the user and the developers, the unreliability of the user, the lack of motivation of both the users and the developers, and the lack of the absorptive and the retentive capacity of the developers and the users respectively. Items were mostly drawn from Szulanski (1996) and were modified to make it appropriate for the context of the current study. Some example items are: 1) Users/system developers were very involved in the initial phase (creation of the project proposal) of the project; and 2) Users/systems developers appear to be disinterested in the initial phase (creation of the project proposal) of the project.

Finally, the third independent variable (determinants of stickiness specific to source and recipient relationship and interaction) was operationalized as the degree of collaboration between the users and the systems developers, the degree of communication between the two stakeholders, the number of meetings held between the users and the developers, and the interpersonal and communication-related skills of either party. Items were primarily drawn from the work of Szulanski (1996). Some sample items are: 1) Collaboration between the user and the system developers was sought actively by the user; and 2) There is a lack of good communication between the user and the system developers, etc.

CONCLUSION

The objective of this research is to examine the factors that create barriers (i.e., stickiness) in the transfer of knowledge during an ISD process. The past ISD research recognizes the existence of stickiness during systems development. However, to our knowledge, nobody has examined this issue through the lens of knowledge management. In this respect, this paper makes a significant contribution to both the fields of knowledge management and ISD.

REFERENCES

Boland, R.J., Jr. (2978). The Process and Product of System Design. *Management Science*, 24:9, pp. 887-898.

Bresman, H., Birkinshaw, & J. Nobel, R. (1999). Knowledge transfer in international acquisitions. *Journal of International Business Studies*, 30:3, pp. 439-462.

Davis, G.B. (1982). Strategies for Information Requirements Determination. *IBM Systems Journal*, 21, pp. 4-30.

Guinan, P.J., Cooprider, J.G., and Faraj, S. (1998). Enabling Software Development Team Performance During Requirements Definition: A Behavioral Versus technical Approach. *Information Systems Research*, 9:2, pp. 101-125.

Holsapple C. W. & Joshi, K. D. (Forthcoming). Knowledge Manipulation Activities: Results of A Delphi Study. *Information and Management.*

Nonaka, I. (1994). A Dynamic Theory Of Organizational Knowledge Creation. *Organization Science*, 5:1, pp. 14-37.

Polanyi, Michael. (1967). *The Tacit Dimension*. Garden City, NY: Anchor.

Simonin, B. (1999). Transfer of marketing know-how in international strategic alliances: An empirical investigation of the role and antecedents of knowledge ambiguity. *Journal of International Business Studies*, 30:3, pp. 463-490.

Szulanski, Gabriel. 1996. Exploring internal stickiness: Impediments to the transfer of best practice within the firm. *Strategic Management Journal*, 17:Winter, pp. 27-43.

von Hippel, E. 1994. "'Sticky Information' and the Locus of Problem Solving: Implications for Innovation," *Management Science*, 40: 4, pp. 429-439.

Walz, D.B., Elam, J.J. et al. (1993). Inside a Software Design Team: Knowledge Acquisition, Sharing, and Integration. *Communications of the ACM*, 36:10, pp. 36.

Zander, U. & Kogut, B. (1995). Knowledge and the speed of the transfer and imitation of organizational capabilities: An Empirical Test. *Organization Science*, 6:1, pp. 76-92.

The Role of the Organizational Context in the Implementation of a Workflow System

Anabela Sarmento
ISCAP – IPP - R. Dr. Jaime Lopes de Amorim, Portugal, asarment@mail.telepac.pt

INTRODUCTION

Companies are adopting Workflow Systems to ensure a better response to the challenges and opportunities of the economic environment.

Workflow Systems (WS), present themselves as one solution able to improve the efficiency and management of organisational processes. They make at one's disposal communication tools allowing collaboration, information share, knowledge and coordination of work. They also support organisational processes and work teams, providing tools to facilitate informal communication, automation and reduction of time of task accomplishment, allowing the realisation of work in a more efficient, effective and creative manner [Khoshafian, 1995; Jablonski, 1996].

Research about these systems has paid much attention to the phase of development and implementation of a system, forgetting what happens after the adoption, that is during the use of it. Also, care has been taken to the technological aspects of the systems, neglecting the characteristics of the organization and the users. Yet, we know that much of the success of the adoption of a system depends, not on the technology but on the context where it is used.

Aware of this fact, I tried to fill this gap, identifying several contextual factors that influence the use of a WS. After building a framework of analysis, I apply it to a case study. I present and discuss the results.

FRAMEWORK OF ANALYSIS

Literature revealed that the adoption and use of a technology can be mediated and conditioned by several factors, namely: (1) Technological Factors, that includes the characteristics of the technology to be adopted and the technology already existing in the organisation; (2) Structural Factors, that means the organisational design, the complexity, the number of hierarchical level, the number of departments, the centralisation or decentralisation of power and decision making, the coordination of tasks, the formalisation of procedures, the design of tasks and jobs and the specialisation; (3) Social and Individual Factors that includes the multidisciplinary work teams, their distribution in time and space, their education, training, work satisfaction, skills and individual characteristics; (4) Political Factors, that means who decides about the kind of technology to adopt, its design and implementation, who is going to use it, with its purposes and objectives; and (5) Cultural Factors, that includes the culture, norms, rules and the reaction to change, and the knowledge and organisational learning capacity [Bolman and Deal, 1997; Bertrand and Guillemet, 1988].

These factors cannot be analysed isolatedly. They interact with each other, influencing the result of the adoption and use of new Information Technology (IT). For example, if people, in the organization, feel that the adoption of new IT will make them loose power, they will develop some obstacles in order not to use it. In an organization with a proactive culture that stimulates change, the adoption and use of new IT will be easier.

METHODOLOGY

Data Collection and Analysis

This framework was applied to a Portuguese company that implemented a WS. This was a longitudinal study. I accompanied the enterprise since it was decided to implement the system till around 9 months after full use of it.

Data collection was done between May 1999 and July 2000. I used observation, document review and semi structured interviews. I collected several documents about the enterprise and also about the process where the WS was going to be implemented. The interviews were done in three different moments. The first one occurred before the adoption of the system. The purpose of these interviews was to know how people worked, their vision of the enterprise and their expectations regarding the system. The second and the third moments occurred one month and between 6 and 9 months respectively, after the beginning of use of the system. The objective of these interviews was to know what kind of changes people had identified and the reasons behind these changes.

The interviews spanned all levels of the company and all the potential users of the system. They were fully recorded and transcribed. I used qualitative techniques to analyse data (Miles and Huberman, 1994), and whenever necessary used the NUD*IST program.

The Organization

Fieldwork was conducted with a company, Alpha Corporation (pseudonym). This organization was founded in December 1985 and it is located in the North of Portugal. In the early days, they copied hospital radiology images into microfilm. Later, around 1996, the company expanded into consulting and programming activities in Electronic Documentation Storing. In 1998, the company developed a Document and Database Filing System, which is part of an Electronic Document Management System that has been internally developed.

Although it started as a family business, this company currently employs 45 workers, whose average age is 28 years old. The staff is now distributed in a linear and functional hierarchical structure with three levels that comprise the following departments: Administrative and Financial (AFD), Commercial, Quality, Research & Development (R&D), Marketing, SAP, Technical Support and Production.

Each department has only one or two employees, except production, which has more than half of the employees of the firm. The top of the hierarchy is composed of three partners to whom all the departments report.

In technological terms, the company is well equipped. Almost all the employees have a college degree, except two members: one from AFD, who has completed secondary school, and the Production Director, who has the 9th grade of secondary school. These two members will be the ones that will use the new system most regularly.

Generally speaking, the employees of this firm are interested, committed and are willing to learn. They help each other whenever needed and do not seem afraid of showing ignorance or expressing difficulties in any situation.

Power and decision-making are centralized in the top of the hierarchy. Internal communication is easy. Informal ties are very important replacing, sometimes, formal relations.

The word that best describes the culture of this firm is technology. This is supported by the area of business, the architecture, the available technologies, the existence of a R&D department, the employee's background and training and by the general attitude towards the development of the company and the maintenance of the company's market share.

The Process

The process chosen to incorporate the WS was the purchase process and in particular the stationery material. This process is composed of two sub-processes: one concerns the internal demand and the other the order to the supplier. In 9 months of full use of the new system there were 73 internal demands and consequently 73 orders. Approximately 75% of these internal orders were made by two employees – the element of AFD and the Production Director. All the other users only made, in the same period of time, one or three internal demands.

The Workflow System

The system adopted was the Metro from Action Technologies, which is based on the work of Medina-Mora, Winograd *et al.* [1992]. This system is web based, which means that the environment where the employees work is similar to an Internet site. This system was chosen mainly because Action Technologies is a business partner of Alpha Corporation, and so access to the material and information needed to develop and implement the system would be considerable facilitated. With this WS, all tasks can be performed from each employee's desk. He /she only has to open the Internet browser and the site that corresponds to the purchase process. From there, he / she can choose to fill in an internal order, see the status of his /her previous orders and check information about his/her purchase behaviour, that is, when and how many internal orders he / she has placed, and the most ordered items.

After filling in the internal order, it is sent electronically to the AFD. The employee of AFD opens up the page of the purchase process daily and checks if there are any internal orders to process. If so, she fills in an order to the supplier by opening the MS Word and the fax program. This operation was not easy at the beginning, as the computer machine allocated to this employee did not have enough memory, and blocked constantly. Whenever the material arrives, she informs her colleagues, electronically or by phone. After picking up the material, the applicant has to open the site again and register his /her satisfaction with the process.

IDENTIFICATION OF ORGANIZATIONAL FACTORS

I identified two types of organizational factors: the constrainers and the enablers of change.

Constrainers

The use of the new WS in Alpha was not implemented entirely without problems. For example, the person in charge of collecting internal orders and of passing the order to the supplier had some difficulties in using the system, as her computer would block constantly, because the system overloaded. Besides, this person also revealed that she had some difficulties in understanding the functioning of the system at the beginning. The requirement of formally finishing any purchase process by expressing satisfaction was especially problematic. This step, although relatively simple, was creating problems because it was seen as unnecessary.

The members of staff who experienced more difficulties in adapting to the new system were those with fewer schooling years. I cannot say for sure that their difficulties were only due to lack of a college education background, as the data available do not allow such an extrapolation. However, the fact that those with a college degree had fewer problems in using the new system does corroborate this hypothesis, which in turn seems to point to the possibility that a college education may help develop some competencies and skills that are easily transferred whenever change and obstacles have to be dealt with.

Finally, some characteristics of tasks may constrain the use of the system. In this case, the purchase process is not crucial to the business and is not performed regularly (except for the element of AFD and the Production Director). Those that perform this task sporadically shown more difficulties in acquiring a work routine than those that do it regularly.

Enablers

In spite of the difficulties described above, there were some factors that seem to facilitate the use of the system. One of these factors is precisely the educational background of the staff members. Most of the employees have a college degree. I would suggest that their educational background seems to allow them to develop some skills and competencies that helped to adapt and respond positively to the new system.

Employee's personality may also play a role in the successful adaptation to the use of the system. Both the member of AFD and the Production Director showed interest and wanted to know how it worked, although they were the ones who experienced more difficulties in learning how to use the system. In fact, of all members of staff, the member of AFD was the one who expressed interest in knowing what the menus were about. She even started to gather information about how many orders she received by person and department and the kind of material most demanded.

Another aspect that seemed to enable the use of this system was precisely the fact that this WS, the Metro, runs in a Web-based platform. To use it, employees only need to know how to navigate in the Internet and understand the reasoning behind this application.

As mentioned above, regular tasks enable the use of the system. Those employees who used the system more regularly (element of AFD and the Production Director) after a while became experts in its use and considered themselves to be so.

Finally, I would like to refer the culture of Alpha as an enabler of change. This enterprise works in a market where changes are rapid, which requires constant updating in order to remain competitive. So, changes are not unusual, but rather inevitable to be able to maintain, and ideally, increase, their market share. Therefore, the predominant ethos of this company helped to create a positive attitude towards change.

It should be noted that these factors are not isolated but interdependent. Moreover, I cannot say that one is more important than the other, as they interact almost simultaneously.

CONCLUSIONS

This paper describes a framework designed to assess the impact of the adoption of a WS in a company and its application to a case study.

Results showed that the organizational factors that constrained or enabled changes in this case were: the frequency of the performance of the task; the characteristics of the WS adopted; the existing technologies; the employees and the culture of the organization. As these factors are interdependent, being the outcome of the adoption of a WS the result of the interaction between all of them. Being aware of which factors might interact beforehand will contribute to a better management of the process of change.

REFERENCES

Bertrand, Y. and Guillemet, P. (1988). *Organizações: Uma abordagem sistémica.* Lisboa: Instituto Piaget.

Bolman, L. and Deal, T. (1997). *Reframing Organizations: Artistry, Choice and Leadership.* San Francisco: Jossey-Bass Publishers.

Jablonski, S. B. (1996). *Workflow Management: modelling concepts, architecture and implementation.* London: International Thomson Computer.

Khoshafian, S. B.. (1995). *Introduction to Groupware, Workflow and Workgroup Computing.* New York: John Wiley.

Medina-Mora, R., Winograd, T. et al. (1992), Action Workflow approach to workflow management technology, *Proceedings of the Conference Computer Supported Cooperative Work (CSCW'92)*, p. 281-288.

Miles, M. and Huberman, M. (1994), *Qualitative Data Analysis*, London: SAGE Publications.

A Learning Process: Some Reflections about AR

Anabela Sarmento, João Batista, Leonor Cardoso, Mário Lousã, Rosalina Babo and Teresa Rebelo
MOISIG
moisig@iscap.ipp.pt

INTRODUCTION

MOISIG is a group of researchers composed of six members who come from different areas of knowledge, as well as from different regions of Portugal. Common interests and goals set them together and push them to go further. This group tries to develop knowledge in the area of Management, Organizations and Information Systems. It has been in existence for two years from now and during this period its members have carried out together several projects concerning their common interests (Cardoso *et al* 2000; Sarmento *et al* 2000a; Sarmento *et al* 2000b; Batista *et al* 2001).

One of the main concerns of the group is to continuously improve the way its members communicate among themselves, as it is difficult to conciliate spare time to meet in person, whenever needed.

Although the group already uses media to communicate, namely email and a mailing list built in yahoo egroups, its members need, in different moments of projects, to be synchronized in time, even if that means not being at the same place.

To solve this problem, the group decided to use a new application based on the peer-to-peer (P2P) approach (Lousã *et al* 2001): the Groove (http://www.groove.net). In order to learn how to use this application, as well as to develop group's communication, it seemed that Action Research methodology (Baskerville 1998) could be appropriate as it implied a reflective process about the results before further intervention.

This paper is organized in the following way: in the next section we will briefly characterize what is Action Research. Then, we describe the methodology used in this case, followed by the outcomes. Finally we discuss the results and point out the solutions that arose after the reflection.

ACTION RESEARCH

Baskerville (1998) describes action research as being a method that merges action and praxis. It is a cognitive process that depends on the social interaction between the observer and those being observed. Action research is a two simple moments process: the diagnostic stage that involves an analysis of the social situation in which the hypotheses are formulated. It is followed by the therapeutic stage that involves experiments. In this stage changes are introduced and the effects are studied.

Action Research can be distinguished by a wide variety of characteristics: the process model, the structure, the typical research involvement and the primary goals. The process model can be iterative, reflective or linear; the structure can be rigorous or fluid; the typical involvement can be collaborative, facilitative or expert, and finally, primary goals can be organizational development, system design, scientific knowledge or training.

METHODOLOGY

We used the canonical action research process model of Susman (1983) (see Figure 1).

This type of Action Research has the following dominant characteristics: it is an iterative model as it involves a repeating sequence of activities, cycling between action activities and problem diagnosis activities; has a rigorous structure, characterised by delineated stages, steps or activities carried out in a sequence or cycle, or selected according to rules or heuristics; the typical research involvement is collaborative as it implies that the researcher is an equal co-worker with the study subjects. As for the primary goals, they can be the organizational development and / or scientific knowledge development and it is possible that both may occur in the same study. In this case, the organizational development is replaced by a group development, as MOISIG is a group and not an organization.

As we can see in figure 1, this model identifies 5 stages: (1) the diagnosis stage, in which the problem is identified and some causes are pointed out; (2) the action planning stage, in which the action to be taken were specified; (3) the action taking stage, that means the implementation of the planned action; (4) the evaluation stage, in which it was determined if the theoretical effects of the action were realised and if these effects relieved the problem; and (5) the specifying learning stage, in which there was a reflection about the results and the learning process as well as the next step to take.

Figure 1: Canonical action research process model of Susman (Baskerville 1998, p. 9)

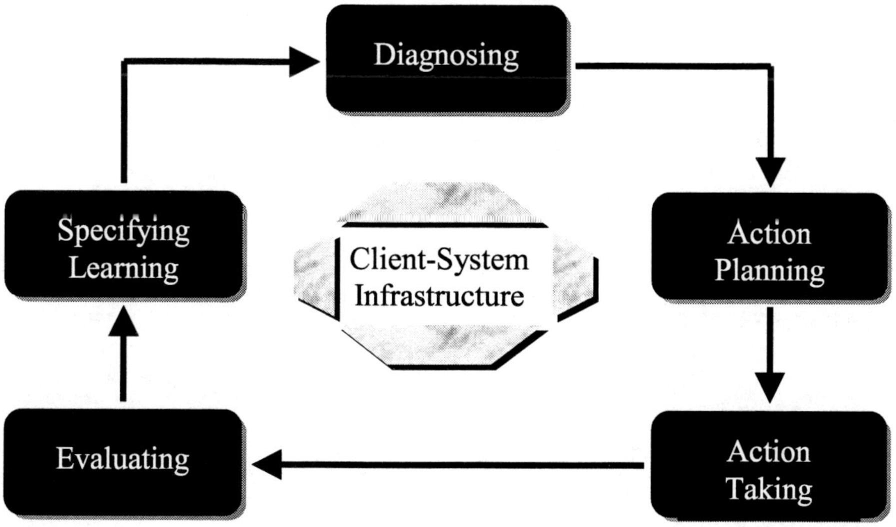

The Diagnosis

The group is geographically dispersed and in order to communicate they use a mailing list and egroups. Many of the artefacts developed by the group are done asynchronously, thus needing a good coordination of tasks and deadlines. There are some difficulties in this process:

- Coordination in the collaborative development of documents. In some circumstances, some elements of the group include changes in the original version of the documents, which implies six new versions almost simultaneously. This discoordination occurs because each member of MOISIG changes the document offline and sends it to the mailing list afterwards;

- The group depends on a particular supplier of e-mail service. As all the messages exchanged are stored in a supplier's computer there's a fear of lack of privacy. Furthermore, as all the members of the group have a TCP/IP connection to the Internet it is difficult to be synchronised. There is also a gap between the moment of sending a message and its receipt.

Action Planning and Action Taking

The group decided to use a new application based on the peer-to-peer (P2P) approach. These kinds of applications do not use an intermediary server. The communication is processed directly from user to user. The application chosen was the Groove (www.groove.net).

Two of the members of the group already knew this application. They decided that the best way to help the other members to learn was to hold a session together in the same physical room. Before the session all the six members filled in a questionnaire about their knowledge about Groove as well as their expectations. At the end of the session another questionnaire concerning the outcomes and difficulties was filled in. The results were then compared. There were another 3 sessions, now each member being at his / her place.

Evaluation

Evaluation was made twofold. On one hand, we evaluated the product and how far it did solved the original problem. On the other hand, we evaluated the use of action research to solve the problem.

Groove

According to the description of this product, Groove is a virtual space for small group interaction. Business interaction in Groove includes capabilities that lend themselves to natural and intuitive groups dynamics. These capabilities include:

- Communication tools – live voice over the Internet, instant messaging, text-based chat and threaded discussion;
- Content sharing tools – shared files, shared pictures and shared contacts;
- Joint activity tools – co-browsing, PowerPoint presentations walkthroughs, live co-editing of Microsoft Word documents, group calendar.

Activity in Groove occurs in a "shared space" – a secure space in which invited "members" carry on conversations. Each Groove shared space is stored locally, on the computers of each of the members of the shared space. When one member adds something new to the space, that change is reflected on everyone's machine – every member of the space remains completely synchronised with all the other members.

After using this application for a while, the group pointed out some difficulties in the use of it:

- Technical difficulties – the full use of this application demands at lot of RAM;
- Synchronisation among users – it is not always easy to schedule a moment to be together in Groove. There were also some difficulties in being in the same created space.
- Costs – as stated above, all the members have a TCP/IP Internet connection, that is, they are not permanently connected. Furthermore, each member pays the calls to the Internet. Thus, each synchronised meeting in Groove can be very expensive.

Approach

The use of the canonical action research seemed adequate for this case. The group identified a problem and tried to solve it. The members planned an action, put it in practice and evaluated the results.

Learning

At the end of this process the group reflected upon the outcomes of the experience, trying to decide if the problem was solved and if they should take another cycle of action.

Generally speaking, the group was frustrated with the use of the application. It was very difficult to synchronise all the members. One of the members could not participate in the virtual meetings as his computer blocked constantly. Groove also consumes lots of resources of the computers in which it runs. This application, in order to run well, needs a computer very well equipped. During the sessions, it was not easy to be together in the same space. Sometimes people were in the space but could not see each other. Briefly, there were some difficulties that took a long time to discover why they were happening and to solve.

The step taken next was to find a machine that could act as a server, permanently connected to the Internet, thus helping all the members to be synchronised (all the members can have, this way, his / her space updated). However, there are not yet results from this experience.

As for the next step in the future, there are two possible ways: (1) to insist in learning how to use Groove and how to use it together, trying to overcome all the difficulties arose, and/or (2) find another application not so heavy and also supporting communication, collaboration and coordination of tasks among group members.

CONCLUSIONS

After diagnosing a problem of communication, this approach revealed to be useful in the action planning and taking. It helped the group to reflect upon the application adopted as well as upon the concept behind it and in the learning that occurred.

Action Research, and its two-moment process (diagnosis and therapeutic) seems to be adequate to help groups (and other entities) to reflect upon problems or subjects and thus helping a learning process to occur.

ENDNOTE

1 The members of MOISIG are: Anabela Sarmento, João Batista, Leonor Cardoso, Mário Lousã, Rosalina Babo and Teresa Rebelo

REFERENCES

Baskerville, R., and Wood-Harper, A. T. (1998) "Diversity in Information Systems Action Research Methods". European Journal of Information Systems 7(2), pp. 90-107.

Batista, J., Sarmento, A., Rebelo, T., Lousã, M., Babo, R. and Cardoso, L. (2001) "MOISIG - a Knowledge Management Example". In Khosrowpour, M. (ed.), *Managing Information Technology in a Global Economy*, 2001 Information Resources Management Association International Conference, Toronto, Canada, May. Idea Group Publishing, Hershey, USA, pp. 922-923.

Cardoso, L., Babo, R., Batista, J., Lousã, M., Rebelo, T., and Sarmento, A. (2000) "MOISIG - A Spontaneous Community of Practice". Proceedings of the First European Conference on Knowledge Management (ECKM), Bled, Slovenia, October, pp. 77-81.

Lousã, M., Cardoso, L., Batista, J., Sarmento, A., Rebelo, T. and Babo, R. (2001) "Relato de uma experiência com uma ferramenta de apoio ao trabalho colaborativo que suporta o conceito P2P". Poster presented at the Second Portuguese Conference on Information Systems, Évora, Portugal, October (the document is in portuguese language).

Sarmento, A., Batista, J., Cardoso, L., Lousã, M., Babo, R., and Rebelo, T. (2000b). "MOISIG: Management, Organizations, and Information Systems Interest Group". Poster presented at the First Portuguese Conference on Information Systems, Guimarães, Portugal, October (the document is in portuguese language).

Sarmento, A., Batista, J., Cardoso, L., Lousã, M., Rebelo, T., Babo, R., Machado, A., and Figueiredo, A. (2000a). "Knowledge Management and Information Systems - Which Relation?". Proceedings of the VIII Congress of Accountancy and Auditing, Aveiro, May (the document is in portuguese language).

Susman, G. I. (1983) "Action Research: A Sociotechnical Systems Perspective". In G. Morgan (ed.) *Beyond Methods: Strategies for Social Research.* Newbury Park, Sage Publications, pp. 95-113.

The Challenges Facing Higher Education in Training the European Workforce for the Information Society

Lee Harris Schlenker
Grenoble Graduate School of Business, France, Schlenker@esc-grenoble.fr

The increased globalisation of industry coupled with rapid technological change has placed increased pressure on both industry and education to devise innovative responses in adapting core competencies to the challenges of the "joined-up" economy.[1] "Helping SMEs to Go Digital" is the most recent of the European Union initiatives designed to prepare European commerce and industry for global competition.[2] One particular focus of these efforts has been to formulate guidelines for education and training on information and communications technologies.

The current contribution explores the scope, the context and the options of higher education in training the European workforce for the challenges of "e-business".[3] The work is based on personal interviews with European senior civil servants as well as representatives from the major European actors in the IT industry and education.[4] This working paper will explore successively the current need of information and communication technology skills, the issues involved in developing these skills, and the needed evolution of business education to adequately address these needs.

SCOPE

If few today doubt the impact of information technology on employment in the European Union, many question the ability of European universities and business schools to provide suitable candidates for industries' current and future needs. A quick survey of market trends establishes the growing demand for skills in information and communications technologies (ICT) , the failure of the market to satisfy this demand, and the economic consequences of the skills gap.

The ICT industries already employ over 4 million people with more than 200,000 related jobs created yearly between 1995 and 2000. ICT creates one in every four new jobs today; in "user industries" the demand for specialists is predicted to double in the next 3 years.[5] In less than 10 years half of all jobs will be in industries that are either major producers or intensive users of information technology products and services.[6]

In spite of these numbers, the growth in employment opportunities have not been met by a corresponding increase in the number of qualified candidates to fill them. In a study originally commissioned for Microsoft, International Data Corporation has predicted that the demand for ICT and e-business professionals outstripped supply by 1.9 million jobs last year and that 3.8 million jobs will remain vacant in 2003 for lack of qualified candidates.[7] The cost of the failure of the market to provide a sufficient supply of candidates has been measured in increasing cost of qualified labor, the deferment of e-business projects, and an increasing demand to recruit foreign nationals.

UNDERSTANDING E-BUSINESS SKILL REQUIREMENTS

While terms like e-business, e-learning and e-commerce have been woven into everyday language, the scope, content and place of electronic business in higher education continues to a subject of lively debate. Before analyzing the issues and challenges facing higher education, this section proposes an operational definition of the concept of electronic business, distinguishes the electronic business from information and communications technologies, and explores what types of skills can be associated with each practice.

Recent efforts in Europe to promote Information and Communication Technology (ICT) skills have focused upon the skills and competencies necessary in the contributing to the production of information and communications technologies. Specific skills include technology design, development, implementation, operation and support.[8] As such, ICT skills are deployed inside a firm's computer services or IS department, or obtained from outsourcing contracts with IT services, products and telecoms companies.

Adding value to business through the use of internet technologies suggests quite a different skill sets tied to aligning the deployment of information technology on a firm's objectives, culture and physical organisation. On the individual level, skills tied to electronic business focus on providing internet enabled business services rendered to organisational clients. Specific job functions calling on e-business skills include the CIO, internet business strategists, product or online service designers, and business unit managers.

On an organisational level, the "successful" deployment of information technologies requires competencies at a number of levels :

- in the workplace (including mastering interpersonal communication, business process improvement, and the strategic use of information),
- in the conception and enrichment of information systems (gauging the proper equation between the physical organisation and the different information architectures),
- in value creation itself (designing enterprise resource planning, supply chain management, client relationship management), and
- in management of the firm (change management, human resource development, the evolution of business models).

E-business "skills" are thus closely tied to how individuals and organisations use technology to meet client needs and objectives. Training programs must focus on how individuals capture, aggregate, distribute, and enrich information for their employees, managers, partners, and clients.

WHICH SKILLS ARE NEEDED IN THE INFORMATION SOCIETY?

For the vast majority of commerce and industry, the question is no longer whether but how to implement information and communications technologies. Corporate spending on training and education reached an estimated $20 billion in 2000, with $3 billion going to universities and the rest to in-house programs and consultants. [9] In spite of these numbers, attempts at e-business training have continued to face stiff challenges :

- Few firms offer training to in-house staff. Employers prefer to hire experienced staff rather than to invest in training. One survey showed that 70% of software engineers had received no recent on-the-job training;[10]
- There is no generally agreed career path for e-business professionals, and little agreement on job titles and responsibilities, making demand for professionals difficult to access.

- There is a mismatch between the skills taught to graduates and the skills needed by industry. There is little dialogue between companies and universities on either the objectives, the content, or assessment of such training.

Will learning about information and communications technology help workers use information technology to produce business value? If a skill can be defined as the ability to do *something* well, what exactly are we trying to do with the electronic business?[11] What is the link between the Internet and sales, between mobile telephones and customer service, between visio-conferences and collaborative working environments? If building business value involves team building, customer service, and quality, should not e-business skills be taught as a means to explore, to develop and to apply these conditions?

When we come to some consensus over pertinent e-business skills, we will still need to analyze how the skills can be transformed into "competencies" directly applicable in the workplace. Not discounting the cultural and conceptual differences in Europe that render common definitions of competencies more difficult still , how can information technologies be used to develop and reinforce the competencies that enhance business skills ?

The confusion between learning about technology and learning to use technology in dealing with business problems has left many perplex. In a survey of European firms for the Europe Community, the Fundacion Tomillo found that technical training was mentioned by top management as a priority almost twice as often as training in customer service, team building, and quality. Paradoxically, learning about information technology appears more of a priority than learning about quality, marketing and sales, outcomes that e-business have been designed to support.[12]

Should a distinction be made between the skills needed in large corporations where information technology is used to improve existing business processes and those skills needed in smaller firms where the basic business processes do not exist? The initiative of the ICT Consortium is an interesting example of a an approach to benchmarking ICT skills across corporations. The consortium has attempted to define skills as a function of the job profiles the participating corporations have identified in information and communications technologies.[13]

In contrast to most corporations the basic business processes tied to sales, distribution, and logistics may be largely inexistent in smaller firms. In such cases, are e-business skills sets tied to the use of information technology to improve internal processes, or to the use of information technology to integrate processes outside the firm itself? This "reality" suggests that the e-business skill sets needed in the SME may be distinctly different than those of the largest corporations.

THE ROLE OF HIGHER EDUCATION

The importance of higher education in training in the European workforce is universally recognized : out of 117 million people aged a least 25 in Europe, 81 million are already in learning establishments..[14] The European Council has recommended a European deadline of December 2003 for all students of all ages to be "digitally literate".[15] This final section will briefly note certain current initiatives, and then explore outstanding issues.

Academic institutions are well aware of the need to adapt their courses to growing demand, and a number of new courses are springing up across Europe. Most major universities and business schools today have added the "e" to subjects as divers as management, commerce, logistics and marketing.[16] Original initiatives include:

- The Copenhagen Business School that for the past three years has a specific "E-commerce institute" based upon a model of having private sector sponsorship to finance this initiative.
- Essex University launched a Master's degree in E-commerce in October 2000. This program is targeted to graduates across Europe who are highly qualified computer scientists and electronic engineers.
- The Grenoble School of Business launched Europe's first "Masters in E-business" back in 1998. In collaboration with ICT suppliers, the school has tried to redesign a coherent curriculum around the managerial, organisational and technological considerations in integrating internet technologies into specific business models.
- Swansea College has launched its Cygnus Online service specifically to meet the needs of employers wanting to improve their staff's ICT skills. This government backed initiative launched to encourage UK workers to improve their networking skills,

As impressive as these efforts are, the speed and pervasive nature of the changes implicit in the Information Society may well require a more fundamental examination of education and training policies. Many institutions find it difficult to adapt their courses as quickly as many employers would like. Several concerns, if left un-addressed, may seriously limit the effectiveness of national and European initiatives in bringing academic curricula up to date:

- Should we be targeting contents, skills or competencies ?
  Most programs are struggling to define a pertinent offer of subjects and contents. As has been argued in this paper, are e-business skills tied to retaining the knowledge of technology or their use in resolving a business problem? Is teaching students about e-business sufficient, or should educational institutions seek to identify and map specific skill sets? Is identifying the skill sets enough, or should schools be recreating the business environment to practice the skills in different contexts and for different objectives?

- How can skills taught in school be transformed into competence applicable in the workplace?
  One fundamental difference between institutional learning and corporate training is that the former is concerned with understanding and the latter with inciting action. Between secondary education, the university and the workplace, which extra-curricular factors influence a student's ability to meet the specific "e-business" requirements of a given job ? Are we talking about end-user awareness, basic programming skills, or the actual use of information technology in commerce, trade and industry? Taken to one logical extreme, is the formal education system the proper place for such training ?

- Which skill sets are we trying to build ?
  Most programs treat e-business skills as a coherent whole Are the ICT skills sets for a secretary working in a SME in Belgium of the same nature as those sought for a site manager on a drilling platform in Norway ? In formulating their product offer, should higher education programs distinguish between small and large firms, and eventually from one industry to the next? Should schools be focusing on developing "e-business" curriculums, or upon the needs and objectives of distinct client segments?

- How can skills be benchmarked to company needs over time?
  Are the current deficiencies of the educational system with regards to the electronic business new, or have they developed over time with the development and use of information and communications technologies ? If the "gap" is the result of an evolutionary process, the definition of ICT skills and competences will continue to evolve in the workplace. What measures for benchmarking the use of information technologies exist today, and will they also evolve to capture the needs of business and industry tomorrow?

- Should schools be offering highly specialized degrees or re-engineering their program offer?
  In the most of the current educational offer behind each "e" hides a "build to stock" philosophy that has traditionally characterized degree programs. Perhaps the reality of e-business implies that higher education should be designing "build to

order" curricula that evolve with client demands. Moreover, higher education could profitably apply information technology to the sub processes of learning (recruitment, skill definition, content development, delivery, assessment and placement) rather than simply as offering content on new technologies. If training the European workforce for the Information Society suggests using information technology to strengthen communities of clients, managers, partners and stakeholders, the traditional classroom may well give way to broader conceptions of the learning space.

ENDNOTES

1 The term has originated in the UK in reference to call for better communication between public and private initiatives so to create a common vision, improve communication, and work toward more consistent legislation.

2 In February 2002 the Commission's Communication on the New European Labour Markets (COM (2001) 116 final) outlined its new strategy for opening the European labour markets for all by 2005. COM (2001) 136 final. http://europa.eu.int/ISPO/ecommerce/godigital/Welcome.html

3 At its simplest e-business can be been defined as the use of information technology to add value to enterprise.

4 Industry representatives have included the Human Resource and Education directors of Apple Europe, Microsoft EMEA, Oracle EMEA, the ICT Consortium, and the EAN (The European Bar Code Association).

5 ...., "Strategies for jobs in the Information Society," COM(2000) 48 final, Communication from the Commission, (Brussels 04.02.2000) : p. 5

6 ...., "Job Opportunities in the Information Society," 1998, Luxembourg: Office for Official Publications of the European Communities, ISBN 92-828-1735-0

7 ...., "ICT Skills in Western Europe", in European Information Technology Observatory (Brussels 2001), p. 23

8 Precise definitions of the corresponding positions and skills set can be found at www.career-space.com

9 International Data Corporation, www.idcresearch.com

10 "ICT Skills", op. cit., p. 23

11 "the ability, coming from one's knowledge, practice, aptitude, etc. to do something well." Infoplease.com

12 "Strategies for jobs in the Information Society," op. cit.

13 ICT consortium was initially composed of BT, IBM, Microsoft, Nokia, Philips, and Thompson-CSF. ICT Consortium, "Generic Skills Profiles," ICT Consortium, ICEL, (Brussels 1999)

14 "ICT Skills" op. cit., p. 58

15 The aim of current efforts is to further accelerate this process by translating "digital literacy" into a set of basic "competencies: mastering of the Internet and multimedia resources; using these new resources to learn and acquire new skills; acquiring key skills such as collaborative working, creativity, multidisciplinary, adaptiveness, intercultural communication and problem-solving

16 The results of a recent worldwide survey conducted by AACSB international indicated that 45.7 % of business school deans and directors have or plan to introduce an MBA concentration in e-business, 46.8 percent an e-business certification programme, and 41.2 percent non-degree executive programs. Shin, Sharon, "The MIS MBA,3, BizEd (January-February 2002) : 25 - 29

Understanding Functional Dependency

Dr. Robert A. Schultz
Professor of Computer Information SYstems, Woodbury University, California
Tel: (818) 767-0888, Fax: (818) 768-5478, bob.schultz@woodbury.edu

In attempting to explain the process of normalization of databases to students, I have noticed that texts differ in small but significant ways in how they explain the concept of *functional dependency*, which is necessary to define and to implement the normal forms.

I think this disparity is due to a problem in the concept of functional dependency itself. Although intuitively clear, it is actually a mixture of two quite different elements:

- Psychological or meaning elements involving dependencies in knowledge —for example, we need to know customer name in order to know customer address. (I will call these intensional elements) .
- Objective elements derived solely from the data about the objects represented in the database in some way reflected in tables. (I will call these extensional elements. The idea is that an extensional element must be based on differences in the way data appear in the table—most notably, patterns of repetition of field values.)

The main motivation for normalization and the normal forms is the elimination of "bad" data redundancies in the database. A tool such as Analyzer in Microsoft Access is able to accomplish this without using any intensional elements or indeed without even considering the meaning of the field names. In logical terminology, its procedures are purely extensional. All that Analyzer uses are patterns of repetition of field values.

We can use repetitions in the data to determine first, second and third normal forms once primary keys are determined. Of course this depends on the data not being misleading. I will discuss whether the following extensional conjecture is true:

THE EXTENSIONAL CONJECTURE

All possible combinations of the data allow normalization (first, second, and third normal form) on the basis of repetitions in the data alone (supposing primary keys are given).

For reasons of space, I will leave aside the "higher" normal forms, namely Boyce-Codd, fourth and fifth normal forms.

My procedure will first be to recap material from standard logical works on the distinction between intension and extension. Then I will examine several sample definitions of functional dependency from popular texts on database design to show how intensional and extensional elements are mixed. Following that, I will examine the issue of whether the Extensional Conjecture is true. I will conclude by discussing the implications for using the concept of functional dependency and the normal forms.

I

The distinction between extensional and intensional elements is familiar in logic. Thus intension has to do with the meanings of the terms involved, and extension with what objects are denoted by or referred to by the terms. In general, if two terms have the same intension or meaning, they have the same extension; but two terms can have the same extension but different meanings or intensions. The classic example is 'the morning star' and 'the evening star' which have the same extension—the heavenly body Venus—but clearly have different meanings or connotations.

It is this last fact which makes intensions difficult to use in mathematical or scientific contexts—in fact we don't have clear criteria for when intensions are the same. The same applies to terms expressing psychological attitudes, such as knowing. I can fail to know that the evening star is the same as the morning star. Yet I cannot fail to know that the evening star is the same as the evening star. What we know about, the objects of knowing, is therefore not extensional but intensional in nature. If we speak about conventions or conventional connections, the result is the same: we are dealing with nonextensional contexts.

We will see that use of the first three normal forms can be extensional in nature. This means that the only features of fields appealed to is extensional—the frequency of their appearance with other fields, and that therefore the meanings or connotations of those fields are not used. This also means that connections between fields having to do with knowledge about the meanings of field names or about business rules or conventions connecting field values are intensional as well.

However, intensional elements may be almost indispensable shortcuts. If we actually had available all the data elements in a database, there would be no question about using extensional methods, for example, the Analyzer function in Microsoft Access. But when the full (extensional) database is not available, we may need to turn to intensional elements to determine functional dependency and hence database design. Let us look at some textbook accounts of functional dependency follow.

II

Textbook definitions of functional dependency differ in various ways. Let us start with a recognized database guru. James Martin's definition of functional dependency is:

> Data item B of record R is functionally dependent on data item A of record R if, at every instant of time, each value in A has no more than one value of B associated with it in record R. [Martin 1983, 208]

This definition seems to be extensional: All one needs to do is to examine the pattern of repetitions in the record. If there are multiple values of B for one value of A in a record instance at any time, then, according to Martin's definition, B is not functionally dependent on A.

Many other authors begin with extensional definitions and then use intensional elements as intuitive shortcuts:

Thus Shelly Cashman Rosenblatt [Shelly Cashman Rosenblatt 1998, 8.16]:

> Do any of the fields in the ... STUDENT record depend on only a portion of the primary key? The student name, total credits, GPA, advisor number, and advisor name all relate only to the student number, and have no relationship to the course number.

Awad and Gotterer [Awad and Gotterer 1992, 221-2] actually define functional dependency with intensional elements:

> A FUNCTIONAL DEPENDENCY occurs when a unique value of one attribute can always be determined if *we know (*my italics) the value of another.

Also Gibson and Hughes:

> A **functional dependency** is a relation that exists between data items wherein data values for one item are used to identify data values for another data item. Stated another way, if you know the value for data item X, you can functionally determine the value(s) for data item Y. [Gibson and Hughes 1994, 501-2]

Allowing the possibility of multiple values is of course incorrect. Otherwise this is a completely intensional definition of functional dependency.

IV

I am inclined to believe that the situation with functional dependency is parallel to that of the intension of a term in general: The most promising modern theory of the relation of intension and extension identifies the intension of a term with its extension in all possible worlds. [Lewis 1969, 171-3] The meaning or intension of a term may indeed be exhausted by the extension of that term in all possible worlds. But we do not have access to all possible worlds. Thus, functional dependency may be fully determined by all possible (extensional) combinations of data. But we may not have access to all possible data combinations.

Thus the Extensional Conjecture is true, but intensional elements may still be useful. The usefulness of intensional elements in determining normal forms lies in the fact that they allow us to anticipate what further data elements will behave like. However, whether a given set of tables is in first, second, or third normal form, at a given moment, depends completely on the extensional pattern of repetitions of data items.

Thus it is possible for a utility such as Analyzer in Microsoft Access to normalize tables without access to the actual meanings of the data items. Actually we can tell that analyzer is using extensional methods when there are "unusual" repetitions in the data and Analyzer makes the "wrong" choice in dealing with them. A Student-Class table

(Class ID, ClassName, DepartmentName, Term,
StudentFirstName, StudentLastName, Grade)

may include data for only one term, the fall term. Analyzer will put the term field in the Student table rather than the Class table. We know it is an "accident" that only Fall class material appears in the student-class table, but Analyzer does not.

V

There are two other related matters which need to be discussed: First, to what extent primary keys are extensional; and second, how this discussion applies to *first* normal form, which, after all, is defined in terms of repeating groups rather than functional dependency.

Analyzer's analysis above raises some of the issues. Since a primary key is defined as a unique identifier, we can have extensional criteria for assigning a candidate primary key: The candidate field(s) must not recur anywhere in the table. From our intensional point of view, Analyzer makes a poor decision in choosing StudentLastName as the primary key. We know that a composite key of StudentFirstName and StudentLastName would be better, and that an assigned ID key would be best. Once again, if we had all the data, Analyzer should get it right.

If one is dealing only with extensional patterns of repetition, functional dependency itself is a matter of repeating groups. Thus we see Analyzer treat all issues such as choice of primary key, repeating groups, and functional dependencies as a matter of repetitions of data within a table. Since these days, all database design is likely to take place in a table environment, the older characterization of First Normal Form as extra subrows within a row can't be directly represented. Instead, to make the data fit in a table, the (formerly) non-repeating information, repeats. Thus in the StudentClass table above, either ClassID-ClassName-DepartmentName-Term could be viewed as a repeating group, or StudentFirstName-StudentLastName could be viewed as a repeating group.

Or, instead, one could simply begin with the table above and check for second and third normal form. Satzinger [Satzinger 2000, 368-372] is very good at doing this based on extensional repetitions in the data. ((summarize))

Alternatively, I will propose what I call "Quick and Dirty Normal Form", which is intended to be an extensional method of reaching third normal form from an initial table in a relational database. It suffers, of course, from our recognized limitation that if the data is incomplete in the wrong way, the results may not be good.

QUICK & DIRTY NORMAL FORM (FOR USE WITH MS ACCESS)

1. Put all fields into one table using "create table by entering data"

1a. Make a couple of backups of the table.

2. Enter a fair amount of data, probably 10-20 records

3. Select or add a primary key. (Access will check for uniqueness.)

4. Use a (select) query to select any group of fields that repeat together, leaving behind only the primary key field(s), with No Duplicates property selected.

5. Rerun the query as a make-table query.

6. Select or add a primary key for the new table

7. Repeat steps 3-5 until only primary keys are redundant when datasheet is displayed.

8. Run analyzer on a backup and compare results.

REFERENCES

Awad and Gotterer (1992) *Database Management.* Danvers, MA: Southwest.

Gibson and Hughes (1994) *Systems Analysis and Design.* Danvers, MA: Boyd & Fraser.

Lewis, David (1969) *Convention.* Cambridge, MA: Harvard.

Martin, James (1983) *Managing the Database Environment.* Englewood Cliff, NJ: Prentice-Hall.

Satzinger, Jackson, Burd, (2000) *Systems Analysis in a Changing World.* Cambridge, MA: Course Technology.

Shelly, Cashman, Rosenblatt (1988) *Systems Analysis and Design,* 3rd ed. Cambridge, MA: Course Technology.

From ERP to Integrated E-Supply Chain System

Keng Siau and Yuhong Tian
University of Nebraska-Lincoln, USA, Tel: (402) 472-3078, Fax: (402) 472-5855, ksiau@unl.edu

ABSTRACT

A company's supply chain consists of all the stages and activities involved in fulfilling customers' requests. The chain extends from designing, producing, promoting, marketing, and delivering to supporting each individual component of the product or service requested by customers. It involves manufacturers, suppliers, transporters, warehouses, and retailers as well as customers themselves.

The purpose of supply chain management is to link all the involved activities in order to provide higher-level products and services to customer at a lower total cost. Products/services, funds, and related information flow along the supply chain. These items are key to success of supply chain management, which makes supply chain information systems critical.

There are two types of supply chain information systems: traditional Enterprise Resource Planning (ERP) systems and analytical supply chain applications. ERP systems are good at providing real-time integrated internal information about the company. On the other hand, ERP has been criticized for its lack of flexibility, notoriously complicated software, high costs and high implementation failure rates. In addition, this software is limited to the operational level and cannot provide many needed analytical functions for supply chain decision-making. As an expedient measure, some analytical supply chain applications or supply chain Decision Support Systems (DSS) are used to process the information provided by ERPs or other operational level systems. The high cost and interoperability problems of having a traditional ERP work with these analytical applications is a very thorny issue for companies looking for a good supply chain management information technology solution.

Furthermore, E-business is quickly becoming the heart of many organizational IT operations that deal with the outside world (suppliers and customers). ERP systems are faced with even more challenges in the e-business era. These challenges include the ability to provide information that can be shared with business partners, suppliers and customers; a necessary focus on both internal and external optimization that fit with extended value chain management; development of the ability to provide functionalities separately yet linked together through the Internet; and development of the ability to be compatible and interoperable with e-business applications. Neither traditional ERP systems alone, nor analytical supply chain applications alone, nor a combination of both, can face the challenges presented by e-business.

A critical question then would be - how do (or how can) organizations construct strong and appropriate information system architectures for supply chain management in this e-business era? This research aims at developing an integrated e-supply chain architecture that combines the benefits of traditional ERP, and the various supply chain applications, and at the same time meets organizational needs in an e-business context. The e-supply chain system not only integrates the company's supply chain, but also integrates with the supply chains of business partners, suppliers, and customers. The e-supply chain system should be secure, flexible, scalable, and interoperable. The enabling technologies for such an e-supply chain system include XML, DCOM, CORBA, SOAP, and .Net. The other features of this e-supply chain system include a further extended supply chain that is enabled by wireless technology. ASP enabled systems are powered by the developing and maturing Internet. Together, these technologies have the potential to revolutionize supply chain systems.

REFERENCES

1. Box, Don "SOAP increases interoperability across platforms and languages" http://www.msdn.microsoft.com/msdnmag/issues/0300/soap/soap.asp
2. Chopra, Sunil, and Meindl, Peter, 2001 "Supply Chain Management- Strategy, Planning and Operation", Prentice-Hall, Inc.
3. Christopher, Martin, 1998 " Logistics and supply chain management-strategies for reducing cost and improving service" Financial Times Professional limited.
4. Hunt, John "Essential Java Beans fast" Springer-Verlag London, 1998, p. 285.
5. Simchi-levi, David, Kaminsky, Philip, Simchi-levi, Edith, 2000 "Designing and Managing the Supply Chain-Concepts, strategies and Case Studies", The McGraw-Hill Companies, Inc.
6. Varshney, Upkar, Vetter, Ronald J. and Kalakota, Ravi "Mobile Commerce: A New Frontier" IEEE Computer, Vol. 33, No. 10, October 2000, pp.32-38.
7. Wang, Wengli, Hidvégi, Zoltán, Bailey Jr., Andrew D., and Whinston, Andrew B. "E-Process Design and Assurance Using Model Checking " IEEE Computer, Vol. 33, No. 10, October 2000, pp. 48-53.
8. "Microsoft MSDN .NET Framework Developer's Guide" downloaded from http://msdn.microsoft.com on Jan, 20, 2002.

Figure 1: Extended supply chain and supply chain flow

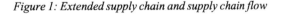

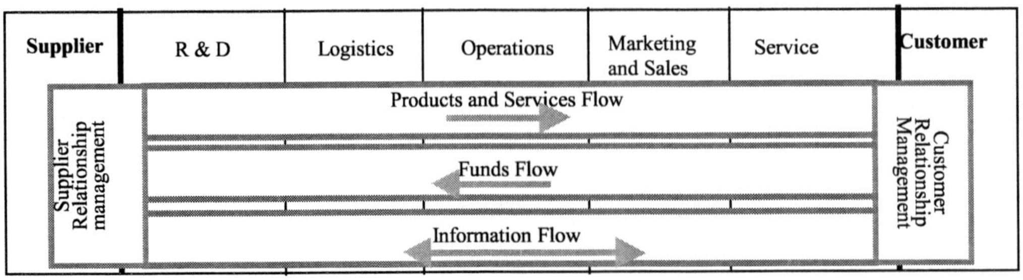

Constituent Relationship Management and E-Government

Keng Siau and Zixing Shen
University of Nebraska-Lincoln, USA, Tel: (402) 472-3078, Fax: (402) 472-5855, ksiau@unl.edu

ABSTRACT

E-government enables people to access government departments and organizations through websites on the Internet, anytime and anyplace. Promising cost efficiency, convenience, responsiveness, and more personalized services, e-government has the potential to make viable and highly productive connections between government and citizens (G2C), government and business (G2B), government and employees (G2E), and government and government (G2G). Implemented correctly, e-government can transform the big government of the Industrial Age into a smart government of the Information Age.

Though the vision of e-government is powerful and compelling, the realities of implementing it are challenging. Among the various technological, managerial, and policy related challenges for making e-government a success, there is a need to rethink how government can be organized from the perspective of its citizens. Unlike traditional government, which is organized around agencies and bureaucracies, e-government in the Information Age will be deployed around the needs of its citizens. This will require rethinking how government needs to be organized from the perspective of its citizens, and will also involve re-engineering how government performs its functions according to the needs of its citizens rather than to the requirements of bureaucracies.

This research is an innovative endeavor to solicit input regarding the possibilities of e-government from the perspectives of citizens and businesses, and to develop strategies to address their needs and expectations in e-government implementations. The research also aims to build value models of e-government based on citizen and business requirements and expectations. In particular, the research questions are: (1) What are the values or features that citizens and businesses want from e-government? (2) How can government reinvent its relationship with the public and view citizens as real stakeholders in the processes of e-government? The findings of this research can help e-government better manage the constituent relationship.

Keeney's (1992) value-focused thinking approach is utilized in the research to conceptualize citizen and business needs and expectations regarding e-government applications. Value-focused thinking is essentially about focusing on the values of interested parties, generating new alternatives and creating proactive decision opportunities. Centered on values, value-focused thinking is a type of complex processing involving three steps. These steps are collecting the values of the involved parties in a specific decision context, identifying sets of objectives from the values collected, and structuring objectives into a value hierarchy of fundamental and means objectives. Specifically, we will conduct initial interviews with citizens, businesses and government personnel in local, state and federal governments, to obtain their diverse views on e-governments, examine the current state of e-government practices, identify and structure e-government objectives, create and clarify alternatives for e-government implementation, and finally build value models on e-government to guide e-government initiatives.

The findings of the research are of significance to government agencies, citizens, and academic researchers. The set of e-government value models provided by the research will serve as a theoretical underpinning to improve our conceptual grasp of what citizens and businesses want in the electronic delivery of government services. The study will reveal the technological and organizational challenges facing governments at various levels and develops recommendations to streamline bureaucratic processes. In short, this research will benefit both academic researchers and stakeholders in e-government applications.

REFERENCES

1. Atkinson, R. (2000) Digital Government: The Next Step to Reengineering the Federal Government. http://www.netcaucus.org/books/egov2001/pdf/digigov.pdf
2. Council for Excellence in Government (2001). E-Government: the Next American Revolution. http://www.netcaucus.org/books/egov2001/pdf/Bluecove.pdf
3. Forrester Research (2000): http://www.forrester.com/
4. Gregory, R. and Keeney R. L. (1994). Creating Policy Alternatives Using Stakeholder Values. Management Science, 4:8, pp. 1035-1047.
5. Keeney, R. L. (1988). Structuring Objectives for Problems of Public Interest. Operation Research, 36:2, pp. 396-405.
6. ———(1992). Value-focused Thinking, Cambridge, Massachusetts: Harvard University Press.
7. ———(1994). Creativity in Decision Making with Value-focused Thinking. Sloan Management Review, Number Summer, pp. 33-41.
8. ———(1999). Developing a Foundation for Strategy at Seagate Software, Interfaces, 29:6, pp. 4-15.
9. ———(1999). The Value of Internet Commerce to the Customer, Management Science, 45: 4, pp. 533-542.
10. Keeney, R. L. and McDaniels, T. L. (1992). Value-focused Thinking for Strategic Decision at BC Hydro, Interfaces, 22:6, pp. 94-109.
11. McDaniels, T. L and Trousdale, W. (1999). Value-Focused Thinking in a Difficult Context: Planning Tourism for Guimaras, Philippines, Interfaces, 29:4, pp. 58-70.
12. Meta Group (2000): http://www.metagroup.com/
13. New Zealand E-government Program: www.e-government.govt.nz
14. Parnell, G. S.; Conley, H. W.; Jackson, J. A.; Lehmkuhl, L. J.; and Andrew, J. M. (1998). Foundations 2025: A Value Model for Evaluating Future Air and Space Forces, Management Science, 44:10, pp. 1336-1350.
15. Pardo, T. (2000). Realizing the Promise of Digital Government: It's More than Building a Web Site. http://www.netcaucus.org/books/egov2001/pdf/realizin.pdf

Students' Perceptions of On-line Courses versus On-Campus Instruction

Judith C. Simon, Lloyd D. Brooks, and Ronald B. Wilkes
The University of Memphis, Fogelman College of Business and Economics, USA
Tel: (901) 678-4613, Fax: (901) 678-2685, {jsimon, lbrooks, rbwilkes} @memphis.edu

ABSTRACT

The recent proliferation of availability of on-line courses and programs has caused some concerns related to ensuring that the time and cost investments provide beneficial results, both to students and the institutions providing the material. Students' perceptions of these programs are likely to affect their interest in enrolling in them. Schools need an awareness of these student perceptions to determine if a need exists for improvements in various aspects, including increased education of the potential students about the sites as well as possible changes in offerings. This study was designed to determine current perceptions of on-line programs of potential students, compared with the traditional on-campus environment.

INTRODUCTION

Many universities are experiencing increasing pressures to offer college courses on-line, partly due to competition with other colleges and universities and offerings available through the business sector. A review of web sites at AACSB-accredited Business schools indicated that a large number of these schools provide courses and complete programs on-line.

Some on-line courses have been implemented so quickly that insufficient time has been available to allow in-depth assessment of the desires, interests, and concerns of their potential direct customers, i.e., students. This study was developed in an effort to identify students' expectations and current perceptions of on-line courses and programs offered by colleges and universities. The results are expected to facilitate effective planning and development of these courses in the future.

DATA COLLECTION METHODOLOGY

A survey instrument was distributed to over 300 students. These students were enrolled in high school Business courses and are assumed to be more likely to be on-line customers for college-level courses than students who are already near completion of a college degree. Additional comparison studies are planned to determine if results are different for students who are currently enrolled in college-level courses in various majors.

Demographic data were collected so that responses could be compared in various ways, including gender. The majority of the study focused on students' awareness of on-line offerings and their current perceptions.

The study addressed students' knowledge and perceptions of on-line courses and degree programs along several dimensions, such as:

- Awareness of availability of on-line courses and degree programs
- Awareness of on-line course offerings in their major
- Awareness of the college's accreditation status
- Awareness of any cost differences of on-line courses and degree programs versus on- campus programs
- Perceived difference in quality of on-line courses and degree programs versus on-campus programs
- Perceived difference in quantity of work on-line versus on-campus programs
- Perceived difference in level of student anonymity on-line versus a campus environment
- Perceived difference in level of one-to-one interaction with instructor on-line versus a campus environment
- Perceived difference in level of one-to-one interaction with other students on-line versus a campus environment
- Perceived difference in difficulty level of work in on-line courses and degree programs versus campus courses and programs
- Perceived difference in fairness of grading by instructors of on-line courses and degree programs versus on-campus courses and programs

SURVEY RESULTS

Demographics

A total of 381 students participated in this study. A large majority were upperclassmen, i.e., high school juniors and seniors, as shown in Table 1.

Table 1: Grade classifications of participants (n=373)

Classification	Percentage of Respondents
Freshman	4.56
Sophomore	24.40
Junior	33.51
Senior	37.53

Regarding gender, a majority of the participants were female, as shown in Table 2.

Table 2: Gender of participants (n=376)

Gender	Percentage of Respondents
Male	41.22
Female	58.78

A high percentage of students (88.97%) indicated that they have access to a computer at home, which could have a direct effect on ability to participate in on-line courses. A comparison of accessibility by gender showed that the difference between genders was slight, as shown in Table 3.

Table 3: Access to a computer at home by gender (n=380)

Gender	Percentage with Access
Male	89.03
Female	88.50

Current Status Regarding Taking On-line Courses

Students were asked to describe their current status regarding taking a course on-line and were allowed to select more than one response. As shown in Table 4, about one-fourth of the respondents indicated that they would not take an on-line course.

Table 4: Current status regarding on-line courses (n=378)

Status Regarding On-line Courses	Percentage of Respondents*
I would not take a course on-line.	24.87
I would consider taking a course on-line.	58.20
I would like to take a course on-line.	28.04
I plan to take a course on-line.	6.35
I am currently taking a course on-line.	0.26
I have completed a course on-line.	0.49

The results for categories shown in Table 4 were also compared by gender, as shown in Table 5. Again, there was very little difference in the results for males versus females.

Table 5: Current status regarding on-line courses by gender

Status Regarding On-line Courses	Percentage – Male	Percentage – Female
I would not take a course on-line.	24.52	24.78
I would consider taking a course on-line.	56.77	58.41
I would like to take a course on-line.	26.45	28.76
I plan to take a course on-line.	6.45	6.19
I am currently taking a course on-line.	0.65	0.00
I have completed a course on-line.	1.94	0.00

Ratings of Issues' Importance

The remainder of the survey had two parts, each with a listing of issues for students to consider. Thirty-eight students failed to respond to a majority of the questions in this part of the survey and were eliminated from further calculations.

In the first section, students were asked to indicate how important each identified issue was to them in deciding whether to take a course on-line or in an on-campus environment. A Likert-type scale was used, with 1 representing "not at all important" and 5 representing "extremely important." A mean was calculated as a basis for determining which issues were considered rather important (defined as a mean of at least 4.0). A majority of the issues had means below 4.0, but none had a mean below 3.0. The issues with a mean of at least 4.0 are displayed in Table 6. The issue with the highest mean as to importance was "knowledge gained."

Table 6: Issues considered important in making course environment decisions

Issue	Mean
Knowledge gained	4.35
Skills acquired	4.29
Access to information (resource materials)	4.20
Time required to complete coursework	4.16
Costs of tuition and fees	4.13
Schedule flexibility to accommodate work responsibilities	4.13

Ratings That a Characteristic is More Likely True for On-line versus On-campus

For the second section, students were asked to consider the same issues as in the previous section but to indicate the likelihood that each issue was a characteristic of an on-line versus on-campus course, with 1 representing "much more likely in an on-line course" and 5 representing "much more likely in an on-campus course." A mean was calculated to identify which issues were considered much more likely in an on-line course (defined as a mean of no greater than 2.0) and which were considered much more likely in an on-campus course (defined as a mean of at least 4.0). A majority of the issues had means below 4.0, but only one had a mean below 3.0. That one issue, "submitting assignments electronically," had a mean of 2.48, which did not place it in the "much more likely" category for an on-line course. The issues with a mean of at least 4.0 are displayed in Table 7.

Table 7: Issues that are much more characteristic of an on-campus course

Issue	Mean
Opportunity for live interaction/discussion among students	4.07
On-campus exams	4.05
Opportunity for live interaction/discussion between faculty and students	4.04

The issues identified as most important were given further review, since those issues were not given particularly strong ratings as either on-line or on-campus options. Table 8 repeats the issues identified as most important that were shown in Table 6 but identifies their means for the comparison of "much more likely in an on-line course" versus on-campus. All had means greater than 3.0, which placed them closer to the on-campus likelihood. Three of these issues considered most important had means that were rather close to 4.0, the value needed to be in the category of "much more likely in an on-campus course" than an on-line course. The issues are listed in the same order of importance shown in Table 6.

Table 8: Important issues related to on-line versus on-campus instruction (much more likely in an on-line course = 1; much more likely on campus = 5)

Issue	Mean
Knowledge gained	3.90
Skills acquired	3.78
Access to information (resource materials)	3.15
Time required to complete coursework	3.33
Costs of tuition and fees	3.85
Schedule flexibility to accommodate work responsibilities	3.10

SUMMARY AND CONCLUSIONS

Most students who participated in this study had access to computers at home, making it easier for them to consider the possibility of on-line coursework. However, no significant differences were found between gender in access level or current status of interest in taking on-line courses.

Students identified some issues that they believed were rather important. They also indicated which issues they believed were more likely to be a characteristic of an on-line course and those that were more likely to be a characteristic of an on-campus course. None of the issues they identified as important were also identified as more likely to be a characteristic of an on-line course.

Perhaps these potential students may not be ready to consider the less traditional on-line option. For example, students rated "knowledge gained" as their most important issue in making this decision and also rated it more likely to be a characteristic of an on-campus than an on-line environment. Institutions wanting to increase the number of on-line students might need to look for documentation of successful results from taking courses in that manner in order to alter this perception.

Some additional advertising might be useful to institutions promoting the on-campus option, as not all students' perceptions represent actual facts. For example, students indicated that higher costs for tuition and fees were more likely a characteristic of an on-campus environment, although the costs are higher for on-line courses at institutions in the participants' local geographic area.

Future students' perceptions should continue to be monitored by institutions wanting to increase the participation of students in on-line programs. If these students' responses are representative of potential students in general, institutions investing significant dollars in on-line programs might want to investigate further the perception that on-campus courses are providing more of the characteristics the students think are important.

Some Notes on Reinventing the Social Contract: A Framework for Understanding Obligation and Responsibility in the Information Age

Robert Joseph Skovira[1] and Frederick G. Kohun[2]
Robert Morris University, Pennsylvania
[1]Tel: (412) 262-8357, [2]Tel: (412) 262-8395, skovira@robert-morris.edu

This paper discusses the notion of obligation and responsibility within the frames of the Social Contract and the Information Age. The essay raises the issue of a moral sense of taking responsibility for one's behavior and what this means to individuals or corporations living in the Information Age, and specifically the Age of eCommerce. In the literature of business ethics, there is a long tradition of discussion of the responsibility of corporations and individuals to the society of which they are a part.

Corporate and individual obligations are derived from a sense of a social contract. The ethos of the Internet, the World Wide Web, and the Information Age contribute to and determine this sense of social contract. Social responsibility and obligation and business practices are linked in the social contract underlying corporate behavior.

The Internet, as the interconnections of people and groups, is an ethos or cultural environment, as our interactions and our conversations demonstrate, even if they are electronic. Where there is a culture, there is a morality, and a sense of social responsibility and obligation. The Internet is a moral context. The idea of virtual community is another way of speaking of the social contract when it comes to ethical behavior.

Cyberspace creates a different social contract (Poster, November 1995, 136). A cyberspace community does not reside in any actual place. Such a community is a socially constructed group within mailing lists, newsgroups, web rings, and links to and from web sites (Negroponte, November 1996, 286). The many discussion lists, news groups, and all of the various web sites are expressive of this. Space and time, a sense of place, no longer holds in digital space. "As we interconnect ourselves, many of the values of a nation-state will give way to those of both larger and smaller electronic communities. We will socialize in digital neighborhoods in which physical space will be irrelevant and time will play a different role (Negroponte, 1995, 7)." The Internet is a new way of communicating and living in virtual communities(Stoll, 1995, 3, 50).

A culture will grow up around the new technology (Gates, 1995, 7-8). The information highway (the Internet and World Wide Web) is redefining our understanding of what counts as documents, who are authors, publishers, where our offices are, what is a classroom, what do textbooks consist of (Gates, 1995, 113).

The information highway, the Internet and World Wide Web, reflects a new social contract. This new social contract is evolving in terms of the so-called netiquette. As the World Wide Web becomes the new town meeting, a new social contract is being created (Gates, 1995, 161). The new social contract is digital and while its major focii are about decentralization and world-wide in scope, the social contract is also about harmony and empowerment (Negroponte, 1995, 228-229). "The Web, in fact, relies on the breakdown of the bounds between private and public; it creates a sense of a large community as well as absolute isolation. The public and private realms become illusion: there is no guaranteed community and no real privacy (Rothstein, April 1996, C21)"

The new social contract is grounded in our digital being. In this cyberworld, informational accessibility is individual and personal (Negroponte, 1995, 164). "In being digital I am *me*, not a statistical subset. *Me* includes information and events that have no demographic or statistical meaning....True personalization is now upon us. (Negroponte, 1995, 164-165)." In this brave new world, the audience is individualistic and personalized.

The Internet is the cybersocial structure of the new digital community. "The true value of a network is less about information and more about community. The information superhighway is more than a short cut to every book in the Library of Congress. It is creating a totally new, global social fabric (Negroponte, 1995, 183)." The interpersonal discussions among people on the Internet turn it into a social construction. "Virtual communities are social aggregations that emerge from the Net when enough people carry on these public discussions long enough, with sufficient human feeling, to form webs of personal relationships in cyberspace (Rheinghold, 1993, 5)."

The Internet's character, however, reflects a sense of cooperation that sometimes comes with a decentralized chaotic organization (Kinney, September 1995, 94). The Internet is an anarchistic social state-of-affairs. "The Internet evolved into a self-contained anarchistic community, with nobody in charge. At the same time, it's promoted as a legitimate conduit for governmental and public communication (Stoll, 1995, 9)." The Internet is considered the ultimate experience of democracy (Stoll, 1995, 31).

From the home to educational institutions to medical institutions to governmental venues to legal circumstances to business organizations, information technology shows up everywhere, in ubiquitous informational appliances. Information technology shows up in our use of cell phones, and pagers. information technology shows up in all manner of software applications: personal and business-oriented. Information technology shows up and transforms people into information workers or knowledge workers (even as information technology deskills). Information technology shows up in email and Internet connectivity changing how we communicate, with whom we communicate, and the frequency of communication. In our increasing reliance upon information technology's presence, we have become dependent on information technology; we are information technology junkies. A cornerstone of this framework is the ability to digitalize anything and everything, and to collect, store, and retrieve anything as wanted.

Information technology is a sociocultural force. As a major sociocultural frame, information technology embodies a set of values that is a catalyst in the transformation of a culture and society. Information technology orients how things are in the world. Information technology provides a new context for living; information technology embodies a set of assumptions and constraints that shape the existential circumstances. This sense of information technology changes the notion of the social contract. Information technology changes the nature of the social; it spans virtual communities, transforms businesses, recreates personal identities.

These technological values represent major shifts in how human problems and issues are resolved. Information technology is a frame of the societal, and is part of the sociocultural dialectic. The dialectic changes to a monologue. This is an overwhelming perspective that like an avalanche carries everything away, utterly changing the cultural landscape forever. As a result, just as information technology is changing our personal views of reality, information technology is a transforming agent of our social lives.

The information age (the information society) is an important aspect of the discussion about social responsibility. The infusion of technology into every aspect of existence gives rise to the notion of technological determinism (Webster 1995, 7-10).

The information society is an interconnected world (Friedman, 2000, 9). The information society is a way of describing the global connectivity of commercial interests, governmental venues, as well as individual and personal ways of being linked around the world (Friedman, 2000, 50). The information society exists globally in the digitalization of all societal and personal affairs (Friedman, 2000, 48-49).

The information society shows up in the ever growing technological presence and use of computer information systems and computer networks. This configuration of information technology changes and determines not only the sociocultural environment, but also human thinking (Webster 1995, 7-10). Information technology reduces the social aspects of human interaction to nothing more than individuals and information flows (Borgmann, 1999, 204-208). The information society is nothing but information and people (Brown 2000, 22). People exist as information entities. Information is the focus of everything; it is everything (Brown, 2000, 31).

The rise and commercialization of the Internet is the most significant event in the construction of the information society. The Internet signals the democratization of information flows globally. Worldwide connectivity is the information society (Webster 1995, 10-13; Friedman, 2000, 77-79).

The information society consists of local informational spaces that become the lived world (lebenswelt) of many individuals (Brown,2000, 39). Cyberspace and virtual reality are both informational spaces. In this world, culture is technology and informational flows (Borsook, 2000, 117). Culture is informational space. The traditional disappears in the information society (Friedman, 2000, 20).

The basic cultural metaphor for the information society is digital. The neighborhoods are digital; physical place is irrelevant (Negroponte, 1995, 228-229). Individuals in the information society are not restrained by national or natural borders. Individuals are not confined to one physical place when they can ride the informational waves to other places in the world (Borsook, 2000, 155).

In the information society, social identities and roles are redefined both locally and globally (Dyson, 1999, 2) Information is personalized; there is an audience of one (Negroponte, 1995, 164). Personal identity is a matter of information. A person can be digitally anyone he or she wants to be. This identity formation is solipsistic (Stoll, 1995, 57-58). The social sensibilities and human bonding that normally help form human personality are not present except informationally. There is no physical social presence or group. Presence is linguistic. Presence is virtual (Brown, 2000, 77). This information is the person in the information society. In cyberspace, existence is in the informative details that presume to capture how a person is in the world. Human identity is informationally constructed (Rheingold, 1993, 169).

The political form of technolibertarianism is an ideology that fosters self regulation and the free market. Any form of government is viewed as repressive and ought to be done away with. The view is that government presents unnecessary obstruction to individuals (Borsook, 2000, 10). The philosophical approach to technolibertarianism is an ethos (Borsook, 2000, 15) that argues for individualism, asocial behavior (Borsook, 2000, 90), self-selection, and self-organization (Borsook, 2000, 212). This ideology embraces digital darwinism and sociobiology (Borsook, 2000, 42, 46)

Social circumstances and personal relationships are the basis for being obligated, being responsible. Collective obligations are norms that structure human interaction and locate human relationships within a moral universe of discourse. Because information technology is a way of human interaction in corporate environments and personal contexts, the use and growth of information technology change collective obligations. Information technology is a cultural force; it is a creator and destroyer of collective obligations and social responsibilities. Information technology changes the social fabric, the social contract.

A social contract results when individuals, for the sake of self-interested preservation, incorporate as a social group to restrain people's natural perversity and propensity to selfishness and conflict. The social contract that results from such incorporation means individuals must give up their perceived natural rights for socially sanctioned rights. Social responsibility and obligation comes only with the agreement to the social contract. The social contract confers the rights of citizenship and the duties—being responsive (responsible) to the now common or mutual interests (Hobbes, 1988, 87-90; Solomon, 1992, 174-175, 191; Solomon, 1993, 182; Halverson, 1972, 60-61).

In conclusion, the Information Age ushered in a hyper paced environment where the traditional notion and application of the Social Contract became challenged. Information technology, particularly the tools of the Internet that includes email and web pages, have taxed our understanding of obligation and social responsibility. The new information media, while perceived as the new frontier where conventions and social boundaries did not exist, fostered a series of new social and philosophical dilemmas. Individuals could communicate ideas and thoughts faster than they could be assessed for potential personal and social damage. The speed and ease by which we exchange ideas does not allow sufficient time to think through potential negative impacts of making thoughts available to thousands (or millions). Furthermore, given the multitude of potential receivers of such thoughts-it is virtually impossible to assess potential impact until it has already happened and taken on a life of its own. The only recourse it to consider the individual's role of Social Responsibility and Obligation. The technology is too pervasive and the new frontier is too big to police. The burden of responsibility is left to the individual-with few alternatives. The focus on self understanding and need for Social Responsibility is the only viable, and ultimately, the only response to the Information Age technological quagmire.

Information Sharing: Competitive Strategy or Cyber Fad?

Donna J. Slovensky[1], PhD, Joseph G. Van Matre[2], PhD and Pamela E. Paustian[3], MSM
University of Alabama at Birmingham, School of Health Related Professions
[1]Tel: (205) 934-1679, [2]Tel: (205) 934-8834, [3]Tel: (205) 975-9376, [1,2,3]Fax: (205) 934-5980, {donnaslo, jgy, paustian}@uab.edu

Linda Roberge, PhD
Syracuse University, School of Management, New York, Tel: (315) 443-3571, Fax: (315) 443-5457, Lroberge@syr.edu

Health care executives face unprecedented challenges in an era of negotiated prices and payer-controlled access to health care services. Many executives pursue technology-based strategies in the belief that like businesses in other industries, health care organizations (HCOs) that fail to recognize the "power and ubiquity of digital technology" (Downes & Mui 1998) likely will disappear from the competitive landscape. Whether the strategic objective is service enhancement or new business development, information technology is viewed as a key enabler, and the Internet has become a powerful corollary. Today, the Internet is pervasive in home, business, and education.

In other industries web-based technologies have been employed to enhance an organization's ability to compete and to reduce the costs of doing business. Among the health related uses of the Internet described are e-mail (Widman & Tong 1997; Eysenbach & Diepgen 1998; Eysenbach & Diepgen 1999; Mandl & Kohane 1999; Furguson 2000; Sands 2000; Taylor 2000), patient education (Richards, Coleman et al. 1998; Dawson, Gilbertson et al. 1999; Helwig, Lovelle et al. 1999; Grandinetti 2000), and disease management (Anon 1999; Cochrane 1999; Peltz, Haskell et al. 1999). Some articles deal with competition and cost issues (Van Brunt 1998; Herreria 1999), while others discuss web site content (Impicciatore, Pandolfini et al. 1997; Winker, Flanagin et al. 2000). Again, the implication is that organizations must either adopt use of the web or be left behind in the new health care environment.

The existence of a web site, however, does not magically improve competitive position. An organization gains competitive advantage when it creates a value-added (from the customer's perspective) product or service that costs less or is better than products or services offered by its competitors. The functionality and utility of a web site must improve the efficiency of information dissemination and exchange, or meet other information needs of key stakeholders for the strategic potential of the technology to be realized. The challenge to strategists is to determine what web-site functionality or content is perceived as value-adding by consumers. This study addresses the question of whether hospitals are using web-based technologies to provide information to key stakeholders, specifically clinical outcomes and other performance data, that could contribute to competitive advantage.

HEALTHCARE INFORMATION STAKEHOLDERS AND HCO PERFORMANCE REPORTING

External stakeholders for HCOs include third party payers, large employers, regulatory bodies, and health plans. The number and diversity of health care stakeholders continue to increase, and the individual consumer is gaining importance as a key stakeholder to provider organizations. Each year the consumer faces increasingly complex health care choices – which health plan, which provider, which facility. Consumers must be knowledgeable about health care delivery systems and understand the limits of science, health care personnel, and our health care resources. Without question, understandable and reliable health care information, including information about quality and comparative performance at the individual provider level is key to consumers' ability to fully exercise their responsibilities.

Aggregated performance and outcomes data or "report cards," may be published as summaries of organization (or health plan) performance on critical indicators of clinical outcomes, customer satisfaction, cost, and process efficiency. The expectation is that consumers will use the data to make informed health care purchasing decisions, whether the buyer is an individual who needs a single diagnostic test, or an employer providing health benefits to employees.

Previous research has suggested that providers view employers and managed care organizations as more important recipients of their report card data than individual consumers (Slovensky, Fottler, & Houser 1998). One argument used to support this position is that most consumers choose a *health plan* from among the three or so selected by their employer, as opposed to choosing a *provider organization*. Therefore, provider organizations frequently prepare report cards to aid negotiations with managed care organizations (MCOs) for approval status on MCO provider panels. However, employers and health plans are responsive to feedback from individual consumers about their satisfaction (or dissatisfaction) with provider organizations. Some plans permit beneficiaries to select their preferred primary care physicians and, thus to some degree, affiliated provider organizations.

In the Internet virtual marketplace, business transactions previously requiring human interactions are replaced with computer systems. Today's consumers perform a multitude of other business transactions independently through computer interfaces, and transactions in health care are not excluded from this way of doing business. In fact, the number of "e-health consumers" is growing much faster than Internet users in general (Bell 2000). Annually, more than 25 million Americans use the Internet to search for medical and health information (Brody 1999), including locating a personal physician or diagnostic services. Thus, making report card-type information available to individual consumers or large purchasers via the Internet could be a value-adding service that attracts new clients and retains current clients.

RESEARCH FOCUS AND METHODS

This research was designed to study web sites developed and maintained by individual hospitals to investigate whether hospitals are using web-based technologies as strategy tactics. We examined the extent to which surveyed sites have incorporated content, and technical and functional features in their web sites that improve client recruitment and service, and thus could enhance the organization's competitive position. Information about the organization, descriptors of the site's technical design and functionality, and the types of information available were captured to construct a picture of how existing websites are used by hospitals to meet the health care information needs of current and potential clients.

The intended utility of a hospital's web site was of particular interest. We questioned whether the site was designed solely as a general marketing tool, or if the organization provided performance data that could help consumers make informed choices among providers in the local market. The latter approach would imply a more strategic focus.

Methodology

A random sample of 300 hospitals was drawn from the 1999 annual membership survey of the American Hospital Association (AHA). The full database included organization-specific items on more than 6,000 hospitals and health systems. Variables describing resource utilization, organizational structures, personnel, hospital services, and finances, were available in electronic format for analysis.

Individual hospital web sites were examined to determine the type, quantity, and quality of information available. Sites were evaluated on a number of dimensions discussed in the report card literature (Goldstein & Florey 1996; Slovensky, Fottler, & Houser 1998; Swain 1999; Walker 1998). Variables examined include the presence of performance data on the web site, the number and type of indicators reported, and whether data were presented in comparison to some appropriate external benchmark. Data also were collected on other variables including technical design features, visual appearance, functionality, content, interactivity, and developer information.

SUMMARY

The ways in which clinical outcomes and other performance information is used by consumers is still relatively unknown, and uniquely defined report cards, particularly those available over the Internet, can be useful to organizations and to their customers. This research explored whether report cards or organizational performance data has become a relatively common feature of hospital web sites, and describes the web-based information products hospitals are creating. The study provides a focused review that helps distinguish between the hype and the reality of how hospitals are currently using web sites to provide useful health care information to consumers. Web sites judged to be examples of "best practices" are identified for the potential to advance the quality of web sites sponsored by other organizations.

REFERENCES

AHA. (1999). About the American Hospital Association. Available www.aha.org; accessed 10/8/99.

Androshick, J. (1999, February 12). A cybercheck on Dr. X. *Forbes*, 132-133.

Anon (1999). Internet-based system keeps diabetics, physicians in touch and patient care on track. *Data Strategy Benchmarks,* 3(4): 59-60.

Bell, H. (2000, April). Going Interactive. *Healthcare Informatics,* 85-86, 88, 90, 92.

Brody, J. E. (1999, August 31). Personal health: Of fact, fiction, and medical web sites. *New York Times on the Web*. Available www.nytimes.com; accessed 9/15/99.

Cochrane, J.D. (1999, May). Healthcare @ the Speed of Thought. *Integrated Healthcare Report*. P. 1-14, 16-17.

Dawson, R., J. Gilbertson, et al. (1999). Pathology imaging on the Web. Extending the role of the pathologist as educator to patients. *Clinical Laboratory Medicine* 19(4): 849-66, vii.

Doctor Errors. (2000, May 8), Editorial. *Wall Street Journal*, p.A22.

Downes, L. & Mui, C. (1998). *Unleashing the Killer App: Digital Strategies for Market Dominance.* Boston: Harvard Business School Press.

Eysenbach, G., & T. L. Diepgen (1998). Responses to unsolicited patient e-mail requests for medical advice on the World Wide Web. *JAMA,* 280(15): 1333-5.

Eysenbach, G., & T. L. Diepgen (1999). Patients looking for information on the Internet and seeking teleadvice: Motivation, expectations, and misconceptions as expressed in e-mails sent to physicians. *Archives Dermatology* 135(2): 151-6.

Furguson, T. (2000). From Doc-Providers to Coach-Consultants: Type 1 Vs. Type 2 Provider-Patient Relationships, The Furguson Report Number 7 · May/June 2000 ,Tom Ferguson, M.D. Available http://www.fergusonreport.com/articles/tfr07-01.htm

Goldstein, D., & Florey, J. (1996). *Best of the Net: The online guide to healthcare management and medicine.* New York: McGraw-Hill/Irwin Professional Publishing.

Grandinetti, D. A. (2000). Doctors and the Web. Help your patients surf the Net safely. *Medical Economics,* 77(5): 186-8, 194-6, 201.

Health care web guidelines offered by new Internet Healthcare Coalition. (1999). *IT Health Care Strategies*, 1(12): 9.

Health site reviews: Site review criteria. Available www.drkoop.com; accessed 10/8/99.

Helwig, A. L., A. Lovelle, et al. (1999). An office-based Internet patient education system: A pilot study. *Journal Family Practice* 48(2): 123-7.

Herreria, J. (1999). America's Doctor Online provides easy access for consultations. *Profiles Healthcare Marketing* 15(1): 31-2.

Hochhauser, M. (1996). Designing readable report cards. *Managed Healthcare*, 8(5): 15-22.

Impicciatore, P., C. Pandolfini, et al. (1997). Reliability of health information for the public on the World Wide Web: Systematic survey of advice on managing fever in children at home. *British Medical Journal* 314(7098): 1875-9.

Institute of Medicine. (2000). *To Err is Human: Building a Safer Health System.* Washington, DC: National Academy Press.

Mandl, K. D. & I. S. Kohane (1999). Healthconnect: Clinical grade patient-physician communication. *Proceedings AMIA Symposium*: 849-53.

Peltz, J. E., W. L. Haskell, et al. (1999). A comprehensive and cost-effective preparticipation exam implemented on the World Wide Web. *Medical Science Sports Exercise* 31(12): 1727-40.

President's Advisory Commission of Consumer Protection and Quality for the Health Care Industry. (1998). *Quality First: Better Health Care for All Americans.* Available: http://www.hcqualitycommission.gov.

Richards, B., A. W. Coleman, et al. (1998). The Current and Future Role of the Internet in Patient Education. *International Journal of Medical Informatics* 50(1-3): 279-285.

Sabherwal, R., & King., W.R. (1992). Decision processes for developing strategic applications of information systems: A contingency approach. *Decision Sciences*, 23, 917-943.

Sands, D. Z. (2000). Using E-mail in Clinical Care, The Informatics Review. March 1, 2000. Available http://www.informatics-review.com/thoughts/index.html.

Shikhar, G. (1998). Making business sense of the Internet. *Harvard Business Review*, 76(2): 126-135.

Slovensky, D.J., Fottler, M.D. & Houser, H.W. (1998). Developing an outcomes report card: A case study and implementation guidelines. *Journal of Health Care Management,* 43(1): 15-34.

Swain, C.E. (1999). Disseminating provider report cards via the Internet. In *Provider Report Cards*, Patrice L. Spath, Ed. Chicago: Health Forum, Inc., 43- 61.

Taylor, K. (2000). The Clinical E-mail Explosion. *Physician Executive* 26(1): 40-45.

Van Brunt, D. (1998). Internet-based patient information systems: What are they, why are they here, how will they be used, and will they work? *Managed Care Quarterly* 6(1): 16-22

Widman, L. E. & D. A. Tong (1997). "Requests for medical advice from patients and families to health care providers who publish on the World Wide Web. *Archives Internal Medicine* 157(2): 209-12.

The Selection, Management, and Use of Information Technologies in Educational Organizations: An Innovation in Collaborative Course Development, Delivery and Evaluation

Ruth V. Small[1] and Pamela Lipe Revercomb[2]
School of Information Studies, Syracuse University, USA
[1]Tel: (315) 443-4511, [2]Tel: (315) 443-4508, {drruth, plreverc} @syr.edu

INTRODUCTION

This evaluation study focuses on the design, development, and implementation of an interdisciplinary course in which students gain knowledge about and discuss issues related to the selection, management and use of information technologies for teaching and learning in a wide variety of settings (e.g., schools, colleges, businesses). The survey course, offered for the first time in fall 2001, was based on the following assumptions:

- Technology literacy is fundamental to the education of citizens of the 21st century.
- Technology integration is fundamentally a human-oriented issue, in the sense that the point is to integrate technology in meaningful ways into the life and work of people; this is especially true with regard to using technology in teaching and learning.
- Technology can provide unique and powerful opportunities to enhance learning and teaching.
- The adoption of information technology will change the way teachers teach and students learn.

This paper describes the collaborative course development process, course objectives, course content and activities, and the results of a formative and summative evaluation, conducted by the researchers. Recommendations for future implementation, including distance delivery, are included.

OVERVIEW

Collaborative Course Development

The development of the new course began as a response to the need to revise and update two masters degree programs, one in the School of Information Studies and one in the School of Education, in order to satisfy current New York State certification requirements for Library Media Specialists and Educational Technologists in schools. These requirements emphasize collaboration among educational professionals to enhance the learning of all students, including those with disabilities and special needs, and specifically collaborative projects that support the use of instructional and information technologies for teaching and learning.

The objectives for developing the new course were to:

- Create an innovative approach to teaching and learning about information technology use in education.
- Encourage collaborative planning and teaching in the areas of information and technology literacy.
- Provide opportunities for students to work collaboratively on school-based technology projects.
- Present first-hand learning experiences from noted practitioners and researchers.
- Teach students to use technology to plan and work cooperatively.

A project team, consisting of one advanced graduate student and one faculty from each school used computer-based collaborative software to support their course development. Initial research was conducted to identify similar collaborative projects and interdisciplinary course development efforts at other institutions. To develop the course content and structure, the team evaluated state certification competencies, educational standards for technology-based learning curricula, and various means of assessing current technology use and instruction.

Guidelines and suggestions for the *process* of developing a course that involves the integration of more than one discipline were found to include the development of the curriculum, course objectives and framework, delivery options, support resources, and evaluation (General Education Proposal, 1977; Course Development for a New General Education Curriculum, 1989; Lambert, 1985; Spicer, 1988). Some research indicated that interdisciplinary courses and teaching tend to be highly innovative, exploring "broad-based social issues that require multiple perspectives," and incorporating a variety of methods and concepts from the disciplines involved (Abell, 1999; Gailey & Carroll, 1993). Other research offered useful suggestions for avoiding the pitfalls they had encountered when first designing an interdisciplinary course (e.g., Ruwe & Leve, 2001). The National Council for Accreditation of Teacher Education (NCATE) and the International Society for Technology in Education (ISTE) recently developed standards and guidelines to be used in support of technology use and integration in professional teacher preparation programs. (Vanatta, 2000).

Results of Planning

Topics to be included in the curriculum were chosen to meet the instructional and information technology needs of students from both schools and in accordance with new State certification requirements. Each class session focused on a different topic. Presentations would include guest speakers who were experts on that subject, fieldtrips to relevant educational sites, and panel discussions. A technology survey (pre- and post-) was developed to measure the students' comfort with and knowledge/use of various educational technologies. The survey was administered at the beginning of the semester, with a re-test at the end. A textbook on education change models was selected and supplemental readings related to specific class sessions were chosen. Assignments and projects were planned, including a collaborative, site-based educational technology project (ETP), preparation of a WebQuest (defined by creator Bernie Dodge of San Diego State University as "an inquiry-oriented activity in which some or all of the information that learners interact with comes from resources on the Internet"), evaluation of a Web site using a specific evaluation instrument, creation of an electronic portfolio, and a final in-class presentation on the results of their ETPs. It was agreed that WebCT would be used as the electronic learning environment for communications, assignment postings, and online discussions.

COURSE DELIVERY

Format

"Information Technology In Educational Organizations," was offered as an interdisciplinary course, designed and taught by full-time faculty from Syracuse University's School of Information Studies and School of Education. Multiple instructional methods were employed, including lectures, discussions, demonstrations, role-plays, debates, labs, field trips, and hands-on activities.

Students were introduced to a wide range of existing and emerging self-contained and distributed technologies, studying them in relation to telecommunications policies, information and instructional services to diverse groups and individuals, research and learning, and collaboration. Online technology was used for communicating, learning, and completing assignments.

Learning Objectives

By the end of the course, it was our expectation that students would be able to:

- Demonstrate an ability to select, manage, and evaluate technologies used in a learning environment.
- Demonstrate an understanding of telecommunications policies that affect the use of technology in schools.
- Describe methods of determining the appropriateness and effectiveness of implementing and using a range of self-contained and distributed technologies within a learning environment.
- Demonstrate knowledge of the impact of technology on information services and instruction.
- Synthesize information presented by a variety of researchers and practitioners in course seminars and readings.
- Successfully complete site-based technology-related team projects for clients.
- Use computer-based collaborative software as one method for team interaction.
- Understand the roles of the library media specialist and the educational technologist in the application of technology for meeting curricular, faculty and organizational needs and requirements; and
- Develop skills in collaboration with other professional staff to support instruction through services that enhance the learning and independence of diverse audiences

Content and Topics

Course content and topics included the management of technology projects collaborative learning technologies, assistive technologies for learners with disabilities and other diverse audiences, evaluation of technology-based learning and electronic resources, digital equity, online instruction competencies, national education databases, asynchronous and synchronous distance learning tools, ethical issues relating to technology use, building online learning communities, knowledge management tools for learning environments, federal telecommunications policies, wireless communications, information technology services and resources for instruction and learning, the impact of technology on the learning environment, technology leadership and videoconferencing systems.

Topics were often covered in several different ways, including speaker presentations, readings, panel discussions, demonstrations, and/or through class role-playing and brainstorming activities. Some of the guest speakers suggested relevant readings so that students would be prepared for discussion sessions after the lectures, or so they would have questions prepared for videoconference sessions.

Technology

The instructors and guest presenters demonstrated and used a variety of technologies to teach the course. The class was held in a state-of-the-art digital classroom containing computer-based presentation technology (including CD, DVD, and Internet connections), multiple cameras for videotaping, videoconferencing and Web casting, and a Smart Board, as well as more traditional classroom technologies (overhead/opaque/video projection system, whiteboards). The technology lab manager for the School of Information Studies demonstrated the new cameras, sensors, microphones, projectors, overhead/opaque desk projector and the remote mouse.

Communication outside of class was conducted using WebCT, a Web-based learning environment. WebCT allows ongoing communication between instructors and students and among the members of student teams to facilitate announcements, class discussions and assignments. Guest speakers and other special sessions of interest to a wider audience (e.g., the entire University, distance students in remote locations, faculty and students at other colleges) were simultaneously broadcast through the Web using Web casting technology. This technology not only allowed remote participants to synchronously view the session but also to interact with the speaker by sending questions and comments via their computers. In addition, all Web casts were archived for future viewing by both students in the class and others.

Speakers and Panel Discussions

Noted guest experts and practitioners participated through presentations (in-person, web cast, and/or videoconference), demonstrations, and panel discussions. Some examples of guest speakers are:

- One of the developers of WELES (Web-Enhanced Learning Environment Strategies), a tool for integrating NASA resources into teaching to inspire science learning.
- An expert on "the digital divide."
- A member of the International Board of Standards for Training, Performance and Instruction's committee developing "Competencies for Online Teaching and Training (COTT)."
- The developers of a "next-generation" online learning tool prototype, combining DVD and Web technology to deliver flexible, modular, multimedia instruction and including such features as video-based case studies, active lesson book marking, and individual note indexing and review.
- A member of the development team for a set of tools for developing effective online instruction.
- The developer of a set of widely used Web evaluation tools for education and business.
- An expert who provides innovative assistive technological needs assessments for people with disabilities.

Field Trips and Labs

A number of fieldtrips allowed students to experience a variety of innovative uses of technology at existing technology-based learning centers and resources located in the Syracuse area. Sites included libraries, teaching centers, academic units, and government-funded national projects. For example, students visited the Information Institute of Syracuse, the collective home of several U.S. Department of Education-funded projects such as the ERIC Clearinghouse on Information & Technology, AskERIC, the Virtual Reference Desk, and the Gateway to Educational Materials (GEM) Project. A 30-workstation lab, next to the digital classroom, was reserved for demonstrations and hands-on activities such as developing WebQuests and evaluating school web sites.

Assignments

The primary assignment was the Educational Technology Project (ETP), which allowed students an opportunity to apply newly learned knowledge and skills to a real situation with a real client. Students worked together collaboratively in teams with site-based educational practitioners to develop and implement solutions to specific technology problems within their organizations. Some examples of projects were:

- Development of a module-based instructional program for a college library's databases.
- Examination of a high school online learning program and determination of the causes of and potential solutions to its high dropout rate.

- Development and implementation of training for elementary teachers using newly purchased technologies (e.g., FlexCam, SmartBoard)
- Planning a professional conference for a university-based organization for school administrators to advance technology use and practice for academic success.

Additional assignments required students to create Web-based learning tools (WebQuests), evaluate educational web sites using an established tool (Small & Arnone's WebMAC Professionalã), and develop electronic portfolios. Students were expected to upload each of the assignments to their student space on the WebCT site. The electronic portfolio was intended as a means for students to organize and present all of their electronic assignments and to provide reflective comments on their experience and growth throughout the course.

EVALUATION

Methods

An ongoing evaluation was integral to course development and delivery. The course development team directed the design of both formative and summative course evaluation. Data were collected from course developers, instructors, teaching assistants, students, and guest speakers. Field-testing using formative evaluation methods occurred at various points as the course was being developed and implemented; feedback guided revisions as the course was in progress (Worthen and Sanders, 1973). After completion of the first offering of the course, data were again collected from all participants (instructors, graduate assistants, speakers, panel members, and students) as part of a summative evaluation effort.

Evaluation data were collected in the following ways:

- Continuous feedback while the course was in progress, focusing on experiences with technology, course materials, assignments, class sessions and other activities via electronic interviews, focus groups, and surveys. [Students were made aware of the fact that the course was new and that their feedback was not only encouraged but also vital to the ongoing evaluation process.]
- Development and use of a series of instruments that evaluate the effectiveness of planning efforts, quality of instruction, attrition rates, use of technology and other resources, learning and affective outcomes, course organization, and impact of student projects on the organizations in which they are conducted.

At the time of the writing of this paper, preliminary evaluation data have been collected and reviewed. Additional data are currently being collected and analyzed from guest speakers and from the standard university course evaluation forms. Complete results will be reported at the IRMA Conference in Seattle in May.

Preliminary Evaluation Results

The instruments used to collect the evaluation data were designed to determine how well the objectives of the course had been incorporated (and met) through assignments, speakers, ETPs, and other class activities. Data were collected through several instruments, including pre- and post-technology surveys, mid-semester evaluations, standard university course evaluations, electronic portfolio (self-reporting) analyses and reflections, and interviews of students, guest speakers, and course developers. At the time of this writing, results are only available for the mid-semester evaluation.

Mid-Semester Evaluation. At approximately the mid-point of the course, students were presented with 12 open-ended questions as a means of collecting their thoughts, reflections and suggestions for how the course was progressing to that point. Questions focused on the following aspects of the course:

- Assignments completed
- Relevance/applicability of topics to their future plans
- Guest speakers
- Using WebCT
- Presentation of educational technologies
- Progress on the educational technology project (ETP)
- Class presentation formats
- Textbook and readings
- Quality of instruction
- Suggestions for improvement

Overall feedback was positive for the assignments, relevance of the topics and content, guest speakers, instructors and teaching assistants. Seventy percent (70%) of the students felt the WebCT presented many difficulties, complaining of having experienced "much frustration" while attempting to upload assignments, being uncomfortable posting to the discussion groups, and having trouble finding things on the site. Students were split 50/50 as to whether the educational technologies were being thoroughly presented, with a unanimous request for more hands-on experience. Information on the progress of their ETPs indicated that 20% of the projects were "going well," 50% were having difficulties scheduling meetings with their team or site supervisors, 30% felt they were not experienced enough to meet the demands of the project, and 20% felt they were confused or unclear about the expectations for the projects.

Although all students agreed that the variety of speakers and formats was a good concept, 40% said they would prefer the course to be less of a survey course and more hands-on or practical activities, complaining that they felt like they were "always an audience." Seventy percent (70%) of the students wanted more focused lectures that would link the speakers to the goals and objectives of the course, suggesting that course instructors might conduct a closing summary after each presentation to stress relevance. Eighty percent (80%) of the students felt the supplemental readings were useful and informative and that the textbook was easy to comprehend, although 30% pointed out that they thought the textbook was "pointless." Final suggestions from 70% of the students indicated that they needed more time in class to work with their ETP teams.

Several steps were taken in response to the feedback from the mid-semester evaluation. In-class demonstrations were given to show students how they would be expected to use WebCT for uploading or otherwise contributing to class assignments. ETP teams met and discussed their progress, problems and other issues with their projects and these were presented for class discussion and suggestions. Discussions and group brainstorming sessions were included in many class sessions following guest speakers. The textbook was used as the basis for several online discussion groups in which students participated by relating the readings to their ongoing ETP experiences.

Recommendations for the Future

Aside from the revisions that will undoubtedly take place after the final analyses of the course evaluation, several conclusions and recommendations have emerged that will be taken into account when presenting the course in the future.

- The educational technology projects were integral for giving the students the experience of working collaboratively with learning technologies.
- Although site/project supervisors attended the first class session to present their projects and were invited to attend the final presentation from their project team, there needed to be a more formal means of collecting feedback from them while projects were in progress.
- Much of the course format will lend itself well to a distance mode of delivery. The use of WebCT for communication and assignment postings is already functioning; many of the guest presentations were done using web casts or videoconferencing with students participating or asking questions live. Panel discussions, hands-on lab work or demonstrations and fieldtrips could be conducted during a limited on-campus residency.
- One potential difficulty with presenting this course in distance mode is the coordination of the ETPs. Students should be provided with guidelines for seeking appropriate sites and supervisors for the projects in their local communities.

CONTINUATION OF THE PROJECT

A Vision Fund Grant for Innovative Instruction from Syracuse University provided funding for the design, development and initial implementation of this course. The focus of this first effort was on a collaborative framework for course development.

To build on initial efforts for further elaboration of both master's curricula, the Schools of Information Studies and Education will continue to collaborate on courses and projects of mutual need and interest. Both Schools strongly support this project and will contribute resources to its continuation. The final project report will include recommendations for expanded collaboration between the two Schools and the development of a model based on lessons learned in order to create meaningful ways to foster interdisciplinary collaboration among academic units campus-wide.

REFERENCES

Abell, Arianne. (1999). Interdisciplinary courses and curricula in the community colleges. *ERIC Digest,* May 1999, ED#429633, 4 pp.

"Course Development for a New General Education Curriculum." (1989). ERIC #ED306844, 29 pp.

Gailey, Joan D. and Carroll, Virginia Schaefer. (1993). Toward a model for interdisciplinary teaching. *Journal of Education for Business*, 69:1, September/October, 1993, pp. 36-39. ERIC #CE525627.

"General Education Proposal, Miami-Dade Community College." (1977). ERIC #ED146957, 26 pp.

Lambert, Leo. (1985). A Discussion of the evaluation of the interdisciplinary seminars program of the honors college at the State University of New York at Oswego. ERIC #ED270049.

Michen, Kathleen S. and Cutting, Alan C. (2000). eEducation: Interdisciplinary crossroads. Research paper: Connecting technology to teaching and learning. ERIC #ED444454, 10 pp.

Ruwe, Donelle and Leve, James. (2001). Interdisciplinary course design. *The Clearing House*, 74:3, January/February, 2001, pp. 117-18. . ERIC #BED101003816.

Small, R.V. and Arnone, M.P. (2000). *WebMAC Professional.* Fayetteville, NY: Motivation Mining Company.

Spicer, Willa. (1988). A core program for the 90's: Changing patterns for instruction. Final Report. ERIC #ED298115.

Vanatta, Rachel A. (2000). Evaluation to planning: Technology integration in a school of education. *Journal of Technology and Teacher Education,* 8:3, pp. 231-46.

Worthen, Blaine R. and Sanders, James R. (1973). *Educational Evaluation: Theory and Practice.* California: Wadsworth Publishing Company, Inc.

Implementing an Enterprise Resource Planning System for the City of El Paso

Adriano O. Solis[1], Karl B. Putnam[2] and Leopoldo A. Gemoets[3]
The University of Texas at El Paso, El Paso, USA
[1]Tel: (915) 747-7757, Fax: (915) 747-5126, [2]Tel: (915) 747-7740, Fax: (915) 747-8618
[3]Tel: (915) 747-7763, Fax: (915) 747-5126, {solis, kputnam, lgemoets}@utep.edu

David Almonte
Office of Management & Budget, The City of El Paso, TX, USA, Tel: (915) 541-4530, Fax: (915) 541-4760, almontedr@ci.el-paso.tx.us

ABSTRACT

This paper reports on a continuing study evaluating the ongoing implementation of an enterprise resource planning (ERP) system for the City of El Paso, and reports on system implementation over the period from September to December 2001. The study aims to identify issues and problems associated with ERP project planning and implementation, particularly in a local government setting, and accordingly provide insights for managing future projects.

INTRODUCTION

Case studies (e.g., Palaniswamy and Tyler, 2000) have shown that firms that have implemented ERP systems have made improvements in inter-functional coordination and business performance at various levels, helping them reduce cycle times, reduce inventories, and share information readily across the organization.

ERP systems, however, are extremely complex pieces of software that require huge investments of financial resources, time, and expertise. Some companies have experienced "horror stories" in implementing ERP systems. Hershey Foods Corporation, in its 1999 Annual Report, declared that implementation of the final phase of its ERP system led to significant problems in the areas of customer service, warehousing, and order fulfillment. FoxMeyer Drug has argued that its ERP system helped drive the company into bankruptcy (Davenport, 1998). In some cases, implementation projects may be poorly managed, with the organization having inadequately trained personnel to install and customize the system.

ERP systems have just started to penetrate the public sector marketplace, and the governments that have implemented them are only starting to enjoy the benefits of such systems (Miranda, 2000). Miranda, however, refers to ERP as "the backbone of digital government," forcing structure and order on diverse transactions and business processes. Sclafani (2000) declares that an ERP system will allow the various functional components of a government agency's overall business system to share the same information, with processes that occur in one functional area automatically kicking off dependent and related processes in the agency's other functional areas—in much the same way that such integration is enabled by an ERP system in an industrial setting.

Miranda (1999) examined the use of ERP systems in the public sector, and identified some obstacles to ERP implementation in government organizations—e.g., turf battles over system ownership; difficulty in establishing project management capabilities, identifying full-time staff resources, and finding experienced implementation partners; failure to recognize limitations of ERP systems.

Some observations and suggestions on ERP project implementation—e.g., the need for top management commitment, cross-functional participation, and effective change management—commonly appear in the limited number of public sector case studies published thus far (e.g., Fontayne-Mack, 1999; Glaser, 1999; Harris, 1999). These observations and suggestions have been made also with respect to ERP projects in the private sector. Others—e.g., a greater difficulty in finding and dedicating full time project staff—may be more specific to the public sector.

THE CITY OF EL PASO: PREVIOUS COMPUTER INFORMATION SYSTEM

With a population of approximately 700,000, the City of El Paso is the fourth largest city in Texas and among the 25 largest cities in the United States. The Director of its Office of Management and Budget (OMB) reports El Paso's operating expense budget to be only 155th among all U.S. cities. Its operating budget for the current fiscal year (September 1, 2001 to August 31, 2002) is about $540 million, based on all funding sources. The City has some 5,800 employees.

Until August 2001, the City of El Paso and the County of El Paso shared a mainframe-based computer information system via an "inter-local" agreement under which an agency called Consolidated Data Processing was formed. The system, based on mainframe technology, consisted of four major subsystems: Financial and Management Information System; Personnel Management Information System; Advanced Purchasing Information System; and Budget Preparation System.

In 1998, the City of El Paso issued a request for proposal (RFP) to acquire a new computer information system to replace the antiquated system. However, it ended up awarding a contract to the original software provider to upgrade the existing system. The upgraded system reportedly led to a multitude of problems.

The City decided to do away with the "inter-local" agreement with the County of El Paso and to seek a new computer information system that would specifically address its financial management and human resources requirements in a timely, effective, and efficient manner. In addition, an Application Service Provider (ASP) arrangement was decided upon, to avoid difficulties in staffing associated with low salary levels in local government service being far from competitive in the market for information technology personnel. Moreover, with the exception of user workstations and internal wiring, computer hardware would be owned, operated, and maintained by the ASP entity. Furthermore, the city was to appoint a Chief Information Officer (CIO) who would take overall responsibility for the development, management, and continuous improvement of the information system. Under the ASP arrangement, the CIO would not have to contend with staffing and hardware acquisition and maintenance concerns, and accordingly would be able to focus on information system development and process improvement.

ENTERPRISE RESOURCE PLANNING SYSTEM

The City issued in September 2000 an RFP for a financial and human resources information system, as well as one for the ASP arrangement. There was no specific reference in the RFP to an ERP system. The intent was to explore the marketplace for a system that would effectively and efficiently address the city's financial and human resources information requirements. While cost was an important factor due to the city's limited financial resources, system capability and flexibility carried more weight than the cost.

After reviewing seventeen responses to the RFP, narrowing the selection process down to three vendors, evaluating presentations and software demonstrations, and undertaking site visits to vendors' existing installations, city officials awarded in March 2001 a contract to PeopleSoft for its ERP solution to the city's financial and human resources management information requirements. The ASP contract was likewise awarded to PeopleSoft, with the system server residing in an "e-Center" located in Pleasanton, California. Everge, a Dallas-based firm that has worked with PeopleSoft on a number of other projects, was selected to oversee system implementation. Separate contracts for Kronos (a time management reporting system) and CORE (a cash management system) were awarded. The Kronos and CORE systems would operate as peripheral processes, by way of modules allowing each product to interface with the PeopleSoft system.

The total direct project cost—inclusive of the ERP software, the ASP, Kronos, and CORE contracts, and the system implementation contract with Everge, but exclusive of additional hardware for system users—is approximately $6 million. The OMB Director estimates that new personal computers and related hardware for various users within the system will cost another $2 million. It is difficult, however, to specify what portion of this latter amount is allocable to ERP system implementation.

ERP SYSTEM IMPLEMENTATION: STATUS, ISSUES, AND PROBLEMS

An Information Technology Director (the city decided to use this in place of the original CIO title) was hired in May 2001; he moved to El Paso from a smaller city in the Northwest. A steering committee—composed of city officials representing the key business process areas of human resources, budgeting, benefits, purchasing, and finance—was constituted in preparation for system implementation. Members of the steering committee chair subcommittees assigned to review, modify, and improve current business practices in their particular areas of competence. In early April 2001, a full-time Project Leader, who is based in the OMB, was designated to head an in-house project team ("core team") that directly interfaces with the Everge system implementation team. The core team membership included one representative each from Purchasing, Human Resources, Finance, and OMB and two from the IT department. An additional representative from OMB would join the core team when the budgeting module is implemented.

An IT professional with a good number of years of experience implementing PeopleSoft payroll, human resources, and ERP systems projects for various clients heads the Everge implementation team.

Implementation: September – December, 2001

The ERP system was targeted to be operational by September 1, 2001—the start of the city's fiscal year. Original implementation plans indicated that, as of that date, the following ERP modules would be up and running: general ledger, accounts payable, accounts receivable, purchasing, fixed assets, projects accounting, human resources, payroll, and benefits management. Also planned to be operational by that date was the CORE cash management system. On the other hand, the Kronos time management system was expected to be in place by December 31, 2001, and the budgeting module by February 1, 2002. In particular, the budgeting module was planned for initial use in preparing the budget for the next fiscal year (September 1, 2002 – August 31, 2003).

The financial management modules of the ERP system (general ledger, accounts payable, accounts receivable, purchasing, fixed assets, and project grants accounting) were actually made operational as of September 4, 2001. However, the fixed assets module will not be in full use until the implications of Governmental Accounting Standards Board statement no. 34 (GASB 34), under which municipalities and other nonfederal governmental units are required to move to the accrual basis required for commercial enterprises, are fully understood and appreciated.

Planned introduction of the Kronos time management system was eventually moved up to September 4, 2001. There were, however, problems with the operation of the system, reportedly arising mainly from a significant number of the "non-exempt" employees (comprising about 90% of city employees) improperly swiping their ID cards through the card readers on reporting for and leaving work—even as such employees had been taught how to do so. Accordingly, a parallel run of the old payroll subsystem was in operation for three additional weeks beyond the planned three initial parallel trial runs.

The CORE cash management system was made operational on September 13, 2001. Insurance enrolment information effective as of January 1, 2002 was updated using the ERP system's benefits management module in the month of November.

Pending Modules

Implementation of the pension module was still pending as of yearend 2001. Planned for implementation in February 2002 is an activity-based costing module. On the other hand, the planned February 2002 implementation of the budgeting module—starting with budget preparation for the 2002-2003 fiscal year—has been postponed to February 2003, applying to the 2003-2004 fiscal year. This postponement will enable the use of a later, Web-based version of the budgeting module. As an interim solution for the 2002-2003 fiscal year, Everge will provide the city with an Excel-based solution.

Other Key Issues and Problems

A number of other key issues and problems have been identified:

- Some members of the core team are not fully dedicated to the ERP project, even as they need to be so (e.g., Fontayne-Mack, 1999; Miranda, 1999). Moreover, the Project Team Leader is not able to exercise proper authority over the core team members, some of whom continue to be on call for other work associated with their home department.
- Some department managers do not assign their "star" performers to take on key user roles in system implementation. The same holds true for personnel assigned to "train the trainer" programs.
- Some department managers do not appear to apply enough pressure on their personnel to ensure that the system is properly used.

REFERENCES

Davenport, T.H. (1998). Putting the enterprise into the enterprise system. *Harvard Business Review*, July-August 1998, 121-131.

Fontayne-Mack, K.N. (1999). Managing enterprise financial system projects: the city of Detroit's experience. *Government Finance Review*, February 1999, 21-24.

Glaser, T.J. (1999). System selection strategies for county governments: the experience of Cook County, Illinois. *Government Finance Review*, August 1999, 19-21.

Harris, J. (1999). Designing change management strategies for ERP systems: observations from Alameda County, California. *Government Finance Review*, August 1999, 29-31.

Miranda, R. (1999). The rise of ERP technology in the public sector. *Government Finance Review*, August 1999, 9-17.

Miranda, R. (2000). The building blocks of a digital government strategy. *Government Finance Review*, October 2000, 9-13.

Palaniswamy, R. and Tyler, F. (2000). Enhancing manufacturing performance with ERP systems. *Information Systems Management*, Summer 2000, 43-55.

Sclafani, J.A. (2000). Think outside the box. *Government Accountants Journal*, 49(2), 18-20.

A Longitudinal Study in Federal and State Cases involving Malpractice, Negligence, Fraud and Misrepresentation

James Spruell and Mustafa Kamal
COIS Department, Central Missouri State University, USA, Tel: (660) 543-4767, {Spruell, Kamal}@cmsu1.cmsu.edu

ABSTRACT

This investigation takes a look at instances of malpractice, negligence, fraud and misrepresentation involving the software acquisition process. The study scope was limited to cases that resulted in either federal or state litigation, and included both the acquisition of custom and mass-marketed software. Examining the litigation has shed significant insight into the underlying ethical issues as well as suggesting options for managerial intervention.

INTRODUCTION

A variety of legal theories exist under which a case involving defective software can be brought to trial. Kaner (1993) classified these as cases involving a breach of contract, a breach of warranty (either express or implied), and those involving strict liability in tort for injury to a person or damage to property. Breach of warranty can involve as express warranty where as breach of implied warranty involves an implied warranty of merchantability and/or a fitness for a particular purpose. Strict liability in tort can involve certainly involve strict product liability, but also conversion, negligence, malpractice, fraud and misrepresentation.

The typical investment in software of a large organization is substantial, and any unethical activities can have a significant impact on the operations of the company, especially if it leads to litigation. We felt a study of this area would be valuable in that

1) The parties involved felt strongly enough about the issues to seek legal redress;
2) The elements and facts are readily available;
3) The consequences (injury to trade marks, reputation), economic injury, etc. are significant enough to warrant managerial actions;
4) Significant management issues will be exposed that are under managerial control that would have avoided or at least mitigated the consequences that led to the litigation.

STUDY SCOPE

This study involved both a qualitative and quantitative survey of litigation brought in federal and state courts involving defective software. Our study period involved the years from 1990 to 2001, and includes legal briefs that have been filed in the last 6 months. We examined 129 cases brought in federal and state courts, with 31 of those selected for further analysis.

The thirty-one cases that were selected were examined in detail to identify the qualitative aspects of ethical and managerial behavior that contributed to the case being filed. Although subjective and interpretive, qualitative analysis provides substantial insight into the unexplored issues involved in litigation. The knowledge gained holds practical implications for the software industry, and adds substantial relevance as to what can be done to avoid being placed in a situation where an organization is vulnerable to negligence, fraud and misrepresentation. As Eisenhardt (1989) has pointed out, this approach both increases the credibility and the rigor of a study.

Overview of Hypothesis 1

The legal theories under which litigation can be brought involving defective software involve either contract law or strict liability in tort. The former involves a broken agreement including breach of contract, breach of warranty, or breach of implied warranty (implied warranty of merchantability or implied warranty of fitness for a particular purpose). Strict liability in tort for injury to a person or damage to property involves conversion, negligence, strict product liability, malpractice, fraud and misrepresentation. We believe that the study period will demonstrate a progressive increase over time in the number of cases involving strict product liability as

1) Contract law often limits remedies to compensatory damages, wherein tort law provides for additional punitive damages.
2) Contracts or agreements can fail for a variety of reasons that do not involve blame, and hence make it more difficult to assign damages where-as tort law is very specific.

Overview of Hypothesis 2

In the case of Bancroft & Masters, Inc. b. Augusta National Inc. the Supreme Court broadly expanded state jurisdiction where geographic or physical contact is lacking. This case opened the door for states to assume jurisdiction where a willful tort was directed against a party in another state. In addition to this many states have enacted legislation dealing specifically with a variety of ethical issues involving software development. As such, we expect that the study period will reveal a longitudinal increase in the number of cases that are being filed initially in state courts (as opposed to federal courts). i.e., responsibility for handling the ethical issues described here-in will be shifted more and more to a local level.

Overview of Hypothesis 3

The majority of cases will reflect that clear managerial control was not exercised to protect the organization from negligence. Specifically we would expect to find inadequate or missing software testing procedures, or at least inexperience at executing those methodologies. With adequate testing in place, the ability to discover negligence in early stages would limit economic and other damages.

Overview of Hypothesis 4

Software can either be acquired through customization, whether via the RFP process or the retaining of a consultant. Conversely the acquisition may be pre-packed software that is purchased off the shelf, obtained as shareware, through bulletin boards, etc.

We expect the nature of the software acquisition to influence the potential for negligence.

The very act of creating custom software whether through hiring a consultant or through the RFP process lends itself to greater managerial control. The presence of a well-defined requirement statement identifying a list of required features, performance issues, etc. would reduce the ambiguity in proving fraud. In other words, the absence of a clear set of requirements lends itself to exaggerated claims, and nebulous performance criteria opening the door to unethical conduct.

Overview of Hypothesis 5

In those instances where performance issues are clearly stated as mtbf, mttr, turnaround time, and throughput will result in fewer claims.

RESULTS AND DISCUSSION

In the 129 cases that we surveyed, we identified very few suits that were brought against the developers of defective software that we would describe as successful. As such, our results strongly support Peter Alces's (1999) suggestion that an implied warrant of merchantability may not be a relevant standard in providing protection in cases where even mass marketed software is relatively unique. Furthermore, he points out that the nature of software development may also make it difficult to talk about fitness for an ordinary purpose. The area is difficult to frame since the purpose of software is intimately tied to the means, the hardware platform and operating system, all designed and implemented in an environment where standards of quality and care are poorly defined.

This environment creates an opportunity for fraud, misrepresentation, and simple negligence to flourish. In the absence of a reasonable probability of success, coupled with the high costs involved in litigation, managerial intervention becomes extremely important.

Our hypotheses were well supported by the qualitative analysis of the cases that we studied. A simple "What is Missing List" would demonstrate that in the cases that we studied that

1) software testing procedures weren't just inadequate, but were altogether missing – if negligence, fraud, etc were evident, discovery occurred after the software was put into production. The importance of acceptance and systems testing may as such be even more important in mass-marketed software than in customized software;
2) clear communication of performance objectives were absent (complaints were stated as this software is slow...not as transactions per second);
3) only one RFP had been utilized;
4) very few instances of customized software made it to court compared with the purchase of pre-packaged software;
5) the custom development of software visa-a-vi the hiring of an external consultant or RFP (Request for Proposal) process represented a small percentage of the court cases.

As previously stated, we suspect that management exercises a greater degree of control in the custom development of the software, thus minimizing the opportunity for fraud, misrepresentation, etc. Managerial inaction greatly contributed to the potential of the organization becoming vulnerable to misrepresentation and/or the distribution of defective or poorly designed software.

Additionally, many warranties were being created on the fly by purchasers in effect relying on the statements of vendors/sales personnel with little technical knowledge of the software. In the absence of a legal defense residing in the implied warranty of merchantability, many cases attempted to formulate a Breach of Contract defense that often failed because of a variety of express warranty disclaimers. The rise in the number of cases alleging misrepresentation, negligence and fraud was sharp (three fold for the years 1995-2001 vs the preceding five years), but few again would we describe as successful. As such a Peter Alces's (1999) warranty of documentation becomes critical.

Based on the results of our findings we formulated ten steps to curb an organization's vulnerability to misrepresentation, fraud, etc. These include...

1. Read the fine print, as dull as it may seem. Many of the court cases turned on the presence of an "express warranty disclaimer".
2. Ensure that relevant documentation is retained. Again, the difficulty of enforcing an implied merchantability of fitness has created the warranty of documentation. Use it.
3. Avoid creating warranties through the creation of false claims, and conversely, be very careful about relying on such claims.
4. Where costs are justified, insist on public demonstrations of the software on the hardware platform that you wish to use.
5. For the purchaser, send a letter of understanding back acknowledging relevant verbal statements that are being relied upon as conditions of the sale.
6. Use a single contact point in working with a vendor.
7. Performance issues should be clearly stated in the contract. Again, not one case had predefined performance criteria.
8. Have an acceptance plan... and execute it.
9. Consider mediation and arbitration clauses in the contract — it's not likely that you're not going to win a legal case...
10. Develop a clear set of requirements, use it, and include the document in the contract.

SUMMARY AND CONCLUSION

Regretfully, our findings clearly suggest that the software industry has won the warranty war when it comes to product liability involving defective software. The cost of litigation and the small probability of success means that management must exercise due care of its own in entering into any software acquisitions. Exercising managerial control, clearly communicating and documenting system requirements, especially functional and performance criteria, can substantially reduce financial vulnerability to fraud, misrepresentation, and outright negligence.

REFERENCES

Alces, Peter. (1999). W(h)ither Warranty: The B(l)oom of Products Liability Theory in Cases of Deficient Software Design. California Law Review, 87:1, 271-304.

Eisenhardt, K.M. (1989). Building theories from case study research. Academy of Management Review, 14: 4 , 532-550.

Kaner, Cem; Falk, Jack; & Nguyen, Hung Quoc. (1993). Testing Computer Software. New York: Van Nostrand Reinhold.

A Usability Model to Predict User Experience in E-Commerce

Adrie Stander and Nata Van der Merwe
Department of Information Systems, University of Capetown astander@commerce.uct.ac.za

ABSTRACT

This pilot study, part of a larger study aimed at building a model using usability factors to predict the e-commerce user experience, looks at the effect of page layout, navigation techniques, security and privacy and perceived usefulness on the user experience.

INTRODUCTION

A large base of research on the usability of computer systems exists. Traditionally this was aimed at optimizing the task performance of expert users (D'Hertfelt, 2000), but the introduction of e-commerce has caused a widening of the focus of HCI to include aspects typically found in marketing and sociology. New fields such as user experience strategy, the design of consumer trust and Captology, the design, theory and analysis of persuasive technologies, are emerging (de Groot, Eikelboom & Egger, 2001), with the actual interaction with the customer becoming of paramount importance.

To date there has been a lack of genuine knowledge about what contributes to effective interactions with online customers, although intuition and previous research (Dholakia and Bagozzi, 1999) suggest that creating a compelling online environment for Web consumers will have numerous positive consequences for commercial Web providers.

Usability techniques can be used to reduce software and e-commerce costs and improve marketability (Gilb, 1988). Web sites that are hard to use frustrate customers, forfeit revenue, and erode brands (Forrester, 1998). Lohse & Spiller (1999) found that poor interfaces and store navigation negatively influence online sales, while Li et al. (1999) found significant positive relationships between online buying behaviour and online channel characteristics such as interactivity. The intention to revisit a website is in part a function of website characteristics (Hoffman et al., 1995) and empirical support for usefulness and enjoyment as drivers of website usage exist (Atkinson & Kydd, 1997). This suggests that website characteristics at least partly determine the frequency and duration of a website visit.

Hurst (2000) predicted that e-commerce sites in the USA would lose several billion dollars in sales during the 2000 Christmas season due to difficulties with the checkout process of these sites while Gartner (1999) points out that studies in the UK and Europe have shown that many users are put off by the failure of Web sites to provide a satisfactory buying process. The popular press suggest a similar situation in South Africa (Van Niekerk, 2001).

CONCEPTS

User satisfaction is seen as the user's perception that a web site has met or exceeded their expectations and is created through the careful design of information content, site usability , security and privacy of the site while taking the characteristics of the intended users into account(Hill, 1997).

The user experience encompasses all aspects of the end-user's interaction with the site. The most important requirement for the user experience is to meet the exact needs of the customer with simplicity and elegance in order that produce e-commerce websites that are a pleasure to use. True user experience goes far beyond giving customers what they say they want, or providing checklist features. In order to achieve high-quality user experience there must be a seamless merging of multiple disciplines, including engineering, marketing, graphical and industrial design, and interface design (Nielsen, 2000).

Usability, often defined as the system's ease of use and throughput (Egger, 1999), is attributed to numerous design factors. Many studies have investigated these factors, but often looked at only a few or even one factor in isolation and with small, well-defined user groups. Often the guidelines developed from these studies are not very useful in normal usability engineering practices (Nielsen & Molich, 1990).

Perceived usefulness, "the degree to which an individual believes that using a particular system would enhance his or her job performance", is a construct of the Technology Acceptance Model (Davis, 1989), often used in research to predict the acceptance of technology.

RESEARCH METHOD

This study looked at how page layout and design, navigation techniques, security and privacy and perceived usefulness influence the user experience of e-commerce website users.

Instrument

The method used by the study entails performing a preliminary classification of usability factors such as colour, navigation technique and functionality for a number of e-commerce websites in South Africa. A web portal then acts as a launching pad for users to access these sites. Upon exit from the site, users are asked to complete a short evaluation to determine the subjective user experience of the website that they accessed. This method holds the advantage that the user's experience is measured immediately after using the site.

Problem Areas

It is difficult to define the norm for the user experience and how it relates to other factors. The user interface, machine factors, cultural factors, individual factors and usability factors are likely to influence the experience. Many user characteristics such as age, experience and gender can also influence the interaction with the website.

The chosen method of data collection employs non-probabilistic sampling and self-selection, therefore it may not be representative of the general population of e-commerce users.

RESULTS

A total of 101 responses , including 72 from university students, covering seventeen web sites from the banking, recruitment, travel, retail and automotive sectors were collected.

Page Design and Layout

It was found that users seem to prefer less saturated colours. While a number of suites used both red and blue, only one got a relatively high rating. This could be attributed to the fact that the colours were less saturated, and so less obtrusive, and that there was less of the colour, rather using the colour to highlight more important areas.

There seem to be a general dislike for background colours. One site had a light blue background, and another had a yellow background and neither got high ratings. On the other hand, a site with an off white background did not get low ratings, which suggests that users do not like coloured backgrounds.

Those sites that were packed with information and did not have much background space showing did not get high ratings. Two sites with a high percentage of content and little background got low ratings while two sites with a high percentage of blank space showing got higher ratings. This suggests that users prefer sites to have some free space so that they are not too busy or full with information.

The one aspect of design that is strongly warned against by many authors is the use of frames, but the researchers did not find any evidence that users do not like them.

Navigation

Web sites that have a high level of clarity and a well defined layout are rated much higher than those sites with a "busy" layout. A greater use of white space i.e. blank spaces on the page, translates into more favourable navigation ratings opposed to those with little blank space.

The pages whose navigation bars were both text and graphics based, also resulted in a favourable perception, by the user, of the site's navigation capabilities. Those web sites that had no navigation bars were rated average or below average by the respondents as these sites used plain links on the page. A possible explanation for this is the fact that the user does not have a feeling of a standard and structured navigation layout and therefore their experience and thus consequent satisfaction are detracted from.

Finally the use of well positioned and clearly defined sub menus have a good effect on a user's satisfaction with the web site, as this provides the user with information in a neat and structured format.

Security and Privacy

Only one site, a bank, got a high ranking for security. This may be attributed to the fact that the design of the web site was extremely professional in comparison to the other sites, creating a sense of security, even though it may not have been one of the most secure web sites.

The general sense of uncertainty could be attributed to the fact that South Africa has an emerging e commerce market, and consumers have not yet adapted to the idea of their safety on the Internet.

There seemed to be no evidence that privacy statements and digital certificates had any effect whatsoever on the perceived security of the sites.

Usefulness

The sites preferred for usefulness had accuracy, reliability and relevance as common characteristics with regards to their information content.

Specifically value added services provided by sites tended to translate into a favourable response from users. This included all the various possibilities and variations that a user might opt for or require whilst using the web site. Much attention was given to the accuracy, reliability and the relevance of the information on these sites in relation to their core business activities.

Conversely the remaining sites were rated lower, due to the fact that these value added services were not present or were present but had no relevance to the web site's core business activities. Specifically this could be seen on some sites that have these so called extras on the site, but are unrelated to any of the core activities performed by the businesses.

Often users did not find the information due to the poor design of the site's navigation.

The User

Since the sample consisted mostly of university students, it did not offer a wide range with regards to age, language and computer experience; therefore no conclusions regarding this could be drawn.

CONCLUSION

Even though based on a limited sample, this study shows that users prefer a user interface with enough white space and a neutral, light coloured background. Standardised navigation bars were preferred over unstructured links for navigation. Privacy statements and digital certificates did not seem to improve the perceived security of the sites, while accuracy, reliability and relevance of value added services helped to create a perception of usefulness.

REFERENCES

Atkinson, M.A., and Kydd, C 1997. *Individual characteristics associated with World Wide Web use: an empirical study of playfulness and motivation.* Database for Advances in Information Systems, Vol.28, no.2, p.53-62.

"*Consumers are ready for e-commerce; Web sites are not.*". 1999. Gartner Research Note. Availble: http:www.gartner.com [30 November1999]

Davis, F.D. 1989. *Perceived usefulness, perceived ease of use, and user acceptance of information technology.* MIS Quarterly, 1989, September, p.319-340.

De Groot, B., Eikelboom, P. & Egger, F.N. 2001. *User or Consumer? Bringing together HCI and Marketing.* CHI2001: Conference on Human Factors in Computing Systems, Seattle (USA), 31 March-5 April 2001.

De'Hertefelt, S. 2000. *Emerging and future usability challenges: designing user experiences and user communities.* Available: http://www.interactionarchitect.com [2 Feb 2000]

Dholakia, U. & Bagozzi, R.P. 1999. *Consumer Behaviour in Digital Environments.* Working Paper

Egger, F.N. 1999. *Human Factors in Electronic Commerce: Making Systems Appealing, Usable & Trustworthy.* Graduate Students Consortium, 12th Bled International E-Commerce Conference, June 1999, Bled, Slovenia.

Gilb, T. 1988. *Principles of Software Engineering Management.* Addison Wesley, Reading, MA.

Hill, N. 1997. *Handbook of Customer Satisfaction Measurement.* Grower Publishing Ltd., England.

Hoffman, D.L., T.P. Novak & P. Chattejee 1995, *Commercial scenario's for the web: opportunities and challenges,* Journal of Computer-mediated Communication, Vol.1, no.3.

Hurst, M. 2000. *Special Report : Design Usability Getting Past Go.* Available: http://www.internetworld.com [15 Dec 2000]

Li, H., C. Kuo & Russel, M. G. 1999. *The impact of perceived channel utilities, shopping orientations, and demographics on the consumer's online buying behaviour,* Journal of Computer-mediated Communication, Vol.5, no.2., December 1999.

Lohse, G.L. & Spiller, P. 1999. *Internet retail store design: how the user interface influences traffic and sales,* Journal of Computer-mediated Communication, Vol.5, no.2., December 1999.

Nielsen, J. 2000. *A definition of User Experience.* Available: http:www.useit.com [14 Apr 2001]

Nielsen, J. & Molich, R. 1990. *Heuristic Evaluation of User Interfaces.* In CHI'90 proceedings, SIGCHI Bulletin, Special Issue, P.249-256.

Van Niekerk, R. 2001. SA *Internetgebruikers oortref verwagtinge : strategiese foute striem die grotes,* Die Burger, 16 January 200, p. 6.

"*Why Most Web Sites Fail.* 1998 " Forrester Research, Available: http://www.forrester.com/ER/research/report/excerpt/0,1338,1285,FF.html [18 April 2001]

Decision Support System for Data and Web Mining Tools Selection

Janusz Swierzowicz
Rzeszów University of Technology, Poland and The University of Information Technology and Management in Rzeszów
Tel: +4 (817) 865-1424, Fax: +4 (817) 856-2519, jswierzowicz@acm.org

ABSTRACT

The system includes a Data and Web Mining Tools database. With this system, the user can distinguish data processing requirements (volume, complexity), data mining requirements (tasks, methodology, domain of data mining), system requirements (scalability, portability, availability, architecture, flexibility of user interface) and economic issues of producer or vendor offers. Some basic descriptions of the system and data mining examples are outlined.

INTRODUCTION

In 1965 Gordon Moore, presented his rule concerning Information Technology development. This rule, known as Moore's law, explains "chip performance doubles every 18 months". Now, this law has been also expanded to include data storage devices. Recent researches on e business carried on by [11] conclude that e-business develops according to Nolan's S curve [12]. E-business hypergrowth has already begun; in North America and Western Europe it started in the year 2000. According to hypergrowth forecast, it will begin during 2005-2008 in Eastern Europe. This e-Business hypergrowth will have strong effects on data resources that are also expanding very quickly. According to current analysis carried out by IBM Almaden Research [10], contemporary Internet resources hold about 100 TB of data. Digital online data exceeds 1EB, digital offline data is about 20EB and analog data capacity is above 300 EB (see Figure 1).

Figure 1: Contemporary data resources

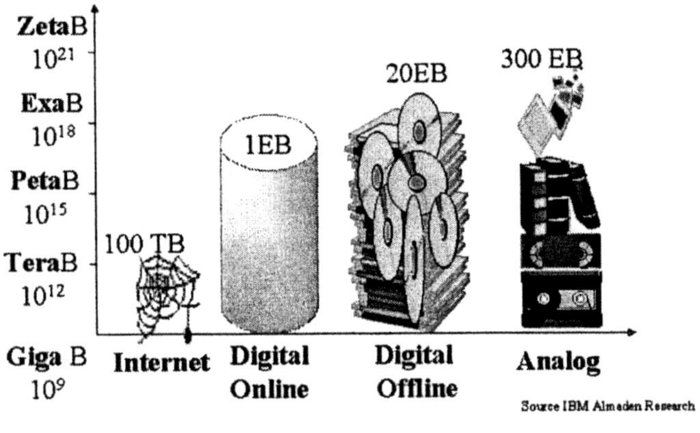

Data volumes are rising at different speeds. The fastest is Internet resources growth – it will achieve the digital online threshold by the year 2006. New projects' goals e.g. CyberAll [1] that is to encode, store and allow easy retrieval of all of the personal information, are further contributing to this growth. In these fast rising volumes of data environment, especial one constant factor seems to be human abilities i.e. human memory capacities ~200 MB [9], reading text 100kB/hour – 6 GB lifetime, spoken text – 40MB/hour ~10 TB and DVD video 2GB/Hour ~8PB lifetime [1]. Another restriction is connected with a human's low data complexity and dimensionality analysis [5].

DATA MINING NECESSITY

One of the results of the inexorable rise of such data volumes and complexity is a data overload problem. It is impossible to solve the data overload issue in a human manner – it takes strong effort to use intelligent and automatic software tools for turning rough data into information and information into profit [2-8, 13-15]. Data mining is one of the central activities associated with understanding, navigating and exploiting the world of digital data. It is an intelligent and automatic process of identifying and discovering useful structures in data such as patterns, models and relations. We can consider data mining as a part of the overall Knowledge Discovery in Data process, which is defined as "the nontrivial process of identifying valid, novel, potentially useful, and ultimately understandable patterns in data" [4]. We have depicted data mining and other steps as a closed loop system in Figure 2.

Figure 2: Data mining cycle

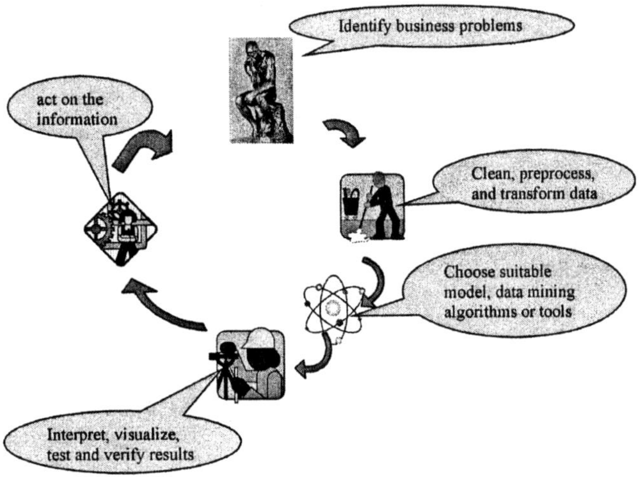

Data Mining should support us as we struggle to solve data overload and complexity issues. With the fastest acceleration of online data resources in the Internet, the World Wide Web is a natural area for using data mining techniques to automatically discover and extract actionable information from Web documents and services, especially in e-business. We have named those techniques of Web Mining that can be broken down into such subtasks as: resource discovery, information extraction and generalization [3, 8]. Web data formats fit into two main categories [6]:

- Web logs data, which are time-stamped records of users' action e.g. access logs, agent logs, error logs, referrer logs, cookie logs, application logs.
- Non-event data (transaction, customer records, demographic databases, site architecture etc.).

We also consider text mining as a data-mining task that helps us summarize, cluster, classify and find similar text documents.

OVERVIEW OF THE SYSTEM

To find suitable software solution the user should determine his requirements according to data processing, data mining, operating system and application domain. The system includes a Web and Data Mining Tools database selected mainly from [7-8] and from the Internet.

Figure 3: An interface of the system

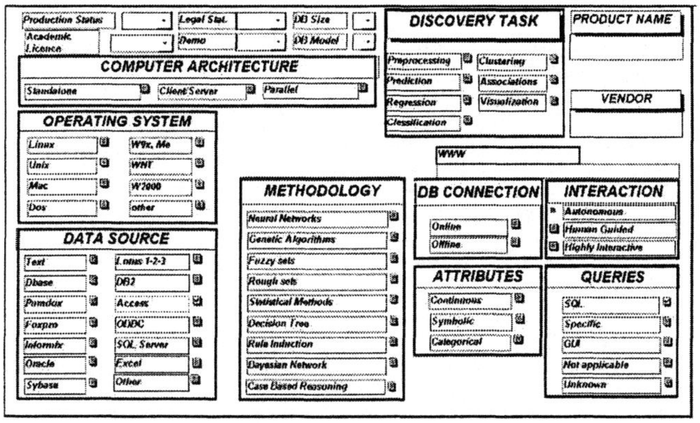

With the system presented in Figure 3, the user can distinguish:

- data processing requirements (data sources, type of database connection, maximum number of handled data, types of handled attributes, data models),
- data mining requirements :
  - goal (Classification, Regression, Prediction, Clustering, Associations),
  - discovery methodology (Case Based Reasoning, Neural Networks, Decision Trees, Rule Induction, Genetic Algorithms, Fuzzy Sets, Rough Sets, Statistical Methods, Bayesian Networks),
  - methodology characteristics factors (Model Training Easiness, Model Understanding Easiness, Model Application Easiness, Model Generality, Model Usefulness, Model Availability),
- domain (Business, Manufacturing, Medicine, Pattern Recognition, Science, Sports, Stocks, Translations, etc.)
- system requirements (operating system, architecture scalability, flexibility of user interface),
- general product characteristics (status of product development, legal product status, manual quality, availability of academic licensing.

Some basic descriptions of the system and examples are outlined below. At the beginning, the user determines a business problem and requirements for data processing, system and data mining tasks. Then the system looks for the best discovery methodology for this task, that are made on the base of the Data Mining Report Card [3], taking into consideration the following data mining methodology characteristic factors:

MAE - Model Application Easiness Factor - explains how simple it is to use a generated model to score a data set,

MAF - Model Availability Factor - explains the number software packages that implement this methodology

MGF - Model Generality Factor - explains if this methodology can be applied to a wide variety of data types and problems,

MTE - Model Training Easiness Factor - explains how much effort is required to build a new model and assertions whether the model requires many data transformations, iterations, manual interventions,

MUE - Model Understanding Easiness Factor- gives the answer to why the model makes the prediction, finds whether it adds insight on the domain and explains the way it arrives at a solution,

MUF - Model Usefulness Factor - explains how good the results produced by the model are and estimates the value of practical results.

Then the system looks for similar business problem determination and for the tools that were used to solve it. Selected tools that were applied in solving previous business problems are adapted to solve the current situation. After selection the user closed loop action for improvement of the system experience is performed.

SOME DATA MINING EXAMPLES

This chapter describes some problems and their solutions with selected data mining tools.

At the beginning, we consider a marketing campaign with a new banking account that was solved with SPSS Clementine [15]. The main business problem was to send offer to customers who are most likely to purchase a new product. The problem was reduced to maximizing the effectiveness of targeting and to decreasing mailing costs. It was solved using Rule Induction and Neural Networks methods with the following steps:

- Select a random sample of customers (who like to buy a new product) for a trial mail campaign.
- Send out a mail offering a new product.
- Record the customers' response.
- Analyze results with DM tool by:
  - Splitting input data on three data sets for training, testing and for evaluation.
  - Selecting items representing data from the object palette.
  - Building a diagram of analytical stream to visualize a business process.
  - Manipulating records and fields.
  - Estimating relationships between variables.
  - Visualizing the data with graphs.
  - Building predictive models using various methodologies e.g. Neural Networks and Rule Induction.
  - Comparing different types of models.
  - Improvement of the Models.
  - Output generation.

An output is a report with customer ID ordered by confidence scores of customers most likely to purchase a new product. The goal of the system i.e.: maximizing the effectiveness of targeting and the reduction of mailing costs are achieved.

The goal of the second example is to find similarities between scientific publications that are gathered in the database. This problem has appeared as one task of Management Information System for Classification of Scientific Achievements [14]. A Memory Based Reasoning algorithm has been applied in this system as follows:

- Data selection: Table *Papers(PaperID, Title,...)*
- Data cleaning : correction of words.
- Data Transformation:
  - Create Table *Terms(TermID, Term, PaperID)*
  - Create Table *Exceptions* and filling up non-content bearing words from the table *Terms*,
    - Delete exceptions from *Terms*
    - Create Table ***LW*** **(*Term*, λ, μ, γ)**

      where: λ- no. of occurrences of the *term* in the table *LW*

      $$\mu = 1/\lambda \quad (1)$$

      $$\gamma = -Ln(\mu)/Ln(2) \quad (2)$$
- Data mining:
  - Distance function determination **d(A,B)** between two points **A** and **B** in data space with following characteristics:

    $$d(A,B) \geq 0 \quad (3)$$

    $$d(A,A) = 0 \quad (4)$$

    $$d(A,B) = d(B,A) \quad (5)$$

    $$d(A,B) + d(B,C) \geq d(A,C) \quad (6)$$
  - For distance function **d(A,B)** determination a relevance feedback score for two papers **δ** was brought into effect as follows

    $$\delta(A,B) = \Sigma\ \gamma\ (A,B) \quad (7)$$

where: **Σ γ (A,B)** –, the weights of the searchable terms in both papers are added together thus a distance function is given as

$$\mathbf{d(A,B)} = 1 - \frac{\delta(A,B)}{\sqrt{\frac{\delta(A,A)^2 + \delta(B,B)^2}{2}}} \quad (8)$$

- Create table **δAB**(ID_A,ID_B, δ(A,B))
- Create table **dAB**(ID_A,ID_B,d(A,B))
- Order **dAB**(ID_A,ID_B,d(A,B)) and show items according to user's determined distance threshold using the SQL parametrical query as follows:

```
SELECT tabDistanceAB.Terms_PaperID AS ID_A,
tabDistanceAB.Terms_1_PaperID AS ID_B, tabDistanceAB.Distance,
Paper.TITLE AS [TITLE_A ], Paper_1.TITLE AS [TITLE_B]
FROM Paper AS Paper_1 INNER JOIN (Paper INNER JOIN
tabDistanceAB ON Paper.ID = tabDistanceAB.Terms_PaperID) ON
Paper_1.ID = tabDistanceAB.Terms_1_PaperID
WHERE (((tabDistanceAB.Distance)<=[Select distance threshold]))
ORDER BY tabDistanceAB.Distance, tabDistanceAB.Terms_PaperID,
tabDistanceAB.Terms_1_PaperID;
```

(9)

- Results

An example of the DM algorithm results with the threshold distance = 0.15 is presented in the table below.

Table 1: DM algorithm results

ID_A/ID_B	Distance	Titles of publications A/B
306/ 371	0,12	On some transformations of the Caratheodory class of functions
		On some subclass of Caratheodory functions and corresponding class of starlike functions
727/869	0,14	Mechanical properties of the two-phase titanium alloys with lamellar microstructure
		The effect of microstructure on the mechanical properties of two-phase titanium alloys

CONCLUSION

Presented system can provide a framework for comparison of different tools considering requirements of processing and mining data as well operating system, domain and economic issues. Current research include the improvement of the search techniques and test of data and web mining tools for compatibility with emergent data mining standards eg. CRISP DM, OLEDB DM, PMML.

REFERENCES

1. Bell G.: A Personal Digital Store, Communication of the ACM, January, 2001/Vol.44, No.1 pp.86-91
2. Berry M., Linoff G.: Data Mining Techniques, John Wiley & Sons, Inc, New York, 1997
3. Etzioni O.: The World Wide Web: the quagmire or goldmine, Communications of the ACM, 1996, November
4. Fayyad, U., M., Piatetsky-Shapiro, G., Smyth, P., and Uthurusamy R.: From data mining to knowledge discovery: An overview. Fayyad, U., M. et al. (ed): Advances in Knowledge Discovery and Data Mining, , AAAI Press/The MIT Press, Menlo Park, CA, pp.1-34, 1996
5. Fayyad, U.: The Digital Physics of Data Mining, Communication of the ACM, March, 2001/Vol.44, No.3 pp.62-65
6. Gaining a competitive edge with Web mining, SPSS Technical Report, 2001
7. Goebel M, Gruenwald L.: A Survey of Data Mining software Tools, SIGKDD Explorations, June 1999, v.1, issue 1, pp.20-33
8. Kosala R., Blockeel H.: Web Mining Research: A Survey, SIGKDD Explorations, June 2000, Vol. 2, Issue 1, pp.1-16
9. Landauer T. K.; "How much do people remember? Some estimates of the quantity of learned information in long-term memory," Cognitive Science, 10 (4) pp. 477-493 (Oct-Dec 1986).
10. Liautaud B.: e-Business Intelligence: Turning Information into Knowledge into Profit, McGraw-Hill, New York, 2001
11. McCarthy J.: The Commerce Threshold, Forrester Research, 2000
12. Nolan R.L.: Managing the Crisis in Data Processing, Harvard Business Review, 1990.
13. Stanfill C., Waltz D.: Toward Memory-Based Reasoning, Communications of the ACM, 1986, December
14. Swierzowicz J.: A Management Information System for Classification of Scientific Achievements, Evolution and Challenges in System Development, Zupancic et al (ed)., Kluwer Academic/Plenum Publishers, New York, pp.735-740, 1999.
15. www.spss/clementine

Inter-organizational Learning and ICT: A Case Study in Sustainability Education

Polly Courtice, Tracey Swift and Lindsay Hooper
University of Cambridge Programme for Industry, UK
Tel: +440 (122) 334-2100, Fax: +440 (122) 330-1122, {Polly.courtice, tracey.swift, lindsay.hooper}@cpi.cam.ac.uk

ABSTRACT

The purpose of this paper is to report on experiential findings regarding a blended learning educational programme for mid-career managers on the subject of sustainability. Using qualitative responses to an evaluation assessment tool after an entire cohort completed the one year course, the paper deepens our insights into factors associated with the failure of ICT. Rather than be deterred, the paper concludes that ICT is still an essential part of inter-organisational learning.

INTRODUCTION

Background Information

This Case Study explores the implementation of ICT in the Sustainability Learning Networks Programme, a University of Cambridge accredited programme launched in 1998 for mid-career executives. Together with the traditional remit of providing instruction for individual learning, a discrete purpose of this course was to facilitate the sharing of learning about sustainability amongst learners from 14 member companies in a learning consortium. A third aim was to embed sustainability literacy within each of the consortium companies. The phrasing of these aims is consistent with the behavioural objectives and desired personal outcomes (Allan, 1996) for learners and their companies. Both work-based action research and learning for the workplace are fundamental to the pedagogy of the course, and our teaching objectives were to use ICT to achieve these learner-centered aims.

ICT was integrated into the design of this programme from its conception. The software and support for this element of the learning Programme were constantly evaluated and refined in order to meet learner needs. However, by the end of the three-year pilot phase (September 2001), the programme has evolved (in response to participant and company demand) to the extent that participants are no longer expected to collaborate, or even communicate online. For new learners joining the course, the Programme's online Workspace is positioned as an information resource, rather than an online collaboration environment.

This paper concludes that the learner-led development away from online collaboration was due to a combination of factors including: the attitudes and motivation of learners (a common inhibitor of ICT adoption in a variety of learner groups; see Cornell & Martin, 1997; and Eccles & Wigfield, 1995), the complexity associated with sustainability (Filho, 2000) and the diversity of initial subject matter expertise. The participant mix was important to establish a safe learning community (Bonk & Cummings, 1998). A critical, yet unexpected finding was that issues of commercial confidentiality also inhibited the success of ICT within this particular learning programme, one that we argue should be taken into consideration in the design and conduct of executive education using ICT.

This paper consists of supplemented highlights of the responses of seventeen students from the first cohort in the Sustainability Learning Networks Programme.

Technology

Lotus Learning Space was used primarily because it provided a relatively user-friendly, internet-based environment for sharing materials, scheduling work, conducting informal discussions and undertaking more formal group work.

A considerable amount of effort has been put into developing the Programme within Learning Space to ensure that the learning objectives could be met as effectively as possible. However, throughout the Programme it has constantly been reiterated that this is just a *tool* to facilitate collaborative working among geographically dispersed programme participants. Although it was requested that the assessed work be submitted via Learning Space, participants were also encouraged to communicate by phone, fax, email or face-to-face if they preferred.

FACTORS ASSOCIATED WITH FAILURE OF ICT

Lack of Familiarity

Failure to use ICT is sometimes associated with lack of familiarity or availability (see for example Williams *et. al,* 2000) and our findings broadly confirmed this. Many of the learners were fairly senior managers within their organisations, and had secretaries to do their typing and send emails for them. They were uncomfortable with a means of communication that involved them sitting down at a computer. However, lack of familiarity with technology was only part of the problem. We found that the attitudes of learners towards ICT in this course were shaped predominantly by their natural mode of communicating in the workplace. Many of the executives were used to participating in face-to-face meetings and preferred to continue this practice, with most project groups arranging 2 or 3 informal meetings in the course of the programme rather than collaborating online.

> *"I have not found the LS to be particularly helpful during the programme... while I think it was a valuable centralised mechanism for storing information, I got the impression you had wanted it to be used more interactively by participants. I am not sure of the reasons for my own discomfort with it. However, the result has been a supplementary reliance on email as a far more effective and efficient means of communicating with other participants and transferring documents. Furthermore, that e-mail communication has only been with other members of my project group – not with other participants."*

Complexities Of Subject Matter

Despite being one of the most widely used scientific terms, sustainability is also one of the most misunderstood constructs (Filho, 2000). Because of the complexity of the subject, learners were not comfortable articulating their thoughts on the subject with the necessary brevity for an online discussion. They preferred to observe in the background, rather than actively participate (Khan, 1998). There was greater comfort over issues of commercial confidentiality when discussing their work face to face when Chatham House rules were in force, but learners were unhappy to share their work on the Programme's Workspace where they felt their privacy was vulnerable to invasion. A further inhibitor was the functional background mix of the learners. Although all the learners were peers in the sense of similar standing in organisational hierarchies, some began the programme with no understanding of sustainability, whereas others were practitioners in related disciplines. The non-experts felt constrained by this difference in intellectual starting points, which was manifested in them not committing their thoughts and work to text on the ICT workspace where they felt they were open to critique.

The Role of Motivation and Assessment

Lack of engagement with ICT was also related to motivation and assessment. None of the learners self-selected for the course, but were nominated to attend on behalf of their companies as part of the learning consortium. They were by no means reluctant to participate, but given that the benefits of the course were aimed primarily at their companies rather than them as individuals, their efforts and enthusiasm were limited to exactly what was required of them i.e. if they weren't being assessed on their participation in online discussions, and if they saw no company benefit in such discussions, they weren't going to make any effort in that direction.

Time Factors

Another factor which impacted on the use of ICT, was the limited amount of time that executives working full-time could devote to developing and completing assessable work. Due to the time constraints associated with their demanding jobs, participants wanted assessable items to be consolidated into 3 major pieces of work, whereas successful ICT implementations typically require participants to complete a range of small tasks online to encourage familiarity and confidence with the medium.

CONCLUSION

It is evident that learners benefit greatly from inter-organisational learning in relation to sustainability, as the following quotes illustrate:

> *"I found the group work invaluable and am trying to implement key actions within my own area of responsibility to drive change from within."*
>
> *"Networking across businesses and the plenary sessions provided insight into how sustainability is tackled within other industries, enabling me to benchmark my company's activities against other organisations/industries."*
>
> *"One of the great benefits of the course has been the interaction with representatives from many diverse companies. Seeing what progress others have made in sustainable development is enlightening. It enables those from more conservative industries or those that are just embarking on the journey to see what is possible and avoid the "Can't Do" mindset."*

ICT seems to be an obvious mechanism for facilitating work-based learning and establishing communities of practice amongst peer groups of executives in different companies and industry sectors. Yet, factors associated with their organisational seniority and the commercially sensitive nature of the information they were required to share in order to participate in group learning were significant in impeding the use of ICT for sustainability learning. Other University educators who wish to use ICT for executive education programmes would do well to consider these findings.

REFERENCES

Allan, J. (1996) "Learning outcomes in higher education", *Studies in Higher Education,* 21, (1), pp93-108.

Bonk, C. J. and Cummings, J. A. (1998) "A dozen recommendations for placing the student at the centre of web-based learning", Educational Media International, 35, (2), pp 82-89.

Cornell, R. and Martin, B.L. (1997) "The role of motivation in web-based instruction", in B. Khan (ed), *Web-based instruction,* Englewood Cliffs, New Jersey, Educational Technology Publications.

Eccles, J.S. and Wigfield, A. (1995) "In the mind of the actor: the structure of adolescents' achievements task values and expectancy-related beliefs", *Personality and Social Psychology Bulletin,* 21, 215225.

Filho, W. L. (2000) "Dealing with misconceptions on the concept of sustainability", *International Journal of Sustainability in Higher Education,* 1, (1) 2000, pp 9–19.

Khan, B. H. (1998) "Web-based instruction (WBI) an introduction", Educational Media International, 35, (2), pp 63-71.

Williams, D., Coles, L., Wilson, K., Richardson, A. and Tuson, J. (2000) "Teachers and ICT: current use and future needs", *British Journal of Educational Technology,* 31, (4), pp307-320.

"Info-Mathics"—The Mathematical Modeling of Information Systems

Andrew Targowski
Professor of Computer Information Systems, Western Michigan University, Department of Business Information Systems
Tel: (616) 375-6860, Fax: (616) 375-8762, targowski@wmich.edu

ABSTRACT

The review of modeling IS techniques, including relational algebra, structured designe, architectural design, and Unified Modeling Language. A new technique "info-mathics" of mathematical description of the hierarchical systems architecture is defined to secure the system reliability and quality. The classification of IS categories and its attributes such as components, structure, relationships, system level, system product, system deepness, system width, system list, system end, and other are presented. Examples of the mathematical notations are provided and their meaning for the practical implications of info-mathics in system analysis and design are indicated.

INTRODUCTION

The design of Information Systems evolves from the art towards engineering as systems evolve from simple to more complex. The introduction of relational databases triggered the application of relational algebra (Merrett 1984). Its application is limited to the database design. The structured designe of systems, introduced in the 1980s, was the step forward after structured programming was offered in the 1970s (Kowal 1988). However, this approach is mostly applied at the level of data flow diagrams at the very low system level, mostly in file updating or transactions processing. The architectural system design was step beyond of DFD and aimed at the large scale-system (Targowski 1990).

The recent trend in system design emphasizes a technique called Unified Modeling Language (UML) (Siau, Halpin 2001). It is aimed at the design of object-oriented software at the level of programming. To design higher-level application systems it is necessary to apply similar techniques as are applied in mechanical or civil engineering, where the main product solution is based on a Bill of Material Processor (BOMP). BOMP lists product components and indicates their assembling sequences (Pawlak 1969). This study presents a mathematical modeling of application information systems leading to the development of a Bill of Systems Processor (BOSP). This is a step of transforming the art of system design into information engineering.

GRAPHIC MODEL OF A HIERARCHICAL INFORMATION SYSTEM

As an example of an information system let's analyze a Hierarchical Management Information System (MIS) which is composed of three systems only:

- Enterprise Information Portal (EIP)
- Enterprise Performance Management (EPM)
- Data Mining System (DMS)

at the following management levels (Figure 1):

- The headquarters level (ex.: General Motors Corporation):
  $HMIS^{c} = \{(EIP^{C}, EPM^{C}, DMS^{C}), R^{C}\}$
  Where R – structure of relationships among systems
- The group level (ex.: Buick-Oldsmobile-Cadillac):
  $GMIS^{G} = \{(EIP^{G}, EPM^{G}, DMS^{c}), R^{G}\}$
- The plant level (ex.: Cadillac):
  $PMIS^{P} = \{(EIP^{P}, EPM^{P}), R^{P}\}$

In the current IS practice the graphic modeling, called also the architectural planning, is the only applied technique. However, in more complex IT environments this technique is limited. The graphic modeling in sciences is superior technique to the scenario technique but inferior technique to the mathematical modeling.

Let's try to generalize an IS definition by applying the mathematical technique.

MATHEMATICAL MODELING OF A HIERARCHICAL INFORMATION SYSTEM

A generalized model of a hierarchical information system is shown in Figure 2. Let's introduce a relation B Ì R, which we will call the direct relationship of a component of a given IS. We will speak that SI(x) is the direct component of SI(y) if:

1. SI(x) is a component of SI(y), which means that SI(x) and SI(y) are in the relation B, and it is noted as:
   B{SI(x), SI(y)},
2. There is no such SI(z), belonging to the set U{SI(z) ÎU}, which is the component SI(y), [SI(z) and SI(y) there are not in the relation B] and whose component is SI(x) [SI(x) and SI(z) there are not in the relation B].

If the set of SI(x) is the direct component of the set SI(y) then we will note it as SI(x) = b{SI(y)}.

The B relation we will call the schema of a system, which can be illustrated in a diagram where circles represent subsystems (Figure 2).

If B{S(x), SI(y)} then the circles representing subsystems x and y we will link by a line from x to y. In such a manner to each system one can subordinate a tree as it is shown in Figure 3. This tree is a graph of all B relations. The system schema means the same as "to be a direct component."

Systems x and y we will call the same (equivalent) if their schema are equal, which means that they have the same components and linked by the same relations.

With every system SI(x) we associate a number l {(SI(x)}, called a **system level** in the following manner:

1. If SI(x) is the end subsystem, then l {SI(x)} = 0.
2. If B{SI(x), SI(y)}, then l {SI(x)} = l {SI(y)} + 1.

Figure 2 illustrates a level of each system. A level of SI is nothing else than a story on which there is a given subsystem in the system schema.

To each system SI(x) we will attribute a number c {SI(x)} called a **system product**, noted in the following manner:

$$\chi \{SI(x)\} = \overline{\beta} \{SI(x)\}$$

where: ' $\overline{\beta}$ {SI(x)} is the number of components of a set b {SI(x)}, which is the direct components of system SI(x).

A system product is the number of direct components.

A **system depth** of SI(x) is the maximal level of its subsystems and we will note it as ¡ {SI(x)}. A system depth is the number of system levels, reduced by 1.

A **system width** of SI(x) is the maximal number of subsystems of the same system level and will be noted as d{SI(x)}.

Figure 1: A hierarchical management information system

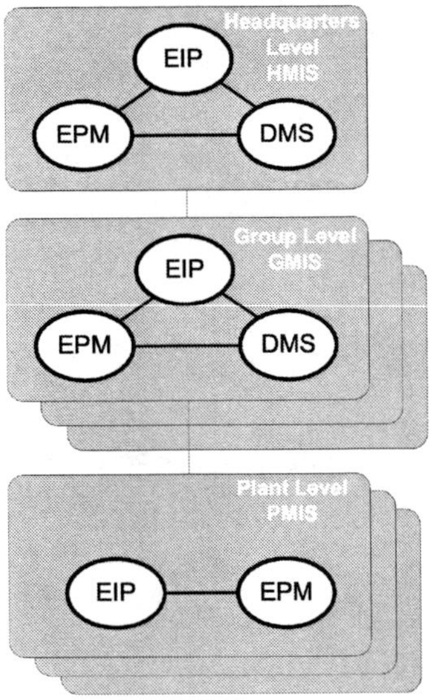

Figure 2: The levels of a hierarchical information system (l=0, l=1, l=2, l=3)

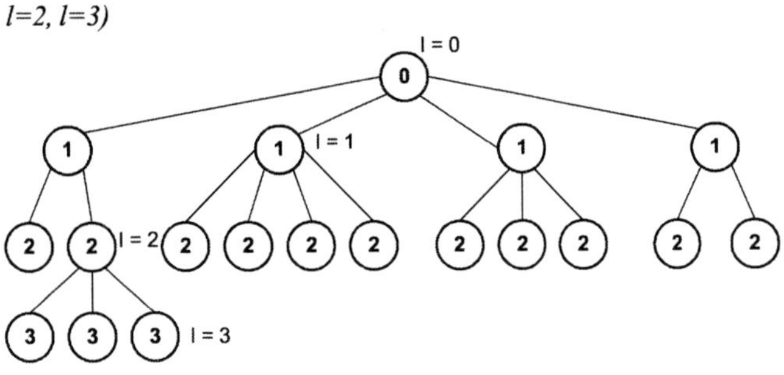

BILL OF SYSTEMS PROCESSOR (BOSP)

Following a concept of BOMP (Bill Of Material Processor) we introduce a concept of BOSP, which is a list of system's components. The condition of defining a BOSP is that the different components should have different names and the same components should have the same names.

1. If SI(x) is a system then $\overline{SI}$ (x) is a name of this system and λ is the number of subsystems of SI(x)
2. If SI(x) is the simple system, then λ SI(x) = SI(x)
3. If SI(y) and $SI(x_1),.....SI(x_k)$ are such systems that

β {SI(y} = $\{SI(x_1),.....SI(x_k)\}$, then λ SI(y) = $\overline{SI}$ (y) $\{\lambda SI(x_1),...SI(x_k)\}$.

This notation means that a BOSP of a simple system is composed of a system name and BOSP, a complex system is composed of a system name and direct components.

Let's consider SI with a name CIS shown in Figure 1. For this system

β (HMIS) = { EIP^c, EPM^c , DMS^c}

β (GMIS) = { EIP^G, EPM^G , DMS^G}

β (PMIS) = { EIP^P, EPM^P }

According to the provider definition, a BOSP of this system will have the following notation:

HMIS [EIP^c, EPM^c ,DMS^c,**GMIS**{EIP^G, EPM^G ,DMS^G, **PMIS**(EIP^P, EPM^P)}]

Figure 3: A tree of a corporate information system

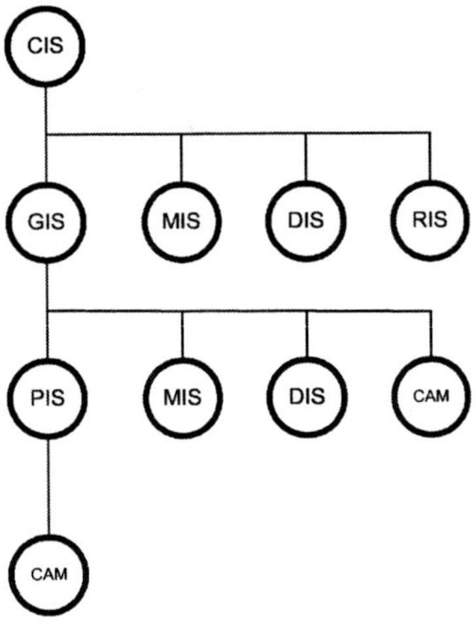

In such a manner a BOSP has been created, which satisfies the above requirements. In this list all subsystems appear. It is easy to recognize subsystems coming to the upper system.

If the parenthesis are eliminated and the number of components is noted in a subscript, then one can define a BOSP in the following manner:

$HMIS_3$ EIP^c_0 EPM^c_0 DMS^c_0 **$GMIS_3$** EIP^G_0 EPM^G_0 DMS^G_0 **$PMIS_2$** EIP^P_0 EPM^P_0

The PMIS' subsystems have only names, because they do not have components. Very often it is necessary to find out what components are directly belonging to the upper system, then the notation can as follows:

$HMIS_3$ EIP^c_0 EPM^c_0 DMS^c_0 **$GMIS_3$**
EIP^c_0
EPM^c_0
DMS^c_0
$GMIS_3$ EIP^G_0 EPM^G_0 DMS^G_0 **$PMIS_2$**
EIP^G_0
EPM^G_0
DMS^G_0
$PMIS_2$ EIP^P_0 EPM^P_0
EIP^P_0
EPM^P_0

In the provided notation, left column determents the notation without parenthesis and components in a row are direct components.

Lets's define a BOSP for an example in Figure 3, where:

CIS – Corporate Information Systems
GIS – Group Information System
MIS – Management Information System
DIS – Dealers Information System
RIS – Retail Information System

CIS_4 GIS_4 MIS_0, DIS_0, RIS_0
MIS_0
DIS_0
RIS_0
GIS_4 MIS_0, DIS_0, RIS_0
MIS_0
DIS_0
RIS_0
PIS_1 MIS_0, DIS_0, CAM_0
CAM_0

The left column contains 10 subsystems, as much as it is shown in Figure 3. Applying the previously defined attributes, one can characterize the CIS as follows:

- System Level: l (CIM)=0, l (GIS)=1, l (PIS)=2, l (CAM)=3

- System Product: $\overline{\beta}$ (CIM)=4, $\overline{\beta}$ (GIS)=4, $\overline{\beta}$ (PIS)=1, $\overline{\beta}$ (CAM)=0
- System Depth: Υ (CIM)=3, Υ (GIS)=2, Υ (PIS)=1, Υ (CAM)=0
- System Width: d (CIM)=4
- End System = CIM (it does not belong to the upper system)
- Simple System = CAM (cannot be divided into subsystems)

Figure 4 illustrates a generalized BOSP for the federated architecture of enterprise-wide systems (Targowski 1990).

CONCLUSION

The presented info-mathic technique of designing large-scale application systems should introduce more order into the sets of enterprise information systems because it is similar to other engineering techniques applied in well developed industries, for example such as the motor or machine-tool industries.

Figure 4: Bill of systems processor (BOSP)

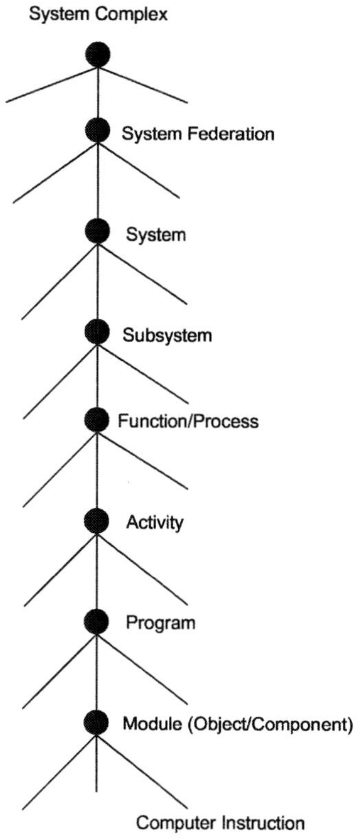

REFERENCES

Kowal, J. A. (1988). *Analyzing Systems.* Englewood Cliffs, NJ: Prentice Hall.

Merret, T. H. (1984). *Relational Information Systems.* Reston, VI: Reston Publishing Co.

Pawlak, Z. (1969). *Matematyczne aspekty procesu produkcyjnego*, Warsaw: PWN.

Siau, K. and T. Halpin. (2001). *Unified Modeling Language.* Hershey, PA: Idea Group Publishing.

Targowski, A. (1990). *The Architecture and Planning of Enterprise-wide Information management Systems.* Hershey, PA: Idea Group Publishing.

The Effectiveness of Frames and an Expandable Table of Contents as User Interface in Hypertext Information Retrieval

Rawiwan Tenissara, PhD
Information Systems Education Center, The National Institute of Development Administration, Thailand, rawiwan@nida.nida.ac.th

ABSTRACT

Difficulties with navigation are common in hypertext documents. Many studies have examined techniques and design strategies to find the proper structure of a hyperdocument whereas others have investigated navigational tools such as overview diagrams, maps, menus, and/or tables of contents that help users navigate through complex hyperdocuments. This study has investigated the effects of table of contents and frames as user interface on user performance and user satisfaction. The result suggests several guidelines for designing complex hypertext information retrieval systems and creating on-line documentation.

INTRODUCTION

Hypertext systems have found various practical applications that can range from on-line documentation, information retrieval systems, to sophisticated learning environments. These applications fall into four general classes: browsing systems, problem exploration tools, macro-library systems, and general hypertext systems (Conklin, 1987).

Hypertext systems, compared to traditional information retrieval systems, provide users with an easy and flexible access to a large amount of information. Hypertext proponents claim that the most salient advantages of these systems are the modularity of information and non-linear access to information through linking (Mohages, 1992).

The primary method for navigating through a hyperdocument is by browsing. However, the limitations of the browsing paradigm were soon revealed when it deals with large hypertext systems. The well-known problems of disorientation and cognitive overload in hypertext systems have been frequently reported and discussed in hypertext literature (Conklin, 1987; Halasz, 1988; Nielsen, 1996).

Providing visual tools, such as overview diagrams or maps, is usually considered an efficient way of helping users navigate through complex hypertext structures (Halasz, Moran, & Trigg, 1987; Yankelovich, Meyrowitz, & Druncker, 1988). However, as noted by many hypertext authors (Bernstein, Garzotto, Paoloni, and Schwab, 1991), designing good overview diagrams for complex structures has proved to be difficult. Overview diagrams may facilitate navigation well in small hypertext systems, but for large systems, overview diagrams might introduce navigational problems of their own (Nielsen, 1990).

Hypertext usage depends on the mental models users have for the system. These mental models, in turn, depend on the conceptual model used by designers to create the system. The system views and navigational tools will be assimilated into a mental model for a system if they are familiar (Marchionini & Shneiderman, 1988). Therefore, designers must know how users seek information in traditional print systems and in the existing electric systems if they are to produce effective interfaces for new systems.

Many readers of books make extensive use of the table of contents and indexes to navigate through a book. They may transfer this experience to using hypertext systems. Table of contents (TOC) shows how the content of a book is related to its structure and provides the terminology of the book grouped in the context of its use (Jacques, Nonnecke, Preece, & McKerlie, 1993). Table of contents is a valuable tool for presenting not only the structure of a hypertext system (Simpson & McKnight, 1990), but the relationships between items within the documents as well. If they are present in hypertext systems, they can provide tremendous help to users.

The interface design for table of contents can vary in hypertext systems. The TOC may be truncated if viewing the response to a query, and may use a fisheye view (Furnas, 1986). An expandable TOC, for example, presents the structure of a hypertext system by employing a fisheye-view method. The expandable TOC, while containing only the highest hierarchical level of headings when a document first displays, allows users to expand each section to its next lowest level and open as many different parts of the table of contents as desired at the same time. Types of interface chosen for table of contents can affect user behaviors, navigation patterns, and ultimately user performance and satisfaction with hypertext systems.

THE OBJECTIVE OF THE STUDY

The objective of the study was to examine the effects of user interface – types of table of contents and frames – on user performance and user satisfaction. To accomplish this goal, a laboratory experiment was conducted using a completely randomized design in which two between-subjects factors were involved.

METHODS

Thirty-six subjects participated in the study and were randomly assigned to four different experimental conditions, e.g., expandable table of contents with single-frame, traditional table of contents with single-frame, expandable table of contents with multiple-frame and traditional table of contents with multiple-frame. Scores obtained in searching and browsing tasks were used as measures of user performance and satisfaction.

RESULTS

The results indicated that expandable table of contents did not lead to significantly better user performance. The users of traditional table of contents performed significantly better than the users of expandable table of contents. In addition, they were more satisfied with the navigational tools than were the users of expandable table of contents. There was no significant difference in user performance or user satisfaction between the multiple-frame and single-frame users. However, the users of traditional table of contents with multiple-frame performed better and were more satisfied with the navigational tools than the users of the other three interfaces. This study suggests a need to further explore how table of contents, frames and a combination of both affect user perception, performance, and satisfaction.

ACKNOWLEDGEMENTS

I would like to thank the study's participants, students at Indiana University Bloomington. Special thanks to Dr. Thomas Schwen, Dr. Samuel Guskin, Dr. Lawson Hughes, Dr. Dirk Van Gucht, Elizabeth Boling, and Dr. Erping Zhu for their valuable support, input and feedback.

REFERENCES

1. Bernstein, M., Garzotto, F., Paolini, P., & Schwabe, D. (1991). Tools for designing hypertextdocuments. In E. Berk & J. Devlin (Eds), *Hypertext / Hypermedia Handbook* (pp. 179-209). New York: McGraw-Hill.
2. Conklin, J. (1987). Hypertext: An introductory and survey, *IEEE Computers, 20,* 17-41.
3. Furnas, G. W. (1986). General fisheye views. *In Proceedings of CHI'86 Human Factors in Computing Systems*, (pp. 12-23). New York: ACM Press.
4. Halasz, F. G. (1988). Reflection on Notecards: Seven issues for the next generation of hypermedia system. *Communication of the ACM, 31(7),* 836-852.
5. Halasz, F. G., Moran, T. P., & Trigg, R. H. (1987). Notecards in a nutshell. *In Proc. Human Factors in Computing Systems* (CHI'87)(pp.45-52). New York: ACM Press.
6. Jacques, R., Nonnecke, B., Preece, J., & McKerlie, D. (1993). Current design in Hypercard: What can we learn? *Journal of Educational Multimedia and Hypermedia, 2(3),* 219-237.
7. Marchionini, G., & Shneiderman, B. (1988). Finding facts vs. browsing knowledge in hypertext systems. *IEEE Computer, 21(1),* 70-80.
8. Mohages, M. F. (1992). The Influence of Hypertext Linking Structures on the Efficiency of Information Retrieval. *Human Factors, 34(3),* 351-367.
9. Nielsen, J. (1990). *Hypertext and Hypermedia.* New York: Academic Press.
10. Nielsen, J. (1996). *Multimedia and Hypertext*: The Internet and Beyond. New York: Academic Press.
11. Simpson, A., & McKnight, C. (1990). Navigation in hypertext: structural cues and mental maps. In R. McAleese & C. Green (Eds.), *Hypertext: State of the Art*, (pp.73-83). Oxford, England: Intellect.
12. Yankelovich, N., Meyrowitz, B. J., & Drucker, S. M. (1988). Intermedia: the concept and construction of a seamless information environment. *IEEE Computer, 31(1),* 81-96.

The Need for Systematic Integration of Legal Considerations in Communications Technology (CT) Management in Contemporary Organisations

James Tunney
Senior Lecture, BA (Law), LLM

INTRODUCTION

CT management is primarily seen as a technical and logistic issue. After the technical and logistical dimension, the accountancy/managerial dimension usually comes next. However, the legal context of CT is extremely important. Because of the focus on the other factors, legal considerations are often considered on an *ex post facto* basis. Often law is perceived to be a reactionary force, and one which need not be considered at an early stage of organisational enterprise. The *Microsoft* antitrust experience revealed that despite its resources, the company was vulnerable to attack for having transgressed very basic rules. Its CT management contributed towards the evidence against it. Indeed, a lack of sophisticated input into the CT management operations may even be the very cause of antitrust breach. When one considers that a company which is found to be in breach of antitrust provisions in the European Union (EU) may be fined up to ten per cent of its gross turnover per annum, considered on a world-wide basis, one can appreciate the benefits of getting it right. This is so irrespective of where the breach occurred, under the notion of 'extra-territoriality' as developed by the European Court of Justice (ECJ).

When one considers in addition, data protection, privacy, freedom of information, defamation, contractual liability, employee protection, trade secrets, copyright, patents and confidential information dimensions, it becomes clear, that many CT management systems will not probably be optimally orientated to deal with them. In many countries, the legal advice in these relatively new contexts will be weak, due to the slowly adapting nature of the national, legal professions. This paper argues that the dynamic, legal context of CT management in contemporary organisations, requires a sophisticated *ex ante* approach.

In view however of the conservative nature and expense of many legal professions and services, it is submitted that it is imperative for organisations involved in CT management to engage with legal discourse in the area of CT. It is imperative for such organisations to build up a proactive, legal-intelligence capability. This capability must be embedded in a practical, adaptive and contemporary way in such organisations. But beyond the operational context, contemporary organisations which are leaders in different fields of CT management must also develop legal information management products. Thus CT management experience, may be turned into commercially saleable products and services. Accordingly, the presently perceived burden of regulation may be turned into opportunities.

This paper will accordingly sketch the relevant legal contours that contemporary organisations operating in a global context must bear in mind, from a CT management perspective. It will then suggest how these considerations should be embedded in the organisation in a prophylactic way. From there it will proceed to illustrate how the adoption of such a strategy should yield benefits, in avoiding liability. It will then suggest how such systems may be turned into products which might be sold.

THE NEED FOR A PROPHYLACTIC APPROACH TO LAW IN MANAGEMENT CONTEXT

It is submitted here that lawyers do not necessarily promote the functionality of legal systems (Tunney, 2000a). Nevertheless law is crucial for the success of business and in the general construction of the context in which information management operates. But lawyers are often trained to think ex post and not ex ante. Thus it is important for users of legal services to encourage ex ante thinking and to engage in it themselves in relation to law.

LAWYERS DO NOT NECESSARILY PROMOTE FUNCTIONALITY OF LEGAL SYSTEMS

That law is perceived to be difficult and complex is not an accident. Professions often promote exclusivity of knowledge to enhance their position and perceived utility. The medical profession has long been accused of this. Their resistance for example hundreds of years ago, to the translation of medical texts into English from Latin, is sometimes cited as characteristic of vested interest triumphing over the 'public' interest. Likewise lawyers can be accused of erecting a wall of incomprehensibility in order to portray themselves as a necessary friend and mediator between a dense and difficult system and a confused citizen or consumer. The fact of restricted practices, has led to all the characteristics of inefficiency and failure to innovate which is associated with market power. Lawyers have been unduly tolerant as a profession of the failures, inadequacies and shortcomings of legal systems. They are not so constructed as to want to reform them too quickly. Unfortunately they have the barely disguised interest that the dentist may have in bad, personal dental hygiene. It is not that the particular professional will not supply a good service when needed (although even this is contestable in a minority of cases). Rather there is a lack of ownership of the system and the circumstances which give rise to the nature and pattern of legal disputes. Dysfunctionality of legal systems is often projected onto politicians or police, while lawyers should have responsibility in view of their pervasive presence in the operation of the legal systems. Another problem is that the failure to innovate by the legal profession may mean that there is an inadequate supply of good quality lawyers in particular areas, such as Communications Technology (CT) and Travel Law, to take two examples.

BUT LAW IS STILL CRUCIALLY IMPORTANT

That legal systems may be dysfunctional, and that lawyers may not have an interest in the functionality of legal systems, does not lead to a conclusion that one should ignore law, particularly as a strategic and operationally relevant force. Law is crucial. Legal rules will always dominate the regulatory environment in which every activity and behaviour takes place. The fact that a particular organisation is unfamiliar with law in a pervasive or specific way does not mean that it can be ignored. 'Ignorance of the law is no excuse,' in law. Employees may be surprised that their bosses have not considered the legal and regulatory environment. That may be because of the dominance of other disciplines and discourses such as accountancy, management, finance or marketing. Organisation 'in-house' lawyers may be preoccupied with housekeeping type legal issues, and have less time for longer-term strategic considerations. But more importantly lawyers are sometimes reactionary and ex post in their way of thinking.

LAWYERS ARE NOT TRAINED TO THINK EX ANTE

Lawyers are not trained particularly to think in an 'ex ante' way, although some might vigorously contest this proposition. Their actual training in the common law world, for example, is often based on the 'case-based' method. In the United States, this has often been associated with Harvard University law faculty. However, teaching by precedents has been long established, and may be traced back in various forms to the very establishment of the common law system in the decades and centuries after the Norman invasion in 1066. The introduction of the case-based teaching system was motivated by good reasons (driven by people such as Langdell), notably the very poor quality of lawyers which had emerged in the US in the late 19th century. It is characterised by the presentation, analysis and critical evaluation of actual cases which have come before the courts. The problem with the case-based method is that it by definition presents a series of situations which in chess terms might be described as ultimate 'endgames.' The fact that they have ended up in court in civil cases almost inevitably means that there has been (what in family law terms might be described as) an 'irreconcilable breakdown' of relations. It is relatively unsurprising therefore if one of the dominant canons in the teaching of law in the common law world, leads to a mindset or world-view which is more focussed on mopping up the spilt milk, rather than preventing it being spilt. While others are told that there is no point in crying over spilt milk, lawyers may be seen to positively smile over it. In general lawyers may be accused of a lack of creativity, despite the creativity of the trial lawyer (Tunney, 2000).

NEVERTHELESS EX-ANTE THINKING AND PREVENTION NEEDS TO BE ENCOURAGED

But that this status quo exists, should not condition those who use lawyers to be negative about how they use them. People who are paying for legal services should require that those who they are supplying them should supply appropriate services. CT has revolutionised the context in which lawyers operate. As writers such as Arthur C. Clarke accurately predicted, it has revolutionised basic grundnorms within law. The basic jurisdictional paradigm itself has been undermined (Tunney, 1998). But more particularly, the legal regulation of CT poses (what might be termed by people such as George Soros as) a reflexive problem for the management of CT itself. As the law moves to regulate CT, the demands put on CT managers will grow exponentially. Bearing in mind the ex post approach of orthodox or conservative lawyers, and the extra burden of the failure of the profession to adequately maintain pace with the conceptual revolution of CT itself, it is probable that those charged with CT management will experience great difficulties in the next decade. There was a curious paradox, that the antitrust litigation in the case of US v Microsoft relied heavily on e-mails as incriminating evidence. The fact that one of the leading CT companies in the world could be so exposed was revealing.

CIVIL LIBERTIES INFORMATION MANAGEMENT IMPERATIVES: FREEDOM AND CHAINS

Freedom of Information (FOI) is an obvious example of a civil liberties type consideration which creates difficulties for information management policies. The general purpose of such legislation is to enable members of the public to obtain access to information to the greatest extent possible, consistent with the public interest and rights of privacy. However it is submitted that non-compliance with disclosure under FOI legislation may be more related to inadequate information management infrastructures rather than a desire to thwart legislative intent. The operation of the FOI Act 1997 in the Republic of Ireland may be being compromised by fragmented policy management (O'Brien, 2002). Apart from compromising legislative intent, the failure to integrate FOI considerations into information management systems could lead to legal liability and adverse publicity. Such a negative spiral could lead to an inappropriately high sensitivity as a result in the organisation which in turn leads to a waste of resources. The consequences of failures to anticipate the operational costs of implementing legislation concerned with information management may be problematic. Universities in Ireland are now citing new information requirements such as under FOI as (well as health and safety and equality) as being responsible for contemporary cash crises (Oliver, 2002). Apart from the costs of failure to implement FOI considerations there are direct costs such as that of employment of FOI officers. Such officers are usually charged with developing procedures and information systems to support compliance with the FOI, assisting in the development of appropriate management policies as well as disseminating information throughout the institution, in addition to promoting awareness and providing guidance to the legislation. However, such particular posts may not be feasible on their own, as many organisations will not be able to afford bespoke posts.

DATA PROTECTION

Analogous to the FOI legislation from an information management perspective is the regime of Data Protection (DP). The substantive content of DP laws is fairly harmonised in the liberal democracies of the world. Organisations such as the Council of Europe have ensured that the principles of DP are fairly well established. Those principles have been further enhanced through other regional legal communities such as the European Union (EU). These communities in turn seek leverage with other regional legal communities and countries, thus embedding the principles. The legal regulation of 'trans-border data flows' adds an extra regulatory hurdle in relation to information for global companies. Thus many countries will be committed legislatively to the principles that information held on computers (and increasingly in manual form) needs to adhere to certain principles. Thus information must be obtained fairly and openly, to be kept only for specified and lawful purposes, be kept accurate and up to date, not be disclosed for incompatible purposes, be adequate and relevant and not excessive and be retained for not longer than is necessary in a secure way. In addition to obligations to register for the user of such data, there will also be subject access provisions to consider. Again a question may arise as to whether there should be a bespoke position in organisations such as universities, to deal with DP. Again the cost of such an approach may seem prohibitive. But what begins to emerge is the need to have either special, dedicated information regulatory management functions or personnel or else perhaps think in terms of a more technological solution.

INTELLECTUAL PROPERTY (IP)

In parallel to the rise of the 'new economy', is the increased importance of Intellectual Property (IP). IP covers patents, copyright, trademarks, confidential information, trade secrets and design. IP is more concerned with respective private rights, although there is a central, public interest dimension. Copyright is the best example of a very relevant context for consideration of law in relation to information management. Napster and Gnutella demonstrated the impact of the threat of technology on copy protection. This has been a ubiquitous interaction going back to the earliest recorded copyright case in 6th century Ireland. The evolution of technology is a relentless spiral which moves in one direction while constantly revisiting elements previously touched. Technological threats court technological solutions. 'Copy circumvention' technology begets anti-copyright protection technology, which begets legal regulation of anti-copyright protection technology, such as in the Digital Millennium Copyright Act 2000 in the US. Bodies such as the World Intellectual Property Organisation (WIPO) have organised complex Treaties to deal with copyright in the on-line environment. However, organisations have shown little pro-activity in the provision of information management tools to help either protect copyright or prevent infringement and liability. Ad hoc organisational reactions will be costly, whether through liability for failure to respect the IP of others or through inadequate exploitation of an organisations own resources.

Recently, awareness of the significance of IP in economic and commercial terms has become wider. It is claimed for example that copyright is now the greatest export of the US, outselling clothes, chemicals, cars, computers and planes, and for instance that Michael Jordan's personal economic value exceeds the kingdom of Jordan's gross national product (Howkins, 2001). The emergence of business-method patents in the US as well as the movement towards 'software patents' presents not only a threat of infringement actions but also an opportunity for firms should they grasp the nettle. However, again the issue of who should become responsible for IP may be difficult. The lawyers will want to be, in certain cases but not in others. Their approach will differ from other professionals for the reasons mentioned above. Other professionals may or may not understand the nature of legal requirements. The possibility for an organisational black hole looms, with selectivity and cherry-picking according to individual interest or based on board-room bias, rather than on a coherent pursuit of institutional interest.

MORE RECENT CONSIDERATIONS: SHIELDS AND SWORDS

As well as these almost 'traditional' CT management considerations there are other emerging ones. In the EU, directives may create information management imperatives which are ignored in the design of IT management systems with peril. While shields must be fashioned to protect companies, it is also worth bearing in mind that other companies will be using CT as a sword. Thus for example CT creates the possibility that convenient trails to liability in the context say of antitrust occur, particularly in contexts where intention is not important as in the Microsoft scenario (Brinkley, 2001)

At the same time there has been a plethora of legislation, particularly in relation to E-commerce. In the EU, there has been recent legislation on 'Distance Selling,' E-Commerce and Electronic Signatures. These may not seem to create overwhelming or insuperable barriers to traders in the EU or elsewhere. However, for the very reason that the E-Commerce directive is a 'framework' legislative measure which creates minimalist regulatory regimes, the courts may be unsympathetic to global organisations which may be subject to, or affected by any of the provisions, but ignored them.

The law of distance selling refers to the protections given to consumers who contract at a distance with the seller of goods and service. It therefore applies to transactions conducted by e-commerce, mail order, telephone ordering and placing an order by fax. In the EU, as well as the E-Commerce legislation one of the main areas of law is *Directive 97/7/EC on the Protection of Consumers in Respect of Distance* Contracts (the Distance Selling Directive). Before this, the consumer had limited specific protection where contracting at a distance. There were some provisions in Directives such as *85/577/EEC to Protect the Consumer in Respect of Contracts Negotiated Away From Business Premises* (the Doorstep Selling Directive). The Distance Selling Directive came into force on 4 June 1997. Member States of the EU were given three years in which to implement its measures. Implementation in the United Kingdom came through a statutory instrument, the Consumer Protection (Distance Selling) Regulations 2000 (S.I. 2000/2334) which came into force on 31 October 2000.

But outside the EU, other regional legal communities such as the Council of Europe (which is far wider than the EU) have been drafting legislation. The new Convention on Cybercrime for example, is perhaps the first major international piece of legislation on cybercrime. Organisations which operate on an international level, which are not informed of its potentially, formative shaping role are surely operated in a strategically impaired mode. In addition to legislative developments are the evolving judicial approaches which must be borne in mind. Thus for example Internet Service Providers (I.S.P.s) may be found liable in the UK for failure to remove defamatory statements which are published on their systems. It would be thus a mistake to automatically apply the reasoning of the US courts to such a context when planning a global strategy in such situations.

SEPTEMBER 11

Even before September 11th, regulatory regimes were beginning to be more demanding of organisations which deal with information management. Thus for example in the UK, the controversial Regulation of Investigatory Powers Act 2000, was seen to effectively co-opt organisations concerned with the transmission of information, into the network of information supply in the national interest through various powers given under the Act to investigatory agencies. The rights or wrongs of such legislation has been well argued by others elsewhere. A lesser degree of attention has focused on concerns for the organisational costs of managing such information. Part of the reason for this has perhaps has been the fragmentation of legal (within law and between law and other disciplines), technological and managerial analyses. Organisations may have to re-organise their information management systems to accommodate increasing executive and judicial demands.

CORPORATE MISMANAGEMENT. ENRON AND AIB

Recent corporate controversies make it clear that the operational complexity of contemporary organisations operating on a global scale requires a re-examination of existing modes of regulation. Enron and AIB losses following other examples of 'rogue trading' such as by Leeson at Barings Bank suggest that regulatory management of contemporary, global organisations must also be considered from a regulatory perspective. Shareholders and investors otherwise will be exposed to unfair risks if there are not systematic diagnostic tools to avoid losses and corporate mismanagement.

FROM THREATS TO OPPORTUNITIES

The fact that law is so complex, that lawyers are reactive, that CT law will necessarily become very difficult to manage and that global systems will lead to global liabilities present great problems. However, as with homeopathy and many systems of 'alternative' thinking, this might instead be looked at positively. Folklore suggests that the cure may come from close to the poison. The fact that CT creates legal problems and that law creates CT problems, suggests that CT could also provide solutions. There will be a growing panopoly of CT products which will emerge in parallel to the exposure of latent difficulties. As diminishing returns are experienced in the investment and production of very basic CT information management systems, the opportunity for more expensive CT systems which have legal considerations embedded in them will grow. CT-Law management systems could be a great, growing market. Already the opportunities presented by computer games technology is being realised (Tunney, 2001)

As well as providing a potentially lucrative market for producers of CT systems, such CT-Law systems could avoid the danger of a multiplicity of costs when dealing with CT services across the world. While the World Trade Organisation (W.T.O.) will liberalise trade in services through the General Agreement in Trade in Services (GATS), high transaction costs associated with different legal systems could outweigh economies of scale and market liberalisation opportunities. Greater use of CT in the management of information will also enhance the general role of regulation in the public interest. Organisations like the World Bank have begun to realise that their worldview may have been dominated on occasions by narrowly mechanistic economic viewpoints, while ignoring institutional imperatives. Thus there should be a demand for institution-enhancing, information-management systems which address and integrate legislative imperatives.

In order to think of the exact nexus between the different systems which underly the task of information management, we might have to critically analyse and evaluate more general senses of information, knowledge and ingenuity. In particular, recent works such as by Homer Dixon (Homer-Dixon, 2001) and discourse on the relationship between social ingenuity and technical ingenuity must be borne in mind.

REFERENCES

Brinkley & Lohr. (2000) U.S v. Microsoft, McGraw-Hill, New York.

Homer-Dixon. (2001), The Ingenuity Gap: How We Can Solve Problems of the Future,

Howkins. (2001) The Creative Economy: How People Make Money From Ideas, Allen Lane, Penguin Press, 2001. p.vii.

O'Brien. (2002). Freedom of information or fumbling of information (Annual ed.): Magill.

Oliver. (2002). University chiefs plan cutbacks to avert cash crisis, *Irish Times* (pp. 2).

Tunney. (1998). *The digital re-mastering of jurisdiction or opportunity for a new paradigm in law.* Paper presented at the BILETA, Dublin

Tunney. (2000a) Notes on the reflexive role of cyberspace, International Review of Law, Computers & Technology. Vol.14, No.2, pages 243-257.

Tunney. (2000). The problematic role of lawyers in the creativity and innovation process. *Creativity and Innovation Management, 9*(4), 222-226.

Tunney. (2001). *Computer games technology and the future of legal education.* Paper presented at the BILETA, Edinburgh.

Factors Affecting The Retention of Women in the South African IT Industry

Nata Van der Merwe and Adrie Stander
Department of Information Systems, University of Cape own, South Africa, nvdmerwe@commerce.uct.ac.za

ABSTRACT

This paper reports on the interim results of a comprehensive study of women in the South African IT Industry. Areas covered are demographics, experience and qualifications, the work environment, discrimination, gender issues, technical abilities and many other issues related to women in the IT industry.

INTRODUCTION

This paper reports on the initial findings of a survey looking at women in the South African Information Technology (IT) Industry. In line with the rest of the world, women represent only 19% of IT employees in South Africa (Jovanovic, 2001).

Worldwide, there has been a strong drive to promote IT as a career for women and to attract them to IT-related courses. As De Palma (2001) points out, there is a wealth of literature available speculating about reasons why so few young women enrol in IT-related courses. Many studies (Myers & Beise, 2001; Cuny & Aspray, 2000) focus on attracting and retaining female students and suggest ways to increase the number of young women preparing for and entering the IT Industry. This groundwork would however be futile if once these women enter the IT industry, effort is not made to ensure their retention as part of the workforce.

Carver (2000) hypothesizes that in order to attract more women to IT, the workplace must have, amongst others, flexible hours, part-time career options, the possibility of reduced work-hours, work-from-home possibilities and childcare facilities. These and other issues related to women in IT are investigated in this study.

Data for the study was gathered from women currently in the IT Industry. The study aims to separate myth from reality in terms of what women want, their perceptions of the industry and what keeps them there, and to recommend employment strategies and management policies.

Due to the comprehensiveness of the survey and space limitations, only selective areas of the survey are reported on.

METHOD

A Web based questionnaire was used to collect data for the survey. To reach as many women in IT as possible, the questionnaire was presented to the IT Industry through an article in ITWeb, an important IT news site for Southern Africa. Women completing the questionnaire were also requested to forward the URL to female colleagues. To encourage participation anonymity was guaranteed. After submission, respondents had the option to provide an e-mail address for further contact, which was stored independently of the questionnaire details. Although the questionnaire was comprehensive in its coverage, questions were designed to be quick and easy to complete. It took on average 10 minutes to complete and was available for a 3-week period from late November till mid-December 2001.

DEMOGRAPHICS

A total of 299 women, representing 9 major industry sectors and 8 of the 9 provincial regions in South Africa responded, with 32% of the respondents from the Western Cape and 61% from Gauteng. These two regions are the economical strongholds of South Africa. Respondents are from across the racial spectrum, with 6% Asian, 6% Black, 5% Coloured and 82% White, while 1% elected the Other-category. The 17% non-white v 82% White respondents is a fair reflection of the racial imbalance existing in skilled jobs in SA.

Woman of all ages took part in the study, with 1% being under 20 years of age and 1% being older than 45 years. 42% of the respondents are between 20 and 30 years of age and 45% between 30 and 45 years. Of concern is the sharp drop in numbers in the over-45 category.

41% of the respondents are single, 44% married, 12% divorced and 3% elected the Other-category. Of the respondents 37% are taking care of children, while 10% care for disabled or elderly relatives.

EXPERIENCE AND QUALIFICATIONS

The average work experience in IT is 9 years, while non-IT experience averages at 5 years. 61% of the respondents have a formal IT qualification, which can be broken down as follows:

- Commercial course 41%
- Technical College 12%
- Technikon (Technical University) 18%
- University 38%
- Postgraduate 24%

Of the respondents 27% hold a recognised industry certification (e.g. MCSE). 31% also have non-IT qualifications.

The fact that the respondents have a number of years experience in IT and are well qualified, contributes to the validity of the survey results.

TYPE AND CONDITIONS OF EMPLOYMENT

Most women (85%) are in permanent positions while 12% work on a contract basis, 2% are self-employed and 1% work part-time or on a freelance basis.

The woman overwhelmingly indicate that flexi-time, work-from-home and equal pay for equal work are very important, while reduced hours is not seen as important. Alarmingly many women (72%) indicate that salaries of women are not on par with male colleagues.

Part-time positions are not attractive, with the respondents agreeing that women in part-time positions are exploited in terms of:

- Less pay for harder work (78%)
- Career advancement and/or promotion (85%)
- Self-development and/or training (79%)

55% of the respondents indicated that they are willing to accept the above to have a more balanced life.

ROLE MODELS AND MENTORS

Although most women (68%) do not have a mentor, more than half of them (53%) act as a mentor. The majority are motivated by women in IT success stories and they strongly agree that women role models are important. Unfortunately, as shown in the next paragraph, management positions are still dominated by men which make women role models a scarcity.

ORGANISATION AND INDUSTRY RELATED ISSUES

The results show that the average number of male team members is 6 and the average number of female team members 3. Management positions are however more male-dominated with 78% of respondents indicating a male immediate superior, and only 22% a female.

Although they are mostly satisfied with the management style of their superiors, they are undecided about the general management style in the organisation.

The majority of respondents (86%) feel there is still gender bias in the IT Industry and 71% agree that employers still have the attitude that women employees will at some stage leave and have a family, with 73% indicating that the fact that a woman could have a family affects her career path.

An alarming 73% indicate that they have experienced discrimination. An industry breakdown indicated that IT-companies (as opposed to Banking or Insurance) are the worst offenders.

86% of the respondents agree that women are under-represented in the IT field, and an overwhelming 94% agree that women are under-represented in the IT executive and management teams. Most organisations (83%) do not have equal representation of male and female managers. An explanation for the sharp decline of respondents in the over-45 age category may be the fact that 70% of respondents report a perceived glass ceiling for women in the industry.

Stress is a factor for women in IT, with 76% indicating that it is stressful to balance work and personal life. However, 63% of the respondents believe that the stress of the IT environment is worth the rewards, with 49% indicating that stress is a factor that will influence them to leave the IT-Industry.

Nearly all respondents (97%) believe that women have special skills that they can contribute to the work environment, but that these skills are not valued by employers (66%).

Most respondents (64%) agree that gender stereotypes influence women's decisions to enter the IT-Industry. While respondents are undecided about being treated differently when getting married (49%/51%), 79% agree that women are treated differently once they start a family or have other family commitments. These perceptions are confirmed by the agreement of the respondents with regard to the status of women in the IT-Industry being influenced by:

- Being a single woman (67%)
- Being a working mother (78%)
- Being an older woman (72%)

Many of the respondents (58%) feel issues faced by women in South African IT are the same world-wide.

PROBLEM AREAS

A number of areas that are often referred to as problem areas were rated by the respondents, in order to establish to what extend these problems are perceived or real. Areas of concern are:

- Time (70%).
- The management style of superiors (61%)
- Sexism (60%)
- The different roles women have (59%)
- Personal and professional trade-offs (58%)
- Training and re-skilling opportunities (54%)
- Higher administrative workloads than male counterparts (53%)
- Lack of childcare facilities at work (53%)
- Family commitments (52%)

Of less concern are:

- Having young children (47%)
- Higher (general) workloads than males (46%)
- Workplace flexibility (40%)
- Academic commitments (34%)
- Community commitments (24%)

SUPPORT

Family

The respondents rated family support as extremely important, and also indicated that they receive a high level of support from their families in areas such as housework, childcare, and on an emotional level. While they are willing to make family sacrifices for career advancement, the respondents are in strong agreement (88%) that male colleagues do not make the same sacrifices for career advancement.

Organizations and Networking

The majority of the respondents (89%) agree that the existence of an "old-boys" network give men an advantage and that women do not network enough (76%). Respondents prefer to network at functions (57%) and conferences (49%), while launches (33%) and the internet (34%) are less popular.

The role of support organisations are rated highly, with 77% indicating that it is important to very important. They overwhelmingly (89%) indicated that they will support female network organisations, with preferences being electronic forums (51%), monthly meetings (51%), and mailing lists (49%), while chat rooms (13%) are clearly unpopular.

TECHNICAL EVALUATION

Contrary to popular belief, women indicated that they do not find the technical environment intimidating. 71% of respondents also do not think that women are less knowledgeable in technical environments and the majority (84%) do not think that women are less qualified to enter technical fields. They overwhelmingly agree (97%) that women need technical skills other than programming, but more than half (59%) feel that their organisations do not do enough to improve the technical skills of women.

CONCERNS

Although most companies in South Africa have affirmative action policies, the low number of non-white respondents (17%) is a matter of concern. Another area of concern is the low number of respondents (1%) in the over-45 age category. This is the age-group where many employees (men) are in senior management and decision making positions and it would be very unfortunate if the IT-Industry is losing women when they have a wealth of experience.

WHAT WOMEN REALLY WANT

In conclusion it was found that contrary to popular belief; women do not want to work fewer hours or part-time and are not overly concerned about child-care facilities at work. Women, however, do want the following:

- Flexi-time
- Equal pay for equal work
- To work from home
- Respect for their technical abilities
- To be valued for the special skills that they can contribute to the work environment

Follow-up research is already underway to investigate the areas of concern and to determine the male viewpoint in order to make the industry more attractive for females.

REFERENCES

Carver, C.L. (2000). *Research Foundations for Improving the Representation of Women in the Information Technology Workforce.* Virtual Workshop Report. Department of Computer Science, Louisiana State University, Baton Rouge.

Cuny, J. and Asprey, W. (2000). *Recruitment and Retention of Women Graduate Students in Computer Science and Engineering.* Computing Research association, San Francisco, June 21-22.

De Palma, P. (2001). *Why Women Avoid Computer Science.* Communications of the ACM, 44(6): 27-29

Myers, M.E. and Beise, C.M. (2001). *Nerd Work: Attractors and Barriers Perceived by Students Entering the IT Field.* ACM SIGPR 2001, San Diego, CA USA.

Jovanovic, R. (2001). *It still pays to be in IT,* (http://www.itweb.co.za) , Accessed 9 March 2001.

E-Divide Issues in Regional Australia

Dr. V. S. Venkatesan and Dr. Ken Robinson
Edith Cowan University, Australia, Tel: 6 (189) 273-8642, Fax: 6 (189) 273-8754, v.venkatesan@ecu.edu.au

ABSTRACT

Computers, Internet and e-commerce are now gaining increased acceptance in daily life and are becoming essential business tools. While the promise that 'e-commerce will literally replace bricks and mortar based transactions' may never be fulfilled, the information technology (IT) sector will continue to grow in future. As in the case of any emerging technology, computers and Internet have the potential to add another divide in the society. Digital divide is now being widely debated in the literature and several countries are taking action to minimise its impact on businesses as well as the general community.

This paper outlines e-divide issues in regional Western Australia. Using data from several in-depth interviews with businesses, trainers and service providers in a small regional town, this paper examines the constraints and business parameters that influence the adoption and non-adoption of computers and Internet by regional businesses. Australia has a high level of computer usage and Internet uptake and, in many respects, Australian results will be applicable to several OECD (Organisation For Economic Co-Operation And Development) countries.

BACKGROUND

The potential for digital divide in the general community and businesses is well recognised in the literature and studies in various countries have highlighted the demographic and social variables that impact on Internet access and the need to bridge this gap (Anonymous, 2000; ArthurAndersen, 2001; Chanda, 2000; Davis-Thompson, 2000; Hoffman, Novak, & Schlosser, 2000; Lieberman, 1999; MRP, 2000; NOIE, 2000; Novak & Hoffman, 1998; UNCTAD, 1998; Veronica, 2000). In Australia, several measures to bridge the divide are afoot and training and computer literacy needs of the community are being examined (MarketEquity, 2001). There is also an increasing recognition that the 'digital divide' issue is not confined to the general community but may impact on businesses as well (CSIRO, 1998; CSIRO, 1999; SETEL, 2001).

Among OECD countries, Australia has one of the highest rates of computer usage and Internet connectivity. According to the National Office of Information Economy (NOIE, 2000), 37% of all Australian businesses are online, ahead of Europe and UK. Australia also compares favorably with other countries in terms of Internet connectivity of consumers and price of Internet access. However, there is a view that the digital revolution in Australia has kept to large cities and regional Australia has not sufficiently benefited from it (Foreshaw, 2000).

In order to appreciate the IT and digital divide issues in regional Australia, it is important to have an understanding of the demographic and business factors that are unique to this area. With most of the Australian population and most business activities concentrated in the metropolitan cities, regional areas are sparsely populated and regional economy still is based on primary industry and local service providers. Vast distance between small towns and communities is another unique characteristic of regional Australia. Small population combined with large distances makes it difficult to provide infrastructure such as telephone or Internet. In recent times, provision of other services such as banking has also been affected.

Some of these constraints, which are rarely felt in large cities, impose a limitation on a business' ability to access and make full use of the Internet and take advantage of e-commerce tools. Such technologies also have the potential to further accentuate the existing disparity in services between metro and rural communities in areas such as access to government services, employment and other information. A preliminary study was undertaken to gather empirical evidence on the IT and digital divide issues confronting regional Australia. This paper discusses the results of such a study.

METHODOLOGY

For this study, a small rural town in Western Australia was chosen. The town was sufficiently away from the metropolitan area as to minimise the influence of being close to a large market. Another factor in the choice of the town was the stability of the community. In depth interviews with a range of businesses and community groups explored various IT related issues. These interviews were recorded, transcribed and common themes were identified.

RESULTS OBTAINED

In all, twenty interviews were conducted, of which half were with businesses and the rest with consumers. Some of these respondents offered their opinion separately as consumers and service providers.

Demographics of the Surveyed Population

Majority of businesses in the area were home based and related to primary production. The number of retail and service based businesses was small. All the responding businesses fell under the small business category employing less than 20 people. Because of the small size of the population, the local market size for any product was limited.

Computer and Internet Access in the Community

- Among the respondents, ownership of computers was around 50% and had increased substantially during the previous 2 years, largely due to the introduction of Goods and Services Tax. Compared to this, about 80% of businesses in Perth, a major metropolitan city in Australia had computers.
- Computers were used mainly for accounting, taxation and basic administrative work. Their use in other areas such as marketing was significantly less.
- About 15 - 30% of respondents were connected to the Internet and its use was mostly for information gathering and email. There were no online transactions.

These results suggest that use of computers and other IT tools in regional Australia may be significantly less compared to that in large cities. The recent increase in computer ownership seems to be the result of government processes. Consequently, it can be argued that awareness of IT may be lacking in small regional communities. In line with this, computer and Internet knowledge of the respondents was found to be at a basic level.

Digital Divide Issues in the Region

Information and infrastructure access has been a key element of the digital divide debate in the literature. The present study identified the following broad themes as relevant to businesses and communities in a regional context.

- Access
  - Physical and technical infrastructure
  - Access to trained personnel and resources
  - Access to current information

- Awareness
  Competition through Internet
- Business processes discouraging the use of Internet.
- Knowledge and training and informal IT networks

Access

- Given the vast distances, sparse population and high cost of telephone service in the regional areas, one would expect cost to be a major problem.
  Businesses did not appear concerned much about the cost factor. Internet access was mostly available at the cost of a local call. However, speed of communication (bandwidth) was identified as a major problem.
- Technical infrastructure and access to skilled personnel emerged as an important bottleneck. Often, businesses did not have information on what IT products were available in the market and lacked local resources to advise them. Further, the remoteness of these business communities from large business centres had a significant effect on the level of service.
- As buyers, these businesses had limited access to external market, thereby reducing their choice of products. To get a wider choice, they had to travel to regional centres incurring additional cost.
- Their search for information online was hampered by time and knowledge constraints. Price and product comparisons, which are often easy in a large market, were difficult for regional businesses, thus restricting their ability to make an informed judgement. Often, the online sources had outdated information which, in turn, reduced their relevance and value. Overall, access to market information was a major issue for these businesses.
- In some community groups, limited access to basic equipment such as a computer significantly curtailed their ability to access essential services such as social security and job network. Added to this was the widening knowledge gap in the use of computers and Internet.
- Rapid changes in technology such as upgrades and new versions of software required users to update their system to communicate with government agencies and others and perform essential operations like banking online. With limitations on financial and technical resources, regional businesses were often left behind.

Awareness

- Some essential services such as banking were available only online. The survival of most businesses operating franchises or agencies in the regional areas was also dependent on their ability to go online to communicate with their parent business. As a result, there was a general awareness in the community that computers and Internet will influence the future.
- However, business owners were not sure that Internet and e-commerce could pose a competitive threat to their business. Many viewed such a threat as nonexistent or being still far away in the future.
- In contrast, majority of consumers interviewed readily opted for 'online' purchase subject to price, payment security and other issues being addressed.

Thus, lack of awareness would have an impact on regional businesses.

Business Processes Discouraging the Use of Internet

- The responding businesses were mostly family owned and small and very few had a separate administrative structure. The owners were also personally involved in the production of goods and services. Under these conditions, their ability to use e-commerce and Internet tools was limited.

Knowledge and Training

- Regional areas lacked a viable mechanism to provide basic training and constant updates. As a result, businesses with simple IT problems often had to seek the help of outside experts incurring additional cost. The informal networks that are available in large organisations were not accessible to regional businesses.
- Diverse and low volume IT knowledge requirements required the business operator to know several things without really gaining expertise in any area.

CONCLUSION

It appears that the IT issues in regional Australia are putting businesses at a disadvantage and conventional IT solutions have limited impact in solving these issues. Instead of opening the external market to these businesses there is a chance that e-commerce could adversely impact on regional areas by adding to the existing constraints on these businesses. Information on the Internet often did not address local business needs. Because of the remoteness of these businesses and communities, the promised benefits of Internet and e-commerce were found to be limited.

LIMITATIONS

In this preliminary study, quantitative data was not collected. The sample was also not randomly chosen. Further work is in progress.

REFERENCES

Anonymous. (2000) Damning the Digital Divide. *America's Network* (October 1).

ArthurAndersen. (2001). *Bringing Power to the People: Governments Worldwide Address the Digital Divide.* Arthur Andersen (April 6) http://www.arthurandersen.com/website.nsf/content/IndustriesGovernmentServicesResourcesDigitalDivide!openDocument.

Chanda, N. (2000). The Digital Divide. *Far Eastern Economic Review* (October 19), 50-53.

CSIRO. (1998). *Australia Could Miss Internet Trade Opportunities* (CSIRO Media Release 98/273). Canberra: CSIRO.

CSIRO. (1999). *Caught in the Web: The Not-So-Lucky Country* (CSIRO Media Release 99/36). Canberra: CSIRO.

Davis-Thompson, D. (2000). *The Electronic Divide: Haves vs. Have Nots* (Spring). Available: http://gany.org/divide.htm.

Foreshaw, J. (2000). Regions miss out as IT keeps to big cities. *The Australian.*

Hoffman, D. L., Novak, T. P., & Schlosser, A. E. (2000). The Evolution of the Digital Divide: How Gaps in Internet Access may Impact Electronic Commerce. *Journal Of Computer Mediated Communication, 5*(3).

Lieberman, D. (1999). *America's Digital Divide - On the Wrong Side of the Wires.* USA Today (November 10).

http://www.usatoday.com/life/cyber/tech/ctg382.htm.

MarketEquity. (2001). *Bridging the Digital divide in Western Australia - An Understanding of WA Computer Literacy Training Needs*: Department of Training and Employment, Western Australia.

MRP. (2000). *Closing the Digital Divide.* Minnesota Rural Partners, Minnesota.

NOIE. (2000). *The Current State of Play - July 2000* . National Office of Information Economy, Canberra.

Novak, T. P., & Hoffman, D. L. (1998). Bridging the Racial Divide on the Internet. *Science* (April 17).

SETEL. (2001). *The Other Digital Divide: E-commerce and Australian Small Business - SETEL Position Paper No 3.* Small Enterprise Telecommunications Centre Limited.

UNCTAD. (1998). *Policy issues relating to ACCESS TO PARTICIPATION IN ELECTRONIC COMMERCE.* Geneva: Report by the UNCTAD secretariat (circulated in TD/B/COM.3/16).

Veronica, C. S. (2000). More aggressive APEC action sought to bridge Digital Divide. *Business World (Philippines) (October 17),* 1-.

Adoption of Internet Technologies and E-Commerce by Small and Medium Enterprises (SMEs) in Western Australia

Dr. V. S. Venkatesan and Dr. Dieter Fink
Edith Cowan University, Australia, Tel: 6 (189) 273-8642, Fax: 6 (189) 273-8754, v.venkatesan@ecu.edu.au

ABSTRACT

Following failures in the 'business to consumer' (B2C) market, 'business to business' (B2B) sector is now seen as offering high growth potential, the assumption being that B2B transactions can take place vertically throughout a supply chain as well as horizontally across similar sized businesses. But very little is known about the number of businesses that are online, their level of online business activities or their experience with Internet technologies. This paper benchmarks the level of adoption of Internet and related technologies by small and medium businesses in Western Australia in 2001. Australia has a high level of Internet uptake and, in many respects, Australian results will be applicable to several OECD (Organisation For Economic Co-Operation And Development) countries.

A study of 193 businesses in a metropolitan City in Australia showed a moderate to high level of computer usage and Internet connectivity. However, the proportion of businesses actively using the Internet for business transactions or generating business through a web presence was significantly less when compared to other conventional tools such as telephone and fax. The Internet was used mostly for information gathering. Factors such as the size or the nature of business did not seem to impact on the level of online transactions. Business owners were also skeptical about the applicability of online transactions to their business.

BACKGROUND

It is now well recognised that the B2C bubble has burst and the earlier growth forecasts in this market may never be reached. A prime reason for this is that such developments were driven by technology with very little input from other disciplines such as consumer behaviour. Added to this was the simplistic thinking that an Internet presence will automatically lead to business transactions. Following the failures in the B2C market, 'Business to business' (B2B) e-commerce is now being projected as the next growth area but there is still a lack of understanding as to what businesses think about the Internet and what has been their experience with this tool and so on. This research examined some of these questions from an Australian perspective. As a precursor, the general industry scene in Australia and the adoption of computer and related technologies by businesses are briefly explored.

The SME sector is considered an important part of the Australian economy (ABS, 2000) and several OECD countries (ABS, 1998; Anonymous, 1996; Chetcuti, 1998; Dunkelberg & Waldinan, 1996; Flynn, Heidi, Baker, & Edmondson, 1998; Timmons, 1990). Australian businesses also have one of the highest rates of computer usage and Internet connectivity (NOIE, 2000), ahead of European nations and the UK. Australia compares favorably with other countries in terms of Internet connectivity of consumers and price of Internet access. However, past studies have indicated that the use of Internet for e-commerce is indeed small in Australia (Akkeren & Cavaye, 2000; Fink, 1998). Several reasons have been attributed to the low level of adoption of e-commerce in the B2C sector and several success factors have been suggested (Dekleva, 2000; Donahue, 2001; Enos, 2000; Rogers, 2001; Sangaran, 2001; Spiegel, 2000). Given the wide disparity between e-commerce growth predictions and the realities, this research attempted to gather empirical evidence from a wide range of businesses on the actual adoption of e-commerce and reasons for such adoption / non-adoption.

METHODOLOGY

In depth interviews with 25 business owners / managers followed by a quantitative study of 800 businesses in an industrial park was done. Quantitative data was collected using a semi-structured questionnaire that was personally delivered to each business in the target area. Responses were obtained through fax or mail or through a personal pick up. Data from the questionnaire was then coded and subject to analysis.

RESULTS OBTAINED

The overall response rate was 24%. Over 90% of the responses were from the owners of these businesses.

Sample Characteristics

About 85% businesses in the sample were independently owned and operated. In terms of size, almost all businesses were in the SME sector. About 60% were micro businesses (< five employees) and about 13% had more than 20 employees, the maximum number of employees being 90. The median turnover (>100,000 to 1 Million), and the turnover profile of businesses surveyed suggested reasonable sized businesses. Almost half of the businesses in the sample were established businesses (median age - 5 years) and had reported 'good' to 'excellent' business growth and profit in the previous two years. These figures are line with the Australian national trend (ABS, 1998). Most businesses surveyed operated within the state and only a small proportion operated interstate or in the international market.

Use of Computers and Internet

- Everyday computer usage was quite high amongst businesses (>80%). Only a small minority (<10%) did not use computers at any time in their business. However, the use was predominantly (85%) for accounting and administration. About 50% of sample businesses used computers for various sales and marketing activities.
- In terms of Internet connectivity, less than 50% of businesses used the Internet regularly suggesting that Internet is still catching on with businesses. About a quarter of businesses surveyed did not have an Internet connection. Over 60% of businesses surveyed had an email address indicating a moderate level of adoption of email.
- More than 85% of sample businesses did not transact any business over the Internet. The remaining 15% generated 10% or less of their business over the Internet. Most business was done over the counter or through phone or fax. In line with this finding, word of mouth emerged as the best medium for generating new customers (49%), followed by other conventional methods such as advertisements (25%) and tenders.
- Businesses were asked to indicate the extent to which the Internet helped in the growth of their business. About 40% of Internet users were of the view that it did not help their business altogether. In 50%, it was found to be somewhat helpful and 10% found it ex-

tremely useful. In effect, only 8% of the businesses surveyed found the Internet extremely helpful. However, the qualitative data suggested that Internet was helpful in searching for information rather than to attract customers or to transact business online.

- As to their future intentions, >50% of those not currently using the Internet indicated that they would use it for marketing or related purposes. This clearly suggests that Internet use is likely to increase in future. However, based on the experience of current users, to what extent will it help in specific areas such as doing business online needs to be seen.
- Knowledge level of users and infrastructure constraints (speed of access, poor bandwidth) did not emerge as major issues for businesses.

Use of Internet for Different Business Activities

Given that the Internet is a medium and can be used for a variety of purposes, businesses were asked to indicate the frequency of Internet usage for specific business activities. This was then compared with the use of conventional technologies. Results are given in Tables 1 and 2.

- Compared to information gathering, businesses used the Internet to a much lesser extent to receive or place orders (17% and 12%, even after taking into consideration 'often' and 'regularly' categories).
- Compared to 50% of businesses that never received orders on the Internet, about 66% never placed orders on the Internet. This suggests a degree of reluctance on the part of businesses to engage in B2B online activities.

These results show that, in general, Australian small and medium businesses do not have any significant level of B2C and B2B transaction. Internet appears to be still in its infancy in the target group of businesses.

Table 1: Use of Internet for different business activities

	Pay bills (%)	Receive orders (%)	Place orders with suppliers (%)	Look for information (%)	Customers come after seeing web site (%)
Never	37.1	50.3	65.7	18.7	51.4
Sometimes	9.3	32.5	22.7	21.3	20.4
Regularly	15.2	13.2	10.0	33.3	19.0
Often	22.5	3.3	2.0	18.7	7.0
Always	15.9	.7	.7	8.0	2.1
Total	100.0	100.0	100.0	100.0	100.0
Missing*	42	42	43	43	51
Total*	193	193	193	193	193

* Figures show actual frequencies

Table 2: Use of conventional technologies

	Phone Take orders (%)	Phone Order supplies (%)	Phone Pay bills (%)	Email with customer (%)	Email within business (%)
Never	6.6	5.3	40.0	34.6	56.4
Sometimes	9.8	5.9	20.5	20.5	9.4
Regularly	15.8	12.2	20.0	22.2	15.5
Often	34.4	32.4	15.1	16.2	8.8
Always	33.3	44.1	4.3	6.5	9.9
Total	100.0	100.0	100.0	100.0	100.0
Missing*	10	5	8	8	12
Total*	193	193	193	193	193

* Figures show actual frequencies

- As Table 2 suggests, conventional technologies and tools such as phone and fax still find wide use in businesses. Compared to about 15% who placed or received orders on the Internet regularly, often or always, more than 80% of these businesses used the phone or fax for similar purposes.
- Likewise, email usage pattern also indicates that businesses are hesitant to use such newer technologies.

CONCLUSION

Results suggest that, though Internet connectivity is high, businesses still prefer conventional phone and fax and use 'online' methods less frequently. This was found to be true for both B2C and B2B activities. One can infer from these results that growth in the horizontal B2B market (transaction among small and sized businesses) may not be as fast as some forecasts suggest. The predicted B2B growth is more likely to be in the vertically integrated market, driven by large businesses. Our results also suggest that business systems have not kept pace with technical developments in IT. Future developments should draw on other business disciplines such as consumer behaviour and technical solutions should be balanced with business processes. Rapid changes in technology could also be contributing to the low level of online activities.

LIMITATIONS OF THE STUDY

These results are not based on a randomly chosen national sample but based on a West Australian sample of businesses. Further, peculiarities of each economy could also limit the generalisability of such results.

REFERENCES

ABS. (1998). *Small Business in Australia* (1321.0). Canberra: Australian Bureau of Statistics.

ABS. (2000). *Small Business in Australia - 1999.* Canberra, Australia: Australian Bureau of Statistics.

Akkeren, J. V., & Cavaye, A. L. M. (2000). *Factors affecting the adoption of E-commerce technologies by small business in Australia - an empirical study.* Paper presented at the ICSB Conference.

Anonymous. (1996). SMEs Top Performers in Manufacturing Sector. *Management Accounting, 74*(6), 5 -.

Chetcuti, V. (1998). Small is Big News in Exporting. *Government of Canada Information Supplement.*

Dekleva, S. (2000). Electronic Commerce: A Half-Empty Glass? *Communications of the Association for Information Systems, 3,* 1-68.

Donahue, T. D. (2001). *What is E-commerce?* T. D. Donahue & Associates. www.strategic-planning-marketing.com/internet/e-commerce, 29/08/01.

Dunkelberg, W. C., & Waldinan, C. (1996). Small Business Economic Trends - June 1996. *Small Business Economic Trends.*

NOIE (2000). *The Current State of Play - July 2000.* The National Office of Information Economy, Canberra.

Enos, L. (2000). Report: B2B Shakeout Yet to Come. *E-Commerce Times* (August 18, 2000), 1-3.

Fink, D. (1998). Guidelines for the Successful Adoption of Information Technology in Small and Medium Enterprises. *International Journal of Information Management, 18*(4), 243-253.

Flynn, J., Heidi, D., Baker, S., & Edmondson, G. (1998). Startups to the Rescue - Throughout the Continent, small companies are where the action is. *Business Week - Industrial / Technology Edition,* 50.

Rogers, J. (2001). Six keys to B2C e-commerce success. *Insurance & Technology, 26*(8), 49-55.

Sangaran, S. (2001). Room for growth in B2B local marketplace. *Computimes Malaysia,* pp. 1.

Spiegel, R. (2000). Loyalty is the final E-commerce Hurdle. *E-Commerce Times,* pp. 1-3, January 17.

Timmons, J. A. (1990). *New Venture Creation: Entrepreneurship in the 1990s.* (3rd ed.). Irwin, Illinois: Homewood.

Against the Trend? Selected Architecture, Selective Outsourcing and Organizational Learning as a Base for a Sustainably Positioned Information Technology Service

Dr. Rüdiger Weißbach
Riesenweg, Germany, Tel: +4 (940) 715-6591, r.weissbach@sh-home.de

INTRODUCTION

Since 1997 I have managed the organizational change of an information technology [IT] service group of a building society in Germany from a first level service group towards a group, whose objectives are now more focussed on strategic aspects and business process support.

As a result of the discussion about business process re-engineering, outsourcing of IT services has been the dominating trend for years, at least in Western Europe. And, of course, it is one possibility to guarantee an operating IT production at calculable costs. But the undiscriminating adoption of this trend tends to reduce IT on a cost factor and neglects the importance of specific IT knowledge for the continuous improvement of business processes. Also, it seems necessary to have a „communication interface" between users on the one hand and the software development and IT production on the other hand. In this situation the question turns upside down: What kind of support can be done by the „communication interface"? What knowledge is necessary to support the processes?

In opposition to leading management trends, we chose an approach focussing on a steady communication between the IT staff and the various departments. In this approach only selected IT services were externalized and the continuing growth of specific IT knowledge became essential.

There is only a small number of publications about IT management in SMEs. So the following ideas are primarily derived from the experience of this work at the building society with about 100 employees and other projects in SMEs.

BASIC SITUATION

At the building society an old self-developed mainframe based application was the core application for the saving contracts and building loan contracts until 1997. Then this application was replaced by another mainframe based application, which was developed by cooperation with other building societies and which is externally hosted. Products of building societies are very complex compared to other financial products. But the business processes are relatively stable. A contract normally lives for 7 to 20 years, therefore long term planning is important. So on the one side, there exists no standard application for the business processes of a building society on the market. On the other side, the complexity of the product and the amount of legal changes makes it impossible for a small company to delevop such a core application on its own.

But beside the core application there are a lot of applications with increasing relevance for lean and customer guided business processes, lika a document management system, the office software, Lotus Notes, software for product simulations, software for cost management and so on. In the building society the organizational support for all applications (except for the mainframe application) and the technical responsibility for all the locally sited systems is concentrated in an IT service group with seven employees.

CONCEPT

The first and most fundamental aspect of the concept is, that there are strong interdependences between the design, the improvement and the re-engineering of business processes on the one hand and the use of IT on the other hand. The importance of the use of IT seems to make it necessary to keep a certain level of technical and organizational skills inside the organization. This knowledge is needed for rating and for transforming and implementing new ideas and IT products, if necessary with external help.

The second aspect is the structure of the user support. Most of the requieries are simple to solve: Forgotten passwords or transaction codes, a simple help for adressing an e-mail and so on. This support does not require special technical skills, but the ability to communicate with the users. A benefit of this communication is the early detection of organizational lacks and training deficits.

A third aspect is the cost reduction for automation and for highly available hardware in the recent years. Tape loaders, RAID systems, servers with redundant power-supplies, management tools and other similar products are now affordable for SMEs. The usage of this techniques reduces operating costs and administration.

The combination of these aspects led to a concept, in which

- the daily technical support and the operating of the local systems,
- the user support and
- the planning, the realization, and implementation of all non-mainframe systems (document archive system, extranet, software for financial planning, ...)

were joined in one group.

Management and Communication

The fundamental objectives of the IT service group are orientated on the following four aspects, which have individual characteristics regarding the cooperation with the various divisions and with the executive board:

Routine Support

The normal support (system administration, first level support) is done either without any communication with the users or triggered by a direct user call.

Current Projects

Projects focussing on technical improvements (system integration, security) only are settled under the direct responsibility of the IT service group.

Projects for business process improvements are done in co-operation with the divisions. These projects are normally managed by a project manager of the respective business division, not of the IT group.

Acquisition, Definition and Preparing of New Projects

Because of the knowledge about actual user and application problems on the one hand and the knowledge about the technical developments on the other hand, the IT service group is able to detect potential solutions and to discuss them with the users and the management. Some of these solutions lead to new projects.

Advancement of Sustainability

The sustainability and the „potential to survive" of the IT service group are advanced by a high flexibility. Thus the group can fulfill new requirements, for example the integration of new applications. Aspects of this concept are:

- building up and securing actual and in future needed skills,
- securing low support costs
- continuing controlling and optimizing of the costs
- accordance to laws, standards and best practices.

This aim influences the make-or-buy decision: Projects which are supporting the business of the company in a specific way, demand the development of inhouse skills. The less crucial the project, the more the decision tends to buying. If the building up of the skill takes a longer time, normally the group combines a first implementation by externals with on-the-job training for the internal staff.

Technical Infrastructure and Support

The *technical infrastrucure* is selected with regard to high standardization, high availibilty and lean administration. New demands from the divisions are analysed concerning to costs and complexity of IT services. If necessary, the demands are modified or refused. Software updates are installed only if absolutely necessary (end of life of older releases, serious bugs). Hardware, especially printers, are selected with special regard to guarantee and on site service.

Concentration on standard products simplifies the work and reduces the dependence on manufacturers or specialized service companies. Intentionally and in contrast to some „philosophies of outsourcing" the *first level support* is done by own employees. This way, the building society maintains the possibility to detect potentials for improvements in technology and processes. So the first level support has a „seismographic function". The second level support is done both by own staff and by external service companies, third level support is mostly done by external service companies.

Skills

The employees need a general *knowledge* (with the ability to further specialize, if needed) which encloses a general IT knowledge, product skills, knowledge about the processes of a building society and about project management.

Every system can be administrated by two or three employees of the building society. In case of absence, no direct substitution by aonther employee is necessary. Rather the organization exploits a certain overlap. Specific knowledge is documented in a Lotus Notes database, which the employees are filling after solving a non-standard problem. With this tool most of the trouble can be solved by all employees in the IT service group, not only by the specially trained staff.

New applications and technical innovations normally are bought as standard applications or developed by externals. The training of the own staff is part of almost all contracts with externals. Aim of this training is to enable the own staff to improve existing applications and develop new applications. This corresponds to incremental software development processes, in which communication between the users and the developers is crucial. Because of the combination of technical and organizational skills the IT service group is also an internal consultant to the divisions and to the executive board.

ACTUAL SITUATION

This concept has led to following situation:

The current technical service (operations, system administration, troubleshooting) is of high quality. It requires about 1.2 employees per 100 users scattered over five locations. The average availability of the applications is greater than 99% (where scheduled maintenance is rated as „not available"). The typical time to identify and to fix a problem is less than 1hour, most of the problems are solved immediately (in a few minutes).

Nevertheess the expenses are about 25% smaller than the costs calculated by outsourcing service providers for a 10-year-contract.

Most of the resources (5.8 employees) are engaged in business related tasks:

- business related user support (for example development of spredsheets for business applications, user training or the transformation of a paper archive into an electronic archive),
- planning, development and implementation of new software products or new releases,
- commercial tasks (cost management, supervision of contracts with service providers).

The skills of the staff are increasing permanently. So in the last years five years knowledge about the following items was built up: JAVA programming, shell script programming, development of Lotus Notes applications, administration of NT, UNIX and telephone servers, and firewall administration.

The rate of personal fluctuation is low (two changes in five years).

The acceptance and the integration of the IT service group into the whole company is high.

RESULTS

- A selected technical architecture and the application architecture lays the foundation for highly available low cost IT. These factors – low cost and high availability – are more important than the immediate adaption of new technologies or of new products / product releases.
- The organization of the internal knowledge diffusion improves the quality of service and flexibility.
- A complete outsourcing would be disadvantageous: The transaction costs would be higher, the potential savings would be relatively low. Instead of a complete outsourcing only selected technical, non business specific services are permanently externalized.
- The continuing feedback between user support on the one hand, planning and project work on the other hand enables broad knowledge about the requirements and allows a focussed project management.
- The combination of general technical knowledge and specific financial knowledge allows a focussed development of the IT infrastructure and an efficient support of business oriented projects.

In principle this concept seems to be transferable to other SMEs. The differences will be in the fraction of the outsourced services. This will mainly be influenced by the service times, the geographical extension of the users, the absolute number of service staff and the complexity of the systems. But the establishment and maintenance of own IT skills is important in any case.

REFERENCES

JENTZSCH, Ric: Getting the Balance Right. Canberra: Proceedings of the 1998 Information Industry Outlook Conference, 7 November 1998. (http://www.acs.org.au/president/1998/past/io98/rghtbl.htm)

RAYMOND, Louis / William MENVIELLE: Managing Information Technology and E-Business in SMEs. Synthesis watch report submitted to Canada Economic Development within the framerwork of the project. Quebec: 2000. (http://www.dec-ced.gc.ca/en/biblio/observatoire/pdf-obs/expanding.pdf)

WEIßBACH, Rüdiger: Supportmanagement einmal anders – Anmerkungen zum Outsourcing bei Anwenderorganisationen. In: MAYR, H. et al. (eds.): SWM'2000 – Fachtagung Software-Management 2000. Wien: OCG 2000:181-186

Building a Genetic Client-Side Data Collection Tool for Web-Based Experiments

Stu Westin
Professor of Information Systems, College of Business Administration, University of Rhode Island
Tel: (401) 874-4202, Fax: (401) 874-4312, Westin@uri.edu

INTRODUCTION

Research studies involving the use of the World Wide Web (WWW) are becoming increasingly common in disciplines such as MIS, Marketing , and E-Commerce. The focus of these studies is quite varied and may involve issues of human factors (e.g., how does download time impact web use?), issues of information processing (e.g., what search strategies are employed in various situations?), issues of information content (e.g., how much detail should be provided in the initial product description in an E-commerce application?), or a myriad of other questions. Regardless of the issue being studied, data collection for online web research often proves to be a vexing problem, and ideal research designs are frequently sacrificed in the interest of finding a reasonable data collection mechanism. The work described here is aimed at addressing this problem through the development of an improved research instrument.

UNDERSTANDING THE PROBLEM

Server-side data collection mechanisms based on Active Server Page (ASP) scripts or the like can prove useful in some circumstances. Consider, for example, the situation where you want to investigate the impact of download time. Using ASP scripts, a delay mechanism can be easily built into a web page so that the server will delay serving the requested page to the client until some precise, predetermined time has passed. Different experimental treatment levels are accomplished by merely manipulating the delay time that is scripted into the web page. Here, the experimental subject, using an ordinary browser, will have the perception that the page is slow to download because of the delay between when the page is requested (e.g., by clicking a hyperlink) and when the page is available in the browser. As another example, consider the situation where you want to study the end user's web search strategy by recording which pages are accessed, along with the sequence of page access. In this case, we need to record the so-called *click stream data*. Again, ASP scripts in the web pages could provide a simple data collection mechanism by logging each page request (page ID, server timestamp) in a server database. In both of these research scenarios, standard web browser software such as Internet Explorer (IE) can be used in the experiment.

In considering the above research problems, it is obvious that client-side data collection mechanisms can be constructed just as easily. In both cases, Java applets, Java scripts, or VB scripts can be embedded into the HTML pages to handle the required tasks, and, again, standard browser software can be used. The only difference in this client-side approach is that the data collection is being handled by the client vis the server machine. Neither approach provides any obvious benefits over the other, although in the client-side approach the web pages could be stored locally and thus WWW or even network access is not required.

One flaw in all of these research scenarios lies in the fact that experimental access must be restricted to a limited set of web pages that have been appropriately scripted for data collection. If the experimental subject is allowed to "wander" beyond this limited set of pages (an activity that is quite fundamental to the nature of the web), then these actions will not be recorded, and the validity of the experiment will be nullified; there will simply be no data collection scripts to execute. Related to this is the fact that all web pages used in the experiment must be developed and maintained by the investigator – a task which can be quite labor intensive if a large number of pages are to be made available. Obviously, the experimental pages should usually be large in number and professional in appearance if external validity is to be maintained.

In some situations the research data can be collected without the use of client- or server-side scripting. Click stream data, for example, can often be gleaned through the use of standard network management software, or through so-called *network sniffers* that can be configured to monitor Internet requests and/or page downloads. In this case the experimental treatment can involve pages other than those created specifically for the research study, and, again, standard browser software can be used for the experiment. The problem here can be in the precision or in the format of the data, as the software was not designed for this purpose. Pages containing multiple frames, for example, may be logged as individual (frame) downloads in some circumstances and as a single page download in others. Client requests that are satisfied through the local cache may not be logged at all.

A problem with all of the data collection methodologies discussed thus far is that they suffer from a lack of experimental control. This lack of control comes from the fact that the instrument with which the experimental subject is interacting (a standard web browser such as IE) was not designed to be used as a research tool.

Consider the situation in which we wish to study WWW use behavior through analyzing click stream data. There are ways of gathering data on page requests or page downloads, as noted above. However, there is no means, short of direct observation, of recording how a particular page was requested. The page request could have come in the form of a click on a hyperlink, but the request could just as easily have been generated automatically through a dynamic action on the page (e.g., *meta refresh*), or through the *Back* or *Forward* buttons in the browser interface. Normal click stream data will not distinguish between these circumstances, so the precise behavior or intentions of the experimental subject can not be determined.

Another problem has to do with the occurrence of multiple windows. Many web sites open hyperlinks in new browser windows, and the savvy experimental subject can even cause this to happen himself (shift-click in IE). The problem here is that the data can not reflect which of the open windows is active when actions occur, or even that there are multiple windows in use. Again, the data can not capture, or misrepresents the behavior in question; true *streams* cannot be traced.

Yet another problem relates to the browser cache. Beyond setting the size of the cache, the experimenter has little control over how or when the cache is used in responding to subjects' page requests. (Note that the cache in IE can not be disabled.) In some circumstances this can introduce systematic error into the data and thus can have a negative impact on the analysis.

TOWARD A SOLUTION

When faced with these and other related problems in a Web-based study, this author set out to find a solution. It was determined that, for maximum experimental control, the experimental manipulations (treatments) and the data collection mechanisms should be as close to the experimental subject as possible. That is, they should be embedded in the browser itself. This led to the development of a custom IElookalike browser for use in Web-based experiments. As it turns out, this is not as complex an undertaking as it might first appear.

The software that we know as Internet Explorer is essentially a software interface surrounding a set of dynamic link libraries (DLLs) that provide the requisite Internet processing functionality. Microsoft, in its *Visual Studio* suite of software development products, provides a software object called the *WebBrowser Control*. This control can be used in Visual Basic (VB) or in C++ applications to add web browsing functionality to the software. The *WebBrowser Control* can be thought of as an object wrapper around the Internet-processing DLLs noted above. The *WebBrowser* object works with the standard event-based model of Windows computing.

Event handlers are provided for all of the major occurrences in an Internet session such as *request to navigate to a page*, *page download complete*, and *request for a new window*. Key data such as URL, Target Frame, and Page Title are available with the events. In some cases, actions can be preempted through a *Cancel* argument in the event handler. One important example of this is the *BeforeNavigate* event handler. This routine fires after a navigation has been requested by the client, but before the request fulfilled. This allows the custom software to inspect and evaluate the situation, and to possibly modify or cancel the request before it is allowed to proceed.

Properties and methods of the *WebBrowser* object can be used to dynamically emulate all of the features of the IE interface such as the status bar, the browser window caption, and the standard buttons (Back, Forward, Stop, Refresh, Home, etc.). In short, an emulation of IE can be built with the inclusion of as few or as many features of the IE interface as are needed in the experimental context.

By developing a custom browser research instrument the investigator is free to include (covertly) all of the requisite mechanisms of experimental control and data monitoring into the browser itself; no external scripting or network monitoring is needed. Timers to control the duration of the experiment or the occurrence of experimental treatments can be embedded into the browser software. Experimental treatment randomization can also be built in. User activity down to the keystroke or mouse-click level can be monitored and recorded with millisecond accuracy if needed. Certain events can also be blocked or modified if necessary. For example, an attempt to open a page in a new window can be intercepted and the page redirected to the initial window. No special (i.e., scripted) web pages are needed, but attempts to "wander" to irrelevant sites or inapposite protocols (e.g., *mailto*, *ftp*) can easily be halted if desired. The cache can be controlled programmatically through calls to the Windows API. Perhaps best of all, once the basic system is developed, modifications and new features are a fairly simple to effect.

CONFERENCE PRESENTATION

In the conference session the author will discuss the requirements of and problems with executing on-line web-based experiments. For the purpose of illustration he will describe the research setting that prompted the development of a custom data collection browser instrument. He will then present the fundamental techniques for building such a browser, including the essential features of the *WebBrowser* object as well as the custom components and techniques that were necessary in the final solution.

For example, the author will demonstrate how to use the Document Object Model (DOM) to allow the *WebBrowser* object to gain access to the descriptive properties (e.g., modification date, referring page) and to the content-related properties (e.g., anchor array, cookie information) of any web page. He will also discuss the special problems involved in implementing a custom, preemptive keyboard handler for the browser, and how these problems can be solved through API calls.

By the date of the conference the software tool will have been used in an experimental setting. Consequently, the presentation will include the all-important problems encountered and lessons learned.

A Pilot Study of Regional Differences E-Commerce Development in UK SMEs

Fiona Meikle and Dianne Willis
School of Information Management, Leeds Metropolitan University, Beckett Park Campus, UK
Tel: 0 (113) 283-2600, Fax: 0 (113) 283-7599, {f.meikle, d.willis}@lmu.ac.uk

ABSTRACT

The UK government has pledged a commitment to making the UK one of the most significant leaders in the E-Commerce marketplace. Despite this SME (Small to Medium Sized Enterprises) adoption of the Internet remains comparably slow with Midland and Northern regions of the UK lagging behind London and South East counties. The aim of this research is to present a pilot study for a situational analysis of e-commerce development within three different Midland and Northern regions, Yorkshire, Nottinghamshire and West Midlands considering key issues and support mechanisms for SMEs.

INTRODUCTION

There were an estimated 3.7 million SMEs in the UK at the start of 2000 [UK online for Business]. The vast majority of these (99%) had less than 50 employees and they provided 45% of the UK non-government employment and 38% of turnover. The International Benchmarking Study 2000 undertaken by the Department of Trade and Industry suggested that only 1.7 million smaller firms were connected to the internet and still less, 450,000 of them were trading online. A later survey by the UK Office of National Statistics (later referred to as ONS) revealed significant variations in e-commerce implementation across the UK with London and the Southeast region "considerably" outpacing Internet sales in other regions. [Saliba 2001] The UK bought $28.6 billion in goods and services, London based companies accounting for $7 billion while regions such as Northeast & East Midlands spending less than $1.5 billion.

METHODOLOGY

Interviews were used as the main data collection method, supplemental data was provided by documentation related to each of the businesses. SMEs were selected from three of the key regions identified by the ONS survey as having significantly less e-commerce activity. Three companies were chosen across three different industries to provide the necessary data for this largely explorative pilot study with a view to identifying potential trends to test in a larger UK wide study. The interview consisted of 25 questions divided into three key sections; e-commerce strategy, project resources and technology. Due to the number and depth of the questions and number of case studies used an interview was considered a more suitable option than questionnaire.

All of the case studies are SMEs that have established an e-commerce service in the last 18 months. Our definition of e-commerce aligns with those set out by the Organisation for Economic Co-operation and Development (OECD) working party on Indicators for the Information Society (WPIIS)

Weavers Wines is a wine and spirit merchant based in Nottingham employing 10 people. Midland Pumps is a pump manufacturer based in the West Midlands and employs 14 people. Both of these companies use clicks and mortar business modes. Furniture 123 is a furniture retailer based in Yorkshire employing 10 people and has a pure play business model.

RESEARCH FINDINGS

E-Commerce Activity

The UK has experienced a proliferation of business use of the Internet in terms of the volume and variety of business processes supported via email, web and other means of information distribution and dissemination. [Duan Y, Mullins R, Hamblin, D, 2000] All three of the case studies have access to the web, a hosted web site and external mail to communicate with customers. All three web sites are categorized as catalogue sites. Level of customer engagement is relatively low. Only Weavers Wines actively sought the integration of legacy systems

The findings to date suggest a lack of B2B e-commerce supported by integrated networks through the supply chain. Comments from those interviewed *'Our suppliers are not geared up to extranet' 'we are not large enough to support that kind of system and we don't have large orders'*

Reasons identified principally cost of development, infrequency of orders and fear of being tied into to a stronger companies system.

E-Commerce Strategy and Managers Perceptions

The research findings to date suggest that manager's perceptions of e-commerce differ significantly,. The managers of the two clicks and mortar companies recognized a need for an alignment between business and e-commerce strategy but both insisted that e-commerce strategy did not take precedence because e-commerce revenues remain relatively minor. The pure play manager answered that e-commerce and business strategy 'are the same for us'.

E-commerce drivers differed greatly. Furniture 123 as the only pure play have built their business model on e-commerce and fundamentally their driver is survival. Weavers Wine's key drivers were a combination of first mover advantage and competitor pressure. Midland Pumps key drivers were competitor pressure. Although Midland Pumps get regular queries and occasional orders from International customers they have never pursued an aggressive e-commerce strategy

Interestingly, although all of those interviewed believe that their e-commerce projects have met their business objectives only Furniture 123, (who track customers activities while on their web site) conduct any formal evaluation or independent appraisal of the effectiveness of their e-commerce activities. All those interviewed maintained sales records but one could not identify which sales were orchestrated via their web site and email as opposed to telephone orders. There is no evaluation of the customer web interface.

Project Resources

All three businesses developed their e-commerce projects using strictly limited resources with no dedicated e-commerce budget. The core applications behind the web sites were developed by a single person usually those interviewed, the CEO or MD. In the case of Weavers Wines the underlying database was developed by the CEO. The web site and application integration was outsourced using 40% of Business Link funding. The underlying architecture for the Midland Pumps web site is their product catalogue. This catalogue was developed by the MD over a period of two to three months and turned into a web site in a very short period of time by a personal friend. The MD was aware of potential funding claims but did not seek any funding due to previous experiences. Even the development of Furniture 123 was initially small scale with the CEO the principal designer supported by a friend within the IT business. The only form of investment came from private investors identified through local networks.

Training and Support Needs

Interview evidence suggests that the businesses discussed are open to any support offered from the private sector but a great suspicion of local and government training schemes. The main area of training is in the development of e-commerce applications and integration of back office systems. At least two of the three interviewed had their web sites hosted by an external party with very little integration of their own systems with another company's web server.

CONCLUSIONS

There is some evidence to suggest that training and awareness raising remains an issue for SMEs, of those interviewed there was a lack of awareness of the options for businesses. One firm in particular showed a lack of awareness of web alternatives to the expensive and standard controlled EDI networks of the previous decades. Two out of the three case studies referred to their work as constantly 'firefighting' and therefore individuals within the business had no time to look at possible initiatives. In particular one individual interviewed stated that the firm's profit margin had decreased substantially, an occurrence throughout their industry resulting in a fear of investing any funds or human resource into a 'blue sky' project

There is some evidence within these preliminary findings that the actual E-Commerce development within SMEs may rely very heavily on the personal networks of the managers There was evidence from two of the firms of heavy reliance on friends who work within the IT industry. Interestingly this included the pure play business.

The results to date suggest a knowledge of government and other independent initiatives for supporting e-commerce development within SMEs but a significant number of poor experiences of using these initiatives. Companies such as Business Link actively approached at least one business on a monthly basis suggesting that SMEs are made fully aware of initiatives offered by local and national government. The findings suggest the need for further research identifying why these initiatives are not working for SMEs, this will include a wider survey of SME experiences and interviews with the businesses such as Business Link.

FUTURE DIRECTION

Evaluation of the work to date indicates that there is scope for further work in this area.

It is intended to expand the number of SMEs interviewed, whilst trying to balance the different categories already identified. The methodology chosen has worked well with a small number of pilot studies, but as each interview lasts in excess of an hour, consideration needs to be given as to whether this is feasible on a wider basis. One possible solution is to reduce the number of questions asked, particularly those covering financial issues which companies were generally not happy to divulge.

As a further step, the UK Department for Trade and Industry will be approached to discover the full range of information and grants available to SMEs and to ascertain how to make this information more accessible to those SMEs who are unaware of what help is available.

REFERENCES

Duan Y, Mullins R, Hamblin, D (2000) '**Making Successful E-Commerce:An Analysis of SMEs Training and Supporting Needs**' Proceedings of the 1st World Congress on E-Commerce Management, Hamilton, Canada

Myers M.D. (1994) '**Quality in Qualitative Research in Information Systems**', Proceedings of the 5th Australasian Conference on Information Systems, pp.763-766

Office of National Statistics, (www.statistics.gov.uk/) Last accessed on 2/10/01

Organisation for Economic Co-operation and Development, (www.oecd.org) Last accessed on 2/10/01

Saliba C. (2001) '**Study:UK Firms Tarry with E-Commerce Adoption**' E-Commerce Times, (www.ecommercetimes.com/perl/printer/13437/) Last accessed on 9/10/01

UK Online for Business (http://www.ukonlineforbusiness.gov.uk/) Last accessed 9/10/01

Porter E.M (2001) '**Strategy and the Internet**', Harvard Business Review, Reprint R0103D, March

Timmers P (2000) **Electronic Commerce, Strategies and Models for Business to Business Trading**, Wiley Series in Information Systems.

Travers, M (2001) **Qualitative Research through Case Studies**, SAGE publications.

Yin R.K. (1994) **Case Study Research; Design & Methods 2nd ed.**, Applied Social Research Methods, Volume 5, SAGE publications

Accounting Information Systems Data Quality: A Critical Success Factors Approach

Hongjinag Xu and Latif Al-Hakim
Faculty of Business, University of Southern Queensland, Australia, Hongjiang.Xu@usq.edu.au, Hakim@usq.edu.au

ABSTRACT

This paper identifies 25 critical factors that affect the data quality of accounting information systems, and reports the results of a large-scale survey of Australian organizations. Analysis of the survey provides some interesting insights into the importance and actual performance of those factors. Results show that the performance ranking of teamwork is low in comparison with the perceived importance of this factor. The survey demonstrates that the input control and nature of the systems play the most important role in the successes of AIS.

INTRODUCTION

Accounting Information Systems (AIS) maintain and produce the data used by organisations to plan, evaluate, and diagnose the dynamics of operations and financial circumstances [1]. With the advent of the information technology age and ever increasing customer expectations, AIS begins to play more of an influencing role than a traditional informing role [2,11]. AIS reports on non-traditional items affecting customer's expectations on quality and costs such as machine utilization rate, non-productive times [8] and increases in wages due to improvement in skills, personnel accident rate, etc. [7]. In addition, to collect and report internally generated information, accountants must report on important external information and monitor the strategy of each rival competitor [8,10]. Such information is important to evaluate the cost advantages which an organization enjoys over its competitors to support its strategic market positions. Similarly, AIS can help in measuring and improving productivity and services [4]. On the other hand, real-world practice evidences that data quality (DQ) problems are becoming increasingly prevalent [9,13,16]. The traditional focus on the input and recording of data needs to be offset with recognition that the systems themselves may affect the quality of data [6]. An accounting information system can be successful only if it can identify and consider the critical factors that influence data quality. It appears that very few attempts have been made to identify the critical success factors for improving data quality of AIS. This paper attempts to fill this gap and aims to study the critical factors that affect data quality in AIS in Australia.

CRITICAL SUCCESS FACTORS

The concept of critical success factors (CSF) was first defined by Rochart [14] as the limited areas in which results, if they are satisfactory, will ensure successful competitive advantage performance for the organization. The CSF approach has become an accepted top-down methodology for corporate strategic planning [4]. It can highlight the key requirements of the top management [3]. One can conclude from literature that identifying CSF forms the first step for developing a roadmap for improving the performance and hence the competitive advantage. Crag and Grand [5] demonstrate the context of competitive resources and illustrate the interrelationship between the competitive resources and critical success factors. Martin [12] points out that CSF combined with computation could effectively improve business strategy planning.

This paper report results of a survey carried out in Australia during 2001. The primary aim of the survey is to determine the criticality of some factors on the data quality and the successful implementation of AIS.

METHODOLOGY

The study consisted of a survey comprising various Australian organizations. It involves constructive interviews with executive to identify the CSFs. The study employs a similar approach to that of Watson and Frolick [17] for structuring the interviews with the executives. Case studies were conducted, which included the interviews to different stakeholders group within each organization. A set of CSFs was then derived by the analysis of the case studies interviews. Systematical analysis was employed to determine the categories that those factors belong to. The study derives these factors from three sets of sources: system factors, human-related factors and industrial factors. The first set includes the nature of the accounting information systems and all the relevant controls. The second set covers levels of management, personnel competency and stakeholders of the AIS. The third set comprises regulations, policies and standards, visions, and external factors.

QUESTIONNAIRE

Based on the interviews, case studies and comprehensive analysis of the literature, we collectively identified 25 factors. The factors were listed in a questionnaire. The first part of the questionnaire provides some definitions of the terms used followed by some preliminary questions to identify the respondent's stakeholder group and collect the general information about their AIS. The third part, which is the main section of the questionnaire, comprises the factors. The respondents were asked to rate each of those factors according to (1) their opinion on the importance of each factors in ensuring DQ in AIS, and (2) the actual performance (achievement) on each of those factors. The importance was on a five-point scale, and the performance was on a six-point scale (Table 2 and Table 3).

SURVEY

A total of 1000 managers of Australian organizations were surveyed. Around 15% of the surveyed managers were found not eligible or not available to answer the questionnaire for various reasons. From the 850 eligible questionnaire recipients, we received 180 completed questionnaires, which makes the response rate around 21%. Figure 1 shows the demographic breakdowns by industry type of the surveyed organization and Table 1 illustrates the organizations' size in term of assets and the annual revenue.

The results show that the majority of the surveyed organizations were from manufacturing and service industries (65%). More than 42% of the organizations have an annual revenue between 10 to 99 million dollars while more than 24% of organizations have more than 100 million dollars. The survey shows that nearly 81% of the recipients were top management while about 15% were middle management (Figure 2).

RESULTS

Table 2 summarizes the results of the survey in relation to the importance of the factors. The table reflects the viewpoint of respondents and shows that *input control* plays the most critical role in the successes of AIS, (see the last column of Table 2). *The nature of the systems* was seen as the second critical factor. Each of these two

Figure 1: Industry type of surveyed organizations

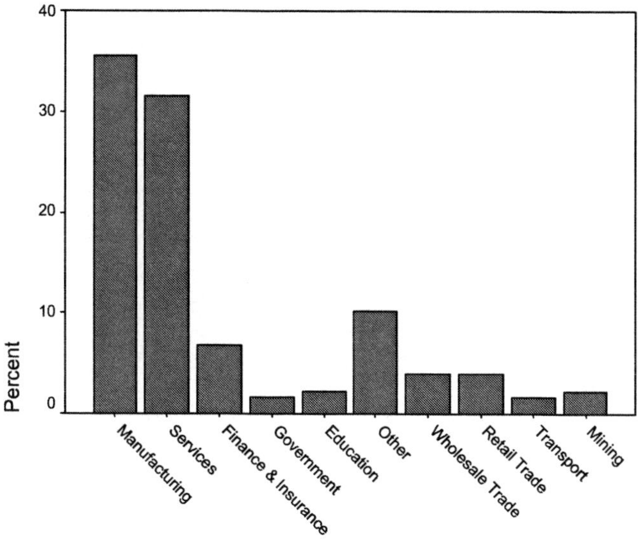

Table 1: The size of the organizations

		The Total Assets	The Annual Revenue
Under $5 million	%	22.7%	13.5%
$5 million to $9 million	%	20.5%	16.9%
$10 million to$99 million	%	32.4%	42.1%
Over $100 million	%	23.3%	24.7%
Not sure	%	.6%	1.7%
Not permitted to disclose	%	.6%	1.1%

factors has a higher rating than the commitment of top management factor which contradicts what is emphasized in most existing literature. Other significant factors are *personnel competency, internal controls*, and *teamwork.*

Table 3 reviews the actual performance of those factors in the organizations. Some of the results are excluded from the consideration because of the high percentage of not applicable responses of those factors. For example, more than 19% of the responses indicate that *DQ managers* do not exist in their organizations. However, the results demonstrate some consistency between the perceived importance of the critical factors and the actual performance of those factors.

An important point to be addressed here is the performance ranking of *teamwork* is lower in comparison with the perception of importance of this factor. One can conclude other important information from the presented results. This will be addressed in future work of the authors.

REFERENCES

1. Anthony, R. S., Reese, J. S. & Herrenstein, J. H. 1994, *Accounting Text and Cases*, Irwin.
2. Bromwich, M. 1990, 'The case for strategic management accounting: the role of accounting information for strategy in competitive markets', *Accounting Organisations and Society*, 15, pp. 17-46.
3. Byers, C.R. and Blume, D. 1994, 'Tying critical success factors to systems development', *Information & Management*, 26(1), pp. 51-61.
4. Chen, T., 1999, 'Critical success factors for various strategies in the banking industry', nternational *Journal of Bank Marketing*, 17(2). pp.83-91.

Figure 2: Level of job responsibility

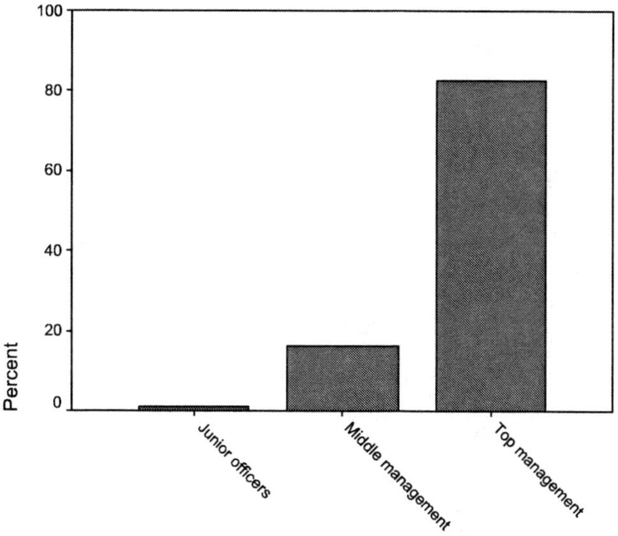

Table 2: The importance of the factors (percentage and mean)

	Not important	Little importance	Average importance	Very important	Extremely	Mean
Top management commitment		2.2%	13.2%	49.5%	35.2%	4.18
Middle management commitment		1.6%	18.1%	50.5%	29.7%	4.08
Education and training	1.2%	3.5%	21.4%	45.7%	28.3%	3.97
DQ vision	2.7%	3.8%	24.2%	52.2%	17.0%	3.77
DQ manager	8.3%	20.4%	21.5%	39.8%	9.9%	3.23
Organizational structure	3.9%	7.2%	29.8%	45.3%	13.8%	3.58
Policies and standards	1.2%	7.6%	21.6%	54.4%	15.2%	3.75
Organizational culture	2.2%	3.3%	15.5%	57.5%	21.5%	3.93
DQ controls	1.1%	2.8%	26.0%	53.0%	17.1%	3.82
Input controls		.5%	9.3%	44.5%	45.6%	4.35
User focus	.5%	1.6%	13.2%	55.5%	29.1%	4.11
Nature of the AIS		1.8%	7.6%	53.5%	37.1%	4.26
Employee relations	1.6%	2.2%	12.1%	56.0%	28.0%	4.07
Management of changes		2.3%	13.7%	60.0%	24.0%	4.06
Measurement and reporting		3.6%	19.8%	49.5%	27.0%	4.00
Data supplier quality management	2.9%	9.4%	31.0%	43.3%	13.5%	3.55
Continuous improvement	.6%	4.5%	24.6%	54.2%	16.2%	3.81
Teamwork (communication)	1.7%	1.7%	11.0%	57.8%	27.7%	4.08
Cost / benefit tradeoffs	3.4%	8.4%	38.5%	39.1%	10.6%	3.45
Understanding of the systems and DQ		2.3%	20.1%	58.6%	19.0%	3.94
Risk management	1.1%	5.0%	24.6%	52.5%	16.8%	3.79
Personnel competency	.6%	2.2%	12.9%	52.8%	31.5%	4.12
Physical environment	.6%	3.9%	31.3%	49.2%	15.1%	3.74
Audit and reviews	2.8%	6.1%	30.2%	43.6%	17.3%	3.66
Internal controls		2.3%	13.3%	56.1%	28.3%	4.10

Table 3: The performance of the factors (percentage and mean)

	Poor	Fair	Good	Very good	Excellent	Not applicable	Mean
Top management commitment	8.8%	17.1%	26.5%	36.5%	11.0%		3.24
Middle management commitment	6.1%	21.5%	31.5%	32.0%	8.8%		3.16
Education and training	14.9%	25.0%	28.6%	27.4%	3.6%	.6%	2.82
DQ vision	16.6%	29.3%	28.2%	19.3%	6.1%	.6%	2.81
DQ manager	13.9%	23.9%	18.3%	19.4%	5.0%	19.4%	*
Organizational structure	10.5%	23.8%	29.8%	21.0%	6.6%	8.3%	*
Policies and standards	9.4%	29.4%	32.9%	19.4%	4.1%	4.7%	*
Organizational culture	13.9%	23.9%	30.0%	26.1%	4.4%	1.7%	2.88
DQ controls	10.6%	30.6%	31.1%	23.9%	2.2%	1.7%	2.82
Input controls	6.6%	15.9%	31.9%	40.1%	3.3%		3.22
User focus	11.0%	25.8%	32.4%	25.8%	4.9%		2.88
Nature of the AIS	7.1%	21.2%	32.4%	32.4%	6.5%	.6%	3.12
Employee relations	11.5%	18.7%	38.5%	25.8%	5.5%		2.95
Management of changes	7.5%	21.3%	35.1%	32.2%	4.0%		3.04
Measurement and reporting	8.0%	24.1%	30.4%	31.3%	5.4%	.9%	3.04
Data supplier quality management	11.2%	30.2%	31.4%	18.3%	1.8%	7.1%	*
Continuous improvement	12.3%	29.6%	35.2%	19.6%	2.2%	1.1%	2.73
Teamwork (communication)	8.1%	19.1%	40.5%	27.2%	4.0%	1.2%	3.03
Cost / benefit tradeoffs	14.5%	35.2%	27.4%	13.4%	2.2%	7.3%	*
Understanding of the systems and DQ	6.9%	29.3%	37.4%	23.6%	2.9%		2.86
Risk management	15.1%	35.2%	27.4%	16.8%	3.9%	1.7%	2.64
Personnel competency	9.0%	18.0%	42.7%	23.0%	6.7%	.6%	3.02
Physical environment	5.6%	16.2%	34.6%	31.3%	11.7%	.6%	3.29
Audit and reviews	15.1%	25.1%	24.6%	24.0%	7.3%	3.9%	*
Internal controls	4.1%	22.7%	34.9%	31.4%	6.4%	.6%	3.15

5. Crag, J.C. and Grant, R.M. 1993, *Strategic Management*, West Publishing, St Paul, MN.
6. Fedorowicz, J. & Lee, Y. W. 1998, ' Accounting information quality: Reconciling Hierarchical and dimensional contexts', February, 1998 Association of Information Systems (AIS) Conference proceedings.
7. Gupta, Y.P. 1988, 'Organizational issues of flexible manufacturing systems', Technovation, pp. 255-269.
8. Hiromoto,T. 1988, 'Another hidden edge- Japanese management accounting', *Harvard Business Review*, July/August, pp.22-26.
9. Huang, Huan-Tsae, Lee, Y. W. & Wang, R. Y. 1999, *Quality information and knowledge*, Prentice Hall PTR.
10. Johnson, J. R., Leitch, R. A. & Neter, J. 1981, 'Characteristics of errors in accounts receivable and inventory audits', *The Accounting Review*, vol. 56, no. 2, pp. 270-293.
11. Kaplan, D., Krishnan, R., Padman, R. & Peters, J. 1998, ' Assessing data quality in accounting information systems', *Communications of the ACM*, February vol. 41, no. 2, pp. 72-7.
12. Martin, J. 1990, *Information Engineering: Book II: Planning and Analysis*, Prentice-Hall, Englewood Cliffs, NJ.
13. Redman, T. C. 1998, ' The impact of poor data quality on the typical enterprise', *Communications of the ACM*, February vol. 41, no. 2.
14. Rochart, J. F. 1997, 'Chief executives define their own data needs', *Harvard Business Review*, 57(2), pp.81-92.
15. Sriram, R.S. 1995, 'Accounting information system issues of FMS', *Integrated Manufacturing Systems*, 6(1), pp.35-40.
16. Wand, Y. & Wang, R. Y. 1996, '*Anchoring data quality dimensions in ontological foundations*', Communications of the ACM, vol. 39, no. 11, pp. 86-95.
17. Watson, H. J., and M. Frolick, 1992, Spring, 'Determining Information Requirements for an Executive Information System', *Journal of Information Systems Management*.

Strategic Decisions in e-Knowledge: An Analytic Network Process

Mahesh S. Raisinghani, Ph.D., CEC *
Graduate School of Management, University of Dallas,1845 East Northgate Drive,Irving, Texas 75062-4736
Phone: 972.721.5173, Fax: 972.721.4007, **Email:** mraising@gsm.udallas.edu

Laura M. Meade, Ph.D.
Graduate School of Management, University of Dallas,1845 East Northgate Drive, Irving, Texas 75062-4736
Phone: 972.721.4072, Fax: 972.721.4007, **Email:** lmeade@gsm.udallas.edu

INTRODUCTION

In a knowledge-based industrial economy, logistics play an increasingly important strategic role for organizations that strive to keep pace with market changes and supply chain integration. Knowledge Management (KM) has been a major topic for management academicians and practitioners alike in the 1990s. A growing number of studies have called for a more holistic, systemic approach to knowledge. It is not simply a 'tool' or 'resource' so much as a social construct. It is a reciprocal, interdependent process of learning arising from knowledge transfer and information flow and communication – a socio-technical perspective which amalgamates the 'dualism' of people and technology (reference source: email communication from Elayne Coakes, Westminster Business School). During his keynote speech at the Information Resources' Annual 1998 Meeting in Boston, MA, Dr. N. Venkatranam discussed how companies manage their knowledge assets and how organizations moved from the Industrial economy to the Knowledge economy. This development led to a shift in the business environment and introduced the new concepts from the knowledge economy as illustrated by the knowledge cycle in Figure 1.

The key is to synthesize the intellectual capital from the tacit and explicit knowledge base of the human mind and the information augmentation provided by applied technologies such as data mining and intelligent software agents. This study focuses on investigating the linkage between the various dimensions of agility, supply chain costs and KM by using the analytic network process in a global telecommunications organization. The overarching strategic organization performance criteria of cost, time, flexibility and quality serve as drivers for this study.

The Internet and e-business have directly impacted supply chain management. With the increasing growth of business-to-business and business-to-consumer avenues the traditional supply chain has been expanded. Business-to- business via e-commerce will reach $5.7 trillion by the end of 2004 or 29% of the dollar value of commercial transactions [3]. Supply chain solutions participants need to leverage their understanding of the physical process combined with the latest technology solutions to provide the necessary visibility and connectivity in the supply chain. The supply chain needs to be able to meet customer's needs as efficiently and effectively as possible.

This paper provides a decision model which assists in determining which construct of KM is most important based on an organization's performance criteria, dimensions of agility and supply chain drivers. The main issue with KM is determining how executives get the insight they need to run their business and how they formalize that insight. Making use of diverse and changing resources has two main objectives. One, in order to substantially benefit from the available technology, the decision maker should be able to efficiently locate and access the needed information/resources in a timely manner. So to begin with there is the goal of providing the library of information and materials, or 'knowledge'. This array of knowledge is by no means static, so maintenance of the system, involving reorganization procedures and continual development of information sources, is necessary.

Figure 1: The Knowledge Cycle

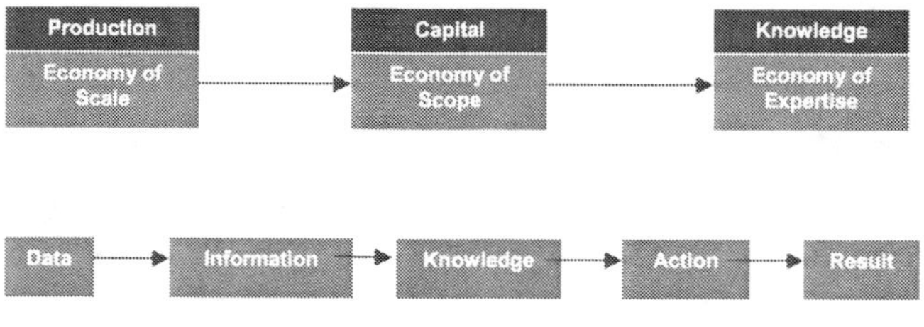

The other essential objective relies more on the human capabilities of analysis and decision-making. The knowledge base must be combined with the ability to effectively and efficiently filter the tremendous amount of data and information so that what is left is truly meaningful packets of knowledge. Software and machines can accomplish this to a point, but the human input and control in the system is the critical component. This, too, should be a continuous and ongoing process. The intent here is not to examine the technical aspects, but to consider the cognitive process needed to develop a useful framework in which to manage our store of knowledge.

RESEARCH CONSTRUCTS AND THEORETICAL FRAMEWORK

The concept of KM concerns the creation of structures which combine the most advanced elements of technological resources and the indispensable input of human response and decision-making. Duhon [7] defines KM as "a combination of technology supporting a strategy for sharing and using both the brainpower resident within an organization's employees and internal and external information found in 'information containers'." The goal of KM is to simultaneously manage data, information, and explicit knowledge while leveraging the information resident in people's heads through a combination of technology and management practices. [7]

Documentum's (a document management company) vice president Larry Warnock describes KM as the "utilization of intellectual capital". Intellectual capital, or knowledge, is the source of innovation that ultimately allows companies to focus on their individual customer. Documentum uses a term called *knowledge chain management* to define the way knowledge is created, shared, and leveraged in context of a business process. The supply chain is the business process by which materials and information move through an organization to deliver the ultimate product to a customer" [27].

KM as operationalized in this paper "caters to the critical issues of organizational adoption, survival, and competence in the face of increasingly discontinuous environmental change. Essentially it embodies an organizational process that seeks synergistic combination of data and information processing capacity of information technologies, and the creative and innovative capacity of human beings" [13].

This definition not only recognizes the discontinuous environment but also the importance of both techno-centric and socio-centric approaches. The traditional view of KM primarily relies on the pre-packaged or "taken for granted" interpretation of the knowledge. Such knowledge is generally static and does not encourage the generation of multiple and contradictory viewpoints in a highly dynamic and ever-changing environment.

Beijerse [2] identifies the following demands on organizations in a knowledge-based economy:

- An increasing complexity of products and processes;
- A growing reservoir of relevant knowledge, both technical and non-technical;
- Increasing competition in an economy with shorter product life cycles, in which case learning processes have to be quicker;
- An increased focus on the core competencies of the firm which have to be coordinated, but letting go less relevant tasks;
- Companies will increasingly have the work done by a flexible workforce, changing workforce, which makes holding on to knowledge and transferring knowledge all the more difficult.

Next we describe the supply chain taxonomy.

A supply chain consists of all stages involved, directly or indirectly, in fulfilling a customer request. The supply chain not only includes the manufacturer and suppliers, but also transporters, warehouses, retailers, and customers themselves. [8 and 24] Some of the functions included in the supply chain are new product development, marketing, operations, distribution, finance, and customer service. If the supply chain process is looked at from a cycle view, all supply chain processes can be broken down into the following four process cycles: Customer Order Cycle, Replenishment Cycle, Manufacturing Cycle and Procurement Cycle [5]. Figure 2 illustrates the KM and supply chain initiatives research model. This is followed by a description of the factor/dimension in each layer represented in figure 2.

The organizational performance criteria consist of traditional strategic organizational metrics such as time, quality, cost, and flexibility ([11], [22]). In order to maintain that the strategy selected relates to the desire to be an agile supply chain, the determinants of agility are also considered.

1. Dimensions of Agility

Due to the pace at which business is conducted the supply chain needs to be able to respond quickly, efficiently and with agility. In

Figure 2: The KM and Supply Chain Initiatives Research Model

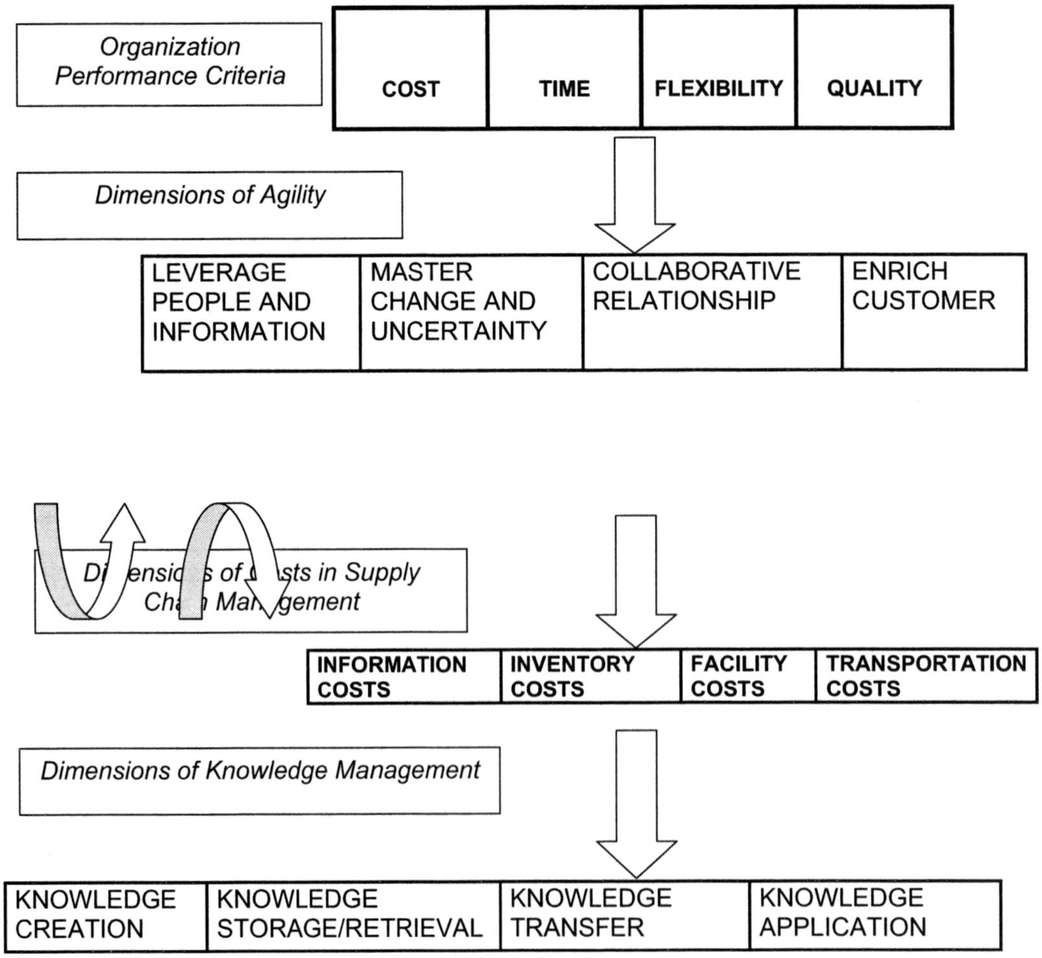

order to be agile; able to respond to unanticipated change, the supply chain must seek to address four main principles 1) Cooperate to Enhance Competitiveness, 2) Enrich the Customer, 3) Master Change and Uncertainty and 4) Leverage the Impact of People and Information [9].

Cooperate To Enhance Competitiveness

Specific benefits of this cooperation include both inter and intra-enterprise benefits:

- Decrease of product development costs, time to market, and risk
- Ethic of trust is built and maintained in order for cooperation to succeed
- Acceleration of technology transfer and an increase in resource availability
- Able to focus on the processes which human and technological resources are best suited.

In order to maximize the potential of this principle, the enterprise needs to utilize existing resources regardless of location in order to bring the product to the consumes as cost effectively and rapidly as possible.

Enrich The Customer

The products of the enterprise need to be viewed by the customer as solutions to a problem. Building long-term stable relationships are based on selling solutions that involve products, information, and services. A relationship between producer and customer will evolve as changes in the environment occur. Products will be able to be designed by the end user, as well as upgraded and reconfigured rather than replaced.

Master Change and Uncertainty

The supply chain needs to be organized so that it can thrive on change and uncertainty. The structure needs to be flexible to allow for rapid reconfiguration of human and physical resources. The following are ways in which to create an environment that embraces change:

- Maintain a skilled workforce.
- Give workers the resources and the authority to respond to changing market opportunities.
- The structure needs to support the linkage of necessary resources within the enterprise as well as between enterprises.
- Foster an entrepreneurial company culture.

Leveraging the Impact of People and Information

Finally, the mechanism, which utilizes cooperative relationships to enrich the customer, is based on the dimension of *Leveraging the Impact of People and Information.* People and information are the agile enterprise's most valued resources. Motivation in employees can be enhanced by distributing decision-making authority. An agile enterprise sells its ability to convert the knowledge, skills, and information embodied in its personnel into solutions for individual customers.

2. Dimensions of Costs in Supply Chain Management

If an enterprise is to exploit the advantages of setting up the supply chain to its full potential, an understanding of the key differences between using the Internet and other channels for the flow of information, products, and funds must be attained. The enterprise needs to identify the value created by using the Internet as well as other channels. Four drivers of the supply chain performance are critical to determining a supply chain's responsiveness and efficiency. These drivers are inventory, transportation, facilities, and information [4]. Inventory includes all raw materials, work in process and finished goods. Transportation is the moving of inventory from point to point in the supply chain and can encompass various modes. Facilities are the places in the supply chain network where inventory is stored, assembled, or fabricated. Finally, information is the data and analysis regarding inventory, transportation, facilities, and customers throughout the supply chain. [6,8,13]

3. Dimensions of Knowledge Management

KM focuses on understanding how knowledge is acquired, created, stored and utilized within an organization. Organizational KM processes that are grounded in the sociology of knowledge and based on the view of organizations as social collectives and "knowledge systems" are as follows: (1) creation, (2) storage/retrieval, (3) transfer, and (4) application [10, 18, 15, and 1]. Learning occurs when individuals create new knowledge by combining explicit knowledge accessed from KM systems, with their prior knowledge, normally in tacit form. These four processes enable end-users, while interacting with their KM system, to generate and share knowledge.

Knowledge Creation

Organizational knowledge creation is generative, where knowledge is actively constructed from information previously stored and new information drawn from the environment. Organizations create new knowledge through social and collaborative processes:

- Action learning—involves working on problems, focusing on the learning acquired, and actually implementing solutions.
- Systematic problem solving—requires a mindset, disciplined in both reductionism and holistic thinking, attentive to details, and willing to push beyond the obvious to assess underlying causes.
- Learning from past experiences —reviews a company's successes and failures, assessing them systematically, and transferring and recording the "lessons learned" in a way that will be of maximum benefit to the organization.

Two important points regarding knowledge acquisition and creation; first, information, whether it is acquired from an external or an internal source is subject to perceptual filters (norms, values, and procedures) that influence what information the organization listens to and ultimately accepts. Second, knowledge acquisition and creation systemically is guided by a firm's core competency strategy. For organizations to meet their strategic objectives, knowledge acquired from multiple sources must self-organize around the firm's key business processes and knowledge domains modeled in a firm's value chain [15]. The principal enabling technologies are data mining, pattern matching, automatic inference, concurrent engineering, process analysis, just-in-time learning and business research [1 and 16].

Knowledge Storage and Retrieval

In order to store and later to retrieve knowledge, an organization must first determine what is important to retain and how best to retain it. Semantic and episodic knowledge about customers, projects, competition, and industry should be structured and stored so the system can find and deliver it quickly and correctly. When structuring knowledge, it is important to consider how the information will be retrieved by different groups of people. Functional and effective knowledge storage systems allow categorization around learning needs, work objectives, user expertise, use of the knowledge, and location (where the information is stored). However, knowledge is not always present in its optimal form, is not available when needed, and is not present where the work activity is carried out. Additionally, knowledge content is often not complete, not current, and not uniform. Some of the key enabling technologies are multimedia databases, query languages, text index, search engines, data mining and storage servers/advanced computer storage technology and document management technology that allow knowledge of an organization's past, often dispersed among a variety of retention facilities, to be effectively stored and made accessible [1].

Knowledge Transfer

Alavi and Leidner [1] have conceptualized knowledge transfer/flows in terms of five elements: (1) perceived value of the source unit's knowledge, (2) motivational disposition of the source (i.e., their willingness to share knowledge), (3) existence and richness of transmission channels, (4) motivational disposition of the receiving unit (i.e., their willingness to acquire knowledge from the source), and (5) the absorptive capacity (i.e., ability to acquire, assimilate, and use knowledge) of the receiving unit. Knowledge transfer involves the mechanical, electronic, and interpersonal movement of information and knowledge both intentionally/formally and unintentionally/informally. Organizations intentionally transfer knowledge by written communications, training, internal conferences, internal publications, job rotation and job transfer, and mentoring. Organizations unintentionally transfer knowledge as a function of unplanned human interaction, i.e. job rotation, stories and myths, task forces, and informal networks. The various levels at which transfer occurs are transfer of knowledge between individuals, from individuals to explicit sources, from individuals to groups, between groups, across groups, and from the group to the organization [1]. Workflow systems, groupware, database, GDSS, video teleconferencing, electronic bulletin boards, discussion forums, knowledge directories, list -servers, and graphics applications are some of the key enabling technologies.

Knowledge Application

Dramatic advances in communications and transportation, has speeded the flow and production of goods and/or services, created increasing demand for these products, and eased the task of managing globally dispersed assets. These factors have all combined to create highly competitive global markets in which change is rapid and companies need to be quick and flexible, but able to retain benefits of both economies of scale and scope. The non-linear, radical and discontinuous changes in the competitive landscape require continual updates to the best practices archived in the knowledge database. How global organizations become aware of their intellectual resources (knowledge) and what programs they implement in order to apply and/or distribute this knowledge, to increase competitiveness, have become a key component in understanding how global companies can leverage their knowledge generating capabilities in creating new opportunities in global markets. Effective KM application promotes an integrated approach to identifying, managing, and sharing all of an enterprise's information assets. Automatic inference expert systems, rule-based/case-based expert systems, workflow systems, workflow automation systems are the key enabling technologies for knowledge integration and application. Next we describe the research methodology and framework used in this study.

RESEARCH METHODOLOGY: THE ANALYTIC NETWORK PROCESS

The research methodology used in this paper is an intuitive approach utilizing quantitative, qualitative, tangible and intangible factors pertaining to the decision of which KM construct is the most important for a given enterprise, based on their organization's performance criteria, the dimensions of agility and the supply chain drivers. The analytic network process (ANP) is capable of taking into consideration multiple dimensions of information into the analysis, a powerful and necessary characteristic for any strategic decision. The ANP is a general form of the Analytic Hierarchy Process (AHP) [21] for decision structuring and decision analysis which was first introduced by Saaty [10]. AHP allows for a set of complex issues that have an impact on an overall objective to be compared with the importance of each issue relative to its impact on the solution of the problem. ANP has also not received as much attention as the AHP model in the research literature (see Meade and Sarkis, [14] for an example application and brief review of other ANP research). ANP does not require the strict hierarchical structure of AHP. The network structure of ANP is defined graphically with two-way arrows (or arcs), which represent interdependencies among clusters or groupings, or if within the same level of analysis, a looped arc. The directions of the arcs signify dependence. Arcs emanate from a controlling attribute to other attributes that may influence it. The relative importance or strength of the impacts on a given element is measured on a ratio scale similar to AHP. The ANP approach is capable of handling interdependence among elements by obtaining the composite weights through the development of a 'super-matrix'. Saaty [21] explains the super-matrix concept as a parallel to the Markov chain process. The supermatrix development is defined in the next section.

Overall, there are six major steps in the ANP process:

1. Develop a decision network hierarchy showing the relationships among decision factors.
2. Elicit pair-wise comparisons among the factors influencing the decision.
3. Calculate relative-importance-weight vectors of the factors.
4. Form a super-matrix (i.e., a two-dimensional matrix composed from the relative-importance-weight vectors) and normalize this super-matrix, so that the numbers in every column sum to one.
5. Calculate converged ("stable") weights from the normalized super-matrix.
6. Determine overall weightings of decision criteria.

Develop a Decision Network Hierarchy

Figure 2 illustrates a high level graphical description of the decision network hierarchy and the general clusters of factors. Many elements are involved in determining the best strategy to select. Of obvious significance are the organizational performance criteria that consist of traditional strategic organizational metrics such as time, quality, cost, and flexibility. In order to maintain that the strategy selected relates to the desire to be an agile supply chain, the determinants of agility are also considered. As discussed above, the supply chain also has four factors (revenue, inventory costs, facility costs, and transportation costs) that determine the responsiveness and efficiency of the supply chain. Their interdependency to the four dimensions of KM needs to be determined.

Pair-wise Comparisons and Relative-Importance-Weight Vectors

Eliciting preferences of various criteria and dimensions requires a series of pair-wise comparisons where the decision maker will compare two components at a time with respect to a 'control' criterion. In ANP, pair-wise comparisons of the elements in each level are conducted with respect to their relative importance towards their control criterion [18]. An example of the pair-wise comparison matrix within the Dimension of Agility *Leveraging People and Information* is shown in Table 1. The decision maker is asked a series of comparison questions and the weightings are then obtained. For this matrix, the decision maker can be asked questions such as: "In terms of *Leveraging People and Information* what is the relative importance of the *Supply Chain Driver* Information as compared to Inventory costs?"

Super-Matrix

ANP uses the formation of a supermatrix to allow for the resolution of the effects of the interdependence that exists between the elements of the system. The supermatrix is a partitioned matrix, where each sub-matrix is composed of a set of relationships between two levels in the graphical model.

Super-matrix Formation and Final Relative Importance Weight Calculation

ANP uses the formation of a super-matrix to allow for the resolution of the effects of the interdependence that exists between the clusters within the decision network hierarchy. The super-matrix is a partitioned matrix, where each sub-matrix is composed of a set of relationships between two clusters in the graphical model. In our model the interdependence exits between the *dimensions of costs in Supply Chain Management* and the *dimensions of KM.*

The next step with the super-matrix evaluation is to determine the final relative importance weights of each of the alternatives. To complete this step and help guarantee convergence, the columns of the super-matrix must be "column stochastic". That is, the weights of each column for the super-matrix need to sum to 1. For convergence to a final set of weights, we raise the normalized (column stochastic) super-matrix to a large power until stabilization of the weights occurs.

The sixth and last step in the ANP process is to take the final results of the converged super-matrix and the eigenvector values from the earlier pair-wise comparisons and calculate the relative importance weight for each KM construct. The construct with the highest value will be the "most important" based on the decision makers' criteria and strategy selected. Therefore, based on the type of strategy being pursued by the enterprise and the importance of their supply chain drivers, the dominant KM construct can be determined. This can then be compared to the overall knowledge management strategy such as codification vs. personalization, and if necessary, the appropriate corrective action taken to align the intent with the implementation of KM strategy.

CONCLUSION

This paper has addressed the need for a strategic decision making tool to assist management in determining which KM construct is most beneficial in the development of an agile supply chain. The ANP process of eliciting information and showing the various relationships requires that management be familiar with the issue and to think of the problem in broader terms. The actual process of going through the decision will help management learn of the various issues related to strategic decisions. The process and model are valuable knowledge and learning tools, not just a mechanism to support a final decision. The model is also flexible enough to incorporate additional criteria with little difficulty, as required by the dynamic and competitive environment and organizational structure.

There are some limitations of the model and what we have presented. One is the knowledge of the decision maker. The decision-maker provides the values for the pairwise comparisons and therefore, the model is very dependent on the perceptual weightings provided by the decision-maker. This risk can be reduced by using more than one decision maker from the same organization and averaging their responses. The decision-maker set needs to include someone in the organization who understands the strategic level of the logistics process and the implications for their company. Second, KM is not just a technology project. KM relies on organizational structures and culture to meet its goals. Therefore, there is a very heavy dependency on the specific organization or at least the specific type of organization, where the KM initiative is being implemented. Thus the generalizability of findings based on our model to other organizations may be limited.

The significance of this study is the development of metrics for measuring the relative importance of a particular dimension based on the application of theoretical concepts from the information systems and management science literature to the modern knowledge economy. It embraces a multidisciplinary and interdisciplinary perspective on the challenge of KM in the context of supply chain strategy by drawing upon perspectives from the domains of strategy, information systems, management science, organizational behavior and organizational development.

This study is intended to raise the level of intellectual curiosity about the link between KM and global supply chain drivers in the modern knowledge economy. The concept of KM in the context of an agile supply chain suggests the creation of structures that combine the most advanced elements of technological resources and the indispensable input of human response and decision-making. The challenge of managing these complex structures has tremendous potential from either the practical, productive viewpoint or the human growth perspective. In a way, the development of a 'knowledge entity' seems to be much like the education of a human being. Both have growing, changing, and unpredictable potential for innovation, each in their own way. Since contextual factors play a critical role in the design of effective KM systems, technical and process solutions need to be customized to fit the organization performance criteria, dimensions of agility and supply chain drivers.

REFERENCES

Available upon request.

Beyond the Search Engine: Perspectives on the Future Models

Mahesh S. Raisinghani, Ph.D., CEC
Graduate School of Management, University of Dallas, 1845 East Northgate Drive, Irving, Texas 75062-4736
Phone: 972.721.5173, Fax: 972.721.4007, **Email:** mraising@gsm.udallas.edu

Robert Scott Dupree, Ph.D.
Director, University of Dallas Library, 1845 East Northgate Drive, Irving, Texas 75062-4736
Phone: 972.721.5000, Fax: 972.721.4007, **Email:** scott@acad.udallas.edu

INTRODUCTION

In traditional library practice, reference librarians are often asked questions that require not only searching for and identifying the proper information but also combining various facts in order to answer them completely. If one is asked, for instance, how many Democrats crossed the picket lines during strikes in Chicago from 1956 to 1980, an accurate answer may or may not be forthcoming, depending on available figures, but it will not be given directly by any one source. What is required, rather, is the ability to search a number of likely sources and compile the facts from them needed to deduce the answer. One might have to look in the records of the Democratic party, in newspaper accounts, in volumes devoted to union activities during the period, and perhaps in books on the labor movement generally. There may well be crucial information in less obvious places. Is it possible to devise a model that might offer this possibility for future researchers, one that could be implemented by a proper approach to the tagging of information as we look towards the next stages of information management and digital libraries?

TAXONOMY OF A SEARCH ENGINE

Over 900 search engines reside on the Internet. Basically, a search engine is a large database of information that is queried with software. There are four basic types of search engines. These include (1) Portals; (2) Keyword (index) searches; (3) Concept (index) searches; and (4) Metacrawler searches.

1. **Portal (directory) search:**

A Directory is a database of sites that is created and maintained manually by humans. A portal presents these sites as a series of categories and subcategories that may be navigated by clicking on the hyperlinks. When a search of a directory is performed, the software searches for the entered text in the names of the categories, subcategories, and the titles of the sites. A portal search is not usually very productive for educational uses. Perhaps the best-known example of a portal is:

• Yahoo!

While you may enter a search string into the search box of a portal, these tools are more appropriately used by clicking on the hyperlinked topic categories. This will provide a set of subcategories. Clicking on a subcategory will yield either a further subcategorization or a set of Internet sites that provide information related to the topic.

Keyword (index) search:

An Index is a database of sites created and maintained electronically by software that searches the Web for publicly-available pages. When a keyword search of an index is performed, the software searches for the text in the titles of the sites, the text within the pages, and any keywords hidden within the codes on the pages. A keyword search is one of the most effective and efficient methods for searching for general information. Examples of keyword search tools include:

• AltaVista

To make best use of AltaVista's searching capability, follow these simple tips:

1. Capitalize proper nouns (not other words)
2. Enclose phrases of two or more words within quotation marks
3. Use a plus sign immediately before a term or phrase to force the inclusion of that item's appearance in the search results
4. Use a minus sign immediately before a term or phrase to exclude the item from the search results

An example of a search string that would look for information about the clock tower known as Big Ben in London, England, and would eliminate information about restaurants and hotels would be:

+"Big Ben" +London -hotel -restaurant

• All the Web's FastSearch

FastSearch claims to have electronically indexed more of the Internet than any other search engine database. To use this tool, follow these simple tips:

1. Enter your search terms into the search box
2. Select (from the popup menu to the left of the search box) whether you wish the results to include *all* of these words, *some* of these words, or the phrase *exactly as typed*

This tool is very fast and efficient in locating relevant information. It even reports the amount of time it took to search its database and report the findings!

• Northern Light

This search tool reports results in a very unique manner. Not only is the result presented as a listing of relevant sites, it is also presented as a collection of categorized findings (folders in the left column of the results screen). Northern Light searches its database (electronic index) of Internet sites and its collection of special documents (available for purchase). To eliminate the search of these "for sale" items, be sure to limit your search with the popup menu next to "Select a source".

Concept (index) search:

A concept search tool features an electronically created database of Internet sites that is searched by artificial intelligence software. The software first parses through your search string to look for concepts (usually synonyms), and then performs the search based on this expanded search. The results may at times be difficult to understand, because terms in addition to the original ones have been employed for the search. Two major concept search tools include:

• Excite

Excite was one of the first search tools on the Internet to feature "natural English" queries. That is, you do not have to structure your search with Boolean operators [see AltaVista above] to accomplish an efficient search. All you have to do is enter words or phrases or sentences into the search box, and let the software do the work for you!

• InfoSeek

InfoSeek, now a part of the "Go" network, offers a feature that allows you to refine your search as you go. Just enter your first term into the box and submit. Then, to refine the search, enter a new term into the box and select "Search within results".

Metacrawler search:

Unlike search tools that search a directory or an index, metacrawler tools have no database of their own. When a search string is entered into one of the metacrawler tools, the software simultaneously searches multiple other keyword and concepts search tools. Representative examples of metacrawler tools include:

• Internet Search Center (IMSA)
• Dogpile
• InFind
• Mamma
• SurfWax

(www.peotone.will.k12.il.us/media/searching.html, 2001)

The general theory behind a concept search is that in any communication the exact choice of word usage may vary between authors, but the underlying meaning is carried by overlapping domains of commonly shared vocabulary. To compensate for the differing vocabulary between an author and a searcher of the document the concept search software looks for all of the possible combinations of intersecting meanings that are present in the search request. Those words that have a significant degree of co-occurrence (i.e., statistically related) with the query words are deemed related within the context of the current database.

Concept Searching allows you to retrieve documents based not on merely lexical meanings but on broader conceptual entities. A good example of this is the intersection of **bear** and **arms** . Individually the words have a greatly diverse set of meanings, but together they have only the *"carrying weapons"* meaning. In another example, a search for "GPS" would also automatically retrieve documents containing the phrase "Global Positioning System". This works both ways, a search for "Global Positioning System" would also find documents containing only "GPS". Also, a search for "Year 2000 problem" would find documents containing the word "Y2K."

The concept search can be a powerful tool in that the concept itself can be a boolean expression. E.g., Intel used the name of a River to name its next generation 64 bit microprocessor chip, Merced. You could define a concept "Merced" so that any time you search for Merced, you are really searching for "Merced and not Merced River".

In the case of Cultural Heritage Information Online, this allows a more targeted search without worrying about using the correct art terminology, and without knowing the field names of the databases to be searched. The user fills in terms in search boxes representing the broad concepts Who, What, When, Where and How. These concepts have been mapped to a number of common Access Points which are the conceptual handles that allow users to pull information from the many repositories of material. These Access Points represent concepts in the museum field, that while well known, may be called different things in different databases. Z39.50 standard for data interchange allows the concept of the search to be presented to the appropriate fields in different databases (http://www.cimi.org/old_site/CHIO/Zquick.html).

In the search illustrated above the user is interested in finding out what Grandma Moses painted, and enters the terms "Grandma Moses" in the Who box, and "Painting" in either the What box or the How box. The software expresses this search as "FIND 'GRANDMA MOSES' IN FIELDS 'ARTIST', 'MAKER', 'CORPORATE NAME', etc., AND 'PAINTING' IN FIELDS 'OBJECT', 'SUBJECT', 'CLASSIFICATION', 'METHOD', etc." This would find only records that deal with Grandma Moses and Painting. The result of this search will be smaller than for a simple searches that is commonly available on the World Wide Web, but will likely contain more relevant information. (www.cimi.org/old_site/CHIO/Zquick.html, 2001)

The DOI Foundation's Digital Object Identifier (DOI) eBook project (www.doi.org/ebooks.html) is part of a far-reaching industry effort to promote the availability of books and other published material in electronic form. DOI is one implementation of a more general method for identifying digital content called the Handle System (www.handle.net). The Handle System was developed by the Corporation for National Research Initiatives, a think tank funded mostly by the Defense Advanced Projects Research Agency and the National Science Foundation. A DOI is just a number consisting of two parts. The first part, the prefix, identifies the original publisher of the material. The word "original" is important, because the prefix is permanent, remaining the same even if the rights to the content are transferred to another publisher. Any publisher can obtain a prefix for a payment of $1,000 to the DOI Foundation.

The second part, the suffix, uniquely identifies the work, which could be a book, a part of a book, or any other text. Publishers are responsible for assigning their own numbers, and they can be in any format. Since every edition of every book currently receives an International Standard Book Number (ISBN), these, perhaps modified to allow sale of partial books, will be used as the suffixes.

DOIs can be incorporated into Web pages much like current links. But instead of pointing to a specific Web location, the DOI sends the browser off to a database, where it retrieves and displays whatever information the publisher chooses to offer. At a minimum, this will be catalog information about the book, but more likely it will also include links to excerpts and to places where you can buy electronic or print copies. Assuming the publishers do their job of maintaining the databases, these centralized references, unlike current Web links, should never become outdated or broken.

In and of itself, the DOI does nothing to prevent copying or collect fees for use. But it can be vital in enabling both. The first step in any rights-management system is positive identification of material and of the rights owner. In the case of shared music, a la Napster, this has proven exceedingly difficult because, as far as computers are concerned, two titles that differ by a single character are two completely different works.

If DOIs are used, typos and variant titles do not matter as long as the identifier code is entered correctly. Second, the DOI system has been designed from the beginning to integrate with existing digital-rights management systems such as InterTrust and with the copy protection schemes of e-book readers such as Microsoft Reader and Adobe eBook Reader. Though a foolproof way to identify the rights owner is not sufficient by itself to make a payments system work, it is a necessary condition (http://www.businessweek.com/magazine/content/01_30/b3742032.htm).

If we look at the procedures involved in textual editing and view them in reverse, we have a kind of preliminary model for moving beyond the search engine. What was the original text for the editor becomes, for the researcher using digital libraries and large bodies of data, the answer to a question. The answer may be as elusive as an author's original text was for the textual editor, but it may in both cases be approximated if there is sufficient information. The textual editor's "tree," inverted, then represents a first stage. But to build such an inverted tree requires that the data be tagged in some fashion so that the process can be automated. From this tree, it would then be possible to establish how close to providing the answer each source might be. At this point, however, some artificial intelligence is required, since the original question must be parsed and divided up into separate units, each of which needs to be identified for type or category and assigned a set of sources for the procurement of data. In our initial example, for instance, the question would have to be divided up into segments that analyze all the concepts implied by "strikes," "picket lines," "Democrats," "Chicago," and so forth. Each of these segments would produce a large number of "variants": does "strikes" refer to baseball, to physical blows, or to labor practice? What aspect of "Chicago" is implied by the query?

Beyond the Present: Some Possible Models for the Future

However, the requirements for a truly conceptual approach that would answer the kinds of routine questions asked of a traditional reference librarian can be extraordinarily complex; in some cases there might not be a single answer or the answer could depend on further elaboration or qualification of details in the question. Nevertheless, even a primitive version of such a tool would be of enormous value to anyone seeking to navigate through huge bodies of irrelevant data in search of at least one answer. Perhaps one way of looking at such a project would be to take some common practice and model procedures on the various steps included in it.

Before printing became sufficiently widespread to dominate the distribution of written materials during the eighteenth and nineteenth centuries, texts were often circulated in handwritten copies. Of course, before the second half of the fifteenth century, all texts were reproduced in this manner. Printing made it possible to fix a text and eliminate many of the errors of repeated transcription by hand. It also made scholars aware of the need to print a definitive text, one that was as close as humanly possible to what the author originally wrote or intended. The various steps towards this goal we call "textual editing." The methodology was worked out and refined over a long period spanning more than three centuries. To this day, the procedure for deciding which text to use in reprinting a book or publishing a manuscript for the first time has remained more or less the same.

The "establishment" of a text to be printed involves certain well-defined steps. Typically, in the case of older texts, there remain numerous versions, none of which can be traced directly to the author's hand—that is, to a manuscript written by him or her directly. In order to edit a historical document of this nature, one is required to search out every version of the text that is extant, compare all of them, and classify them in some fashion. Then one establishes a base text, using for it the version that is either oldest or seems most likely to be closest to what the author intended. Next, all the other versions of the text are compared with the base and discrepancies noted. Sometimes, however, the base text is erroneous (because of a transcription error) and needs to be corrected by reference to one of the other surviving versions. Thus, a later and seemingly less accurate text may contain a word or phrase that is obviously the right one and must be substituted for the corrupted part of the base text. And so it goes. The editor makes a thorough comparison of all versions and adjudicates, on a case by case basis, each time there is a discrepancy in wording among them. Editing at this point involves making informed decisions about which phrasing to adopt. The various "readings" or alternate versions of a word or phrase are tabulated and presented in the form of an *apparatus*, which is usually presented at the bottom of the page to which they refer. These differing versions of a word or phrase are called "variants." Eventually, manuscripts that are too far removed from the original to be useful and removed from this compilation, and only those that seem to offer independent lines of derivation from the original are kept. Nevertheless, a thoroughly bad manuscript could still retain a version of the text in some instances that is closer to the original than is the best one.

A helpful way of assessing the value of each variant is the preparation of a tree chart, an attempt to show in graphic form which manuscripts or printed copies were derived directly from the author's original and which were secondary, tertiary, or even further removed from it. This rhizome-like representation, which resembles a genealogical table, allows the editor to see at a glance how far removed a given variant is from the original text and therefore to gauge the likelihood of its correctness

The manuscripts are grouped into "families," and the "descendants" or copies are arranged generationally into a *stemma codicum*, which might look something like this:

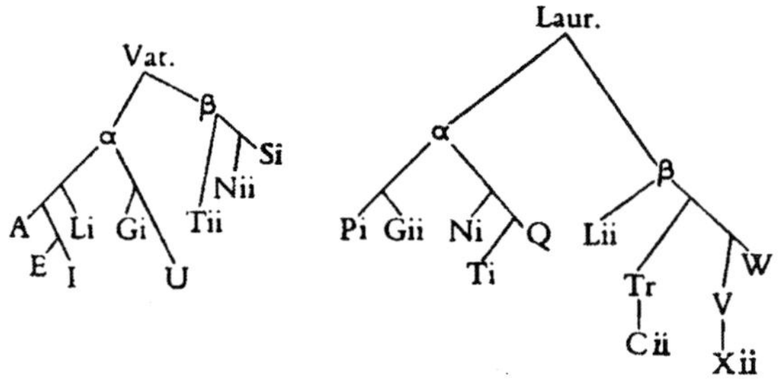

This instance is taken from an edition of the ancient Greek poet Theocritus (3rd century B. C. E.) published in 1952. Some thirty or so separate poems are involved, and not all are present in every manuscript, thus further complicating the editor's task. In addition, the earliest manuscripts date only from the 13th century C.E., so that a gap of well over 1500 years separates the originals from the copies. However, Theocritus is quoted in texts by other ancient authors, so that there are independent, if fragmentary versions of individual poems that may be older and more accurate than the surviving complete texts. The final version arrived at by A. S. F. Gow in his edition of Theocritus' works is, accordingly, an attempt at reconstruction, not a text that corresponds to any surviving copy.

Viewed in reverse, then, the *stemma* is like a search for the answer to a question with multiple elements, such as the example of the striking picketers. The answer will have to be constructed from available data as filtered through the requirements of the query. Such a diagram might look something like this:

Answer (a number)
1965-1980
Non-Chicago Chicago
Democrats Non-Democrats
Strikers Non-Strikers
Picketline-Crossers Non-Picketline-Crossers

The "picketline crossers" are like a word that has survived intact through a series of recopyings of documents and can be traced back to the original because it occurs uniformly throughout the tree. But how would this concept be tagged?

The answer is at hand in traditional print indexing, which is labor-intensive and requires knowledge of a certain kind. Fortunately, a skilled indexer can do an excellent job on a manuscript without any specialized acquaintance with its subject. Professional indexing is a service that has been routinely available for authors and publishers for many years. If we look at a well-executed index from a printed book, we are likely to find entries like the following:

Modifiers, defined, 453; classified, 453-467; in the sentence, 97-103; dangling, 182, 333-339; misplaced, 183, 590; restrictive and non-restrictive, 419-430; punctuation of restrives and non-restrictives, 647-649; proper placing of, 348; squinting, 412; substantive, 570.

What is noteworthy about this venerable practice is the presence of fine distinctions that are nevertheless evident from the context. As we have learned in the decades devoted to artificial language and the attempt to accomplish such simple deductions as must be arrived at from ordinary actions ("He went into the room" implies a doorway that is entered), indexing presupposes a knowledge that is not only contextual but often consists of lexicographical distinctions that are understood but reside between the lines and are usually unstated. They reside, in fact, at the intersections of several concepts. To go beyond the search engine, we must find a way to apply the *stemma* approach to finding an answer to the conceptual distinctions that are present in traditional indexes. Until then, we will continue to find the indexes in the backs of our printed books to be necessary adjuncts of our ability to find every word in a document.

REFERENCES

Availability upon request

Abstracts

A Review of Survey Research in Knowledge Management

Daniele Chauvel and Charles Despres
e^cKM: The European Center for Knowledge Management
Graduate School of Business, Marseille-Provence, France
Tel: +3 (349) 182-7800, Fax: +3 (349) 182-7921
eckm@esc-marseille.fr

The concept of Knowledge Management (KM) has grown and gathered importance in the field of business management. Some 10 years after its introduction, KM has a role in MBA and PhD curricula, is a keyword in bibliographic databases, forms the conceptual nucleus of a developing literature, is sought after by leading firms and readily prescribed by all the major consultants. KM is increasingly positioned as a viable approach to the New Age of business and a growing number of professionals and academics are working to elaborate its principles and application technologies.

The developmental path that KM is following is unexceptional for sociologists of science. We argue that the development of scientific knowledge is largely a sociological phenomenon involving the dynamics of power, communities and social facts. Social psychology rather than "Truth" provides the ways and means that lead a community to create the distinction between bunk and "Reality." KM is a new domain that integrates fields of endeavor uncharacteristically found together, hence its fuzzy nature. We now appear to be entering a second phase of development where the rhetoric and the thinking are winding around more coherent themes.

Agreement on problems and heuristics is a key to such coherence. A key indicator is found in the tools that a field deploys to generate knowledge about its knowledge, and one such tool set are surveys conducted to determine current practice, establish benchmarks and track developments. This article takes the self-referential nature of survey research as its starting point. The knowledge generated by these tools is an artifact and informative, but the nature of the tools themselves is also informative with regard to the conceptual foundations of the thinkers in the field. The purpose of this paper is therefore as follows:

1. To identify the surveys that have been conducted in KM between 1997 and 2001;
2. To analyze these surveys for the major themes that they evoke;
3. To determine from this review and analysis the topics that appear to be major preoccupations in the field of Knowledge Management, those receiving little or no attention, and to project future developments in the field.

Our research program identified surveys conducted in KM between 1997 – 2001, identified the conceptual foundations of these surveys through thematic deconstruction, and determined the conceptual dimensions that appear to be major and minor preoccupations. This developed a framework of six bipolar dimensions that account for the organizing logics employed in this set of surveys. This framework is pressed against previous research in which Despres & Chauvel (2000) identified the structuring devices used in conceptual models of KM. We conclude by making projections for future thinking in Knowledge Management given the view it appears to be taking on itself.

When It Comes to Selling a Proposal, Appearance Does Matter!

Nancy J. Johnson, PhD
Associate Dean of Business
Capella University, Minneapolis, Minnesota
Tel (home): (612) 333-8910
Tel (work): (612) 252-4365, or 1-888-CAPELLA, ext. 365
Fax: (612) 399-0730
johns024@tc.umn.edu and/or njohnson@capella.edu

When preparing a proposal for a major IT expenditure, the preparers are often perplexed in trying to decide how much time to put into the final printed presentation document. The relative influence value of the various aspects of the IT project evaluation by funders (e.g., reputation of the project champion, the political and strategic value of the project, the appearance of the document, the oral presentation to the funding decision makers) is not known absolutely. Multiple types of financial evaluations are done on the estimated costs and paybacks, however the evaluators are often skeptical of the accuracy of the estimates rendering the calculations useless. The decision to fund a project is often based on illogical, unquantifiable factors such as the perceived history of past project successes/failures, the reputation of the sponsor, or the perceptions of the relative merits of the other projects competing for development dollars.

This problem of not knowing what the funders really want exists in both the private sector as well as in the public sector. A study was conducted on four years of major IT proposals presented to the State of Minnesota legislature by various state agencies. The content and format of 51 proposals was evaluated against the funding eventually received, and 35 in-depth interviews were conducted with key proposal preparers, evaluators, and funders. The content and presentation format of the proposals was compared to the actual funding received. The results of the interviews were analyzed statistically and also stratified by the role of the interviewee.

The results showed a strong correlation between the appearance of the proposal and the resulting funding. Other measurable factors surrounding the proposals were considered and analyzed, however the strongest correlation for receiving full funding was the quality of the appearance of the proposal. The better prepared and presented the proposal was, the more likely it was to be funded fully. The legislators are similar to the funding committees in any organization in that they are made up executives with little IT acumen and training. When faced with the inability to critically analyze the content or portent of a proposal, people fall back on appearance as a tool to differentiate quality. The results of the research demonstrated that common sense observations about decision makers prejudice held true.

What does this result mean for proposal preparers? The more time invested in the research and preparation of a proposal, the greater the chance of receiving funding. Many other types of factors outside of the preparer's control may hamper the success of funding, however presenting a poorly done proposal reduces the chances of getting any funding at all.

EIS Information: Use and Quality Determinants

Manal M. Elkordy
Alexandria University, Egypt
melkordy@hotmail.com

Omar E. M. Khalil
University of Massachusetts
okhalil@umassd.edu

Since information is essential to organizational learning and competitive advantages, an understanding of the factors that affect its usage is critical. EIS are assumed to provide improvements in the quantity and quality of information made available to executives from internal and external sources. EIS use may be influenced by their quality, the extent to which users believe that the information generated by the EIS available to them meets their information requirements.

Although there is a substantial body of evidence suggesting that user perceptions are important determinants of information use, there is considerably less work directed at examining factors that may influence such perceptions. Information systems research models and past research suggest a number of factors that believed to influence perceived information quality, including user training, system sophistication, ease of use, perceived usefulness, IS maturity, user participation, and user involvement.

However, EIS information quality received little attention as a construct in past empirical information systems research. Information quality was often treated as a component of the general measure of user satisfaction. On the other hand, there is a need within the IS community to have a better understanding of the factors that may influence the users' perception of EIS information quality. The research model of this study was designed to investigate the relationship of EIS information use to EIS information quality and the possible impact of ease of use, user involvement, information systems (IS) maturity, and system sophistication on EIS information quality.

The information of an EIS that is perceived to be easier to use and less complex has a higher chance to be perceived positively by its users. User participation in EIS development efforts is expected to enhance his/her perceived information quality through the intervention of a need-based psychological component (i.e., user involvement). A more mature IS function should be in a better position to design, implement, and operate better quality EIS, and users are expected to have a more positive beliefs about their information quality. Finally, system sophistication, e.g., availability of EIS functions, is expected to positively influence information quality. These expectations were stated in the form of research hypotheses.

Data were collected from 216 UK executives. EIS information quality was found to positively influence EIS information use, and EIS information quality, in turn, is positively influenced by ease of use, user involvement, IS maturity, and EIS sophistication. Ease of use was the strongest determinant of EIS information quality, followed by user involvement, IS maturity, and system sophistication.

The findings suggest that information quality is an important determinant of information use, which ultimately leads to organizational learning. EIS information quality, in turn, can be enhanced by fully or partially manipulating factors such as ease of use, user involvement, IS maturity, and EIS sophistication. The practical implication of the findings is that providing EIS information with higher quality encourages more EIS use and enhances the usefulness of the systems in the eyes of their users. This emphasizes the importance of EIS as a source for high quality information that enables executives to stay atop the ever-changing external and internal business environment.

A Web-Based Appointment Scheduling System for a Major Health Center

Yousif Mustafa
Assistant Professor, Department of Computer Information Systems
Central Missouri State University
Tel: (660) 543-8647, Fax: (660) 543-8465
Mustafa@cmsu1.cmsu.edu

Larry Hedden
Ryan Witt
Jermy Carty
Mustafa Kamal

Inspired by the success of implementing the e-commerce for car rentals and airline seat reservation, where customers have the ability to reserve the car of their choice or book on the flight of their choice via the internet at any time of their convenience, we have simulated the implementation of e-commerce and apply it to the healthcare industry. In this paper, we describe a case study where we have developed an Internet-based system for scheduling appointments with physicians at a local medical center. The system, just like Avis.com for example, allows patients to login via the Internet, create their profile, browse through a list of physician names, view their specialties, read a synopsis of their practices, even look at their personal photographs, and submit a review of any physician in the center. After selecting a physician, the patient views the physician's calendar, and select the time slot of his/her convenience to schedule an appointment without the need to call during business hours, or hold for a nurse. The system will empower patients and enable them to act as proactive "Customers" rather than passive "patients" by providing them with the power of "screening" their physicians in order to make an informative selection. Patients can also modify their profile, cancel or reschedule an appointment. Finally, the system will give patients the flexibility to ask their physicians to e-mail a prescription to their pharmacy whether the pharmacy is around the block or in Hawaii where the patient caught a cold while vacationing.

The Digital Divide: A Psychological Perspective

Helen Partridge
Associate Lecturer, School of Information Systems
Faculty of Information Technology, Queensland University of Technology, Australia, Tel: 6 (173) 864-9047
Fax: 6 (173) 864-1969, h.partridge@qut.edu.au

Based in its ethos of "information for all" the public library community in both Australia and the United States has been actively involved in bridging the Digital Divide. Public libraries have invested time and money to develop programmes and resources aimed at bridging the information and technology gap in community. These programmes and resources have been developed based on the current understanding of the Digital Divide. An understanding that has been developed primarily from a socio-economic perspective. Very few studies have considered the social, psychological or cultural barriers that may contribute to the Digital Divide. This paper will outline a research project aimed at exploring the psychology of the Digital Divide. The research will use the Social Cognitive Theory by Bandura[1] to examine the psychology of the information and technology gap in community. This theory postulates that a person will act according to their perceived capabilities and the anticipated consequences of their actions. Participants in the study will be novice Internet users drawn from public libraries in the United States and Australia. Self-administered surveys will be used for data collection. This research will assist organisations such as public libraries in developing strategies for bridging the emerging information and technology gap and will lend support to the existence of a Social Digital Divide as proposed by Harper[2].

Beyond the Boundaries of the Sacred Garden: Children and the Internet

Dr. Marian Quigley and Dr. Kathy Blashki
School of Multimedia Systems, Monash University
Australia, Tel: +6 (139) 904-7159/ +6 (139) 904-7118
Fax: +6 (139) 904-7125
{marian.quigley, kathy.blashki}@infotech.monash.edu.au

A 1999 study revealed that in Australia, approximately 2/3 of 6-17 year olds were Internet users and preferred it to books, radio and Pay TV. In November 2000, the Australian Bureau of Statistics reported that approximately 50% of Australian children aged 5 to14 had gone online in the past year. The Australian Government has responded to community concern about the possible harm to children posed by the Internet by establishing legislation (January, 2000) which requires ISPs to take 'all reasonable steps' to ensure that access to prohibited material is denied.

Concern about children and the Internet is the latest in a ritual cycle of moral or media panics surrounding new technologies. Such panics often focus on children and are related to adult anxieties surrounding the transgression of boundaries including those between adult/child, private/public, and work/leisure. They are also founded on technological determinist accounts of media and an essentialist view of childhood that sees children as particularly susceptible to media effects. According to this view, childhood is seen as residing in a mythical past 'Golden Age' that is now considered to be under threat by technological development.

The authors of this paper argue that the Internet, as other media before it, plays an important role in the socialisation of the young and that children need to be recognised as active – and often sophisticated - participants rather than passive recipients of multimedia texts and messages. In any case, as the sociologist David Buckingham points out, the proliferation of new technologies, together with the increased fragmentation of audiences, now render almost impossible the 'pro tection' of the young by the adult members of electronic societies. His claim is supported by a recent Australian study by Nightingale, Dickenson and Griff (2000) that highlights the important role media play in the transition from childhood to adulthood along with children's adeptness in circumventing adult control.

The path toward autonomy and full participation in the socio-political world is a continuum: one that is increasingly bound up with, and dependent upon, engagement with multiple and varied media texts. Consequently, there needs to be a shift away from the current emphasis on restriction and protection, to a focus on communication and consultation between adults and children.

The Role of Provider Side Variables in the Adoption of a Government Electronic Submission Program

Niya Werts, MHES, MS and Dr. Gerald Canfield
University of Maryland Baltimore County
Tel: (410) 455-3206, Fax: 410-455-1073
{nwerts1, canfield}@umbc.edu

With the advent of digital government, government institutions are primary change agents for innovation. The task at hand for any entity promoting an innovation is how to gain acceptance and adoption of the innovation. Government faces the challenge of disseminating intra-organizational change, as well as a fundamental change in the way business is conducted with citizens and the private sector. One way in which government regulatory agencies have augmented their interactions with the private sector is offering electronic submission alternatives to formerly paper based processes. An exploration of factors contributing significantly to voluntary adoption becomes particularly important to regulatory entities when electronic alternatives have potential benefits for both the agency and the industry.

To date, much of the research on organizational innovation adoption focuses on the characteristics of the potential adopter as predictors of adoption behavior. However, this view of adoption research can be criticized for furthering the "individual blame bias" discussed by Rogers (Frambach, 1993; Rogers, 1995). Rather than further promote this type of bias, Frambach suggests an integrated model of adoption in which supply side variables are examined for their role in technology adoption. Supply side variables are those aspects of marketing and promotion that providers of a technology innovation have control of (Frambach, 1993). Analogous to the customer-supplier context, governments dealing with industry customers may also employ a number of strategies to promote the use of certain technologies as it moves toward the reality of digital government. King, Gurbaxani, Kraemer, Raman, and Yap examine institutional actions in information technology innovation from a "supply push-demand pull" context where government influence and regulatory actions converge (1994). They list 6 institutional actions to promote technology: (a) knowledge building, (b) knowledge deployment, (c) subsidy, (d) mobilization, (c) standard setting, and (d) innovation directive. By attempting to promote, adopt, and diffuse technology, the six institutional actions closely resemble supply side launch strategies. In the public sector context, the term "provider side variables" may be more appropriate. A cross-national meta-analysis of government efforts to promote electronic data interchange (EDI) revealed that King et.al.'s provider side institutional actions can be clearly observed in many instances, and the quality of those actions may strongly influence the success or failure of EDI initiatives (Damsgaard & Kalle, 1996).

The focus of the present research is the effect of provider side variables on adoption of an electronic submission program offered by the Food and Drug Administration's Office of Generic Drugs (OGD) for the filing of Abbreviated New Drug Applications (ANDAs). Currently, only a third of ANDAs submitted have an accompanying electronic component. While an electronic filing mandate does not presently extend to the FDA's industry partners, electronic filling will eventually become required (Levin, 2000). Voluntary compliance by industry now could allow for much needed feedback and suggestions that may create greater ease in the transition from paper based to paperless submission. A preliminary case study investigation of two generic drug companies revealed that mobilization, standard setting, and knowledge deployment may have a significant role to play in voluntary adoption behavior. The pilot test for a quantitative survey methodology is currently being conducted to query sponsor research organizations about both organizational demographic information and subjective ratings of OGD performance in five of King et.al.'s six institutional actions.

The study's findings can potentially make a contribution to the present adoption and diffusion literature by examining the role of provider side variables on innovation adoption. A scholarly investigation of the role of provider side variables will contribute to a more holistic model for innovation adoption research. A contribution can also be made to the public administration literature by examining King et.al.'s well-cited institutional actions, which have not been extensively explored in an empirical sense. Additionally, a study of this kind can add to the growing body of literature specifically relating to electronic government.

E-Commerce: A Matter of Trust and Control

Yi-Miin Yen, University of Alaska Anchorage
Tel: (907) 786-4117, Fax: (907) 786-4115, afmyy@uaa.alaska.edu

The rise of the Internet as the medium for E-Commerce has changed many of the company's business applications. The needs of successful implementation of E-Commerce applications must be viewed as part of an overall integrated solution to an organization's business requirements. A broader business needs, goals and advantages of developing E-Commerce applications need to be considered and analyzed while many business processes are required to be reengineered. These changes in businesses as well as in technologies introduce risk that could be minimized through effective internal control implementation and review. The purpose of this paper is to provide internal auditors and the management the general guidelines of developing internal control procedures that should follow the system development life cycle (SDLC) approach and be designed and implemented simultaneously with the development of the Internet-based business applications. In addition to describe the fundamental objectives and characteristics of the Internet-based internal control, this paper also discusses many of the design, implementation and monitoring issues important to managers and auditors in developing the internal control systems.

Re-engineering College Instruction using Web-based Technologies: The Experiences and Recommendations of Some College Professors

C. Shayo, PhD
Information and Decision Sciences Department
California State University, San Bernardino
Cshayo@csusb.edu
R. Santiago, PhD
Director, Technology Research Center
California State University, San Bernardino, Rsantiag@csusb.edu
F. Lin, PhD
California State University, San Bernardino, Flin@csusb.edu

The Internet and other web-based technologies are offering new opportunities for delivering on-campus and off-campus courses. College professors are in different stages of taking advantage of these new opportunities. Some professors have just started embracing web-based technologies, while others have more than four years experience. Some professors have used evolutionary approaches by slowly embracing those aspects of web-technologies they felt comfortable with—thus matching their teaching styles and philosophies to the technology; yet others have allowed the technology to radically change how they teach. Should teachers use an evolutionary or revolutionary approach to integrating web-based technologies in their teaching? How much effort do they perceive is required to master the web-technologies? What is their work backlog (visible and invisible) in terms of what they think remains to be learned or mastered?

This study surveyed 30 instructors who were different stages of adapting web-based technologies and documented their experiences and recommendations.

Information Technology and Technical Efficiency in the Constant Elasticity of Substitution Stochastic Production Frontier

Winston T. Lin
State University of New York at Buffalo
School of Management, Tel: (716) 645-3257
Fax: (716) 645-6117, mgtfewtl@acsu.buffalo.edu

Benjamin B. M. Shao
Arizona State University - Main Campus
College of Business, School of Accountancy and Information Management, Ben.Shao@asu.edu

Information Technology (IT) has become increasingly important in a business organization and the effect of IT investments on technical (or productive) efficiency has recently caught a great deal of attention (Lin and Shao, 2000; Shao and Lin, 2000; Shao and Lin, 2001; and Shao and Lin 2002). Productive efficiency is a useful economic performance measure, different from profitability (e.g., Cron and Sobol, 1983; Dos Santos et al., 1993; and Hitt and Brryjolfsson, 1996, among others), productivity (e.g., Weill, 1992; and Dewan and Min, 1997), consumer surplus (e.g., Bresnahan, 1986; and Hitt and Brynjolfsson, 1996), quality (e.g., Mukhopadhyay et al., 1997), operative efficiency (Banker et al., 1990), and Tobin's *q* (Bharadwaj et al., 1999).

This study is devoted to examining the relationship between IT investments and technical efficiency based on the constant elasticity of substitution (known as CES) stochastic production frontier model. The primary objective of this research is three-fold: one, to re-assess how IT investments affect technical efficiency; two, to re-examine the productivity paradox; and three, to analyze how IT impacts the five important parameters associated with the CES production process (Chiang, 1974; and Kmenta, 1986), namely, the efficiency parameter, the distribution parameters, the returns-to-scale parameter, and the substitution parameter.

Since the CES stochastic production frontier models have never been applied in the literature of management information systems as a methodological basis, we expect the empirical results to be both interesting and challenging. Some preliminary results seem to point to these expectations. One implication of the preliminary results is that the productivity paradox may hold in some sense, somewhat contrary to the conclusion reached by Lin and Shao (2000) and Shao and Lin (2001a, 2001b). For example, when the labor (L) factor is replaced by the IT stock (I) factor, with the capitol (K) variable being kept unchanged, the technical efficiency decreases from 0.8124 to 0.4487. Another implication is that while the impact of IT investments on technical efficiency is positive, the IT investments factor is less important than the labor variable. A third implication is that the substitution between capital and labor differs from that between capital and IT investments in sign and magnitude as well. A final evidence is that the pair of K and L and the pair of K and I in the CES production process result in substantially different estimates of the efficiency parameter (1.9678 vs. 16.3987), the distribution parameter (0.2065 vs. 0.9676 to K, 0.7935 to L, and only 0.0324 to I), the returns-to-scale parameter (0.9696 vs. 0.7138), and the substitution parameter (-0.1814 vs. 0.7250).

The data used in this study are the same as those used in the work by Hitt and Brynjolfsson (1996), Dewan and Min (1997), Lin and Shao (2000), Shao and Lin (2000), and Shao and Lin (2001a, 2001b). Some reasons why the same data set is used are that it facilitates a meaningful comparison of the results with those reported in previous research and that the data are the most comprehensive set available at the firm level for evaluating IT business value at the present time.

As pointed out in Lin and Shao (2000), the data source for the IT-related data is the International Data Group (IDG)/Computerworld surveys of information systems (IS) spending by large U.S. firms, conducted annually during the period 1988 to 1992. The survey focuses primarily on large Fortune 500 firms. About two-thirds of these firms belong to the manufacturing sector and the rest is from the service sector. More detailed information of the data set can be found in Hitt and Bynjolfsson (1996), Dewan and Min (1997), Lin and Shao (2000), Shao and Lin (2000), Shao and Lin (2001a, 2001b).

The Taylor's series expansion is applied to the original CES production function to derive estimable frontier models. All the empirical results will be obtained using the LIMDEP statistical package software in two steps. The first step calls for the ordinary least-squares (OLS) estimates to be used to serve as the starting values for the variance parameters for the frontier models. In the second step, the maximum likelihood estimation (MLE) method is applied, using the OLS estimates obtained in the first step as the initial values. If the OLS residuals are positively skewed, the MLE is halted (Waldman, 1982). Otherwise, the residuals are computed by the formula given by Jondrow et al. (1982), and productive efficiency is measured by the formula given by Lovell (1993, p. 20).

References Available Upon Request

E-Books and Libraries: The Challenge of Hardware and Software Inconsistencies

Les Lynam
Central Missouri State University
Tel: (660) 543-8795, Fax: (660) 543-8001, Lynam@libserv.cmsu.edu

Electronic text has become a standard form of communication, yet the term Ebook conjures many different images and definitions dependent on who is using the term. Libraries have long been central figures on campuses and in communities, chiefly in acquiring, classifying, storing and disseminating texts. For decades, this process changed little as books and journals were the chief forms of information acquired. Although there have been some ripples, such as microform storage, video-recordings, and other "non-book" formats, the current state of Ebooks has librarians hoping to find some standard that can be a useful tool now, and not obsolete in just a few months.

A serious gap exists between publisher and the library's mission to store and deliver information. The book, as ink on bound pieces of paper, exists in a media to disseminate information in a one to one ratio of book to reader. While many readers can read the same book, serially, rarely is a single physical book read simultaneously by more than one person. Thus, the publisher is able to sell many units of a published work and make a profit from publishing. While it is possible to photocopy a written work, it is not generally cost effective to duplicate full copies of a text that contains hundreds of pages. This is not the case with text in electronic format. Storage of an electronic book is minimal. The time it takes to copy an entire book from one file to another is nearly instantaneous. Transport over thousands of miles via the internet is fast and cost effective. Everything is in place to support an efficient and effective dissemination of ebooks, except for profit and protection of intellectual property rights.

Publishers are experimenting with ways to make the purchase of an ebook fit the one-to-one ratio of purchased book to reader. There have even been some successful models, which even some book selling chains have embraced. One such model allows a person with an electronic reading device (in this example an RCA REB1200) to connect to a bookstore over a phone line, select an ebook, purchase it, and nearly instantaneously have the text transferred to this handheld reader. No trip to a brick and mortar store required. A combination of software and hardware features allows this purchaser to rapidly have access to a desired book, and though rapidly transmitted, the encryption prevents it from being transferred to another reading device or mass distributed (pirated). This follows the desired effect of having one purchaser reading one single purchased book which ensures that the publisher can still profit from publishing titles. At the same time, it totally fails to fit into the model of a library purchasing a book with the goal of supplying it to many readers without expecting payment from them.

IT Trends and Issues: How to Evaluate the Individual Versus the Global Information Services?

Solidoro A. Elisabetta
Università degli studi (DISA, Trento, Italy)
Mühlebachst. 15 , 6340 Baar , CH

Apparently the trend and issue of IT (Information Technology) are defined by the application of its tools to the fields of B2B (Business to Business) and C2B (Consumer to Business). Between the two main applications of IT and AI there is a *preferencial direction* which seems to be the B2B.

Recently the *mobile phones* are an example of application of PDA technolgies.

It is *reasonable* to think that these applications are much more near to the consumer than to the business, also if they are used by managers and business people.

Given this *dual dimension* of the application itself, it is easy to end up with a question: using the IT for a particular goals or task can generate *inconsistencies* with the structure and aim of the whole system[1]?

More specifically is it possible to properly fullfil the needs of the final users (with their personality and culture, so as *non rational behavior*), by *guaranteeing the requested quality*, and in the meanwhile keep the electronic system efficient and effective?

This question is similar to the general question that an economist can ask:

- Is the individual in a Pareto efficient market equilibrium really satisfied from the final allocation?
- Is the system *therefore* a perfect syntesis of all its components or is it for some reason a separated entity?

Because of the already existing literature on the *optimal design mechanism*, the question is also implicitly *mentioning* tools such as Internet and all the software (already existing and/or that could be created) used to connect the entities or nodes, and which is quite similar for some aspects to the economic system with all its elements and rules.

The paper will try to describe the particular components of the information systems (or MAS), the PDA, and than in the following it will concentrate on the content of the information they are providing and the contribution to the individual and social benefit.

PDA means Personal Digital Assistent and it is a programm used to support the user in performing particular tasks, which are *repeated and frequent.*

The application in the field of the *mobile phoning* is mainly referred to the opportunity of using the internet and manage the e-mail account.

The model that will be created in the paper have to clarify the relationship between the individual behavior and the necessity of the whole system, in terms of *services reliability,* and to consider a measure of the information content and of the change in user's utility caused from a given information/knowledge.

Usually it is said that the knowledge or the technology is a factor of positive change for the national economy. But it is quite difficult to find an elaborated and complete model of the economic environment itself so that it is quite difficult to *evaluate its goodnes* and the impact on the real economy.

The model I have to *depict* have to consider the relevance of the information and the maintanability of the system, in order to highlight the prospective evolution for the initially showed evidence of a specifical trend in the technologies and, furthermore, to finally solve a typical and contradictory dilemma (also in the real world): the satisfaction of individual versus collective needs.

Panels

The Next Phase of Web-Based Education

Moderator: A. K. Aggarwal ,Lockheed Martin Research ProfessorUniversity of Baltimore, Baltimore MD 21201 USA

Panelists:
Ron Legon, Provost, University of Baltimore, Maryland
S. Valenti, Professor, Computer Science Dept., University of Ancona, Italy
Minnie Yen, Professor, University of Alaska, USA
Jim Toner, Professor, University of Maine, USA

Web-based education (WBE) is changing the concept of education. During the first phase of WBE in the late 1990's, researchers were trying to define the concept itself. Though WBE may be known by different names, such as distant education, web-education, cyber-education, networked learning or E-learning, it is typically defined as a learning environment that provides education on-line with little or no face-to-face contact. A complete course may be offered on-line with no human contact. From a student's perspective, the only requirement is a PC and access to the Internet. Many web-based teaching models have been suggested. In these models, courses use the web as a "part" or as a "supplement"—or are entirely web-based. For-profit and non-profit universities in the U.S. are offering a variety of courses, diplomas and degrees. Several universities have recently graduated their first students and are waiting for corporate input about the quality and know-how of these virtual students.

The obvious question for the next phase is: where do we go from here? Anything that is so easily accessible can create quality and control problems. It raises fears about the value of an on-line degree that has typically been associated with mail diplomas. It has the potential of bringing in profiteers with little or no knowledge of the subject matter, and providing an education that may sell diplomas on demand. There are no established governing bodies that are certifying these programs. There are checks and balances in place to ensure "quality control" in a traditional learning environment, but this is not the case with WBE—at least not in the same format. Other questions arise: is it sufficient to simulate a face-to-face environment on the web? How can we ensure that quality is not sacrificed for profit? How should students be evaluated on the web? What is an optimal class size? Is WBE for everyone? How can we monitor for-profit organizations that could potentially sell diplomas?

This panel will discuss issues related to the second phase of WBE in terms of quality control. Several academicians and administrators will share their thoughts and experiments in this area.

More Truths About Distance Learning

Discussant: Dr. Sorel Reisman
College of Business and Economics
California State University
Tel: (714) 278-3325, sreisman@fullerton.edu

Discussant: Thomas F. Bennett
Federal Government - Defense Information Systems Agency
Arlington, Virginia, Tel: (703) 882-1227, bennettt@ncr.disa.mil

The purpose of this session is to continue the discussion that began at IRMA International Conference in Toronto, in 2001 where an experienced panel of distance learning experts introduced and discussed controversial technical, instructional, and administrative issues related to the delivery of business school courses via the World Wide Web. As in Toronto, discussants will deal with and answer and solicit questions regarding issues that they and audience participant have encountered working alone, with other instructors, and with administrators concerned with Internet-based delivery of instruction.

Distance learning, as a means of reducing costs of delivering instruction, has captured the imagination of many higher education administrators. The appeal of collecting limitless tuition without an increase in the costs of constructing and maintaining bricks and mortar facilities appears to be the economic factor driving these fantasies. However, from the perspective of instructors, the truth is otherwise.

Issues that will be discussed in this session include:

- The effort involved in preparing for distance learning classes; e.g. – is there more up front work required to prepare a course for distance learning?
- The time commitment to deliver a course; e.g. – do instructors spend more time, less time, or strange times when they oversee classes of distance learners?
- The appropriateness of the medium for business curricula; e.g. – are some topics better or worse suited to the use of distance learning?
- Demographic issues; - e.g., are all students at all levels suitable candidates for learning via the Web?
- Integration of multimedia in the learning experience; e.g., are audio and video preferred, useful, or distractions?
- Appropriate and inappropriate instructional tools; e.g., do email, chat, or video conferencing functions make teaching/learning easier or more difficult, and for whom, the instructor or the student?
- Instructional delivery systems; e.g., should you build your own or should you use vendor systems, and at what cost?
- Legal issues; e.g., what materials can you legally put in a course, who owns a developed course, is it possible to earn royalties from a course you developed?

Additional topics, comments, and observations will be solicited from the audience providing for a lively session on this very controversial but important topic.

Women in Information Technology: A Vanishing Resource

Panel Chair:
Donald J. Caputo, Ph.D., Chair
Assoc. Professor, Computer & Information Systems
Robert Morris University, Pennsylvania
caputo@robert-morris.edu, caputo@rmu.edu

Panel Presenters:
Frederick J. Kohun, Ph.D.
Assoc. Dean, School of Information Systems
Robert Morris University, Pennsylvania
Kohun@robert-morris.edu

Jeanne M. Baugh, Ed.D.
Assoc. Professor, Computer & Information Systems
Robert Morris University, Pennsylvania
baugh@robert-morris.edu

Sharon N. Vest
School of Computer and Information Sciences
University of South Alabama
vest@cis.usouthal.edu

Arlene Eisenman-Palka, M.S., M.B.A
Chair, Information Technology
Bay Path College
Massachusetts, apalka@baypath.edu

Women today are standing at the threshold of unprecedented opportunity in the field of Information Technology. At the very moment that a large unmet demand for IT practitioners exists, approximately one-half of the American work force is largely declining the offer. The Information Technology Association of America estimates the number of IT jobs languishing at a staggering 840,000 total. Though women in IT earn 60% more than women in other occupations, their numbers have dropped from 40% in 1986 to 29% today. The White House Council of Economic Advisers notes that women are leaving the IT field at twice the rate of men. Preceding these dismal statistics is the fact that the number of women majoring in technology-related fields in college has steadily declined over the past ten years.

Robert Morris University of Pennsylvania recently hosted a gathering of Information Technology professional women comprised not only of Pennsylvania participants, but also practitioners from other states in the mid-Atlantic area. These corporate representatives ranged from mid-level Information Technology managers of small and medium-sized companies to the CIO of a large multi-national corporation. The stated purpose was to identify and classify the reasons for the decline of the female presence in today's diverse technological-based enterprises.

This IRMA panel, comprised of selected members of the Pennsylvania gathering, will seek to explore, clarify, and integrate the findings and suggestions of the corporate community and, hopefully, suggest answers to the question "What do Women Want" in the technology field. We will focus on the topics of e-commerce, pay discrimination, "glass ceiling" barriers, family issues, flex time, mentoring programs, educational resources, prevailing attitudes toward women, and the underutilization of the unique qualities that women would bring to the workplace.

Interestingly, current government statistics reveal that web-based entities are creating an environment that is rapidly assimilating women into career positions that did not exist a few years ago. Internet companies have produced not only more entry level jobs for women, but far greater numbers in upper management echelons. In fact, a critical mass of women IT executives appears to be on the near horizon.

Additionally, the educational component of the original convocation was meshed into a fact-finding initiative, seeking to integrate and balance the needs of the corporate sphere and its collegiate counterparts. This component was comprised of professors and administrators from four colleges and universities that have fostered special ties with the workplace environment.

Not surprisingly, a curricular focus also surfaced during the discussions. It became apparent that an important objective in dealing with the overall problem of declining female representation in Information Technology is that of designing curricula at the undergraduate and graduate level of universities that would match the needs of the corporate world.

Thus, our panel will be describing, examining and comparing a selection of existing and emerging integrative curricular approaches to the pervasive but solvable paradox of the vanishing resource of women in Information Technology.

IT Education Roundtable

Panel/Workshop/Tutorial Chair(s):
Eli B. Cohen (chair)
Informing Science Institute & Leon Kozminski School of Entrepreneurship and Management
Santa Rosa, California, eli_cohen@acm.org

Panel/Workshop/Tutorial Participants:
Joao Batista, Departamento de Engenharia Informática
Pólo II - Pinhal de Marrocos, Portugal
jbatista@dei.uc.pt

Tom Bennett
APPS Inf. Mgmt
Defense Information Systems Agency
bennettt@ncr.disa.mil

Dennis Bialaszewski
Prof of MIS
Indiana State University, D.Bialaszewski@att.net

Linda Knight
DePaul University
School of Computer Science, Telecommunications & Information Systems, Illinois, lknight@cti.depaul.edu

Jintae Lee, Associate Professor
Systems Division (Campus Box 419)
University of Colorado, jintae@colorado.edu

John Mendonca
School of Technology, Purdue University
West Lafayette, Indiana, JaMendonca@tech.purdue.edu

Xun Yi
Information Communication Institute of Singapore
School of Electrical and Electronic Engineering
Nanyang Technological University, Singapore, exyi@ntu.edu.sg

The Information Resource Management Association has provided a great service to the IRM community through its IRMA/DAMA model curriculum. Since its inception, the model curriculum has undergone continuing revisions. The roundtable is composed of selected members of the IRMA IT Education Committee, which is again revising and bringing up to date the IRMA/DAMA model curriculum.

The primary purpose of the roundtable is to solicit from those attending 1) ideas on changes they would like to see in the revised curriculum, and 2) feedback on ideas the committee is currently considering.

The members of the IT Education Committee taking part in this roundtable demonstrate the wide range of views and needs of our constituency, from academia to industry, and from educational institutions around the world. Below is a small number of the issues the committee is dealing with:

- The changing curriculum, from IT to OB/OD specialists, combined programs in IS, CS, IT
- Industry-university collaboration through course partnerships
- Potential for continuing education (particularly part-time programs) in IS/IT education.
- Issues in programming Language Selection
- Helping students achieve Real-world experiences
- What do we teach now as introduction to our field?
- Challenges being faced by developing countries
- Future of Business education in times of "just in time learning"
- How Web based education affects the delivery and teaching of IT

- Influence of the local culture on IT education
- IT Beyond the B-school
- Transitions into Tomorrow's workforce of Knowledge Workers
- Educating (future) general managers for IT
- IT Enabled constructivist and collaborative learning
- Teaching IT Management online
- Teaching research methods to MS in IS students.
- "On-line education - it's psychology, not technology"
- Teaching Case teaching, at a distance
- The role of on-line learning in a formal educational program
- The Importance of Faculty Development in the Updating of IS Courses

A secondary purpose of this session is to draw together individuals (from the roundtable and the audience) who have similar interests with an eye toward working together on IT Education research projects.

Information Systems and Organisational Change: Issues in Change Management and Process Re-engineering

Panel Chair
G. Harindranath, Royal Holloway, University of London, UK

Panelists
Gurpreet Dhillon, University of Nevada at Las Vegas, USA
Gerald Grant, Carleton University, Canada
Sherif Kamel, The American University in Cairo, Egypt

This panel will examine key issues in the area of information systems and organisational change. In particular, it will address the themes of process re-engineering, process institutionalisation, and change management using case studies from a number of countries such as the UK, US, Canada and Egypt. A brief outline of the contribution from each of the four panellists is given in the following:

RE-ENGINERING HEALTHCARE: LESSONS FROM A UK CASE STUDY

G. Harindranath, Royal Holloway, University of London, UK
g.harindranath@rhul.ac.uk

This paper presents a case study of a US$ 30 million project to establish a new form of rapid healthcare service delivery within the context of a highly politicised National Health Service Hospital Trust in the United Kingdom. This project involved large scale business process re-engineering, including the redesign of long-established healthcare procedures and the development of sophisticated new information systems through a unique partnership between the public sector and a number of private sector companies (a software developer, a facilities manager, a hardware vendor and a builder). This paper suggests a political model of information systems development and business process reengineering.

POWER, IS IMPLEMENTATION AND CHANGE IN A NEVADA DEPARTMENT OF MOTOR VEHICLES CASE

Gurpreet Dhillon, University of Nevada at Las Vegas, USA
dhillon@unlv.edu

Based on a case study of an IT-enabled change project at Nevada DMV, this paper argues that that good project management goes far beyond the technical development of a system, and that it is far more important to understand the softer human behavioral aspects of the analysis, design and management of systems. The paper sensitizes researchers and practitioners alike to the importance of interpreting various dimensions of power and their importance in an information technology enabled strategic change initiative. It also presents a particular way in which a complex concept of power can be applied to analyze particular situations.

PROCESS INSTITUTIONALISATION

Gerald Grant, Carleton University, Canada
gerald_grant@carleton.ca

Many organizations have embarked on enterprise systems implementation efforts without giving sufficient attention to process transformation. Preliminary data from both research and practitioner sources seem to suggest that the realization of benefits of enterprise system implementation are to a large extent predicated on the institutionalization of process approaches. Since a large number of companies in the United States and Canada have implemented or are in the process of implementing enterprise systems, we are interested in finding out the extent to which process-orientation is being institutionalized within the organizations.

CHANGES IN THE BANKING SECTOR USING ICT: CASES FROM EGYPT

Sherif Kamel, The American University in Cairo, Egypt
skamel@aucegypt.edu

The information and communication technology revolution has led to tremendous changes in the Egyptian retail banking industry over the last two decades, including significant investments in advanced banking technologies. This case provides an analysis of the retail banking business in Egypt highlighting the progressive changes in electronic delivery channels and payment systems coupled with an in-depth analysis of the customers' acceptance and attitude with respect to using the already existing traditional methods versus venturing into newly introduced technology-based systems offered by their banks.

The Role of IT Faculty in Assessing Academic Technology Initiatives

Panel Chair:
Dr. Charles A. Morrissey
Irvine, California, Tel: (949) 854-6912; Fax: (949) 854-3015
cmorriss@pepperdine.edu

BACKGROUND

One of the most challenging and critical issues facing higher education is the need to assess the benefits from their burgeoning growth and investment in instructional technology. While this topic has been researched and analyzed over the past few years, there is little evidence of emerging assessment criteria, models or standards for such evaluation.

EDUCAUSE's 2000 Current Issues panel this topic framed the question "In what ways can the progressive innovations in information technology enhance the outcome of our educational efforts across the full spectrum of the University's missions?"

Scholars of the academic technology movement continue to make significant contributions to understanding the full complexity of this topic. However, Green's (1999) cogent summary that "we do not yet have clear, compelling evidence about the impact of information technology on student learning and educational outcomes", and Barbara Yentzer (1997), director of the National Education Association's Center for Education Technology, observations that " the concept that computers and networking can enhance learning is largely a matter of faith" continue to reflect the general consensus of these papers.

PANEL OBJECTIVES

This panel will provide a forum for IT faculty to voice their position, and share experiences, in examining what role IT faculty should play in guiding their institutions to meet this complex challenge. An extensive list of references and web links will be provided to attendees.

REFERENCES

References Available Upon Request.

Research Issues for the Unified Modeling Language and Unified Process

Panel Chair
Jeffrey Parsons
Faculty of Business Administration
Memorial University of Newfoundland, Canada
Tel: (709) 737-4741, Fax: (709) 737-7680
jeffreyp@mun.ca

Panelists
Brian Dobing
Faculty of Management
University of Lethbridge, Canada
Tel: (403) 329-2492, Fax: (403) 329-2038
brian.dobing@uleth.ca

Keng Siau
Department of Management
College of Business Administration
University of Nebraska-Lincoln
Tel: (402) 472-3078, Fax: (402) 472-5855
ksiau@unl.edu

TBA
Analysis and Design Task Force Representative
Object Management Group

PANEL OBJECTIVES

The Unified Modeling Language (UML) is widely accepted as a standard for use in object-oriented software development. It has attracted a wide following and has generated a large number of practitioner-oriented books covering the many modeling constructs that make up the language.

Currently, the UML is undergoing a major revision that will result in version 2.0, targeted for adoption by the Object Management Group (OMG) in 2002. This revision is driven by a subset of the practitioner community of organizations that develop object-oriented systems.

The objective of this panel will be to discuss whether and how the academic community might contribute to the evolution of the UML toward a "better" modeling language. UML evolution has been driven by the ad hoc concerns of specific UML proponents who belong to the OMG. A key focus of the panel will be to examine whether there are potential benefits to evaluating the UML from one or more theoretical perspectives, or by basing UML enhancements on broadly based research on problems encountered by UML adopters.

ISSUES TO BE COVERED

The panel chair will open by introducing the panelists and giving a brief overview of the motivation for the panel and the panel format.

A member of the OMG Analysis and Design Task Force will provide a brief history of the UML and outline the process by which changes to the UML are made. The primary focus will be on possible avenues for academic research to impact on this process.

Brian Dobing will discuss reactions to UML from a practitioner perspective, including issues identified in a survey of UML adoption. This will include issues related to the justification of the models that make up the UML, the transition between models, and how application of these models varies among practitioners.

Keng Siau will discuss empirical studies on UML. The studies will look at the complexity of UML, the problems students encountered in learning UML, and the evaluation of UML using different empirical techniques. The objectives of these studies are to provide a better understanding of UML and its various diagramming techniques, to investigate how the various diagramming techniques complement/conflict with one another, and to provide input to the evolution/revolution of UML.

PANEL MEMBERS

Jeffrey Parsons is a Professor at Memorial University of Newfoundland. His research interests include theoretical analysis of the role of object-orientation in systems development, and empirical studies of problems encountered by UML adopters.

Brian Dobing is an Assistant Professor at the University of Lethbridge. His research interests include object-oriented systems analysis and development. He has also worked closely with practitioners and consultants using UML.

Keng Siau is an Associate Professor at the University of Nebraska at Lincoln. His research interests include empirical evaluation of modeling methods.

The panel will include a fourth member, who is actively involved with the Object Management Group's revision of the UML. Given the length of time before the IRMA conference, we have not yet been able to confirm a specific person for this role on the panel. However, we have a number of contacts with OMG members involved in the UML revision, and expect we will be able to find someone from the Seattle area to participate.

Asynchronous Collaboration of a Business Computer Graphics Course

Herbert F. Rebhun, Ph.D.
Professor—Computer Information Systems
University of Houston-Downtown, Texas
Tel: (713) 221-8052, Fax: (713) 226-5238
rebhunh@uhd.edu

Christiana Birchak, PhD
Associate Professor-English
University of Houston-Downtown

Jean DeWitt, PhD
Associate Professor-Speech
University of Houston-Downtown, Texas

INTRODUCTION

To prepare students for success in the new millenium, universities should consider encouraging interdepartmental, computer-mediated collaborations. By exploring new technologies for use in human communications the student will not be bound by time/space, students forge partnerships in a multicultural world and develop guidelines for operating in cyberspace.

Representing the colleges of business and humanities, these authors over a five-year period of time collaborated in this asynchronous activity. Although our disciplines are diverse, we shared a commitment to technology as a tool for creativity and to a teaching philosophy.

BACKGROUND

The 9500+ University of Houston-Downtown (UHD) students are nationally recognized for their diversity. The average age of our undergraduate, commuter students is 26.5. The participants in our collaborative reflect the ethnic diversity characteristic of the UHD students: 32.1% Hispanic, 25.6% Caucasian, 27.8% Black, 11.5% Asian, and 2.8% International.

Beginning in the fall of 1997, Computer Information System (CIS) majors in the junior Computer Graphics in Business course were selected by the instructor and arranged so that there was always an attempt to have a mixture of the UHD ethnic diversity on all teams. The business students were paired with students in an upper-level English course and used HyperStudio to create a CD-ROM prototype entitled "Gulliver in Cyberspace." The following semester, spring 1998, the multimedia collaboration was expanded to include a colleague in speech communication. Located at a satellite campus, the University Center in The Woodlands, Texas, students in this semester's collaboration created PowerPoint presentations concerning women writers of the 18th, 19th, and 20th centuries.

For the spring 1999 term, the same three faculties expanding our delivery systems as students developed multimedia presentations on issues arising from the Y2K problem. The Business and Professional Speech course was taught again at the University Center. The Computer Graphics in Business was an evening ITV section beamed from our downtown Houston home site to the satellite campus, and the English class— Feature Writing was a face-to-face morning class at the home site. Each of the 10 teams developed a 20-25 minute PowerPoint presentation relating to the impact of Y2K on a specific sector of society.

During the Spring 2000 the Computer Business Graphics course was being offered via ITV from both the home campus and at the University Center. The English class was Writing for the Sciences course. The teams again developed a 20-25 minute PowerPoint presentation using the topic of medical diseases.

The most recent activity is during the Fall 2001. The English class was again joined by the Speech class and the face-to-face CIS Business Graphics class. This term the students are preparing material that would permit the offering of on-line help sessions for students throughout the university to learn and practice with the various graduate admission exams needed for entrance to any type of graduate school from an MBA to MA in the Arts to Law School or to Medical School.

In all semesters the CIS students received downloaded storyboard material and suggested references from the English class. They also received downloaded WAV files from the speech class that introduced the topic and named the various team members. The business computer students then took the material and either created an entire Power Point and Web presentation or modified downloaded material to create the final project.

COLLABORATIVE LEARNING

Our goal in reconfiguring this collaborative for several semesters was to enrich the opportunity for computer-mediated learning at UHD, creating ultimately a model for the urban university with a multicultural, undergraduate student population. Such need arises as faculty and students merge the process of active learning with the technological tools that foster asynchronous collaboration. Instead of relying entirely on the traditional lecture mode, faculty members expand their teaching strategies to promote increased student participation.

INTERDEPARTMENTAL COMMUNICATION

Over the various semesters, and as the technology field progressed, the faculty and the students constantly modified the shared learning environment. The faculty introduced several modes of communication. During the first year HyperStudio and IntraKal were used to both permit the sharing of files among the various team members and as a classroom management software. The students in all the classes were required to become familiar and use e-mail as the primary method to communicate with each other and the other class's team members. In addition, all classes had been introduced or reintroduced to PowerPoint slide capabilities. The computer class had previously spent three to four weeks designing and writing web pages using HTML and thus was expected to use this knowledge in their joint project.

In subsequent semesters, the computing students moved the web activities to Front Page and currently to Dreamweaver. The use of Power Point is still the major common source in the file sharing process.

Students analyzed, synthesized, and evaluated the research material on various topics. The digital interchanges necessary to transform data into information required discussion, writing, and reflecting. As students from different departments negotiated meaning in digital space, they drew on their unique skills, interests, and knowledge. For instance, the team that developed "The Liability of the Y2K Millennium Bug" consisted of several students who worked part-time in law offices

Students seemed to appreciate the importance of sensitivity to communication in digital space. Generally, the non-CIS students were eager to use technology for communication. One student commented, "This group project was the most interesting one I have encountered in any class. It was highly challenging but applicable to today's business world. Computers have revolutionized communication in the workplace. We no longer pick up the phone and call our colleagues; we e-mail them. This is why this project was so important. Most companies would argue that virtual teams are a necessity because of their efficiency and effectiveness. But are they really effective?"

The use of the PowerPoint software and creating web pages either through Front Page, Dreamweaver or direct HTML code was very valuable to the computer students and generally adopted (at least in using PowerPoint) by the English students. The need to include the reasons behind requiring this software is well known to all of us in the business instruction field. This software was available at all sites and the need to be concerned over licensing issues was never an issue.

CONCLUSION

Despite the problems that have arisen over the past five years the results presented by students in their various projects have been generally at a level that is truly satisfying. The students, despite some of their complaints, all admit that the results were very rewarding. Preparing students for the competitive workforce is part of the UHD mission statement. Using technology across distance and time has enabled the students to develop team-building skills that reflect real life challenges: deadlines, group cohesion, communication building skills, and interpersonal conflicts. A project that requires specific expertise from multiple persons necessitates collaboration across disciplines.

International Program in Educational Technology between Duquesne University and the University of Ulster: "Setting Everyone Up For Success"

Author and Panel Member
Dr. Linda C. Wojnar
Assistant Professor, Duquesne University
School of Education
Distance Learning
Pittsburgh, Pennsylvania

Other Distinguished Members of the Panel

Course Participants
Mr. Richard T. Wallace
BECTa Expert Consultant
Vice-Principal
Ballyclare High School
County Antrim
BT39 9HJ

Ms. Mary Mallon
Advisory Teacher for Mathematics
Craigavon Teachers' Centre
Craigavon BT65 5BS
Tel: 0 (283) 834-2467

Duquesne University:
Dr. Larry Tomei
Instructional Technology Program Coordinator
Assistant Professor, Duquesne University
School of Education
K-12 Strand
Pittsburgh, Pennsylvania

Dr. William Barone
Duquesne University
Chair, Dept. of Instruction & Leadership
School of Education, Pittsburgh, Pennsylvania

University of Ulster:
Dr. Anne Moran
Dean, School of Education
University of Ulster at Jordanstown
Newtownabbey, Co. Antrim, BT37 0QB

Northern Ireland Administrators:
Mr. Joe Martin
Chief Executive
Western Education & Library Board
Omagh, CO. TYRONE, BT79 0AW

Mrs. Marie Martin
International Officer
Western Education & Library Board
Omagh, CO. TYRONE, BT79 0AW

Mr. John Anderson
Education Technology
Strategy Coordinator
Department of Education for Northern Ireland (DENI)
Mobile: + 440 (790) 991-2012
tel and fax: +440 (284) 062-6455
john.anderson.deni@nics.gov.uk

Ireland Institute of Pittsburgh:
Sr. Michelle O'Leary
President and Founder of the Ireland Institute of Pittsburgh
Regional Enterprise Tower, Pittsburgh, Pennsylvania

Dr. Mary Catherine Conroy-Hayden
Director, School Performance Network
Consultant for Ireland Institute of Pittsburgh
Pittsburgh, Pennsylvania, Tel: (412) 201-7400

The overall objectives of the eleven member panel discussion are to provide an overview of the innovative International MSc Program in Educational Technology; to critically discuss and evaluate the effectiveness of the International MSc Program partnering Duquesne University in Pittsburgh, Pennsylvania, USA and the University of Ulster in Northern Ireland; to assess the program's impact on both participants and staff who were involved; to provide the evolution and lessons learned from this initiative that would be beneficial to any educational setting who desires to design similar programs.

The methodology will include case stories from administrators and educators. Course participants will share their case stories, excerpts of their coursework and transcript dialogue from online discussions. The panel will begin their reflections by describing how an informal discussion of the Distance Learning Strand content led to an agreement for the selection of 17 participants to obtain a master's degree that prepares educators to teach in an online environment incorporating both synchronous and asynchronous components. Course participants represented all of the Northern Ireland provinces. Visiting Northern Ireland and experiencing the culture and context of the workplaces for each participant in the program in February 2001 influenced the leadership and direction for all course content and all tutor preparation within the program. The commitment of the University of Ulster's Dean to send two tutors to Pittsburgh and her commitment to maintain continuity of instruction that began in Pittsburgh was another key component to the success of the program.

Some additional topics that will evolve in the panel discussion are: role of the Ireland Institute, management of change processes, building communities of learners, establishing trust and relationships, celebrating the value of diversity, strengths of collaborative learning, stimulating learning processes and accenting the benefits of a mixed mode program provision combining online with face-to-face interaction, while concentrating on the pedagogical and psychological perspectives of online learning. The instructional design of the Distance Learning Strand was designed as a holistic approach to learning; all courses and projects in each of the courses were to be a part of the final project in the capstone course.

In conclusion, the panel will assess and evaluate the benefits of the program for the two universities, focusing on the professional development of all staff that were involved, the effective development of partnerships with professionals external to the universities, the impact of the program on the strategic planning of ICT in Northern Ireland for the future, and the value of a residential study abroad component of the program.

The partnership demonstrated that trans-Atlantic links are as strong as ever. This program was all the better for overcoming obstacles in the early stages of implementation, some were overt and predictable, while others were learned along the way and handled in "real time." Participant evaluations unanimously echoed that the same experience and growth could not have taken place if all coursework was taught in their homeland.

Tutorials/Workshops

LEZI

Prof. Eng. Mario A. Bochicchio
Software Engineering & TeleMedia Lab (SET-Lab)
University of Lecce, Italy
Tel: +39 (083) 232-0216, Fax: +39 (083) 232-0279
mario.bochicchio@unile.it

Eng Nicola Fiore
Software Engineering & TeleMedia Lab (SET-Lab)
University of Lecce, Italy
Tel: +39 (083) 232-0216, Fax: +39 (083) 232-0279
nicola.fiore@unile.it

Eng. Antonella Longo
Software Engineering & TeleMedia Lab (SET-Lab)
University of Lecce, Italy
Tel: +39 (083) 232-0216, Fax +39 (083) 232-0279
antonella.longo@unile.it

Most modern multimedia applications are complex to conceive/design, and their development process can become rather expensive in terms of time, knowledge, specific techniques, complex graphics, animations, high quality video and audio. The attempt to reduce costs or to shorten production times could easily cause poor quality results [1-3].

Nevertheless, in particular niches, specific kinds of multimedia applications can give good quality results, even with short production cycles and at low cost. We are referring, for example, to good teachers, who speak easily, explain using images and slides, show objects, write on the blackboard and use their mimic to better grab and hold the attention of their students. Those lessons can be easily transformed in good quality multimedia applications for both on-line and disk-based distribution with small effort.

Unfortunately, a few hours' lesson can produce a big amount of digital contents (video, texts, audio, pictures, etc.), difficult to manage.

LEZI authoring environment has been designed to simplify this technical task and to supply teachers/lecturers with a tool to operate at a higher level than conventional authoring tools.

Lezi is a tool useful to effectively tranform a traditional conference/lesson in a powerful multimedia application based on a very simple and regular structure.

This 3 hours' workshop is addressed to educational hypermedia titles' authors, such as teachers, lecturers, business managers, who are not able to pay publishers due to too expensive production and the small number of readers.

Lezi enables these niche categories to develop their ideas and to publish their works on CD/DVD or on the Web, with animations, sounds, music and other multimedia features without requests for deep technical knowledge

The workshop is structured in 4 parts:

- **applicative contexts and examples** to illustrate the benefits and the importance of the tool in educational and distance learning contexts; this part is aided by some applications already developed (Metaponto, The Museum of the Environment, etc.)
- **fundamentals of video production and shooting techniques**: after the description of the different video production tools and their impact on the look of the final product, it's explained the different techniques of capturing moving images on videotape, how to convert them to PC format, how to edit and manipulate them to yield maximum effect when presented to the viewer
- **lessons' editing with Lezi** where functionality is showed
- **session of practice** where participants are given the chance to try the authoring tools.

References Available Upon Request

Current and Emerging Trends in Mobile / Wireless Commerce

Workshop Leader
Dr. Candace Deans
Associate Professor of Information and Technology Management
Thunderbird – The American Graduate School of International Management, Glendale, Arizona, Tel: (602) 978-7608

Mobile commerce and wireless technologies are becoming increasingly significant in the strategic planning and business model implementations of companies today. The wireless revolution will impact business in much the same way as the .dotcom era of electronic commerce. This workshop will address current issues facing corporations today, emerging technologies that will impact the direction of future innovation, and what appear to be emerging trends for the future. The workshop will also address issues of how to best incorporate this content into the existing curriculum.

Global trends in mobile commerce indicate that the United States is not currently taking the lead. Europe and Japan are currently leading in this realm with Japan's successful i-mode initiative and Europe's lead in mobile phone penetration. Most of the rest of the world have higher mobile penetration than personal computers. Cultural differences are also playing a role in the acceptance of mobile technologies. With the advent of 3G technologies we will likely see an acceleration of commercial applications as well as new implications for current business models.

Business model issues will be discussed in the context of how to create value for customers in this new mobile world. Currently no killer application exists for mobile commerce. Just as with electronic commerce, most of the current applications are in the business to consumer domain. Business to business applications, however, will likely be where the money will be made. Companies will need to draw on the lessons learned from the dot.coms. The mindset will need to focus more specifically on short-term profits and business models that emphasize relationships.

Mobile commerce can be viewed as a continuing piece of electronic commerce to be incorporated into the existing electronic commerce strategy. We will discuss some of the issues to consider and how emerging technologies will play a role in how this plays out in the long- term.

Information Technology Workforce Development— A Partnership with Community Leaders, K-12 Faculty, and University Faculty

Wayne Moore, Professor/Chairperson
Technology Support and Training
Eberly College of Business and Information Technology
Indiana University of Pennsylvania, Tel: (724) 357-5647
Fax: (724) 357-3013, moore@iup.edu

Karen Rivosecchi, Link-to-Learn Project Director
in IT Workforce Development
Indiana University of Pennsylvania, Tel: (724) 357-6493
Fax: (724) 357-6200, krivosec@iup.edu

Together with local and regional industry partners and K-12 institutions, Indiana University of Pennsylvania has formed an alliance to respond to the shortage of IT professionals—IUP Information Technology Workforce Development Project. Through this alliance, efforts have been focused on five major areas: curriculum alignment, student recruitment and retention, infrastructure improvements, faculty professional development, and educational access. Partnership activities in the five areas enhance and expand current programs as this alliance looks at innovative approaches to solving the IT workforce shortage. At the start of the project's second year, student activities have been coordinated and hosted, professional development activities for secondary and post secondary faculty have been provided, and resource materials to provide career information and promote IT career opportunities have been developed.

Attendees will receive ideas and resources that can be easily replicated in their communities. The success of this project is due primarily to the cooperative effort of the faculty in the three IT programs at IUP—computer science, management information systems, and business technology support. While all three are IT programs, each attracts students with distinct interests, aptitudes, and personality types. By demonstrating a breadth of career opportunities in IT, many students are able to identify the appropriate program for them.

The partnership has used a multi-faceted approach to reach a variety of audiences. The project advisory committee comprised of industry, K-12 and post-secondary representatives, has provided the guidance and input for the design of successful initiatives. Infrastructure improvement was the foundation of the project. Grant funds along with local funding supported the implementation of a digital production studio that provides opportunities for students and faculty to access state of the art technology. Additionally, this multi-media technology is used as the platform in the development of IT career promotional resources, i.e., web site, logos, informational videos, posters, marketing tools, and multi-media presentations.

Activities developed in partnership with K-12 institutions provide opportunities for secondary students to visit IT areas on campus and meet with post-secondary IT students and industry representatives. Post-secondary student retention is aided by their involvement in the enrichment activities. Opportunities include: IT summer institute, IT career day, ThinkQuest for 6th grade students, and specialized programs developed based on school district requests.

A better working relationship between the three IT departments—Business Technology Support, Computer Science, and Management Information Systems has been developed by reviewing departmental mission statements and curriculum. Under-enrollment in the IT areas is often due to students' lack of knowledge and sometimes-stereotypical views of these professions. To address these issues efforts have been focused on providing a wide variety of IT career information at all educational levels. The resources that have been developed through this IT workforce development project will allow conference attendees to replicate these approaches as they meet their communities' needs.

A Rich Storehouse for the Relief of Man's Estate? Education for Knowledge Management Workshop

Mark Brogan, Philip Hingston and Vicky Wilson
School of Computer and Information Science
Edith Cowan University, Western Australia
Tel: +61 (809) 370-6299, Fax: +61 (089) 370-6100
v.wilson@ecu.edu.au

INTRODUCTION

The School of Computer and Information Science at ECU has made a commitment to teaching Knowledge Management (KM) and has developed a Master's suite of courses in KM that will take their places with existing postgraduate LIS and IT courses offered by the School in February, 2002. As part of this process, the School engaged in debate with other academics and industry practitioners about the contribution that the IT and LIS disciplines can make to KM. Part of that process was the development of a questionnaire that surveyed respondents' opinions on the structure and content of such a course and their attitudes to KM in general.

At the time of writing, data gathering has not been completed to our satisfaction, as time and cost restraints restricted our initial survey population to local (Western Australian) respondents involved in IT-related industries. This meant that the number of respondents was small and the limited industry sectors surveyed introduced some bias into the results that we obtained. It is our intention to regard this initial survey as a pilot and to try to gather further responses both via the web and from other sources.

As part of the IRMA 2002 conference, we would like to conduct a workshop in the form of a focus group session, where we will request the participants to comment on the validity of our conclusions so far and to discuss a series of points developed from our initial research questions.

OBJECTIVES

The objectives of this workshop will be:

1. To gather data from academics and industry practitioners on the nature of KM body of knowledge and the contribution that the IT disciplines have to make to that body of knowledge;
2. To gather informed opinions on the nature of the course that we

have developed and on whether it adequately covers the needs of students studying in this area;
3. To gather informed opinions on future directions for research into KM.

RESEARCH QUESTIONS

The specific research questions that we would like the focus group to address are:

1. Do you agree that KM can be defined as a hybrid discipline that encompasses the three elements of People/Technology/Processes, as described by Collison and Parcell in our paper? (Copies of the paper will be supplied to participants)
2. If not, how would you change this definition?
3. 'Knowledge Computing' has been defined as 'the construction of Knowledge Management systems informed by a body of discipline knowledge inherited from information science and computer science'. Do you agree with this definition?
4. If you do not agree with this definition, in what way would you alter it?
5. Do you agree with the model of the relationship between Knowledge Management and Knowledge Computing presented as figure 1 in our paper?
6. If you do not agree, in what way would you modify that model?
7. Do you agree that the model presented as figure 2 in the paper accurately maps the required curriculum for KM education as it presently stands?
8. If you do not agree, in what way would you modify the model?
9. Do you feel that the research questions identified by the OECD adequately cover the requirements for research in this area?
10. If not, what other research questions would you add to this list?

The workshop will be conducted by Vicky Wilson, who is one of the researchers in the Information and Knowledge Management Research Group at Edith Cowan University.

Doctorial Symposiums

ERP Systems Implementation and Management Theory

Joseph Bradley
Central Washington University
College of Business – Department of Accounting
Ellensburg, Washington, Fax: (509) 963-2875
BradleJo@cwu.edu

ABSTRACT

This study examines the critical success factors for implementing enterprise resource planning systems in the framework of classical management theory. An earlier study (Sneller, 1986), identified critical success factors in the implementation of materials requirements planning systems (MRP). Since this study, software vendors have enhanced the functionality of MRP systems, first by developing manufacturing resource planning systems (MRP II) and subsequently by developing enterprise resource planning systems (ERP). As a result of expanded functionality, implementation of such systems affects a wider portion of the business enterprise than operations and logistics. The present study partially replicates and expands Sneller's work to determine the critical success factors for ERP systems. Sneller surveyed material managers, as MRP dealt with their functional areas. This study surveys functional managers to reflect the wider organizational impact of ERP functionality. Sneller used a two dimensional view of success, this study uses a six dimensional view. Upon completion, this study will define the critical success factors that lead to the successful implementation of an ERP system.

INTRODUCTION

Businesses around the world are spending approximately $10 billion per year on enterprise resource planning systems and about the same amount on consultants to install these systems. (Davenport, 1998) The magnitude of this expenditure makes knowledge of the factors most likely to result in successful ERP systems implementation an important topic for analysis. Managerial and economic resources are scarce in all firms. Determination of critical success factors will help management in allocating resources appropriately.

RESEARCH PROBLEM

The main research question is: What are the critical success factors for a successful ERP implementation? Additional questions to be investigated are:

- Does prior organizational experience with a major systems implementation, such as MRP or MRP II, change the critical success factors?
- Within the manufacturing sector, are the critical success factors different for different types of industries?

LITERATURE

The literature relating to the following topics is examined.

- The evolution of ERP
- Why firms adopt or do not adopt ERP
- Critical success factors found previously
- The applicability of the functions of management theory to the implementation of complex systems
- Success measurement

While practitioner literature on ERP abounds, academic literature is sparse. Practitioner literature, while rich in observations and anecdotes, generally lacks the rigor of empirical research. Where specific ERP literature is not available, general management information systems literature is examined.

For consistency with prior MRP research, the Koontz operational planning model is used. This model defines the management transformation process as consisting of planning, organizing, staffing, leading and controlling.

Planning. The relevant literature on integration of information systems planning and business planning suggests that higher levels of integration may lead to successful implementation outcomes.

Organizing. The use and reporting level of a project manager are related to successful implementation outcomes.

Staffing. The amount of training, the use of testing with training and inclusion of business process training in addition to software specific training are related to successful implementation outcomes.

Leading. Executive support is generally regarded as critical to the development and implementation of management information systems. Champions may be important to the implementation of information systems, such as ERP, due to their ability to bring about the needed organizational change.

Controlling. Steering committees are the common method of control for information systems projects. Gupta & Raghunathan (1989) found that steering committees had a large impact on achievement of planned goals and integration of IS into business, a major issue in ERP implementation.

METHODOLOGY

This section will identify specific hypotheses for testing the individual functions of managers: planning, organizing, staffing, leading and controlling. Where feasible the hypotheses developed by Sneller for testing MRP systems implementation will be used. In areas where the expanded functionality of ERP systems requires or where the literature addresses new issues, new hypotheses will be added or substituted.

Planning

Hypothesis I. The level of integration of IS planning and business planning is positively related to improved implementation outcomes. Variables tested include degree of IS/BP integration, common vision of role of IS, and mutual understanding of IS/BP objectives.

Organizing

Hypothesis II. Organizing the ERP implementation project under the direction of a project manager ("PM") whose sole responsibilities are project implementation is positively related to implementation success. Variables tested include use of a PM, percentage of PM's time devoted to implementation project, and importance the project versus other business objectives.

Hypothesis III. An organizational structure in which the Project Manager reports directly to the business unit's senior manager is positively related to project success. Variables include reporting level of PM, use of matrix organization, percentage of project members time devoted to project, and degree of support given by business units senior manager.

Staffing

Hypothesis IV. Staffing the project manager position with an individual with extensive business experience is positively related to implementation success. Variables include years of ERP systems experience, years of project management experience, motivation, and rewards.

Hypothesis V. Use of an ERP consultant for guidance in the system implementation process is positively related to implementation success. Variables examined include percentage of time consultant used, phase of project used and whether the consultant was the PM.

Hypothesis VI. The quantity and quality of training and the use of testing are positively related to the success of the implementation project. Variables tested include importance of training, timing, quality, and use of testing, and percentage of budget for training.

Leading

Hypothesis VII. CEO involvement in the planning and implementation of ERP systems is positively related to improved implementation outcomes. Variables include perceived level of CEO involvement.

Hypothesis VIII. The existence of a champion is positively related to the success of the implementation project. Variables include use of champion, organizational level and ability to overcome user resistance.

Hypothesis IX. Management's effectiveness in reducing user resistance to change is positively related to improved implementation outcomes. Variables include management awareness of user resistance, communication of need for system, and ability to reduce user resistance.

Controlling

Hypothesis X. The use of a steering committee that: a.) is headed by the CEO and b.)meets at least every four weeks is positively associated with project success. Variables tested include the use of a steering committee, frequency of meetings, and rank of chairperson.

Data Collection

Two methods will be used to test these hypotheses, a questionnaire and case studies. Companies surveyed will include manufacturing companies, the largest user group of ERP systems. Firms with sales in excess of $500 million will be selected will be selected from the Harris Manufacturing Database or a similar database.

Questionnaire

The survey questionnaire consisted of 50 questions grouped under the titles Background, Planning, Organizing, Staffing, Leading, and Controlling.

Expected Outcomes

The questionnaire responses will be summarized for demographic characteristics. The first ten questions address implementation success measurement-systems quality, information quality, use, user satisfaction, individual impact and organizational impact. Two success variables will be developed. The first variable will describe the project as successful or unsuccessful and be used in the discriminant analysis of each hypothesis. The second will be a continuous dependent variable to be used in performing multiple regression analysis for each hypothesis.

Based on the success variables, responses will be separated into two categories: successful and unsuccessful implementations.

The data testing of each hypothesis will be evaluated using the following statistical techniques, which were used in the earlier MRP study (Sneller, 1986).

1. Responses for successful and unsuccessful implementations will be compared using the t-test for significance. This test will be used to determine statistically significant differences between the means of the responses of the implementations classified as successful and those considered unsuccessful.
2. Multi-variate regression analysis with the continuous success variable as a dependent variable will be determined. This analysis identifies the best combination of independent variables to predict the dependent variable, success.
3. Multi-variate discriminant analysis with the dependent variable for success will be conducted. This analysis is useful in identifying the ability of the independent variable to predict membership in a group, i.e., successful or unsuccessful.

The expected outcome of each hypothesis is discussed below:

Planning

Hypothesis I. Level of integration of IS planning and business planning.

The support of this hypothesis will inform management of the necessity of including IS planning as an integral part of business planning. The most important lesson to be learned from this hypothesis is that the tasks of business planning and IS planning are inseparable and better integration will lead to more successful ERP implementations and improved business performance.

Organizing

Hypothesis II. Organizing under the direction of a project manager whose sole responsibilities are project implementation.

The project manager's sole responsibility should be the project.

Hypothesis III. Project manager reports directly to the business unit's senior manager.

The reporting level of the project manager is a signal of top management support and a positive relationship to project success is expected.

Staffing

Hypothesis IV. Project manager's business experience.

Most problems encountered in ERP implementation are organizational rather than technical. Extensive business experience of the project manager is expected to enhance implementation project success.

Hypothesis V

(a). Quantity and quality of training.

(b). The use of testing during training.

Support will indicate that training is critical to project success and often inadequately provided for in implementation plans

Hypothesis VI. Use of an ERP consultant.

Sneller found no relationship between the use of consultants in MRP implementations and project outcomes, raising the question of the effectiveness of such expenditures

Leading

Hypothesis VII. CEO involvement in planning and implementation of ERP systems.

This hypothesis tests one of the strongest theories supported in the literature. The Sneller study concluded, "MRP system implementation will probably not succeed without the support and involvement of senior management" (Sneller, 1986)

Hypothesis VIII. The existence of a champion.

Both management literature and systems literature support the role of a champion. A significant relationship between project success and a champion will inform management of the importance of this role.

Hypothesis IX. Management's effectiveness in reducing user resistance.

As change issues overshadow any technical issues in implementation projects, management's ability to overcome resistance is a major factor in project success.

Controlling

Hypothesis X. The use of a steering committee that is a.) headed by the CEO or other non-IS executive and b.) meets regularly.

A steering committee head that is from the top management team and not an IS manager will demonstrate management support and commitment to the project and be more effective in addressing business issues such as business process reengineering and change management.

Stage of this research

This research is based on my dissertation proposal at Claremont Graduate University. I expect to defend my proposal and to commence data gathering during the winter 2002 quarter.

Feedback Sought

Selection of sample. I plan to use a relatively large sample of manufacturers, but expect a modest reply percentage. The Sneller study used a very small sample (150 firms) in a single industry but had a high response rate. Which approach is likely to be more successful?

International dimension. Would it improve the study to add an international dimension? Can it be done without greatly expanding the scope or cost of data collection?

Data Analysis. Will path analysis of my independent variables yield useful results and possibly lead to development of a model?

REFERENCES

Davenport, T. H. (1998). Putting the Enterprise into the Enterprise System. *Harvard Business Review, 76*(4, July-August), 121-131.

Gupta, Y. P., & Raghunathan, T. S. (1989). Impact of Information Systems (IS) Steering Committees on IS Planning. *Decision Sciences, 20*(4), 777-793.

Sneller, M. L. (1986). *Application of Classical Management Approach to the Implementation of Material Requirements Planning Systems.* Unpublished Dissertation, Claremont Graduate School, Claremont. CA.

The Information Needs of Heritage Establishments in the United Kingdom (Doctoral Research)

Alan Brine
Department of Information Science,
Loughborough University, Loughborough, LE11 3TU
Tel: +440 (150) 922-3078, Fax: +440 (150) 922-3994
a.c.brine@lboro.ac.uk

ABSTRACT

In the United Kingdom (UK) heritage establishments are a large part of the tourism and leisure market. Heritage encompasses a wide variety of establishments including historic houses, historic gardens, heritage centres, town centres, countryside and museums. The UK has a vast amount of cultural resource in this respect and the research intends to concentrate on establishments that are known as the "built heritage" in the UK. More specifically we are looking at properties that are managed by organisations or individuals and are often described as "historic" or "country houses" and that have years or centuries of history attached to them. Millions of visitors annually visit properties to experience an insight into earlier periods of history.

Heritage establishments appear to have little access to information resources, unlike other small or medium sized businesses (SMEs), which may have ready access to local business networks. It is necessary to ascertain the role, if any, other organisations have in providing information to them. UK bodies including English Heritage and the National Trust (NT) have information resources available that may aid heritage establishments in running their businesses.

Drawing a composite picture of information usage within heritage establishments through the research enables comparisons and analysis to be carried out to determine the mismatch in information needs and information use. Some establishments may fulfill their needs by being part of larger organisations, such as the NT. Those that are independently run by a trust or by their owners may have no support of this kind. The research seeks to uncover which sources are used in the running of heritage establishments and whether these meet their actual information needs.

Building on the empirical work it is intended to make recommendations on gaps in their information provision and suggest methods for the management of their information. This may include more effective use of information technology to manipulate their information systems or the introduction of policies and strategies that enables effective management of information resources within the establishment. Ultimately efficient information management or knowledge management should lead to an improvement in the business' effectiveness.

STAGE OF RESEARCH

The research is currently in its early stages. Appendix 1 shows the timeframe for the complete PhD. The literature is currently being reviewed to determine the extent of work that has already taken place within the field. The initial survey is due to be piloted before the end of 2001. Initial contact with organisations is being progressed over the next month to establish possible pilot sites as well as convincing them of the merits in taking part in the survey. The full survey of establishments begins at the end of the year and continues through the beginning of 2002 when many establishments will be closing to the public for the winter months. Analysis of these initial survey results will have taken place and further case study interviews will then be underway by the spring 2002.

OBJECTIVES

The aim of the research is to ascertain the information needs of heritage establishments through surveying the information requirements of a discreet, but sufficiently large and representative sample of places to discover the varying functions that perform in the running of the business.

Further to this we will also investigate their actual practice and use of information to determine where there are gaps in their information provision.

There are five objectives resulting from these aims. These are:

- Discover the information needs of the properties;
- Identify the "actual" information being used at establishments;
- Reveal sources of information used in the operation of heritage establishments;
- Determine gaps in heritage establishments' information needs;
- Propose alternative sources, and methods of information management, including information technology, to increase the efficiency and effectiveness of heritage businesses.

This leads us to the following hypotheses against which the research will be measured:

1. Heritage establishments are very diverse in their management, but despite this they have common information needs.
2. The wide variety of activities taking place at heritage establishments means that they have a wide range of information needs.
3. Heritage establishments appear not to have adequate internal information services to ensure dissemination of information.
4. Current information sources are not adequately fulfilling establishments' information needs.
5. There is scope for collaboration and co-ordination in assuring and maintaining the flow of information to heritage establishments.
6. There is scope for the improvement of information management within heritage establishments.

LITERATURE REVIEW

The review so far has already revealed a lack of research on information needs and management of information within the heritage industry. The review framework has therefore been built on the following foundations:

- information needs within SMEs;
- information flows within SMEs;
- models of information use to support business;
- the construct of the heritage, (and information), environment.

The remit of heritage establishments is often more diverse than any small or medium sized company and their information needs may be more complex than similar sized businesses in the UK.

Using the information needs and flows of SMEs as a grounding for the work to be carried out within heritage establishments provides us with a benchmark against which to determine heritage establishments needs.

Information needs are being reviewed in SMEs in general, as there is little in culture and heritage literature on this aspect. Investigations so far indicate that there is work on information use in museums, which have some related functions to heritage establishments.

A discussion on leisure, heritage and culture, as defined by authors such as Hewison and Yale, will take place to clarify the environment heritage establishments operate in.

Further discussion looking at historic/country houses and their operations in an attempt to draw conclusions on the facilities they are providing that necessitate appropriate use of information resources. This should result in a "map" which details the operations that take place in heritage establishments.

Reviewing literature on national and regional heritage organisations has given an indication on how larger organisations help properties with their information needs. Models, such as the centre-periphery model discussed by Schon, are being reviewed to enable a discussion on the centralised versus local provision of information. Certainly heritage establishments are so diverse that both will arise in the survey results.

A thorough review of the literature enables us to determine whether the research project needs to be altered in any significant way to achieve the desired outcomes.

RESEARCH METHODOLOGY

There are a wide variety of heritage establishments across the country that provide different functions and belong to different heritage organisations. To find out their information needs, it is necessary to select a large sample that will be surveyed to gain quantitative data from which the hypotheses can be tested against. Further qualitative data is to be collected by surveying a smaller number of sites and heritage organisations to further test the hypotheses. The research will consist of a number of different methods of data collection to elicit information on heritage establishment information needs. The methods to be employed will be a paper questionnaire, followed by interviews of both heritage organisations, and a subset of heritage establishments to act as case studies.

The sample of heritage establishments is:

- drawn from 2000 historic properties in Hudson's "Historic Houses and Gardens";
- stratified to ensure regional coverage and representation of heritage organisations.

The survey includes:

- a pilot phase to ensure questions will retrieve data necessary for the analysis of information needs at heritage establishments;
- questionnaire revision;
- approximately 1000 questionnaires to ensure enough returns for a representative sample, (minimum 335), taking into account non-responses;
- follow-up to ensure return of surveys;

preliminary data analysis as questionnaires received.

Parallel interviews with both national and local heritage organisations will be conducted at this time to provide data enabling information provision by heritage organisations for property managers to be determined. It may provide perspectives on information not being used to its full potential, and enable the formulation of more incisive questions for heritage establishment case studies.

The results of the questionnaire survey will pinpoint properties to approach as case studies. The case studies shall include:

- an appropriate selection of properties;
- on-site interviewing of property owners/managers.

Analysis of both quantitative and qualitative data from the selected sample of heritage establishments is to be carried out. This includes the three datasets; the property information needs and resources surveys; the property case studies; heritage organisation interviews.

Coding, recording and tabulation of the questionnaire survey data will reveal patterns in the data, enabling conclusions to be drawn. Analysis of interview data will be performed by segmenting and categorising the results, to enable the data to be divided into issues and themes when the process is concluded. From these it is possible to interpret the data and draw conclusions on the research hypotheses.

The collation and analysis of the data makes it possible to determine gaps between the information needs of heritage establishments and the actual information used in their operations. The analysis may pose more questions needing answers or that indicate the need for further research.

EXPECTED OUTCOMES

At the end of the research it will be possible to test the hypotheses and identify the gaps in the information requirements of heritage establishments.

The survey should provide a set of information sources that could act as a guideline or resource guide that could be used by property managers as a first step in addressing their information needs. It should also be possible to determine whether there are any untapped sources of information that are readily available for properties from external or internal sources.

A list can then be drawn together to enable establishments to take any measures that would make their business more effective and efficient. This will include better use of information management, (including better use of resources); better organisation of resources; and effective use of information technology to enhance use of information. Beyond the management of information it would be appropriate to make recommendations on information policies and strategies that would enable a more far reaching and effective use of information resources for heritage establishments, including co-operation between establishments on a national or regional level.

Although many questions will be answered by the research, many more will be raised. As this is an area of that has seen little research, many facets of information management remain to be addressed for heritage establishments.

Ultimately the research will determine the information needs of heritage establishments and shall inform the LIS community regarding the differing needs of this little researched industry.

RESEARCH TIME SCHEDULE

	2001						2002												2003											
	J	A	S	O	N	D	J	F	M	A	M	J	J	A	S	O	N	D	J	F	M	A	M	J	J	A	S	O	N	D
Literature review	■	■	■	■	■	■	■	■	■	■	■	■	■	■	■	■	■	■	■	■	■	■	■	■						
Determine sample				■																										
Questionnaire drawn up				■	■																									
Pilot questionnaire					■																									
Establishment contacted			■																											
Questionnaire sent out						■	■																							
Interviews in heritage orgs.										■	■	■	■	■	■	■	■													
1st year report													■																	
Data input								■	■																					
Questionnaire analysis								■	■	■	■																			
Case studies shortlist made											■	■																		
Draft case study script											■	■																		
Case study interviews													■	■	■	■	■													
2nd year report																									■					
Transcribing																■	■	■												
Analysis of case studies																		■	■	■										
Draft conclusions																							■	■	■					
Draft report						■	■	■	■	■	■	■	■	■	■	■	■	■	■	■	■	■	■	■	■	■	■	■	■	■
Submission																													■	■

Author Index

3 New Journals

Official publications of the Information Resources Management Association

Available January 2003!

International Journal of Distance Education Technologies

Editors-in-Chief: Shi-Kuo Chang, University of Pittsburgh, USA
Timothy K. Shih, Tamkang University, Taiwan

A new journal produced by Idea Group Publishing, International Journal of Distance Education Technologies provides a form for research in distance learning and distance education, in the categories of Communication Technologies, Intelligent Technologies and Educational Technologies.

ISSN: Pending; eISSN: Pending; Price: US $185.00; Frequency: Quarterly

Journal of Electronic Commerce in Organizations

Editor-in-Chief: Mehdi Khosrow-Pour
Information Resources Management Association, USA

Journal of Electronic Commerce in Organizations, new from Idea Group Publishing, is dedicated to electronic commerce and provides a worldwide view of all aspects of the subject, from impacts on consumer behavior to the development of e-commerce technologies.

ISSN: Pending; eISSN: Pending; Price: US$185.00; Frequency: Quarterly

International Journal of IT Standards and Standardization Research

Editor-in-Chief: Kai Jakobs
Technical University of Aachen, Germany

New from Idea Group Publishing, The International Journal of IT Standardization Research aims to advance knowledge and research in all aspects of IT standards and standardization in modern organizations, by including contributions from a wide array of disciplines, including computer science, management, business, and social science, among others.

ISSN: Pending; eISSN: Pending; Price: US $145.00; Frequency: Semi-Annually

---

To subscribe or for more information on these new publications, contact:

Idea Group Publishing
1331 E Chocolate Avenue
Hershey PA 17033-1117, USA
cust@idea-group.com